T0317464

Infrastructure as an Asset Class

Founded in 1807, John Wiley & Sons is the oldest independent publishing company in the United States. With offices in North America, Europe, Australia and Asia, Wiley is globally committed to developing and marketing print and electronic products and services for our customers' professional and personal knowledge and understanding.

The Wiley Finance series contains books written specifically for finance and investment professionals as well as sophisticated individual investors and their financial advisors. Book topics range from portfolio management to e-commerce, risk management, financial engineering, valuation and financial instrument analysis, as well as much more.

For a list of available titles, visit our Web site at www.WileyFinance.com.

Infrastructure as an Asset Class

Investment Strategy, Sustainability, Project Finance and PPP

Second Edition

BARBARA WEBER
MIRJAM STAUB-BISANG
HANS WILHELM ALFEN

WILEY

This edition first published 2016
© 2016 Barbara Weber, Mirjam Staub-Bisang and Hans Wilhelm Alfen
First edition published 2010 by John Wiley & Sons, Ltd

Registered office
John Wiley & Sons Ltd, The Atrium, Southern Gate, Chichester, West Sussex, PO19 8SQ, United Kingdom

For details of our global editorial offices, for customer services and for information about how to apply for
permission to reuse the copyright material in this book please see our website at www.wiley.com.

Library of Congress Cataloging-in-Publication Data

Names: Weber, Barbara, 1968- author. | Staub-Bisang, Mirjam, 1969- author.
  | Alfen, Hans Wilhelm, author.
Title: Infrastructure as an asset class : investment strategy, sustainability, project finance and PPP / Barbara Weber,
Mirjam Staub-Bisang, Hans Wilhelm Alfen.
Description: Second edition. | Chichester, West Sussex : John Wiley & Sons, 2016. | Series: The Wiley finance series |
  Includes bibliographical references and index.
Identifiers: LCCN 2016004044 | ISBN 9781119226543 (hardback)
Subjects: LCSH: Infrastructure (Economics)–Finance. |
  Investments–Management. | Public-private sector cooperation. | BISAC:
  BUSINESS & ECONOMICS / Finance.
Classification: LCC HC79.C3 W43 2016 | DDC 388/.049–dc23 LC record
available at http://lccn.loc.gov/2016004044

A catalogue record for this book is available from the British Library.

ISBN 978-1-119-22654-3 (hbk) ISBN 978-1-119-22656-7 (ebk)
ISBN 978-1-119-22655-0 (ebk) ISBN 978-1-119-22657-4 (ebk)

Cover Design: Wiley

Set in 10/12pt Times by Aptara Inc., New Delhi, India
Printed by CPI Group (UK) Ltd, Croydon, CR0 4YY

C9781119226543_291121

Contents

List of Figures

List of Tables

Preface

Investors and governments globally continue to express strong interest in infrastructure, yet for different reasons. Governments have ever-rising, partially urgent needs for new infrastructure and the maintenance of existing assets, which are the backbone of any society and hence strongly determine its quality of living. Investors search for yields in order to meet their long-term liabilities faced with a seemingly continuing low-interest rate environment. Infrastructure investments may be part of the solution.

At the same time, awareness of time-critical sustainability questions in general, and environmental or climate issues in particular, seem to have reached a tipping point. Governments, NGOs and financial institutions as well as institutional investors, such as insurance groups and pension funds, have joined forces internationally to address these major challenges and agree on sustainability goals.

Given the above, governments, societies, and investors alike are particularly interested in (renewable) energy-related and social infrastructure assets. This second edition addresses this interest with new sector sections on renewable energy, energy transmission and storage (electricity, natural gas, district heating), as well as social infrastructure (hospitals, schools, administrative facilities). Sustainability aspects related to infrastructure investments are addressed throughout the book, in all subsectors and in the investment process. Furthermore, it includes a new section on infrastructure benchmarking, which will prove useful to many investors and their advisors.

Last but not least, all relevant economic data and statistics, which have changed since 2010, when the first edition was published,[1] have been updated. In a number of instances, the new data required new interpretations of the overall situation.

The purpose of this book is to comprehensively guide investors who are considering investing, or already invest, in infrastructure through the basic and advanced essential concepts of infrastructure investing. These include an understanding of the market and how closely related sustainability aspects are with the market, as well as any investment decision, benchmarking, possible investment approaches, organisational and contractual models and structures, characteristics of the most important infrastructure sectors and subsectors, general, sector-specific and project-specific risk assessment (including ESG factors), and project finance.

To this end, we unite the pressing topics of infrastructure investments, sustainability, project finance and public–private partnerships (PPPs). For this, we systematically process and classify a compiled basis of theoretical information and illustrate it with examples and case

---

[1] *Infrastructure as an Asset Class*, Barbara Weber and Hans Wilhelm Alfen, John Wiley and Sons, 2010.

studies relevant to practitioners in industry, finance, international organisations and various areas of the public sector. We discuss the differing objectives and expectations of the many parties involved in infrastructure provision and investing. Specific attention is given to risks surrounding infrastructure assets and investments, which is reflected by a new chapter dedicated to risk.

With this book, we predominantly address the needs of advanced readers to deepen their knowledge and to receive up-to-date industry information, while we seek at the same time to meet the expectations of comparatively inexperienced readers who may want to take a closer look at the potential of infrastructure investment for their institutions. The book answers key questions, such as:

- How is infrastructure defined? Which sectors/assets are classified as infrastructure, how are they categorised and what are the differences between them?
- What are the characteristics of infrastructure as an asset class?
- How is a sustainable investing approach to infrastructure assets applied?
- What are suitable infrastructure investment strategies and approaches for different types of investors?
- How are suitable benchmarks for infrastructure investments defined and developed?
- What ESG risk factors need to be considered in new infrastructure projects and operating assets alike? What tools are available for assessing ESG risk factors?
- How are direct and indirect infrastructure investments categorised and evaluated?
- Which organisational structures and business models exist to finance infrastructure projects with private capital?
- Which risks do these structures and models entail and how can the risks be addressed?
- How should assets be structured in order to best allocate the risks in the context of an investment?

In addition to background knowledge and information on the latest developments in the individual subject areas, we provide specific instructions and concrete proposals on the approach to adopt when assessing and making investments in infrastructure assets, whether directly or via investment funds (indirect investments). This includes the analysis, structuring and implementation of project finance, which is at the core of almost any infrastructure investment.

The contents of this book are based on the practical experience and broad theoretical knowledge of the authors. To this end, this second edition benefits greatly from the knowledge of our new co-author Mirjam Staub-Bisang, who helped us address sustainability and environmental, social and governance (ESG) matters. Throughout the book, we illustrate how to incorporate them in every infrastructure investment decision. Hans Wilhelm Alfen, the co-author of the first edition, contributed a new section on social infrastructure to this edition in addition to the revision work completed on a number of key sections.

A Note from the Publisher

The landscape of infrastructure investing has changed profoundly since the publication of the first edition of this book. As a result of these changes the second edition has been fully revised and updated, but also much expanded.

The book's lead author Dr Barbara Weber and Dr Staub-Bisang, who joined the team as a co-author in order to complete this work, have been responsible for the vast majority of the updating and revision throughout this volume. They are responsible for all new content in this volume, with the exceptions noted below.

Prof Dr Hans Wilhelm Alfen, the co-author of the first edition, ably supported the project. He is primarily responsible for Section 1.3, the entirety of Chapter 3, as well as Section 4.1, 4.2, 4.3 and Section 4.7. Section 5.1 and Chapter 6, parts of which are originally based on Prof Dr Alfen's research, have been substantially and substantively revised by Barbara.

Acknowledgements

We would like to thank David Brugman, MSc Climate Change and Sustainable Development, De Montfort University and Björn Wündsch, Dipl.-Ing., Bauhaus-Universität Weimar, who both assisted us greatly in writing and editing this second edition. We would also like to thank Paolo Alemanni and Hadrien Guillemard for their valuable contributions to the new energy sections as well as Reto Michel for his contribution related to data of listed infrastructure investments.

We are also very grateful for the last minute support and engagement of Stefan Weissenböck and Oliver Werth during the final stages of the book.

Further, we would like to thank all our colleagues in the industry, from representatives of pension funds and insurance companies, corporate and public investors in infrastructure, through to fund managers, placement agents and journalists, who kindly supplied information on their companies and information about current and historical developments in the infrastructure market. Their contributions have been an important factor in improving the quality of this book and ensuring that it is up to date and state of the art.

Acknowledgements

About the Authors

Dr. **Barbara Weber** is Founding Partner of B Capital Partners AG, an investment advisory firm focused on building institutional infrastructure portfolios of all shapes – direct and (secondary) fund investments, equity and debt. It offers related strategic and asset allocation services to institutional clients as well. Barbara is also a member of the investment committee of the Swiss pension funds' infrastructure platform IST3. She has over 19 years of direct and fund investment experience in these areas gained with Dresdner Kleinwort Benson, Poly-Technos and, since 2003, B Capital Partners AG. She previously worked for the private-sector development group of the World Bank in Washington, DC on Russia. Barbara wrote her PhD in Economics at Harvard University and University of St. Gallen. She holds an MSc in Business and Operations Research from Warwick University and a postgraduate degree in International Relations from Mannheim University. She continues to lecture at various universities and is the author of several books and articles on infrastructure investing.

Dr. Mirjam Staub-Bisang is CEO of Independent Capital Group AG, an investment management firm focused on sustainable investing and real estate investments in Switzerland. In addition, she serves as a non-executive director on the boards of several public and private companies and as a trustee and member of the investment committees of several institutions. She counts over 16 years of investment experience across asset classes, which she gained in senior positions in asset management and private equity among which at Commerzbank and Swiss Life. She holds a Ph.D. in Law from the University of Zurich, and an MBA from INSEAD. In 2009, she was elected a Young Global Leader of the World Economic Forum. Mirjam Staub-Bisang authored the standard work *Sustainable Investing for Institutional Investors* (Wiley 2012) and is a contributing author of several other finance books and publications.

Prof. Dr.-Ing., Dipl.-Wirtsch.-Ing. Hans Wilhelm Alfen is Head of the Chair of Construction Economics at the Bauhaus-Universität Weimar in Germany and General Manager and founder of Alfen Consult GmbH, Weimar. He has more than 20 years' practical experience in developing and investing in infrastructure as well as researching and teaching in more than 25 countries in Africa, Asia, Europe and Latin America. Before joining the Bauhaus-Universität Weimar, he worked in leading positions in the construction as well as in the consulting industry. He is significantly involved in the German PPP standardisation process as researcher and advisor. He has contributed to a long list of national and international publications.

Introduction

BACKGROUND AND OBJECTIVES

The quality and volume of infrastructure has a positive effect on the attractiveness, competitiveness, sustainability and economic growth of countries, cities and municipalities. Infrastructure opens up new business opportunities and promotes trade as well as the expansion of existing economic activity. It also improves the standard of living of the public by giving people access to essential resources, such as water and electricity, schools, hospitals and markets. This is even more true if the development of infrastructure is done in a sustainable way.

Notwithstanding, around the world – in highly developed industrialised nations, high-growth emerging economies and developing countries alike – there is a growing gap between the acute need for new or modernised infrastructure, maintenance and overhaul measures and the actual level of investment and current expenditure, as evidenced by crumbling bridges, broken highways and leaking water pipelines. The public sector, which is traditionally responsible for infrastructure, frequently claims to have a number of other priorities that prevent it from investing the necessary funds in closing this gap, which is so vital for societies in terms of furthering development and prosperity.

Institutional financial investors with a long-term perspective, such as insurance companies, pension funds, sovereign wealth funds, endowments and foundations, are increasingly investing in infrastructure assets, therewith joining strategic investors such as construction, energy and utility companies who have done so for decades. This is because (conservatively structured) infrastructure investments provide attractive returns in a low-interest-rate environment and, additionally, serve to diversify and thus improve the risk-return profile of an investor's overall investment portfolio on account of their low correlation with traditional asset classes.

The volume of private capital in infrastructure is expected to increase significantly in the future and to a certain extent will be essential to help close the aforementioned funding gap for the public sector and ensure further economic growth. This holds in particular for emerging economies.

Going forward, investors in (new) infrastructure assets need to consider rigorously and factor in sustainability and ESG aspects such as environmental risks (e.g. climate change and natural resource scarcity), as well as social and governance risks (mainly) in emerging economies in their investment decisions.

The market for infrastructure is vast and, contrary to popular belief, the range of potential infrastructure investments is extremely broad, which presents challenges and opportunities for most investors. While they appreciate the enormous market potential and the possibly excellent fit of the asset class with their own investment goals and their existing portfolio, they may lack a sufficient overview of the infrastructure market and/or insight into suitable investment opportunities and their related risks. Furthermore, institutional investors with a sustainable investing mandate may miss clear information and tools for assessing and integrating sustainability considerations in their investment process as well as related risks in their overall risk analysis of infrastructure projects. All of the above make it challenging for investors to take the right investment decisions for their individual strategies and existing portfolios.

This book offers a way out of the dilemma, providing investors with the necessary theoretical knowledge and background information as well as practical examples to help further their understanding of the key aspects of infrastructure investments with a particular focus on appropriate organisational structures, finance, benchmarking and sustainability.

As a minimum, professional investors should have a sufficient understanding of the infrastructure sectors and the corresponding markets and industries along with the relevant legal, contractual, institutional and commercial conditions – which can vary significantly from region to region and sector to sector – to allow them to identify inherent project-specific risks and to determine their prospective risk-return profiles. This is particularly important if the sectors in question have been dominated by the special rules and restrictions of the public sector in the past and are being opened up to the investment conditions required by private investors only on a gradual basis.

This brings us to a basic, yet vital, question: what exactly is infrastructure? We discuss the applicability and validity of various definitions of this term in detail in Section 1.3, but for now it is sufficient to note we use the following common and practical definition throughout this book:

Infrastructure generally describes all physical assets, equipment and facilities of interrelated systems and the necessary service providers, together with its underlying structures, organisations, business models and rules and regulations, offering related sector-specific commodities and services to individual economic entities or the wider public with the aim to enable, sustain or enhance social living conditions.

Typical examples of infrastructure include roads, airports, ports, oil and gas networks, energy generation, including renewable energy (e.g. wind, solar, hydro, biomass), water supply, waste water and waste disposal as well as social infrastructure, which includes public facilities such as schools, hospitals, administrative buildings and social housing.

Many investors are interested in the comparatively stable and predictable current income with moderate volatility and risk relatively independent of macroeconomic conditions, which is generated by a certain subset of infrastructure assets – return features shared by real estate or long-term, fixed-income investments. The long-term nature of infrastructure investments allows pension funds and insurance companies to use them to match the maturity structure of their liabilities. Infrastructure assets with this return profile are the driving force behind infrastructure's reputation as an attractive asset class – a hybrid with characteristics of debt, equity and real estate.

Although infrastructure investments certainly can have this comparatively low-risk profile, it is not necessarily so, and unless structured accordingly such investments can entail significant risks similar to those of investments in traditional companies. For any potential investment, these risks must be identified and assessed carefully.

To this end, we provide a fundamental understanding of infrastructure in general, the differences – in some cases significant – between infrastructure measures and key performance indicators (KPIs) within a sector and the various infrastructure sectors themselves.

A new section on benchmarking allows readers to assess the performance of infrastructure investments against a suitable benchmark. The suitability of a benchmark is determined primarily by the desired risk-return profiles and characteristics.

The systematic procedures and analytical tools we propose, enable readers to understand and evaluate both direct investments in infrastructure assets and indirect (fund) products along with their complex underlying project finance structures. Taken together, they allow the assessment of the risk-return profiles of the respective infrastructure investments.

Given that risk-return analysis, assessment and structuring are at the core of infrastructure investing, the main risks of infrastructure assets are discussed comprehensively in an individual chapter in this new edition. The risk analysis and assessment flows right into, and is among the most important input factors for, structuring the project financing, which itself is a crucial part of the financing of infrastructure assets involving the private sector.

Project finance has a number of benefits compared with traditional forms of financing; however, it also requires a deep understanding of financing structures and complex analytical approaches. All in all, a successful project finance fundamentally depends on the ability to develop the appropriate contractual structure for the respective sector in terms of optimal allocation of risk among the parties involved, financing and value added, competition/regulation and the possibility of private-sector involvement. *It is the contractual structure that predominantly determines the risk-return profile of each individual infrastructure asset.* To this end, the book guides readers step by step through the various phases of project analysis, using practical examples, and provides an introduction to concrete financing instruments and techniques.

This book is aimed at the following groups in particular:

- Financial investors, e.g. insurance companies, pension funds, fund managers and banks;
- Strategic investors, e.g. construction, operation and supply groups, technology suppliers and facility managers;
- Public authorities responsible for infrastructure in the various sectors, in particular ministries of construction and regional building authorities, including their budget departments, as well as ministries of finance and legal supervisory institutions such as audit courts;
- Public and private infrastructure companies, e.g. power suppliers, water supply and disposal companies, airports and railroad companies;
- International organisations, e.g. The World Bank, EIB, OECD, which seek to support and incentivise infrastructure investments on the part of the private sector.

The book's in-depth theoretical basis also makes it suitable as a textbook for students.

STRUCTURE

Conceptually speaking, we have divided this book into three parts. The first part consists of Chapters 1 and 2. In Chapter 1, we provide an overview of the international infrastructure market with a particular focus on demand for infrastructure assets and the expected capital requirements. This is followed by an introduction to sustainability and the need for sustainable infrastructure. Chapter 1 concludes with an overview of the most important infrastructure sectors, the country-, sector- and project-specific characteristics influencing the risk-return profiles of the infrastructure sectors (and hence any respective investments) and a discussion of their general cross-sector characteristics.

Chapter 2 begins with an overview of some of the most experienced and/or largest global infrastructure investors. We then provide an introduction to infrastructure as an asset class by going through a substantial body of research in this field and discussing the main investment characteristics of the asset class – stand-alone as well as in comparison with and in relation to other asset classes. We conclude that infrastructure comprises a broad variety of assets, and hence appears to be a hybrid between bonds, real estate and (private) equity, which should indeed be considered an asset class on its own.

Given its variety, benchmarking (especially unlisted) infrastructure is challenging. This new edition addresses this problem by guiding investors through the basics of benchmarking and offering them a selection of potentially suitable benchmarks depending on their individual investment strategy.

Chapter 2 continues by making the case for sustainable investing in infrastructure, starting with the history and definition of sustainable investing and how it is framed within the larger investment spectrum. This is followed by an introduction to the ESG factors that are crucial to assessing the sustainability of an infrastructure investment. Chapter 2 concludes with an overview of the different approaches to infrastructure investing, that is via listed as opposed to unlisted assets and direct as opposed to fund investments. It then focuses on unlisted assets, and in particular fund investments, because they represent the entry point to the infrastructure market for most investors.

The second and third parts of the book focus on direct invesments only. Accordingly, Chapter 3 provides investors with an investment evaluation framework for direct assets. Referred to as the 'organisational model', it gives a structured overview of the various approaches to develop and organise infrastructure delivery with a particular focus on private investments. The aim of our model, which distinguishes between privatisation, partnership, business, contractual and financing sub-models, is to allow investors to analyse and classify individually any infrastructure investment opportunity on the basis of its ordinary components and its general, technical, economic, financing and legal/contractual key determining factors. In order to facilitate this classification, we list the common types of organisational models around the world. This enables investors to better understand and internationally compare, for example, the ownership and/or involvement of the partners and stakeholders and their contractual relationships, the payment mechanisms, incentive structures and resulting flows of funds, as well as the risks and risk allocation. In order to help the reader understand this highly complex model, we make use of examples from around the world.

Chapter 4 describes the typical characteristics of most infrastructure sectors and subsectors, that is transport and traffic (including road, rail and water transport/ports as well as air transport), water supply/disposal, solid waste management, renewable energy generation (leaving out traditional energy generation), energy transmission/distribution networks and storage (electricity and gas), as well as social infrastructure. We break down the discussion of each of these sectors into five areas: organisation, financing and value added, competition/ regulation, private sector involvement and sustainability considerations. These aspects seem to be – consistently across all sectors – the most relevant for investors when it comes to analysing and conceiving the impact the particular economic and legal environment of the respective sector may have on the long-term viability of their individual investment. The detailed discussions of the selected sectors seek to raise the reader's awareness and understanding of the general approach of how to identify and assess the sector-specific factors, their interdependence and interaction with country- and project-specific aspects as well as their overall influence on individual investments. The approach can be transferred easily to any other infrastructure sector.

In the third part of the book, Chapters 5–7 continue to deal with direct investments in infrastructure assets and their evaluation, with a particular focus on risks and the financing of such assets with project finance – in its pure private-sector form as well as in PPPs.

Chapter 5 discusses comprehensively general and project/asset-specific risks prevalent in the context of infrastructure investments that need to be identified, analysed, evaluated and ultimately allocated to the project parties involved. The accurate identification and understanding of risk is central to any investment decision, they form the basis for the implementation of appropriate (contractual) structures that provide protection for investors.

Chapter 6 contains an introduction to the basics of project finance, including the main participants, cash flows and contractual relationships, followed by an extensive discussion of the project finance process broken down into individual phases.

Chapter 7 addresses the various kinds of capital and financing instruments that are used (or that can be used) within and beyond project finance. Further, it introduces selected European and national government support institutions that support infrastructure projects and programmes in various forms.

CHAPTER 1

Infrastructure – An Overview

High investment and maintenance costs for infrastructure assets are a heavy burden on public budgets. As a result, over the last four to five decades all OECD (Organization for Economic Cooperation and Development) countries have steadily reduced their level of infrastructure investment both in absolute and relative terms. This situation is enhanced by the consequences of a severe global financial crisis and the enormous challenges facing infrastructure assets caused by climate change.

In response to this situation, a number of governments have sought to identify new ways of financing adequate infrastructure facilities despite (or even because of) this dearth of state funding, demonstrating a change in attitudes. In almost all of the countries concerned, the outcome has been cooperation with the private sector with a view to ensuring continued domestic economic productivity even in the face of growing populations and insufficient public budgets. Ultimately, the quality of a country's available infrastructure is a vital factor in its future economic growth and, hence, must have first priority.

Already today, around the world, a significant proportion of infrastructure assets are in private hands. This is especially true for the telecommunications sector, to a lesser extent for power generation, transmission and storage and even less for transport, water, waste, and social infrastructure. It is expected that private money will continue to flow into these sectors because governments lack the means to finance and maintain publicly-owned and operated infrastructures, owing to pressure on budgets and tax-raising capacity. At the same time, in an ongoing low interest rate environment, investors will keep looking for attractive, long-term, low risk investment opportunities as presented by many infrastructure assets.

Most Western countries as well as several emerging economies in Asia, the Middle East and Eastern Europe, have implemented extensive legislation to open up the possibility of infrastructure investments by the private sector. For its part, the private sector has recognised the financial benefits of funding, constructing and operating/holding infrastructure assets, whether in the form of long-term concessions or by way of permanent ownership.

Before infrastructure is defined and its general characteristics addressed in some detail, the following section provides a brief overview of the size of the infrastructure market and its investment requirements.

1.1 DEMAND FOR INFRASTRUCTURE

Significant demand for investments in both economic and social infrastructure assets exists around the world. This is because public infrastructure projects/assets in areas such as traffic, supply and disposal, health and social care, education, science and administration are some of the key location factors and growth drivers of any economy. Although governments are responsible for investments in new and existing infrastructure assets, and hence are in a position to influence positively the economic development of their countries, the combination of economic upturn, insufficient investment in these sectors and the inadequate, even most basic, maintenance of existing ageing facilities over the past decades has led to a considerable imbalance between supply and demand when it comes to infrastructure assets. This has been exacerbated by population growth and an increased demand for constructing, modernising or replacing existing assets, which in turn leads to higher costs. The global investment shortfall in infrastructure is estimated to be at least US$1 trillion per annum (WEF, 2014a). The World Bank estimates this excess demand at 1.3% of global gross national product (GNP) (World Bank Database, 2015). Meanwhile, the gap between the need for infrastructure investments and the ability of national budgets to meet this demand is continuing to widen throughout the world.

In less prosperous developing countries and emerging economies, demand for infrastructure investments continues to focus on primary care and utilities in particular. Funding for the development and operation of such projects, most of which are constructed on greenfield sites, has always been scarce. In the past, these requirements have largely been financed with the assistance of development subsidies and multilateral sponsor organisations, while private investors rarely got involved. However, this situation is changing dramatically at least for those emerging economies with dynamic economic growth. In countries such as China and India, infrastructure projects financed with private investment are becoming increasingly common as a means of meeting the vast capital requirements for the construction of basic infrastructure. The same applies to the transitional economies of Eastern Europe, where initially the main focus has been on privatising state-owned enterprises.

Yet, established industrialised nations are also facing growing financial challenges when it comes to providing efficient infrastructure facilities. Their existing infrastructure (brownfield), which is generally well constructed, must be operated, serviced, maintained, modernised and adjusted to meet current requirements, including environmental and social standards. These assets often entail new construction, renovation, expansion or conversion measures. Due to demographic change, this sometimes even requires the dismantling and fundamental redesign of the relevant assets.

One particular challenge is financing the construction and operation of international, cross-border infrastructure facilities that are extremely important for the integration of international economic communities, as evidenced by the examples of the Trans-European Transport Network (TEN-T), the Trans-European Energy Network (TEN-E), and the Trans-European Telecommunications Network (eTEN).

All country types – developing, emerging and industrialised – have a financing gap of some sort that they need to close. However, there are considerable differences in terms of the political, legal and economic conditions and requirements for closing this gap with the aid of private capital. One particular consideration is the substantial variation in economic growth combined with the national debt and existing tax and contribution ratios of the respective countries. Industrialised nations often show low levels of growth and rapidly dwindling scope for financing infrastructure via new borrowing or further increasing the burden on taxpayers and users. Therefore, it is important for these countries to realise efficiency benefits through the expansion, maintenance and operation of the existing infrastructure. As a consequence, these countries can only get hold of extra cash by making savings in their bureaucratic structures, in other words they need to cover future expenses by reforming their already overburdened administrative machinery and adjust their budgets accordingly. In this context, value-for-money comparisons (effectiveness and efficiency) – both between infrastructure assets of the same kind and/or in the same sector as well as conventional procurement vs. private-sector participation/partnerships – play a decisive role. This is even more crucial once governments aim to attract private capital to fill the financing gaps.

In contrast, the financial liquidity aspect is considerably more important in high-growth countries, because the required infrastructure needs to be available for use as quickly as possible – 'whatever the cost' – in order to not only meet urgent needs but also further support economic growth. In a scenario reminiscent of the post-World War II economic boom in Germany, the aim here is to offset the resulting new (government) debt with growing revenues generated in other areas. In both cases, though, the acquisition of private capital to supplement governments' efforts is one of the primary objectives.

Building on this qualitative analysis of the demand structure, the following paragraphs aim to quantify the costs for these infrastructure requirements to some extent.

According to estimates by the World Bank, global operating and maintenance costs for existing infrastructure assets alone amount to 1.2% of global GNP, almost equal to the excess demand for new investments of 1.3% mentioned earlier (World Bank Database, 2015). These costs may be due in part, although by no means exclusively, to overall rising raw material costs.

The growth in healthcare costs and pension obligations owing to an ageing population accompanied by reduced tax receipts has led to a further deterioration in the financing options available to governments. In high-tax countries, such as Germany or Scandinavia in particular, tax increases are not a feasible option for funding infrastructure assets. Using fixed-income securities as alternatives has a negative impact on the public purse and the financial rating, plus it can be used to finance only an extremely limited number of projects. In short, the current public policy and regulatory and planning frameworks in most countries appear inadequately equipped and structured to tackle the multifaceted challenges facing infrastructure development in general and sustainable infrastructure in particular over the next 25 years.

According to the comprehensive two-volume *Infrastructure 2030* OECD study published in 2006/2007 – this is still the only study of its kind to which all newer studies keep referring – government spending on infrastructure in OECD countries amounted to 2.2% of GNP between 1997 and 2002, compared with 2.6% in 1991–1997 (OECD, 2006, 2007). Figure 1.1 illustrates this development, broken down by a selected number of OECD countries over a period of 30 years from 1970 to 2002. With the exception of the US in 2002, the ratio of government infrastructure spending to total spending in the respective countries declined or stagnated over the same periods. A more recent OECD report on transport infrastructure only shows that investment rates for OECD countries have decreased even further from 2002 to 2011, floating between 0.8 and 0.9% of GNP (OECD/ITF, 2013).

Figure 1.2 compares the key European Union (EU) countries as well as all 15 EU countries over a 30-year period. It shows a substantial downward trend in public investment in the EU from 1970–2003 as well, not only in relative but also in absolute terms. A 2015 report illustrates a continuation of this trend with public investment in infrastructure for the (now) 28 EU countries in 2013 down by a further 11% compared to 2010 (Ammermann, 2015).

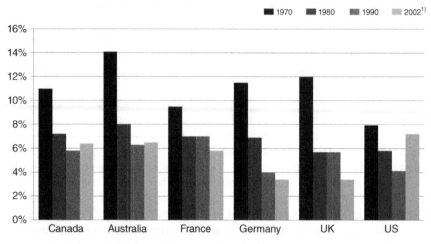

1. Note: US Data for are not available

FIGURE 1.1   Government infrastructure investments as a percentage of total outlays in
OECD countries
Source: OECD (2006)

According to estimates contained in the *Infrastructure 2030* OECD study 2006/2007 and
a 2013 report by McKinsey (McKinsey Global Institute, 2013), the need for infrastructure
investments – including additions, renewals and upgrades – has increased so significantly at
a global level that investments totalling some US$60 trillion will be required between 2013
and 2030 in order to improve the key infrastructure facilities around the world in line with
requirements. This corresponds to around 3.5% of global GDP annually. Although the OECD

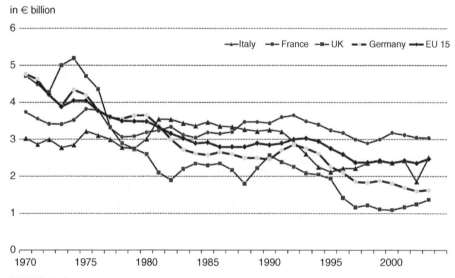

FIGURE 1.2   Infrastructure investments of EU governments
Source: OECD (2006)

study fails to provide details of the assumptions underlying these estimates and whether the investments constitute a politician's wish list or essential requirements in the respective countries, there is no reason to doubt the prevailing trend. According to the study, the 30 OECD member states have to invest more than US$600 billion a year in electricity, road, rail and water infrastructure from 2005 to 2030. Infrastructural improvements in the energy sector alone were forecast to total around US$4 trillion over the next 30 years. The modernisation and expansion of water, electricity and transportation systems in the cities of Western Europe, the US and Canada are expected to cost some US$16 trillion. In developed countries, there will also be a need to completely replace existing facilities and make additional new investments to meet rising demand.

Figure 1.3 presents the estimated spending requirements on infrastructure over time in the OECD and BRIC countries broken down into selected sectors.

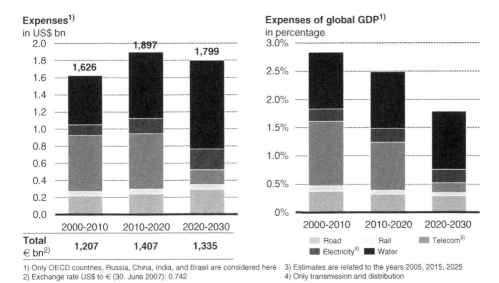

1) Only OECD countries, Russia, China, India, and Brasil are considered here 3) Estimates are related to the years 2005, 2015, 2025
2) Exchange rate US$ to € (30. June 2007): 0.742 4) Only transmission and distribution

FIGURE 1.3   Estimated average annual infrastructure spending in OECD and BRIC countries (new and replacement investments) in selected sectors, 2000–2030, in US$ billion as a percentage of global GDP
Source: UBS (2006)

In high-growth countries, the imbalance between capital supply and demand is many times greater. Estimated annual investments of 5–9% of GDP would be necessary to maintain the projected growth in these countries and facilitate the projected investment needs of US$460 billion over the coming years. According to the OECD, none of the countries concerned will be able to implement these measures without the support of the private sector. Globally, infrastructure investments will need to increase by 60% over the next 18 years to meet demand, following the 2013 McKinsey report cited above. A 2014 report from Swiss Re estimates that annual global infrastructure spending needs to increase from US$2.6 trillion in 2011 to around US$4 trillion by 2030 (Swiss Re, 2014).

There may be some debate as to the precise investment volumes needed. The high level of global demand for infrastructure investments and the inability of governments to cope with

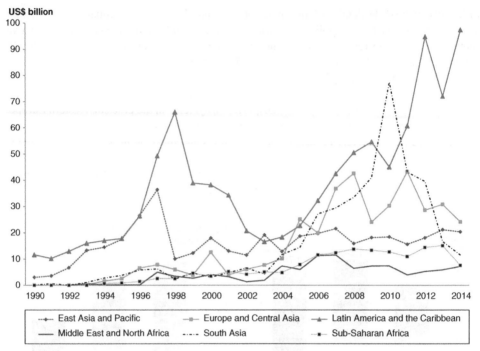

FIGURE 1.4   Investment commitments to infrastructure projects with private participation by region, 1990–2014
Source: Private Participation in Infrastructure Project Database (2016)

the level of capital and expertise required are undeniable. While public spending in essential infrastructure has been reported to continuously decrease, the share of private infrastructure investments has increased steadily. Over recent years, the volume of private investments in infrastructure in general, and especially in variants of public–private partnership (PPP) models, has risen across most regions (Figure 1.4). This is particularly evident in more recent years. It illustrates the general investment commitment to infrastructure projects with private participation, according to PPIAF (Public-Private Infrastructure Advisory Facility). Privatisation of state assets has been an important driver of this development. Since the 1980s, more than US$1 trillion of assets have been privatised in OECD countries and infrastructure has consistently taken centre stage. Aggregated figures for the period from 1990 to 2006 demonstrate that almost two-thirds of all privatisations in the OECD area related to utilities, transport, telecommunications or oil facilities. Over a similar period, some US$400 billion of state-owned assets were sold in non-OECD countries, approximately half of which were infrastructure-related (OECD, 2006, 2007).

Another indicator for the growing interest of private infrastructure investments is the share of private investments in listed infrastructure assets, the total stock of which increased fivefold from US$465 billion in 2000 to US$2.3 trillion in 2013 (Elliott, 2009; AMP Capital, 2014) – see Section 2.3.1 for further information.

Commitments to unlisted infrastructure funds are a further indicator. According to an infrastructure report by Probitas Partners, annual fundraising increased rapidly from US$2.4 billion in 2004 to US$39.7 billion in 2007 before dropping to US$10.7 billion in 2009 following the financial crisis (Probitas, 2014). Since then, annual investing has recovered strongly.

According to Preqin, a provider of infrastructure market data, 144 unlisted infrastructure funds were seeking aggregated capital commitments of $93 billion as of January 2015 (Preqin, 2015a).

Although investments in European infrastructure have not returned to pre-financial-crisis levels (US$7.5 billion in 2014 compared to US$10.1 billion in 2007) (Preqin, 2015a, b), the region still remains a global giant with respect to infrastructure investment offerings. Based on a recent report by Linklaters, investments have been strongest in the UK and northern Continental Europe while in southern Europe private infrastructure investment has crumbled since the financial crisis (Linklaters, 2014). Yet, foreign investors quadrupled their investment activity in European infrastructure from 2010 to 2013 (especially investors from Canada, China/Hong Kong, the Golf Cooperation Council [GCC] region, Japan and South Korea). Canada alone has invested over US$13 billion in Europe's infrastructure in the last three years. Notwithstanding, European investors still accounted for almost 75% of infrastructure acquisitions on the Continent during the same period. The report also notes that Europeans' share in global infrastructure investing has diminished from more than half in 2006 to just a quarter in 2013.

Funding investments of the magnitude stated above via tax increases is neither feasible nor sensible. By governments cooperating more often with the private sector, which is obviously interested in getting involved, the necessary repairs, modernisation work, operating, maintenance and new construction of infrastructure assets can be largely achieved in the medium to long term without significant tax hikes or additional borrowing for societies. Needless to say, private investors alone are not the solution. A long-term shift in the spending priorities of governments, increased user finance and more efficient infrastructure management will have to happen in parallel. Here, too, greater cooperation between the public sector and private investors will make an important contribution.

1.2 SUSTAINABILITY AND INFRASTRUCTURE

Sustainability and infrastructure share a common goal: to meet the current and long-term needs of society. It is not surprising that in a world of increasing resource scarcity, social unrest, population growth, ageing societies and climate change, sustainability and infrastructure are intrinsically interconnected. How we select, design and manage infrastructure systems today will play a key role in how such systems affect society and the environment now and for years to come. This in turn will have consequences for the exposure of infrastructure assets themselves to environmental, social and governance (ESG) risks.

Environmental risks relate to, for example, physical damage to infrastructure assets from climate-change-induced environmental hazards such as storms or floods, pollution and environmental degradation, changing regulations to curtail CO_2 emissions and the contamination of the environment. Violations of human rights, consumer protection rights, rights of indigenous populations, operational health and safety regulations and unfair competition are examples of social risks potentially affecting an infrastructure project or asset. Governance risks result from unethical behaviour (e.g. corruption), a lack of the rule of law in a country and governance structures or management systems that create conflicts of interests between the management and stakeholders of an infrastructure project.

The growing importance of sustainability considerations presents investors with new risks and opportunities. ESG factors are increasingly relevant both for shaping corporate reputation as well as for determining the long-term financial viability of infrastructure assets. At the same

TABLE 1.1   Quick reference guide to sustainability content

Section	Title	Page	Topics covered
1.2.1	Sustainability and sustainable development – a brief history	8	Background and key milestones for sustainable development
1.2.2	The need for sustainable infrastructure	9	Facts and figures supporting sustainable approaches to infrastructure development
2.2	Sustainable infrastructure investing	56	Introduction to sustainable investing and ESG factors, including examples of ESG assessment and benchmarking tools
4.1–4.7	Characteristics of selected infrastructure sectors and subsectors	114–258	Summaries of *sustainability considerations* at the end of each infrastructure sector sub-section
5.2.4	Environmental, social and governance (ESG) risk	270	Discussion of ESG risks (especially climate change) in infrastructure investments
5.2.5.2	Renewable energy regulations	280	Risk of changes in renewable energy regulations on clean energy investments
5.2.5.3	Stranded (fossil-fuel) assets	281	Risk of climate change policies on the valuation of fossil-fuel assets
5.4	Sector-specific risks	291	Sector-specific ESG risks

time, sustainability-themed, investable infrastructure assets such as renewable energy plants, resource-efficient water supply facilities and climate-change-resilient transportation systems and buildings all have a positive impact on sustainable development.

Given the key role of sustainability for the centuries and societies ahead of us, we will re-address sustainability aspects and considerations throughout this entire second edition in order to illustrate ESG (risk) factors to investors and help them incorporate them into their infrastructure investment decision-making process. Table 1.1 provides a quick reference guide for locating all sustainability (ESG) related content throughout this book.

1.2.1   Sustainability and sustainable development – a brief history

In the realms of ecology, sustainability describes how biological systems (such as watersheds, ocean fisheries and forests) remain diverse and productive over time. Yet, since its early beginnings, the concept of sustainability has encompassed more than just the need to preserve nature. By the start of the 18th century, intensive logging for the mining industry and smelting of ores had resulted in an acute scarcity of timber, threatening the livelihood of thousands in Saxony (today's Germany). The region's mining administrator, Hans Carl von Carlowitz, fought this threat by introducing the principle of sustainability that limited the felling of timber to the number of trees that were expected to grow back. This became the first clearly formulated concept of sustainability in forestry, acknowledging the intrinsic relationship between natural resource management, human well-being and economic prosperity. In more general terms, it recognised the interconnections between the environmental, social and economic aspects of sustainability.

It was not until the late 1900s, however, that the term 'sustainable development', that is the relationship between human development and environmental sustainability, was defined on an international level. In 1987, the World Commission on Environment and Development (WCED), under the chair of the former Norwegian prime minister, Gro Brundtland, famously defined the sustainable development:

> *'Sustainable development is the development that meets the needs of the present without compromising the ability of future generations to meet their own needs.'* *(WCED, 1987).*

Over the last two decades, there have been a number of international agreements and declarations addressing the need for sustainable development.

- In 1992, the United Nations (UN) Conference on Environment and Development in Rio de Janeiro (the Earth Summit) adopted two milestone frameworks for sustainable development: *Agenda 21*, an action plan related to sustainable development, and the *Convention on Biological Diversity*, which focused on the conservation and sustainable use of biological diversity.
- The *Kyoto Protocol* of 1997 committed industrialised nations to binding targets to reduce CO_2 emissions by 5% compared to 1990 levels by the year 2012.
- In 1999, the UN launched the initiative *Global Compact*, which embraced guiding principles for human rights, labour and environmental protection and established a system of sustainable principles for business enterprises.
- In 2000, the UN adopted the *Millennium Declaration* (or *Millennium Development Goals*), with the aim of ensuring the well-being of future generations. A new set of UN *Sustainable Development Goals* are currently being developed to replace the Millennium Goals, which expire in 2015.
- The UN Climate Change Conferences in 2009 and 2010, which had all governments in attendance, including those of the US and China, committing to the goal of limiting global warming to 2°C above pre-industrial levels and to take further measures to combat climate change.
- Lastly, in November 2014, the Intergovernmental Panel on Climate Change's (IPCC) *Fifth Assessment Synthesis Report* warned that 'climate change is a threat to sustainable development' and that avoiding such a threat will require 'substantial emissions reductions over the next few decades and near zero emissions of CO_2 and other long-lived GHGs [greenhouse gases] by the end of the century'.
- In December 2015, the COP21, also known as the 2015 Paris Climate Conference, reached an agreement to pursue efforts to limit the global temperature increase to 1.5°C.

1.2.2 The need for sustainable infrastructure

Progress in sustainable development will depend in large part on the development of sustainable infrastructure. It is estimated that by 2050 the world population will reach 9–10 billion (UN, 2015a). By then, three billion people (40% of today's global population) will be brought into the 'middle class' (Bloomberg Business, 2012). This will result in a significant demand for new energy, water, social and transportation infrastructure.

To this end, the OECD estimates that the current, business-as-usual approach to infrastructure development will lead to unsustainable increases in both water consumption (55%) and energy demand (85%), ending in a potential collapse of the global water supply and dangerous

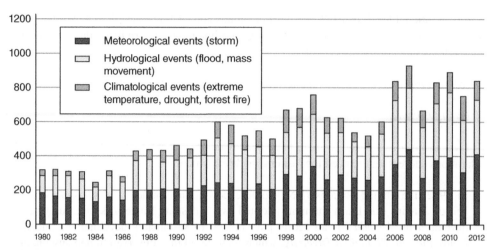

FIGURE 1.5 Weather-related catastrophes worldwide 1980–2012
Source: Munich RE (2013)

climate change-driven events, such as extreme heatwaves, increased frequency and severity of storms, increased river flooding and rises in sea levels (OECD, 2012). In fact, environmental risks such as water scarcity and weather-related catastrophes have been on the rise over the last several decades. For example, Figure 1.5 illustrates the rapid surge in weather-related catastrophes over three decades. Such extreme weather events can lead to increased risks to the physical integrity and functionality of infrastructure systems (see Section 5.2.4.1).

In conclusion, constraints from economic development, global population growth, resource scarcity, human rights and labour issues and climate change will require a 'change of strategy', a shift towards consequent sustainable infrastructure development. A condition for this to happen is that investors in infrastructure integrate sustainability considerations as a matter of course in any decision-making process. See Section 2.2 for further discussion on this topic.

1.3 DEFINITION AND CHARACTERISTICS OF INFRASTRUCTURE

The term 'infrastructure' was originally used in the military context to refer to military assets such as barracks and airfields. Relatively recently, it has come to mean the necessary organisational backbone supporting an economy. However, a huge variety of definitions has been suggested by national agencies, national and regional governments, academia, dictionaries and of course the financial community, and infrastructure can, as a result, encompass all things to all people. This approach is hardly a useful way to define infrastructure, but instead clouds the ability of investors, governments and their citizens to understand, advocate and direct capital towards these assets (Fulmer, 2009). Therefore, this section provides an overview of various definitions of the term with the aim to reach a single definition to be used in this book.

One of the broadest definitions of 'infrastructure' can be traced back to Jochimsen (1966), who focuses on infrastructure's role in the development of a market economy. To this end, he considers not only economic and technological elements but also social and cultural aspects in the equation. Accordingly, he describes 'infrastructure' as:

> *the sum of all material, institutional and personal assets, facilities and conditions available to an economy based on the division of labour and its individual economic units that contribute to realising the assimilation of factor remuneration, given an expedient allocation of resources. The term material infrastructure stands for the sum of all physical assets, equipment and facilities and the term institutional infrastructure points to the norms and rules, which develop and are set in a society over time; in addition, the term personal infrastructure is used to encompass the number and qualities of people in a market economy.*

With this definition, Jochimsen refers back to the works of List (1841) and Malinowski (1944/2006). Jochimsen focused on these issues because a central question in economic policy was, and still is, to determine the conditions necessary for the development and growth of a market economy as well as the various required types of infrastructure.

In turn, the narrowest definition (or understanding) of infrastructure is found within the financial industry. Given the focus of this book, this definition is of particular interest and therefore is addressed in more detail here.

The key factor for any investor is ultimately not the specific infrastructure sector or supply characteristics of a physical infrastructure asset but rather its specific risk-return profile, which largely depends on the various characteristics of the respective investment opportunity. For this reason, the financial industry took it upon itself to define infrastructure on the basis of certain economic and financial characteristics (see Section 2.1). However, the characteristics they introduce effectively only apply to a small subset of the universe of real infrastructure assets in existence, namely the conservatively structured ones. These characteristics are:

- *Key public service.* Infrastructure assets meet key public requirements in everyday life, such as the provision of water, energy, mobility, communications, education, security, culture or healthcare, making them a basic prerequisite for economic growth, prosperity and quality of life.
- *Low elasticity of demand.* Owing to their fundamental functions, demand for such infrastructure services is relatively independent of industry cycles and economic performance even when prices increase (e.g. owing to inflation adjustment regulations), stable (i.e. subject to low volatility) and predictable (e.g. due to long-term contracts).
- *(Quasi-)monopoly situation with high barriers to market entry.* Infrastructure assets are hard to duplicate on account of the high start-up investment costs for the construction of a water, electricity or telephone network, for example. After commissioning, the cost of providing each additional service/product unit (e.g. a new connection to the water supply or an extra unit of electricity supply) is comparatively low. This combination of circumstances means the barriers to market entry are high. Accordingly, these kinds of infrastructure assets have little or no competition.
- *Regulation.* In situations with little or no competition, regulatory authorities perform a corrective function on the market (e.g. by fixing prices or providing minimum payments guarantees). However, a regulated market per se does not necessarily eliminate the market risk for the provider. The best example of this is the telecommunications market.

■ *Long service life.* Infrastructure assets have service lives of as much as 100 years or more. There are many historical examples with significantly longer lives, such as the Roman aqueducts. In addition to the physical and technical life of an asset, however, a key factor is its economic life, which may be even less than five years in the case of laboratory or medical facilities. For investors, the amortisation of their investments over the economic life of the asset is important.

■ *Inflation protection.* Infrastructure assets may provide a natural hedge against inflation, because revenue from infrastructure investments is often combined with inflation adjustment mechanisms, whether through regulated income clauses, guaranteed yields or any other form of contractual guarantees. Project income generated via user charges (e.g. toll roads, public utility plants) rather than availability payments is usually tied to GDP or the consumer price index (CPI).

■ *Regular, stable cash flows.* Infrastructure assets that possess the characteristics listed above generally have stable, predictable and in most cases inflation-adjusted long-term revenues that can survive economic downturns and cycles and support a significant credit burden.

Although these generalised characteristics serve as an indicator of the potential attractiveness of infrastructure investments as a whole, only *some* infrastructure assets of the available universe conform strictly to these characteristics. There are just as many 'real' infrastructure assets that meet them only in part. In other words, infrastructure assets *may* have the comparatively low-risk, in some cases bond-like, characteristics highlighted by the financial industry. Not every real infrastructure asset, however – be it greenfield or brownfield – possesses these characteristics, and in particular the associated risk-return profile. Notwithstanding, they are all infrastructure assets.

This inconsistency – not to say misrepresentation – has led to considerable confusion among investors who – in real life – are effectively confronted with all kinds of infrastructure assets, the characteristics of which go unsurprisingly beyond the financial industry's 'definition'. In the opinion of the authors, this definition is not only short-sighted but also risks misleading investors who are less familiar with infrastructure as an asset class.

Hence, what the financial community needs is a realistic, practical and pragmatic definition of infrastructure that considers all kinds of assets and all the aspects mentioned above rather than denying their existence.

Further, it would be salutary at this point to remember that the modern general linguistic usage of the term 'infrastructure' identifies it with *material* infrastructure, that is *physical* assets such as roads, ports, utilities and the like (Frey, 1978). Although Buhr (2007) generally agrees with the practical focus on material infrastructure, he classifies it by initially concentrating on the physical and social needs of human living, in order then to deduce the required infrastructure output (e.g. water, energy, heat, light) and the associated physical assets (material infrastructure).

Following a similar line of thought, Fulmer (2009) finds that 'inconsistencies and sector-specific biases abound ... common threads run through the myriads of definitions. Nearly all mention or imply the following characteristics: interrelated systems, physical components and societal needs'. A sample definition is:

> *'The infrastructure supporting human activities includes complex and interrelated physical, social, economic, and technological systems such as transportation and*

energy production and distribution; water resources management; waste management; facilities supporting urban and rural communities; communications; sustainable resources development; and environmental protection (American Society of Civil Engineers, 2015).'

Aiming to come up with a practical definition that integrates the common themes of systems, physical assets and societal needs, Fulmer (2009) concisely suggests:

'the physical components of interrelated systems providing commodities and services essential to enable, sustain, or enhance societal living conditions'.

Following this brief overview of the variety of definitions and understandings of infrastructure prevalent in the market, this book also seeks to address 'only' material infrastructure and its underlying structures, organisations, business models, rules and regulations. This includes all physical assets, equipment and facilities of interrelated systems and their necessary service providers offering related commodities and services to the individual economic entities or the wider public with the aim of enabling, sustaining or enhancing societal living conditions (see Figure 1.6).

Economic infrastructure				Social infrastructure
Transport	**Energy**	**Water**	**Communication**	

Land
– Roads
– Rail networks
– Public local
  transport
 	
Water
– Inland waterways
– Sea
– Canals (e.g. Suez)
– Ports
 	
Air
– Airport services
– Airline services
– Air traffic control
 	
Multimodal
– Inland terminals
  (road/rail-freight)
– Cruise terminals
	Generation Conventional
	– Coal
	– Oil/gas
	– Nuclear
	Renewable
	– Solar
	– Wind
	– Water
	– Biomass
	– Geothermal
	Transmission/Distribution
	– Electricity
	– Gas
	– Oil/fuels
	
	Storage
	– Electricity
	– Gas
	– Oil/fuels
	
	District Heating
		Supply
		– Domestic
		– Industrial
		Sewerage
		– Rain water
		– Domestic
		  wastewater
		– Industrial
		  wastewater
		
		Waste
		– Domestic waste
		– Industrial waste
			Telecommunication
			– Fixed networks
			– Mobile networks
			– High-speed
			  internet
			– Towers (cell &
			  broadcast)
			Space
			– Satellite network
			– Observation
			Other services
				Health
				– Diagnostic
				– Therapy/treatment
				– Care
				– Rehabilitation
				– Elderly housing
				Education/Culture
				– Schools
				– Student housing
				  (campus)
				– Libraries
				– Theatres
				– Museums
				Sport
				– Recreational
				– Professional
				Public administration
				– Offices
				– E-government
				Security
				– Prisons
				– Police
				– Defence

FIGURE 1.6   Infrastructure: sectors and subsectors

1.3.1   Differentiation of terms: project – asset – facility

Infrastructure projects, assets and/or facilities exist in the form of strictly public, public and private or private ownership structures. By definition, private investors may only invest in infrastructure projects or assets in the public/private or pure private space. An investment in a newly founded public/private partnership usually takes the form of a project (e.g. a PPP-project) whereby the private partner obtains a concession, a licence or any other kind of PPP-contract from the public partner (and owner) for a specific period. In a purely private structure, the focus is on assets or facilities whereby one or several private partners (will) own the infrastructure asset in question. The following explanation serves to explain why and how this book differentiates between these three terms: project, asset and facility.

The terms 'asset' and 'facility' represent the physical objects of the 'material infrastructure' (i.e. the physical road, power plant, school, etc.). As such, they form part of the 'built environment' of the economic and social infrastructure, and the investor becomes a full or partial owner of the existing (or future) asset/facility. The difference between asset and facility seems to be more a question of use of language in different professional disciplines. Whereas architects and engineers, especially in real estate, tend to talk about facilities, the finance industry seems to prefer the term 'asset'. Because this book forms part of the finance literature, it predominantly, but not exclusively, uses the term 'asset' rather than 'facility'.

Investment in infrastructure projects primarily differ from those in infrastructure assets as in the former, the investor does not necessarily become the full or partial owner of the assets in question. Rather, the investor invests in or finances the provision of an asset – i.e. the development and construction as well as its operation and maintenance – and in exchange is granted either the revenues generated by the project or a regular payment (for example availability payment) from the principle during the course of a clearly defined project. In PPP projects, for example, the private investor usually 'only' becomes shareholder of a 'project company', which in turn is responsible for the provision of the assets for a certain period. The ownership of the assets remains with the public partner. In addition, projects have a time limit by definition. Accordingly, the investment in an infrastructure project ends with its termination determined by the project contract.

As a consequence of the particular ownership status of the private investor and its defined time limit, infrastructure projects require a structure with which private investors can generate sufficient revenue during the project life to satisfy their return requirements. They cannot sell the assets at the end, because they typically do not own them in the first place. In contrast, investments in assets don't have such a defined ending and hence do not have this formal requirement. While their official lifetime may come to an end, the asset remains (physically) in existence and the investor remains the owner of the asset, with which it can do what it wants.

Unfortunately, in the general linguistic usage, the terms 'project' and 'asset' are not as neatly differentiated. Irrespective of ownership and a defined termination, the term 'project' is often used during development and construction of an asset. Once the asset is (physically) built and goes into operation – which often coincides with the point in time it is sold on to investors – the same project (asset) is labelled 'asset' from then on. Needless to say, this makes matters complicated and sometimes confusing. The confusion goes on with the term 'project company', which is often also used in situations where the term 'asset company' (which does not exist as such), 'company' or 'SPV' (special purpose vehicle) would have to be used to be precise. This book cannot solve this problem but tries to be consistent by referring to 'project company' only, when the term is used in the narrower sense. Otherwise, it refers to '(project) company', 'company' or 'SPV'.

This book cannot ignore the general linguistic usage of the term altogether. Hence, it aims to find a middle way while being as precise as possible.

1.3.2 Characteristics

On the basis of this broadly accepted definition of infrastructure outlined above and a short explanation as to how to differentiate the terms 'project', 'asset' and 'facility', Figure 1.7 shows how infrastructure in that sense can be further broken down on the basis of its country-specific, sector- and subsector-specific and project/asset-specific characteristics.

Country-specific characteristics generally describe the legal, political, institutional, economic, financial and entrepreneurial framework and the conditions of competition with a tangible influence on any asset, and hence any investment in such assets. These may vary significantly from country to country and therefore cannot be discussed in detail in this book. However, the various international examples discussed throughout the book are intended to provide at least an insight into them. In addition, sectors or subsectors and their specific structural, regulatory and contractual conditions and, in particular, the project/asset- and transaction-specific characteristics are extremely important.

The sector- and subsector-specific characteristics, listed in Figure 1.6, may vary considerably from country to country. Certain aspects, however, apply to all sectors alike and hence may be addressed on a cross-sector basis, as it is done in this chapter from Section 1.3.3 onwards. In Chapter 4, these and other characteristics are discussed in detail on a subsector level.

In addition to the country- and sector-specific characteristics, notable project-, asset- and transaction-specific characteristics and risks may influence the risk-return profile of an individual infrastructure project/asset in a particular sector and country. These are addressed in detail in Chapter 5 and Chapter 6 in conjunction with the discussion of the most important

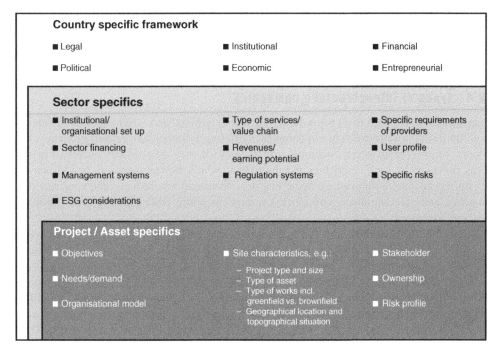

FIGURE 1.7   Country-, sector- and project/asset-specific characteristics

risks facing infrastructure assets (Chapter 5) and the project finance structures that are most commonly used or required to finance direct investments (Chapter 6).

The following sections provide an initial insight into the universal, cross-sectorial aspects of infrastructure provision and some key determining factors behind investments in infrastructure.

1.3.3 Cross-sector characteristics

Figure 1.6 (Section 1.3 above) gives an overview of the most important infrastructure sectors and their subsectors. Each of these infrastructure sectors – and often also their subsectors – are subject to individual structural, regulatory and contractual conditions with which investors should intensively familiarise themselves prior to any investment (see also Figure 1.7). A knowledge of the responsibilities and the distribution of functions within the public administration, the existing financing structures and sources of revenue, the existing privatisation models and their structures and procedures and the specific legislative framework, norms, standards and other rules and regulations, which may vary significantly between the individual sectors and subsectors and from country to country, is essential for a successful investment. In addition, investors must examine the individual infrastructure elements or value chain elements of a sector in terms of their consistency with the investors' overriding investment strategy, the corresponding revenue and earnings structure and the compatibility of the interfaces with other components within the integrated value chain. Examples include the network, passenger and goods transportation services and stations owned by railway companies. The transportation services are often privatised, whereas the network and the stations remain in the hands and under the control of the government. This requires a precise definition of the allocation of functions, responsibilities, risks, mutual requirements and interfaces. Potential investors should also be aware of the specific competitive structures in the respective sector, including any regulatory systems that may be in place.

1.3.4 Types of infrastructure companies

Financial investors (such as pension funds, insurance groups, and sovereign wealth funds) generally invest in infrastructure via companies offering infrastructure-related products and services, which operate as self-contained entities. As such, they are primarily interested in the profits generated by such companies and the risks to which they are exposed. In addition to the return on capital employed, strategic investors (corporations from e.g. the construction, real estate, and telecommunications sector) examine the profits from additional value to their own core operations.

Infrastructure companies can be broken down into three types: (i) project companies, (ii) operating companies and (iii) service companies, depending on their typical business purpose.

Infrastructure project companies have a business purpose that is closely linked to a specific project in terms of location, timing and functions. A typical example would be a PPP road project between points A and B, under which the construction, financing/investment and operation is transferred to a company that is specially formed for this purpose for a period of, for example, 30 years under the terms of an agreement with the characteristics of a contract for work and services, with ownership returning to the public-sector principal at the end of the contractual term.

This company may have an exclusively private-sector shareholder structure or may have both public- and private-sector shareholders. Typical (first-time) investors include strategic investors such as construction groups or infrastructure operating companies (discussed below), which expect to generate a profit from their core operations in addition to the return on their capital. Financial investors often – though not always – invest after the ramp-up phase, replacing the strategic investors in part or in full. Ownership of the infrastructure assets commonly remains with the public-sector principal or is transferred to the company only for the term of the contract. The remuneration structure, that is the future sources of revenue from the company (for the investors), may include one of the following:

- *Fixed availability fees:* to be paid by the principal, usually the government, via the state budget depending on the performance of the contractual services, under which the investors are exposed solely to performance risk.
- *User fees:* the project company obtains a concession granting it the right to levy fees in order to finance the contractual services – including the investments – via the users of the asset or services provided; in this case, investors are exposed to demand risk as well as performance risk, although this may be cushioned to a greater or lesser extent by government guarantees, depending on the respective circumstances and contractual agreements.
- *User-driven payments:* availability payments by the principal, paid from the public budget and linked to usage (e.g. frequency and/or intensity of use, see also Section 3.3) or a combination of availability fees and user fees in order to align incentives and optimally meet project service quality and/or financial viability.

During the tender process of a new project, which is still partially or fully owned by the public sector, investors are in competition for this project. Once any single or group of bidders win the tender, their project company is likely to face little or no competition on the open market. In case such project companies are subject to direct-user payments, projects are usually fee-regulated in order to protect users from a potentially monopolistic situation. Infrastructure project companies are becoming increasingly common around the world, with examples found in practically all infrastructure sectors.

In contrast to pure project companies, *infrastructure operating companies* have an essentially unlimited scope in terms of timing and location. Rather than concentrating on a specific project or asset, they generally focus on one (e.g. utilities) or several (e.g. multi-utility companies) infrastructure sectors. These purely private or mixed-ownership companies invest in infrastructure assets and perform comprehensive infrastructure services on their own account and their own responsibility with a direct (contractual) relationship with the users, who ensure that the asset and/or service is financed via user charges. They also invest in infrastructure project companies. In contrast to project companies, operating companies are established as permanent entities and generally also own at least those infrastructure assets that they are permanently responsible for operating; as such, they are exposed to both performance and demand risk.

Private infrastructure operating companies often arise from enterprises that were originally in the public sector, whether as the result of an initial public offering (IPO) or the auction of some (partial privatisation) or all (full privatisation) of the shares in the existing enterprises by way of a public tender. Privatisation is often driven by the need for additional capital to renovate or expand the company's existing infrastructure assets. The involvement of private investors also seeks to achieve more efficient structures and improved performance on the part of the company. These companies are, in most instances, in direct competition with other similar companies on the market. Where monopoly situations exist, the respective companies are subject to regulation with regard to the services they need to offer and the pricing policy they need to follow in the respective markets at the very least. Notable examples include power suppliers, such as E.ON and EDF; water suppliers, such as Veolia and Suez; waste disposal companies, such as Sita (Suez) and Remondis; and telecommunications companies, such as Vodafone and Telefonica, as well as global providers of transport infrastructure, for example toll roads (e.g. Vinci, Abertis), airports (e.g. AviAlliance, Fraport) or port terminals (e.g. APM Terminals, Hutchinson Port Holdings).

Infrastructure service companies focus on one or more service categories in one or more infrastructure sectors and perform these services in exchange for contractually agreed fees. Examples include consulting, construction and facility management companies and other companies or service providers, for example Techem, which specialises in recording data on energy and water consumption in Germany. Generally speaking, this type of company does not invest in infrastructure in its own right, does not perform any cross-lifecycle infrastructure services and hence is not exposed to any of the corresponding performance or demand risks. However, their service range is always subject to a relatively large degree of pressure from competing companies.

Following the definition of infrastructure outlined above, in this book infrastructure service companies are not considered part of the 'asset class infrastructure'. They are described only in order to clearly delimit them from the other types of infrastructure companies.

As can be seen above, any infrastructure investment decision must take into account the type of company in question and its specific infrastructure involvement. It is also important to examine the infrastructure sector in which the company is primarily active. To this end, it is essential to become familiar with the characteristics of the individual infrastructure in order to be able to assess in particular the specific risks arising as a result. This is especially important for infrastructure project and infrastructure operating companies, owing to the particularly long term of their involvement and the fact that they are usually backed by a substantial amount of initial equity. It is somewhat less crucial for infrastructure service companies, which can be replaced or move in and out of a project relatively easily.

1.3.5 Role of the private sector

A growing number of infrastructure assets are being operated by or in cooperation with private investors and operators, for example energy transmission assets or assets under long-term (PPP) concession agreements. However, the nature and extent of the private sector's involvement and the individual business models vary significantly between the different infrastructure sectors and subsectors. Private-sector participation in 'public functions' involving private investment may range from PPP models based on long-term contractual arrangements through to full material privatisation, under which private providers operate an asset on a permanent and independent basis in competition with other private-sector or, in some cases, public-sector providers.

Certain sectors are naturally unsuited to the full range of privatisation models (for a detailed description and discussion of the different privatisation models – formal, functional and material privatisation, see Section 3.1). In the road sector or certain fields of social infrastructure, for example, there are practically no examples of full privatisation anywhere in the world; instead, a highly diversified range of PPP models exists. Publicly dedicated roads, military and police facilities, correctional service facilities and educational establishments are usually owned by the public sector and required to remain as such by law. The energy and telecommunications sectors, in contrast, both have been fully privatised in a number of countries. The large number of airports privatised over the past 15 to 20 years use both PPP models and full or partial material privatisation models. In some sectors, private and public structures exist alongside each other at every stage of the value chain, for example where individual private operators use the public rail network in exchange for track charges, individual private port terminals are granted concessions by the public-sector operators of the main port facilities, or waste water is transported via the public sewer system to a private sewerage treatment plant. In the waste sector, however, these priorities are harder to distinguish. For example, although the private sector's involvement in Spain and Germany focuses on waste disposal, particularly in the form of incineration plants, waste collection in Sweden is largely performed by private companies and disposal is primarily organised by the public administration (PSIRU, 2006).

As well as the boundaries and opportunities inherent to the system, aspects such as tradition, public-sector mentality and existing structures that are often difficult to change may serve to promote or restrict the use of the full range of existing organisational models, or even prevent the possibility of private investment in public infrastructure altogether.

This discussion makes apparent the significant sector- and country-specific variations in the models used for private-sector investment. There is very little standardisation with regard to the chosen business models or even the underlying contractual models. On the contrary, some of the models and structures that have evolved have their own terminology and are essentially impossible to compare. An internationally understood and accepted, cross-sector standardisation would be highly desirable, not to mention extremely useful to investors. To this end, Chapter 3 of this book in particular systematically records, defines and classifies the known privatisation, partnership, business, contractual and financial models that can (or indeed should) be combined and structured to an overall organisational model for every individual infrastructure project/asset.

1.3.6 Value chain elements

The individual elements of the value chains of the various infrastructure sectors can be broken down into two types: (i) movable and immovable assets belonging to the service range offered by the respective subsector and (ii) the service range itself.

Movable assets, such as locomotives and carriages in the rail sector or ships in the water transport sector, and immovable assets, that is fixed buildings and physical structures, represent the actual investable assets as independent elements of the value chain. These are combined with additional elements such as planning, construction (erection and provision of equipment), financing, and constructive and operational maintenance (comprehensive overhaul measures and ongoing maintenance respectively). Constructive and operational maintenance are often aggregated as the operation of infrastructure assets.

The elements associated with the realisation and operation of movable and immovable assets exist to a greater or lesser extent for every type of infrastructure service and differ only in terms of the type of asset involved. The providers of such services include engineering offices, construction firms and facility managers for the performance of technical functions, and financiers, that is investors and banks, for investment and financing. These parties frequently offer cross-sector services rather than specialise in a specific type of infrastructure. For example, larger engineering offices and construction firms may perform planning and construction services for roads, airports and railways as well as hydropower plants, water mains and sewage treatment plants.

Investors can be broken down into pure financial investors, primarily interested in the return on the equity or debt they invest (also called institutional investors), and strategic investors, who expect, in addition to a financial return, various forms of value chain elements from the aforementioned services. Accordingly, financial investors largely invest across various sectors, primarily driven by risk and return considerations (for further detail, see Section 1.3.8), whereas strategic investors tend to limit themselves to those sectors that are strategically relevant to them. As such, the latter group derives its total return from a mixed calculation.

The associated services – often provided by the strategic investors themselves – can vary significantly from sector to sector and require wide-ranging knowledge and expertise. Depending on the perspective adopted, entire sector- and subsector-specific elements of the value chain can be broken down into individual elements or combined to form a value chain in a more or less aggregated or differentiated form. For example, the water sector consists of water supply, waste water disposal and, owing to its environmental relevance, watercourse maintenance and expansion. In turn, the supply of (drinking) water is composed of the elements of catchment, collection, storage, preparation, distribution (to the domestic or industrial supply point) and billing. Each of these individual elements can also be broken down further. As such, the differences between the service ranges offered by each infrastructure company are just as pronounced.

For investors, this knowledge and the resulting opportunities for structuring their investments are important, because different individual or combined service ranges can allow them to leverage different elements of the value chain, and hence access a different risk level and related return or yield potential. Investments may also seek (i) to leverage additional upside potential by expanding or, in some cases, (ii) concentrating the activities of the company itself. Expansion or concentration processes may relate to a specific region or customer base or to the value chain as a whole and are usually structured following three diversification principles.

In the first case, known as *horizontal diversification or integration*, companies offering the same or similar elements of the value chain are combined with a view to expanding market share, that is realising economies of scale and increasing market power. Returning to the example of the water sector, horizontal integration is particularly relevant because of the existence of natural monopolies. With almost no exceptions, business combinations are implemented with the aim of expanding regional service areas.

In the second case, known as *vertical diversification or integration*, a company expands its activities to deepen its value chain by incorporating additional elements. This may affect the depth (e.g. expansion of capacities for the realisation of components/services within a production or service process that were previously procured externally) or breadth (e.g. expansion of product or service range) of the value chain or the number of steps in the value chain (e.g. the upstream or downstream integration of individual consecutive elements in the value chain).

A further option in the infrastructure sector is *lateral diversification*, in which companies connect elements of entirely unrelated value chains. Common examples include multi-utility companies in the private sector and public or semi-public utilities, which may offer a wide range of supply, disposal and transport services or bundle all three service areas. In particular, the network infrastructures for water, electricity, gas, transport, telecommunications, etc., and the potentially largely identical customer bases of these otherwise extremely different sectors, may offer significant synergy potential and hence provide a strong incentive to bundle services in this way.

Financial investors may also want to apply general corporate objectives, which are pursued typically by strategic investors when considering whether to make an investment. Strategic investors principally make investments in order to achieve one of the following:

- Meet additional (internal or external) demand/requirements (new and/or expansion investments).
- Compensate for technical and/or economic obsolescence (overhaul/replacement investments).
- Leverage additional efficiency potential within an element (streamlining investments).

They base their investment decision either – in the case of a PPP project – on the corresponding tender requirements or – in the case of a pure private project/asset – on internal considerations. Depending on the maturity of a project or asset, one or multiple objectives may apply in the course of a certain contract period.

1.3.7 Greenfield versus brownfield investments

In the context of infrastructure investing, a distinction is usually made between greenfield and brownfield investments, otherwise known as 'project development and operational assets' or primary and secondary projects respectively. These classifications reflect the specific (project/asset) risks associated with their different development stages. Investors tend to assume that the risk of a greenfield investment is always higher than that of a brownfield investment. As we will see, this is generally a safe assumption to make. In specific cases, however, it may be surprising to learn that selected greenfield investments have a level of risk similar to that of brownfield investments (see also Weber, 2009).

This book defines greenfield (or primary) projects as assets that are constructed for the first time at a specific site. They may be in the planning, development, financing or construction stage. In contrast, brownfield or secondary projects/assets are already operational and/or have a predecessor of some description at the same location. These projects may involve the reconstruction, renovation or expansion of existing assets. In other words, the key differences lie in the maturity of the asset and the available asset-specific experience, which is significantly less in the case of greenfield projects. This may lead to a considerably higher degree of uncertainty and risk on the cost and revenue side.

The cost-side risks of greenfield projects primarily relate to planning, development, the receipt of approvals and environmental permits, public acceptance and construction and operation, particularly where new and unproven technologies are used; compare the construction of a new hydropower plant with the expansion of an existing plant to install additional turbines, for instance. On the revenue-side, demand and price uncertainty constitute the primary risks. This applies in particular to user payment projects (see Section 1.3.9 and Section 3.3). They can only be fully identified once the facility has been taken into operation. For example, toll roads in comparatively undeveloped areas are considered significantly more risky than comparable projects, which replace existing road connections with proven high volumes of traffic. Even in the latter case, however, the acceptance/usage and price risk remains if the previous road was toll-free and there is a corresponding lack of historical data with regard to price sensitivity of users. The revenue risk of greenfield projects with revenues, which are covered partially or entirely by public funds and/or guarantees from trustworthy institutions should ideally be eliminated by way of the project (contractual) structure (again, see Section 1.3.9).

By contrast, brownfield projects relate to existing, operational assets that have already gone through the greenfield/development phase. All the risks related to the development phase or to environmental issues, public acceptance, the approval process, commissioning, technology and initial demand will have been dealt with already at the brownfield stage. The main residual risks are operational risk, regulatory risk and market risk, to a lesser extent geographical, political, legal and ESG risk. However, some of the typical greenfield risks may reappear if extensive replacement or expansion measures become necessary, such as the demolition and reconstruction of an existing facility.

As a matter of principle, existing assets are comparatively easy to evaluate (e.g. in terms of demand, operation and maintenance, ESG issues) on the basis of historical data and past experience. However, certain risks, which, for example, may result from operating an asset, such as contamination or hidden defects may become highly relevant for investments in brownfield infrastructure assets.

A further important difference between greenfield and brownfield investments is that investors in greenfield projects do not generally return a profit on their investments in the first years of the development and construction phase but instead are merely required to make payments. Initial capital is only returned when the respective facility is operative (resulting in a so-called 'J curve', which is typical of cash flows from private equity investments). Investors, which are predominantly interested in (increasing) the IRR accept this J curve and the generally higher risk associated with greenfield compared to brownfield investments because they can participate in the potentially high appreciation of value of the asset in this phase and possibly generate higher returns as a result (see also Section 1.3.8).

By contrast, brownfield assets in good condition with long-term contracts will ideally offer stable, predictable current cash flows from the very start in the form of dividends or interest payments in a similar way to real-estate or fixed-income products. As a result, they tend to be particularly suitable for risk-averse yield-driven investors, whereas greenfield projects are more appropriate for capital-gain or growth-style investors who are prepared to take additional risk (see also Section 1.3.8 and Chapter 2).

However, it would be a mistake to conclude that necessarily every brownfield investment has low-risk, bond-like returns. The risk profile of brownfield assets exposed to full market risk (demand or price) or in poor condition – for example owing to their age, inadequate main-tenance, weak management, heavy usage and/or financial distress because of, for example, high leverage or no long-term contracts – may be quite high and the return/cash flow profile very unpredictable and unstable. In this case, the aim is to generate additional value through signing long-term contracts, which reduce or even eliminate the market risk or through oper-ational improvements, repairs and capacity expansions, new forms of use or financial and/or contractual renegotiations and restructuring, for example.

1.3.8 Yield-driven versus IRR-driven investors

All investors in infrastructure generally share certain financial goals, they do not form a homogeneous group by any means and their individual interests may differ when it comes to investing in infrastructure assets.[1] In addition to differing individual risk-return profiles reflected in the selection of certain countries, sectors, stages of entry, currencies and the like, the targeted cash flow profiles, which are mostly closely linked to the investors' investment horizon for such assets, may differ as well.

When making infrastructure equity investments, strategic and financial investors generally pursue one of two overriding financial objectives, or a combination of the two: (i) ensuring a stable, high level of current income (yield) and/or (ii) ensuring the greatest possible return on equity (see also Sections 1.2 and 7.1). To this end, a distinction can be made between primarily yield-driven and IRR-driven investors.

Yield-driven investors, which include insurance companies, private and corporate pension funds, sovereign wealth funds, charitable foundations and so on, typically have a long-term (buy-and-hold) investment horizon with no short- or medium-term intention to sell the asset in question. They rely purely on the current yield in the form of dividends and interest on share-holder loans, e.t.c. They will be referred to as 'yield investors' throughout the book. Typically, IRR-driven investors have a short- to medium-term time horizon of two to approximately seven years. Such investors include the resale value of the asset at the exit into their overall return calculation and are – mostly – prepared to forego early and/or current cash flows while holding the asset. Development and construction (greenfield) assets are a case in point. This category of investor includes strategic investors, investment funds managed by professional investment managers as well as any institutional investor with a similar short-term investment focus. They will be referred to as 'IRR investors' throughout the book. Naturally, this categorisation provides an indication only; combinations and exceptions exist in either group of investors.

Among the reasons for these differing investment interests is that yield investors tend to need a stable, long-term income in order to match the maturities of their assets with the maturities of their liabilities (e.g., pension obligations, life insurance), not least due to the strict requirements of the financial authorities and the regulatory bodies (see also Section 1.2). Typical approaches include investments in long-term government bonds with a term of 10, 20 or even 50 years, as well as real estate. However, government bonds are comparatively unattractive – if not simply insufficient from a return perspective – in periods of low interest rates and flat yield curves. Equity investments in conservatively structured, long-term infrastructure may offer an alternative with an acceptable risk level (sometimes they entail even primarily sovereign risk) and a current income (yield) superior to that of government bonds and/or real estate. Long-term (high-yielding) infrastructure bonds are another alternative (i.e. see Section 7.3. 'Debt').

Short- to mid-term oriented, return maximising IIR investors in contrast, require, and hence are attracted by, the possibility of an early exit (an investment horizon of two to seven years). For IIR investors to invest in an asset, they need the option to sell their interest in it after a certain date prior to e.g. the end of the project lifetime or prior to the repayment of the debt, without jeopardising the long-term success of the entire project/asset or the financing, if any. As a matter of principle, the following exit strategies may come into consideration for equity investors in infrastructure: sale via the secondary market, a trade sale or an IPO (see Section 7.1 for further detail).

---

[1]To this end, Section 6.3.2.2 'Equity providers' discusses the, in some cases differing, *strategic* objectives of strategic investors and institutional financial investors. This section continues by focusing on the differing *financial* objectives of equity investors.

Recently, financial investors are increasingly involved in the development, structuring and implementation of infrastructure from the very start (see also Section 6.3.2.2 'Equity providers'). Their early involvement brings additional structuring expertise to the table, particularly with regard to financial considerations, and is instrumental in making the realisation of many new projects possible. It also increases the likelihood of a smooth sale from strategic investors to financial investors at a later point in time of the investment because the structure will be generally suitable for financial investors.

1.3.9 Sources of revenue and financing

Revenue of some sort is required in order to finance infrastructure investments and the subsequent operation of the respective assets, whether from public or private sources. In most countries, financing and operational functions of infrastructure are housed with different public-sector offices depending on the infrastructure asset in question. In a purely state-based system, revenue is generated from taxes and duties that may be sector-specific (e.g. motor vehicle tax in the road transport sector) or general (e.g. income tax) as well as direct-user payments, which are naturally sector-specific in their nature (e.g. tolls, water charges, waste collection charges). In general, government revenue/expenditure systems are based on the principle of general budget appropriation, meaning that all sources of revenue are initially aggregated – in the form of the public budget – before being allocated to the individual area-specific budgets on the basis of corresponding negotiations. This applies equally to general and sector-specific taxes, duties and user charges. Irrespective of the principle of general budget appropriation, some countries earmark certain proceeds for a specific purpose, for example revenue that can be directly allocated to a specific sector – whether in the form of taxes, duties or user charges – is also dispensed in the same sector, that is on a sector-specific basis. Such revenue does not reach the general public budget, but instead remains in the budget of the respective sector. One typical example is road funds, which are generated from fuel duty, motor vehicle tax and, where applicable, toll revenue, that is without being fed into the wider public budget at any point.

The clearest case of earmarking is when a government grants a private infrastructure investment operator the long-term right to apply the user charges from a project directly to cover any project costs (investment costs, current expenses, interest on capital, repayment of debt and equity), and to generate a return. In this case, it could be said that the earmarking is not only sector-specific but also project-specific. This sums up the government's perspective.

For private infrastructure investors, there are two basic sources of revenue: user finance or, where this does not exist on a project-specific basis or is unavailable to the investor, budget finance paid by a public-sector principal as a regular fee (see also Figure 3.5 in Section 3.3). Internationally, a number of subsectors are largely user-financed, particularly water and power supply, but also public transportation by rail, sea or air. The disposal sector is less clear-cut, because some countries still do not charge for waste or wastewater disposal.

Opinions also differ when it comes to the road transport infrastructure. User charges are traditionally levied in a number of countries, at least for high-priority roads. A distinction is made between mileage-based tolls and time-dependent charges in the form of vignettes (toll stickers). User financing for social infrastructure facilities is a further sticking point. Although users in some countries pay charges to a greater or lesser extent, such as school and university tuition fees in the education sector or direct fees charged by doctors, hospitals or other institutions in the healthcare sector, such facilities are mostly financed only by cost allocation systems that frequently pose problems in terms of collection when it comes to the private (re-)financing of individual facilities. Even in the case of (mass) sport and cultural institutions, the revenue generated is almost always insufficient to cover the costs incurred. In certain sectors, such as the administrative, security/military and penal systems, such kinds of revenue streams are unthinkable in the first place.

There is no need to rule out the possibility of private investment just because a user-financed approach is impossible or inadequate. However, such assets must ultimately be financed by the public budget, for example in the form of PPP measures. These regular service- and/or performance-based payments by the public sector, acting as a principal of its project-executing agency, to the private operating investor of a PPP project are also referred to as 'availability payments' (see Section 3.3.1).

User finance naturally entails a great financial risk for private investors, particularly if the revenue risk is passed on to the investor in full. These risks result from the uncertainty that is inherent in the long-term revenue forecasts. As such, it is important to make an accurate estimate of future volumes and demand (e.g. traffic or refuse volumes, power or water demand), as well as future prices and charges. In infrastructure markets, the long-term development of both of these parameters is influenced by a number of factors over which private infrastructure investors naturally have little or no control. For example, volume development is generally determined by macroeconomic and economic policy factors or changes in legislation rather than by user behaviour falling within the investor's sphere of influence, and prices are often driven by the applicable regulations and not by the operator's pricing strategy.

These revenue risks do not apply if the private operator and investor are remunerated in the form of availability payments from the public budget. In this case, the relevant factors are the operator's performance with respect to the contractually agreed standards and, in particular, the creditworthiness of the public-sector principal in terms of its ability and willingness to meet its payment obligations. Payments by the public-sector principal are generally governed by a complicated set of funding instruments that varies significantly from country to country. However, it is sometimes difficult or impossible to reconcile the specific subsidy conditions associated with the respective 'pots' with private investment. This naturally also entails risks for the investor that must be identified and actively managed to the greatest possible extent. In some cases, it may even be necessary to amend legislation or administrative regulations in order to enable the required compatibility.

1.3.10 Competition and regulation

Whenever there is a fear of market distortion or even market failure in an economic sense, for example natural monopolies or other forms of restriction on competition of common assets, the government can and must intervene in the form of regulation. Market regulation therefore describes the body of all rules and regulations used by the government to this end. This is achieved through the issue of statutory provisions and ordinances that serve to limit the effect of market forces while ensuring legal security and reducing information and transaction costs. In other words, it is important to achieve a suitable degree of regulation and employ the right systems and methods. These responsibilities are generally assigned to regulatory authorities.

A regulatory authority is a government body involved in determining competition policy in a similar way to an anti-trust authority, but with more extensive duties. Anti-trust authorities are usually responsible for the ex post control of markets, whereas regulatory authorities are primarily created for ex ante control of economic sectors in which ex post control is insufficient to maintain the required degree of competition. Regulatory authorities are characterised by far-reaching instruments of ex ante control, such as price and product approval, they operate on an industry-specific basis and are generally found in markets with a tendency for monopoly situations, such as line- or network-based sectors in which the creation of parallel networks is either undesirable or economically unfeasible. This typically includes the telecommunications, post, rail, broadcasting, gas and power markets. Regulation is also essentially indispensable in the water and aviation markets as well as the toll road sector.

Within the European Community, the national regulatory authorities are obliged to implement the relevant EU directives.

At a global level, a distinction is made between various regulation systems based on their impact:

- *Volume regulation:* where the number of competitors in the market or the production volume is controlled by the number of licences and concessions that are required for market entry, for example. Service obligations and prohibitions on activity are also used in order to increase the attractiveness of a market by determining its scope.
- *Price regulation:* which seeks to achieve a specific price level. Fixed prices and price floors and caps are used to set absolute limits. Potential measures also include cost tariffs that specify the relevant price calculation procedures and the imposition of individual prices that cannot be changed without the approval of the responsible regulatory authority.
- *Rate of return regulation:* which sets a limit on the return on capital employed.

Additional regulatory procedures, some of which are sector-specific in nature, are described in detail in Chapters 3 and 4.

This introduction to infrastructure definitions and characteristics illustrated the most important general, non-sector-specific characteristics of infrastructure assets, including some of the financing issues that are relevant for investors. As such, it forms the basis for investments of institutional investors, and in particular financial investors (in contrast to strategic investors).

In the following chapter, the first objective is to explain and position infrastructure as an asset class. To this end, various research reports are analysed and discussed, focusing on risk and return as well as portfolio diversification issues. Second, the concept of sustainable infrastructure investing in general, and in sustainable infrastructure in particular, is presented along with an introduction to ESG (risk) factors and benchmarking. The final section of that chapter discusses the wide range of different investment approaches – with a focus on unlisted infrastructure funds – and concrete tools for their evaluation.

CHAPTER 2

Infrastructure Investments

Most of the infrastructure products that come to the market advertise the advantageous characteristics of infrastructure assets for institutional investors' portfolios. Their comparatively inelastic demand profile, for example, means they are largely unaffected by fluctuations, of moderate volatility, in the economy as a whole and have stable and foreseeable current income streams with built-in inflation hedge, and little correlation to other asset classes, providing for diversification of the entire portfolio. However, given the target returns most products market, it is questionable how such supposedly conservative assets can possibly meet these targets. Is there a free lunch, after all? While the answer to this question was obvious to insiders from the start, it took the financial crisis of 2008/09 for everybody else to realise the answer should be a clear 'no'.

This idealised view on infrastructure assets is essentially driven by the financial industry, especially by product and index providers, who took it upon themselves to redefine infrastructure, conveniently, as an asset class on the basis of certain favourable economic and financial characteristics that suited their needs and purposes (see Section 1.3). This 'definition', however, captures effectively only a subset within the universe of infrastructure assets on the market, namely the relatively low-risk assets, which do indeed exist. It excludes a substantial part, if not the majority, of infrastructure assets to which only some of these favourable characteristics may apply with the respective implications for their risk-return profiles.

This (mis)representation of infrastructure assets has led to considerable confusion among investors, because it created expectations that often could not and/or would not be met given the kind of investments made, investments that have the potential to meet the high return targets marketed initially. As a case in point, during the subprime crisis, significant casualties of infrastructure assets were observed. Assets that were (sold and) bought as conservative, low-risk assets turned out to be, de facto, quite risky because they did not possess (or only partially possessed) the above characteristics. As a consequence, the stability of their cash flows was lower, their volatility as well as their correlation with the equity markets was higher than predicted and they followed the downward rally together with the rest of the market to a greater or lesser extent.[1]

---

[1]Please note that most true low-risk assets decreased in market value during the crisis as well. The main difference is that their market values appreciated again because investors convinced themselves that their underlying contracts were solid. After all, the cash flows/dividends of these assets were not affected.

In other words, in order to be able to meet high-target returns, which are indeed achievable in the infrastructure market, fund managers, not surprisingly, usually will need to reach out to the high(er)-risk infrastructure assets. While from the outside, conservative and risky assets may look alike, a closer look 'inside the asset', especially on the contractual obligations of the involved parties, eventually reveals that in order for these assets to provide the potential for higher returns they generally are exposed to more risk. Accordingly, costs and revenues are less predictable, and less stable, than initially propagated. In short: their risk-return ratio is higher than initially propagated. Hence, it is not 'what you see is what you get' but 'what you don't see is what you get' (see also Weber, 2009).

Notwithstanding, many investors, especially pension funds, insurance companies and sovereign wealth funds, see the enormous potential of the growing infrastructure market, as illustrated in Chapter 1. Hence, they look for investment opportunities in this space. Most of them search for the stable, long-term, inflation-adjusted returns above government bonds to match their long-term liabilities. Increasingly, they also require the inclusion of environmental, social and governance (ESG) criteria. However, not all of them overview the market with its different investment opportunities – be it direct or indirect – or have the capability in house to look 'behind the scenes' of these assets, to investigate the significant differences between them and to examine the different risk-return profiles of the fund/investment opportunities offered to them respectively.

The aim of this chapter is therefore threefold: (i) to examine whether, and if so why, infrastructure can be considered an asset class in its own right, (ii) to introduce the concept of sustainable investing and how it is applied to infrastructure investments and (iii) to illustrate the different investment approaches to infrastructure. The chapter starts with a brief overview of some of the large and relatively experienced infrastructure investors in the market. It then focuses attention on the risk-return differences between both assets within the infrastructure asset class as well as related asset classes. By doing so, it differentiates between listed and unlisted infrastructure. It continues discussing the impact the industry sector has on the risk-return profile of an asset and the extent to which infrastructure serves to diversify an investor's portfolio as a whole. In this context, it illustrates the difficulty of benchmarking unlisted infrastructure and suggests ways to address the issue. The second part of the chapter re-introduces the concept of sustainable infrastructure investing as well as why and how to go about including ESG criteria in the investment decision. The third part of the chapter elaborates on how to invest in infrastructure – listed versus unlisted and direct versus indirect (via funds) – ultimately focusing on unlisted, indirect fund investment opportunities. In this context, the most important peculiarities concerning the evaluation of infrastructure fund investments are explained, including the suitability and appropriateness of their terms and conditions. A detailed discussion of the evaluation of direct investments takes place thereafter in the following chapters.

2.1 INFRASTRUCTURE AS AN ASSET CLASS

Infrastructure assets offer a wide variety of risk-return and cash flow profiles, theoretically ranging from highly conservative bond/fixed income-style asset profiles through to investment opportunities that are comparable to (private) equity. These are explored and discussed in the following sections.

2.1.1   Investors in infrastructure

Over the past decade, there has been a tangible rise in interest in infrastructure investments among pension funds, insurance companies and sovereign wealth funds, as well as foundations and endowments. This is because in addition to the potentially stable income stream and conservative risk-return profile, infrastructure investments may also offer a wide range of social and political benefits in their respective region under certain circumstances, which can be of interest to pension funds and insurance companies in particular. Furthermore, certain infrastructure assets will meet the sustainability investment criteria (see Section 1.2), with which institutional investors are increasingly obliged to comply.

Australian and Canadian pension funds were the first to gain extensive experience in this asset class and now invest up to 15% of their assets in infrastructure. However, the average for both countries is 'only' around 5% (Inderst and Della Croce, 2013). Initially, most had been doing so primarily indirectly, via listed funds (the 'Australian Model') and successively also via closed-end funds, or then by investing directly into infrastructure assets. The largest direct investors in infrastructure are Canadian: OMERS (Ontario Municipal Employees Retirement System) via its specially created investment company Borealis, CPP (Canada Pension Plan), OTPP (Ontario Teachers' Pension Plan), the Caisse de Dépôt et Placement du Québec, and PSP Investments, some of which have invested in infrastructure since 1997. Nowadays, they all employ large teams of experts (engineers, economists, bankers, lawyers) to operate their direct investment activities at home and abroad. At the end of 2014, OMERS had total assets of C\$70.2 billion (up C\$5.2 billion on 2013) and an allocation to infrastructure of 15% (C\$9.8 billion). OTPP maintains its target allocation of 7.7% (C\$11.7 billion) based on total assets of C\$154.5 billion (up C\$13 billion on 2013). CPP with C\$219 billion (C\$183 billion in 2013) of assets under management entered the market several years later. Notwithstanding, its infrastructure investments amounted to 6.1% (C\$13.3 billion) at the end of 2014 with no explicit target allocation. CPP has built up its team for direct investments globally over recent years, and they can be expected to remain one of the key players in the future. The Caisse de Dépôt et Placement du Québec is an equally large player with C\$225 billion (C\$200 billion in 2013) of assets under management and C\$10.1 billion invested in infrastructure by the end of 2014, which represented 4.9% of their assets. PSP with C\$94 billion of assets under management (C\$77 billion in 2013) has also advanced to a serious and active direct investor globally with a 13% long-term target for infrastructure. Table 2.1 lists the investments, allocations and returns of various pension funds.

European financial investors started to become interested in infrastructure much later but have caught up astonishingly during the past few years. In 2013, reportedly 65% of institutions made their first commitment to the asset class. Most European investors allocate, on average, 4.6% of their total assets into infrastructure, which is close to the average investment of Canadians or Australians (October 2014; Preqin, 2014a). However, 48% of Europe-based infrastructure investors are still below their target allocations for this asset class, suggesting that they will likely increase their infrastructure investments in the near future.

During the past six years, following the publication of the first edition of this book, many European participants got involved. Only a few are mentioned in the following due to space restrictions. The two Dutch pension funds ABP (with APG as its internal asset manager) and PGGM belong to the first, largest and most active infrastructure investors in Europe. With assets under management in 2014 of €343.8 billion (up €44 billion from 2013), ABP/APG currently devotes 1.6% of its total asset investments to infrastructure (€5.4 billion) with a target

TABLE 2.1 Infrastructure investments, allocations and returns of selected pension funds

Pension funds	Total AuM 2014 (2013)	Infrastructure investment 2014	Infrastructure allocation 2014 (mid-term target)	Return 2014 (benchmark)	Return 2012/2013
CANADA					
Ontario Teachers (OTPP)	C$154.5bn (C$140.8bn)	C$12.6bn	7.7%[1] (n.a.)	11.8% (10.1%) 10.1% (5.9%)[2]	10.9% (2013)
OMERS (Borealis)	C$70.2bn[3] (C$65.3bn)	C$14.4bn[4]	14.7% (n.a.)	10.0% (7.7%) 12.7% (9.6%)[5]	6.0% (2013)
CPP[6]	C$219.1 (C$183.3bn)	C$13.3bn	6.1%[7] (n.a.)	16.5%	10.1% (2013)
Caisse de Dépôt et Placement du Québec[8]	C$225.9 (C$200.1bn)	C$10.1bn	4.9%[9] (n.a.)	12.0% (11.4%)	12.6% (2013)
PSP	C$93.7 (C$76.1bn)	C$6.0bn	6.4% (13%)	9.4% (4.6%)	
AUSTRALIA					
Future Fund	A$100bn (A$89bn) (2012–2013)	A$20bn	7.8%[10] (7.4%)	13.9% (7.5%)	15.4% (2013) 2.1% (2012)
QIC	A$70.6bn (A$70.3bn)	A$5.8bn (31 March 2015)	n.a (n.a.)	6.8% (GFI Alpha)	10.6%(2013)
IFM Investors[11] (30 June 2015)	A$57bn	A$23bn[12]	n.a.	10%[13]	8.8%[14]
State Super[15]	A$40.3bn (A$38.2bn)	A$4.9bn (Balanced)	10%	10.0% (Balanced)	13.7 (2013)
Australian Super	A$78.3bn (A$65.3bn)	A$7.8bn[16]	13% (Balanced)	13.9% (Balanced)	15.6% (2013)
Unisuper	A$42.7bn (A$36.3bn)	A$4.3bn[17]	5%[18] (n.a.)	13.8% (Balanced)	15.9% (2013)
HESTA	A$28.7bn (A$24.2bn)	A$2.7bn[19]	10% (Core Pool)	13.2% (Core Pool)	14.8% (2013)
Telstra Superannuation Scheme	A$15.5bn (A$13.5bn)	A$433m	4.3% (Balanced)	15.8% (Balanced)	16.9% (2013)
MTTA Superfund	A$7.5bn (A$6.9bn)	A$779m (directly managed)	15% (Balanced) (n.a.)	12.2% (Super Balanced)	–1.0%(2013)
Military Superannuation Pension Fund[20]	A$4.9bn (A$4.0bn)	A$603m[21] (A$320m)	Long term: 10% (Conservative), 2% (Growth Option)	12.5% (5.6%)	–1.0%/4.9%

EUROPE				
ABP[22] (via APG, 2014 data)	€343.8bn (€299.9bn)	€5.4bn	3%[23] (n.a.)	14.5%	6.2% (2013)
PGGM – NL[24] (2013 data)	€154bn (€134bn)	€4.5bn[25] (2015)	5–6% (n.a)	n.a.	n.a.

Notes:

[1] Estimate calculated based on 23% allocation (exposure goal) for real assets (real estate and infrastructure) where historic investment data shows infrastructure representing about 33% of total real asset investments.

[2] 10.1% (5.9%) for infrastructure portfolio only.

[3] Represents net assets. AuM in annual report includes third party capital, debt, and other liabilities.

[4] Represents exposure value – assumed to be equal to invested capital.

[5] 12.7% (9.6%) for Borealis infrastructure portfolio.

[6] http://www.cppib.com.

[7] Represent the actual percentage of total net investment (Statement of Investment Asset Mix).

[8] http://www.lacaisse.com/en.

[9] Benchmark portfolio composition.

[10] Allocation percentage includes timberland.

[11] http://www.ifminvestors.com/.

[12] This is the NAV of the Global and Australian Infrastructure Funds. Does not include undrawn investor commitments.

[13] 10% return target, net of fees and investment-level taxes, over rolling 3 year periods.

[14] Gross, local currency, since inception, investment-level returns for the Global Infrastructure Fund

[15] http://www.statesuper.nsw.gov.au/.

[16] This number is expected to double in the next 5 years.

[17] Property and infrastructure combined.

[18] Property and infrastructure combined.

[19] http://www2.hesta.com.au/update/2014/04/16/you-have-a-stake-in-some-of-australias-most-important-infrastructure-assets/.

[20] http://www.militarysuper.gov.au.

[21] Based on Growth (default) fund AND includes infrastructure and property.

[22] http://www.abp.nl/.

[23] Strategic allocation of investment portfolio to asset classes (2014 Annual Report).

[24] http://www.jaarverslagenpggm.nl/.

[25] https://www.pggm.nl/english/what-we-think/Pages/Three-awards-for-PGGM.aspx.

Source: Annual reports (numbers according to respective company's fiscal year, which varies considerably between March 2013 and Dec 2014) plus additional information obtained directly from pension funds

allocation of 3%. Following the Canadian and Australian strategies, ABP/APG and PGGM initially invested only in funds. However, over time they have both established a team allowing them to make direct investments in individual infrastructure projects.

Notable Scandinavian pension investors – including the Swedish buffer funds AP3, AP4 and AP6, the Danish ATP, PensionDanmark, Industriens Pension, PKA and PFA pension, as well as the Finnish Ilmarinen and VER – got involved in infrastructure fund and/or infrastructure direct investments. In Germany, the largest infrastructure investors tend to be insurance groups with few exceptions, like the BVK (Bayerische Versorgungskammer), which only invests indirectly via funds. The two largest active insurance groups are Allianz Group with €488 billion assets under management (Allianz, 2015a) and MEAG with €256 billion assets under management (MEAG, 2015), the asset manager for Munich RE (the largest reinsurance group in the world) and its subsidiary, the ERGO Insurance Group. In the UK, many of the largest pension funds such as British Airways, British Rail, Hermes, the London Pension Funds Authority (LPFA) and the Universities Superannuation Scheme (USS), to name just a few, have combined assets of €125 billion and currently invest 1.4–5.4% of total assets in infrastructure (2014).[2] Not all of them have dedicated infrastructure teams, though. Further, the UK government launched a dedicated infrastructure investment initiative at the end of 2013 with very ambitious, maybe slightly unrealistic, infrastructure investment goals. Part of this is the PiP initiative, comprising a group of British pension funds who try to use economies of scale by screening and investing jointly. In Switzerland, most notably, several Swiss pension funds joined forces to set up an infrastructure platform (IST3), which is comparable with the PiP in the UK. While many Swiss pension funds are also invested individually – such as the corporate pension funds from Migros, Novartis, Roche, SBB, Swiss Post and Zurich Insurance, and public pension funds such as the cantons of Aargau, Luzern, and Lausanne – only one large Swiss insurance group, Swiss Life, has built up a sizeable, dedicated team.

As of Q1 2014, US public pension funds with an infrastructure allocation or the intention to invest in infrastructure had an average current allocation of 1.9% and a target allocation of 4% (Preqin, 2014b). These include CalPERS, TIAA–CREF, Alaska Permanent Fund Corporation, CalSTRS, Municipal Employees' Retirement System of Michigan, Oregon PERS, Washington State Pension Plan and the World Bank, to mention just a few.

Sovereign wealth funds in the Middle East and Asia are also heavily invested in infrastructure and are expected to continue to invest large volumes and establish corresponding teams. Examples include ADIA (Abu Dhabi Investment Authority), ADIC (Abu Dhabi Investment Council), China Investment Corporation (CIC), the sovereign wealth funds of Kuwait, Qatar and the like. ADIA, with total assets of US$589 billion (2014), currently invests 1–5% in infrastructure, while ADIC, with total assets of US$90 billion, targets investments in Europe with a focus on utility companies (Sovereign Wealth Center, 2015).

The limited capital under management of most investors dedicated to infrastructure investments and the necessary size to put together and finance a high-class direct investment team in-house means, relatively speaking, there will be few influential players with large proprietary teams. Apart from this, experience shows that even these investors are short of access to suitable direct investment opportunities since they need to invest large sums of capital per

---

[2]Based on 2014 annual reports with USS €50.3 billion, (5.1%), British Airways €11.7 billion (5%), British Rail €20 billion (4%), Hermes €42 billion, 5.4%, City of London €1 billion (1.4%).

annum. Hence, one way or the other, they all work together with advisors, who help them source deals and execute the transactions.

2.1.2 Risk-return profiles of unlisted infrastructure investments

What return can institutional investors expect from unlisted infrastructure investments and at what risk? The available data is still poor; history can offer little guidance. The following sections seek to help and give an indication.

The extremely broad range of infrastructure assets around means that the risk-return profiles of these assets are correspondingly varied. As such, it is difficult to draw general conclusions about the investment profile of infrastructure investments without making a precise differentiation between the various possible investment types.

Notwithstanding, in order to provide useful information on the key data of infrastructure in the context of a wider investment portfolio and to benchmark it with other asset classes, it is necessary to analyse and understand the risk-return profile of infrastructure investments and their volatility, their correlation with other assets classes, etc. The problem is that empirical data, such as historical returns, volatilities, correlations, default rates, is scarce and, consequently, suitable, stand-alone standardised benchmarks for infrastructure investments are not available (yet). Both are required for the typical statistical models and tests used in the context of asset/liability studies. This makes it difficult for investors to analyse and integrate infrastructure as an asset class in their asset and liability management (ALM) analyses and their portfolios, respectively, in a meaningful way. The severity of this issue was illustrated in a decision by the European Insurance and Occupational Pensions Authority (EIOPA), which refused to reassess risks related to infrastructure assets (as a separate asset class) owing to the lack of data and transparency.[3] Such a signal is not particularly helpful, especially in light of the fact that institutional investors globally are struggling to find a way to invest in infrastructure, which is in line with regulatory requirements.

Some initiatives, such as establishing a comprehensive database for unlisted infrastructure and suitable benchmarks, have been kicked off in the relatively recent past, predominantly led by some of the largest institutional infrastructure investors. Although most initiatives are still in their infancy, they are helpful and clearly heading in the right direction.

2.1.2.1 Listed infrastructure – an indicator for unlisted? As an approximation to the reality of infrastructure risks and returns, an important effort has been made to assess infrastructure as an asset class in its entirety with the aim to provide investors with potential points of reference for investments in general and ALM studies in particular. To this end, research about historical risk and performance characteristics of infrastructure has been published, usually referring to the data from the (still relatively small number of) listed infrastructure indices. (It should be kept in mind that these indices are in most instances established by banks, which also act as product providers.)

---

[3]However, as of 2015, EIOPA is exploring the possibility to introduce a specific standard formula treatment for a category of infrastructure investments in order to ensure current regulations (such as Solvency II) are properly accounting for the specific risk-return profiles of long-term infrastructure investments (EIOPA, 2015).

Attempting to approximate investor risk in unlisted infrastructure using listed infrastructure data will most likely lead to unsatisfying results, though. First, listed assets in general have different correlation and volatility characteristics from unlisted assets. This is true not only for infrastructure but also, for example, for private equity. Second, the universe of listed infrastructure companies used to build infrastructure indices rarely has any pure infrastructure project companies or assets. Instead, it contains a wide range of infrastructure operating or service companies active in the infrastructure sector in various forms (see Section 1.3.4). The majority of these listed stocks, therefore, have none or only a few of the characteristics of conservatively structured infrastructure assets described above with the beneficial effects on portfolio diversification postulated.

Against this background, it is unsurprising that the results of research studies, some of which are listed in Table 2.2, vary considerably, owing to the number of (mostly unavoidable) approximations of actual data, and inevitably limit their information value.

Naturally, when comparing research from different studies, it is impossible to keep the period under observation constant. At the same time, it is well known that the period chosen has an important impact on the results. This is why most studies included in this overview observe as similar time periods as possible and are as up-to-date as possible, dated around 2012–2013 or even 2014, thus including not only good investment years but also bad ones, like the years of the financial crisis. Not surprisingly, this resulted in lower average returns and increased average volatility during the observation periods when compared to the data presented in the first edition of this book published in 2010.

2.1.2.2 Unlisted infrastructure – lack of data

Having criticised the data on listed infrastructure and its usefulness as indicator for risk-return profiles of unlisted infrastructure, it is even more difficult to find robust performance statistics of unlisted infrastructure investments, let alone data series over a meaningful period, data on the actual risks, revenue drivers, cash flows and terms of infrastructure investments in general. There are various reasons for this situation. First, and most importantly, it is the lack of transparency that is typical of unlisted investments. Investment data are usually proprietary and not made public by investment managers and/or investors. Partly as a result of this, independent service and information providers, like those that have existed for a number of years in the fields of private equity, and to a lesser extent project finance lending, have not been able to publish separate infrastructure reports, owing to a lack of sufficient long-term data (so far only Australia has unlisted data series of >15 years) and access to these kinds of data.[4] Second, very few collecting points for these kinds of data have been established to date, again owing to both the usual quarterly reporting of unlisted investment vehicles plus the overall, still relatively short, history of unlisted infrastructure investments and investment vehicles – Australian, Canadian and Dutch fund and/or direct investments being the exception. In part, it is also because infrastructure can be broken down into a large number of subsectors. The rather diverse profiles of these subsectors mean that their performance etc. is difficult if not impossible to compare, even more so when the assets are aggregated on a fund level. Last but not least, infrastructure, like

---

[4]In late 2014, MSCI released the IPD Global Infrastructure Direct Asset Index, the first of its kind for tracking investment performance of infrastructure on a global scale. Further, some of the largest infrastructure investors around the world are working on establishing a jointly accessible, mutually useful database.

TABLE 2.2 Performance and volatility of infrastructure funds and indices

Type	Source[1]		Institution/Author/Index	Period	Region	Annual Return (%)[2]	Volatility (% st. dev.)[3]
Unlisted Funds	Academic	2007	Peng and Newell (2007)	1995–2006	Australia	14.1	5.8[4]
		2010	Finkenzeller, Dechant and Shepherd (2010)[5]	1994–2009	Australia	8.2	3.8[2]
		2011	Hartigan, Prasad and De Francesco (2011)	1998–2008	UK	6.5	n/a
		2011	Newell, Peng and De Francesco (2011)	1995–2009	Australia	14.1	6.5[2]
	Industry	2004	Macquarie[6]	1995–2002	Australia	19.2	n/a
		2006	Colonial First State[7]	1996–2006	Australia	13.5	n/a
		2010	Colonial First State[8]	2001–2010	Australia	11.0	n/a
		2013	Mercer/CFS[9]	1995–2013	Australia	11.8	5.9
		2015	JPMorgan[10]	1995–2014	Global	7.0	7.5
Listed Funds	Academic	2007	Peng and Newell	1995–2006	Australia	22.5	7.9[5]
	Industry[11]	2015	Duet Group	2004–2014	Australia/NZ	10.70	29.44
		2015	Cohen & Steers Infrastructure Fund	2004–2014	Global	9.63	26.40
		2015	Lazard Global Listed Infrastructure Fund	2005–2014	Global	11.09	14.76
		2015	Macquarie Infrastructure Corporation	2004–2014	US	14.95	63.52
		2015	Macquarie Korea Infrastructure Fund	2002–2014	Korea	7.52	18.65
Listed Indices	Index Provider[6]	2015	ASX Infra Index T	2003–2014	Australia	10.14	16.79
		2015	Dow Jones Brookfield Global Infrastructure Index	2002–2014	Global	14.66	14.34
		2015	Macquarie Global Infrastructure Index	2000–2014	Global	8.75	15.28
		2015	MSCI World Infrastructure Index	1998–2014	Global	2.30	15.98
		2015	S&P Global Infrastructure Index	2001–2014	Global	7.20	15.98
		2015	S&P Emerging Mkt Infrastructure NTR	2002–2014	Emerging Markets	17.22	18.93
		2013	UBS Global Infrastructure & Utilities 50-50 Index	2002–2012	Global	12.2	15.0

Notes:

[1] Except where otherwise noted, all data are from OECD (2014a), p. 25.

[2] Monthly return for listed funds and indices (industry sources), annualised since inception.

[3] Daily volatility for listed funds and indices (industry sources), annualised since inception.

[4] Huibers (2012).

[5] Methodology: portfolio allocations are optimised by using an algorithm that accounts for downside risk rather than variance. An Australian dataset comprising stocks, bonds, direct real estate/infrastructure and indirect infrastructure is applied for portfolio construction.

[6] Macquarie Global Infrastructure Index (NBIM, 2013).

[7] Colonial First State (2007).

[8] Colonial First State (2010).

[9] Mercer/CFS (Colonial First State) Unlisted Infrastructure Index (NBIM, 2013).

[10] JPMorgan (2015).

[11] Selection of the largest listed infrastructure funds based on market capitalisation as of October 2015, Bloomberg.

any other asset class, is faced with issues of reliability of performance data used in publicly available marketing material, usage of different assumptions, data sets and benchmarks, as well as the lack of agreed performance reporting standards.

Notwithstanding these data shortages, Peng and Newell (2007) were among the first in the academic field to solidly, comparatively analyse listed and unlisted infrastructure investments in Australia, where the data situation is best. Over a period of 10 years (1995–2006), they compared the risk-adjusted performance of 16 listed infrastructure companies (with assets of A\$55 billion), 16 listed infrastructure funds (with assets of A\$27 billion) and 19 unlisted funds (with 144 infrastructure assets of A\$4.5 billion). They found that for listed infrastructure the average return was 22.4% and the volatility was 16.0%, which compared to a 14.1% return and a 5.8% volatility for unlisted infrastructure. More recent academic papers from Newell, Peng and De Francesco (2011) and Finkenzeller, Dechant and Shepherd (2010) report surprisingly differing average returns/volatility for unlisted infrastructure in Australia of 14.1/6.5% (1995–2009) and 8.2/3.8% (1994–2009) despite covering almost identical periods on the identical region (see Table 2.2).

The limited data available on unlisted funds are based mainly on Australian funds, for the above-mentioned reasons. For various periods between 1994/5 and 2015, the returns ranged from 6.5% and a staggering 22.5%, with volatilities between 3.8 and 16.2% (Table 2.2). This compares to returns of listed indices (2002–2014) ranging from 4.0 and 12.6% with a volatility range of 8.6–13.7%. To the best knowledge of the authors, no research of comparable quality is available for Europe or North America, simply because of the often-cited lack of data. Notwithstanding, in late 2014 MSCI released the IPD Global Infrastructure Direct Asset Index, which is the first of its kind for tracking investment performance of infrastructure on a global scale. At the time, it comprised 132 investments (US\$49 billion) with exposures in Australia (44%), Europe (43%) and North America (8%) and weighted towards the transport (47%), power (24%) and water sectors (22%) with an average annualised return over the last five years of 13.4% (no volatility data available to the authors).

2.1.2.3   Risk-return profiles and industry sectors   Most infrastructure studies illustrate the risk-return profiles of infrastructure investments broken down by industry/sector. This way of approaching infrastructure assets, however, can be problematic. Therefore, this section critically discusses some of the analytical approaches that are widely used in risk-return studies. Chapter 3 presents a more comprehensive approach to assessing the risk-return profile of infrastructure projects/assets in any given sector that the authors believe allows for a more suitable categorisation than by industry/sector, thereby better reflecting the wide variable risk-return profiles of this asset class.

The various infrastructure subsectors, their degree and kind of regulation and, in particular, their seemingly endless range of sector and transaction-specific contractual structures mean that there is no such thing as a uniform risk-return profile within any given infrastructure sector (Weber, 2009). This is the case even without considering additional dimensions, such as the various stages of investment (e.g. greenfield vs. brownfield), geographies and the like, which increase the complexity even further. Notwithstanding, repeatedly studies aim to classify the risk-return profile – as well as the yield profile – of infrastructure assets according to their various (sub)sectors (see Table 2.3 for an example).

Table 2.3 and similar kinds of tables of common risk-return profiles actually tend to oversimplify the complexity of infrastructure investing for they fail to account for the broad

TABLE 2.3 Simplified illustration of subsector risk-return profiles

Infrastructure Types	3-year Equity IRR (% in AUS$)	Expected Cash Yields (% in AUS$)	Risk
Social	9–11	4–12	Medium
Regulated	11–12	6–10	Low
Rail	12–13	8–12	Medium
Airports/Ports	11–13	5–10	Medium
Power Generators	12–14	4–12	High
Toll Roads/Greenfield	13–15	3–5	Medium/High

Note: IRR = internal rate of return.
Source: AMP Capital (2014b)

variety of assets found within a single sector. They suggest that the identity of the sector or the fact that a market is regulated provides sufficient evidence to determine the corridor for the expected risk-return profile of an asset or project. This is a severe mistake, which is still commonly made by (inexperienced) investors. Strictly speaking, the sector alone does not allow any conclusions to be drawn about the risk-return profile of an asset. An analysis of the individual case is always necessary. Also, a regulated market cannot be automatically equated with low risk. This is particularly apparent in the regulated telecommunications market, which embodies an extremely high level of market risk. There may also be a variety of regulations within the same sector across geopolitical boundaries (e.g. high-voltage electrical transmission, gas networks, rail transport networks).

Instead, the contractual structure has a major impact on the risk-return profile of an asset/project. This is because each contractual structure with its various contract partners represents a unique risk profile comprising risk factors pertaining to, among others, revenue and cost, credit, construction and operations, including maintenance, as well as political and regulatory risk, and has its unique risk allocation among the contractually involved parties.

Hence, it is the combination of the aforementioned influencing factors and characteristics – and *the contractual structure in particular* – that ultimately determines the risk-return profile of an investment. Therefore, it is possible for investments with similar physical asset characteristics to appear identical on the surface (e.g. two road or power plant projects) yet to have entirely different risk-return profiles resulting from their underlying contractual structure and risk allocation (Weber, 2009). This is illustrated in Figure 2.1.

Figure 2.1 aims to demonstrate, once again, that the risk-return profile of an infrastructure asset is not predominantly determined by the sector but that it depends in large part on the geography, stage and contractual structure in which it is embedded and the risks that the private partners take on. As such, similar physical assets in a sector can deliver an IRR ranging from around 5 to well above 15%. The case with the least risk, categorised as 'I. Operational – Availability/FIT based – No market risk' in Figure 2.1 represents, for example, an operational asset with an availability-based PPP structure, not too highly leveraged, in which a recognised public body in a politically and fiscally stable country is the contractual partner of the private parties. As a consequence, the private sector takes little or no market (demand and price) risk. From day one, the asset generates a long, stable and predictable cash flow for the duration of the contract period, which is reduced only if either the operator is not able to maintain

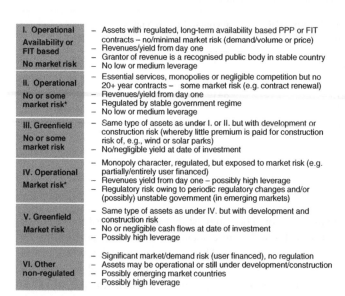
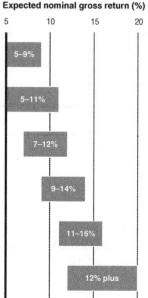

Expected nominal gross return (%)

| | | 5 | 10 | 15 | 20 |

I. Operational
Availability or FIT based
No market risk
 – Assets with regulated, long-term availability based PPP or FIT contracts – no/minimal market risk (demand/volume or price)
 – Revenues/yield from day one
 – Grantor of revenue is a recognised public body in stable country
 – No low or medium leverage
5–9%

II. Operational
No or some market risk*
 – Essential services, monopolies or negligible competition but no 20+ year contracts – some market risk (e.g. contract renewal)
 – Revenues/yield from day one
 – Regulated by stable government regime
 – No low or medium leverage
5–11%

III. Greenfield
No or some market risk
 – Same type of assets as under I. or II. but with development or construction risk (whereby little premium is paid for construction risk of, e.g., wind or solar parks)
 – No/negligible yield at date of investment
7–12%

IV. Operational
Market risk*
 – Monopoly character, regulated, but exposed to market risk (e.g. partially/entirely user financed)
 – Revenues yield from day one – possibly high leverage
 – Regulatory risk owing to periodic regulatory changes and/or (possibly) unstable government (in emerging markets)
9–14%

V. Greenfield
Market risk
 – Same type of assets as under IV. but with development and construction risk
 – No or negligible cash flows at date of investment
 – Possibly high leverage
11–16%

VI. Other
non-regulated
 – Significant market/demand risk (user financed), no regulation
 – Assets may be operational or still under development/construction
 – Possibly emerging market countries
 – Possibly high leverage
12% plus

* not an availability based PFI/PPP or clean energy FIT based asset/project

FIGURE 2.1 Drivers of assets' risk and return profiles
Source: B Capital Partners

and operate the asset as contractually agreed or the operating costs are higher than projected because, for example, the wear and tear of the asset dramatically increases – both rather manageable risks.

An asset classified as 'IV. Operational – Market risk', on the other hand, exhibits a riskier profile, because although the asset is operational and regulated it is exposed to market risk. In most instances, market risk is the single biggest risk for a private concessioner/owner followed by political/regulatory risk. Therefore, while these two types of assets are both operational – that is brownfield, regulated, and may look identical from the outside – their risk-return profiles differ significantly (see also Weber (2009) for further elaboration).

An additional, frequently used measure of risk is that of debt default rates. Infrastructure investments generally tend to benefit from low debt default rates. Moody's has analysed and compared investment-grade[5] cumulative default rates of corporate infrastructure[6] debt vs. non-financial corporate (NFC) debt issuers from 1983 to 2012 (see Figure 2.2). Although default rates were initially similar, cumulative default rates for infrastructure tend to level off as a project matures, whereas NFC cumulative defaults continue to increase, being around 50% greater than those for infrastructure debt after 10 years.

---

[5]The vast majority of corporate infrastructure debt (81%) is investment grade.
[6]The main sub-sectors, by sample size, within corporate infrastructure debt are: regulated utilities (63%) and unregulated utilities (9%) of corporate infrastructure, remaining other utilities (19%) and remaining other corporate infrastructure or non-utilities corporate infrastructure (8%).

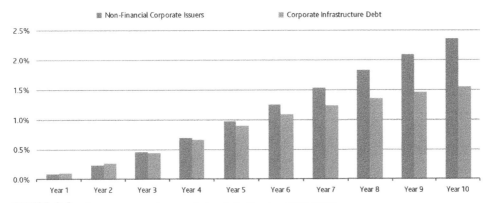

FIGURE 2.2   Investment-grade cumulative default rates, 1983-2012
Source: Moody's (2012)

One often-cited reason for the superior performance of infrastructure over corporate bonds is the fact that banks analyse infrastructure bonds, which are based on project finance principles, more rigorously and cautiously than corporate bonds. That is, they have to base their credit decision primarily on the future cash flows of the (new) project company rather than being able to rely on the assets of a corporate issuer, with which they consider themselves to be familiar and/or have a longstanding relationship, which needs to be honoured (see also Section 6.1). Also, certain infrastructure project companies may be less exposed to economic fluctuations than 'regular' corporates that are (more) exposed to market risk, making them relatively crisis-resistant (e.g. natural monopolies). Last but maybe not least, average corporate infrastructure debt trading prices tend to be around 40–45% higher than those for NFC issuers, suggesting that the former may be 'overpriced' in the first place, in the sense of not fully reflecting all the risks of the corporates.

In any case, these results, which are based on long data series, are clearly an argument in favour of investments in infrastructure, be it in the form of equity or debt.

Moreover, when infrastructure debt does default, the recovery rates are much higher compared to those for corporate debt – with the exception of senior unsecured debt of unregulated utilities (Table 2.4) – confirming the sounder (credit) risk profile of project finance debt underlying most infrastructure transactions (see Chapter 6).

TABLE 2.4   Recovery rates for defaulted corporate infrastructure debt, 1983–2012

Sector	Senior Secured	Senior Unsecured
Regulated utilities	$82.52	$59.16
Unregulated utilities	$60.96	$41.45
Others	$65.93	$60.05
Average corporate infrastructure debt	$68.72	$53.01
Average non-financial corporate issuers	$49.30	$36.50

Source: Moody's (2012)

Supporting the above, infrastructure debt has a lower volatility than corporate debt, as depicted in Figure 2.3, which compares notch-weighted rating volatility.[7]

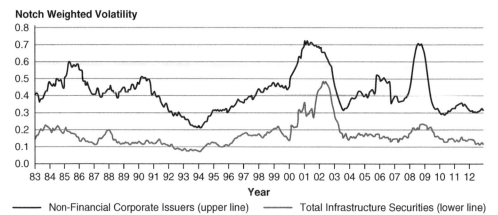

Notch Weighted Volatility

FIGURE 2.3   Rating volatility for total infrastructure securities and non-financial corporate issuers
Source: Moody's (2014)

When comparing the performance of infrastructure against other asset classes, the lack of established performance benchmarks for infrastructure investments does not help. Given the risk-return bandwidth of infrastructure and the well-known general difficulties of benchmarking unlisted assets, this is not surprising. Defining the right benchmark depends heavily on factors relating both to the asset/liability profile of the investor and, of course, the investment goals pursued with the infrastructure investment strategy (e.g. yield or capital gain, see also Section 1.3.8). The next section elaborates on possible approaches to benchmarking the performance of infrastructure assets, being well aware, though, that this is still early days.

2.1.3   Benchmarking infrastructure investments[8]

Institutional financial investors use benchmarks to compare the financial performance of their investments with the market. Accordingly, a benchmark can be defined as the relevant market with which the performance of an investment is compared. Typically, a financial benchmark is an index of similar listed securities. In the case of listed infrastructure assets, the indices displayed in Table 2.2 in Section 2.1.2.1 may serve as suitable benchmarks for investors depending on their specific investments. Such indices, however, are of limited use for the performance measurement of unlisted infrastructure assets. As, for reasons mentioned in the previous section as well as the next paragraph, indices based on standardised, actual performance data of unlisted infrastructure assets do not (yet) exist. Therefore, investors lack industry standards for benchmarking and monitoring both the financial and sustainability performance of their

---

[7]Notch-weighted volatility: this metric is constructed by adding the notch-weighted downgrade rate and upgrade rate together. These metrics are computed by taking the number of notches (e.g. alphanumeric rating movement of a credit from Aaa1 to Aaa2) and dividing it by the number of outstanding ratings. Because of this construction, the volatility rate can at times exceed 100%.

[8]Unless otherwise mentioned, sources for this section on benchmarking include: Weber B. (2013), EDHEC (2014), EDHEC (2013) and CFA Institute (2012).

infrastructure assets. In the absence of such standards, a range of approximate financial benchmarks is used by some investors, and yet none by others. The first sustainability benchmarks are just in the process of being developed. They are touched upon in Section 2.2.3.2.

2.1.3.1 Structuring/developing a benchmark

In theory, there are various ways to structure a benchmark for unlisted infrastructure. In practice, though, investors are confronted with multiple challenges, of which the three most important ones seem to be that (1) benchmarks require a reliable data universe to work with, (2) benchmarks need to fulfil certain criteria, among which are replicability and investability and (3) returns need to be attributable. First, insufficient data are due to (i) little and short publicly available performance data series (e.g. only Australia has performance data dating back over 15 years for unlisted infrastructure), (ii) a broad investment universe within infrastructure with an equally broad range of investment strategies (comprising a wide range of different risk-return profiles, which would need to be itemised in order to compare the performance of individual investments/assets) and (iii) a lack of coherent performance measurements by investors. Second, replicability/investability (a typical requirement of a benchmark) is an equally difficult condition to meet because the above-mentioned insufficient data universe of publicly available, tradable assets make it challenging, if not impossible, to construct a replicable, meaningful index/benchmark. Third, a classic return attribution to active management relative to an industry benchmark is merely impossible for unlisted infrastructure assets because infrastructure investment styles are often broad and the quantification of benchmarks subjective as well as backward looking.

2.1.3.2 Benchmarks currently in use

Out of necessity, many financial investors use a simple, straightforward approach and benchmark their investments against absolute return expectations and/or inflation (CPI) plus a margin.[9]

However, some investors pursue a more sophisticated approach that considers overall asset allocation goals, investment strategy, risk profiles of underlying assets, performance expectations, etc., when specifying a benchmark. Table 2.5 illustrates selected benchmarks as used by selected financial investors.

2.1.3.3 A strategic approach to benchmarking

While absolute performance and CPI-related infrastructure benchmarks are convenient and easy to use, they may be of little value or even misleading if investors select them based on the wrong parameters, for example physical characteristics rather than the risk-return profiles of the individual assets.

Professional investors eventually need to take a strategic, more informed approach to benchmark selection. A strategic approach to benchmarking infrastructure assets requires the specification of a benchmark, which is appropriate, i.e. that is able to measure if the main investment goals (e.g. return target given a certain risk profile) of the investment strategy are met. This means *benchmarks need to match the investment strategy with its individual risk-return specifications. The physical characteristics of the asset itself are of minor importance* (see Section 2.1.2.3).

---

[9]In the early days of unlisted infrastructure investing, institutional investors often applied listed infrastructure indices as benchmarks mainly because of a lack of alternatives. Nowadays, none of the experienced infrastructure investors does so. See also Section 2.1.4 for a discussion of correlations between listed and unlisted infrastructure.

TABLE 2.5 Examples of benchmarks used in the industry

Investor	Benchmark
Insurance companies	
Australian insurance company	Absolute return (8%) + coverage of internal management costs
German insurance (predominantly life insurance)	Government bond + margin (5%)
South European Insurance (diversified)	Absolute return (6.5%) unlevered, post tax
Pension plans	
British Columbia Investment Management Corporation (bcIMC)	8% absolute return with adjustments for asset, country, and currency risks
Caisse de Dépôt et Placement du Québec	50% S&P 500/TSX + 25% S&P 500 + 25% MSCI EAFE Index
California Public Employees' Retirement System (CalPERS)	CPI + margin (5%)
A Canadian public pension	Government bond + margin (4–5%)
CPP Investment Board (CPP)	Calculated on an investment-by-investment basis
European Public Pension	CPI (Harmonised Index of Consumer Prices [HICP]) + margin (n/a)
Municipal Employees' Retirement System (MERS) of Michigan	Barclays Aggregate Bond Index
OPSEU Pension Trust (OPTrust)	CPI + margin (5%)
Ontario Teachers' Pension Plan (OTPP)	CPI + margin (4%) + sovereign spread (where CPI is based on country and currency of investment)
PSP Investments	CPI + bond return + equity premium (inflation adjusted infrastructure risk premium and infrastructure cost of capital – 2014 annual report)
UK Public Pension Fund	CPI (Retail Price Index (RPI)) + margin (5%) (used across all alternative assets)
Borealis Infrastructure (invests on behalf of OMERS and other institutional investors)	Absolute return set at the beginning of the year based on operating plan

Note: The authors do not know whether the institutions listed are still using the indicated benchmark by the time this book is published.
Source: Weber B. (2013) and CFA Institute (2012)

Benchmarking infrastructure assets, like any other asset, can be viewed as a three-step process:

i. Define the infrastructure investment strategy, specifically its desired target risk-return profile(s); it is possible for one infrastructure strategy to have two or three different sub-strategies with distinct risk classes and related return targets, if required or more suitable;

ii. Select a suitable benchmark and specify margin if appropriate – do so for every risk category, if applicable;

iii. Measure the performance of the infrastructure asset – after having assigned it to the respective risk category, if applicable – against the relevant benchmark.

i. Define the infrastructure investment strategy Investors ideally develop their infrastructure investment strategy based on their overall long-term investment strategy and asset allocation. To this end, they are advised to consider the relevant investment criteria in the context of infrastructure investing and the related questions listed in Table 2.6. These criteria may help investors to define their infrastructure investment strategy and, most importantly, to carve out the related risk-return profile(s). Investors are encouraged to address and form an opinion about each of the investment criteria in order for their infrastructure investment strategy to be sufficiently precise while leaving enough flexibility (i.e. a large enough universe) for its actual implementation (i.e. the asset picking).

In addition to the risk and return profiles, reflected in the selection of certain countries, sectors, stages of entry, currencies and the like, the cash flow profiles of any particular strategy are usually of paramount importance for investors and are closely linked to their investment horizon. Essentially, investors can be categorised into (primarily) yield-driven investors ('yield investors') and IRR-driven investors ('IRR investors'), see Section 1.3.8 for further information.

TABLE 2.6 Infrastructure investment criteria – questions and considerations

Investment Criteria	Questions/Considerations
Risk profile	Which kinds and scales of risks am I able or prepared to take?
Return profile	Given the risk profile, what are the short and long-term return expectations for both annual running yield and IRR?
Cash flow profile	Timing of cash flows Preferred cash flows (e.g. capital gains at exit vs. annual yield) Interest vs. dividend payments (consider tax and/or regulatory implications)
Investment horizon	Long-term vs. short-term holding period
Inflation protection	Relevance of real vs. nominal returns, which is predominantly driven by elasticity of demand and structure of investors' liabilities (e.g. pension fund vs. life insurance vs. reinsurance liabilities)
ESG criteria	(Industry specific) exclusion criteria (e.g. military) to be applied, if any
Stages of investments	To be considered from the point of view of both the cash flow profile (greenfield generally has no immediate cash flow) and/or the risk profile (greenfield has additional risks)
Currencies	Hedging costs
Leverage	To be considered from both a risk and a return point of view
Geographies	Political and regulatory risks, currency exposure
Liquidity	If liquidity is of utmost importance, unlisted infrastructure may be the wrong investment approach to start with
Diversification	Specify across which aspects/categories of risk and for which purpose
Control of assets	Kind of control usually required for listed investments Which control rights, if any, for which purpose? Under which circumstances are more control rights required and of which kind?

When addressing these questions and considerations and when specifying the investment criteria, investors may want to pay attention to and/or have a clear opinion about the following selected, seemingly sophisticated but possibly important, issues, which are frequently overlooked:

- *Post tax vs. pre-tax returns:* equity returns in the form of dividends or capital gains tend to be measured after tax, while bond returns (interest payments) are discussed based on their coupon value. For tax-exempt investors (as many are, e.g. pension funds), a distinct pre- and post-tax consideration is not relevant. For the majority of investors, however, it is.
- *Leverage:* equity returns are mostly geared, while debt returns are not.
- *Inflation protection of debt vs. equity:* the vast majority of debt – infrastructure and corporate alike – is not inflation linked. Equity returns of infrastructure assets, in contrast, very often are (even up to 100%), hence providing a significant protection against inflation risk, which debt does not.
- *Absolute vs. relative return targets:* the structure of the liabilities of an investor usually determines its desired/required profile of future returns – absolute vs. relative. Insurance companies, for instance, typically need to lock in absolute returns because in their, for example, life insurance contracts with customers they commit to absolute amounts to be paid out. In a possibly deflationary environment, inflation-linked returns would backfire. The liabilities of pension funds, that is the pensions, in contrast, are linked to inflation, which can go up or down. Therefore, pension funds should have a strong preference for inflation-linked returns. In a deflationary environment, their liabilities would decrease accordingly.
- *Country risk:* depending on the country risk, a higher or lower return for a certain investment may be appropriate. In case the country in which an investment is located differs from that of the investor, it needs to be decided which country determines the benchmark. Is it the geographic location of the asset or of the investor? Good arguments for both may be possible.

ii. Select a suitable benchmark and margin   Once the most important parameters of the investment strategy have been defined, a suitable benchmark must be identified or developed that captures the most relevant characteristics of the investment strategy. If appropriate, in addition a margin needs to be specified that reflects the risk level.

Investors may have creative and unusual ideas regarding benchmarks. As a starting point, possible benchmarks are listed below, which may be more or less suitable for individual investors, depending on the infrastructure strategy they pursue:

Selected benchmarks

- Absolute return
- CPI + margin
- Real estate (index) + margin
- Bond yield + margin
- Peer group
- Listed infrastructure + margin
- Listed equity + margin
- Asset mix + margin

For additional information on these benchmarks, please refer to Table 2.7.

TABLE 2.7 Matching selected benchmarks to exemplary risk-return profiles

Benchmarks		Absolute return	CPI + margin	Real estate + margin	Peer group	Listed infra + margin	Listed equity + margin	Asset mix + margin	Bond yield + margin
Risk-return profiles	Description								
Low risk (core)	Long term, stable, predictable yield, inflation protection	yes	yes	yes	yes	no	no	no	yes
Medium risk (value add)	Medium/long term, some stable yield and capital gain, some inflation protection	yes	no	yes	yes	y/n	y/n	yes	no
High risk (opportunistic)	Short/medium term, little yield, capital gain, no/little inflation protection	yes	no	no	yes	yes	yes	yes	no

Generally, investors expect to be compensated for taking additional risks over risk-free investments (e.g. government bonds of politically stable countries) by a margin. Likewise, they expect to be compensated for taking additional risk over the risk inherent in the assets, which is represented or reflected by the benchmark. Which margin(s) over the benchmark – if any – is/are considered appropriate is a direct function of the benchmark chosen and the previously defined risk-return profile(s) of the investment strategy.

The margin can be specified further and ultimately quantified by approximation, taking into consideration the risk premium paid for comparable risks. For example, the geographic/country risk of an asset located in an emerging market country can be approximated by the interest rate differential and thus the risk premium paid between developed and developing markets, respectively. The currency risk is reflected by the hedging costs between two currencies, which again are based on the interest rate differential of two currency markets. The illiquidity risk can be approximated by the higher return expectations for, for example, private equity (or debt) over listed equity (or debt) investments. Consequently, the return expectations of low-risk, core investments in developed countries (e.g. availability-based toll road PPP) are significantly lower than for high-risk, opportunistic investments in developing countries (e.g. user-paid toll road with full market risk).

As a rough and initial guidance for investors as to which benchmark may fit with which kind of investment strategy, the matrix in Table 2.7 matches a low-, medium-, and high-risk investment strategy with selected benchmarks (for detailed information on infrastructure investment risks, please refer to Chapter 5). Most importantly, the matrix illustrates with 'yes' and 'no' which infrastructure benchmark is considered suitable for measuring which investment strategy. Not every benchmark – with or without a margin – can be applied to measure adequately every infrastructure investment strategy. This is due to the diverse characteristics of infrastructure assets in many dimensions.

iii. Measure the performance of the infrastructure asset against the relevant benchmark
Once one – or several, as the case may be – suitable benchmarks have been identified for a – or several – risk-return profile(s) within a particular investment strategy, the historical and/or expected performance of each infrastructure asset in the portfolio can be measured against the relevant benchmark. For this exercise to be meaningful and to fulfil its purpose, investors need to ensure that the investment characteristics of the asset in question, most importantly the risk-return profile derived from, for example, the stage, contractual structure, currency, sector, etc., matches the one of the benchmark.

When measuring an asset's performance against the benchmark, the following aspects may be relevant and, if so, should be addressed carefully:

- *Match benchmark and vintage period.* When calculating and comparing returns relative to a benchmark, it is crucial to always match the period over which the benchmark returns are calculated to the period over which the asset/portfolio returns are calculated.
- *Match benchmark and valuation frequency.* With a portfolio of illiquid assets, investors are well advised not to publish new performance results relative to the benchmark more frequently than new valuation data for their assets are actually available.
- *Contemplate cost–benefit trade-offs.* In establishing a system of benchmarks and valuation protocols for unlisted assets, the cost and benefits of having a highly time- and resource-intensive process with more frequent points of measurement needs to be weighed against a less burdensome and more straightforward process with fewer points of measurement.
- *Track the business plan.* It is difficult to know how to interpret the early performance of a long-term investment. Investors should put emphasis on tracking the performance of the investment relative to the initial business plan (i.e. tracking operational targets, performance milestones and deviations from base-case financial model projections).
- *Revalue conservatively.* There are risks if illiquid asset values are marked up (or down) too quickly on the book before performance is unequivocally demonstrated (CFA Institute, 2012).

2.1.3.4 Advantages and disadvantages of different benchmarks   Selecting a reasonably suitable benchmark for unlisted infrastructure assets and specifying an appropriate margin, if applicable, are challenging tasks. Table 2.8 illustrates some advantages and disadvantages of selected benchmarks. While not conclusive, it may serve to guide investors in their search for the right benchmark and margin that suit their particular organisation and their individual investment strategy.

2.1.4 Portfolio diversification through infrastructure

In addition to the risk-return profile and benchmarking of an individual investment, another issue of interest is the extent to which infrastructure – just like any other asset class – serves to diversify an investor's portfolio as a whole. Simply put, diversification is achieved by

TABLE 2.8 Possible benchmarks for infrastructure

Benchmark	Advantages	Disadvantages
Absolute return target (fixed)	– Commonly used benchmark – Easy to use, i.e. measurable and achievable if set properly	– Not investable – Not inflation linked – Very subjective since dependent on individual cost of capital – Reliance on historical data dangerous as investment market changes over time – Long term absolute return targets impossible
CPI + margin (real)	– Commonly used benchmark – Easy to use – Captures inflation by definition – Well suited for low risk, long term, steady infrastructure strategies	– Not investable – Long-term view of the CPI required – Different CPI if asset is located in different country from investor
Real estate + margin (real)	– Usually strongly inflation linked – Well suited for esp. social infrastructure due to similarity of risk drivers and cash flow profiles – Long data series available	– Not easily investable – Not commonly used – Not suitable for majority of infrastructure assets – Terminal value usually constitutes high component of valuation – Volatility of listed real estate does not represent unlisted infrastructure – Listed real estate correlates more with other listed equities than with unlisted infrastructure
Peer group comparison (real)	– Inflation inherently captured – Allows identification of alpha – Performance measure over short intervals possible	– Not available due to lack of suitable data – Data sets of peer portfolios would need to be stratified into different risk-return categories to provide like-for-like comparison – Lack of coherent performance measurement – Performance data usually confidential

(continued)

TABLE 2.8 (Continued)

Benchmark	Advantages	Disadvantages
Listed infrastructure (equity) + margin	– Easy to use since data available – Investable, e.g. S&P, Macquarie, Dow Jones Brookfield, UBS – Partially inflation-linked depending on assets represented in index	– Market volatility of esp. low-risk infrastructure not well represented by listed infrastructure (see also real estate) – Listed infrastructure correlates more with any other listed equities than with unlisted infrastructure – Most infrastructure indices have significant bias towards energy generation infrastructure
Listed equity + margin	– Easy to use since data available – Investable (plenty of indices) – Partially inflation-linked depending on industries represented in index	– Market volatility of esp. low-risk infrastructure differs strongly from listed equity – Listed equity correlates somewhat with high risk and badly with low-risk infrastructure
Asset mix + margin	– Partially inflation-linked – Risk of infrastructure between various asset classes	– Not easily investable – Not commonly used – Short term possibly low correlation as infrastructure not well correlated to most other asset classes – Correlation difficult to interpret, due to variety of return drivers of equity, fixed income, real estate and infrastructure – Definition of asset mix may not properly reflect asset mix of actual infrastructure portfolio
Bond yield + margin	– Commonly used – Easy to use since data available – Well suited for low-risk infrastructure	– Not inflation linked (very few exceptions) – Inflation link can be achieved at price of duration mismatch, i.e. buy short term bonds and roll over

TABLE 2.9   Inter-asset correlation matrix (Q3/1995–Q2/2006)

	Composite infrastructure	Listed infrastructure	Toll roads	Airports	Utilities	Unlisted infrastructure	Real estate	Listed equity	Bonds
Composite infrastructure	1.00								
Listed infrastructure	0.86*	1.00							
Toll roads	0.85*	0.99*	1.00						
Airports	0.38*	0.40*	0.26	1.00					
Utilities	0.82*	0.42*	0.42*	0.14	1.00				
Unlisted infrastructure	0.31	0.36*	0.36*	0.26	0.16	1.00			
Real estate	−0.08	0.03	−0.01	0.36*	−0.21	0.26	1.00		
Listed equity	0.15	0.21	0.14	0.54*	0.01	0.06	0.14	1.00	
Bonds	0.57*	0.38*	0.38*	−0.03	0.57*	0.17	−0.12	−0.21	1.00
Inflation	−0.20	−0.22	−0.22	−0.23	−0.12	−0.27	0.10	−0.09	−0.25

Note: ∗ Significant correlation (p < 5%).
Source: Peng and Newell (2007)

combining so-called uncorrelated assets in the portfolio (i.e. assets which tend to change in value independently of each other) or, more specifically, by combining assets that have different risk and return characteristics and an asset price that does not depend on the same economic drivers. A measure commonly used in the context of portfolio diversification is the correlation of returns.

Correlation analyses are relatively easily done for listed infrastructure indices. This is because they typically not only have a fairly long track record of over 10 years but also, more importantly, their valuations are priced on a daily basis, like listed equity and bonds. Therefore, they provide a wealth of data points over the years, unlike unlisted infrastructure, which is usually only valued quarterly.

2.1.4.1   Cross-sector correlation   One of the first comprehensive analyses of unlisted infrastructure data series was undertaken by Peng and Newell (2007). Using quarterly data from Australian assets throughout in their 11-year analysis (1995–2006), they found that the different sectors within infrastructure are relatively little correlated among each other with only utilities and toll roads showing a significant correlation (0.42) (see Table 2.9).

This observation is supported, while not as strongly, by more recent research from RARE (2013) based on 12 years of performance data points from listed infrastructure assets (2000–2012), which show that except utilities, electricity and gas, which are naturally related industries, most correlations only range between 0.45 and 0.65 with the exception of communication, which correlates even less (see Table 2.10).

2.1.4.2   Inter-asset correlation   Unlisted infrastructure shows a low correlation with other asset classes, according to Peng and Newell (2007), with –0.06 against equity, 0.17 against bonds and 0.26 against direct property (see Table 2.9) – all correlations are

TABLE 2.10 Cross-sector correlation matrix (2000–2012)

2000-2012	Airport	Communications	Electric	Gas	Logistics	Diversified utilities	Railway	Seaport	Toll road	Water
Airport	1.0									
Communications	0.30	1.0								
Electric	0.63	0.26	1.0							
Gas	0.52	0.14	0.77	1.0						
Logistics	0.58	0.40	0.61	0.47	1.0					
Diversified utilities	0.41	0.17	0.79	0.75	0.47	1.0				
Railway	0.55	0.22	0.59	0.62	0.50	0.49	1.0			
Seaport	0.65	0.18	0.62	0.64	0.49	0.45	0.61	1.0		
Toll road	0.69	0.35	0.64	0.61	0.52	0.46	0.58	0.69	1.0	
Water	0.45	0.19	0.53	0.59	0.36	0.49	0.36	0.51	0.48	1.0

Source: RARE (2013)

TABLE 2.11 Inter-asset correlation matrix, 2001–2013

	US bonds	US equities	Listed infrastructure	Hedge funds	Private equity	US core real estate	OECD core infrastructure
US bonds	1.0						
US equities	−0.7	1.0					
Listed infrastructure	−0.3	0.8	1.0				
Hedge funds	−0.6	0.8	0.8	1.0			
Private equity	−0.4	0.8	0.9	0.8	1.0		
US core real estate	−0.2	0.1	0.3	0.2	0.4	1.0	
OECD core infrastructure (unlisted)	−0.2	0.0	0.1	0.2	−0.1	0.2	1.0

Note: JPMorgan Global Real Assets (GRA) approximates the different assets classes as follows: US Bonds: US Bonds – Barclays Global Aggregate Index; US Equities – MSCI World Total Return Index; Listed Infrastructure – Macquarie Global Infrastructure Total Return Index (covers publicly listed infrastructure funds in 48 markets around the world); Hedge Funds – HFRI Diversified FoF Index; Private Equity – Burgiss Private Equity Index; US Core Real Estate – BRE/IPD/JPMAM-GRA Modeled Series; OECD Core Infrastructure – JPMorgan GRA Research Modeled.
Source: JPMorgan (2015)

statistically insignificant on a 5% level, though. This compares with 0.21, 0.38 and 0.03 for listed infrastructure, respectively. It is worth pointing out that:

- Listed and unlisted infrastructure correlate only moderately with a value of 0.36 (statistically significant), highlighting once again that listed infrastructure cannot be used as approximation for unlisted infrastructure in an investment portfolio.
- Listed infrastructure correlates statistically significantly, yet fairly low, only against bonds (0.38), underlining that certain kinds of listed infrastructure investments can diversify a bond portfolio; in this data set, the results seem to be driven by the utility assets in particular, which show a moderate correlation (0.57) to bonds.
- Counterintuitively, the returns of listed infrastructure companies used in this study correlate only little (0.21) against listed equity, with the exception of airports (0.54). Utilities and toll roads show no significant correlation.

JPMorgan (2015) undertook a similar 12-year analysis with global data and for a later period (2001–2013) based on daily data for US bonds, US equities, listed infrastructure and hedge funds, and quarterly data for private equity, US core real estate and OECD core infrastructure (see Table 2.11). Its results differ partially substantially from Peng and Newell (2007), underlining once again the challenging data situation and the potentially high impact the chosen time period may have on the results. In particular, global listed infrastructure investments correlate very highly against US equities (0.8), as one would expect, and negatively against US bonds (−0.3). JPMorgan (2015) confirmed the results found by Peng and Newell (2007), that unlisted infrastructure neither correlates with listed equity (0.0 vs. 0.06 Peng and Newell, 2007) nor with bonds (−0.2 vs. 0.17 Peng and Newell, 2007). The article does not state whether these correlations are statistically significant on a 5% level, which leads us to conclude that they are not statistically significant. Unlisted and listed infrastructure correlate

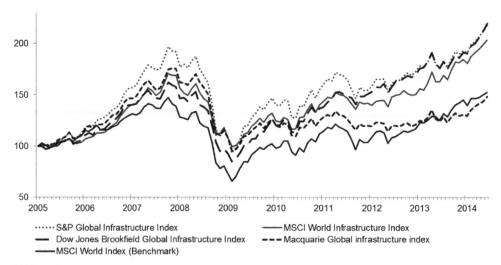

FIGURE 2.4   Total return infrastructure indices and MSCI World (Q1/2005–Q1/2015), rebased to Q1/2005
Source: JPMorgan (2015)

only with 0.1, supporting once again the results of previous studies that listed infrastructure is not a good approximation for unlisted infrastructure.

For comparison purposes and to put the correlation results of listed equities against listed infrastructure of the two studies above in perspective: if one correlates listed infrastructure assets of different, global, publicly listed infrastructure indices[10] against listed equities (MSCI World) over a 10-year period from Q1 2005 until Q1 2015, high correlation coefficients of between 0.85 and 0.96 result (see Figure 2.4).[11] This compares with Australian data, represented by the S&P ASX Infrastructure Index for listed infrastructure and the broad Australian stock market index ASX 300 for listed equities, over the same period (0.74).[12] These results suggest that Australian-listed infrastructure correlates highly with listed equities in contrast to the findings of Peng and Newell (2007). It stretches the context of this book to analyse the possible reasons for these contradicting outcomes. The authors suspect they are primarily caused by the different time periods and the different proxies used for listed infrastructure.

Both studies mentioned above (Peng and Newell, 2007; JPMorgan, 2015), as well as other studies[13] show no or little correlation of unlisted infrastructure with listed equities and bonds, suggesting a high diversification potential of unlisted infrastructure. Notwithstanding, there is a general tendency to underestimate volatility and co-variances and to overestimate the diversification potential of unlisted real assets, for example private equity, unlisted real estate and unlisted infrastructure. Wide agreement among researchers of private markets exists that the intensity of a correlation is caused to some extent by the frequency of measurement, in other

---

[10]S&P Global Infrastructure Index, Dow Jones Brookfield Global Infrastructure Index, MSCI World Infrastructure Index, Macquarie Global Infrastructure Index.
[11]JPMorgan Asset Management – Global Real Assets (2015).
[12]Bloomberg, accessed 12 October 2015.
[13]For example, Credit Suisse (2010), AMP Capital (2014b), Colonial First State (2014).

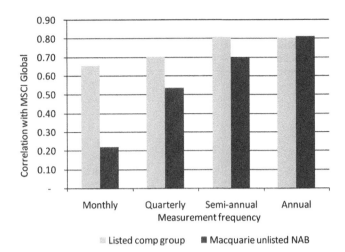

FIGURE 2.5 Correlation of listed and unlisted infrastructure with the MSCI World (2002–2008)
Source: RARE (2009)

words many data points (daily, mark to market observations of listed assets) tend to produce higher correlations than a few data points (quarterly or annual, mark to model observations of unlisted assets). This effect can be exacerbated by serial correlation (autocorrelation) as unlisted assets are valued by appraisal (mark to model). That is, valuation results of previous appraisals can be indicative of the valuation results of future appraisals, hence resulting in very stable returns.

RARE (2009) also took a closer look at the effect of valuation frequency on correlation results. Its results suggest that the low correlation between returns of unlisted vs. listed assets, be it listed infrastructure or listed equities, may indeed be largely driven by the measurement interval (see Figure 2.5). Essentially, it found that the correlation differences largely disappear, when the measurement interval increases, to this end RARE reduced the data points derived from monthly data to quarterly, semi-annual and annual observations (RARE, 2009).

Additional issues with correlation measures as approximation for diversification are the exact definition of returns (e.g. gross or net of fees, pre- or post tax) and the stability of correlations over time (for this aspect, see also Peng and Newell, 2007).

2.1.4.3 Unlisted infrastructure improves risk adjusted-portfolio return

The usefulness or even suitability – and therefore the information value – of correlation analyses as a basis for ALM studies in particular are strictly limited in light of the quality of the data available. However, it can be observed that listed infrastructure is affected by general stock market volatility. Also, the inclusion of especially conservative, unlisted infrastructure assets in a wider portfolio of equities, fixed-income securities, real estate and other alternative asset classes seems to have a clear positive effect on the diversification and risk-return profile of a portfolio. This holds even during difficult markets, as is shown by JPMorgan (2015), which assessed the impact of adding 2, 5 and 10% of a diversified unlisted global infrastructure allocation to a traditional portfolio's risk-return profile. Capturing a 20-year period (1995–2014),

TABLE 2.12 Impact of different infrastructure allocations to an existing portfolio

	Existing portfolio allocation	+2% to global infrastructure	+5% to global infrastructure	+10% to global infrastructure
Global equities	30%	30%	30%	30%
Global bonds	60%	58%	55%	50%
Property	5%	5%	5%	5%
Alternatives	5%	5%	5%	5%
Global infrastructure	0%	2%	5%	10%
	100%	100%	100%	100%
Expected return*	4.2%	4.4%	4.7%	5.2%
Expected income*	2.0%	2.0%	2.1%	2.2%
Historical return	7.0%	7.1%	7.3%	7.7%
Historical volatility	7.5%	7.5%	7.5%	7.5%
Estimated Sharpe ratio	0.36	0.39	0.43	0.49

Notes: (1) The allocation to global infrastructure is assumed to be taken from the global bonds allocation. (2) The Long-term Strategic Global Infrastructure Allocation is assumed to be 75% OECD core/core+ infrastructure and 25% Asian infrastructure. (3) The expected returns are derived from JPMorgan internal estimates of respective asset class returns. (4) Sharpe ratio assumes a risk-free rate of 1.5% and is estimated based on asset class target return assumptions and historical (annual) modelled 20-year (1995–2014) volatility (standard deviation of historical annual returns). (5) The portfolio attributes stated in the above table are for illustration purpose only. (6) The portfolios assume annual rebalancing.
Sources: Bloomberg, MSCI, Barclays, Burgiss PE, CBRE, IPD, UBS and JPMAM-Global Real Assets.
Source: JPMorgan (2015)

which includes the years of the financial crisis, JPMorgan found that unlisted infrastructure increased portfolio returns and the Sharpe ratio significantly (see Table 2.12 and Figure 2.6).[14] Generally, the greater the value of the Sharpe ratio, the more attractive the risk-adjusted return.

2.1.4.4 Infrastructure – an asset class For institutional investors, the issues raised in this section (2.1) are not merely academic but crucial for their investment decisions. They need to find a way, for example, to assess infrastructure investments correctly, benchmark them, model them in asset-liability studies, truly understand their diversification potential in a portfolio and integrate them into strategic asset allocation and risk budgeting exercises. One thing is certain: more research will need to be done in this field. An overall agreed-upon definition and categorisation of infrastructure assets and the specific mix of risk premia used across infrastructure investments are crucial elements in the analysis.

Overall, the long-term lifecycle of infrastructure assets and – providing the requisite contractual structure – their long-term, predictable stable income can be similar to that offered

[14]The Sharpe ratio is the average return earned in excess of the risk-free rate per unit of volatility or total risk. Generally, the greater the value of the Sharpe ratio, the more attractive the risk-adjusted return.

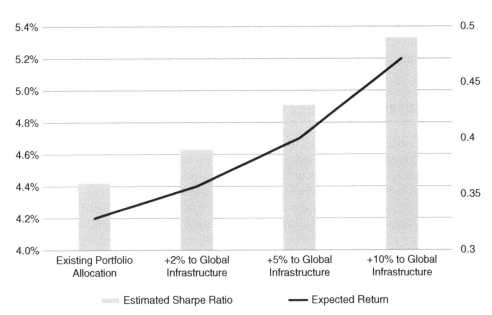

FIGURE 2.6   Effect of infrastructure allocation on expected return and estimated Sharpe ratio of a portfolio
Source: JPMorgan (2015)

by real estate assets or fixed-income securities. The inherent inflation protection offered by many infrastructure assets may also make them an interesting alternative to inflation-protected government bonds, corporate bonds, mezzanine and high-yield debt. However, infrastructure investments can also offer (private) equity-style returns with the respective volatility and risks involved. To this end, infrastructure shares similarities with all three asset classes. With which of these three most similarities are shared ultimately depends on the specific infrastructure asset in question and cannot be generalised.

On the basis of the limited available data and the above analyses, infrastructure appears to be a hybrid form of real estate, private equity and fixed income and can be considered as a separate asset class, even though it does not exhibit a homogeneous profile. This, however, is equally true for the other three asset classes mentioned, and even more so for hedge funds for that matter, every single one of them spanning a wide spectrum of investment strategies when analysed in detail. At the same time, it can be demonstrated that infrastructure cannot be sub-categorised as a mere adjunct of any of the other asset classes. Its inclusion in a wider portfolio will increase the diversification of the portfolio and as such reduce its risk-return profile.

> *Infrastructure appears to be a hybrid form between real estate, private equity and fixed income that can be considered to represent a separate asset class.*

The remainder of this chapter is structured as follows: Section 2.2 explains why and how to include sustainability in infrastructure investing. Section 2.3 provides a brief overview of how to approach infrastructure investing, focusing on infrastructure funds. The remainder of the book concentrates on direct investing into the assets themselves. Given the demonstrated necessity to analyse each and every infrastructure asset individually in order to assess its risk-return profile, Chapter 3 presents an analytical framework to do so. Chapter 5 serves as a 'risk-analysis guide' throughout any infrastructure investment process.

2.2 SUSTAINABLE INFRASTRUCTURE INVESTING

Sustainable infrastructure is in the interest of everybody. Global investments in infrastructure, such as energy generation and transmission, water supply and sanitation facilities, transport networks, as well as social infrastructure, will play a key role in determining how successful societies will be in meeting the immense social and environmental challenges of our time, such as eradicating poverty, managing natural resources sustainably and curtailing dangerous climate change. Sustainable infrastructure will benefit societies, governments, and investors alike because they all have an interest in well-functioning and well-governed social, environmental and economic systems: societies because they rely on them and they affect their quality of life; governments because they will need to invest less into these assets in the long run and/or the assets will be particularly effective and/or efficient, and investors because 'healthy', futureproof assets produce stable, long-term financial returns over the life of the investment.

This chapter introduces the concept of sustainable investing and how it can be applied to private infrastructure investments.

2.2.1 Concept of sustainable investing

As markets become increasingly interconnected globally, the effects of environmental and social pressures resulting from food, water and energy scarcity, access to natural resources, climate change, environmental disasters and demographic change increasingly affect investors around the world. Sustainable investing stands for an investment approach that acknowledges the full spectrum of risks and opportunities resulting from these global challenges and includes them in the overall investment decision. The following sections provide some information on the origins and history of sustainable investing, a working definition and an overview of different approaches to sustainable investing as well as relevant market data.

2.2.1.1 Origins of sustainable investing   The concept of sustainable investing has its roots both in the civil rights/anti-war movement and the environmental protection movement of the 1960s and 1970s. In those days, students demanded more ethical business and investment practices, for example calling for the boycott of companies that produced military weapons and requesting equal rights and safer conditions for workers. During this same period, a growing concern over the impact of industrial pollution, ignited by Rachel Carson's milestone environmental book *Silent Spring* (1962), led to the founding of the first Earth Day and the creation of a number of national environmental agencies such as the United States Environmental Protection Agency (US EPA) in 1970 and the German Federal Environment Agency in 1974, reflecting an international movement towards better protection of the environment and human health. The Three Mile Island nuclear power plant accident in the US in 1979 followed by the catastrophic Chernobyl nuclear power plant disaster in Ukraine (in the then Soviet Union) in 1986 further heightened public concern about the large-scale environmental and human health risks associated with modern industrial practices.

In 1989, the *Exxon-Valdez* oil tanker accident, in which over 10 million gallons (41 000 litres) of spilt crude oil damaged over 2100 km of coastline, was a catalyst for re-evaluating current risk assessment practices in industry. In that same year, the US-based international organisation Ceres was established by a small group of investors with the explicit purpose of promoting sustainable business and investment practices. In 1997, Ceres launched the Global Reporting Initiative (GRI), now the de facto standard for sustainability reports of companies worldwide.

However, it was not until the 21st century that sustainable investing became a mainstream movement in itself. Some milestones in this movement are:

- 2003: Ceres creates an investor network on climate risk (INCR) to establish a business and fiduciary case for integrating sustainability criteria into mainstream investment analysis. By 2015, this network has grown to 100 institutional investors managing US$11.8 trillion in assets.
- 2004: A group of industry experts develops the Darmstadt Definition of Sustainable Investments, which comprises three components of sustainable investing:
  - Economic: Profits based on long-term strategies that are not corrupt, do not threaten basic human needs and increase economic value.
  - Environmental: Profits consistent with increased resource productivity, renewable resource investment, recycling and reuse of materials and the workability of global and local environmental systems (e.g. rainforests, oceans).
  - Social and cultural: Profits consistent with the development of human capital (employment education, work/life balance, etc.), of social capital (gainful employment, responsible corporate citizenship) and of cultural capital (cultural diversity, civil rights, societal integrity).
- 2006: The UN launches the Principles for Responsible Investment (PRI), a global initiative to promote the integration of ESG issues into investment analysis and decision-making processes. The initiative has been very successful and as of September 2015 counts 1378 signatories (asset owners, investment managers, service providers) representing US$45 trillion in assets under management (www.unpri.org).
- 2011: A work stream dedicated to supporting signatories in implementing responsible investment policies and processes in infrastructure investments was formally established. Support tools include case studies, webinars, discussion papers and in-depth guidance documents (www.unpri.com).
- 2015: Specifically in relation to infrastructure investments, Ceres' Clean Trillion investment initiative, highlights the need for global investments of US$44 trillion in clean energy to limit global warming to 2°C and to avoid the worst effects of climate change. As such, the initiative prompts investors to increase their investments in and around clean energy significantly and requests policymakers to adopt policies that stimulate such investment - including energy efficiency, renewable energy infrastructure and clean transportation - and that put a limit and price on greenhouse gas emissions.

2.2.1.2 Working definition of sustainable investing
Sustainable investing can be viewed as a comprehensive approach to investment analysis, decision-making and engagement, which includes full consideration of ESG risks and the related opportunities that can affect investment returns. It is not a new method of investing but it purposely broadens the scope of traditional risk analysis and management. The goal is first to identify these ESG risks

and then prevent or mitigate and manage them to the benefit of shareholders and stakeholders. Examples of common ESG risk factors are:

- Environmental: climate change risk (physical and regulatory risks), hazardous waste, contamination, resource scarcity (water and other natural resources), environmental degradation;
- Social: human rights, labour rights, consumer protection, local communities;
- Governance: governance structure/management systems, rule of law, government relations, corruption, compensation structures (management, employee, incentives).

Terms such as '(socially) responsible investing', 'sustainable investing' and 'impact investing' are all used in the financial world to describe the process of accounting for ESG risks factors in the investment process with a view to creating sustainable value for society. While socially responsible investing adds an ethical perspective and takes additional values such as fairness and justice into consideration, impact investing reflects the fact that investors accept higher risk and/or lower returns in order to make a positive impact on society. The term 'sustainable investing' walks the middle path with investors focusing on reducing long-term ESG risk and making a positive impact on society.

Ceres defines 'sustainable investing' as 'investing to meet the needs of current beneficiaries without compromising the ability to meet the needs of future beneficiaries' (Ceres, 2013). For pension funds, for example, this definition translates into sustaining their ability to meet their multi-generational obligations.

SUSTAINABLE INVESTING

In this book, we use the term 'sustainable investing' to describe an investment approach that explicitly acknowledges environmental, social and corporate governance (ESG) factors and integrates them into the investment process with the purpose of reducing risk and embracing opportunities, hence enabling a positive, lasting impact on society.

2.2.1.3 Sustainable investment strategies Sustainable investing is driven by the growing awareness of investors that the integration of ESG issues – mainly in asset allocation, investment selection, portfolio construction as well as shareholder engagement and voting – is fundamental to assessing the value and the expected risk and return of a portfolio of assets over the medium to longer term.

There are different approaches to sustainable investing, mainly (i) positive and negative screening strategies, (ii) ESG integration, (iii) thematic and impact investments, and (iv) shareholder engagement (Staub-Bisang, 2012). The spectrum of sustainable (and responsible) investing spans from conventional investing (focus on financial return with little consideration of ESG factors) to philanthropic investing (no required financial return), with 'sustainable and responsible' and 'thematic' and 'impact' investing located in between these two extremes. Figure 2.7 provides a schematic overview of the different sustainable and responsible investment approaches, which can be applied to all asset classes. They are discussed further below, including the related terminology. The figure deliberately does not include the category 'shareholder engagement' as this strategy by definition can only be applied to listed equities.

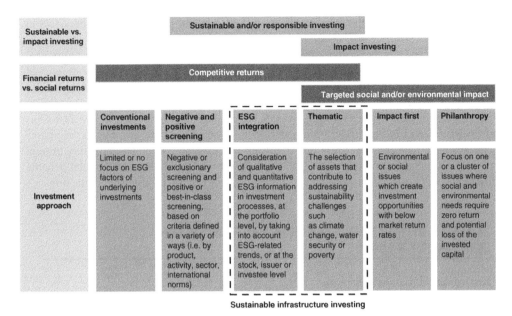

FIGURE 2.7 Sustainable investment approaches and strategies within the investment spectrum
Source: Modified from UN (2015b)

Institutional investors with a sustainable investment approach naturally focus on investment strategies, which provide competitive or market returns – mainly screening, ESG integration and thematic investments – while so-called impact first investments, which focus on environmental or social issues accepting below market returns, if necessary, are left to charitable foundations, private high-net-worth investors and family offices specifically. Institutional investors, for example pension funds, are obliged to maximise long-term risk-adjusted investment returns owing to the fiduciary duty of both their trustees as well as their asset managers and consultants (e.g. the US) (UNPRI, 2015).

First, screening strategies encompass negative/exclusionary screening and positive/best-in-class screening. Negative screening aims to avoid, and therefore excludes, investments in business sectors or practices from the investment universe that do not correspond to predefined ESG standards or certain minimum standards based on international (e.g. OECD, ILO) norms. The reasoning for this approach is that capital should not be made available to industries or companies that are harmful to the environment or society as a whole. As opposed to negative screening, positive screening strategies focus on investments in securities or assets selected for positive ESG performance relative to industry peers. The best-in-class approach creates, first of all, a sustainable, investable sub-universe meeting certain sustainability criteria. And then, the financially most promising securities or assets out of this sub-universe are selected.

Second, ESG integration stands for the systematic and explicit inclusion of ESG factors into traditional financial analysis with the goal of reducing and mitigating ESG risks. The inclusion of ESG factors in the investment process adds a valuable dimension, which has been shown to have no negative impact on financial returns; on the contrary, many studies could demonstrate the positive effect on the long-term performance of the assets in question.[15]

Lower risk and equal or better long-term performance result in a superior risk-return profile, that is long-term, risk-adjusted investment returns of ESG investments over conventional ones. For this rational and convincing reason, a growing number of investors now include ESG factors in their investment decisions. An excellent primer on how to incorporate sustainability (ESG) risks and opportunities into the investment decision-making process is *The 21st Century Investor: Ceres Blueprint for Sustainable Investing* (Ceres, 2013). This breaks the phases of a sustainable investment process into a 10-step process, integrating sustainability criteria across all asset classes and investment strategies. Further, it highlights the potential benefits of including ESG risk factors in the investment process. They are summarised in the box.

BENEFITS OF INCLUDING ESG RISK FACTORS IN THE INVESTMENT PROCESS

Environmental analysis reveals:

- Business impacts on environment throughout the product and business life cycle
- Portfolio vulnerability to regulatory changes and preparedness for climate change
- Strategies for sustainable energy and resource use, and greenhouse gases reductions
- Investment opportunities based on adaptation strategies and sustainable solutions

Social analysis reveals:

- A company's commitment to human rights, health and safety and supply chain risks
- Investor awareness to substandard labour practices and community values
- A company's reputational risk and risk of losing the licence to operate

Governance analysis reveals:

- The strength of a company's management systems and its accountability practices
- Board and management commitment to social and environmental performance and ethical business practices
- Accountability at the board and C-Suite levels for anticipating and managing risks
- Alignment of policies to sustainability, diversity, gender equality and transparency

Source: Modified from Ceres (2013)

Third, thematic and impact investments focus on specific investment themes or sectors with an economic potential while pursuing dedicated environmental or social goals, such as water protection, support of renewable energy, clean technologies or micro-finance. Thematic investments can be classified as impact investments to the extent that their primary intention

---

[15]For a comprehensive overview, see the meta study by Mercer (2009); additional studies are Morgan Stanley (2015) and TIAA-CREF (2014).

TABLE 2.13   Growth of sustainable investment assets by region, 2012–2014

	2012	2014	Growth
Europe	$8758	$13 608	55%
United States	$3740	$6572	76%
Canada	$589	$945	60%
Australia/NZ	$134	$180	34%
Asia	$40	$53	32%
Total	$13 261	$21 358	61%

Note: Asset values in billions
Source: GSIA (2015)

is to benefit society as a whole. However, the explicit aim is to generate returns that are in line with financial markets. So-called impact first investments focus on environmental or social issues 'first', with investors accepting below market returns, if necessary.

Fourth, shareholder engagement describes the strategy of using shareholder power to influence corporate behaviour, be that through direct corporate engagement and dialogue (i.e. communication with senior management) or shareholder activism in the proxy process, filing shareholder proposals guided by comprehensive ESG guidelines.

All strategies, except shareholder engagement, can be applied to a larger or lesser extent across all asset classes; the latter is limited to equity investments per definition.

Globally, the market for sustainable investable assets has grown dramatically over the past years. In Europe alone, which still represents the largest market for sustainable investment strategies, it grew more than 20-fold from less than €0.5 trillion in 2002 to over €13 trillion in 2014 (Eurosif, 2014; GSIA, 2015). According to the 2014 Global Sustainable Investment Review (GSIA, 2015), the global market for sustainable investments expanded by more than 60% from 2012 to 2014, with most of the growth accountable to investors in the US, followed by Canada and Europe (see Table 2.13). The three regions account for 99% of global sustainable investing assets, with 64% in Europe alone, followed by the US, with 31%.

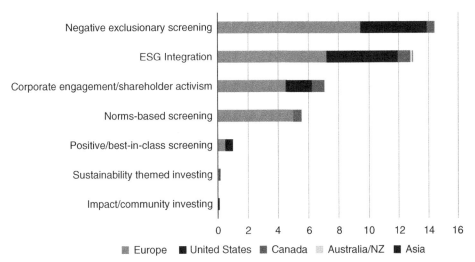

FIGURE 2.8   Sustainable investment assets by strategy and region (2012–2014) in USD trillions
Source: GSIA (2015)

Moreover, Figure 2.8 illustrates that the most important sustainable investment strategy globally in terms of investment volumes is negative screening/exclusions (US$14.4 trillion), followed by ESG integration (US$12.9 trillion) and corporate engagement/shareholder action (US$7.0 trillion). Geographically, negative screening is the dominant strategy in Europe, ESG integration is most important in the US, Australia/New Zealand and Asia in asset-weighted terms.

2.2.2   Why invest in sustainable infrastructure?

Investors may apply sustainability criteria to infrastructure investments for a number of reasons, some of which will be addressed below. Improved competitiveness of economies and societal benefits, as well as resilience to climate change – while possibly not immediately measurable – are likely to become crucial to investors in the long-term and are hence among the main reasons. Improved risk-return profiles of investments are clearly of primary interest to all investors in the short and the long term.

2.2.2.1   Improved economic competitiveness and societal benefits   Applying the above-mentioned sustainable investment principles to infrastructure assets and projects – that is the consideration of ESG factors in the infrastructure investment process – is highly relevant for the competitiveness of an economy. This holds in particular because infrastructure can be an important driver in addressing some of the most systemic development challenges of today's world such as social stability, rapid urbanisation, climate change adaptation and mitigation, and natural disasters. Without an infrastructure that supports green and inclusive growth, countries will not only find it harder to meet unmet basic needs but also struggle to improve competitiveness (World Bank, 2012a). Sustainable infrastructure is not only a key component of a functioning economy it also forms the backbone for livelihoods for billions of people, and has the potential to contribute significantly to achieving a more sustainable world. Indeed, the UN Open Working Group on Sustainable Development also recognises the potential of infrastructure in its proposal of Sustainable Development Goals (SDGs) by requesting sustainable and resilient infrastructure in two of the 17 SDGs that have been passed by the UN Sustainable Development Summit 2015 in New York. This underlines the potential power of infrastructure to drive sustainable development, which should be in the interest of any responsible institutional investor.

For instance, an EU report estimates that €270 billion in annual EU investments will be needed for development in low-carbon energy supply, energy efficiency and infrastructure, which could also provide additional societal benefits such as annual fuel savings of €170–€320 billion and monetised health benefits of up to €88 billion per year by 2050 (European Commission, 2013a). With respect to global water supply and disposal needs, a WEF report ranks scarcity of fresh water first in the top 10 systemic global risks affecting society that could result in a worldwide breakdown in economic, social and environmental systems (WEF, 2015). On this subject, a UN report concludes that, by 2025, fresh water demand will increase by 50% in developing nations with two-thirds of the world population living under stress water conditions (UN, 2013).

Private investors are seen as playing a key role in helping to meet social needs by investing increasingly in sustainable infrastructure. For example, the Peruvian government recently announced it was seeking US$19 billion in private equity investment to help improve access to portable water and sanitation across the nation (Bloomberg Business, 2014a).

In light of the above, it becomes apparent that for institutional investors globally sustainable investing no longer is just a means to tick the sustainability box for marketing or reputational reasons. Rather, they now increasingly consider it a vital component of comprehensive risk assessment to ensure that ESG issues are accounted for and addressed during the entire life of an investment. For example, a number of global investment firms that invest in infrastructure, including some of the largest and most renowned pension funds globally (AIMCo, APG, ATP, Aviva, CalPERS, Mirova, OTPP, PGGM) now include ESG issues as a core component of their investment process (see also GRESB Infrastructure in Section 2.2.3.2). *They view such risks as material, having a significant impact on the long-term risk-adjusted financial return of their portfolio.* To this end, CalPERS (US$307 billion), for instance, announced in May 2015 that, from now on, it will require all of its managers to identify and articulate ESG issues in their investment processes. The degree to which ESG risks are accounted for by external asset managers will factor into the selection and contracting of external managers, as well as influence how relationships are maintained and managed. (Top1000funds, 2015).

2.2.2.2 Resilience to climate change There is a growing interest among infrastructure investors to assess specifically the resilience of an infrastructure asset to climate change risks. The European Investment Bank (EIB), for example, has developed several sector strategies, which include applying cost-effective, appropriate adaptation measures to infrastructure assets in locations with a risk of significant adverse impacts from climate change and increased frequency of extreme weather events. Many commercial banks also include climate change risks in their due diligence processes by now after having been engaged in adaptation research over a number of years.

With respect to private investors, a 2012 survey by the Global Investor Coalition on Climate Change (representing institutional investors in Europe, North America, Australia, New Zealand and Asia) found that for the 84 investors surveyed (representing over US$14 trillion in assets), the risk from climate change increasingly influences their investment activities. Over 80% of asset owners and almost 70% of asset managers viewed climate change as a material risk across their entire investment portfolio and nearly 100% of asset managers and 80% of asset owners incorporated climate change risks and opportunities into their due diligence and investment analysis processes (Mercer, 2013). Among the top climate risk factors identified were regulatory changes relating to greenhouse gas emissions, government support schemes, physical impacts and corporate governance policies for climate change.

2.2.2.3 Improved risk-return profile Adaptation measures to mitigate climate change risk (e.g. protective constructions to reduce physical damage to assets caused by storms or floods), resource efficiency measures to prepare for future higher costs for scarce resources (e.g. water) and compliance with current and future environmental regulation potentially result in higher upfront investment cost. These higher costs occur at a time when the specific long-term implications and related costs of climate change are still difficult to quantify for any individual asset.

Notwithstanding, such costs are likely to be offset by immediate cost savings (e.g. lower energy and water use) and the benefit of future proofing an asset against such risks while its returns should remain (at least) the same. In other words, such adaptation measures improve the risk-return profile of the asset in question as already indicated above. Consequently, sustainable infrastructure assets, which will be able, for example, to withstand the potential physical impacts from climate change and/or to conform to future regulatory standards not yet known, are projected to be able to demand higher valuations than those that are not.

Other examples of ESG risks to which the same (economic) rationale applies, are: environmental risks (e.g. hazardous waste, pollution from operations), social risks (e.g. substandard labour practices, poor relations with local communities) and governance risks (e.g. unethical management practices, corruption). They bear significant reputational risks and the risk of losing the licence to operate.

In conclusion, sustainable infrastructure can provide at least the same functions and services as conventional infrastructure and yet offers additional benefits to all three main stakeholders, namely society as a whole by contributing to a better quality of life, to governments by easing their balance sheets, and to investors by improving the risk-return profiles of their infrastructure investments. With the market opportunity for private infrastructure investments being so apparent, the economic and reputational benefits to long-term investors of owning de-risked and future proofed assets should need no further comment.

2.2.3   How to invest in infrastructure sustainably

There are different ways to invest in infrastructure in a sustainable way while targeting market returns. Based on the terminology introduced in Section 2.2.1.3, the most practical, and hence promising approach is considered to be 'ESG integration', that is the inclusion of ESG (risk) factors in the investment process for infrastructure investments across all sectors (see Sections 4.1–4.7 for a detailed discussion of selected infrastructure sectors). Targeted 'thematic investments' with the specific purpose of addressing sustainability issues such as climate change or resource scarcity are also seen as a suitable approach. The economic relevance of the latter is growing, but only applies to a fraction of the entire investable infrastructure universe, yet. It is therefore not covered in a separate sub-section below. Both approaches share the goal of reducing ESG risks while making a positive contribution to society. At the same time, they may increase the chances of providing long-term, stable market returns to institutional investors, which will enable them to meet their fiduciary obligation of maximising long-term risk-adjusted investment returns.

2.2.3.1   ESG integration in infrastructure investing   By their very nature, investments in infrastructure always either actively affect the environment or society or are affected by it, positively or negatively. Accordingly, ESG risks related to infrastructure can be classified in two main groups: first, infrastructure that has a significant impact *on* the earth and society (generally and globally) and therefore should be built in a sustainable way respecting the environment and, second, infrastructure that is vulnerable *to* ESG factors, such as physical damage *from* climate change.

Examples for negative impacts on the environment and society from operating an infrastructure asset are environmental degradation and pollution, human rights issues (labour law issues), health and safety risks for workers and/or the local communities or unethical management practices (mainly corruption). Examples of ESG risks that affect infrastructure projects and assets are mainly physical and regulatory risks resulting from climate change, but also can be related to, for example, resource scarcity/natural resources constraints (water, clean air), pollution, population growth and ageing societies (see Section 2.2.1.3).

Depending on the type and location of the infrastructure asset in question, these kinds of ESG risks are more or less likely to materialise. The (ideally early) integration of ESG factors in infrastructure investment decisions and processes in addition to traditional economic and specifically financial considerations seeks to minimise the potential negative impacts and their (financial) consequences (damage/loss) resulting from such ESG factors. Further, there is always an inherent reputational risk to be considered by all project partners.

On the positive side, infrastructure assets that account for and reduce exposure to risks from ESG factors may provide additional societal benefits in support of sustainable development while meeting corporate and institutional sustainability goals – as well as improving the risk-return profile of the assets.

Whether considering investments in infrastructure projects/assets in traditional sectors or in those aimed at providing a specific sustainability benefit (thematic and impact investments, see Section 2.2.1.3), asset owners and their stakeholders (e.g. beneficiaries of pension funds, governments) increasingly want to assess, measure, rate and partially also benchmark not only the financial, but also the sustainability performance and risks of any infrastructure project or asset they own or consider to acquire. To this end, the next section provides an overview of several approaches and tools to assessing and rating the sustainability of infrastructure investments.

2.2.3.2 Sustainable infrastructure assessment and benchmarking

Awareness of ESG issues and their potential risks is of little use unless investors have the means to effectively evaluate and measure such risks in order to subsequently take an educated decision as to how to eliminate or mitigate them or possibly to abstain from the investment altogether. Currently, no global, universally agreed ESG standard exists for assessing and benchmarking the sustainability performance of infrastructure assets or projects. Yet, an internationally coordinated ESG (risk) assessment and benchmarking approach is in the long-term interest of all stakeholders in infrastructure as it could support more informed investment decisions by making different investments comparable along both financial and sustainability/ESG attractiveness.

A number of sustainability assessment tools (guidelines, frameworks, rating systems) that have been initiated and supported by various kinds of stakeholders – including development banks, international organisations and institutional investors as well as independent research providers, academic institutions and non-for-profit organisations – are available to infrastructure investors. The breadth and depth of such tools varies and they continue to expand at a rapid pace. We hence recommend that investors do their own research to ensure they have access to the most relevant and most suitable ESG assessment tools available for their particular needs.

Notwithstanding this, below we provide a selection of ESG assessment tools (available at the time this book went to press) the authors considered most suitable for infrastructure investors. Many of them were developed for use in a particular country, region or sector and therefore may have sustainability criteria that are weighted towards the key sustainability issues of a particular geographic area or sector. However, although the ESG assessment tools listed here vary in scope and complexity, they all share the common goal of supporting investors in incorporating sustainability (ESG) issues, benefits and risks into their infrastructure assessment, which in turn should help them to benchmark their assets in question.

Common to all providers is the use of a set of criteria to measure and rate sustainability performance throughout the lifecycle of a project or asset, if applicable. Many of the sustainability assessment criteria are similar to those currently used in popular sustainability/green building rating systems such as LEED (US), BREEAM (UK), and DGNB (Germany). Some of the assessment tools (or rather their providers) have a clear focus on risk management with the goal of supporting investors in identifying and assessing potential ESG risks (see Section 5.2.4 for a comprehensive discussion of ESG risks). Others have the explicitly stated goal to develop as a (standard) sustainability benchmarking instrument. Given the limited scope of

most tools and the fact that all of them are still in the early stages of development, their use
for proper benchmarking is currently limited.

CDC Toolkit on ESG for Fund Managers (UK)

The easy-to-use ABC rating system contained within the detailed, 184-page toolkit allows
for a quick assessment and benchmarking of each (ESG) risk type. It also includes
detailed references to international standards including those of particular importance in
the infrastructure sector. Although designed primarily for private equity fund managers
investing in emerging markets, this toolkit is also appropriate for infrastructure investors.
It has been developed by CDC (www.cdcgroup.com), the development finance institution
owned by the UK government's Department for International Development. See Appendix
A for sample page from rating system.

Envision Sustainable Infrastructure Rating System (North America)

Envision is a planning, design and evaluation tool for rating the sustainability of any
kind of infrastructure project (http://www.sustainableinfrastructure.org/rating/index.cfm).
It provides a scoring framework for grading the community, environmental and economic
benefits of infrastructure projects using 60 criteria, or credits, divided into five sections:
quality of life, leadership, resource allocation, natural world and climate and risk (see
Appendix B for complete credit list). The goal is to assess the costs and benefits over
the project's lifecycle, evaluate environmental benefits, achieve sustainability goals and
possibly get public recognition (Envision award). To that extent Envision also aims to
become a benchmarking tool, investors can self-assess, that is rate different projects and
compare their sustainability performance.

Envision has been developed in a collaboration between the Zofnass Program for
Sustainable Infrastructure at Harvard University and the Institute for Sustainable Infrastructure (ISI). The rating system was designed primarily for use in North America by
a wide stakeholder group, including infrastructure owners, design teams, community
groups, environmental organisations, constructors, regulators and policy makers.

Business Case Evaluator and AutoCASE risk analysis tool (for Envision)

The Excel-based Business Case Evaluator (BCE) and the cloud-based AutoCASE plug-in
for Autodesk Infrastructure Design Suite both help convert Envision sustainability metrics into a quantitative risk-based cost–benefit metric (www.impactinfrastructure.com).
In doing so, these tools allow owners and investors to monetarily measure the costs and
benefits associated with sustainable infrastructure investments. As of March 2015, ver-
sions of these tools were available only for storm water projects. However, new modules
are in the works for highways, buildings and other types of infrastructure. The BCE is a
cost-free, public-domain tool, whereas AutoCASE is commercial.

Global Infrastructure Basel (GIB) Sustainable Infrastructure Grading

This tool provides owners of infrastructure projects (at any stage) with a sustainability
assessment and rating metric focused on developing countries (www.gib-foundation.org).
The ESG performance of any project is graded relative to a GIB-defined benchmark in 10
categories (e.g. accountability, transparency, poverty responsiveness, resource protection,
shared incentives, sound financial mechanisms). This produces a sustainability rating that
allows investors to identify the strengths and weaknesses (and the related ESG risks)
of a project and compare the sustainability performance of different projects relative

to each other and the (subjective) GIB benchmark. GIB is currently (as of September 2015) in the process of developing a new voluntary sustainability standard for sustainable and resilient infrastructure (SuRe) based on the GIB Sustainable Infrastructure Grading self-assessment tool.

GRESB Infrastructure, Netherlands

GRESB Infrastructure is an investor-led assessment tool that allows investors to undertake systematic assessment and aims to offer sector-specific benchmarking of the sustainability performance of their infrastructure assets (www.gresb.com). It seeks to develop and establish a consistent framework for investors to collect and compare key ESG factors and related performance metrics across assets globally. The framework is aligned with international reporting frameworks, such as the GRI and PRI. GRESB provides benchmark reports that contain peer group comparisons for each ESG theme; alternatively, investors can selectively compare results for individually specified categories (e.g. region, sector). The eight founding institutional investors are AIMCo, ATP, Aviva Investors, APG Asset Management, CalPERS, Mirova, OTPP and PGGM Investments, with US$1.5 trillion in assets under management.

Infrastructure Sustainability Rating System (Australia)

This Australian-based Infrastructure Sustainability Rating System uses a framework of six themes and 15 categories to evaluate an asset or project (www.isca.org.au). The goal is to obtain a rating for existing assets or to help integrate sustainability measures in infrastructure projects from the planning phase. See Appendix C for an overview of themes and categories. Although economic performance is currently not included in this rating system, the addition of this feature is currently under review (August 2015).

International Infrastructure Support System (IISS), Switzerland

The main objective of IISS differs from the ones mentioned above for it is designed as a public project management tool enabling public-sector agencies to raise the quality, consistency and transparency of the public sector's infrastructure project preparation and, as such, improve their project preparation activities down to a subsector level (www.sif-iiss.org). The assessment and management of ESG factors form part of the overall project management. IISS has been set up and is actively supported (as funding and technical partners as well as leading private-sector investors and operators) by a group of multinational development banks: African Development Bank, Asian Development Bank, Banco Nacional de Desenvolvimento Econômico e Social, Development Bank of Southern Africa, European Bank for Reconstruction and Development, Inter-American Development Bank and the World Bank Group. IISS is run by the not-for-profit Sustainable Infrastructure Foundation (SIF) headquartered in Geneva, Switzerland.

All of the tools listed above support investors in assessing their projects and assets under sustainability aspects, yet only few – and mainly the more recent initiatives – provide or have the ambition to provide some sort of benchmarking tool as well. As of now, they all rely on self-assessment or (subjective) assessment by some kind of 'expert committee', and not on objectively measured sustainability performance data. Notwithstanding, they may give a first indication where things could be heading.

By definition, benchmarking requires a 'standard', with which individual objects, here greenfield projects or brownfield assets, can be compared. Currently, such a standard does not exist, owing to a lack of standardised sustainability performance data, collected for infrastructure projects/assets globally across regions and sectors. Moreover, in contrast to financial benchmarks, which tend to be based on purely quantitative parameters related to risk and return, sustainability performance data are multifactorial and only partially quantifiable. Qualitative data always include the subjective bias of the observer.

In summary, important ground has been covered already in the context of the benchmarking of unlisted infrastructure assets in general, and benchmarking them along sustainability criteria in particular. Notwithstanding, it is still in its infancy and remains a major challenge for years to come. Apart from benchmarking, additional challenges remain with sustainable infrastructure investing.

2.2.4   Challenges of sustainable infrastructure investing

Despite the potential triple-win situation of sustainable infrastructure investing – society, governments, investors – there are barriers to investors entering certain infrastructure sectors. An OECD report identified three main barriers unique to sustainable, low-carbon investments (Kaminker et al., 2013). The first barrier results from the lack of strong, stable, predictable environmental, energy and climate policies regarding carbon pricing; renewable energy support schemes, such as feed-in tariffs; and fossil fuel subsidies. In this context, in September 2014, just prior to the UN Climate Summit in New York, a coalition of 348 global investors representing over $24 trillion in assets issued a Global Investors Statement on Climate Change. The initiative called on government leaders to provide stable, reliable and economically meaningful carbon pricing to help redirect and scale up low-carbon and climate protection investments while phasing out fossil fuel subsidies (Investor Platform for Climate Change, 2015). The second barrier concerns unintended policy impacts, such as domestic tax credits for clean energy investments that do not benefit tax-exempt or foreign investment funds. The third barrier is caused by the lack of suitable financial vehicles for sustainable investments. For example, the emerging green bond market, which finances sustainable infrastructure projects in developing countries, currently has too few issuances that meet the investment grade requirements of institutional investors (see Section 7.3.2.1 for more on green and climate bonds).

An additional challenge to sustainable infrastructure investing relates to the fact that institutional asset owners need to justify the immediate cost of futureproofing infrastructure with (difficult-to-quantify) benefits during the investment term (or the life of the assets), resulting from lower risks and/or cost savings. They need to demonstrate to stakeholders (e.g. beneficiaries of a pension fund and governments among others) that they can expect at least the same risk-adjusted return with sustainable infrastructure investments compared to conventional ones. Immediate cost savings related to a lower use of resources (e.g. water, energy) are easily understood and accounted for. Lower long-term ESG risks – be they physical risks to the asset, regulatory risks or financial and reputational risk from negative impacts on the environment or people (e.g. workers, local communities) – are difficult to quantify, as outlined above, especially if they do not materialise during the life of the asset or the investment term. The long-term value of potential benefits from sustainable infrastructure, such as cleaner air and water or functioning environmental ecosystems, is even harder to determine. However, the worse pollution and its detrimental effects on society and human health will get and the more frequent climate-change-induced weather hazards (e.g. storms, floods) will strike, the more likely it is that investors and stakeholders alike will appreciate and account for the benefits of futureproof, sustainable infrastructure assets. In addition, the more hard data related to risk and return of sustainable investments gets collected over time, the more evident the financial benefits are expected to become. In the meantime, investors are likely to be more motivated by direct cost savings (e.g. resource efficiency measures, subsidies).

Given this book approaches sustainable infrastructure investing from a general infrastructure investor's perspective, for whom risk analyses are at the core of investing, further insight into how to integrate sustainability considerations, namely ESG risk assessment, into the sector as well as general and project/asset-specific risk analyses is given in Chapter 4 for each individual infrastructure sector covered in this book, and in Chapter 5 (Risks), respectively.

2.3 APPROACHES TO INFRASTRUCTURE INVESTING

Institutional investors follow a number of approaches to invest in infrastructure. A general distinction should be made between listed and unlisted investment opportunities. Although both ultimately involve investments in infrastructure, they have certain fundamental differences in their investment profiles. These are reflected to a greater or lesser extent in their investment characteristics within a portfolio (see Section 2.1 for a detailed discussion).

2.3.1 Listed infrastructure investments

Listed infrastructure comprises a wide range of investment possibilities. Investors may buy the shares and debt of individual infrastructure companies on the stock exchange or investment funds or index certificates, which bundle a number of individual infrastructure assets and/or companies or debt (see Table 2.14).

The range of available listed infrastructure investment opportunities not only covers all sectors, stages and geographical locations but also takes in the entire value chain, including project developers, building contractors, operators, suppliers, customers, utilities, etc.

TABLE 2.14   Listed infrastructure investment opportunities

Direct investments in listed infrastructure securities (equity and debt)	Listed infrastructure investment funds
– Shares of companies that own and/or operate infrastructure assets (e.g. utilities or toll road operators) or that are otherwise active in the infrastructure sector (see Section 1.3.4) – Bonds of the same companies	– Open- or closed-ended funds/indices that invest in individual listed infrastructure project companies (this is relatively rare in its purest form) and/or in 'infrastructure operating or service companies' (see Section 1.3.4) – Funds that invest in unlisted infrastructure assets and/or 'infrastructure companies' or 'infrastructure debt (bonds or loans)' – Hybrid funds that invest in listed and unlisted infrastructure assets, 'infrastructure companies' or infrastructure debt (bonds and loans)

2.3.1.1 Direct investments Both institutional and private investors have been shareholders of listed infrastructure companies since the early days, mainly in the utility, communication, transport and energy sectors. In fact, as of 31 December 2014 utilities represented 3.6%, telecommunication 4.1%, transportation 2.9% and energy 7.4% of the Bloomberg World Index.[16] In addition, many infrastructure operating companies, namely concession and construction companies, have invested directly in infrastructure assets for decades. The performance of some of the largest European concession and construction companies has been very mixed over the last 15 years (until end of 2014), ranging from losing more than 50% to almost tripling in value.[17] For instance, Fomento de Construcciones y Contratas and Sacyr-Vallehermoso S.A. have lost 21 and 45% over 15 years, respectively, while Abertis and Vinci have increased in value by 253 and 297%, respectively. For comparison, the MSCI Europe Index rose 30% during the same 15-year period.[18]

Investors may also choose to invest in corporate bonds and project bonds of the aforementioned sectors, which are often (de facto) government backed, or else in government-backed securities such as tax-exempt US municipal bonds. Infrastructure bonds are a typical means of financing specific infrastructure projects (e.g. Eurotunnel) or a number of projects fulfilling certain investment criteria (e.g. bonds issued by development banks, green bonds; see Section 7.3.2.1 for further discussion). In the UK, for example, PPP/PFI (public finance initiative) bonds are well accepted for financing public infrastructure projects. The attractiveness of infrastructure bonds is largely driven by both their generally long duration of 20 to 30 years, which appeals to investors with long-term liabilities such as pension funds, life insurance companies and sovereign wealth funds, and their interest rates, which are generally higher than those of the government bonds of the respective country – the margin can be up to around 3% for senior debt even when government backed (Institutional Investor, 2014).

Yet the performance dispersion of (senior) infrastructure bonds can be high, because bond yields depend on the overall interest rate environment, the credit rating of the issuer, government guarantees and project-specific risk premia. Nevertheless, the performance of global infrastructure debt as represented by the Dow Jones Brookfield Global Infrastructure Broad Market Corporate Bond Index[19] or the S&P Municipal Bond Infrastructure Index[20], for example, is solid and may be used as a performance indicator with annualised returns in US dollars over 10 and five years[21] of 2.5 and 5.0% for the former and 4.4 and 4.8% for the latter.

---

[16]Bloomberg, accessed 1 October 2015.
[17]Performance for 5/10/15 years until 31/12/2014 for: Abertis Infrastructure S.A. (33%/65%/253%), Actividades de Construction y Servicios S.A. (−17%/72%/268%), Acciona S.A. (−38%/−14%/0%), Atlantia S.p.A. (23%/14%/230%), Bouygues S.A. (−18%/−12%/−52%), Fomento de Construcciones y Contratas S.A. (−46%/−55%/−21%), HOCHTIEF AG (9%/144%/76%), Sacyr-Vallehermoso S.A. (59%/−69%/−45%), Vinci S.A. (15%/87%/297%).
[18]Performance for 5/10/15 years until 31/12/2014 for MSCI Europe: 53.3%/76.1%/30.3%.
[19]The Dow Jones Brookfield Global Infrastructure Broad Market Corporate Bond Index is a market-value-weighted index that tracks the performance of corporate debt issued by infrastructure companies globally (i.e. electric, gas, water and multi-utilities, oil and gas storage and transportation, airports, roads and rail tracks, marine ports and services); www.spindices.com, accessed 25 November 2015.
[20]The S&P Municipal Bond Infrastructure Index is a market-value-weighted index that consists of bonds in the S&P Municipal Bond Index that are related to infrastructure issued by a US state or local government or agency www.spindices.com, accessed 25 November 2015.
[21]Until 13 October 2015; S&P Indices, www.spindices.com, accessed on 12 October 2015.

2.3.1.2 Fund investments Over the last decade, many infrastructure funds and investable indices have been listed. A number of them were delisted or acquired by other funds in the wake of the financial crisis. Today, the investable universe for listed equity funds is made up of around 250 listed infrastructure equity funds with assets of more than US$100 million.[22] There are only a few listed instruments that invest directly in unlisted infrastructure assets. The vast majority are actively managed, open-ended funds (e.g. mutual funds, unit trust), which invest in listed infrastructure companies globally. They focus on income generation, capital appreciation or both. Over 100 ETFs track global infrastructure indices.[23] While some funds have a sector focus (e.g. utilities, communication, transportation or exploration assets in the oil and gas sector) or a geographic focus (regional, country), most of them have a global investment mandate.

The largest listed infrastructure equity fund has a market capitalisation of over US$6 billion, fewer than thirty funds have a market value of more than US$1 billion and approximately 100 funds pass the US$100 million mark.[24] Dedicated infrastructure investment vehicles are listed on different stock exchanges globally, including New York, Toronto, Sidney, Singapore, Luxemburg and Dublin. Their combined market capitalisation amounts to close to US$60 billion.[25]

Also, the composition of infrastructure indices varies significantly: while the Australian infrastructure index S&P ASX Infrastructure provides exposure to listed Australian infrastructure companies from two distinct clusters only, transportation and utilities, excluding energy, the S&P Global Infrastructure Index includes all three clusters, tracking 75 infrastructure companies altogether. The constituents of the Dow Jones Brookfield Infrastructure Index are pure play infrastructure companies from around the world (including emerging economies) and across all sectors, including, for example, energy exploration assets. The Macquarie Global Infrastructure Index provides exposure to infrastructure companies globally, yet with a strong focus (more than 50% weight) on electricity generation and distribution.[26] Constituents of the MSCI World Infrastructure Index are limited to mid- and large-cap securities from developed markets with over 25% exposure in the telecommunications sector.[27] These few examples of some of the infrastructure indices with the longest track records show the large dispersion in exposure investors get with different indices. The index composition and the related market exposure (e.g. exposure to energy prices for energy exploration assets) are critical for investors, both for investment and benchmarking purposes (for benchmarking see Section 2.1.3).

There are close to 50 dedicated listed infrastructure bond funds, which tend to be small compared to listed infrastructure equity funds with almost none of them managing more than US$100 million, the majority being under US$50 million. Many energy projects are partly financed with high yield bonds, which represent a sizeable share of the high yield bond market. Bonds of infrastructure companies (e.g. utility, transportation, telecommunication, energy sector) represent a high share of high yield bond indices (e.g. over 25% of the BOFA Merrill Lynch Global High Yield Index).[28] The surge of labelled green bond issues (i.e. bonds

---

[22]Bloomberg, accessed on 12 October 2015.
[23]Bloomberg, accessed 12 October 2015.
[24]Bloomberg, accessed on 13 October 2015.
[25]Bloomberg, accessed on 7 October 2015.
[26]FTSE100, www.ftse.com, accessed 7 October 2010.
[27]MSCI, www.msci.com, accessed 13 October 2015.
[28]Bloomberg, accessed on 20 February 2016.

with proceeds officially earmarked to finance projects devoted to climate protection, such as low-carbon investments and climate adaptation) as well as other environmental protection measures led to the first dedicated green bond funds to come onto the market in 2013 (see Section 7.3.2.1).

Listed instruments offer immediate access to the market and allow investors to establish globally diversified portfolios easily with relatively small investment amounts. Funds that invest in listed infrastructure-related securities, especially the higher capitalised ones, are reasonably liquid with decent trading volumes. Funds that invest in unlisted infrastructure assets, however, typically experience reduced liquidity, which is usually a function of the terms of the structure (i.e. notice periods, quarterly or yearly redemption terms, lock-up periods and amounts). In times of market volatility, especially the latter-listed instruments tend to trade at significant discounts to the net asset value (NAV) of their underlying assets. As a result, listed instruments allow investors to adjust their investment strategies at short notice – which goes, however, (the authors note) against the explicitly stated concept and goal of most institutional investors, which is to seek long-term investments in infrastructure assets with their predictable long-term contractual cash flow profiles to match long-term liabilities.

The downside of listed liquid instruments compared with unlisted ones is their (compared to unlisted infrastructure) higher level of volatility and their relatively high correlation with other asset classes, listed equity in particular (see Section 2.1.4, Table 2.10 and Table 2.11 and Figure 2.6). As a case in point, during the financial crisis the value of listed infrastructure investments dropped in line with the global equity markets. While the MSCI World lost 39% between October 2007 and June 2009, the S&P Global Infrastructure Index lost 38%. During the same period, the NAV of 10 of today's largest listed infrastructure-focused funds lost close to 34% of their peak value on 31 October 2007.[29] Most funds took between three and four years to recover their losses, in line with investors in global equity markets, while some never made it back up.

This volatility can be attributed not only to their daily tradability but also to the fact that, with some exceptions, investments in liquid infrastructure instruments do not constitute investments in individual, unlisted infrastructure project companies, which may be largely independent of economic developments, but rather in infrastructure operating or service companies that are active in the wider environment of the infrastructure sector (see Section 1.3.4). As such, their investment characteristics resemble more those of typical listed companies being exposed to economic swings as demonstrated above (see Section 2.1).

But even listed infrastructure funds that invest solely in individual, unlisted infrastructure project companies with stable, safely contracted revenue streams that are largely independent of economic developments (see Section 1.3.4) are still exposed to the (occasionally irrational) fluctuations on the capital markets and hence their at times extreme volatility. This volatility can be attributed mainly to the mark-to-market requirements of investment instruments traded on the stock exchange, which will reflect the day-to-day investment and economic climate. Moreover, it must in part be ascribed to very high leverage levels of these funds and/or their underlying portfolio companies, which increases and in some cases multiplies their exposure and vulnerability to capital market fluctuations.

---

[29]The 10 were: 3I Infrastructure Plc, Cohen & Steers Infrastructure Fund, DUET Group, HICL Infrastructure Company, Macquarie Infrastructure Corporation, Macquarie Korea Infrastructure Fund, Renaissance Global Infrastructure Fund, Lazard Global Listed Infrastructure FD, LO Macquarie Infrastracture-CHF, PG Listed Infrastructure I-A.

This painful truth was experienced by some fund managers and investors during the financial crisis starting in 2007, with investment funds trading far below their carrying amount (NAV), and thus testing the theory that infrastructure investments are recession-proof. Certain highly leveraged transactions – leverage was increased with sophisticated financial engineering techniques (non-recourse borrowing, securitisations, accreting swaps and mezzanine financings) to supplement plain-vanilla bank loans and project bonds, but also thanks to the expansive use of monoline insurance and a robust market for syndicated bank loans – faced financial trouble, forcing infrastructure funds and concession companies to initiate distressed asset sales to reduce debt levels. Babcock & Brown as well as Macquarie were the most prominent examples at the time, with the former going into insolvency as a result of extremely highly leveraged infrastructure assets in their portfolios. In some cases, the assets and/or funds were not only very highly leveraged but also financed with rather short maturities, which forced them to refinance at the midst of the financial crisis. Last but not least, management teams of listed investment entities – whether funds or discrete investments – naturally focus on managing for the share price in the immediate future, which may or may not conflict with longer-term investment returns on the assets. This conflict of interest can be addressed with long-term incentive structures.

In summary, the characteristics of listed infrastructure investment instruments do not reflect those of unlisted infrastructure investments. As a result, the diversification effect offered by listed infrastructure assets on a portfolio level is much less pronounced than by unlisted infrastructure (see Section 2.1.2.2 for an extensive discussion). Given that many investors are interested in infrastructure precisely because of this diversification effect, the authors focus on unlisted assets in the remainder of this book.

2.3.2 Unlisted infrastructure investments

Investors seeking exposure to unlisted infrastructure assets may buy shares and/or tranches of debt of individual infrastructure companies in private placements or via open-ended (evergreen structure) or closed-ended investment funds with a limited term (see Table 2.15). As most investors new to the asset class are likely to choose to invest with

TABLE 2.15   Unlisted infrastructure investment opportunities

Direct infrastructure investments	Infrastructure investment funds
– Direct investments in individual unlisted infrastructure assets/ projects or 'infrastructure companies' via equity or debt (see Section 1.3.2)	– Open-ended (evergreen, periodically opened for investors) and closed-ended investment structures or funds that invest in individual unlisted infrastructure projects, operating or service companies via equity or debt (see Section 1.3.4) – Hybrid funds that invest in individual listed and unlisted 'infrastructure project, operating or service companies' via equity or debt – Infrastructure funds of funds, which invest in closed-ended (and in some cases also open-ended) infrastructure funds (equity only)

an experienced investment manager by investing in a fund, much of this section focuses on evaluating and selecting infrastructure funds.

2.3.2.1 Characteristics and challenges

The number, and for that matter the range, of unlisted investment opportunities for institutional investors – both in assets/projects directly and in investment funds via equity or debt – has increased steadily over recent years and is expected to increase even further (see Section 1.1 for information on the market of unlisted infrastructure funds).

Unlisted investments typically require a significant initial capital allocation, relatively high fees in the case of fund investments and, naturally, provide limited liquidity. Access to suitable unlisted investment opportunities – especially direct ones – is among the most important considerations for any investor. Investors who decide to access the infrastructure asset class via unlisted assets need to choose between direct investments or indirect investments via funds or tailor-made managed/separate accounts. The former requires them to be willing and capable (in terms of resources, experience, networks etc.) to undertake direct transactions. For an increasing number of predominantly large pension funds and insurance groups the advantages of investing directly in unlisted infrastructure assets/projects outweigh the extra effort by far (see Section 2.1). They often do so in partnership with other investors, be it fund managers, like-minded financial investors or corporates such as construction firms. The majority of financial investors and essentially close to all new investors in the market tend to approach infrastructure as an asset class indirectly, that is via some kind of investment fund or managed account. Fund of funds (FoF) structures seem to get squeezed out of the market due to the additional layer of fees and, hence, high overall fees.

Investors increasingly consider direct investments as a superior model for investing in the asset class thanks to, among other reasons, less fees and, hence, potentially higher financial net returns. As a rule, direct investments come with lower fees (or no fee) when compared to funds. These fees need to be weighed against the costs of hiring a financial advisor for a managed account and/or on a deal-by-deal basis, or employing a professional full-time team with all the necessary infrastructure investment experience and skills though (see Section 2.3.3). Investors who have multiple of billions to allocate, as some of the very large pension funds do, are likely to benefit from a direct investment approach. Most investors, though, are of a smaller size and therefore are well advised to go through funds or, preferably these days, tailored managed accounts, the investment strategy of which meets their investment needs exactly. The idea is that funds/managed account investments confer several benefits, most importantly an experienced and well-networked management or advisory team to source suitable and good investment opportunities. This approach allows investors to gain experience and learn about the asset class while reducing their risk, because the diversification offered by investment funds and tailor-made managed accounts traditionally offers a lower overall risk of loss or default than direct investment in single infrastructure assets/projects. Given that the fund market is still relatively young (compared to private equity), with resulting short performance histories for most fund managers and advisors, the challenge is to pick not only a good manager or advisor – which is difficult enough – but also those whose investment strategies and/or capabilities fit with the ones of the investors'.

Fund investments, however, entail additional specific risks that do not necessarily apply to direct investments. These have been experienced in recent years by quite a few explicitly conservative institutional investors, who made – in cases inappropriately high – initial investments in infrastructure funds that ultimately did not pursue the desired conservative investment profile as stated in their marketing documents but instead took clearly risky positions to those in the know. Not surprisingly, in the falling markets experienced in especially 2007/2008, many of these funds did not deliver the stable annual cash yields which were initially propagated. This did not apply to the asset class as a whole though, but was driven by the assets chosen by the fund managers in question.

It is probably fair to say that investors not only might have wanted to blame the fund managers but should have done a better due diligence on the managers and their strategies ahead of time. To what extent and how managers and their funds can be assessed in advance to a reasonable extent is discussed separately in Section 2.3.2.3.

Given this experience, some investors who are new to the asset class may be hesitant about investing in infrastructure, owing to a lack of knowledge and experience, the shortage of data and the resulting lack of benchmarks. However, if they still wanted to engage in the asset class they are confronted with, and supposed to find answers to, questions such as:

- What kind of infrastructure investment strategy fits their requirements in the context of their asset allocation?
- What type of assets can fulfil these requirements?
- Which investment approach should they take given their current personnel resources and their ability to scale up in the future?
- Which fund managers pursue and actually implement an investment strategy that truly meets their needs?
- Do they understand how the different fund managers assess investment opportunities and which ones they invest in as a consequence?
- Do they understand the various conflicts of interest between fund managers and themselves?
- Do they understand the relevant advantages and disadvantages of fund investments and a tailor-made managed account?
- Do investors understand the significant difference between co-investing with fund managers vs. likeminded financial investors?
- Which tasks of the investment process can or should be outsourced?

These questions and many others are addressed throughout this book.

The remainder of this section focuses on unlisted fund investments only. Managed accounts are only mentioned separately where diverging from fund investments. Direct investments are addressed in-depth in Chapters 5–7 following a detailed description of the various existing infrastructure (business) models and sectors in Chapters 3 and 4, which both seek to enable a better understanding of how the asset class ticks.

2.3.2.2 Universe of infrastructure funds
As the universe of investable infrastructure funds increases, so too does the amount of investment strategies available to investors, and hence the level of complexity when it comes to selecting the most suitable investment funds for a defined investment strategy. Generally speaking, unlisted fund investments allow investors to achieve diversification by investing for a period of several years in one or more well-diversified or specialised funds and their respective assets that best suit their requirements. In order to understand the main differences between these various infrastructure funds, Table 2.16 illustrates some of their key distinguishing features of unlisted infrastructure

TABLE 2.16 Range and distinguishing features of unlisted infrastructure funds

Feature	Variations
Fund size	150 million – 8 billion
Currency	€, US$, GBP, etc.
Term	10 years/25 years/evergreen plus extensions
Investment period	3–5 years, ongoing (in case of evergreen)
Manager	Independent/part of a corporate or bank (captive)
Fund set up	Closed-ended, open-ended (evergreen)
Geography	National/Europe/US/OECD/emerging markets/global
Industries/sectors	Individual sectors, e.g. (renewable) energy, ports, social infrastructure/selection of sector(s)/PPP (across sectors)/all sectors
Investment stage	Greenfield/brownfield
Degree of regulation	Low/medium/high
Contractual security	Long/medium/short term
Type of investment	Equity/mezzanine/debt
Team	Existing/new
Target/source of return	Yield: 5–12% (cash flows); IRR: 8–20% (capital gains)
Risk profile	Low/medium/high

funds. The features and their variations presented are examples only and not intended to be a conclusive list.

Similar to private equity funds, infrastructure funds may pursue different investment strategies. So far, the large funds are predominantly positioned as generalists pursuing a broad bandwidth of assets and taking responsibility for their weighting (e.g. geographies, sectors, stages, risk profiles) within the fund in line with their PPMs. Some funds, however, have a narrower focus, such as on a certain investment stage (greenfield and/or brownfield), geographical location (individual country, Europe, US, OECD, emerging markets) and/or sector (individual sectors, e.g. only [renewable] energy, ports, airports or social infrastructure; a selection of sector[s]; only PPPs [across sectors]; all sectors) accompanied by different sizes, terms and structures. Infrastructure funds generally have a volume of €300 million or greater because their target transactions mostly require substantial amounts of capital. Few exceptions are niche players, such as those investing purely in, for example, development assets or smallish PPP social infrastructure. These kinds of funds tend to be as small as €150 million.

Closed-ended funds have a specific term (currently in most cases between 10 and a maximum of 25 years) with extension options, whereas open-ended funds generally take the form of evergreen structures with an unlimited term. For evergreen funds to be able to keep investing over time, they raise fresh capital in capital increases from new or existing investors according to previously specified terms. Likewise, existing investors are allowed to exit the fund at certain times as long as they follow certain rules. A standard fee structure such as that used in private equity does not exist for infrastructure funds, because a uniform fee structure would not adequately reflect the variety in the investment strategies – with different risk-return profiles – pursued by fund managers and demanded by investors, the underlying assets as well as the heterogeneity of overall fund terms. (These and others aspects are further discussed in Section 2.3.2.3.)

At the time this book goes to press (March 2016), the vast majority of funds still have a 10- to 12-year term and follow a rather broad investment strategy. It can be observed, however, that focused/specialised niche funds are increasingly coming to market that target certain regions and/or sectors or specific risk and return metrics, allowing for fine-tuned investment strategies on the part of investors. Compare, for instance, a UK-focused, availability payment-based, secondary-PPP investment strategy with a term of 25 years to a growth-led airports-only strategy with a term of 10 years. Both funds invest in infrastructure assets. One, however, invests in a long-term predictable contract structure without market risk, a very low political/regulatory risk and an annual distribution-driven return profile, whereas the other takes substantial market (price and demand) risk and aims for a quick exit after a few years, resulting in high IRR-based returns. Investors aiming for the former may not want to have the latter included in their portfolio and vice versa.

The large range of risk and return profiles of infrastructure assets and the partially very specific investment goals of investors imply that it is not always advantageous for the investor to let the fund manager – or the FoF manager as the case may be – blend the infrastructure assets and the risks attached to them. Although blending and diversification provide some benefits, pure, narrowly defined investment strategies have clear merits as well. Again, if an investor aims for low-risk assets and a predictable annual cash yield only, there is little advantage in a fund manager blending such suitable assets with high-risk, capital-gain-driven ones.

Along these lines, for most investors it would probably be advisable first to define a clear investment strategy that suits their needs and then, very selectively, to pick only funds that focus exactly on these discrete areas of interest within the infrastructure universe. One solution for investors is to work with tailor-made, non-discretionary managed accounts and/or an independent investment advisor. The advantage of such an approach is twofold. First, by setting up a managed account, there is a high chance of the advisor actually implementing the investment strategy as specified by the investor, because the latter can keep control over the assets purchased for the portfolio. Second, while investment advisors may undertake nearly the same services as fund managers, they do not take discretionary investment decisions, but rather the final investment decision remains with the investor upon presentation of the investment opportunity in question. While such an approach is clearly more work-intensive for the investor than 'only' picking funds, the extra effort may well be worth it. The following section addresses some of the most important aspects to consider when investing in infrastructure funds and includes some obvious conflicts of interest between investors and fund managers.

2.3.2.3 Evaluating infrastructure funds It is clear from the description above that the evaluation and selection of infrastructure investments at fund level is not a trivial matter. Generally speaking, fund investments offer the benefits of diversification, the investment expertise of the respective fund manager and access to attractive investment opportunities. However, in addition to the primary risk arising from the quality and the respective performance of the underlying fund portfolio, investment funds also entail risks at the fund manager level that must be addressed before an investment in a fund can be made. This section provides a brief overview of some of the key aspects to be addressed as part of a systematised, stringent and diligent fund investment process. See Figure 2.9 for an illustration of the main steps and areas of due diligence involved.

In the private equity literature, a rich body of publications exists that describes the general due diligence process for a fund investment in great detail (see, for instance, Meyer and

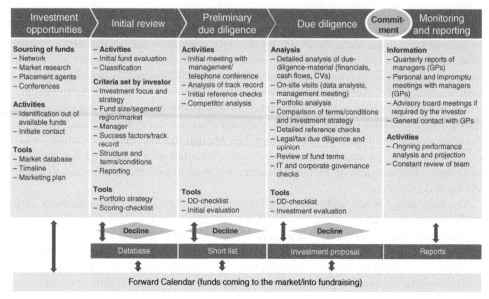

FIGURE 2.9 Fund investment process
Source: B Capital Partners (2016)

Matthonet, 2006). Because the due diligence process behind a private equity fund investment is very similar, except for a few aspects, to that for an infrastructure fund investment, the following discussion primarily focuses on infrastructure fund-specific aspects and risks. The following sections should not, however, be taken as a complete and comprehensive due diligence list, neither for private equity nor for infrastructure funds; they only highlight some of the most important due diligence aspects to be considered.

Manager risk   Manager risk is probably the most important risk factor arising in conjunction with fund investments because the investor is contractually locked in with the manager for the entire term of the fund (> 10 years). At the same time, manager risk is probably the most difficult to evaluate, because it can neither be assessed nor quantified easily. Please note that while the advisor risk is in the same category it is nowhere near as severe, since advisory contracts, by definition, can be terminated more easily. In addition, the investor has more control over the investments taken given that advisory mandates are non-discretionary by definition. Ultimately, investors must rely on a manager's/advisor's capability to identify, professionally evaluate and resolve/mitigate all significant risks affecting transactions that are planned or those that have been conducted (for more information, see in particular Chapters 3, 4 and 5). As such, it is worth spending time and money on manager/advisor due diligence.

It is important to select the best fund manager(s) for the determined investment strategy within the desired target (sub-)segments. For this, it is indispensable first to gain an overview of the entire universe of existing managers and funds. The authors estimate the universe of infrastructure investment funds to currently comprise approximately 425 managers and well over 1000 unlisted infrastructure funds globally.

One can easily lose track of or miss out on some of these fund managers. Especially small and/or new independent managers regularly fall through investors' nets because they often only passively screen investment funds (i.e. looking at what 'comes through the door' by email or mail) and do not proactively and systematically search the market as a whole. This happens despite the fact that some of the small and/or independent managers may be qualitatively very good if not better or more suitable for the investment objective of the investor. In other words, even when investors select the best investment funds that they have examined, by definition, there is statistically a high probability that this selection will lead to a suboptimal result if they have not analysed the entire investment universe of available funds in the first place. This point cannot be stressed enough!

Accordingly, investors entering this asset class for the first time are strongly recommended to perform a thorough and proactive research of the entire funds universe in their respective area of interest or to consult an advisor with the relevant experience. Good investment advice – like good legal or tax advice – is generally worth the time and expense, because the superior return achieved by the selection of a high-quality fund manager who pursues an investment strategy that genuinely suits the needs of the respective investor easily outweighs the cost incurred. Moreover, the opportunity cost of being locked in with the wrong fund manager needs to be accounted for as well.

The goal of manager due diligence is first to identify those managers whose invest-ment strategy (e.g. risk profile, cash flow profile [yield and/or IRR driven], targeted sec-tors, stages, geographies, degree of specialisation and diversification, investment horizon) essentially reflects the investor's requirements. The next question is whether there is a suffi-ciently large universe for the respective investment strategy; that is, are there enough potential investable assets in the target segment? If this can be shown, it must be ensured that the man-agers identified do indeed have access to the best transactions in the targeted market segments (via their networks). Furthermore, the team needs to have the specific skill set required to pursue the anticipated investment strategy – that is to identify, acquire and successfully man-age the right kinds of assets in order to generate corresponding returns for the investor. For instance, in the case of greenfield infrastructure investments, the manager should demonstrate in-house, hands-on experience of developing greenfield infrastructure projects. This includes being able not only to assess projects at the development stage but also to bypass the rising costs of competitive tenders and to provide the benefits from de-risking the assets as they move through the development phase through to operation (see Chapter 5 for more on risk analysis).

Although one cannot eliminate the risk that a manager will be unable to generate the promised returns, this risk decreases significantly if the manager meets the following condi-tions, especially if:

- The manager can demonstrate previous operational and investment experience (track record) in the target segment, including the sale of companies to the extent relevant for the investment strategy.
- The management team has worked together successfully in the past and gathered relevant (investment) experience as a team as well as individually.
- The team can reasonably demonstrate that it possesses the necessary expertise, network and resources to continue to find projects/assets offering value-added at attractive prices in the target markets in the future.

Fund managers are often subject to investment pressure and incur substantial due diligence costs in the project analysis phase. Therefore, investors must ensure that the manager is interested in working efficiently yet carefully, not foregoing any costs required to evaluate the risks of a transaction in detail. At the same time, they need to watch out that the manager does not pay excessive purchase prices for the assets solely to build up a portfolio quickly. Contractual structures must align, as much as possible, the interests of all participants at both the fund and the project level so as to eliminate any of the potential conflicts of interest outlined in this section.

Last but not least, as well as analysing all the formal aspects of a manager, including ESG, legal, tax and IT aspects, investors must obtain a sufficient number of relevant references from proficient and trustworthy persons that ideally go above and beyond the reference lists provided by the managers.

Strategy drift   Strategy drift describes the risk that the fund manager will fail to adhere to the agreed investment strategy, for instance the manager invests in transactions or, in the case of an FoF manager, single fund managers who provide a lower or higher risk profile and/or different cash flow profile with a lower target current yield/IRR than initially stated. This can have severe, undesired consequences for the investor. For instance, if current income was essential for an investor on the basis of its internal investment guidelines or simply its liquidity situation, and the manager was primarily selected because of its promise to invest only in transactions that generated current income from the outset, any deviation from this strategy resulting in no current income in the first years could cause serious problems for the investor. This could be the same in the case of a shift in geographical location, currency, industry, etc. Strategy drift is also undesirable because the new strategy adopted by the fund manager may already be covered by other managers whom the investor considers better suited to pursue the respective strategy.

Although it may not constitute a strategy drift in the conventional sense, an equally problematic scenario can emerge if an investor sets specific investment requirements, (e.g. related to ESG aspects) that the manager initially accepts but subsequently fails to observe to a sufficient extent, resulting in potentially negative tax, regulatory, ethical, reputational or other consequences for the investor. Therefore, it is important to discuss such requirements in advance and ensure that they are legally enshrined in the contracts or at least in a side letter.

Term and disposability   The investment term of infrastructure funds, especially those of earlier vintages, are still largely based on those of private equity funds, that is 10 or 12 years plus a two- or, in some cases, up to plus a four-year extension period. As mentioned previously, this term structure is suitable only for (private equity-style) infrastructure investment strategies with the primary objective of generating capital gains by selling the assets after three to five years of following them and then to set up a successor fund for new investments once the current fund is fully invested. However, these comparatively short terms are not suitable for investors seeking to invest in long-lived infrastructure assets, on account of their stable cash flows. For example, many yield-oriented investors with a long-term investment horizon are not interested in having to sell high-yielding assets with a remaining life of 20 years after three to five years simply because the term of the fund, which bought the assets, is limited to 10 years. This problem can be resolved with longer fund terms or evergreen structures. Notwithstanding, funds offering longer terms or evergreen structures are still the exception despite the fact that such structures suit the requirements for long-term yield-oriented investors. Yet, they pose different problems, which are discussed in more detail later in this section.

Some funds with a relatively short-term structure meet the desire of investors for a longer asset-holding period by allowing them to take a majority vote at the end of the (e.g. 10-year) term on whether to sell the assets to third parties, float them on the stock market or retain them by, for example, extending the existing fund structure repeatedly or indefinitely. Investors who are interested in selling their fund interests are always given a corresponding exit opportunity. Investors are naturally also permitted to buy the assets, which are sold out of the fund, themselves, whether individually or as a group, and to continue to operate them independently or via a manager. However, these scenarios are less than ideal because they create conflicts of interest within the investor base and with the manager. Also, their long-term viability has yet to be demonstrated as, so far, few funds have been converted into longer-term structures.

There is probably no such thing as the optimal fund structure for infrastructure funds, because the range of infrastructure assets is so diverse that no single structure would be suitable for all of the asset types, let alone the large variety of investor preferences. This is not a problem per se, providing that the chosen fund structure matches the fund's investment strategy. Generally speaking, 'short', private equity-like terms are appropriate for capital-gain-oriented strategies, such as dedicated greenfield funds, the objective of which is to follow projects through their development and/or construction phase and sell them rather quickly afterwards with target returns that are similar to private equity in some cases. The same applies for direct investments in operational infrastructure companies with typical (private) equity profiles, commensurate market risks and/or high restructuring requirements, etc. similar to the kind of transactions usually conducted by private equity investors. By contrast, longer-term or evergreen structures are more suitable for yield-oriented strategies in healthy operating assets with a stable current income, for example certain kinds of transmission and distribution networks (electricity, water, oil and gas pipelines), renewable energy generation plants and (availability-based) PPP assets (transport or social infrastructure).

Accordingly, the term – that is the fit of the term with the declared investment strategy of a fund – may turn out to be an essential investment criterion when considering a specific fund investment. It is important to note that any considerable change in the term of a fund requires the fee structure and performance-based payments to be adjusted accordingly – not only in height but partly also in kind – to reflect the implications of the new terms. This can be a challenging task.

Fees In the same way as their terms, the fees of infrastructure funds are still oriented towards the relatively uniform fee schemes of private equity funds. However, increasingly, investors and fund managers alike acknowledge that a 'one size fits all' approach does not adequately reflect the range of underlying infrastructure assets, cash flow profiles and fund terms. Investors who seek conservative investment opportunities do not generally wish to pay private-equity-style fees for bond-style returns and eventually start to demand alternative fee solutions. At the same time, irrespective of the varying asset profiles, the time and effort required by managers to identify and make good infrastructure investments is comparable to that required for private equity investments in many cases, particularly when it comes to assets that are, for example, still in the development stage or require restructuring before they can generate an adequate return.

Generally, there is no fundamental reason not to apply the established fee structure of private equity funds in the infrastructure environment with fund terms of 10–12 years and target returns of 15–20% IRR. Private equity funds typically charge a management fee of 1.0–2.0% on the committed capital during the investment period (three to five years). This is when the fund manager generally incurs the highest costs, owing to the investment activity performed. For the remaining approximately five to seven years of the fund term, a management fee of 1.0–2.0% on the invested capital is typically charged, with the absolute payments on the part of the investor decreasing proportionally with the divestments of assets out of the fund. It is the successful divestments of the assets that generate the desired capital gains for investors.

For fund terms of up to 25 years, and even more so for evergreen structures, with no or only a very slow reduction in the capital invested over time, managers cannot justify fees of this nature and extent, either in terms of the actual time and effort expended or the returns generated. On this point, a recent OECD study noted: 'One of the key areas of tension in the unlisted infrastructure equity market has been a conflict of interest between investors and fund managers over fund fees and terms and conditions. The fees charged by managers for core infrastructure have been in the past often excessively high, resembling private equity fees, despite private equity returns being higher' (OECD, 2014a). The reason the invested capital may not decrease at all or only slowly is that investors care to hold their assets for good (or until the end of the 25-year term) with no intention to sell (beforehand).

The performance fee must also be adjusted so that it reflects the nature of the underlying assets and the investment objectives of the respective investors. The typical IRR-based performance fee for PE fund managers (15–20%, rarely 30% of the performance over a specified hurdle) is appropriate only to a limited extent, if at all, for funds with terms of 20–25 years or evergreen funds that seek to generate constant yields. Why this is the case can be illustrated best with the above-mentioned example of investors who invested for a long-term, steady, inflation-linked income stream to match their liabilities: most are unlikely to be interested in selling their high-yielding, long-term assets from their portfolio even if they can achieve an attractive price for it today. The main reason is the reinvestment risk, that is the risk that investors will not be able to reinvest the returned capital in an equally well-performing asset any time soon. A fund manager, in contrast, who is incentivised via a performance fee based on the IRR has every incentive to sell an attractive, high-yielding asset quickly – even more so if there are indeed few assets of that quality in and/or likely to come to the market soon, because this will drive up the selling price.

The good news is that these conflicts of interest are known and predictable and can be solved to a large extent by altering the terms and conditions. A yield-based performance fee based on an annual, bi-annual or even tri-annual performance basis or a combination of IRR- and yield-based performance remuneration, for example, may be far more suitable for a long-term, buy-and-hold, yield-driven investment strategy. One has to be careful, though, not to create the next conflict of interest by introducing a hurdle on the yield. The fund manager may now be incentivised to squeeze every bit of cash out of the assets in the portfolio early on in order to reach the yield hurdle. This issue can also be solved, however: first, as long as the lifetime of the fund is very long, the manager cannot afford to work the assets too hard because it needs their yields over time; second, introducing a cap on the yield sharing will incentivise the manager to smooth the yield stream over the lifetime of the fund rather than sell many assets at a time or squeeze them too heavily.

In this context, the payment of an IRR-based performance fee to the manager once the entire portfolio is sold and the fund is liquidated – as is typical for private equity funds – presents a problem for funds with extremely long terms, because the timing of the reward is too far in the future from a motivational perspective for the manager, and potentially also in terms of manager life expectancy. Furthermore, this would cause an unsolvable problem for evergreen structures. An intra-year, yield-based performance fee as suggested above is therefore advisable to provide the fund manager with a reasonable performance incentive. These kinds of performance fee structures are slowly being accepted in the market.

However, if one does not work with a yield-based performance hurdle that can be measured easily at the end of each defined period but rather with an IRR or a NAV base, the fee becomes rather difficult to compute. It raises the question of how to value the underlying assets/portfolio companies appropriately at each payment date. Realistically, such a situation would require 'independent' valuers employed by the general and limited partners to reach a corresponding agreement. Not ideal.

However, investment decisions should not be made solely on the basis of the level of fees. As a matter of principle, the quality of the manager is more important than negotiating the lowest cost. It is also more important that the agreed structure of the incentive mechanisms match the respective investment strategy and the underlying assets in order to ensure a true alignment of interests between the investor and the manager, as discussed above.

Illiquidity risk   Like private equity funds, unlisted infrastructure funds are exposed to the risk of limited liquidity and disposability. However, this risk is often exaggerated. There is now an active secondary market for infrastructure assets and funds. Funds with partially or fully financed, solid assets that generate stable, current income are in demand with secondary investors and change hands for remarkable prices in some cases. While the liquidity of such assets clearly cannot be compared with market-traded equities, the disposability risk is relative. First, many listed funds have theoretical liquidity only because of very low trading volumes. Second, liquid listed funds/assets may lose value over night when markets become volatile. Hence, even though the fund or asset might be tradable, by the time investors decide to sell, any obtainable offer price would most likely be at a steep discount to NAV. Third, most institutional investors explicitly state that they are interested in infrastructure assets with the view to holding them for 10–20 years or longer in order to match the maturity structure of their liabilities. When this is the stated objective, there is little reason to seriously worry about whether the asset is tradable on a daily basis.

Comparability/benchmarking   Infrastructure investments are still thin on the ground and have a comparatively short history, even in countries such as Australia, Canada and the UK. This raises the question of how best to measure and compare/benchmark the performance of existing fund managers. Despite new research papers in this area and notable advancements compared to six years ago when the first edition of this book was printed, the pool of reliable performance and cash flow data about historical transactions remains limited and relatively unreliable. In light of the most commonly used, yet often still suboptimal benchmarks listed in Section 2.1.3, and the valuation methods applied for the underlying transactions, performance and volatility, as well as correlation figures offer little in the way of information value. In short, there are still no internationally accepted or standardised benchmarks for infrastructure, meaning that an individual analysis of the assets and the expertise of the respective managers is even more important. The fact that the bandwidth of infrastructure assets is so wide and the heterogeneity of assets within the sectors and subsectors so high – for all the reasons mentioned above – clearly does not help to identify meaningful benchmarks. Notwithstanding, the industry is working on it and the first reasonably solid propositions are on offer in the market.

Political/regulatory risk   Private investments in infrastructure are never purely private; they always have a governmental and a societal side to them. Different stakeholders have different interests and get involved at various levels throughout the lifetime of the investment. Pressure groups and NGOs may become vocal, and politicians may prefer to take a short-term view when elections are coming up. As a consequence, these complex settings comprise a number of risks (see Chapter 5 for further details and examples).

A lack of wide-scale acceptance for the private ownership and/or operation of assets that were previously held by the public sector (whether through a PPP or full privatisation) could lead to problems. Public acceptance in the UK, Australia and Western Europe (to the extent experience exists) has been largely positive to date. However, vocal opposition against, for example, private finance initiatives (equivalent to PPP) is prevalent in the UK, using a number of arguments: lack of transparency, increasing costs, a build-up of huge off-balance-sheet liabilities for future taxpayers, excessive returns for the financial industry, etc. (EIB Papers, 2010). The possibility of similar opposition and difficulties in other countries or sectors cannot be ruled out.

Furthermore, political disputes between national and state governments are almost inevitable when it comes to cost and revenue distribution of such assets, and related debates can lead to significant project delays. Depending on the nature of the contract, delays on this scale may have an adverse effect on the returns obtained by private investors. Along these lines, Nigel Wilson, CEO of Legal & General, a FTSE 100 UK financial services company, stated that the 'single largest risk to economic progress remains the persistent backdrop of political and regulatory uncertainty'. In referring to the UK government's much-trumpeted National Infrastructure Plan, as little more than a '£375 billion wish-list', Wilson stressed that there can be extreme political risk as government leadership and priorities change over time. 'You can invest and find that the rules have changed' (Osborne, 2014).

The takeover of key infrastructure assets by foreign (private) investors may be exposed to severe public criticism in, and may lead to governmental action of, the host country. In Canada, the 'strategic asset' argument has been used to try to block several recently proposed foreign infrastructure investments, for example Warren Buffett's Berkshire Hathaway Energy's proposed takeover of AltaLink, an electricity company with significant transmission assets in the province of Alberta. The acquisition is being opposed by some, using the argument that transmission is a 'strategic asset' that should remain in Canadian hands (Mintz, 2014).

A different form of political risk arises when governments fail to meet their prior commitments to transactions, for example in the form of credit guarantees or guaranteed payments for the performance of specific services (such as availability payments for motorways or feed-in tariffs [FITs] for renewable energy). Whereas this type of political risk used to be a consideration only in emerging markets or countries without democratic governments, the financial crisis and the ongoing crisis in Greece mean there is now also some doubt as to whether governments in certain OECD states will be able and/or willing to meet their obligations. In this context, another risk type that had been largely ignored is the default of established insurance companies that are responsible for insuring all aspects of infrastructure transaction risks, including political risks.

There are also substantial regulatory risks, particularly in highly regulated sectors such as transport, (renewable) power transmission and supply and water supply/disposal, most of which are driven by political considerations. Changes in regulatory conditions, for example the imposition of reduced consumer prices or increased competition through the break-up of monopolistic/oligopolistic structures, may have a pronounced impact on a project's revenue, growth and operating margins. This can make a project under examination unattractive for private investors. For example, Michaela Koller, director general of industry lobby group Insurance Europe, said that European insurers' role as long-term investors may be hurt by the new Solvency II regulations, which require companies to 'hold inappropriately high amounts of capital against their long-term investments' (see Section 5.2.5.1). Koller went on to note that 'this will make it more expensive for insurers to invest in long-term government and corporate bonds, as well as growth-stimulating activities, such as infrastructure projects' (Bloomberg

Business, 2014b). In the case of changes in regulation after an investment is conducted, it may have an extreme adverse effect on the original business case. One prominent example is the sale of the Norwegian gas transmission network Gassled from Statoil (Norwegian government-owned) to a group of foreign investors (Abu Dhabi sovereign wealth fund, German insurer Allianz, the Canada Pension Plan Investment Board and Canada's Public Sector Pension Investment Board) in 2012 (Reuters, 2014). Only a few months after the closing of the transaction, the Norwegian government changed the regulation dramatically, decreasing the allowed return by around 90%. Another remarkable example in an equally trustworthy country is that of the airport operator BAA in the UK, which, having operated a total of eight airports for a number of years, was forced to sell at least two of its British airports within a defined period. (See the first example box in Chapter 3.)

As well as leading to lower-than-expected returns, an investment in a project that is the subject of public dispute may result in damaging the investor's reputation. Another reputation risk concerns the corruption of people involved in infrastructure projects, be it as corporate managers or government officials (regulators, legislators, judiciaries, etc.).

Legal and tax risks Depending on the investment project and the country-specific regulations, certain legal and tax issues apply that need to be identified and resolved ahead of a transaction. Therefore, a professional legal due diligence of any infrastructure (fund) investment taking into account the provisions of investment and tax law is always required. This book does not elaborate on such risks, because they vary significantly depending on the respective country and the kinds of, as well as the specific legal and tax set up of, the investor in question.

Good fund managers must be able to anticipate all of the above and similar risks at an early stage and either resolve them in a convincing manner with the aid of their network or recognise that, owing to the non-transparent and uncertain conflict scenario, a given project involves so many uncontrollable or irresolvable risks that it may be better to abstain from investing in the first place. Chapter 5 provides a detailed overview of all general and project/asset-related risks of an investment.

2.3.2.4 Direct investments/co-investments Direct investments in infrastructure assets allow a highly customised and targeted investment strategy. However, investing directly is not only capital-intensive but also labour- and resource-intensive. The implementation of a direct investment programme requires a significant number of experienced investment professionals with considerable expertise in the different fields of infrastructure, a proven track record and extensive networks in the relevant investment segments and target markets. The cost of maintaining a suitably qualified in-house team is considerable and only worthwhile for truly large financial investors, or clubs of investors, with assets under management running into the tens of billions and for traditional strategic investors.

Most financial investors are unable to perform direct investments without external support because they lack the necessary investment volume in order to deploy adequate professional resources. In this view, some specialised infrastructure advisors offer their services on the basis of tailor-made managed accounts or even on a deal-by-deal basis. Such an approach allows the investor to control the investment decisions while 'in-sourcing' the infrastructure transaction and management experience from the advisors (see Section 2.3.2). Alternatively, a number of funds offer investors the opportunity to co-invest, that is enabling them to invest in selected transactions directly alongside their fund(s). Both approaches allow investors to learn about the asset class and the relevant steps in the investment due diligence process alongside their advisors or fund managers. A benefit of co-investing with fund managers is the reduction in the overall cost burden, because fund management fees are generally not charged on co-investments, or are at least reduced. However, there are also drawbacks to and/or conflicts of interest when co-investing with fund managers. First, in most cases, the investor will only have the right to be offered co-investment opportunities if he invests in the fund in the first place. The overall investment strategy of the fund may not match the requirements of the investor, possibly only for selected assets. Second, by definition, the fund manager will only select and offer assets for co-investment that suit the investment strategy of the fund – and not necessarily the investor's strategy (selection bias) – and are too large for the fund manager to digest alone. Third, it is in the discretion of the fund manager to decide on the leverage of the asset. This is often higher than the desired leverage of conservative financial investors, who increasingly prefer to buy assets with little or even no leverage for reasons of risk reduction and higher capital deployment. Fourth, the fund manager will typically have to exit the asset at the end of the term of its fund. If the investor has a longer investment horizon and wants to hold the asset for good, it can only buy it in the regular competitive sale process unless the term of the fund is extended (see 'Term and disposability' in Section 2.3.2.3).

Another (and arguably better) way of co-investing that entails significantly less conflicts of interest may be with like-minded financial or possibly also strategic investors in a 'club-deal' structure. Such an approach eliminates the need to invest in a fund with an unsuitable investment strategy, it solves the selection bias, it allows joint agreement between the investors on the leverage (higher leverage requirements can be dealt with on the level of the respective investor) and it enables the group of investors to hold the asset as long as they want irrespective of fund term considerations. Infrastructure advisors provide their services to investors who aim to undertake club investments but lack the necessary in-house skills and/or resources to do so.

Section 2.3 demonstrates that, for most investors, investments in unlisted funds and/or managed accounts are effectively the most sensible way to become familiar with the infrastructure asset class. The section explains the key aspects of investment fund analysis, including how to approach the evaluation of an investment management team and its investment strategy and how to start tackling the analysis of direct investments as well as the main terms and conditions of an infrastructure fund.

The problem remains, however, that selecting the right fund (or FoFs) is non-trivial and difficult without knowing the entire fund universe and without the ability to evaluate the existing underlying projects/assets or the investment pipeline to a sufficient extent. However, project/asset-specific considerations, such as sector, stage, geographical location, condition and market, play an important role, as does an understanding of the structures and contractual arrangements underlying these projects/assets (e.g. long-term purchase/supply agreements, government guarantees, insurance for specific risks). This is because the existence and the characteristics of these criteria largely determine the risk-return profile of a project/asset.

As such, the stated objective of this book is to provide investors with additional theoretical know-how and practical examples in the following chapters – some of which go into considerable detail. This information will enable a deeper understanding of the key aspects of infrastructure investments, including their complex (project finance) structures, thereby allowing investors to analyse the risk-return profiles of individual projects/assets in the portfolio or pipeline. This knowledge may be useful not only when assessing the quality of a fund manager but also, most importantly, when selecting an advisor or conducting co-investments or direct investments at a later date.

CHAPTER 3

Organisational Model

E valuating private investments in infrastructure on the basis of comparing different sectors, countries or stages of development (greenfield versus brownfield), as is frequently observed, is clearly insufficient. Instead, a more comprehensive analysis of the most important country-, sector- and project-specific characteristics of infrastructure projects as well as of existing infrastructure assets is required during any investment due diligence. To this end, Section 1.3 provides an initial systematic overview that is elaborated on further in this chapter.

Country-specific characteristics will not be systematically investigated further beyond Section 1.1 and the various international examples throughout the book, owing to space limitations. Sector and subsector characteristics are set out in detail in Chapter 4. This chapter focuses on project/asset-specific characteristics – most of which are listed in Figure 1.7. They are discussed in the context of a complex 'organisational model' that provides a universally applicable description of any relevant organisational model that is applied internationally for infrastructure projects and assets, being aware that country-specific variations may exist. While this 'organisational model' focuses on project development, it can also form the basis for due diligences of existing assets.

Globally active investors have a fundamental interest and need in being able to identify and demarcate clearly different organisational models of infrastructure projects/assets and their individual determining factors. They seek to describe them and, in particular, analyse them irrespective of how they may be designated at a national level. On closer inspection, it becomes apparent that such an (overall) organisational model can be considered composed of or 'determined' by various self-contained, describable sub-models – the privatisation model, the partnership model, the business model, the contractual model and the financing model – as shown in Figure 3.1.

3.1 PRIVATISATION MODELS

Privatisation often has negative connotations. This can be seen from the use of phrases such as 'selling the family silver' when discussing the sale of public assets or 'privatisation of profits and nationalisation of losses' in reference to the privatisation of production processes or services that were previously performed by the public sector. In its essence, however, the term 'privatisation' describes nothing more than the highly complex procedures for the

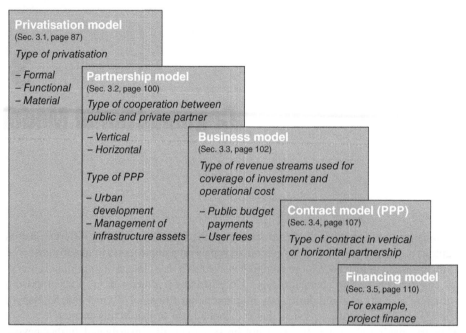

FIGURE 3.1   Determinants of the organisational model

transfer of assets and/or functions from the public sector to the private sector. This may involve a simple procurement process, such as the purchasing of planning, consulting, construction or facility management services that were previously performed in-house in 'force account' by the public authorities, or different degrees of privatisation of an entire service provider, such as Deutsche Bahn in Germany or Thames Water in the UK. Whether this holds positive or negative consequences for society as a whole cannot be generalised but should be investigated on a case-by-case basis.

The same reaction can be observed in the case of Public Private Partnerships (PPPs). Until today, the term 'PPP' has been associated with very different things, the misleading confusion with privatisations being only one example.

3.1.1   Privatisation versus PPP

One essential reason for the confusion between privatisation and PPP is certainly that, if compared internationally, the historical development of PPP, and the understanding of what PPP actually is, shows very different patterns in different countries. The term 'PPP' was first used in the US in the 1960s to refer to typical urban development projects involving private investors. This concept spread across the world and is structured as follows. Larger cities, in particular, may seek to ensure the involvement and assistance of private investors in order to develop brownfield and fallow sites for use that adequately reflects the aims of urban planning while offering a commercial interest for the investors. The public authorities generally provide the land on which the private partner uses its capital to develop, construct and market the real estate and the corresponding infrastructure, taking into account the relevant urban planning standards and other public requirements, but applying its own ideas and at its own risk. The partnership is formed with more of a long-term perspective than a time-limited approach with the goal of a joint concept of urban development. Depending on the structure, a mixed-form or purely private company is formed for the project.

PPPs then became known globally as a method of procurement for the public sector among others in the area of social infrastructure and infrastructure management. Initially developed into a standardised form as a result of the Private Finance Initiative (PFI) in the UK in the 1990s, it was taken up throughout the world in various forms and is becoming increasingly popular both as an alternative procurement option for the public sector and as a good investment opportunity for private investors. The key characteristic of this kind of PPP is the transfer (for a limited period) of integrated services relating to the planning, construction, financing, maintenance and operation of public infrastructure (lifecycle approach) that were previously performed by the public sector to private partners. The main objective is to generate efficiency gains in the provision of services. However, another stated aim – with varying priority – is to bridge liquidity bottlenecks on the side of the public authorities when performing urgent construction or modernisation tasks of infrastructure that are needed and/or requested by members of the public and other users of these assets.

In summary, the main characteristics of a PPP defined in this manner are:

- Lifecycle approach;
- Generation of efficiency gains through the appropriate assignment of functions;
- Real risk transfer to the private sector with balanced risk allocation;
- Creation of incentive structures for and leveraging of innovation potential of the private sector through results-oriented performance description and remuneration;
- Use of private expertise and capital;
- Long-term relationships on a partnership basis and, in particular, governed by contractual provisions;
- Rules/regulations set by public bodies.

The above characteristics describe how the PPP concept is interpreted in many countries that use this method of procurement and have developed it further on a country-specific basis. Canada, Australia and a number of European countries have established a similar kind of PPP understanding among official government bodies as presented in the following box.

PUBLIC–PRIVATE PARTNERSHIP (PPP)

PPP is a long-term, contractual cooperation between the public and private sectors for the economic execution of public tasks under which the necessary resources (e.g. expertise, equipment and facilities, capital, staff) are bundled in a joint organisational relationship and any project risks are allocated appropriately to reflect the risk management expertise of the project partners.

Source: German Federal Ministry of Transport, Building and Urban Affairs (2003)

Based on this understanding, a PPP is an alternative method of procurement for the public sector that, in contrast to conventional methods, is based not on the batch procurement of individual elements in the value chain of a public function, including the in-house provision of certain components, but rather on the performance of integrated cross-lifecycle services. In the real estate and infrastructure sectors, PPPs integrate the planning, construction, finance, investment, maintenance and operation phases. These services are performed on the basis of long-term cooperation between the public and private sectors that requires the conclusion of comprehensive contractual provisions. Ideally, the public partner should be responsible for performing sovereign functions and those that generally form part of the provision of subsistence, including:

- Determining demand, i.e. determining what needs to be provided and where, the dimensions, functionality and quality thereof, and the financial scope;
- Public approval measures and procedures, not necessarily including the preparation of the required documentation;
- Organising and ensuring competition 'around the market', i.e. the tender and award process for the desired services, and – where possible – 'within the market', e.g. regulating any monopoly situations that arise as a result of the long-term PPP contracts;
- Monitoring the performance of the private partner.

In contrast, the private partner assumes responsibility for all operating functions that can generally be performed more economically in a market economy structure than in the public sector. This may require the unbundling and subsequent restructuring of packages of functions that have evolved within and are geared towards government structures, as well as the corresponding resources.

The definition above also shows that the 'make or buy' decision in a PPP transfers not only the respective functions and tasks but also, in particular, the associated risks. The aim is not to transfer as many risks as possible but to achieve a balanced risk allocation. Unforeseeable risks that cannot be influenced by the project participants inevitably lead to uneconomical solutions from the perspective of the public and private partner.

This thought leads to the core of what a PPP actually is, according to the understanding of the authors: a method of procurement used by the public sector with the primary aim of generating efficiency gains compared with conventional methods. These must be identified, systematically expanded during project development and, ultimately, contractually guaranteed. They must be sustainable over the term of the contract, which means they should retain their value compared with a theoretical conventional solution even in the case of the unforeseeable events that inevitably occur over such a long timeframe.

It is notable that in many countries a systematic PPP standardisation process and a common understanding of PPP have been established only in some infrastructure sectors (e.g. in Germany only in the road transport and social infrastructure sectors). In other sectors, such as water supply and sewage, energy or waste disposal, PPPs and the corresponding understanding and terminology have historically developed in different ways. This experience is typical for many countries in Europe (e.g. France, Italy, the Netherlands, Spain) and around the world.

In Asia, Latin America and Africa, the generation of efficiency gains using PPP as a method of procurement tends to be less important than the pure financing aspect. This applies, in particular, to direct user-financed PPPs such as toll roads or water supply and disposal projects. Often driven by budgetary constraints, the clear priority is to obtain private capital for the implementation of infrastructure measures – in some cases, regardless of the cost. High-growth countries such as China and India, which were experiencing a boom that is comparable to the economic boom in Western Europe in the 1960s and 1970s, can and must be able to afford this approach in order to meet the huge need for infrastructural development. The resulting debt can be presented as an investment in future generations to a greater extent than would be possible in countries with low long-term growth rates.

The member states of the European Community established rules for new indebtedness as part of the Maastricht Treaty's Excessive Deficit Procedure (EDP). This regulation also affects infrastructure investments. One particularly relevant aspect concerns the circumstances under which infrastructure investments should be included in public debt or treated as 'off balance sheet'. The latter can generally be assumed in the case of full material privatisation, whereas for partial material privatisation, and PPP models in particular, the precise circumstances must be taken into account when performing allocation. Guidance on this matter has been provided by Eurostat, as outlined below.

MAASTRICHT TREATY: EXCESSIVE DEFICIT PROCEDURE

In 2004, Eurostat, the Statistical Office of the European Community, decided the following treatment of assets covered by PPPs in national accounts (Eurostat, 2004): If the construction risk and either the default risk or the demand risk under a PPP are clearly and comprehensively transferred to the private partner, the assets covered by this PPP may not be classified as government assets and hence may not be recognised as a deficit within the meaning of the Maastricht criteria. According to the decision, this applies to concessions in particular and in addition for all projects under which the government is the main purchaser of the services supplied by the partner, independent of whether the demand originates directly from the government itself or from third party users, as is the case for some social and transport infrastructure. Since 2011, with the enactment of the Protocol on the Excessive Deficit Procedure under the Maastricht Treaty, EU governments have had to take into consideration the impact of PPPs on government debt and deficit on a European statistical treatment level. For national accounting purposes, each European country enjoys the freedom to consider PPP projects either as government or as non-government assets. This regulation reduces incentives to create off-balance-sheet shadow budgets for large-scale infrastructure investment but instead leads to the transparency of national debt on an EU level.

If projects are to be considered non-government assets in national accounts, it must be demonstrated that the construction risk has been fully and comprehensively transferred to the private partner. For example, this condition is satisfied if the payments by the government to the private partner are made taking into account the effective state of the assets (e.g. payments only begin upon termination of construction). It must also be examined whether the default risk and/or the demand risk is borne by the private partner. If the government is entitled to significantly reduce the amount of the regular payments owing to inadequate performance by the private partner, the default risk is considered to have been transferred to the private partner. Demand risk is transferred to the private partner if fluctuations in demand not attributable to the behaviour of the private partner result in a tangible decrease in the private revenue generated. A detailed examination of every individual case, however, needs to be conducted in order to establish whether the respective project constitutes a PPP in accordance with the EU regulation, taking into account all the risks transferred to the private partner and the guarantees issued by the government.

The term 'PPP' still means different things in different countries and even sometimes within one country when comparing different national infrastructure sectors. The only way to find some common ground in terms of the basic understanding of PPPs as a concept under these circumstances would be to refer to each and every form of cooperation between the public and private sectors as a PPP, irrespective of whether it involves functional or material privatisation, was commissioned or initiated independently, governed by contractual provisions or a loose association, with or without the involvement of private investment, etc.

As this is not particularly helpful for public bodies or private infrastructure investors when it comes to performing due diligence, however, a more concrete description of the precise relationships is required. The severe negative economic consequences of such an unorganised approach were also recognised by the European Investment Bank (EIB), which responded to this problem by launching the European PPP Expertise Centre (EPEC) in 2011 based at the EIB in Luxembourg. It provided some degree of harmonisation in terms of the basic understanding and terminology, at least in Europe, and connected the existing PPP expertise centres in the various European countries. The objective was to form a network for the intensive exchange of experience (see Section 7.4.3 for further information). As of 2015, 35 public institutions (from 30 different countries) are members of the EPEC network. A major step towards the objective of harmonisation of the European PPP process has been achieved through the publication of the EPEC *Guide to Guidance* as well as various activities of capacity building, policy and programme support among the member countries. Essentially, EPEC activities and guidelines aim to reflect the different understanding of PPP within the countries or infrastructure sectors, while forming a sort of PPP umbrella for further development and harmonisation of this form of procurement across Europe.

Meanwhile, this book seeks to solve the problem in a pragmatic and practical way by taking a different approach. It accepts the existing differences – the described historical developments aside – that may have specific political, legal or organisational causes as inevitable for the time being and will not even try to find another definition of PPP, most probably one even less commonly acceptable and applicable than the existing ones. Instead, the 'organisational model' allows for systematically analysing and categorising every individual complex scheme of private-sector participation (PSP) internationally, irrespective of whether the project type is called a PPP. This is achieved by breaking it down into its type of privatisation, partnership, business, contract and financing model, thus making it transparent and comparable, particularly concerning inherent risk allocation. This approach allows the description of any individual form and definition of public infrastructure procurement, and therefore to understand infrastructure projects based on their individual characteristics as well as type of privatisation applied.

The following three sections describe and differentiate between three types of privatisation: (i) formal privatisation, (ii) functional privatisation and (iii) material privatisation. The key characteristics used to distinguish between these forms of privatisation are:

- *The nature and extent of the transfer of functions to the private sector:* A distinction is made between sovereign functions and the provision of subsistence, which are not transferable, and largely operative functions, which can be transferred, particularly if there is sufficient competition and no other evidence of market failure exists.
- *Allocation of the 'provision function':* This relates to the question of who is responsible for determining demand; for infrastructural assets, this means which of the partners is responsible for determining where and when capacity should be established and maintained and what its dimensions and quality should be.
- *Ownership interests:* In the majority of forms of privatisation discussed in this book, ownership of the respective physical structure remains with the public sector for legal and, in most cases, constitutional reasons (prohibition of ownership transfer) even if the functions, regarding what the infrastructure offers to the user, have been transferred to the private sector to the greatest possible extent.
- *Duration of privatisation:* Privatisation is often limited to a defined period after the transfer of functions, i.e. the public sector assumes responsibility for the transferred functions at the end of the term or puts them out to tender again.

Figure 3.2 provides an overview of the various types of privatisation in terms of the characteristics described above.

Type of privatisation	Transfered tasks					Provision function	Ownership		Duration
	Design	Finan-cing	Invest-ment	Build	Ope-ration		Public	Private	
Formal privatisation: 'public entities in private clothes'									
legally ...	private business model					public	100%		unlimited
financially	private financing (company)					public			
Functional privatisation: 'the private partner as the assistant of the public'									
outsourcing ...	... of single delegable tasks/services					public	100%		limited
	... of comprehensively integrated services						x%	x%	
Materially privatisation: transfer of ownership / provision function									
partial material privatisation	joint venture					public/private	x%	x%	umlimited
full material privatisation	sale of shares to private investors					private		100%	

FIGURE 3.2   Main characteristics of various types of privatisation

3.1.2 Formal privatisation

Formal privatisation describes the transformation of an administrative public entity into a company under private law, typically in the form of a limited corporation. The public sector remains the sole shareholder. As such, this procedure involves a purely legal privatisation. If the company obtains finance from non-public sources, it can also be described as financial privatisation. In global terms, formal privatisation is probably the most widespread form of privatisation in the infrastructure industry and can be found in all infrastructure sectors. The objective is usually to outsource the departments responsible for a specific infrastructural task from the public authority in order to form a legally and economically independent entity. Legal privatisation is often preceded by bundling in the form of public law institutions (e.g. special public agencies) or other strictly public law company structures. However, formal privatisation often also serves as the precursor to a more extensive material privatisation, whether in part or in full, by way of an initial public offering (IPO) and/or the sale of shares to strategic or financial investors. The box briefly describes a number of typical companies that underwent different degrees of privatisations in different countries, which means some were only formally privatised while others proceeded further to material privatisation (which is discussed in Section 3.1.4).

EXAMPLES OF PRIVATISATION PROCESS

Deutsche Bahn AG (DB AG, DBAG or DB) is the German national railway company, a private joint stock company (AG) that is 100% owned by the Federal Republic of Germany (formal privatisation). Based on the 'Bahnreform', it came into existence via outsourcing to 'Deutsches Eisenbahnvermögen' and the subsequent formal privatisation in 1994 as the successor to the former state railways of Germany, the Deutsche Bundesbahn of West Germany and the Deutsche Reichsbahn of East Germany. After several further steps of internal reforms between 1999 and 2007, a long-term goal of the company and the shareholder was a partial material privatisation by selling shares on the stock market. This has been a subject of highly controversial political discussion in Germany for a long time and a decision has not been taken until now. One of the main questions is whether a partial material privatisation of the rail system should be carried out with the railway network (integrated model) or without (split model).

Heathrow Airport Holding (former British Airports Authority), formed in 1965, has been the owner of Heathrow, Gatwick, Stansted and Prestwick airports since 1966. The Airports Act 1986 saw the formal privatisation of the British Airports Authority as a public limited company. Since then, the new company has been known as BAA. As part of its subsequent continuing material privatisation process, BAA went public through an IPO a year later, in 1987. In 2006, the company was taken over by Ferrovial and delisted from the Stock Exchange (example is continued in Section 4.1.4.4).

ASFiNAG, founded in 1982 as a 100% subsidiary of the Austrian Federal Republic (formal privatisation), took over the tasks of design, financing, construction, maintenance and operation of the whole Austrian highway network, with a length of approximately 2100 km, from the responsible public administration. In 1997, the company got the usufruct right of all properties and assets of the primary road network that continued to be owned by the Federal government as well as the right to collect tolls on this network. Since ASFiNAG does not get any financial support from the public budget, the aim of the transfer of these additional rights was to strengthen the company's creditworthiness. Aside from conventional forms of procurement under the formal privatisation, ASFiNAG also tenders PPP road projects within the Austrian road network. These projects are functional privatisations in comparison to ASFiNAG itself. Hence this example shows a multi-layer privatisation concept of public infrastructure asset management (example is continued in Section 3.6).

Brisa Auto-Estradas de Portugal SA, a government-owned corporation, was formed in 1972 (formal privatisation). Thereafter, Portugal initiated a range of major investment projects for the expansion of its high-end road network. After that, Brisa's privatisation process continued towards a partial material privatisation by selling shares on the stock market. It was contracted with the construction, financing, maintenance and operation of the Portuguese highway network. To this end, it was given the right to collect tolls from road users. Between 1997 and 2001, the Portuguese government sold all its shares to private investors in several tranches (example is continued in Section 3.1.4).

France With the previously state-owned highway companies SANEF (Société des Autoroutes du Nord et de l'Est de la France), ASF (Autoroutes du Sud de la France) and APRR (Autoroutes Paris-Rhin-Rhône), the French government pursued a similar strategy in 2005, selling the shares it still held in the concession companies after the IPO to private investors (in this case strategic) investors (example is continued in Section 3.1.4).

The primary motivation for formal privatisation is to escape the restrictions involved in public revenue, collective bargaining, administrative provisions, etc., in order to offer services more efficiently than could be achieved in a purely public-sector administrative structure. However, experience has shown that this is only possible to an extremely limited extent, if at all.

From a regulatory perspective, for a formally privatised company to enter into competition with a functional private sector is not advisable, as fair competition cannot generally be guaranteed and the market equilibrium may be disturbed. As such, formal privatisation should be seen as a preliminary step towards material privatisation in the near future, whether in part or in full (see below). For private investors, formal privatisation is interesting only to the extent that it may be the precursor to partial or full material privatisation (see examples above and in Section 3.1.4).

3.1.3 Functional privatisation

Functional privatisation describes the transfer of functions that were previously performed by the public sector in its own right to a private company for a specified period. When functions relating to buildings and physical structures are transferred, this typically includes planning, construction and/or infrastructure asset management services such as cleaning and servicing. The term 'outsourcing' has also established itself for this form of privatisation.

Functional privatisation includes PPP models – or at least those meeting the definition used in this book – the services of which are 'comprehensively integrated', bundled and awarded by way of a PPP contract concluded for a long, individually defined term (lifecycle approach). Accordingly, a functional privatisation always occurs when the provision function (as defined in Section 3.1 above) and, typically, ownership of the physical structure remain with the public sector. One exception is the build–own–operate–transfer (BOOT) model, under which ownership is transferred to the private operator during a limited contractual term, mostly for tax reasons (see the Athens example). Partnership models and respective examples are extensively described in Section 3.2, as are business models in Section 3.3.

ATHENS INTERNATIONAL AIRPORT

One prominent example of a BOOT model is the airport in Athens. The Greek government holds a majority interest of 55% in Athens International Airport SA (primarily in the form of land), whereas private shareholders with a combined interest of 45% were responsible for the planning, construction and operation as well as financing the necessary investments until the transfer to the government after the concession period of 30 years (including the five-year construction phase). The concession was granted in 1996. Owing to the success of this project, the Greek government expressed its interest in a partial sale of its shares via the Stock Exchange in 2009. At the same time, the public authorities enjoyed the annual profit share generated by the airport. The question of whether there should be a trade-off of a one-time receipt through the sale of shares versus annual yields is regularly discussed in the Greek parliament. However, a date for the IPO has yet to be determined and no decision to sell a part or all shares has been yet taken by the government (AviAlliance, 2014).

3.1.4 Material privatisation

As long as a market is functional, that is there are no market distortions or even market failure in an economic sense, it is safe to assume that a function can be transferred to the market in full. Among other things, this means that the competitive environment determines the appropriate prices and quality for use of the functional services, thereby ensuring optimal provision for the users of the respective infrastructure asset. This scenario also serves as a clear indicator that the respective function does not form part of the core tasks of the government, at least from a market economy perspective. However, material privatisation should also be largely irreversible, with all the consequences, advantages and disadvantages this entails in both good times and bad. The government is required to intervene only in a regulatory function using the instruments at its disposal where there is evidence of market failure or market deficiencies, such as external effects or safety aspects. In certain cases, subsidies may also be a suitable means to do so while at the same time benefiting from private structures to the greatest possible extent.

The key characteristic of material privatisation is that, in addition to comprehensive functional transfer, ownership of the assets necessary to perform those functions is also transferred on a permanent basis. This constitutes a de facto divestment on the part of the government. Accordingly, the provision function is generally also transferred from the public to the private sector, that is the capacity and prices of infrastructure provided are subsequently determined primarily on the basis of the interaction between demand and supply. In this scenario, the government withdraws to all practical extents from an entire infrastructural function that it previously performed. Therefore, in contrast to functional privatisation, material privatisation always involves the formation of a new private company (as is the case in formal privatisation as well), if only to demarcate clearly the privatised operations.

A distinction is made between full and partial material privatisation based on the extent to which a public partner retains an interest in the company after privatisation. Partial material privatisation can be further broken down into majority and minority interests, depending on the interest held by the public sector in the jointly-owned private company. Full privatisation means there are no longer any public partners involved as shareholders. That is why only partial material privatisation results in a 'horizontal' partnership with the private sector on a permanent basis (see Section 3.1.3).

As evidence of market failure often exists for infrastructure – a reason for the state having to remain involved in some way – genuine cases of full material privatisation (i.e. 100% privatisation on a permanent basis) rarely occur in the public infrastructure sector. It is fair to say that the most extensive material privatisations around the world can be found in the telecommunications and energy sectors. Even in these cases, the public sector generally attempts to retain some influence over the company as owner by way of a golden share. In the event of full material privatisation, the government can and must exercise its influence in the form of legislation, regulation or similar whenever public interests, such as those of users, are threatened. The box featuring the privatisation of Deutsche Telekom is an example of an extensive material privatisation.

DEUTSCHE TELEKOM AG

Deutsche Telekom AG developed quickly from a former administratively organised monopoly company to an innovative, dynamic and competitive service company with international ambitions. By 2014, it had become the biggest vendor of telecommunication services in Germany and – judging by its sales revenues in that year amounting to €62.7 billion – one of the biggest telecommunication companies worldwide with a presence in more than 50 countries and 228 000 employees (as per 31 December 2014). It has its origin in the former publicly owned Deutsche Bundespost of postal and telecommunication services. Until the national postal and telecommunication reform in 1989, the Federal Ministry for Postal Services and Telecommunication was the headquarters for the entire sector.

In Step I of the reform, Deutsche Bundespost was split into three independent companies: Deutsche Bundespost Telekom (telecommunication services), Deutsche Bundespost Postdienst (postal services) and Deutsche Bundespost Postbank (banking services). However, these companies still had one common management board with the political and sovereign tasks remaining in the Federal Ministry for Postal Services and Telecommunication (formal privatisation).

Step II of the national postal and telecommunication reform – implemented on 1 January 1995 – was the transformation of the three companies into independent joint stock companies: Deutsche Telekom AG with its daughter companies being responsible for telecommunication services, Deutsche Post AG for postal services and Deutsche Postbank AG for banking services. Step II of the reform also ruled that Deutsche Telekom AG had to be listed on the stock market by 31 December 1999 – which it did in 1996 with the majority of its shares being held privately. The process took place in three steps: (i) IPO – DT 1 – in November 1996, (ii) second public offering – DT 2 – in June 1999 and (iii) third public offering – DT 3 – in June 2000. Throughout, the share of the Federal Republic decreased from 100% to 74% after the first stage, to 65% after the second and reduced finally to 58% after the third stage. The takeover of American mobile phone providers VoiceStream and Powertel on 31 May 2001 reduced the share of the government further as the purchases were paid in cash and by swapping shares.

The shareholder structure of Deutsche Telekom AG (as per 31 December 2014) is as follows: Public float 68.3%, KfW Group (Reconstruction Loan Cooperation, which trades part of the government's shares on behalf of the Federal Republic) 17.4% and the Federal government 14.3%.

Further examples of material privatisation in the transportation sector include the afore-mentioned privatisation process of the Heathrow Airport Holding, (former BAA) and, to a lesser extent, Düsseldorf Airport in Germany (both examples are detailed further in Section 4.1.4.4), as well as Autobahn TankRast GmbH, Germany's leading service provider on service areas along the Autobahn. Nevertheless, the majority of full or partial material privatisations within the transportation sector involve airports or harbours. To a certain extent, this can be explained by the fact that there is significantly greater competition among airports or harbours than between other transport carriers.

Full material privatisations rarely occur in infrastructure sectors other than energy, telecommunication and specific transport (airport, harbour), as mentioned above, and prac-tically do not exist at all in the road transport sector (except for roadside services). Among other things, this may be due to the fact that, particularly in road transport, the sale of land to the private sector is very uncommon almost everywhere in the world – roads are always public assets. Furthermore, it is almost impossible to rule out the existence of monopoly situ-ations in this subsector. Therefore, functional privatisation models in the form of time-limited concessions (BOT models) without transfer of ownership are the appropriate and usual way of involving private investors in road sector projects (for more details regarding the different models applied in the road sector refer to Section 3.3).

This applies also to France (SANEF, ASF and APRR) and in Portugal (Brisa). In Section 3.1.2 these are presented as formally privatised infrastructure companies (i.e. as private legal entities being in full state ownership) that were materially privatised later on (i.e. shares have been gradually transferred to private ownership through a subsequent sale). However, strictly speaking, they only represent concession companies created for a special purpose, for a temporary period and without ownership of the assets, but having the usufruct right of the physical infrastructure assets that enables them to design, finance, build, maintain and operate these assets according to the contractual requirements. After the concession periods, which may vary significantly from between 20 years and 90 years, the functions performed by the concession companies are returned to the government. The latter may choose to put them out to tender again. The process of privatisation of the infrastructure management company (responsible for a certain part of the network, i.e. through a concession) has to be distinguished from the concession itself awarded to the special-purpose company (SPC) that signs responsibility for a certain project or part of the network over. The SPV has been and keeps being independent of the legal status of the management company (formally or materially privatised) and the composition of its shareholders (public or private). Within the classification system developed in this book, SPVs must be (with respect to the temporary concession) ultimately categorised as functional privatisations. The Brisa example describes the development of Brisa, SANEF, ASF and APRR as infrastructure management companies and their privatisation process from formal to material privatisation (see Section 3.1.2 for the first part of these examples).

BRISA

By the end of 1981, the formally privatised Brisa (Auto-Estradas de Portugal SA) was granted its first concession involving the construction of around 390 km of highways. The government held 90% of the shares of the company directly and a further 10% indirectly, with CGD (a state-owned bank) and IPE (a government institution) each holding 5%. Between 1997 and 2001, the state-owned shares were sold in four tranches. The government sold 35% of its shares in 1997, 31% in 1998, 20% in 1999 and 4% in 2001 (totalling 90%). The main shareholders of Brisa had been José de Mello, Abertis and the Arcus European Fund I (former Babcock & Brown European Infrastructure Fund). Around 35% of the shares were freely traded on the open market (Brisa, 2009). In 2012, Tagus Holdings successfully launched a takeover bid for all Brisa shares. As a consequence, Brisa officially was delisted from Euronext on 12 April 2013 (Brisa, 2013). The concession of Brisa motorways ends in 2035.

After a partial material privatisation, the French government reduced its shares in the highway companies SANEF (to 76%), ASF (to 54%) and APRR (to 70%). The sale was conducted in several tranches, most of which were implemented via the stock exchange. Hence, most of the nongovernmental shares were in free float. In late 2005, the French government decided to sell its remaining shares in the form of a public tender procedure to strategic and/or financial investors. The successful bidders were Abertis for SANEF (1743 km), Vinci for ASF (3124 km) and a consortium comprising Eiffage SA, Macquarie Infrastructure Group (MIG) and Macquarie European Infrastructure Fund (MEIF) for APRR (2260 km). The transaction generated total revenues of €15 billion for the French government.

Similar transactions had already been conducted in Italy (e.g. the privatisation of Autostrade) and in Spain (e.g. the privatisation of the airline Iberia).

3.2   PARTNERSHIP MODELS

When distinguishing between the various privatisation models, it becomes evident that not all forms of privatisation necessarily include a legal involvement on the part of the private sector. Figure 3.3 shows, for example, that there is no private partner as shareholder – and consequently no PSP in the case of formal privatisation and, at the other extreme, no public partner in the case of full material privatisation, under which the private sector acts alone in the market. Consequently, PSP or partnerships between the public and the private sector exist only in functional privatisations in the form of outsourcing and partial material privatisation, as highlighted in Figure 3.3 with dark shading.

In this classification, a distinction is made between horizontal and vertical partnerships in structural terms. In the case of functional privatisation, reference is also made to contractual (vertical) and institutional (horizontal) PPPs. Accordingly, Figure 3.4 illustrates the structural differences between these two functional partnership models and the horizontal partnership arising from partial material privatisation. It should be noted that horizontal partnerships in functional privatisations are also called 'institutional PPP' (or 'institutionalised PPP' in the EU Green Paper on PPP; European Commission, 2000a). Nevertheless, in order to distinguish clearly between partnership models without or with only temporally limited ownership (functional privatisation) and those with permanent transfer of ownership (material privatisation) from the public to the private sector, in this book models of partial material privatisation are still called 'horizontal partnerships', but not PPPs.

In both cases of PPPs, that is contractual and institutional, a principal/agent relationship is entered into with an SPC formed specifically for the respective (project) purpose under the terms of the PPP contract, which functions as a contract for work and labour or as a

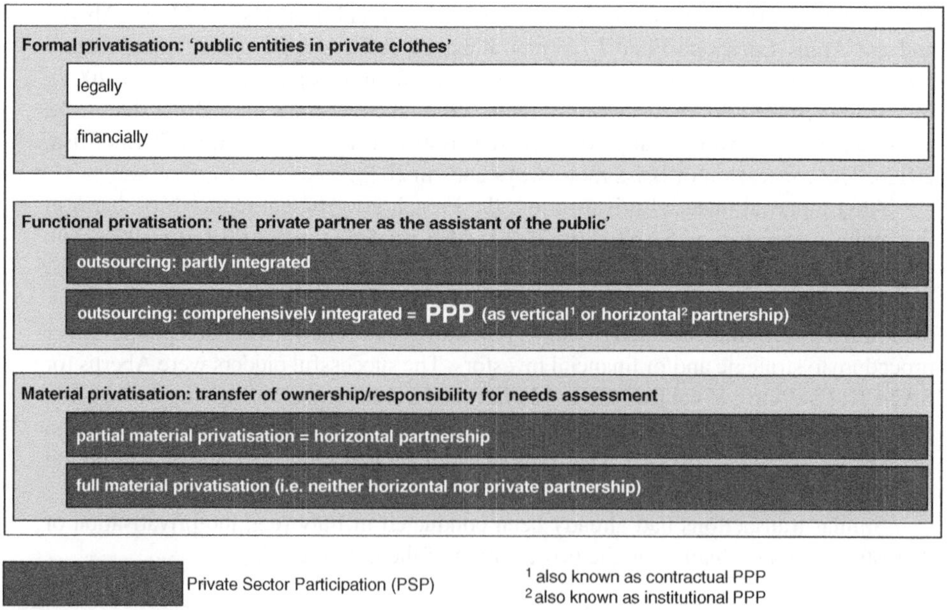

Formal privatisation: 'public entities in private clothes'
legally
financially

Functional privatisation: 'the private partner as the assistant of the public'
outsourcing: partly integrated
outsourcing: comprehensively integrated = PPP (as vertical[1] or horizontal[2] partnership)

Material privatisation: transfer of ownership/responsibility for needs assessment
partial material privatisation = horizontal partnership
full material privatisation (i.e. neither horizontal nor private partnership)

Private Sector Participation (PSP)   [1] also known as contractual PPP
                                            [2] also known as institutional PPP

FIGURE 3.3   Privatisation with and without private-sector participation

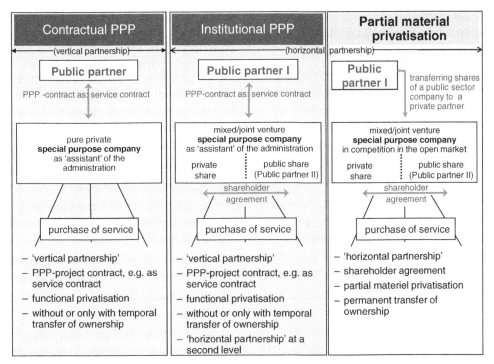

FIGURE 3.4 Structures of partnership models

service agreement. In contrast to (purely) contractual PPPs, where the agent is a (purely) private project company, the public sector retains a share in the project company in the case of institutional PPPs, whether in the form of the public-sector principal itself or another public-sector institution through a shareholder agreement in place among the two parties on the SPC level. A separate description of the typical business and PPP contract models is provided in Sections 3.3 and 3.4.

Take another look at Figure 3.4: the horizontal partnership shown on the right-hand side of the figure as a partial material privatisation describes the participation of public-sector and private-sector partners as co-shareholders of an infrastructure project company that designs, builds, finances, maintains and/or operates an infrastructure asset. In practice, there are predominantly two ways in which this type of partnership may be established. In the first case, an infrastructure project is put out to tender as a BOO (build own operate) contract (see Figure 3.7). The tender conditions specify that the public sector intends to participate in the project company to be formed jointly by the partners after award and contract signing.

In the second case, an already existing project company wholly owned by the public sector/government seeks a private investor as a shareholder. Shares are then sold either to a private strategic partner by way of tender or auction or widespread by way of IPO. There may be various reasons for taking this approach; however, the most common scenario is that capital is required for the expansion or renovation of an infrastructural facility. A further objective may be a desire to integrate the expertise of a private operator into the existing organisational structure and transfer some of the risks to the private partner.

For example, following the fire disaster in 1996, Düsseldorf Airport looked for a buyer to take up 50% of the shares, perform and finance the renovation and conversion work and operate the airport permanently in cooperation with the public-sector partner (for more information, see the box in Section 4.1.4.4). In terms of financing, partial material privatisation models use common financial techniques such as mergers and acquisitions as well as IPOs on the stock market.

In all cases of horizontal partnerships, be they PPPs or partial material privatisations, the public sector can generally control the degree of its influence over the provision function in the wider sense and the transfer of functions on the basis of its shareholding as set out in the partnership agreement. To this end, the business risk remains with the public sector to the same extent. If the aim of obtaining private investment is to achieve a clear separation of risks and risk spheres between the public and private partners, this can generally be achieved more effectively by entering into a vertical partnership, for example, with one of the PPP business and contract models described in Sections 3.3 and 3.4 rather than a horizontal partnership agreement. The influence that the public project execution agency wishes to exercise can generally also (and sometimes should) be set out in the underlying (PPP) contract.

3.3 BUSINESS MODELS

The two key aspects to be taken into account when evaluating a business model are the revenue side (i.e. the available sources of revenue, the amount of revenue and the corresponding remuneration mechanisms) and the cost side. The following highly simplified discussion focuses solely on the revenue side. In contrast to the cost side, which largely depends on the infrastructure services to be provided, on the revenue side two fundamentally different, alternatively applicable sources of revenue exist that may be used for the same kind of infrastructure services: 'budget-financed' and 'user-financed'. In general, that means every business model remuneration is based on direct user payments, availability payments from the public budget or a combination of both (see Figure 3.5). For 'user-financed' models, it is crucial

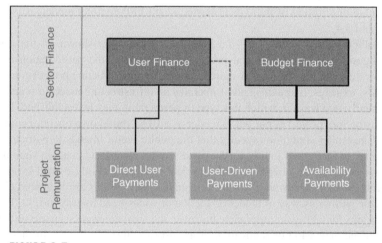

FIGURE 3.5 Business model – sources of revenue and remuneration structure

to distinguish between 'direct user payments' (e.g. user toll) and 'user-driven payments' (e.g. shadow toll) payments. User-driven payments typically form a mixture of budget payments that are directly linked to the actual use of an asset even though the user does not notice it. As such, they increase the risk-return profile of the asset compared to pure budget (availability based) payment models.

The above shows that the source of revenue is highly relevant when it comes to the assessment of the risk and potential yield of a project. Notwithstanding, in most instances, the private partner can determine the source of revenue and the concrete configuration of the remuneration structure only to a limited extent, if at all. The most common international business models are discussed in the following sub-sections.

3.3.1 Availability payment models

In the case of availability payment models, the private partner receives a fixed remuneration that is generally budget financed and payable by the principal at regular intervals, based on specific task and service level agreements. Examples are:

- *Performance-based payments* corresponding to the services set out in the specifications or list of services;
- *Availability-based payments* corresponding only to the availability of premises, areas, facilities, equipment, etc.;
- *Volume-based payments* corresponding to the consumption of water, electricity, gas, etc.;
- *Results-based payments* corresponding to contractually agreed (optimisation) targets.

Fixed remuneration is used mainly in the area of social infrastructure. The following sections provide examples of typical budget-financed business models.

3.3.1.1 PPP owner model The PPP owner model is used extensively for infrastructure assets for which a transfer of ownership to the private sector is not applicable by law in the respective country, such as the renovation and/or new construction and expansion of schools or other social infrastructure assets as well as road infrastructure. As such, this model combines the turnkey construction or renovation of buildings or facilities and comprehensive facility management during the subsequent operating phase, which may have a duration of 20 to 30 years, depending on the investment volume. In contrast to the contractual models described below, ownership of the buildings or facilities generally remains with the public partner acting as the principal and landowner or is transferred back to the public partner on completion by act of law.

Analogous to the PPP purchaser model described below, the private partner receives a monthly or annual fixed regular fee depending on the availability of the asset, which is financed by the budget and covers all its investment costs, operating costs, any risk premiums and its profit. The private partner bears no market (demand and price) risk on the income side. However, it retains a limited element of demand risk on the cost side as the operating and maintenance costs depend on the volume of use (e.g. for transport infrastructure in the form of heavy goods vehicles). The risk can be mitigated through an agreement of compensation payments in the event that the usage of the asset significantly exceeds the forecast that is part of the contract. For example, in the case of Norway's E39 project the actual traffic is 20% above the traffic forecast.

During the individual project phases, the risks are primarily borne by the contractor. Only the realisation risk and demand risks on the cost side remain with the principal. The main difference between the PPP owner model and a BOT concession model is the demand risk that is transferred in the case of the latter to the private partner (e.g. in the case of swimming pools, retirement homes, student housing), which will then be classified as direct-user payment remuneration.

3.3.1.2   PPP purchaser model

The PPP purchaser model involves turnkey construction and comprehensive facility management during the subsequent operating phase, which takes usually between 20 and 30 years. During the term of the contract, the building is owned by the contractor. The services to be performed by the contractor include design/planning, construction, financing and operation. At the end of the contractual term, ownership is transferred to the public-sector principal (transfer/utilisation). As in the PPP owner model, the contractor receives a monthly or annual availability fee that covers all its investment costs, operator and other operating costs, any risk premiums and its profit. This fee is paid from the public budget.

During the individual project phases, the risks (design/planning, construction and financing) are primarily borne by the contractor. Only the risk of accidental destruction (risk of loss and price risk) is generally transferred to the principal prior at the start of the operating phase. The principal also bears the risk arising from the economically viable use of the asset during the project term and its utilisation after ownership is transferred at the end of the term (realisation risk).

3.3.1.3   PPP lease model

The PPP lease model describes the turnkey provision of an asset owned by the contractor by way of a real estate lease and the performance of comprehensive facility management during the operating phase, which is usually between 20 and 30 years. In contrast to the PPP purchaser model, the principal is usually either granted a purchase option for the residual value of the building, which is calculated when the contract is concluded, or given the opportunity to extend the lease. Variations may include agreements on heritable building rights or sale and leaseback concepts.

The services to be performed by the contractor again include the design/planning, construction, financing and operation of the property. In contrast to the PPP purchaser model, however, planning and construction do not form part of the contractually agreed obligations of the contractor but instead are a condition of the contractor's duty to make the asset available for use. As in the case of the PPP purchaser model, the contractor receives a regular monthly fee for the services provided paid via the public budget. This fee is generally based on a partial payout calculation of the investment costs (including financing costs).

During the individual project phases, the risks are primarily borne by the contractor. Owing to the structure of the contractual model as a real estate lease in accordance with decrees issued by the fiscal authorities, the risk of loss and price risk associated with the asset in particular remain with the contractor. In contrast to the PPP purchaser model, the realisation/utilisation risk is also borne by the contractor unless the principal exercises its purchase option.

3.3.1.4   PPP tenant model

As in the case of the PPP purchaser model, the PPP tenant model describes a combination of the turnkey provision of a building owned by the contractor and the performance of comprehensive facility management during the operating phase, which is usually between 20 and 30 years. Like the PPP lease model, transfer of ownership to the principal at the end of the contractual term is not compulsory; instead, the principal may be granted a purchase option or an option to extend the rental agreement. Unlike the PPP lease model, however, the purchase price when the purchase option is exercised is based not on the residual value calculated on conclusion of the contract but on the market value of the property at the date on which the option is exercised. Variations may include agreements on heritable building rights or the separation of land and building ownership through the conclusion of pseudo-component agreements.

As is the case for the previous models, the PPP tenant model may also be used for existing assets owned by the private contractor and requiring renovation. The services to be performed by the contractor again include planning, construction, financing and operation. The contractor receives a regular monthly fee via the public budget from the principal for the services provided. This fee is not based on a full or partial payout calculation of the contractor's investment costs but instead is calculated on the basis of the standard market rent for similar properties and the contractor's operating and other costs.

During the individual project phases, the risks are primarily borne by the contractor. As the contract takes the form of a rental agreement, the risk of loss and price associated with the asset remains with the contractor as the landlord. The realisation/utilisation risk is also borne by the contractor unless the principal exercises a purchase option. Particularly when no purchase option is granted, the model constitutes a normal tenancy, albeit with additional facility management services, and should therefore be classified as a full material privatisation model (see also the international designation DBROO in Figure 3.7 in Section 3.4) rather than a functional privatisation.

3.3.2   User-driven payment models

User-driven payment models are a combination of budget and user finance. The revenue required to cover the investment and operating costs is paid via the public budget, but directly linked to user demand, that is use of the respective assets or services. The public remuneration of these models is typically based on:

- *Usage-based payments*, which can be further broken down into:
  - Frequency of use, such as the shadow toll for roads or fees that reflect the number of users of a swimming pool, a sports hall or another public facility;
  - Intensity of use, such as in the case of shadow tolls, whereby diverging 'shadow rates' apply based on axle loads or emissions.

The characteristic feature of all user-driven payment models is that the demand risk is softened because users' consumption behaviour is not influenced by (changes in) price. This is the case because users do not even know the price. They are not charged directly on usage but the public contract partner pays the bill 'in the background'. Accordingly, the price risk stays with the principal who, however, also is the one who negotiates the price with the operator in the first place. The following sections provide examples of user-driven payment models that are typical for transport infrastructure PPP projects.

3.3.2.1   Shadow toll model   The transfer of functions and risks under the shadow toll model used in various European countries, particularly the UK, Finland and Portugal, is essentially the same as under the availability payment model. The shadow toll model is also budget-financed. However, as the operator is remunerated by way of a traffic-based 'shadow toll' rather than a fixed fee, as in the case of an availability-based payment model, the operator takes the traffic risk (frequency and intensity of use) under this model, which naturally determines the revenue side. The traffic risk is still lower than in the case of the BOT concession model (see Section 3.3.3) because only the traffic volume risk is transferred to the contractor. In the UK, the traffic volume risk of shadow toll models is reduced because of the introduction of 'traffic bands'. These bands typically constitute four areas within which the shadow toll revenue is constant irrespective of the exact traffic volume within them. This arrangement ultimately serves to limit the traffic volume risk transferred to the private partner.

3.3.2.2 Active management model   The active management model is a combination of the availability model and the shadow toll model. It allows the principal to set an incentive framework for the private contractor to achieve performance and usage-based results, for example in terms of road safety, active road management or average speed of vehicles. One can find these innovative remuneration schemes in the UK. It allows the principal to take advantage of value-for-money potential when investing in infrastructure projects that are purely budget financed.

3.3.3 Direct-user payment models

Direct-user payment models obtain the revenue required to cover the investment and current operating costs directly from user fees such as tolls, charges, entrance fees or rents. The characteristic feature of these models is that the market risk is determined by the level of demand, which in turn varies with the willingness of the prospective users to pay a certain fee. The level of the fee depends to a large extent on the level of competition in the respective usage situation. A distinction is made between:

- *Compulsory usage*, e.g. compulsory connection to the water network, where users have no choice but to obtain their water supply from the local provider (monopoly situation);
- *(Quasi-)compulsory usage*, e.g. when there are no alternatives to using the services offered or the available alternatives are unattractive; typical examples include bridges over or tunnels under rivers that cannot be crossed in another manner within an acceptable distance (quasi-monopoly situation);
- *Free choice of usage in a competitive environment*, e.g. when the user can choose between several telephone providers or a shorter toll road compared with one or more longer non-toll roads within an acceptable distance.

The level of competition ultimately influences the degree of regulatory interventions, which together determine the risk-return profile of the project/asset. Generally speaking, the greater the level of competition, the better the functionality of the market in terms of the self-regulation of prices. The lower the level of competition, the greater the need for external regulation (see also Section 1.3.10), which may serve to increase or reduce the market risk depending on the circumstances. Private investors must assess for themselves which scenario – regulation or competition – they consider embodies the greater risk and the greater yield potential.

In the case of a combination of budget- and user-financed sources of income, the user fees charged are often supplemented by performance-based or availability-based elements, for example in the form of contractual penalties, which could also be regarded as project-specific regulation measures. Contractual penalties may serve to offset the lack of quality incentives that arise in monopoly situations in particular. On the other hand, low user fees (e.g. road transport or student housing) that are insufficient to cover the actual cost of a service may be supplemented by the government due to social considerations in the form of upfront grants, continuous subsidies or guarantees.

A typical direct-user payment model for infrastructure PPP projects/assets is the BOT concession model (DBOT).

The BOT concession model involves the transfer of a concession for planning/design, construction, financing and operation to the private partner. This type of business model can also be combined with any of the other business models presented above. Accordingly, the principal may or may not obtain ownership of the asset. The operating phase typically varies between 10 and 30 years.

This model can be found in all sectors in which direct-user payments are applicable, that is generally in the transportation, supply and disposal sectors, but also in the area of public real estate, for example sports facilities, swimming pools, exhibition grounds, healthcare facilities, student housing or retirement homes. The principal grants the contractor the right to cover its costs by levying fees or charges to be paid by third parties for the use of the asset. If a project proves to be unprofitable because of insufficient demand or a certain lack of willingness or ability to pay, but is still a desirable project from a socio-economic perspective, the principal may commit itself to contributing subsidies to the ongoing operation of the project or even providing upfront grants in case the project lacks financial viability before it is realised.

The risk allocation among the partner of the project depends on the contractual model with which the BOT concession model is combined, as well as the terms and conditions of the individual contracts (see Section 3.4).

The BOT concession model is characterised by the fact that the contractor generally bears the full or at least the majority of the market (price and demand) and usage risk during the operating phase. The concessionaire is granted the right to levy user fees for the duration of the concession, although this right may be limited to individual/specific user groups. It is extremely rare for the concessionaire to be completely free to determine the amount of the fee (e.g. a toll) to be levied. The public-sector principal – controlling the regulatory body – often prescribes limits or even determines the amount of the user-fee in case the user-fee-based infrastructure assets constitute a natural monopoly. For the concessionaire, it makes an important difference to know the price of use (user-fee to be levied) in advance when calculating the project rather than only after completion of construction and prior to commissioning, determined by the public sector, for example on the basis of corresponding legislation.

3.4 CONTRACTUAL MODELS

This book can provide only an overview of the various contractual models for the planning, realisation and operation of public infrastructure that are common throughout the world. Because of its international relevance owing to investor interest, this overview focuses on PPP contractual models that embody as extensive a lifecycle approach as possible in terms of the nature and extent of the transfer of functions and risks from the public to the private sector, and private financing, in particular (see also Figures 3.2 and 3.3). Even though the

PPP = [functional privatisation, comprehensively integrated services]	
(D)B(F)OT	*(Design) Build (Finance) Operate Transfer Concession*
(D)B(F)OOT	(Design) Build (Finance) Operator Own Transfer
DBFO(T)	Design Build Finance Operator (Transfer)
(D)B(F)OOT	(Design) Build (Finance) Operate Own Transfer
DBLOT	Design Build Lease Operate Transfer
DB(F)ROT	Design Build (Finance) Rent Operate Transfer Contracting

Application typically in the areas of:
- Social infrastructure
- Economic infrastructure

FIGURE 3.6   Contractual models comprehensively integrated

respective contractual characteristics are globally largely uniform in terms of the need for regulation and the content thereof, the names used for such complex contractual models are extremely heterogeneous. In an international context, however, the models are often designated using letters that reflect the services transferred under the scope of the respective contract. Unfortunately, this system is not used in a consistent way either, because the abbreviations for the different models do not necessarily show all letters of the services transferred, as shown in detail in Figure 3.6 and Figure 3.7. The individual letters used here stand for the following services:

- 'D' – Design
- 'B' – Build
- 'O' – Operate or Own
- 'T' – Transfer
- 'L' – Lease
- 'R' – Rent
- 'F' – Finance

This systematic contract model description forms the basis for the overviews contained in Figure 3.6 and Figure 3.7, which are primarily used in the social infrastructure and economic infrastructure sectors (especially in road transport). However, international experience has shown that these basic models can essentially be transferred to all infrastructure sectors, with sector-specific characteristics primarily being reflected in the respective contractual provisions of the individual projects/assets.

Figure 3.6 summarises the PPP contractual models used in functional privatisations and Figure 3.7 shows the models used in (partial) material privatisations, that is horizontal partnerships. It is important to repeat that the above does not constitute a complete overview as a number of intermediate forms of contractual models used internationally are too inconsistent

(Partial) Material Privatisation	
(D)B*(F)*OO	(Design) Build (Finance) Operate Own Funding of SPC
BDB*(F)*OO	Buy Design Build (Finance) Operate Own Shareholder of SPC (Purchase of Shares) with the obligation to invest
DB*(F)*ROO	Design Build (Finance) Rent Operate Own Renting including Facility Management

Application typically in the areas of:

- Social infrastructure
- Economic infrastructure

FIGURE 3.7   (Contract) models of the material privatisation

and varied to be included in this systematic approach. In many cases, they are applied on a national and/or sector-specific basis only.

The additions to the established abbreviations (shown in parentheses in Figure 3.6 and Figure 3.7) describe common deviations from the system of categorisation and are intended to prevent potential misunderstandings. The 'BOT model' in Figure 3.6, for example, as the best-known user-financed operator model internationally, frequently also contains significant design/planning components and in all cases private finance. Therefore, the abbreviation predominantly used is not entirely correct or complete, for it does not reflect all services performed under this scheme. This also applies to other contractual models. Accordingly, a 'D' for design and an 'F' for finance have been added to the relevant cases in Figure 3.6 and Figure 3.7, either directly or in parentheses. For the same reason, a 'T' has been added to the DBFO/shadow toll model to show the transfer that regularly takes place in this model, even though this is not included in its standard international abbreviation.

Figure 3.8 illustrates PPP contractual models introduced in Figure 3.6 and Figure 3.7 to show the relation between risks taken and value-added in the various business models and contract types. This allows investors to understand the principles behind the different risk-return profiles that one will find among infrastructure assets. While the composition of the list of models as well as the designation and individual characteristics of the models themselves are principally based on their application in Germany, it is rather straightforward to transfer the main principles applied to other countries and their individual legal and contractual frameworks.

The main characteristic that all these PPP models share is the lifecycle approach. They, hence, include the planning, construction, financing, operational and realisation phases. The main differences among them relate to the allocation of ownership before, during and after the contractual term and the allocation of the realisation risk, that is the risk of further usage, sale, rent, lease or any other kind of utilisation of the infrastructure asset after termination of the PPP contract. In terms of the nature of the remuneration provided to the private partner and the structure as a horizontal or vertical partnership, the models may be combined with

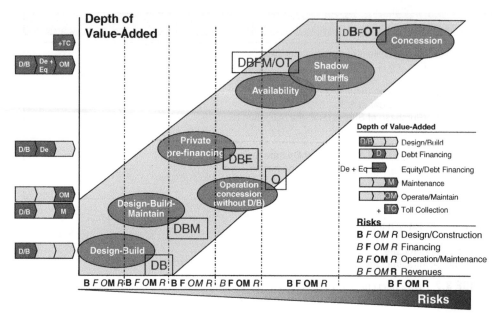

FIGURE 3.8   Contract types by value-added/risk profile
Source: Weber, Alfen and Maser (2006)

the user-financed BOT concession model and/or the institutional PPP model. The contracting model, which is based on specific tasks or sections of an asset, has a special status as a form of functional privatisation.

3.5   FINANCING MODELS

After explaining the various PPP models, the ownership interests and the remuneration structure, one of the key determining factors in the organisational model is the financing of the respective infrastructure project/asset and its detailed structuring. Apart from equity being required in any financing, project finance loans are the most common debt financing model used internationally.

A financing alternative are bonds where creditworthiness is linked to both the economic power of the project and the creditworthiness of the principal/issuer. Traditional corporate finance may also be used in conjunction with partial privatisation. The topic of financing, and project finance in particular, is discussed in detail in Chapters 6 and 7.

3.6   INTERIM SUMMARY – VARIOUS 'PRIVATISATION PATHS'

The information presented in the previous sections shows that there are essentially two different development trends with regard to privatisation (referred to here as 'privatisation paths'). One is based on the forms of functional privatisation and is characterised by increasing private

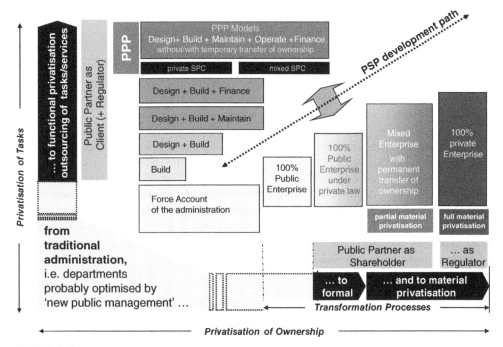

FIGURE 3.9   Path of privatisation

sector involvement in the various functions and steps in the value chain within the lifecycle of a physical infrastructure asset. As such, this can be seen as a growing 'privatisation of tasks'.

The other path is initiated by a public-sector institution that performs specific functions relating to a physical infrastructure asset and is seeking to involve private partners as shareholders and providers of capital. This form of privatisation ultimately leads to (partial or full) material privatisation when ownership is transferred, and therefore can be seen as a 'privatisation of ownership'.

Figure 3.9 illustrates these two development paths taking two directions:

- Functional privatisation, from the outsourcing of simple functions to the complex, cross-lifecycle PPP model with the contractual variations described above (privatisation of tasks);
- Partial or full material privatisation, generally via the aforementioned bundling of functions within a public legal institution and subsequent formal or material privatisation (privatisation of ownership).

These paths include at their roots various forms of public-sector formation and reorganisation, which relate to the term 'new public management'.

These trends towards growing privatisation are accompanied by trends in the opposite direction. In addition, interim models spanning these two fundamentally different directions do exist. One example is the aforementioned formally privatised ASFiNAG in Austria (see Section 3.1), which, as principal, also awards concessions for highway projects to strategic investors. This would be considered a functional privatisation according to the classification introduced in this book.

ÖSTERREICHISCHE AUTOBAHNEN-UND SCHNELLSTRASSEN FINANZIERUNGS AKTIENGESELLSCHAFT (ASFiNAG)

ASFiNAG was formed in 1982 as a company of the Austrian federal government. Since 1997, ASFiNAG has been able to raise loans because of its usufructuary rights while the land and facilities are still owned by the Austrian federal government. It is also entitled to levy user fees. ASFiNAG is responsible for the planning, financing, construction, maintenance and operation of the entire Austrian motorway and highway network (with a total length of 2000 km). It is financed by the earmarked revenue from vignettes (toll stickers), mileage-based tolls for vehicles > 3.5 tonnes gross vehicle weight (GVW) and the collection of special tolls in its own right. Besides the infrastructure management services provided by ASFiNAG, it tenders concession projects. For example, as part of the 'PPP Ostregion' project, ASFiNAG and the consortium Bonaventura (HOCHTIEF PPP Solutions GmbH, Alpine Mayreder Bau GmbH, Egis Projects SA) have signed a concession agreement followed by the financial close in December 2006 (ASFiNAG, 2009). This was the first PPP highway project in Austria awarded by ASFiNAG. The consortium that forms the SPC is responsible for the planning, construction, financing and operation of the A5 motorway (Nordautobahn) and sections of the S1 (Wiener Außenringschnellstraße) and S2 (Wiener Nordrandschnellstraße) highways forming part of the Vienna city ring road. The consortium is remunerated by shadow toll (30%) and availability payments (70%) starting with commission of the stretches of the road (ASFiNAG, 2014). In conclusion, ASFiNAG as an infrastructure management entity is considered a formal privatisation according to the classification of this book, whereas the projects they tender (i.e. 'PPP Ostregion' project) would be considered as functional privatisations.

Before turning our attention to the topics of infrastructure finance and sustainable infrastructure investments, Chapter 4 provides a detailed description and analysis of selected infrastructure sectors and subsectors. An in-depth understanding of the infrastructure sectors and how they work will serve to supplement the information already provided and place it in a wider context. It will also allow a better comprehension of the explanations and analytical steps discussed in the following chapters on financing and sustainability.

CHAPTER 4

Characteristics of Selected Infrastructure Sectors and Subsectors

Investors may want to familiarise themselves with the characteristics of the various sectors and subsectors of infrastructure that determine the risks and rewards of their investment activity and the corresponding prospects for success (see also Section 1.3). This book aims to sensitise readers to the aspects private infrastructure investors must observe and assess by describing the typical characteristics of the most important infrastructure sectors and subsectors. The discussion of each of these sectors is broken down into five topics and always follows the same logic: (i) characteristics and organisation, (ii) sources of revenue and value chain elements, (iii) competition and regulation, (iv) private-sector involvement and – new to this second edition of the book – (v) sustainability considerations.

These five topics seem to be (consistently across all sectors) the most relevant for investors when it comes to analysing and conceiving the impact the institutional, legal and contractual environment of a particular sector may have on the long-term viability of an individual investment. This sector discussion aims to raise the reader's awareness and understanding of the general approach to identifying and assessing sector-specific factors, their interdependence and interaction with country and project/asset-specific aspects (see also Figure 1.6 in Section 1.3) as well as their overall influence on individual assets and, hence, investments.

The final selection of the sectors discussed in this book is the result of careful consideration. The stated goal was for them to be different and diverse to provide as broad a picture as possible to the reader as well as being relevant to those interested in private investment. As a result, this second edition of the book covers more sectors than the first one. In addition to transport and traffic, including road, rail, water transport/ports and aviation, as well as water supply, sewage and waste disposal, which were already covered in the first edition, it also includes renewable energy generation (solar, wind, hydro, biomass), both electricity and natural gas transmission networks and storage, district energy systems, including heating and cooling, and social infrastructure (for a comprehensive overview of the key infrastructure sectors refer to Figure 1.6 in Section 1.3). Valuable aspects of, and examples from, all sectors can be found throughout this book.

By systematically analysing each sector along the five topics mentioned above, this chapter also seeks to provide a basic understanding of sector-specific risks, which will be essential for any investment – be it debt or equity – in any kind of infrastructure asset (for an in-depth discussion of risks in infrastructure investing, please see Chapter 5).

4.1 TRANSPORT

4.1.1 Cross-sector characteristics

The transport and traffic sector comprises various carriers of traffic and modes of transport that are interdependent and in competition with each other. In highly developed industrialised countries, users seeking a transportation solution between two locations – whether for passenger or goods transportation – almost always have the choice between cars, trains and aircraft as modes of transport or road, rail, air and potentially also water as carriers of traffic. Although these all have their own distinctive characteristics, it is clear they cannot be analysed independently of each other. As such, investors in one of these subsectors would be well advised not to lose sight of the competing subsectors and their various interdependencies. With this in mind, this section will initially present and discuss a number of cross-sector aspects followed by an analysis of the individual subsectors.

4.1.1.1 Structure of the transport sector   The transport sector can be broken down into the following subsectors:

- *Land transport* involving road and rail transportation (see Section 4.1.2 and Section 4.1.3, respectively);
- *Air transport* with the corresponding flight services in the air, ground services at airports and air traffic control (see Section 4.1.4);
- *Water transport* involving national and international shipping on canals and natural waterways and the corresponding port facilities (see Section 4.1.5).

Telematics is relevant to almost all subsectors, because it is expected to increasingly influence the management of the transport sector. Telematic systems largely use telecommunication data and satellite services. In addition, they may present attractive private investment opportunities in themselves. Transport in (outer) space has existed for some time now, particularly in the form of satellites. To date, however, these have primarily been used for observation and research purposes as well as telecommunications and other services, such as GPS, weather and other geo-data, rather than for transportation purposes in the narrower sense. Although satellites are subject to growing interest on the part of private investors, they are mentioned here only for the sake of completeness, particularly since the SpaceX corporation shows how private investment contributes to space transport services.

4.1.1.2 Structure of demand   In a world that is growing ever smaller, mobility not only is a commodity that is in increasing demand but also represents one of the most important topics of national and international political agendas. Accordingly, it is undeniable that the corresponding infrastructure, such as roads and highways, railway lines, waterways and other shipping routes and airports, remains one of the key location factors and growth drivers of any economy. At the same time, aspects such as the necessary degree of mobility, preference among carriers of traffic and the necessary scope and location of concrete infrastructure construction measures are the source of considerable controversy, not least because of sustainability considerations such as their consumption of dwindling natural resources and other environmental considerations like CO_2 emissions.

Accordingly, new transport construction projects have become – not unreasonably – the most difficult public infrastructure measures to obtain approval for, apart from power plants and landfill sites, particularly in more densely populated *industrialised nations*, and are characterised by stringent requirements, long and unpredictable approval periods and a correspondingly high level of potential follow-up costs. Industrialised countries are less focused on achieving a significant expansion in their transport infrastructure, but instead are seeking to close gaps and, in particular, perform substantial maintenance and renovation work combined with potential (natural) resource efficiency improvements. In Germany, for example, the maintenance of the primary land transport network already accounts for more than 65% of the master plan's budget for the domestic transport sector (German Federal Ministry of Transport and Digital Infrastructure, 2012). Whether and to what extent the existing transport infrastructure can be maintained and managed more efficiently with the aid of private operators and capital contributions from private investors is another important debate. It takes place in light of the strained budget situation and the other considerable challenges faced by the public sector, such as how to adjust social and healthcare systems to reflect demographic changes.

Notwithstanding this, in all industrialised countries, the existing transport infrastructure – unlike some of their other infrastructure sectors – is capable of covering the costs of the necessary additional investments as well as current operating and maintenance costs. In some cases, it even generates significant excess revenue.

It goes without saying that the demand situation for transport infrastructure in *developing and emerging countries* is rather different. These economies are still, to a large extent, working on the provision of a basic infrastructure, meaning that the potential investment volume is high. While individual transport users in dynamic emerging economies such as China and India probably have sufficient economic power and growing purchasing power to finance such investments, less developed countries are lacking both. Private investment in these sectors, which generate revenue exclusively in the national currency, is further exacerbated by the lack of functional local capital markets.

Given the prominent public status of transport infrastructure, political, legal and institutional changes represent a significant risk factor for private investors in any country. Discontinuities in national and, in particular, regional transport policy, transport-specific legislation or administrative responsibilities and structures generally, may have a serious impact on costs (e.g. in the form of adjustments to technical standards, security requirements, environmental standards). They can also have an impact on revenues, which are generated via traffic volumes multiplied by price e.g. the selection of new projects affecting traffic flows in the existing transport infrastructure, fundamental changes in priority among the various carriers of traffic with a corresponding impact on the modal split or in the attitude towards mobility in general. Any discontinuities of this kind obviously may seriously affect the revenue situation of project developers and asset owners alike.

4.1.1.3 Initiation and realisation of transport projects

Almost everywhere in the world, demand for transport infrastructure and the list of concrete measures to be realised in future are identified, reconciled and prescribed on the basis of political resolutions and long-term master plans for the transport sector as a whole. The decision as to which of the existing project ideas should be implemented and in which order is generally based on a cost–benefit analysis. This analysis compares not only the direct costs of the measure (e.g. the investment), operating and maintenance costs in particular and the direct benefit for the transport user (i.e. cost and time savings and improvements in comfort) but also positive and negative 'external effects' such as employment, the environment, health and security. Such master plans are not limited to new construction or expansion projects but increasingly also include measures for the maintenance of the existing network in accordance with the demand situation, at least in developed industrialised countries.

In addition, the criteria by which transport measures are prioritised by the governments within transport master plans do not necessarily reflect the yield-oriented criteria of investors, meaning that government priority lists can serve only as an indicator to investors at best.

4.1.1.4 Organisation of the transport sector   Overall responsibility for the transport sector, including needs assessment, transregional spatial planning, approval and monitoring of the preparation and implementation of measures, preparation of the relevant legislation, budgeting and other sector-specific sovereign functions across all transport subsectors, lies – in almost all cases – with a corresponding (transport) ministry at central government level. Additional governmental, semi-governmental or private operational structures may exist below this level. Their structural organisation can vary significantly between countries and subsectors, which is why road, rail, air and water transportation are addressed separately in the following sections. For investors, the resulting responsibilities, rules and regulations for the respective project/asset in question are crucial to their assessment and ultimately, their financial success. For concession agreements, for example, this means it is important to stipulate the interfaces with other authorities as well as with the principal itself.

4.1.1.5 Sources of revenue in the transport sector   Transport infrastructure may be financed from the public budget and/or user charges, irrespective of whether the relevant project is a public or private undertaking (see also Section 1.3.6 and Section 3.3). Table 4.1 illustrates the relevant potential sources of revenue for the transport sector. A distinction is made between general government revenue and transport- (sector) and road transport-specific (subsector) revenue. Whereas road and air transport are generally self-sufficient, that is they collect enough revenue to cover their specific costs and often generate excess revenue, the rail sector typically makes a loss and hence must be subsidised. This is due to its particularly costly infrastructure as well as the ticket prices that are frequently imposed on account of political and social policy considerations.

4.1.1.6 Telematics in the transport sector   Transport telematics are intelligent technical solutions using new information, communication and routing technologies, in some cases on an intermodal basis, to help manage the high traffic volume. Solutions of this nature have become increasingly important to ensure that the various forms of mobility are coordinated efficiently and as environmentally friendly as possible, for the individual and the economy as a whole.

Accordingly, there have been a large number of impressive developments and private investments in this field over recent years. Intermodal applications include urban and state-wide traffic management with the aim of optimally allocating traffic volumes to the respective carriers and enabling forward-looking transport information and control. Telematics

TABLE 4.1 Sources of revenue and financing in the transport sector

Public budget	– Tax
	   – direct (income, capital yields, net worth, etc.)
	   – indirect (value added, etc.)
	– Customs duty
	– Charges, fees (social welfare, etc.)
	– Fees (user, residents, etc.)
	– Other revenues

(Transport)
Sector-specific revenues
	– Sector specific taxes, charges, fees
	   – for consumer goods (e.g. fuel)
	   – for transport services (e.g. airport services)
	   – VAT on consumer goods and services
	– User charges (e.g. charges for public transport, rail, ship)
	– other revenues (e.g. sales of airports or rail companies)
	– Retail/franchising/commercials in airports and rail stations etc.)

Subsector-(roads and highways) specific revenues	– Subsector specific taxes, charges, fees
	   – for consumer goods (e.g. fuel, vehicle ownership tax)
	   – for road-specific services (e.g. telematics services, traffic management)
	   – VAT on consumer goods and services
	– User charges (e.g. toll, vignette, congestion charges)
	– Other revenues (e.g. incomes of privatisations, concession fees of petrol stations and test areas, commercials)

applications exist for road transportation, public rail and bus transportation, shipping and aviation.

The most prominent example is probably the European civil satellite navigation system, Galileo. This independent, highly-accurate positioning and timing system is intended for use in various navigation applications in the aviation sector, safe navigation using electronic charts in the shipping sector, train routing and tracking systems in the rail sector, route guidance in the road sector and intermodal applications for monitoring the transportation of dangerous goods and tracking cargo, among other things. Implementation, including funding on a purely private basis, ultimately failed after a number of attempts. It is expected to be completed by 2020, solely using public funds. The cost of development will be around €5.3 billion and will be divided between the European Union (EU) budget and the ESA.

Generally, satellite navigation is an attractive growth market. According to the European Commission, the global market for satellite navigation products and services reached a volume of €141 billion in 2012 and is growing by around 10% each year (Oxford Economics, 2012). By 2020, this market is expected to rise to as much as €240 billion.

Although Galileo has not as yet received any capital from private telematics investors, the objective is still to attract substantial private investments in the subsequent operation of the system. Almost more important for investors, however, is the fact that telematics and corresponding future developments may be one of the key innovation and efficiency drivers in all subsectors of the transport industry in future, and hence they are likely to offer vast potential. Albeit, telematics is not considered infrastructure but a service provided within the infrastructure sector.

4.1.2 Road transport

4.1.2.1 Characteristics and organisation
National road networks are generally broken down into road categories. A distinction is typically made between primary, secondary and sometimes also tertiary road networks. Primary road networks are mainly used for transregional and transit traffic. The primary road network frequently differs from the secondary and tertiary network in terms of its construction: for example, primary roads often have several lanes in each direction of travel and a separation between the two directions, have flyover crossings (instead of crossroads or junctions) and are separated from the secondary and tertiary network through dedicated slip roads, at least in developed industrialised countries. Such roads may be referred to as 'national highways' or 'motorways'.

The secondary and tertiary road network generally consists of various other road categories. Here, too, road classification depends on the type of traffic – transregional, regional or inner-city – predominantly using the roads. Accordingly, a distinction may be made between state roads or regional highways, regional or rural roads and municipal or urban roads.

The respective road category often makes it clear who is responsible for planning, construction, financing, maintenance and operation. For example, primary road networks generally fall within the responsibility of corresponding government ministries but are administered by separate executive organisations acting on behalf of the ministries. One typical example is the Highways Agency in the UK – a model that is used in a number of other countries, particularly in the English-speaking world.

In contrast, the relevant public-sector bodies (region, state, county, municipality, etc.) are responsible for the secondary and/or tertiary road network, although investments and their funding often remain assigned at the government level. In this way, responsibility for performing the relevant functions, that is the operational implementation of the construction, maintenance and operation of roads, may lie with the federal states or regions in the case of state/regional roads and highways, counties or municipalities in the case of regional/rural roads and city authorities in the case of municipal/urban roads, but the corresponding funding is still provided centrally by the national budget. Responsibility for planning may also remain with the higher-ranked public-sector body.

For the most part, the allocation of responsibilities and the performance of the relevant functions for road networks are governed by corresponding legislation. For example, the French government resolved to reassign the responsibilities for its national roads as part of its legislation on decentralisation. Since then the regions are responsible for around 20 000 kilometres of the 38 000 kilometres of national road network in future. The central government only retained responsibility for roads with a significant national status and toll roads, most of which are operated privately under long-term concession arrangements (Eurofound, 2005; Fayard, Gaeta and Quinet, 2004).

In some cases, the various responsibilities for funding and performing the relevant functions result in conflicts of interest between the individual participants in terms of long-term conceptual planning, the provision of their own resources and the recognition of residents' demands and economic interests. These may affect the interests of private investors to a significant extent. This is particularly critical when concession agreements contain arrangements with the concessionaire that are not binding for other public-sector authorities. The more prevalent federal government and administrative structures are in the respective country, the more frequently this problem is encountered. For example, under the first tunnel concessions to be issued in Germany in the 1990s for the Warnow Tunnel in Rostock and the Herrentunnel in Lübeck, the respective city authorities were the principal (concession grantor), whereas the start-up funding was provided from federal and EU budgets as a subsidy, and planning permission and an ordinance prescribing the level of the tolls to be charged were issued by the federal state as the regulatory authority. Although the resultant interfaces are governed by a corresponding treaty, this is largely insufficient to meet the demands of investors.

4.1.2.2 Sources of revenue and value chain elements Road transport infrastructure can be both budget- and/or user-financed. In the vast majority of cases, the road infrastructure is funded by the general public budget (i.e. from general government revenues, see Table 4.1). In a number of countries, however, the primary road network at least may be financed by user charges levied by the public or private operators in the form of a toll based on mileage (monetary unit per kilometre) or a period depending on the respective toll sticker or vignette (monetary unit per unit of time). These revenues could be accounted within the general public budget or could be earmarked either for the overall transport sector or exclusively for the road subsector (see also Section 1.3.9). In the case of the road sector, 'earmarking' may be (i) directly project-specific or (ii) performed indirectly on a subsector-specific (e.g. via a road fund such as ASFiNAG in Austria) or a sector-specific basis.

The revenue from road sector-specific sources (see Table 4.1), which primarily consists of fuel duty and motor vehicle tax and/or user charges (tolls or toll stickers/vignettes), often exceeds the costs in this subsector. The excess revenue is then channelled into less profitable but more politically opportune local and/or long-distance passenger transportation projects or even areas outside the transportation sector that are considered to be more important. Stakeholders of the profitable road transport sector regularly attempt to ensure that the excess revenue is earmarked. The principle of general budget appropriation as described in Section 1.3.9, however, makes this impossible and allows earmarking only for user charges under privately financed projects. Both of these charge types are generally only levied in the primary road network or for the use of special structures, for example tunnels, bridges or unusual routes, such as mountain passes. In contrast to vignettes, toll collection in the secondary and tertiary network is essentially impossible, owing to the lack of an adequate vehicle capture and collection system, at least based on the current state of the art.

Vignettes such as those used in the Austrian and Swiss highway networks represent a substantially simpler technical solution. They can be purchased at almost every petrol station and entitle a vehicle to use the vignettes-based infrastructure an unlimited number of times within a specific period. This eliminates the need for the collection and registration of user data. On the other hand, vignettes allow traffic to be directed to a far lesser extent than mileage-based tolls. They also allow less differentiation than direct tolls; although a distinction can be made according to the vehicle type, number of axles, emission class, etc., a charge scale based on the respective day of the week, time of day or frequency of use that allows for better traffic control and – which is even more interesting for private investors – for a better price differentiation is practically impossible to enforce. For the same reasons, private operating investors consider vignettes a less attractive source of revenue for financing their investments and current costs, making it extremely rare for them to be used for this purpose.

In practice, only mileage-based tolls are used. However, the collection of such tolls is technically complex and expensive, particularly when requirements in terms of the collection rate and the protection of user data are high. A number of technical solutions exist to this end. The simplest and most widespread is collection at toll plazas. Electronic toll collection systems that do not break up the flow of traffic are growing in popularity: they reduce the space and, in particular, staffing requirements at toll plazas.

TABLE 4.2   Advantages and disadvantages of various financing sources in the road infrastructure sector

Financing resources	Advantages	Disadvantages
Direct road user charges		
Tolls	– Direct relationship to usage, flexible (different tolls for different daytimes, vehicles, etc., possible) – Easy to earmark – Economically beneficial on congested roads	– Can be costly to implement – Can be politically difficult to accept – Because of diversions, economic benefits of road are reduced, if road is not congested
Vignette	– Easy to implement – Easy to earmark – Cheap to implement	– No direct relationship to usage
Indirect road user charges		
Fuel tax	– Easy to implement – Cheap to collect	– Direct relationship to road usage only via fuel consumption – Earmarking politically difficult
Vehicle ownership tax	– Easy to implement – Cheap to collect	– No relationship to road usage – Earmarking politically difficult

Source: Euromed Transport Project (2008)

The most modern and efficient system in the world at present is still probably that used to collect tolls for heavy goods vehicles on the 12 000 km German motorway network, which currently generates revenue of around €4.3 billion a year. This system was developed, realised and (project) financed and is now operated under the terms of a 12-year PPP contract, which was extended in 2015 for three more years until July 2018. It is satellite-based, meaning the need for toll plazas is eliminated altogether; however, registration is required prior to initial use. This system is also used to collect tolls on the secondary road network.

Simpler solutions, such as in Canada, register vehicles by photographing their registration plate and bills are sent out by post. However, data protection legislation makes this kind of solution impracticable, in particular in many European countries. For the German-type solution, vehicles must be fitted with an on-board unit that allows payment transactions to be conducted in an untraceable manner. The system only identifies toll evaders. In Europe, there are concentrated efforts to achieve standardisation for the interoperability of electronic toll road systems within the European Community (EC), because European travellers cannot be expected to observe different systems in the longer term.[1] Table 4.2 summarises these various alternatives.

---

[1]Directive 2004/52/EC of the European Parliament and of the Council was passed with the aim of standardisation.

PPP models in the road transport sector may be financed via availability payments or user-driven payments from public funds or direct user charges. Only in the two latter cases does the operator bear the revenue risk (see also Section 3.3). In this subsector, the risks primarily consist of traffic volume and toll rate, as well as to a lesser extent toll collection technology risks relating to the toll capture and collection system. In other words, the overall revenue risk comprises the risk that:

- The actual traffic volumes will be less than forecast in the various toll rate classes.
- The forecast toll rates cannot be collected in practice, because they would otherwise unintentionally force users to seek other solutions, are rejected by the regulatory authorities or are difficult to implement owing to political considerations.
- The toll collection system is permanently available and functional, i.e. it can be ensured that all vehicles are recorded correctly and broken down into the corresponding toll rate classes.
- All outstanding payments are initiated.
- All payments are actually collected, i.e. payment can also be demanded from toll evaders and bad debtors retrospectively via a functional dunning system.

As such, it is essential that investors obtain reliable traffic or revenue forecasts and/or consider implementing appropriate risk allocation mechanisms in conjunction with the principal (concession grantor), familiarise themselves with the details of the existing regulatory system with regard to pricing and plan, and implement an adequate and functional toll capture and collection system. For investors, the latter is an important cost factor in the project development phase that, depending on the system, could offer optimisation potential in terms of both investing and operating costs totalling as much as 10% of the total project costs. When weighing up any savings in the toll capture and collection system, however, investors should be aware that this is a key factor in guaranteeing what could be their only source of revenue.

Table 4.3 shows the elements of the value chain of the road transport sector together with the corresponding investment opportunities.

Within this value chain, the most important elements relate to the provision and management of the road network, including planning, construction and maintenance of the various categories of road transport engineering works, into which the primary investments in this area are channelled.

The other value chain elements listed – such as traffic management, traffic data collection, telematics services and toll collection – are part of the road transport operation. The construction of petrol and service areas also forms part of the value chain of traffic infrastructure in a wider sense. On the German motorways, for example, even this area was publicly administered until the end of the 1990s, before being transferred in full to a private investment syndicate in a tender procedure and hence fully materially privatised. The company now operates under the name Tank & Rast GmbH.

GERMAN AUTOBAHN TANK & RAST GMBH

The operator of almost 90% of the service areas along the German motorways is a good example of the privatisation of a former state-owned company. After having been part of the federal ministry responsible for transport and traffic, the state-owned public limited company was established in 1994 as a formal privatisation with the German government being the sole shareholder. In 1998, a consortium of two private equity houses (Apax Partners and Allianz Capital Partners) and Deutsche Lufthansa AG acquired the company for a price of around €600 million after an EU-wide tender procedure. At the end of 2006, the three shareholders sold the company to the British private equity company Terra Firma, having cancelled an envisaged stock market flotation. Only six months later, the European Infrastructure Fund of RREEF, a subsidiary of Deutsche Bank AG, purchased 50% of the shares of Tank & Rast. In August 2015, the company was sold on to a consortium of Allianz, MEAG, a subsidiary of Munich RE, OMERS (via its investment vehicle Borealis) and ADIA, the sovereign wealth fund of Abu Dhabi, for the price of €3.5 billion.

Since being materially privatised in 1998, about €500 million has been invested in the modernisation and extension of service and rest areas as well as in the improvement of service quality. With approximately 340 petrol stations and around 370 service areas (including 50 hotels), Autobahn Tank & Rast is still the leading provider of services on German motorways. In recent years, Tank & Rast started cooperating with well-known food services brands such as Barilla, Burger King, Nordsee, McDonald's, Segafredo and Lavazza.

Although there has always been a high level of private value chain elements in the planning and construction stage, due to the involvement of planning offices and construction

TABLE 4.3   Road traffic infrastructure – value chain elements and investment opportunities

Roads

Value chain elements	Investment opportunities
Road network – Provision and management of road infrastructure	– Roads/bridges/tunnels – Drainage systems – Retaining walls – Other engineering works and secondary infrastructure – Maintenance depot including road cleaning
Operation – Traffic management/control	– Traffic management systems and equipment
– Traffic data collection	– Traffic data collection system
– Telematics services	– Telematics service system
– User charge collection	– User charge collection system (e.g. toll stations)
– Fuelling, parking and resting	– Petrol stations – Service areas/rest stops – Hotels/motels

firms, the maintenance and operation of road infrastructure remains in the public domain in most countries, and investments in particular are traditionally conducted by the public sector. In these countries, the integration of the value chain has, in many cases, taken hold with the emergence of PPP projects. This is because such value chains require complex services, including the necessary investments that can be provided by private operators.

In contrast, countries such as France, Italy and Spain have a long tradition of private construction, operation, maintenance and financing of road infrastructure. In South Africa, too, all areas of the value chain in the national road network are covered by SANRAL (South African National Roads Agency Limited), which operates largely independently of its sole shareholder, the National Department of Transport. SANRAL can draw upon various sources of finance, including public funding for non-toll-road sections and indirect funding from toll revenue by granting concessions. SANRAL also has the option of generating funds on the capital markets by issuing bonds (SANRAL, 2009).

As mentioned earlier, telematics services are increasingly forming part of the value chain in the road transport infrastructure sector. Functions that are already used intensively in road transportation include traffic guidance systems aimed at increasing road safety and improving the traffic flow. The digital channel TMC (Traffic Message Channel) allows drivers to receive traffic reports tailored to their individual requirements. A number of individual telematics products and services are also increasingly establishing themselves on the market, such as the navigation and fleet management, traffic information, road condition and weather information, vehicle accident and breakdown and driver assistance systems developed by the industry. From a technical perspective, the toll collection systems described above (in a different context) are also classified as telematics systems.

4.1.2.3 Competition and regulation

Prices and tolls in the road network are determined by supply and demand to an insufficient extent. Direct competition within the road transport infrastructure is rarely possible, because there is usually no parallel infrastructure with the same features and characteristics. It is even more unusual for users to have the choice between several toll roads – a decision that would be taken on the basis of the expected price/performance ratio in a traditional functional market. From a government perspective, this makes it even more important to institute and enforce (price) regulation with regard to tolls in particular, especially if the tolls on the respective road sections are not collected by the government itself but by private operators in a monopoly scenario.

The tolls collected are usually broken down into various price bands. A pricing distinction is almost always made between different classes of vehicles. Classification may be performed on the basis of the number of axles, the weight, length and/or height of a vehicle, the number of trailers or, most recently in some countries, the emission class. It is also possible to offer special rates or discounts to specific groups of users, such as commuters who use the section of road frequently, public service vehicles or – as is common in South Africa, for example – the unemployed. A distinction may also be made between peak (rush hour) and off-peak (non-rush-hour) traffic. All of the price bands must generally be agreed with the relevant regulatory authority as prescribed.

Under a concessionary arrangement, pricing and the pricing structure are supplemented by additional aspects that may be relevant in terms of competition or regulation. For example, it is relevant whether a toll is collected only on the stretch of the road for which the concession is granted or whether it applies across the entire road network, and whether it is collected by the concessionaire itself or determined and collected by the public sector and subsequently passed on to the concessionaire. The date on which the toll is initially calculated – that is prior to the investment phase or only when operations begin – and the degree of flexibility in determining the toll structure are also subject to different provisions in many countries. These aspects are highly relevant to investors when performing risk analysis. For example, it may be in the interests of a concessionaire to charge a lower toll rate in the first few years after a new toll road is commissioned (i.e. the ramp-up phase) as a kind of 'try-out price' in order to convince users of the attractiveness of the road with a view to increasing the toll at a later date. Although this can significantly stabilise the (project) finance or even make it possible in the first place, it may also contradict the strict principle of cost-based pricing or the equal treatment of all users over time. The extent to which this is still possible ultimately depends on the regulatory framework of the respective country.

In general, the complexity and rigidity of regulation differs significantly around the world. In the UK, for example, concessionaires are largely free to determine the amount of toll to be levied. By contrast, the tolls charged by concessionaires under the 'F-model' in Germany are determined by the public sector in a corresponding toll ordinance (*Mautverordnung*). This is based on general fee legislation, that is the principle of cost origination (based on cost documentation) and/or equivalence (based on the principles of equal treatment and intergenerational justice) without the existence of any precise rules for determining tolls. In the case of the first concessions to be granted under the F-model, this led to a degree of legal uncertainty for investors and is likely to happen again for future projects granted under the F-model, since no clear rules have been established as of now. In Italy, the various private motorway operators can enter into negotiations with ANAS, the public regulatory authority responsible for granting concessions, if they wish to increase toll charges. This process takes into account (i) the tender process, (ii) forecast traffic volumes, (iii) inflationary adjustments and (iv) the concessionary's yield expectations (Albalate, Bel and Fageda, 2007).

4.1.2.4 Private-sector involvement Around the world, roads are generally seen as a 'common asset' and hence fall ultimately within the responsibilities of government bodies. In particular, ownership of the roads themselves typically remains with the public sector for this reason. Even in countries such as France and Italy, where the management of extensive portions of the motorway network is performed by private or privatised companies – a situation often incorrectly referred to as privatisation (see also Section 3.2) – this still only takes the form of time-limited concessions that return to the government at the end of the contractual term. This arrangement serves to ensure that the road transport infrastructure is always implemented in accordance with the priorities of the government and not solely on the basis of investor considerations. By implication, then, only those sections or sub-networks of the overall road network where the decision-making criteria of the government and investors largely coincide can be transferred to private custody for a given period.

As it is getting increasingly difficult to finance the extensive requirements in the transport sector solely via public budget, private investors are becoming ever more involved in this infrastructure subsector. This is demonstrated by the growing number of privately financed projects and programmes.

The various forms and some examples of private-sector involvement in the road transport infrastructure are arranged systematically and described in detail in Sections 3.2 and 3.3. As explained there, only PPP models involving functional privatisation – that is availability payment, user-driven payment and direct user payment (e.g. as in BOT projects) models as concessions (and no real material privatisation models) – are relevant and of interest to investors.

These PPP models are used for individual, usually expensive, road infrastructure projects such as bridges and tunnels, sections of road, road networks and sub-networks, and across almost all road categories. User-financed BOT models as concessions are generally implemented for sections of road or sub-networks within the primary road network, particularly where tolls are already charged on this network in the respective market, such as in European countries, including Italy, France, Spain and Portugal. In particular, the operation of sub-networks may be an attractive option for private operating companies, because this allows sections of roads with lower toll revenue and/or higher costs to be compensated by sections with higher toll revenue and/or lower costs. This serves to spread the revenue and cost risk in accordance with the portfolio approach. However, there are also examples of individual construction projects in the secondary and tertiary road network, particularly in cities and large urban areas.

User-driven payment models currently exist, for example, in the UK, Finland, Germany and Portugal. Individual elements of the remuneration system have also been implemented in Austria with the aim of ensuring a more efficient allocation of revenue risk between the public-sector principal and the private-sector operator. PPP availability models are becoming increasingly popular in the secondary and tertiary road network, particularly at the municipal level. Among others, one of the first examples includes urban roads in Portsmouth (UK) and the 460 km municipal road network in the Lippe district (Germany), which were awarded in the form of long-term availability models with performance-based remuneration.

Alongside the PPP models, various efforts are under way to implement privatisation in the area of road maintenance and operating services. The first example of full privatisation in Germany was TSI (Thüringer Straßenwartungs- und Instandhaltungsgesellschaft mbH & Co. KG), which is described in the following box.

TSI (THÜRINGER STRASSENWARTUNGS-UND IN STANDHALTUNGSGESELLSCHAFT MBH)

The privatisation process of TSI began with the traditional conversion of the formerly state-owned enterprises to form a private limited company (GmbH), that is, formal privatisation. In 1996, TSI was formed as a fully state-owned company by the Free State of Thuringia with a view to subsequent privatisation. This move was unique within the Federal Republic of Germany in that it marked the first occasion in which a federal state had eased a substantial burden on its budget by cooperating with a regulated market economy service provider. In 2002, all the shares in the company were transferred to private ownership in a public tender process. TSI GmbH has developed into a full-service provider of road operation services, which it offers to the public administration as well as private companies and institutions.

4.1.3 Rail transport

4.1.3.1 Characteristics and organisation The rail sector is a typical network industry. There is usually only one network, that is the rail network on which all trains travel, and no additional parallel network. This inevitably results in a monopoly situation requiring regulation. A distinction is generally made between rail infrastructure companies, which own their own network, and rail-operating companies, which operate the networks and/or the passenger and/or goods trains using them. In this context, network operation is defined as the provision of (transport) services for passengers and/or cargo. As such, it goes without saying that there are significantly more rail-operating companies than rail infrastructure companies.

These two functions, that is the provision of the infrastructure and the (transportation) services, may be integrated and performed by the same company or two or more companies. Both of these organisational models as well as various hybrid forms exist around the world. In Germany, for example, Deutsche Bahn AG (DB AG) is responsible for both network infrastructure and operation. DB AG – whose sole shareholder is the German government – is in competition with other rail-operating companies. France, by contrast, has seen a formal separation of rail infrastructure companies and rail-operating companies. Société Nationale des Chemins de Fer (SNCF) is the operator for passenger and goods transportation, whereas Réseau Ferré de France (RFF) is responsible for operating the French rail network. However, both companies are ultimately owned by the French government.

The first example of a systematic separation of both functions in Europe was implemented in the UK. As is well known and can be read in the 'British Rail' example, however, the resulting privatisation of the infrastructure company Railtrack was quite a regrettable chapter in the UK's history of privatisations.

BRITISH RAIL

Until 1994, the state-owned British Rail was responsible for the railway infrastructure as well as for the operation (the carriage of passengers and goods) of Britain's railway network. In 1993, the Railways Act required the following reorganisation of the railway industry in the UK: (i) the separation of transport operation from railway infrastructure, (ii) the introduction of a franchise system for regulated passenger rail transport, (iii) the privatisation of the freight rail transport business and (iv) the privatisation of the infrastructure. As a first step, the new infrastructure manager Railtrack became the sole owner and manager of the entire railway infrastructure including tracks, signalling, electrification, stations, depots and shops and was listed on the London Stock Exchange. Subsequently, in 1995, the freight rail transport was completely privatised and taken over by four private freight train operators that had to buy operating licences for this purpose. They owned the rolling stock and operated in a competitive market environment. In parallel, 25 private passenger-train-operating companies were established and regulated under a franchise system.

The (separate) privatisation of the infrastructure with Railtrack as the private infrastructure provider turned out to be a major problem for the whole privatisation process. After three serious train accidents, mainly caused by cutting maintenance costs for economic reasons, Railtrack had to replace hundreds of kilometres of damaged track and pay compensation to train operators. Both compensation and investments led to a financial crisis and Railtrack declared bankruptcy in October 2001. Subsequently, the government replaced Railtrack with Network Rail in March 2002. Network Rail is a not-for-profit company limited by state guarantee. It took over the ownership and management of the rail infrastructure. Hence, the railway infrastructure in the UK is de facto re-nationalised.

Although usually there are no parallel rail networks in direct competition, the wider rail system may include networks operated by one or more companies that offer synergies. In the same way as the road infrastructure, the rail sector can be broken down into lines for transregional and cross-border traffic and lines for regional traffic. All these lines can generally be used interchangeably by train companies/operators without any interfaces. In some cases, however, there may be incompatibilities at national borders due to differences in track gauge, power systems or points systems. Regional trains more frequently use transregional lines than the other way round. This is because regional rail networks are not generally as developed as transregional networks, meaning that trains cannot reach the same (high) speeds.

For the same reason, some countries have dedicated networks that are reserved for high-speed trains, such as for the TGV (Train à Grande Vitesse) in France, the AVE (Alta Velocidad Española) in Spain, the Shinkansen in Japan and so on. However, different fares serve to create a certain degree of competition within the network – or, more accurately, between the various categories of sub-networks – because users may have a choice between the more rapid, and often more comfortable, transregional route or the less efficient regional route between two locations. In many countries, regional rail transportation is commissioned by the respective region (public-sector body) and transferred to private or public rail-operating companies in a competitive process. The respective network remains in the hands of a dominant public rail infrastructure company that may also perform operating services, albeit in competition with a large number of other rail-operating companies, including private providers. This 'owner-tenant model' is particularly widespread in North America.

In addition to related networks with the same owner, individual rail lines – whether or not connected to the national rail network – may be privately owned. Typical examples include industrial railways and special goods lines (particularly for the transportation of raw materials from the place of extraction to the port of export), as well as (rapid transit) connections to airports, trade fair grounds and tourist attractions.

Rail-based local public transport systems form a separate category. Examples such as the London Underground and, increasingly, metro systems in the major cities of Latin America and Asia show that local public transport can offer private investment opportunities; however, city transport being by itself a major topic, which falls outside the scope of this book, it will not be further discussed.

Rail infrastructure companies require rail-operating companies to pay track charges for the use of their tracks. These charges may vary depending on: (i) the type of track (e.g. high-speed tracks), (ii) the nature of transportation (passengers or goods) or (iii) the time of day. As most countries only have one rail infrastructure company that provides the infrastructure to a number of rail-operating companies, government regulation is often necessary, particularly if the rail infrastructure company also offers passenger and goods transportation services in competition with other rail-operating companies.

Broadly speaking, the following three basic organisational models are found internationally (OECD/ITF, 2008):

- *Vertical integration* – the infrastructure and all operational services are provided by one company; this is the most common model around the world.
- *Vertical separation* – the infrastructure/rail infrastructure company is fully separated from the operator(s)/rail-operating companies; introduced for the first time (in its purest form) in the UK, this is the future model recommended by many experts for Europe.
- *A combination of both models* – also known as the owner-tenant model; this is the dominant model in North America, but is also found to a lesser extent in other countries such as Germany.

There is a fourth, more theoretical, model: vertical integration combined with horizontal separation. In this case, a number of companies exist alongside each other, operating individual lines or sub-networks as rail infrastructure companies and rail-operating companies in a vertically integrated manner without acting in direct competition. These organisational models give rise to different value chains, as discussed in the next section (4.1.3.2).

The rail sector competes with other carriers of traffic but is also linked to them on an intermodal basis via connections with road and sea transportation as well as aviation. At the interfaces with the road and sea network, movable infrastructure systems (combined cargo) and immovable infrastructure systems (cargo transport centres) are used to unload and reload the goods transported by rail. These systems also represent investment opportunities that should be mentioned, but will not be described in detail at this point. Connections with the aviation sector exist in the form of railway stations that have been constructed at most of the world's airports.

There is an entirely different, but no less important, interface with the energy sector. On the one hand, the providers of transportation services are dependent to a large extent on energy prices, and particularly electricity prices. On the other hand, raw materials for energy production are largely transported by rail. In commodity-rich developing countries in particular, energy companies may therefore establish or invest in the rail infrastructure in order to reduce their storage capacity and transport the raw materials they extract at cost.

4.1.3.2 Sources of revenue and value chain elements A separate analysis of the respective sources of revenue is advisable, not least because of the separation of rail infrastructure companies and rail-operating companies demanded by the EU, which is increasingly taking hold.

Investments in the primary and secondary rail infrastructure (see Table 4.4) are comparatively expensive and rarely worthwhile, because passing the cost on to the passenger would likely lead to an undesirable shift in usage.

In most cases, the national governments provide the majority of the funding for the construction, expansion and replacement of the rail infrastructure from the public budget in order to serve the general good and meet transport requirements to an adequate extent. The rail infrastructure companies themselves are generally responsible for servicing and maintenance, which are primarily funded by the revenue they generate from track charges. The same applies for stations, which are financed via the charges paid by rail-operating companies for stopping at a given station. Retail revenue is increasingly also used. In the same way as airports, large

TABLE 4.4 Railroad traffic infrastructure – value chain elements and investment opportunities

Railroads	
Value chain elements	**Investment opportunities**
Railroad network	
Provision and management of infrastructure	Primary infrastructure (superstructure)
	– Track network
	– Signalling
	– Electrification
	Secondary infrastructure (substructure)
	– Embankments
	– bridges/tunnels/retaining walls
	– other secondary infrastructure
Operation	
Trains operation	Rolling stock
– Passengers	– Locomotives
– Cargo	– Carriages
Services	
– Gateways	– Railway stations
	– Cargo-handling stations
– Retail/catering	– Necessary facilities
– Other services	– Necessary facilities

railway stations in particular are developing into shopping malls, making them interesting for developers and investors alike. Track charges may vary depending on speed, the type of transportation (passengers or goods), the frequency of use of the respective line and the time of day/day of the week.

Rail-operating companies generally finance their operations from direct user charges, that is, the revenue generated from passenger and goods transportation in the form of ticket prices (fares) (see Section 3.3.3 for detail). In regional transportation in particular, government grants may be used to subsidise ticket prices if these would otherwise have to be unreasonably high in order to cover the operator's costs in full. However, rail-operating companies also have the option of generating revenue not from direct user fares but by offering the transportation services to regional transport companies and/or associations in the required capacity at a fixed price. In this case, the transport association bears the demand, i.e. the utilisation risk in its role as principal who collects the ticket revenues, which usually do not cover the costs incurred. For their part, the rail-operating companies 'only' bear the performance risk, that is the risk of being able to provide the required capacities in the prescribed quality at all times.

Rail companies with comprehensive vertical integration essentially cover the entire value chain in the rail transport sector, from the planning, construction and maintenance of the network including all equipment, via the operation and management of the network on behalf of their own transport department and other rail-operating companies, through to passenger and goods transportation services (including loading services) and on-site delivery where applicable. They also develop and operate stations and own logistics companies. Owing to the significant energy costs involved, they may even act as their own energy producer and supplier.

By contrast, companies with vertical separation focus either on network construction, maintenance and servicing in the role of a rail infrastructure company or on passenger and goods transportation in the role of a rail-operating company. Even if these companies remain wholly owned by the government – as is the case in e.g. France – this separation opens up the rail operation market to competition, particularly from other transport service providers.

In addition to the primary components of the rail sector value chain as described above, the area of telematics has established itself as a further value chain element over recent years. This includes the systems briefly listed below, which represent value chains on their own and hence may offer interesting investment opportunities but the features of which mean that they are not considered material infrastructure according to this book's definition and hence not discussed further:

- Computer-based operating guidance systems for the optional initiation of measures at the control centre. This allows the early identification of operating disruptions, the coordination of remediation measures and the provision of corresponding information to passengers;
- Electronic timetable information systems (e.g. DELFI) allowing route, time and price information to be obtained at information posts and on home computers;
- Dynamic passenger information systems providing precise information on current bus and train arrivals and departures, current parking space availability, etc.;
- Cashless payment systems;
- Needs-oriented local public transport systems, including fleet management systems, satellite-based vehicle tracking systems or in-car digital maps;
- Wireless-only control and safety technology for train management and safety within the rail network (route allocation and distance control), i.e. without fixed signals.

4.1.3.3 Competition and regulation Competition within the rail network relates primarily to tracks and track access charges. Accordingly, regulation in this sector focuses on this area, but may also include wider aspects such as the granting of licences and safety-related or administrative considerations. The ultimate aim of regulation is to ensure that all rail infrastructure companies – regardless of their market position – offer the rail-operating companies and other authorised users, such as freight forwarders and shipping agents, non-discriminatory access to the entire rail infrastructure, that is not only to the tracks themselves but also to service facilities such as stations, maintenance facilities, ports and sidings.

Quite often, regulation is undertaken by the ministry of transport. This is the case in Belgium, France and Spain, for example. By contrast, Germany, the UK and the US have special regulatory authorities that are also responsible for other network industries. In the US, the Surface Transportation Board performs comprehensive regulatory functions for all areas of surface transportation (rail, road, water and pipelines, but not airports). In addition to price regulation, it is responsible for approving company mergers and disposals and granting planning permission for new tracks. In Germany, the Bundesnetzagentur (Federal Network Agency) acts as a cross-sector regulatory authority (electricity, gas, telecommunications, post, rail) with responsibility for supervising competition and non-discriminatory network access. In the case of the rail network, this relates to the rail infrastructure, and therefore the regulation of track charges and the corresponding scope of services as well as the fares charged by rail-operating companies. In contrast, functional supervision and the corresponding regulatory aspects are performed by the responsible functional ministry.

TABLE 4.5 List of the 10 largest European railway companies

Company name	Country	Length of network (km)	pkm (millions)
DB	Germany	33 426	88 407
SNCF	France		83 907
ATOC	United Kingdom		61 768
FS	Italy	16 723	38 611
Renfe Operadora	Spain		23 753
SBB/CFF/FFS	Switzerland	3 73	18 231
NS	Netherlands		17 018
PKP	Poland	18 942	11 865
ASTOC	Sweden	10 744	11 842
SNCB/NMBS Holding	Belgium		10 974

Source: CER (2015)

Table 4.5 shows the 10 largest European railway companies based on the number of passenger kilometres (pkm) in 2015 (CER, 2015).

Needless to say, Table 4.5 lists only a fraction of all rail-operating companies in Europe. In addition, in most countries there are a vast number of small railway companies that operate on a regional basis and hence rarely compete with each other on the same routes. In Germany alone, there are more than 360 (small) rail-operating companies in the passenger sector. In other countries, too, there are a large number of competing rail-operating companies: 44 in Switzerland, 54 in the UK, 40 in Italy and 60 in Poland, for instance (CER, 2015). Very few countries have only one national rail-operating company, these include Finland, Ireland, Lithuania and Slovakia (IBM – Business Consulting Services, 2006). The national players occupy what is essentially a monopoly position in the transregional market.

Goods transportation is a different story. There is generally a far greater degree of competition between the various rail-operating companies, including on the same routes.

4.1.3.4 Private-sector involvement

Rail infrastructure has a long tradition of private-sector involvement. In the early days of rail transportation, a number of lines were constructed and operated by private companies, although most were subsequently nationalised.

Today, national railway companies are usually publicly owned because of the monopolistic nature of the rail network infrastructure. Notwithstanding, several companies have been formally privatised and mostly operate as stock corporations. Removing this monopoly to an extent by separating the network and operation functions was previously seen as impracticable on the grounds of technical and safety considerations. This separation has only become possible because of the extensive technical development in terms of both infrastructure (e.g. routing systems) and trains. This explains why, over recent years, governments have increasingly sought to separate infrastructure and operation – in some cases successfully – with a view to ensuring greater competition and private investment in the system.

Despite these obstacles, there are also some genuine cases of private-sector involvement in the rail transport sector. A growing number of fully or partially privatised rail-operating companies have appeared in the operating sector, entering into competition with each other and the relevant state-owned rail-operating companies. In addition, various major international providers offer rail services throughout the world. In contrast, the rail infrastructure sector is home to typical PPPs, largely budget-financed availability models or, less frequently, direct-user financed BOT models. The latter are mainly used on individual lines, such as airport connections or high-speed routes, and – with the exception of inner-city projects – are comparatively rare when it comes to entire networks or sub-networks.

Examples of PPPs involving planning, construction, financing, maintenance and operation include the high-speed line in Taiwan and the Arlanda Express in Sweden.

THE ARLANDA EXPRESS

In order to create a high-speed rail link between Stockholm Central Station and Arlanda International Airport, a functional tender process was conducted for the construction, operation and maintenance of the line, around 40 km in length, in 1993. Construction started in 1995 and the line was commissioned in late 1999. In addition to private capital, the public sector provided significant funding for the necessary start-up investments. The concessionaire (A-Train AB) financed its operations through the sale of tickets, meaning that it bore the revenue risk, among other things. The original shareholders of the project company A-Train AB were the construction firm NCC/Siab (44%), GEC-Alstom (29%), Vattenfall (20%) and Mowlem (7%). On 9 July 2014, Portare 1 AB (Portare) acquired 100% of the shares in the company which owned A-Train AB. The vendor was Macquarie European Infrastructure Fund, which had owned the company since 2004. Portare is owned by State Super and Sunsuper, which are two large Australian pension funds, and SAFE, which represents China's State Administration of Foreign Exchange and manages the foreign exchange re-serves for the People's Bank of China. The concession agreement has a term of 45 years and expires in 2040 (Arlanda Express, 2015; Källenfors, 2005).

Probably the best-known PPP project in the area of rail infrastructure is the Channel Tunnel, the (in)famous rail connection between the UK and the European continent under the English Channel, which had to be rescued from bankruptcy several times. The Channel Tunnel Rail Link (CTRL) between the English entrance to the Tunnel and London was also implemented as a PPP, although this was somewhat more successful. The ambitious new high-speed rail line projects in France are also scheduled to be realised with private finance in the form of PPPs. Another well-known PPP rail project is the HSL-Zuid in the Netherlands.

HSL-ZUID

The Dutch government simultaneously granted two PPP project tenders for the construction and operation of HSL-Zuid, a 125-kilometre-long high-speed rail line between Amsterdam and the Belgian border. A tender for the construction and maintenance of the line for a period of 30 years (2006–2031), including a five-year construction phase, was granted to Infraspeed BV (a consortium composed of Fluor Infrastructure, Royal BAM Group, Siemens Netherland, and the British investors Innisfree and HSBC Infrastructure) on the basis of an availability model. Siemens sold its shares in 2011 to Innisfree. One notable characteristic is that the Dutch government conducted a conventional tender process for the substructure, meaning that the PPP project was limited to the superstructure. Under the availability model, the private operator had to meet an availability target of 99.46%. If this target was not achieved, payments would be reduced or, in the case of availability of less than 90%, suspended altogether (Freudenstein and Obieray, 2005). The second PPP project involved a 15-year concession for the operation of the same line and was granted to the High Speed Alliance consortium (Dutch Railways [NS] and Royal Dutch Airlines [KLM]). The concession began in 2008 (HSL-Zuid, 2009).

4.1.4 Air transport

4.1.4.1 Characteristics and organisation

Far more than any other method of transportation, aviation is dominated by international considerations such as security regulations, standards and provisions, the monitoring of aircraft movements and airspace, agreements between countries and alliances between airlines and airports, as well as global demand, the corresponding aircraft movements and transregional airport hubs. This global background is one of the reasons why this traditionally stable growth market has shown clear signs of vulnerability in recent times, for example during the financial and economic crisis or isolated external effects such as epidemic outbreaks or terrorist attacks. Aviation remains, however, a long-term growth market. Passenger traffic growth picked up momentum from 2009 onwards and is expected to grow over the next 10–15 years annually by around 5 to 6% (Airbus, 2014; Boeing, 2015), thereby outstripping the global economy as a whole. These forecasts are primarily based on the growing private and commercial demand for mobility around the world, which is the result of the increasingly globalised division of labour and the expected wealth growth in Asia and Eastern Europe in particular. Flying is also becoming appreciably cheaper because of the successive liberalisation of the market. This in turn is driven by privatisation and the resulting increased competition across almost all value chain elements, as well as technological innovations and efficiency improvements in the management of air and ground capacities. The latter includes more efficient air traffic control, growing market penetration by low-cost airlines and significant capacity expansions in terms of both aircraft and airports.

Counterarguments to this thesis are the trend towards saturation in key aviation markets, increased fuel costs, the rising cost of air traffic control, environmental taxes, dwindling public acceptance because of environmental awareness, increasingly difficult approval procedures for major airport projects, shifts to other carriers – particularly for regional transportation.

Aviation is characterised by a variety of trends involving significant investment that are global in nature, and hence extremely relevant for the respective national situation:

- Alliances between international airlines with the aim of generating economies of scale and network effects;
- Focus on international hubs for transit passengers, particularly in the Asian and European regions with few major airports, and on point-to-point flights in the polycentric US market;

- Use of wide-body aircraft offers growing capacities, such as the A380 on long-distance point-to-point routes between Asia and Europe or the US;
- Harmonisation of air traffic control through the standardisation of control systems and the launch of new technologies, such as Galileo in Europe, as well as the more efficient demarcation of the individual air traffic control zones independently of national borders;
- Appearance of low-cost carriers in terms of their number and capacity, which started in the US and has since spread via the UK and Continental Europe to the Asia-Pacific region. In addition, traditional carriers adopted parts of the low-cost carriers' business model or founded low-cost subsidiaries. This business model is based on the systematic generation of (i) economies of scale in the service range as a result of the optimisation of business processes and resource management as well as market power with a focus on regional airports in particular and (ii) additional demand above and beyond that previously covered by established airlines through the resulting extremely low ticket prices that can be adjusted flexibly to reflect the utilisation of the respective aircraft; accordingly, the target group is price-sensitive travellers seeking point-to-point flights between large and medium-sized cities;
- Market liberalisation is increasing at a national level but remains inadequate in many respects when it comes to international development. This relates in particular to the political and administrative aspects of the Global Open Skies project, such as adherence to rights of transportation for the protection of national carriers, their subsidisation, anti-competitive conditions for all parties in terms of fares and other competitive provisions, security standards, etc.;
- Growth in competition because of (i) the optimisation of slot allocation, e.g. the trend away from 'grandfathering' for long-term slot-holders in favour of procedures aimed at ensuring improved utilisation, such as use-or-lose provisions, peak load pricing or auctions at market-clearing prices with high competitive allocation efficiency, and (ii) the requirements of international anti-trust authorities with regard to dominant market positions, which are increasingly occupied by the three major strategic alliances between international airlines, i.e. Star Alliance[2] (27 airlines/number of passengers 641.10 million/ turnover US$179.05 billion), oneworld[3] (16 airlines + 30 associated service companies/ 512.8 million/US$143 billion) and SkyTeam[4] (20 airlines/602 million).

The aviation market as a whole as compared with other infrastructure sectors is characterised by a significant degree of disintegration between the various value chain elements. With some national variations, the main value chain elements and their global providers are currently largely independent of each other. These primarily include:

- Aircraft production and maintenance and aircraft manufacture as the most capital-intensive resource for air services;
- Airlines as the providers of air services;

---

[2]http://www.staralliance.com/en/about, accessed 15 August 2015.
[3]https://de.oneworld.com/news-information/oneworld-fact-sheets/oneworld-at-a-glance/, accessed 15 August 2015.
[4]http://www.skyteam.com/de/About-us/Press/Facts-and-Figures/, accessed 15 August 2015.

▪ Airports and airport operators, which can be broken down into providers of (i) aviation services – typically including terminals, runways and ground-handling services – and (ii) non-aviation services, consisting of all commercial activities found at modern airports.

Private investment is commonplace in all three of these areas. As in the case of the other sectors and subsectors discussed in this chapter, this section focuses on the immovable, material infrastructures, that is airports rather than services.

International airports generally fall within the scope of the government, which is responsible for the planning, approval, construction and financing of airports. The relevant regions/municipalities are responsible for smaller, mostly regional airports. Although there are countless examples of private investment in small airports, it is the major international airports that are more interesting for investors. Therefore, the following section focuses on international airports.

International airports can be broken down into primary and secondary airports with the former playing an important role in international air traffic. However, secondary airports have enjoyed considerable growth over recent years, benefiting from the strain on capacity at major airports and the ongoing increase in slot prices. Primary airports include hub or transfer airports, that is airports at which a large number of passengers merely transfer to another flight in order to reach their final destination. The origin and destination airports are classified as secondary airports or, if they are small, tertiary airports. A final category is so-called quaternary airports, which are mostly served by a small number of low-cost carriers only.

The majority of airports around the world are owned either directly or indirectly by the respective government, region or municipality. Indirect ownership means an airport is administered by a superior public institution that is responsible for a number of airports. These institutions or the airports themselves mostly have a private law structure; however, the government is often the sole shareholder. At the same time, various airports around the world have either been fully or partially materially privatised.

4.1.4.2 Sources of revenue and value chain elements

Airports are mostly financed by a combination of internally generated funds (direct user financed, see Section 3.3.3) and government grants. Paying users of airports primarily include airlines and passengers, as well as visitors using only the commercial services.

Revenue from airport operation can be broken down broadly into revenue from aviation, including the corresponding land- and airside ground-handling services, and non-aviation revenue from commercial services on the ground. This classification is based on the primary value chain elements described in detail below. Revenue from aviation includes the fees paid by airlines for take-off and landing, use of the terminal and aircraft parking, as well as revenue generated from concessions for centralised or decentralised ground-handling services such as baggage handling and aircraft refuelling and maintenance. In some countries, passengers are also charged airport fees.

Non-aviation services offer a wide range of revenue sources. Typical examples include all forms of retail, for example shopping, food and drink, as well as hotels, conference and office facilities, car parking, car rental and other commercial services aimed at passengers and visitors. These have become increasingly important for airports as a means of covering their costs. Cynics may suggest that modern airports are little more than 'shopping malls with runways attached'. The fact of the matter is that non-aviation services can account for more than 50% of the total revenue of the average airport – and the figure for airports such as London Heathrow is significantly higher – with implications on the risk-return profile.

Compared with other infrastructure sectors, the aviation value chain is highly extensive and complex. In the same way as for the aforementioned infrastructure sectors, Table 4.6 provides a systematic – but by no means exhaustive – overview of the key value chain elements and allocates them to the corresponding investments. Value chain element services include the services provided by airports (aviation and non-aviation), airlines and air traffic control.

The aviation value chain includes all the activities and services relating directly to the handling of actual air traffic and the accompanying auxiliary services. Among other things, this includes:

- the provision and management of general infrastructure, such as:
  - the runway system, including aprons and taxiways, hangars, etc.;
  - passenger terminals, including gates, customs, immigration, health and security services and passenger check-in and boarding;
  - cargo terminals, including loading and warehousing facilities;
  - the central operational infrastructure, i.e. the airport facilities on which ground-handling service providers are dependent, such as refuelling systems, baggage conveyor systems.
- landside ground-handling services, including passenger services such as baggage handling, check-in and cargo services, such as acceptance and loading;
- airside ground-handling services, including maintenance, flight operation and security functions as well as aircraft loading and unloading, internal cleaning, catering, pushback, bus transfers and passenger handling;
- provision/management of central operational infrastructure, i.e. the airport facilities on which ground-handling service providers are dependent, such as refuelling systems and baggage conveyor systems.

Generally speaking, aviation value chain elements involve ensuring smooth airport operation in close cooperation with the airlines as well as the end-to-end optimisation of the passenger flow, cargo handling, overall airport logistics and security.

Non-aviation goods and services – such as retail outlets, hotels, conference and office facilities, car rental, car parking – are primarily used by passengers and their companions when leaving or arriving at the airport, although particularly attractive offerings may be used by airport visitors independently of the aviation side, such as conference/office facilities.

A final area of interest is the connection to the transport infrastructure, which consists of personal and public transport connections such as roads and railways, parking spaces and taxi ranks.

The use of state-of-the-art technology, and particularly telematics applications, is extremely advanced in the aviation sector. Such technology is used primarily to increase aviation safety, such as the European air traffic management organisation EUROCONTROL, which performs a pan-regional air traffic control function for the airspace and uses telematics to reconcile the planned air traffic volume (demand) with the relevant aviation safety provisions. Movement guidance and control systems are also used to increase the capacity, safety and efficiency of vehicle movements on the airport's premises.

TABLE 4.6 Air traffic infrastructure – value chain elements and investment opportunities (authors' own source)

Airports		Airlines	
Value chain elements	**Investment opportunities**	**Value chain elements**	**Investment opportunities**
Aviation		**Provision and management of airplanes**	**Airplanes for** – Passenger – Cargo
Provision/management of – general infrastructure – central operational infrastructure	– Terminals – Run- and taxiways, aprons – Hangars – Passenger/cargo terminals – Refuelling systems – Conveyor systems – etc.	**Passenger services** – Sale of tickets – Services on board – After sale service – Security on board – Other services	Necessary facilities, systems and equipment
Landside ground services – Passenger handing – Cargo handling	Systems/equipment for – Check-in and boarding – Baggage handling – Guidance – Acceptance and loading	**Cargo services** – Acquisition – After sale service – Security on board – Other services	Necessary facilities, systems and equipment
Landside ground services – Passenger handling – Cargo handling	Systems/equipment for: – Maintenance, flight operations, security – Loading and unloading – Push back – Bus transfers – Cleaning/Catering	**Air traffic** – Pilots – Passenger care	Necessary facilities, systems and equipment
		Maintenance and repair of airplanes	Necessary facilities, systems and equipment
Non-aviation		**Air traffic control**	
Commercial services	– Retail outlets – Hotels – Conference and Office – Facilities – Car rental/car parking – etc.	**Value chain elements** – Air and ground control – Navigation services	**Investment opportunities** Necessary facilities, systems and equipment

4.1.4.3 Competition and regulation   The competitive situation in the airport sector can be broken down into the aforementioned categories of primary, secondary, tertiary and quaternary airports.

As hubs, primary airports and the dominant airlines at these airports – such as Lufthansa/Star Alliance in Frankfurt, Finnair in Helsinki or American Airlines in Dallas, to name just a few examples – mainly compete with other international hubs and their established airlines or alliances. If fees increase at a hub and the established airline is required to increase ticket prices as a result, transfer passengers generally have various options in terms of selecting a different airline that offers the same connection via an alternative, lower-priced hub. For example, there are eight different daily routes from Berlin to New York with various airlines. Hubs often compete with each other even within an alliance or the same airline, such as the competition between Munich, Zurich and Vienna within Star Alliance for connections to Eastern Europe.

For secondary and tertiary airports, which mostly serve as the origin and/or destination (O&D) airports, the competitive situation depends to a large extent on the overlap between the catchment areas of neighbouring airports, and in particular major airports. Although O&D passengers are particularly sensitive to increases in airport fees, this only affects demand if there are alternative airports nearby from which they can reach the same destination at a lower cost.

Additional competitive factors in the airport sector include private and public transport connections to urban and suburban centres, parking, attractiveness for airlines and, to a certain extent, attractiveness and comfort for passengers, for example owing to short handling times or entertaining facilities in waiting areas. In other words, the more pronounced these competitive factors are, the greater an airport's market power – and hence the more scope it has in terms of increasing the fees charged to airlines and, ultimately, passengers.

This market power is generally at its least pronounced among quaternary airports. Such airports are comparatively dependent on a small number of interested airlines – mostly low-cost carriers – and are forced to offer particularly low airport fees that sometimes fail to cover their costs and hence are often the subject of regional subsidies.

The intermodal competition posed by personal transport and local public transport must also be taken into account, although this mainly affects airlines serving domestic routes and connections with neighbouring countries and hence also affects corresponding airports.

Not all airports are subject to price regulation. The need for price regulation for take-off and landing, use of the terminal and aircraft parking depends in particular on the market power of the respective airport. In England, for example, prices are regulated by the UK Civil Aviation Authority (CAA). The CAA assesses the market power of airports and if an airport passes the market power test under the Civil Aviation Act 2012 it regulates the airport with an economic licence. Currently, Heathrow and Gatwick are licensed. Licence conditions include a price cap on Heathrow's charges on airlines, the enforcement of commitments Gatwick made to its users and requirements about the operational resilience at both airports (Civil Aviation Authority, 2015). For further information regarding Heathrow Airport Holding, refer to the corresponding box in the next section (4.1.4.4).

Price regulation may take various forms. A distinction is made between cost-plus regulation and price cap regulation. In turn, both methods can be combined with the single or dual till principle.

Cost-plus regulation gives little or no incentive to cut costs and can expose public institutions to a certain conflict of interests, because the regulators of a given airport are often also its shareholders. In their ownership role, they have an interest in generating additional revenue, and hence charging relatively high prices, whereas their regulatory function requires them to ensure that prices remain at an appropriately low level.

In the case of price cap regulation, the operator is given an incentive to increase its profit by improving productivity during the respective regulatory period. As such, the incentives for efficiency gains and cost reductions are more pronounced than under traditional cost-plus regulation.

The single till principle includes regulation for both aviation and non-aviation services, whereas the dual till principle relates solely to aviation services.

4.1.4.4 Private-sector involvement Private-sector investments in airports are prevalent around the world. These are undertaken in various forms from horizontal partnerships and concessions through to partial and full material privatisation.

In Germany, for example, partial material privatisation models are most common. The first German airport to be partially privatised was Düsseldorf Airport, which was previously jointly owned by the federal state of North Rhine-Westphalia (NRW) and the City of Düsseldorf.

DÜSSELDORF AIRPORT

Flughafen Düsseldorf GmbH was formed in 1927 and now is the third-largest airport in Germany. Following a fire in 1996 that affected the terminal building, the NRW state government resolved to sell its 50% share in the airport company to a private investor owing to the significant investment volume required. In an EU-wide tender process, in 1997, the Airport Partners GmbH consortium, consisting of HOCHTIEF AirPort GmbH (HTA) (60%) and the Irish state-owned airport operator Aer Rianta International (40%), acquired the shares for €180 million (City of Düsseldorf, 1997). Under the terms of the acquisition, the strategic investor was required to return the airport to full functionality in a short period as part of the 'airport 2000 plus' project. Between 1997 and 2003, Airport Partners GmbH invested around €390 million in extensive construction measures. Close to the airport terminal the private investors realised a 23-hectare business park development. The partial privatisation allowed the airport to return to normal operations rapidly. The 50% private interest in the airport was then held by HTA (20%), HTAC (HOCHTIEF AirPort Capital, 10%) and Aer Rianta (20%). The remaining 50% is still held by the City of Düsseldorf. HTA was sold to the Canadian pension fund PSP on 1 January 2013. Non-aviation services currently account for 37% of the airport's total revenue (AviAlliance, 2015a).

Frankfurt Airport is the only German airport to be partially materially privatised by way of an initial public offering (IPO). This was conducted in 2001 following the legal formation of Fraport AG. As part of the stock exchange placement, around 29% of the shares were transferred to a wide range of private investors.

The global airport sector is characterised by a shift from government control to profit-oriented companies, a process that often involves privatisation. The new (private) owners increasingly include global companies, such as the largest British airport operator Heathrow

Airport Holding (formerly BAA), TBI plc,[5] Macquarie Airports Group (Australia), AviAlliance and Fraport AG (Germany).

The development of the portfolio held by AviAlliance, which now consists of six airport interests, is typical of this type of strategic infrastructure investor. In 2005, AviAlliance in its role as provider of financial services to HTA, attracted institutional investors by establishing one of the first airport investment partnerships together with Hastings Funds Management Ltd (Australia), Caisse de Dépôt et Placement du Québec (Canada) and KfW IPEX-Bank (Germany). AviAlliance later took over interests from HTA, and its portfolio now includes interests in Athens, Budapest, Düsseldorf, Hamburg and Tirana international airports (AviAlliance, 2015b).

Fraport AG, in contrast, acts as a strategic investor itself as part of its growth strategy. As a result, it has become a global airport operator. Fraport offers a wide range of services and invests in a number of projects and airports. For example, it is active as a ground-handling service provider at airports such as Vienna, Brussels, Hong Kong, Lisbon and Jacksonville, and provides airport security services at more than 30 locations (via its fully owned subsidiary ICTS Europe Holdings BV). It performs terminal management at Antalya Airport, Turkey (a BOT project in which Fraport owns 50% of the shares in Antalya Airport International Terminal AS), human resources management for a BOOT project in Athens and airport management in Lima, Peru (a BOT project with a concessionary term of 30 years and an option to extend for a further 10 years, with Fraport owning 70.01% of the shares in the project company).

One of the few examples of full material privatisation is the British Airports Authority (BAA). BAA was or seemed to be a success story of privatisation until the UK Competition Commission interfered and forced BAA to sell three of its airports. For more details, see the 'Heathrow Airport Holding' example.

HEATHROW AIRPORT HOLDING

The Heathrow Airport Holding (formerly British Airports Authority, BAA) was established by the passing of the Airport Authority Act 1966, to take responsibility for three state-owned airports: London Heathrow Airport, London Gatwick Airport and London Stansted Airport. In the following years, BAA acquired responsibility for Glasgow International Airport, Edinburgh Airport, Southampton Airport and Aberdeen Airport. As part of Margaret Thatcher's moves to privatise government-owned assets, the Airports Act 1986 saw the formal privatisation of BAA as a publicly limited company listed on the London Stock Exchange. The initial capitalisation of BAA plc was £1225 million. In the early 1990s, the company sold Prestwick International Airport.

In July 2006, Grupo Ferrovial led a consortium that took over BAA for £10.1 billion (US$20 billion). As part of the transaction, BAA was delisted from the London Stock Exchange (it had been part of the FTSE100 index) on 15 August 2006. Successively, BAA expanded into international operations, including retail contracts

---

[5] Founded in 1972 in the UK by Thomas and Bailey under the name of Thomas Bailey Investments (TBI) as a property development company that ultimately focused on airports, TBI was acquired by Abertis (90%) and Aena International (10%) in 2005.

at Boston Logan International Airport and Baltimore–Washington International Thurgood Marshall Airport (through its subsidiary BAA USA, Inc.) and a management contract with the City of Indianapolis to run Indianapolis International Airport (as BAA Indianapolis, Inc.).

In 2007, the UK Competition Commission (UKCC) investigated BAA after a report by the Office of Fair Trading into business practices at the airports was published. UKCC's key complaints focused on the monopoly position, which had made BAA complacent about responding to airlines and passenger needs. In 2009, UKCC ordered BAA to sell three of its seven UK airports within two years: Gatwick, Stansted and either Glasgow or Edinburgh, with Gatwick and Stansted being the second and third biggest airports in London, respectively. In October 2009, BAA sold Gatwick Airport to the infrastructure fund Global Infrastructure Partners (GIP) for £ 1.5 billion. This was well below the level sought by Ferrovial on the grounds that bidders encountered problems raising the debt finance from banks in the middle of the global financial crises. In 2012, Edinburgh Airport was sold to GIP as well, the same year that BAA changed its name to Heathrow Airport Holdings.

4.1.5 Water transport

The water transport sector consists of ports, which are primarily used for the transhipment of cargo, and the waterways (e.g. rivers and canals) on which goods are transported.

Private investment generally focuses on port facilities, with the exception of a few largely historical, albeit spectacular, examples, such as the Suez Canal. Therefore, this section adopts the same focus. To start with, however, the topic of inland waterways shall be discussed briefly, not least because these are naturally important in terms of connecting ports with the interior of a country. As such, the expansion of inland waterways will be particularly relevant in emerging and developing countries where these are little developed, and will inevitably be realisable only with the help of private investment. The revenue potential of waterways is low, however, compared with the relatively high level of construction investment required. As a consequence, inland waterway investments almost inevitably require budget-financed models in order to attract private capital.

Water transport is primarily associated with the following characteristics: (i) the transportation of commodities and bulk cargo and (ii) environmentally friendly, low-cost transportation. Especially inland waterway transport is a competitive alternative to road and rail transport in terms of both energy consumption and noise and gas emissions. Its energy consumption per km/tonne of transported goods is approximately 17% of that of road transport and 50% of rail transport (European Commission Mobility and Transport, 2015). In addition to transport, waterways can perform many different functions, including:

- Power generation;
- Fishing;
- Leisure and recreation;
- Domestic and industrial water supply;
- Drainage (flooding) that may generate additional benefits and/or revenues.

TABLE 4.7 Traffic infrastructure of waterways – value chain elements and investment opportunities (authors' own source)

(Inland) Waterways	
Value chain elements	**Investment opportunities**
Network infrastructure	
Provision and management of infrastructure	– Naturally waterways – Canals – Bridges and other engineering works – Locks – Hoisting devices – Other secondary infrastructure
Operation – Traffic data collection – Telematics services – Fuelling	– Traffic data collection system – Telematics service systems – Tank farms

While none of these is related to transport and hence will not be discussed further here, this functional range is one of the main reasons waterways are largely owned by the public sector and administered by public institutions.

Waterways are a 'natural' monopoly in the true sense of the word: the majority of waterways are formed by river courses, with only a small number created artificially, and their use partially depends on the weather. For example, navigation can be restricted at high or low water. The fact that most waterways are formed by natural rivers does not mean their usage is possible without further investment. Quite the opposite, in fact: the natural water flow often means steps have to be taken to make rivers navigable in the first place. This may include deepening the navigation channel, constructing locks, hoisting devices and pumping stations, or straightening watercourses. With some regional exceptions, the waterway network is wide-meshed compared with the road network.

Like the value chain of the road sector, the majority of value chain elements lie in the provision and management of the infrastructure for commercial and, to a lesser extent, private users. Further information is provided in Table 4.7, which, however, does not contain the value chain elements of the transport service providers operating *on* the waterways.

With very few exceptions around the world, the necessary funding for waterway infrastructure is provided by the public sector. This does not apply to the value chain elements of the transport service providers operating on the waterways.

Revenues may be generated in different forms of shipping levies for the use of waterways and facilities, for example fees for the length of waterways used, lockage per passage or bridge tolls. The amounts charged may vary depending on the size of the ship, the weight and type of the goods being transported or, in the case of passenger ships, the maximum passenger capacity.

After this brief discussion of (inland) waterways, which are neither considered attractive nor, in most instances, possible investment targets for private investors, the rest of the chapter – as already explained above – concentrates on ports.

TABLE 4.8   List of the 10 largest international ports worldwide (World Shipping Council, 2013)

Rank	Port	Country	Million TEU
1	Shanghai	China	33.62
2	Singapore	Singapore	32.60
3	Shenzhen	China	23.28
4	Hong Kong	China	22.35
5	Busan	South Korea	17.69
6	Ningbo-Zhoushan	China	17.33
7	Qingdao	China	15.52
8	Guangzhou	China	15.31
9	Jebel Ali	Dubai	13.64
10	Tianjin	China	13.01
11	Rotterdam	Netherlands	11.62
12	Dalian	China	10.86
13	Port Kelang	Malaysia	10.35
14	Kaohsiung	Taiwan	9.94
15	Hamburg	Germany	9.30
16	Antwerp	Belgium	8.59
17	Keihin ports	Japan	8.37
18	Xiamen	China	8.01
19	Los Angeles	USA	7.87
20	Tanjung Pelepas	Malaysia	7.63

Note: TEU = twenty-foot equivalent unit (represents total port throughput, including loaded and empty TEU)

4.1.5.1 Characteristics and organisation

Ports can be broken down into seaports and inland ports. The main difference is that seaports are located on the coast and are predominantly used to process international trade, making them extremely important industrial locations from a regional and economic perspective. In contrast, inland ports are situated on a waterway (river, lake or canal) and are used primarily for the national, but to a lesser extent also the international, transhipment of goods and as an interface between the various modes of transport. Table 4.8 lists the 20 largest international ports. Although this table suggests that major port investments have been done and will come up mostly in emerging markets (especially across Asia), a large number of significant, albeit often smaller, port constructions and investments for specific kinds of ships, for example, have been made in the recent past and will be required across Europe and North America.

Figure 4.1 shows the impressive development of international maritime trade and gives an impression of the competitive situation in the market. In particular, to cope with the continuous growth in worldwide container handling in the last 20 years has necessitated the finding of appropriate ways to realise the investments necessary – often by involving private capital and using the organisational models described below. Even though the financial and economic crisis led to a reduction in general port handling in 2009, the industry recovered relatively quickly and, since then, a continuous growth in port handling has been realised.

Based on the primary cargo type, a distinction is made between ports and port terminals for: (i) containers, (ii) dry bulk cargo (sand/coal), (iii) liquid bulk cargo (gas, oil) and (iv) break bulk cargo (wood).

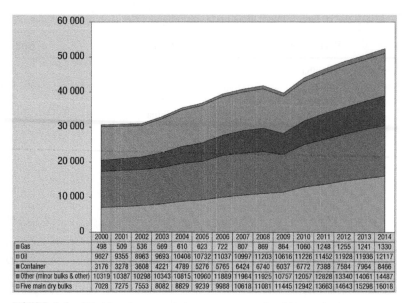

	2000	2001	2002	2003	2004	2005	2006	2007	2008	2009	2010	2011	2012	2013	2014
▨ Gas	498	509	536	569	610	623	722	807	869	864	1060	1248	1255	1241	1330
▨ Oil	9627	9355	8963	9693	10408	10732	11037	10997	11203	10616	11226	11452	11928	11936	12117
▪ Container	3176	3278	3608	4221	4789	5276	5765	6424	6740	6037	6772	7388	7584	7964	8466
▨ Other (minor bulks & other)	10319	10387	10298	10343	10815	10960	11889	11984	11925	10757	12057	12828	13340	14061	14487
▫ Five main dry bulks	7028	7275	7553	8082	8829	9239	9988	10618	11081	11445	12942	13663	14643	15298	16018

FIGURE 4.1   World seaborne trade in cargo tonne-miles by cargo type,
2000–2014
Source: UNCTAD (2014)

A local port authority is usually responsible for port operations, including port manage-ment and, in some cases, the construction and maintenance of the entire port infrastructure (waterways, locks, piers, roads, railways, etc.) and the provision of special (terminal-based) infrastructure, for example quay walls and cleared building plots. The superstructure of ports, that is terminal buildings including cranes, storage surface, warehouses/depots, facilities for production and processing and so on, are provided and managed either by the local port authority itself or by private port operators. In most countries, ports form an integral part of the national transport concept for which the relevant government ministry is responsible. In particular, its responsibility includes the provision of seaward access routes and inland connections such as waterways, roads and railways.

Four basic organisational models are used for ports around the world depending on (i) the extent of private-sector involvement, (ii) the owners of the infrastructure and (iii) the owners of the superstructure. These organisational forms are (World Bank, 2007; Euromed Transport Project, 2008):

- Public service ports;
- Tool ports;
- Landlord ports;
- Private service ports (fully privatised ports).

Public service ports are ports with a strictly public structure. All services are performed by the port authority, which owns both the port infrastructure and the superstructure (see Table 4.9). The port authority charges user fees for its services and performs a regulatory function. The number of public service ports in Europe and in the US is limited in comparison

TABLE 4.9   Port infrastructure – value chain elements and investment opportunities (authors' own source)

Ports

Value chain elements	Investment opportunities
Infra- and Superstructure	
Provision and management of infrastructure and superstructure	Primary infrastructure
	– Waterways
	– Quay walls and piers
	– Roads/rail infrastructure
	– Locks
	– Protection, e.g. breakwater
	Secondary infrastructure
	– Dry/floating docks (repair)
	– Information system
	– Refuelling installations etc.
	Superstructure
	– Terminals including cranes
	– Storage surface
	– Warehouses/depots
	– Facilities for production/processing etc.
Services	
For ships	
– Traffic control and security	– Necessary facilities
– Navigation services	
– Towboat	
– Repair	
For cargo	– Necessary facilities
– Discharge/charge	
– Logistic	
– Storage	

to many developing countries where public service ports have a share of approximately 70% in the market (Sorgenfrei, 2013).

The main difference between tool ports and public service ports is that, in the case of tool ports, the public-sector port authority owns the entire port infrastructure, including the superstructure, but services on ships in port are performed by private operators. The port authority leases the superstructure facilities to the private operators for this purpose. This constitutes a normal lessee–lessor relationship. Accordingly, the material risks of the investment remain with the port authority, which is entitled to charge for the services provided. In addition to providing the superstructure, the port authority remains responsible for regulation.

Landlord ports are the most widespread organisational model. As in the previous models, the port authority is the owner of the port infrastructure. Private port operators lease this infrastructure from the port authority under long-term agreements and construct the necessary superstructure mostly in the form of terminals. The long-term agreements are usually concluded as concession arrangements, that is the private investor/port operator has to recover the cost arising from the investment and the operation of the facilities by the fees levied from the individual terminal users. Accordingly, unlike tool ports, the private operators bear the investment risk as well as the risk of facility operation. The port authority remains responsible for all regulatory functions, as well as the physical expansion of the port area and the provision of the underlying port infrastructure.

In the case of fully privatised ports (private service ports), the port infrastructure and the land are privately owned. However, the public sector may hold shares in the private port authority (i.e. in the form of a horizontal partnership) in order to ensure that public interests are protected.

In the last three cases the private partner bears the market/demand risk (i.e. the risk the services offered are actually marketable) but, depending on the investment amount and/or the conditions of the lease contract, with different (usually increasing from tool to fully privatised ports) consequences.

4.1.5.2 Sources of revenue and value chain elements Essentially two types of port user fees exist: fees for infrastructure usage and fees for port services (direct user finance, see also Section 3.3.3). Fees for port infrastructure usage include harbour dues, quay usage fees, demurrage and storage fees and flat-rate fees for the unloading and disposal of ship waste. Regarding fees for the use of port services, not all services are voluntary; certain fees must be paid e.g. whenever a port is entered, including fees for piloting and towing, the use of road and rail facilities and other terminal-based services. The fees charged are based on the size or dimensions of the respective ship.

As described above, the port authority (under the landlord model) often issues concessions to port operators/investors (i.e. concessionaires) for the various terminals of a seaport. These (terminal) operators can then charge their own fees for loading, unloading, demurrage and storage. In addition, the port authority (owned by the responsible government body) is obliged to provide the public infrastructure on the port site and the necessary funding. The port authority also has the option of levying rental or lease payments from the (terminal) operators by issuing concessions.

The value chain in the port subsector is highly diversified. It ranges from the provision of the primary and secondary port infrastructure (see Table 4.9), which is the main focus of this section, through to shipbuilding at the port itself. As for the other sectors, the value chain for the port infrastructure can be broken down into planning, construction, operating, maintenance, financing and realisation. These functions are generally assigned to the port operators, which are responsible for expanding and maintaining the waterways within the port and the cranes and warehousing space necessary for processing ships.

The port operators, whose main task is to ensure the rapid transhipment of goods, also perform additional services for ships, some of which run in parallel to the unloading and loading of goods.

Telematics systems are widely used within the shipping sector, particularly in busy international waterways and within ports. Depending on their functions, these systems are primarily employed for traffic monitoring, consulting and regulation with the aim of increasing safety. Traffic monitoring forms part of the information system that provides key data (e.g. status reports) to all parties. The primary feature of traffic consulting is navigation support, in which information, advice and recommendations on navigation are provided to individual ships with respect to routing and taking nearby traffic into account. This system is supported and supplemented by traffic regulation services, which seek to identify potential hazards in advance and prevent them through measures designed to change the traffic flow.

4.1.5.3 Competition and regulation The decidedly international nature of seaports (in particular) means regulation at the national level is insufficient. Accordingly, the regulatory framework in this sector is increasingly prescribed by, for example, the EU. In its *Green Paper on Sea Ports and Maritime Infrastructure* published in 1997, the EU sets out provisions for establishing the conditions for competition between ports and port service providers. The key content of this Green Paper includes: (i) ports and the common transport policy, (ii) financing and charging for ports and maritime infrastructure and (iii) port services. This is reflected in the current focus of the EU's policy on seaports, which includes the liberalisation and harmonisation of intra-port competition, the regulation of public subsidies and port fees and the integration of seaports into the Trans-European Network (TEN).

At national level, the individual EU member states are responsible for ensuring the functionality of seaports. This responsibility primarily relates to the expansion and maintenance of seaward access routes and inland connections.

One example of a centralised regulatory authority at national level is the Indian Tariff Authority for Major Ports (TAMP). Formed in 1997, TAMP is solely responsible for the 12 major ports in India. As well as regulating the prices of port services, it sets out guidelines for the calculation of lease payments for the land on port sites that is leased by private port operators.

TABLE 4.10 Examples for the organisational models of private-sector involvement in the port sector

Types of port	Public service port	Tool port	Landlord port	Private service port
Type of privatisation	Commercialisation or corporatisation	Functional privatisation	Full material privatisation	
Ownership of infrastructure	Public	Public	Public	Private
Ownership of superstructure	Public	Public	Private	Private
Terminal operation	Public	Private	Private	Private
Examples (some ports in developing countries)	Colombo[1,2] (Sri Lanka) Nhava Sheva[1,2] (India) Dar es Salaam[1,2] (Tanzania)	Chittagong[1] (Bangladesh) Banjarmasin[3] (Indonesia) Cebu[3] (Philippines)	Rotterdam[1,3] (Netherlands) New York[1] (USA) Singapore[1,3,4] (Singapore)	Some ports in the UK[1] and New Zealand[1]

Notes:
[1] *Source*: World Bank (2007).
[2] In transition towards a landlord port structure.
[3] Asian Development Bank (2000).
[4] Since 1997.

4.1.5.4   Private-sector involvement   In the port sector, all operating services can be transferred to private companies. The degree of private-sector involvement is determined by the organisational form of the port. For example, private companies are naturally involved in public service ports to an extremely limited extent, primarily focusing on the performance of construction works and other services to order. Under the tool port model, too, the private involvement is limited and investment risk remains with the port authority. By contrast, the landlord port model involves significant private investments as well as the transfer of material operating risks to the private operator.

Table 4.10 contains a schematic overview of the various forms of private-sector involvement in the port sector.

Internationally, the landlord port is the most common organisational model. Major port/terminal operators include APM Terminals, Hutchison Port Holdings (HPH) and PSA, each of which operates terminals worldwide.

PORT OPERATING COMPANIES

APM Terminals, with revenues of over US$4.45 billion in 2014, it is part of the AP Møller Maersk Group of Copenhagen, Denmark, and serves over 60 of the world's container shipping lines with terminal operations in 58 countries. The APM Terminals Global Terminal Network of 73 operating port facilities provides the container shipping community with port capacity, operational expertise and infrastructure investment. The company invested US$723 million in new ports and port projects in 2008, complementing 2007's investments of US$850 million (APM Terminals, 2009). In August 2015, APM announced the acquisition of the 11 terminal portfolio of Barcelona-based Grup Maritim TCB, which will significantly increase the APM Terminals global terminal network in Europe and Latin America, increasing overall annual container throughput capacity by 4.3 million TEU (Twenty-foot Equivalent Unit). The deal will see APM Terminals buy into Grup Maritim TCB's portfolio for an undisclosed sum. It acquires the stake from Spain's largest shipping and logistics group Pérez y Cía, which currently controls the assets (Port Finance International, 2015).

Hutchison Port Holdings (HPH), founded in 1994, is a leading port investor, developer and operator with interests in a total of 319 berths in 52 ports, spanning 26 countries throughout Asia, the Middle East, Africa, Europe, the Americas and Australasia. HPH also owns a number of transportation-related service companies. In 2008, the HPH Group as subsidiary of the diversified Hutchison Whampoa Limited (HWL), handled a combined throughput of 82.9 million TEU worldwide. The HPH Group now has ports and related operations that span the entire logistics chain, providing customers with a full range of benefits that include container storage and repair, container tracking, general and bulk cargo transfer, warehousing, marine shuttle services and other related services. The HPH Group directly invests in hubs that serve large hinterlands and that either already support international trade or have the potential to become key transport centres (HPH, 2015).

PSA Corporation Ltd – PSA's principal business is the provision of integrated container terminal services, including multipurpose terminal services. PSA's other businesses include PSA Marine. PSA was formerly the Port of Singapore Authority, a statutory board regulating, developing, operating and promoting the port of Singapore's terminals. In 1996, PSA's regulatory functions were handed over to the Maritime and Port Authority of Singapore. PSA Corporation Limited was subsequently incorporated in 1997 as the corporate successor to the Port of Singapore Authority to manage and operate its terminals and related businesses. In December 2003, PSA International became the investment holding company for PSA's businesses in Singapore and worldwide. PSA International is fully owned by Temasek Holdings. With its flagship operations in PSA Singapore Terminals and PSA HNN, PSA participates in 27 ports in 16 countries across Asia, Europe and the Americas handling a total of 65.4 million TEU globally in 2014. For the financial year 2014, it reported consolidated revenues of S$3.83 billion and a net profit of about S$1.4 billion. To meet the future growth of global trade and the long-term needs of its customers, PSA is developing Pasir Panjang Terminal Phases 3 & 4 – the first set of berths began operations in 2014. When fully completed (by the end of 2017), the new terminals will boost Singapore's total container-handling capacity to 50 million TEU per year (PSA International, 2015).

The most extensive private-sector involvement is naturally prevalent in ports that have been materially privatised, whether partially or in full. Material partial or full privatisation is frequently performed through a public auction of shares that were formerly held by a public port or terminal operator to strategic or financial investors or, as in the case of Hamburger Hafen und Logistik AG (HHLA), by way of an IPO. Since going public in 2007, around 30% of the shares in the terminal operator HHLA have been in free float, with the majority (70%) remaining in the ownership of the Free and Hanseatic City of Hamburg. The primary aim of the IPO was to generate funds for the necessary expansion of the port infrastructure on the capital market. The total volume of the IPO was around €1.2 billion.

4.1.6 Sustainability considerations

Transportation conveys substantial socioeconomic benefits by increasing mobility for passengers and freight. At the same time, though, transport activities are associated with growing levels of environmental externalities the most important ones being environmental and social impacts related to climate change, air, water and soil quality, noise, biodiversity and land take (Tahzib and Zvijakova, 2012). For a comprehensive overview of environmental, social and governance (ESG) risk, please refer to Section 5.2.4.

4.1.6.1 Environmental The transportation industry is exposed to physical and regulatory risks resulting from climate change, as climate-change-induced, extreme weather events can affect infrastructure assets, while activities of the transportation industry may contribute to climate change. Natural hazards – such as storms, heatwaves, flooding and rising sea levels and temperatures – affect transport infrastructure and can result in long-term shifts in transportation usage patterns resulting from large-scale demographic changes (relocation) and changes in tourism travel (ground, sea and air). The projected increase in the frequency and intensity of extreme weather events such as heavy rain and snowfall, heatwaves and cold spells, cause flooding, icy roads, poor visibility and physical stress on infrastructure that can lead to damages, injuries, transport disruption and delays and related financial losses. Weather-related stress is responsible for 30–50% of current road maintenance costs in Europe (€8 to 13 billion a year) alone, while about 10% of these costs (€0.9 billion a year) are connected to extreme weather events (European Commission, 2013a). Marine ports, as well as roads, airports and other infrastructure located close to coasts, may be prone to extensive damage owing to an increase in frequency and intensity of offshore storms striking land. Inland shipping may also be affected by changes in snowpack melt and precipitation, resulting in river flooding or, in the case of drought, limited mobility, owing to extreme low water conditions.

COPENHAGEN-RINGSTED HIGH-SPEED RAILWAY LINE

When planning to expand the track capacity between Copenhagen and Ringsted on Zealand, the Public Transport Authority carried out a climate-change impact assessment for the project with a goal of determining a future rail track's robustness to climate change over a 100-year operating period (Danish Ministry of the Environment, 2015). The results presented show, on the one hand, that especially increased precipitation and increased water flow in watercourses can significantly affect railway constructions. Particularly relevant is an expected 20% increase in the intensity of rainfall in heavy downpours by the year 2100 with the respective implications for the size of railway drainage ditches. Consequently, the new track between Copenhagen and Ringsted will have a 30% greater capacity for water flow than the current norm, which will allow water to flow quickly enough and prevent it from building up and eroding the railway construction. On the other hand, environmental factors related to climate change such as increasing temperatures, rising sea levels and rising groundwater are not expected to have a significant impact for the project in question. The project is expected to be completed in 2018.

Activities of the individual and public transport are polluting the atmosphere. Every year, several million tonnes of gases are released into the atmosphere, including lead (Pb), carbon monoxide (CO), carbon dioxide (CO_2; not a pollutant), methane (CH_4), nitrogen oxide (NO), nitrous oxide (N_2O), chlorofluorocarbons (CFCs), perfluorocarbons (PFCs), silicon tetrafluoride (SiF_4), benzene and volatile components (BTX), as well as heavy metals (zinc, chrome, copper, cadmium) and particulate matters such as ashes and dust (Tahzib and Zvijakova, 2012). These emissions are connected to climate change, yet to what extent is still subject of debate. Some of these gases, particularly nitrous oxide, also contribute to harming the stratospheric ozone layer, which protects the surface of the earth from ultraviolet radiation (Tahzib and Zvijakova, 2012).

Transportation is the second-largest source of global greenhouse gas (GHG) emissions, responsible for almost a quarter of all CO_2 emissions from fossil fuel combustion. The International Energy Agency (IEA) estimates that the transport sector could contribute up to 21% of the global GHG emission reductions needed by 2050 in order to limit global warming to within 2°C (IEA, 2013a). In addition, ground transportation contributes significantly to local air pollution and poses serious risks to public health both in developed and developing nations, hence investments in sustainable, low-carbon transport infrastructure (such as electrical rail systems) can have multiple ESG benefits (Ang and Marchal, 2013).

Public and private transportation activities and, in particular, marine transport significantly affect surface and groundwaters, biodiversity and wildlife.[6] Emissions of cars and aircrafts can result in acid rain, which damages buildings, reduces agricultural crop yields and causes forest decline. Fuel, chemical and other hazardous particulates discarded from aircraft, cars, trucks and trains or from port and airport terminal operations (e.g. de-icing) can pollute surface waters, oceans and wetlands. Waste, oil spills, ballast waters and dredging related to marine transport affect the marine environment. While the environmental problems caused by waste and oil spills are more than obvious, ballast waters acquired in one region may contain invasive aquatic species that can disrupt the natural marine ecosystem. The deepening of harbour channels by removing sediments from the bed of a body of water (dredging) hamper marine biological diversity; coastal transport and shipping facilities cause soil erosion and contamination. Highway construction or lessening surface grades for airport and port developments results in the loss of fertile and productive soils. The use of toxic materials by the transport industry leads to soil contamination (e.g. chemicals used for preservation of railroad ties or fuel spills).

Transportation significantly affects biodiversity: the development of land-based transportation has led to deforestation and drained land, thus reducing wetland areas, driving out water plant species. Restricting and removing the plants growing next to roads and railways has led to new species different from those that originally grew in the areas. Many animals have become extinct as a result of changes in their natural habitats and a decrease of ranges (e.g. game crossings which are cut by roads and railways).

In summary, public and private transportation activities with means of transport that are moved by fossil fuels of some kind are harmful to the environment and contribute to its degradation. These issues are addressed by a growing body of environmental regulations. Investors in transportation assets may want to focus on futureproofing their fleets by investing in lowering harmful emissions.

4.1.6.2 Social Despite the obvious benefits of transportation such as increasing mobility and connecting communities, transportation may have significant negative impacts on society, in particular on human health and safety but also on the built environment in the context of cultural heritage.

Health risks such as cancer and cardiovascular, respiratory and neurological diseases are associated with toxic air pollutants. Particulates emissions (dust) may lead to respiratory problems, skin irritations, eye inflammations, blood clotting and various types of allergies. Smog adversely affects quality of life, while acid precipitation damages historical buildings and affects the attractiveness of tourist sites. Noise, an inherent characteristic of transportation, negatively affects life quality with noise levels above 75 dB seriously hampering hearing and affecting human physical and psychological wellbeing. Increasing noise levels have a negative impact on the urban environment reflected in falling land values and loss of productive land uses (Rodrigue, 2013).

Transportation facilities influence not only the urban landscape but also social and economic cohesion (e.g. when new transport facilities such as elevated train and highway structures cut across an existing urban community). Moreover, major transport facilities can create physical barriers, emissions, impact built heritage and hence affect the quality of urban life.

Poor occupational health and safety in transportation infrastructure may lead to disruptions, temporary shutdowns and lower productivity, and related economic loss, as well as

---

[6]For a detailed list of environmental effects see Tahzib and Zvijakova (2012) and Rodrigue (2013).

brand damage owing to the potential loss of customers, poor community and union relations and difficulty to attract and retain new staff (AMP Capital, 2013c).

4.1.6.3 Governance   Governance as applied to sustainability involves the management of issues that are inherent to the business model or common practice in the industry and are in potential conflict with the interest of broader stakeholder groups (government, community, customers, employees). Examples are regulatory compliance, lobbying, safety management, supply chain and resource management, conflict of interest, anti-competitive behaviour, corruption and bribery. All modes of transportation pose safety risks, either from mechanical failure or human error, and cause many fatal accidents. Accordingly, a key governance issue is how health and safety issues are handled by the leadership team (e.g. management of working hazards and accidents) with employees, authorities and the wider public. Regulations and public relations involving the impact of accidents on the public and the environment can damage a company's reputation and consequently affect its financial performance, while the global nature of marine shipping and logistics services exposes companies to an elevated risk of corruption. Moreover, the auto and airlines industries are faced with high unionisation rates in a very competitive environment (Lavigne-Delville, 2014).

4.2   WATER SUPPLY AND SEWAGE DISPOSAL[7]

4.2.1   Characteristics and organisation

Water is essential to the survival of all living creatures. In no other infrastructure sector is the gap between demand and investment requirement as (life-)threatening as in the water sector. Access to clean water is a basic human necessity. This fact makes the water sector particularly important, especially in areas where water is naturally scarce or unavailable for regular use and, in particular, unsuitable for consumption by humans or animals.

Globally, 1 out of every 9 people (750 million) has no access to safe, clean water and 2.5 billion (over one-third of the planet's population) have no access to proper sanitation facilities. An average of 840 000 people – many of whom are children – die every year from the consequences of dirty drinking water or inadequate waste water disposal, and the majority of illnesses in developing countries are attributable to poor water, waste water and hygiene facilities (Water.org, 2015).

Water is a key prerequisite for human and economic development, and for maintaining ecosystems (OECD, 2009). Global water crises – from drought in the world's most productive farmlands to the hundreds of millions of people without access to safe drinking water – are viewed as the top systemic global risk based on impact on society for the next decade that could result in a worldwide breakdown in economic, social and environmental systems (WEF, 2015). The UN estimates that already by 2025 fresh water demand will increase by 50% in developing nations with two-thirds of the world population living under stress water conditions (UN Water, 2013).

The availability of this precious commodity is also vital to agriculture, and hence the food supply, as well as industry and commerce. As such, those responsible for the water supply are often faced with significant challenges, even in parts of the world with sufficient water

---

[7]The terms 'sewage' and 'waste water' are used synonymously throughout this book.

resources. Despite the ambitious resolutions of national and international decision-makers in terms of setting supply targets, global issues such as climate change, the growing pollution of the environment and the sustained increase in the world's population are threatening to exacerbate the problem rather than ease it.

These problems are particularly serious in developing and emerging countries, where even the most basic infrastructure is often unavailable, meaning that a staggering degree of investment would be needed to make a tangible improvement. However, the capital requirements for the urgent maintenance of the often-antiquated infrastructure in industrial countries, particularly in the area of waste water disposal, are no less substantial. This is even more the case when taking into account the additional conversion and expansion work necessary to reflect demographic changes and migratory effects, as well as the more stringent quality and environmental standards, particularly in Europe and other OECD countries.

Only 2.5% of the earth's water is not salt water and only 0.3% is suitable for human use (UN Water, 2014a). Globally speaking, human consumption of this 'blue gold' is split between agricultural uses (around 70–75%), industrial and commercial uses (around 20%) and domestic uses, particularly drinking water (around 5–10%; OECD, 2006). This consumption forms part of the natural water cycle, which describes the vertical and horizontal circulation of water in all its states of matter between the sea and dry land. The processes involved include evaporation, precipitation, infiltration and runoff (see Figure 4.2). Water

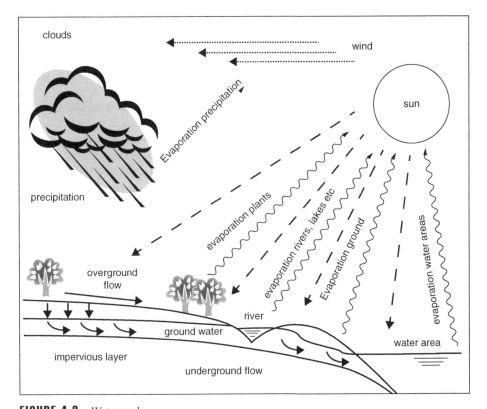

FIGURE 4.2 Water cycle

circulation processes are triggered by solar energy and gravity. No water is lost in the course of the cycle.

Water for human use is extracted from the cycle at springs and wells, from lakes and rivers or directly from groundwater sources, subjected to technical and chemical treatment depending on the water quality and stored in reservoirs in some cases. It is then distributed to consumers via water disposal and supply networks by way of gravity and/or pumps, where it is further distributed within internal systems depending on its planned usage, consumed and returned to the public system as waste water.

The waste water generated is routed via canalisation networks to a sewage treatment plant for biological or chemical treatment before being fed back into the natural water cycle. Any residue, for example in the form of sewage sludge, is subject to further treatment where necessary and disposed of or reused depending on its substance. The majority of rainwater seeps into the ground, although some reaches the canalisation network via land, surface and road drainage systems. Canalisation networks may take the form of separate or combined systems. In separate systems, rainwater and waste water to be treated are carried in separate sewers, whereas the same pipes and channels are used in combined systems.

The processes described above represent the typical scenario in developed industrialised countries and, ideally, in cities in developing and emerging countries at present. In many countries, particularly in rural areas, the required network and treatment infrastructure is still highly inadequate or, in some cases, entirely unavailable. This means the quality of drinking water is often not guaranteed and waste water is returned to the natural water cycle without being treated, with corresponding consequences for people and the environment. On the other hand, the transferability of this system to developing and emerging countries in terms of their infrastructural development and, even its sustainability for industrialised countries is disputed and currently under scrutiny. In the areas of waste water treatment and disposal in particular, the search is on for decentralised solutions that are less dependent on capital-intensive network structures.

The specific investment costs (in relation to total life cycle cost) in the water and waste water sector are particularly high compared with other infrastructure areas in general, averaging around double the costs required in the energy sector and other infrastructure sectors, assuming the same level of operating costs. Accordingly, the capital requirements represent a particular challenge for governments worldwide. Corresponding to OECD estimates (OECD, 2006), the necessary global annual investments in water and waste water systems were expected to amount to around US$800 billion in 2015, and to rise to around US$1040 billion annually by 2025. However, there is considerable variation in the figures cited by the relevant literature. In contrast to the OECD forecasts, more recent estimates are significantly lower, with annual capital requirements of US$500–600 billion from 2013 to 2030 by McKinsey in 2013 or even 'only' US$171–205 billion per year up to 2050 (David Lloyd Owen being quoted in 2011 in OECD/World Water Council, 2015).

Further challenges in the water sector include dealing with inefficient organisational and management structures and mismanagement, which can result in substantial technical and economic losses, for example following leakage in the supply and disposal network. This problem is by no means limited to developing and emerging countries. Average leakage rates are relatively low in Germany (7%) but remain quite high in England and Wales (19%), in France (26%) and Italy (29%) (OECD, 2011). In the UK in the 1980s, some 30% of all water was lost from water distribution systems (see the 'Regulation of Thames Water Utilities' example). According to OFWAT (the Water Services Regulation Authority), the leakage rate in

London was approximately 25% in 2015 (OFWAT, 2015), which is extremely high compared with the rest of Europe but entirely normal for developing and emerging countries. The infrastructure of the approximately 50 000 public water works in North America is up to 100 years old and urgently requires renovation. Here, too, leaking pipes lose an estimated 2.6 trillion gallons (approx. 9.8 trillion litres) of drinking water every year (Cohen, 2012), and the incentive structures for consumers to conserve water resources are often insufficient. All in all, there is a critical need for action that is increasingly putting pressure on political and administrative authorities.

THAMES WATER UTILITIES

In 1989, Thames Water Utilities Ltd was established as a public limited company under Prime Minister Margaret Thatcher. Private capital mainly from US pension funds and London investors was invested to refurbish the dilapidated water and sewage system. The London water network consisted of 32 000 km of pipelines for drinking water and 64 000 km of sewers, all having been kept on a low technical standard for the last 150 years since their construction – with the subsequent damage being substantial. Roughly 30% of the drinking water seeped into the ground and water pressure in the pipelines constantly varied. Water quality declined because air penetrated the pipes and because of the withdrawing of waste water. Thames Water became the UK enterprise most frequently sued for environmental crimes. Following the privatisation of London's water supply, the service became even worse and the lines of the privatised water and sewage system of London deteriorated yet further.

In 1999, the German Energy Group RWE bought Thames Water. The deal made RWE the largest water and waste water enterprise in the world at that time with eight million customers for drinking water and 15 million for waste water in the London region. RWE's intention was to develop new international markets as a global player. As such, it avoided urgently needed investments and instead undertook only some measures to ease the situation.

Under Tony Blair, a regulatory authority was finally established (OFWAT, or the Water Services Regulation Authority). OFWAT is the economic regulator of the water and sewerage industry in England and Wales. It acts independently from the government and aims to provide consumers with value for money. OFWAT sets the tariffs individual water companies can charge their customers, and aims to protect the standard of service customers receive from their supplier. It forced RWE to invest €714 million into the drinking water pipelines and €470 million for the sewers between 2005 and 2010. These investments could not be passed on to customers and at the same time OFWAT limited the annual return to 6%. RWE considered these returns rather unattractive and took the opportunity of bullish capital market conditions in 2006 to sell Thames Water to the consortium Kemble Water, led by the Australian investment bank Macquarie.

During RWE's ownership, Thames Water significantly underperformed and was identified by OFWAT as one of the worst performers in the sector for leakage and customer service. After Macquarie bought Thames Water in 2007, the aim was to refocus the company on its core regulated business and implement a 'back to basics' strategy, which led to a significant improvement in the group's operations, reversing years of underperformance. Within 15 months, Thames Water demonstrated significant improvements in every key area of operational performance, including an improved water supply, a reduction in leakage and a reduction in sewerage flooding. It achieved a significant reduction in operating costs (7% compared to the previous regulatory period) and its Overall Performance Assessment score (a comprehensive measure of performance used by OFWAT) increased from 342 to 416.8 (out of a maximum of 437.5 in March 2010). The group spent an average £1 billion per annum in capital expenditures and its regulatory capital value grew by 19%, from £6.5 billion in March 2007 to £7.7 billion as of March 2010.

In 2009, the good news was clouded by the announcement that Thames Water was being fined £125 000 for pollution of the River Wandle in 2007 (Environment Agency, 2009). Since then, OFWAT has fined Thames Water several times and Cathryn Ross, chief executive of OFWAT, said on the BBC in 2014: 'It's only fair that when companies make mistakes they put it right and make sure customers are not out of pocket' (BBC News, 2014). In 2015, Thames Water outperformed regulatory targets for leakage reduction for the ninth year in a row. The overall leakage is down by a third since 2004 (OFWAT, 2015).

Due to the high cost structure in the water sector and political efforts to ensure socially acceptable prices for water meeting a basic human need, water and, in particular waste water, prices rarely cover the corresponding costs (at least in full) anywhere in the world. However, there is a strong global trend towards obtaining a greater financial commitment on the part of consumers to close this gap, which would also serve to promote consumer awareness of how best to conserve water resources.

The high level of sunk investment costs and the decreasing average cost to the operator for each additional household connected to the network (economies of scale) mean that the water sector is a natural (regional) monopoly.[8] This is not expected to change substantially in the near future, because it is highly unlikely that innovation and technical progress will open up the possibility of an entirely network-independent water supply. The water sector naturally offers fewer investment/innovation opportunities than the telecommunications sector, for example, where radio communications have led to intense competition between an adequate number of

---

[8] Dams and reservoirs, for example, are typically size-based on the reasoning of economies of scale; a small dam and reservoir might cost less in total, but would have higher costs per unit of water storage. Similarly, the additional cost of sewer pipes to bring sewage from large areas to a single waste water treatment plant rather than to two smaller plants has often been justified by the lower unit cost of treating sewage at a larger plant. Diseconomies of scale are also possible, which is why some water systems are horizontally fragmented. For example, sewer systems in flat terrain are often smaller in size than in sloping terrain because it is more difficult to move water over large distances when the terrain is flat. Discharge to natural watercourses at many, rather than a few, locations is rational, and administrative boundaries tend to correspond to the boundaries of the underground pipe system. Also, small management units may have administrative cost advantages over larger units when systems are simple and areas are sparsely populated or in case companies have different management priorities and objectives.

providers in what was formerly a monopolistic environment. Natural monopolies mean that government intervention is essential, particularly in the case of basic supplies. Accordingly, the water sector is also characterised by the fact that functions are performed by the state to a large extent, as well as by a relatively extensive need for regulation.

In emerging markets, the picture is different. Data from the World Bank indicate that private investments in water projects are four to five times more likely to default or be cancelled compared to investments in other infrastructure sectors. Between 1990 and 2014, 27% of water projects with private participation became distressed or were cancelled, compared to 5% of energy projects and 7% of transportation projects (World Bank, 2015a).

The key characteristics of the water sector can be summarised as:

- Water and the related services are essential for life.
- The withdrawal and consumption of water forms part of the natural water cycle, the anthropological disturbance of which is inevitably detrimental to humans and nature alike.
- The (organised) water sector around the world, or at least the water supply, is almost exclusively user-financed. At present, however, the prices charged for water supply and disposal rarely cover the corresponding costs.
- Passing the full cost on to the consumer would require exorbitant price increases in most cases, thereby leading to social hardship. Therefore, the water sector is a prominent example of an area requiring budget-financed subsidies and political intervention (see also Section 3.3.3).
- The necessary infrastructure facilities within the water sector are extremely capital-intensive; to date, only highly-developed countries have been able to establish them to the extent required to ensure an adequate water supply to the population.
- The (highly capital-intensive) water supply and disposal network structures in particular make the water sector a natural monopoly that requires regulation.
- In some countries, the water sector offers (vast) potential for efficiency gains through fundamental reconsideration and, where appropriate, conversion to tailored solutions within the familiar process chain, organisational and business models involving private investment and management structures as well as technical innovation.

The typical organisational structures in the water sector are as follows: water systems have traditionally been governed at municipal, regional and subnational levels. Water systems are often local or regional in scope, performing abstraction, treatment and delivery within relatively small areas compared with the distance that other utilities (such as telecoms or energy) may travel. Although water regulations are typically introduced at a national level, governance over water supplies and systems is usually performed at a municipal level. Water and waste water services have historically been a function of the municipal government, with some financial assistance from national governments that usually remain ultimately responsible for the overall policies as well as the legal, political, economic and organisational framework.

This structure is the reason the boundaries between water supply and waste water disposal systems and their organisational structures are often determined by areas of political or administrative responsibility rather than the location of watersheds or river basins. This inevitably leads to inefficiencies within the water sector. Therefore, a 'river basin approach' is used more and more around the globe and is explicitly supported by the EU in its Water Framework Directive (WFD) (European Commission, 2000b).

Such an approach considers all the water falling into one river basin or watershed and manages the needs of all residents in the watershed. This will require more supra-municipal levels of coordination and government and will help to manage all water inputs, extraction, loss and in-stream uses in the entire river basin system. Regionalised water systems in general can take advantage of managing water systems across many municipalities to reduce costs, share expertise, improve performance, enhance the security of water supply in uncertain climate conditions and address as well as manage water systems on a more appropriate watershed scale. In addition, management at a river basin level may have advantages in terms of water resource planning, demand management, infrastructure development, financing and other functions.

4.2.2 Sources of revenue and value chain elements

The main source of revenue for financing the water and waste water sector are the water and waste water charges paid by consumers (direct user-financed, see also Section 3.3.3). Pricing structures show many variations and may involve both fixed and variable components. In Chile, for example, charges vary according to geographical location, seasonal factors and consumption levels. Different prices may also be charged depending on whether the users are commercial enterprises or private households. Consumers in developing and emerging countries are often subsidised directly. One exceptional source of revenue is the pre-paid water (PPW) system that is prevalent in a number of African countries. This scheme is based on devices that use pre-paid cards to limit the consumer's water consumption to the volume paid for in advance (Johannessen, 2008).

A further source of revenue is the charges levied by network owners for the use of their network by other water providers in the form of wheeling rights.

Transparency and public involvement in decisions about rate increases are important issues in the water sector. Rapid and substantial increases in water rates can cause strong social and political reactions. Public protests and political demonstrations over price increases have occurred in many places around the world. Therefore, rate increases need to be clearly tied to communication and public involvement efforts. There is abundant evidence that people – even those on low incomes – are willing to pay for water and sanitation when the services are reliable and the cost of delivering those services is reasonably transparent, socially acceptable and understandable to customers. This suggests that the dissemination of detailed information about improvements in services, and the capital investments required to realise those improvements, is essential to the public's acceptance of increases in overall water prices.

With regard to value chain elements in the water sector, a fundamental distinction is made between water supply and waste water disposal. The corresponding functions are often performed by different institutions. In the highly decentralised German water sector, for example, around 6000 companies are active at a municipal level in each of these subsectors. Table 4.11 shows the typical value-chain elements and the assets requiring investment in each case distinguished in water supply and sewage disposal.

Water supply is composed of water catchment, transportation, treatment, storage, distribution, connection and billing. The chain begins with investment in the realisation of a water extraction plant, which must be constructed with the capacity required to achieve needs-oriented extraction in the future. Water is transported from the source via the pipelines to treatment plants, where it is treated as necessary in order to obtain the desired water quality. The storage of treated water allows sharp daily or seasonal fluctuations in demand to be absorbed. Water is then distributed to the connections in private households, agriculture, industry or

TABLE 4.11 Infrastructure for water supply and waste water disposal – value chain elements and investment opportunities

Water supply and sewage disposal systems

Value chain elements	Investment opportunities	Value chain elements	Investment opportunities
Water supply		**Sewage disposal**	
Catchment – Surface water – Groundwater	Water catchment facilities Surface water: – Water towers – Barrages – Fonts Groundwater – Wells	Handover waste water	(Necessary investments done by users)
Treatment	– Treatment plants	Transport	Regional and supra-regional separate or combined sewer systems
Storage	Natural and artificial water reservoirs: – Storage lakes – Deep basins – Fire water reservoirs – Water towers	Treatment	Decentral: separation installation (e.g. for oil and grease) Central: Sewage treatment facilities for: – Mechanical/physical – Organic – Chemical treatment
Distribution	Distribution network – Pump stations – Booster stations – Pressure pipelines – Gravity sewers – Control armatures – Hydrometric installations – Inspection manholes	Discharge of waste water, recovery, removal	Gaining streams Agriculture Disposal sites Combustion plants
Connection	– House service lines		
Billing	– Meter devices		

commerce. Depending on the local conditions, the order of the individual phases may vary or certain phases may not form part of the process, for example if the water extracted already meets the relevant quality requirements. In countries with an inadequate or non-existent network infrastructure, tankers often perform the function of water distribution to unconnected areas.

Sewage disposal is composed of transportation (after handover from the users), treatment and discharge of waste water or removal. After water is used, the resulting waste water needs to be disposed of. Waste water is directed to sewage treatment plants for physical, mechanical, biological and chemical treatment via regional and supra-regional separated or combined sewer systems. The treated water is then fed back into the natural water cycle. Depending on its composition, any residue may be used for agricultural purposes, taken to landfill sites or incinerated in combustion plants.

4.2.3 Competition and regulation

The water sector, a network industry, effectively constitutes a natural monopoly. Natural monopolies do not require nationalisation per se and, based on past experience, if nationalised, it does by no means guarantee an efficient price/volume outcome. Some kind of regulatory intervention on the part of the government is necessary, however.

From an economic perspective, water supply and sanitation utilities are considered services of general economic interest. Their economic regulation, hence, pursues three main objectives (Marques, 2010):

- Protect the interest of customers with regard to public service obligations;
- Promote efficiency and innovation;
- Ensure (water supply and sanitation) service stability, sustainability and robustness.

Following these objectives, essentially three regulatory models have been established across the world, with minor national or regional variations. These models are the 'English model', the 'French model' and the 'public operator model' (which is sometimes referred to as the German or Dutch model) (Marques, 2010).

The English model accepts the general existence of monopolies and aims to minimise their negative impacts by external regulation. This external regulation is usually defined by public authorities on a national level and administered by local or regional public authorities (Kraemer and Jäger, 1997). In many countries, a number of different regulatory authorities exist, which have an impact on water utilities. For example, in the UK there are three major regulatory authorities – the Environment Agency (responsible for water quality and resources), Drinking Water Inspectorate (responsible for the water quality delivered to customers) and OFWAT (responsible for the economic regulation of water utilities).

Typical micro-economic regulation instruments are based on profit cap regulation and/or time-period-based price regulation. Both forms of regulation may be based on the regulatory asset base (RAB) or performance point systems. These forms of micro-economic regulation follow the objective to allow water utilities to achieve a suitable operational profit.

A potential issue with the English model, which may come up in especially relatively immature water infrastructure markets, is the well-known 'principal-agent dilemma'. The regulatory authorities, by definition, have less insight and information than the utilities they control (so-called information asymmetry). This may lead to what is known as the 'Averch–Johnson effect'. The effect describes the risk of creating inefficiencies of resource allocation owing to potential over-capitalisation incentivised by a return on capital regulation (Averch and Johnson, 1962).

The French model uses market-based self-regulation through regular competitive tendering instead of a permanent regulatory authority. This approach is based on time-based contracts between municipalities and water utilities. Within these contracts, services and prices are determined and usually cover aspects of operation, strategic planning, investments and financing. The respective contract period could be up to 25 years. The regular competitive tenders of the concessions in question aim to limit profits to private investors resulting from these contracts (Wackerbauer, 2003).

Usually, the public authorities keep certain rights to influence the activities of the water utilities during a contract period in respect to urban technical development. Both the English and the French model have in common that they promote de facto the formation of large-scale vertically-integrated water and construction companies.

For the public operator model the term 'regulation' is somewhat misleading, since there is no external supervision by a regulatory body over a water utility. Instead of external regulation, the public interest and objectives of regulation, as described above, are secured via shareholder rights of public authorities, which partially or fully own such utilities. Municipalities are involved in the process of service delivery, therefore information asymmetries as described in the English model between public authorities and water utilities are limited (Wackerbauer, 2003).

The separation of the monopolistic network operations and other operative services, where competition is possible, intend to minimise the risk of inefficiencies caused by the respective regulator. The regulatory aspect of the network operation (natural monopoly) is addressed by establishing public companies (formal privatisation), which only need to cover their actual running costs via service fees. They have no objective to generate a profit. All other related services may be subject to market competition.

Although these three different models of regulation described above form the basis of most models in the water industry and are universally accepted in the water sector, many intermediary variants exist across the globe. While in certain countries the water sector has a limited degree of horizontal integration, serving only a few households (e.g. Denmark or Finland), in other countries they are characterised by a high level of horizontal integration, serving thousands of households (e.g. the UK). Hence, the country-specific situation requires selecting and adjusting the mode of service delivery and regulation.

4.2.4 Private-sector involvement

Despite its high investment costs, the water sector is highly attractive to private investors, due to the 'safe bet' scenario. This results from the specific demand situation and the ultimately high degree of price elasticity on the part of consumers, the need for substantial investment and the technical challenges (both of which reduce the number of potential bidders), the relatively low operating costs and the potential for efficiency gains. While the returns offered are often comparatively low because of relatively safe regulatory frameworks, in many instances they are accompanied by an entirely adequate risk profile. Therefore, in most industrialised countries, the water sector provides a steady and stable rate of return that makes it attractive to risk-averse investors (Gurría, 2009).

Different forms of private-sector involvement have emerged in the water sector, ranging from the purely public (with only some single services contracted to private companies), via a mixture of public and private structures, through to the purely private. As explained in Sections 3.1 and 3.2, these forms of private-sector participation are difficult to compare across countries, because the designations and terminology as well as the underlying structures are handled very differently from country to country. This statement is particularly true for the water sector and for the waste sector (see Section 4.3).

There are a number of purely public examples, for instance in the US and Canada, where the constructed water infrastructure assets are fully owned and operated by public entities. France and Germany have allowed the development of *régies* (French) and *Regiebetriebe/Eigenbetriebe* (German) (Graetz, 2008), where the utility belongs to the municipality and has no legal identity. As such, these entities are not (yet) formally privatised but do have a separate budget. This model is now criticised, typically in the EU, as being opaque. However, the model of formal privatisation also exists in Germany. In this case, a so-called *Eigengesellschaft* with a city or another public-sector body as the sole shareholder acts as the owner and operator of all assets.

A scenario where the systems themselves remain purely public but a private company provides management services to the public utility in return for a fee, and potentially also a performance bonus, is referred to as the 'management contract' model.

Dutch water companies often have mixed public–private ownership, with private investments in and public operation of assets and profit sharing up to 50% of the dividends in a structure that constitutes either a type of institutional PPP (e.g. as a temporary concession) or a partial material privatisation if the partnership is permanent in nature and the ownership of the assets lies with the company. A similar model also exists in Germany, known as the *Kooperationsmodell*.

A wide range of models provide for the continued full public ownership of all assets but involve more or less integrated, lifecycle-oriented services (design, construction, various degrees of operation and maintenance) for a certain period, with or without an investment obligation for the assets and with or without the transfer of user financing-related risks (water or waste water charges), to purely private project companies formed especially for this purpose.

'Operating contracts' and design–build–operate (DBO) schemes for procuring new assets without the involvement of private finance are becoming more common in cases where commercial risks are not intended to be transferred to the private service provider. Under most of these contracts, the public entity collects payments from customers (direct user-financed, see Section 3.3.3) or raises revenue from other sources (budget-financed), and pays the contractor for its services in the form of a regular (performance-based, for example, availability) fee. In the French *affermage* model, the private partner retains a user-driven (consumption-based) fee for the same business that is not generally equal to the customer tariff but instead is based on the volume of water sold (i.e. a type of user-driven model, 'shadow fee'). Under a design–build–operate–finance (DBFO) scheme, the private partner also finances the investments and is paid in the form of an availability payment or a user-driven payment (e.g. shadow fee).

A variation of the French *affermage* model is sometimes referred to as the 'lease model'. In this model, publicly-owned assets are leased to the private operator. The operator pays a fee for the use of the assets, which is then recovered from customers (direct user-financed model) as part of the water or waste water service charge.

Concession and franchise agreements as well as divestitures are often similar to design–build–operate–transfer (DBOT) schemes, insofar as the concessionaire or franchisee is granted the right to design, build and finance a new system or to operate an existing system and make minor improvements and collect revenues from the customers (direct user-financed model). Concessions often include the exclusive right to construct new assets, whereas franchises tend to be more limited in this respect. In the case of concessions and franchises, ownership of the respective system remains with the public. By contrast, in the case of divestitures, the concessionaire owns the assets until the end of the agreement.

Today, private-sector participation models in the water sector are quite common around the globe and have a relatively strong presence in high- and middle-income countries. The vast majority of private contracts have been granted in urban areas. This trend is most marked in East Asia, where some concessions and various BOT and service deals are managed by international private companies. China has been perceived as a potential growth market, and national private enterprises play and will continue to play an important role in other areas, such as Latin America and Eastern Europe. In contrast, low-income and poor countries such as sub-Saharan Africa, South Asia and the Middle East are not attracting much interest from private capital other than in management contracts, since political risks are quite high and willingness (or ability) to pay for services is at a very low level.

In 2010, around 10% of global consumers received water from private companies. However, a 2014 report by the Transnational Institute indicates that in higher-income nations there has been a significant trend towards the municipalities taking back ownership of previously privately-held water and sanitation services. According to the report, between 2000 and 2014, 180 water systems were reportedly 're-municipalised' by cities and communities in 35 countries, including Buenos Aires, Johannesburg, Paris, Accra, Berlin, La Paz, Maputo and Kuala Lumpur. There were 36 cases in high-income countries with over 100 cases in the US and France alone. Those in developing countries tended to be bigger cities than those in richer countries (Transnational Institute, 2014). There are different reasons that contribute to this overall trend, which could be seen as part of a continuous cycle of political intervention for and against private-sector involvement within the water sector, which result sometimes in a higher or lower number of investment opportunities.

Only a few transnational corporations (TNCs) are well established in the water sector. With about 19 companies – all based in OECD countries – holding the majority of contracts, the market is highly concentrated; for example, one company has more than 25 million customers on four continents (OECD, 2006).

THAMES TIDEWAY TUNNEL LTD (TTT)

TTT is a regulated utility company that designs, constructs and has financed a 25-km sewer tunnel needed to prevent untreated sewage discharging into the tidal River Thames in London. The planning decision was taken in 2014, with the main works to start in early 2016 and with completion envisaged by 2022/23. The company has its own licence with revenues determined by the regulator OFWAT, and will collect bill payments for the tunnel via Thames Water. Thames Water will continue to provide water and waste water services to its customers as it does now. Investors were invited to bid for TTT in a competitive procurement process run by Thames Water. This process is a new way of forming a utility company and as such could be seen as a private–private partnership.

Thames Water was responsible for securing planning consent (referred to as a Development Consent Order) and acquiring the land needed to construct the project.

The cost of the project will be borne by Thames Water's 15 million customers through an average increase in annual charges of up to £70–£80 per household, on 2011 prices, excluding inflation. The increase will be introduced gradually between 2014 and the early 2020s as the project is developed and constructed. Once completed in 2023, Thames Water will operate the facility as an integral part of the London sewage network and will be responsible for its day-to-day maintenance. Around £1.4 billion of the Thames Tideway Tunnel's construction cost will be financed by Thames Water and £2.8 billion by TTT Ltd, which in turn is financed by private investors; predominantly (UK) pension funds but also the German Allianz insurance, and Swiss investors, among others. Thames Water will fund development costs, enabling works and interface works.

> TTT will enter into contracts with construction companies for three areas in east, west and central London to build the project. When formed, the company will receive support from government against exceptional risks. This will reduce the cost of the project (Thames Tideway Tunnel, 2015).

4.2.5 Sustainability considerations

The most important ESG issues of water supply and disposal relate to climate change, water scarcity, urbanisation, pollution, poor governance and risk to human health. In this section, we will focus on sustainability considerations to the extent they are relevant for investors in water supply and disposal infrastructure, rather than on general sustainability issues related to water. For a comprehensive overview of ESG risks, please refer to Section 5.2.4.

4.2.5.1 Environmental   Climate change warms the atmosphere and alters the hydrological cycle. It is effectively changing the amount, timing, form and intensity of precipitation and the flow of water in watersheds, as well as the quality of aquatic and marine environments. Climate change affects the quality of water resources and, as a consequence, public health and safety.

The potential impacts from climate change will further stress existing water supply and disposal systems. Impacts include water scarcity in some regions owing to changes in snow pack and seasonal runoff patterns, saltwater intrusion in groundwater aquifers from rising sea levels, water supply and sewage systems vulnerable to flooding and extreme precipitation events (e.g. dam breaches) and failure in storm water systems owing to increased rainfall and resulting runoff. More frequent heavy rains can increase the amount of runoff into rivers and lakes, polluting them with sediment, trash, animal waste pollutants and other materials, thus making water supplies unusable, unsafe or in need of treatment. In coastal areas, rising sea levels affect freshwater resources as saltwater moves into freshwater areas, while drought may cause water resources to become more saline as freshwater supplies from rivers are reduced, both effects resulting in an increased need for desalination (EPA, 2015a).

On the water supply side, in many areas climate change may lead to an increase in water demand putting additional pressure on shrinking water supplies. This presents a challenge for water resource management to meet the needs of stakeholders, that is growing communities, farmers and ranchers, energy producers, manufacturers and, last but not least, sensitive ecosystems (EPA, 2015b).

Perhaps one of the most significant, recent examples of regional water scarcity is the severe drought that has persisted in the state of California over the last five years (2010–2015). With water reservoirs at 5% of their normal seasonal level, the state government proposed regulations in April 2015, which provided emergency relief to drought-stricken cities and communities, including food aid and drinking water and put state-wide mandatory water restrictions in place (Gambino, 2015). In addition, it earmarked hundreds of millions of dollars to fund long-term projects involving water recycling, conservation awareness and flood control projects.

In addition, water is wasted. Owing to crumbling infrastructure, drinking water and waste water systems face increasing challenges in maintaining and replacing their pipes, treatment plants and critical technology. Even in developed countries, 30–40% of urban water supply is currently lost through seepage and poor infrastructure (McKinsey, 2009) (see also Thames

Water case study in Section 4.2.1). In the US alone, an estimated 14–18% of daily water use, or over 20 million of cubic metres of treated water, is wasted every day (CNT, 2013). Further adding to water scarcity is the inefficient use of water, especially in agriculture, which consumes more than 70% of fresh water globally.

On the water disposal side, the main environmental risks relate to pollution and environmental degradation. It is estimated that over 80% of all waste water worldwide (90% in developing countries) is currently neither collected nor treated (UN Water, 2014b). Sewage that is dumped into water bodies, such as rivers or lakes, or in estuary or coastal areas creates a human health hazard and can negatively affect aquatic ecosystems. While the application of sewage sludge can address potential deficiencies in soil fertility, plants and animals as well as positively affect biodiversity of fauna and flora (e.g. use of sewage sludge as an agricultural fertiliser), excess levels of pollutants reduce the biodiversity of terrestrial and aquatic flora and fauna (SNIFFER, 2008). In addition, the contamination of urban groundwater by sewage leakage is a topic of public and regulatory concern. In Germany alone, an estimated 100 million cubic metres of waste water leaks every year from damaged sewerage systems into the soil and the groundwater, and the main source of groundwater contamination stems from chloride and nitrogen compounds (Eiswirth and Hölzl, 1997).

In order to prevent or limit environmental damage and to mitigate the risks related to water scarcity, there is an urgent need for sustainable water supply and disposal infrastructure assets. Futureproofed water infrastructure assets intended to be resilient against physical impact from climate change, and adaptable to climate-change effects (e.g. water treatment plants and sewage systems that can deal with extreme climate situations), should be resource efficient (e.g. no leakage of fresh water) and not pollute the environment (e.g. leakage of waste water). In addition, the environment and intact ecosystem services can build resilience to climate change and reduce vulnerabilities in communities and economies. Hence, they need to be protected. Well-functioning watersheds, intact floodplains and coasts provide water storage, flood control and coastal defence (IUCN, 2009).

4.2.5.2 Social Given the current circumstances, water resources will be exhausted in many areas in the foreseeable future. In less than two decades the demand of water is expected to exceed supply by at least 40% (water gap) (McKinsey, 2009). Already today, residents of areas exposed to temporary water scarcity feel the stress during exceptional droughts (e.g. southern California and São Paulo in 2014). In China, the situation is severe: 60% of China's close to 700 sprawling cities do not have enough water and 110 of them (among them major cities such as Beijing and Tianjin) are suffering from serious shortages (China Water Risk, 2010). The recently completed South–North water transfer pipeline should help mitigate those effects.

The expected shortage of water is exacerbated by population growth and urbanisation and presents one of the gravest risks to humanity. Moreover, 750 million people, or approximately one in nine people, around the world lack access to safe water (UNICEF, 2014), and as a consequence are exposed to increased health risks such as malaria, cholera and schistosomiasis as well as diarrheal diseases caused by water polluted with microorganisms whereby most victims tend to be children.

A topic of concern is increasing water prices. Water is seen as a fundamental right from which poorer people should not be excluded. Water prices in the US, for example, rose by 90% on average from 2006 to 2010; in some areas, they almost tripled over the same period. This is due to increasing demand, maintenance and, partially, energy costs, failing infrastructure, faulty metering as well as flat-out theft, which costs money (CNT, 2013).

Investors in water supply and sewage infrastructure assets are exposed to significant reputational risks (and the related financial damage) if such infrastructure presents health hazards to populations and communities resulting from, for example, polluted drinking water or waste water contaminating groundwater or if the water supply infrastructure cannot provide clean water at affordable prices. Sharply rising water prices are the subject of much political debate.

As with any infrastructure operation, there are health and safety risks (and the related reputational risks) for workers of water treatment plants, particularly in connections with exposure to hazardous substances. This applies especially to countries with poor labour standards and environmental regulations.

4.2.5.3 Governance The UN states in its first *World Water Development Report* (2003) that the water crisis is essentially a crisis of public governance – which private investors cannot change, yet are affected by it – with societies facing a number of social, economic and political challenges as to how to govern water more effectively (UN, 2003). Water governance is defined as the established political, economic, social and administrative systems and processes related to the development and management of water resources and services (OECD, 2009). How a country manages its water resources strongly impacts the health of its people, the success of its economy, the sustainability of its natural environment and its the relations with its neighbours (Rogers and Hall, 2003).

The political and institutional context of a country shapes the provision and governance of its water systems and affects different stakeholders at different levels. While the government carries the overall responsibility for water provision, in many countries private sector companies are in charge of managing water, allocating resources and organising service provision to a certain extent. Governance issues relate to the decision-making processes about water use, extraction, storage and discharge, as well as the allocation between competing uses, including allocations to maintain basic environmental ecosystem services (World Bank, 2006). In many countries, the unclear roles and responsibilities of the people and organisations involved in water governance, territorial fragmentation as well as limited capacity at the local administrative level prevent effective water management (GWP, 2015). Particularly in areas of water scarcity, governance issues arise from the involvement of different stakeholders, such as state, regional and communal governments, multi-stakeholder/basin organisations, community-based organisations, the private sector and civil society. Different users (e.g. private households vs. corporate sectors) and different types of use (e.g. private households, agriculture, industry, tourist development, ecosystem services) result in overuse of aquifers and surface water.

Water governance issues are very relevant to investors in the sector, especially as infrastructure investments are long-term by nature. In addition, general governance issues need to be considered, in particular corrupt business and administrative practices, weak public and corporate governance structures, management incentive systems and the rule of law, including its enforceability, particularly in emerging economies.

4.3 WASTE DISPOSAL

4.3.1 Characteristics and organisation

'Waste' can be described as raw materials that are in the wrong place. This serves to illustrate the importance of the waste sector, given that the vast majority of the items that enter the materials cycle will become waste in the short, medium or long term. According to the European Commission, 2.5 billion tonnes of waste are generated in Europe every year. This corresponds to approximately six tonnes per head of population. The largest waste producers are individual households and commercial enterprises, industry, agriculture, construction and demolition, mining and quarrying, and power generation (European Commission, 2010). In Europe, the volume of resources consumed that are classified as waste in accordance with the generally accepted definition rose from an average of 60 kg per person per year in 1950 to approximately 480 kg today (Eurostat, 2013). Waste has become a hot topic because populous, high-growth economies such as China, India, Russia and Brazil are expected to reach similar volumes in the medium term. The smaller nations of Africa, Asia and Latin America are also undergoing a process of industrialisation. Thus, the waste sector faces the particular challenge of having to respond to the inevitable scarcity of resources, due to their limited nature and the burden on the environment, while simultaneously ensuring the management of the waste. As such, the waste sector around the world – like the water and energy industries – is under pressure to evolve and innovate because of sustainability considerations such as global environmental protection and resource conservation.

'Waste' is a catchall term for objects, substances, residues and leftovers that have lost their value for their users, who therefore no longer wish to keep them. From a legislative perspective, waste constitutes anything that is thrown away. In other words, everyone who creates waste and wishes to dispose of this waste must observe the corresponding statutory provisions.

A large amount of waste can be recycled or even reused, meaning it does not need to be sent to a combustion plant or landfill site (Umweltdatenbank, 2009). Waste comprises several categories, as illustrated in Figure 4.3. This diagram shows only the most common forms of municipal waste owing to the different and, in some cases, highly specific characteristics of industrial, construction and demolition waste. Producers are defined as all people or organisations whose activities generate waste and/or who treat, combine or otherwise process this waste in such a way as to change its nature or composition (European Commission, 2006).

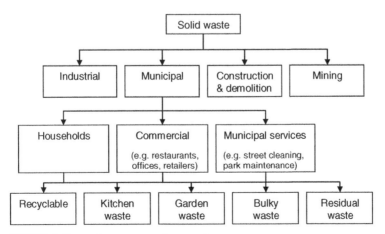

FIGURE 4.3   Major sources and types of waste
Source: Kleiss (2008). Reproduced by permission of T. Kleiss

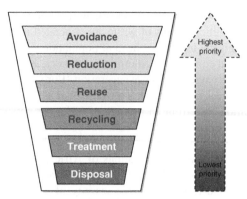

FIGURE 4.4   Waste management hierarchy
Source: Adapted from Kleiss (2008)

The key functions and areas of responsibility in the waste sector are:

- Creation of the legal framework for waste disposal, and the corresponding ordinances (definitions of waste, abandonment and disposal, recycling requirements, reacceptance obligations, municipal statutory law, fee legislation, approval procedures for waste treatment plants, etc.);
- Recognition of the volumes, types, composition and origin of waste (methods of investigation, toxicological evaluation);
- Strategic waste sector planning (local, regional, national), development of waste sector concepts and plans including all relevant aspects and phases of waste management;
- Waste collection, transportation, recycling and disposal, including the monitoring of these processes and the monitoring of landfill sites after their closure;
- Permanent search for waste prevention opportunities, e.g. through advice and consulting.

The performance of these functions may be organised in various forms and allocated to different public offices and private companies. Notwithstanding, there is a globally recognised waste hierarchy (see Figure 4.4). This hierarchy serves to facilitate optimal waste management from an environmental perspective by presenting the options for dealing with waste in the order from most preferable to least preferable. The higher a strategy is ranked within the hierarchy, the more positive its impact in terms of the environment and resource conservation.

The top of the diagram is formed by waste avoidance, followed by waste reduction. These approaches conserve energy and resources by not expending them in the first place. Reuse also prevents the consumption of resources for new production; however, this depends on the extent to which the properties of the product and/or materials are suitable for reuse. The question of the 'secondary market', that is whether there is sufficient demand for recycled products, is also relevant. This level of the hierarchy is followed by recycling strategies, waste treatment and disposal.

Broadly speaking, the creation of waste indicates that the relevant systems and processes are not optimally designed. In economic terms, it makes little sense to spend money and resources on both the creation process and the subsequent disposal process. The question whether concepts that are seen in nature, such as the 'cradle-to-cradle' model, could also be applied to the waste generated by humans is a topic of ongoing research. Under this approach, waste is considered equivalent to food. The cradle-to-cradle concept is based on the intention to develop highly-profitable products, the components of which are suitable for circulation in biological and technical nutrient cycles, and thereby have a positive impact on the environment and health at the same time. This contrasts with the 'cradle-to-grave' model, in which the material flows relating to a product are often designed with little concern for resource conservation, and where materials and products often disappear into landfill sites or incinerators or are even accumulated in ecological systems at the end of their natural life, never to be seen again (EPEA, 2009). These approaches also serve to underline the vast potential for innovation within the waste sector.

European waste policy follows the principles of the waste hierarchy. Environmental protection and hence waste legislation form part of the core responsibilities of the EU. In order to harmonise the requirements on waste prevention, recycling and environmentally sound waste disposal within the EC, the EC has issued a number of directives and regulations since 1974, making an important contribution to the development of waste legislation in its member states. The EU Waste Strategy (1997) and Waste Prevention and Recycling Strategy form the strategic backbone of this development. The Waste Framework Directive is the central EU directive on waste, representing the general area of European waste law that sets out the definition of waste, waste disposal measures and the producers and owners covered by the legislation, as well as the general obligation of the member states to prevent waste and ensure its environmentally sound recycling and disposal.

In Europe, the waste hierarchy began to be established as political credo in most countries in the mid-1980s and formed the basis for national Waste Management Acts. The fundamental environmental policy principles are: (i) the precautionary principle, (ii) the polluter pays principle and (iii) the cooperative principle. These principles are reflected in the responsibility borne by product manufacturers, who are required to address the environmental impact and potential risks during the lifetime and disposal phases of their products in their role as polluter ('precaution'). In conjunction with the other parties involved in the process – producers, distributors, consumers, disposal and recycling companies and government offices ('cooperation') – manufacturers are obliged to establish a system that minimises the adverse environmental impact and maximises the continued utilisation of the goods in question (recycling, reuse).

A further key element is the Packaging Ordinance. Companies that manage their own disposal obligations and dual systems must recycle a certain proportion of the packaging they put into circulation (for companies that manage their own disposal) or declare (in the case of dual systems). The recycling rates are the same for both variants and depend on the respective material. Waste glass, waste paper, old clothes, compost and biodegradable waste, packaging, bulky waste and special waste are collected from private households separately and taken for recycling by the public waste disposal authorities or private waste disposal companies.

In developing and emerging countries, there is often still a distinct shortage of waste management services, with conurbations and, in particular, rural areas not yet connected to the system to a sufficient extent. In the poorest countries, waste collection services may only be provided to some 10–40% of the inhabitants of a city. In middle-income countries, the waste disposal system reaches 50–85% of urban inhabitants. Despite the recommendations of the waste hierarchy, however, the majority of the waste collected is simply taken to the nearest landfill site without any effort to apply one or more alternative strategies. A further complicating factor is that these landfill sites often lack the necessary horizontal sealing, meaning that pollutants from waste and conversion processes can find their way into the groundwater and nearby bodies of water.

The key characteristics of the waste sector can therefore be summarised as:

- Extremely relevant in terms of the environment and resource conservation;
- Global agreement on the waste hierarchy as a strategy;
- Waste as a 'product of value' has a wide range of origins and potential uses;
- A high degree of international variance in terms of waste production volumes and management systems within the waste sector;
- The need for comparatively restrictive legal and institutional conditions at a national level in order to implement the strategies imposed at an international level;
- A large degree of innovative potential in both technical and organisational terms.

In light of these facts, it is not surprising that the waste sector is generally considered a public function. Accordingly, the organisation of the waste sector is largely dominated by the public sector. At the same time, there is a comparatively high level of private-sector involvement around the world, which is positive, providing they are structured correctly and with a sense of proportion. As in other infrastructure sectors, the identification and strict separation of sovereign and delegated functions is a good starting point.

The option of allowing services to be performed in a more or less comprehensively integrated manner, either by public companies or with the assistance of the private sector acting as agents, is only feasible with delegated functions. In its role as principal, the public sector always retains responsibility for identifying demand, specifying the remuneration mechanisms and monitoring the correct performance of the services due. However, the fact that these functions remain with the public sector does not necessarily mean that it pays the private companies directly for services rendered. The charges collected from waste producers such as households and industry may also flow directly to the private service provider under the terms of concessionary arrangements (direct user-financed).

Waste disposal is largely seen as a municipal function and hence falls within the responsibility of the relevant municipalities. This responsibility remains unaffected even if individual steps in the value chain are delegated to private companies. The waste sector in the EU member states is organised along these lines. Responsibility for waste disposal from households and commercial enterprises remains with the relevant municipalities and the corresponding associations that have been formed between municipalities for various reasons. The public authorities are free to decide whether to perform the relevant tasks themselves or to contract private companies to this end. It is more common for private companies to be contracted with the collection of recyclable materials than regular household waste. Potential institutional arrangements involving cooperation between the public and private sector could include concessions, mixed-ownership companies, leases, trading partnerships or cooperatives where share capital is only partially held by the relevant municipality (Gaßner and Kanngießer, 2002).

WASTE DISPOSAL IN THE UK

Until early 2000, the waste market in the UK has been a special case in Western Europe: it represented one of the least developed markets with a dependency on landfill at over 70%, the reason being that landfill generates considerably lower immediate costs in comparison with alternatives such as incineration or gasification of waste. Of a total of 28.2 million tonnes of municipal waste produced in 2000/01, 79% (23 million tonnes) was landfill. Just 12% was recycled or composted and 8% was incinerated with energy recovery. At the same time, with the waste being produced in the UK growing by approximately 3% every year, this was one of the fastest growth rates for waste in Europe (Greenery Theme, 2008).

The EU Landfill Directive of 1999 aims 'to prevent or reduce as far as possible negative effects on the environment, in particular the pollution of surface water, ground-water, soil and air and on the global environment, including the greenhouse effect, as well as any resulting risk to human health, from the landfilling of waste, during the whole life-cycle of the landfill' (European Commission, 1999). It required the UK to reduce landfill use by 65% between 1995 and 2020, and was brought into force in the UK on 15 June 2002, as the Landfill (England and Wales) Regulations 2002. Only since then has the UK begun seriously to work on finding new waste solutions and moving away from the traditional reliance on landfill even though it had introduced some kind of landfill tax in early 1996, which at the time represented the first ever environmental tax in the UK.

The applied landfill tax in the UK worked such that the standard rate per tonne of waste charged increased every year from its introduction by £8 until 2014. Since June 2015, the tax stands at £82.60 per tonne and has a floor of £80 until 2020. In addition, utility companies are required to generate a certain percentage of their electrical power from non-fossil fuels (the biodegradable portion of the biomass from waste qualifies as such). This portion of non-fossil-based power receives one or, depending on the technology applied, two Renewable Obligation Certificates (ROCs) per megawatt hour of generation, which can be traded, and the value of which depends on the demand in the market.

According to EU legislation, since October 2007 pre-treatment of waste is required, meaning that all non-hazardous waste (including commercial and industrial) has to be pre-treated before it can go to a landfill site (pre-treatment has to comprise physical, thermal, chemical or biological processes), which considerably increases the cost of landfill. The purpose of this treatment is to change the characteristics of the waste to reduce its volume or its hazardous nature, facilitate its handling and/or enhance its recovery (Greenery Theme, 2008).

The combination of these measures, despite the wholesale energy market standing only at around £37/MWh (price March 2016), makes certain, selected waste to energy plants an attractive business case for private investors. Private capital usually recognises interesting investment opportunities when they are put in place. The total value of the UK waste management market is currently assessed at around £12 billion. The sector is expected to expand, with the UK Treasury forecasting growth of 3.1% for waste management and 4% in recovery and recycling on an annual basis (UK Waste, 2014). This situation illustrates once more that it is in the hands of the regulator to make a market attractive or unattractive for private investors to enter.

WASTE SEPARATION IN GERMANY

Waste separation is given particular attention in Germany. The company Duale System Deutschland GmbH (DSD) operates the most widespread German waste separation system. As one of a total of nine service providers, the company runs a nationally approved dual system for the collection and subsequent recycling of waste packaging. DSD does not collect, transport and sort waste packaging itself, but instead contracts other waste disposal companies to perform these tasks by way of tender. To this end, the Federal Republic of Germany is divided into service regions for which interested waste disposal companies can submit individual bids. Industrial enterprises who wish to place the Grüner Punkt (Green Dot) symbol on their products in order to signify that they can be recycled via the DSD system must pay a corresponding licence fee to the DSD.

4.3.2 Sources of revenue and value chain elements

Like the water sector, the waste sector is primarily financed by user charges (direct user-financed, see Section 3.3.3), as well as government subsidies (budget-financed, see also Section 3.3.3). Fee systems may have a single-tier or multi-tier structure. Multi-tier systems may allow, for example, for basic or flat-rate fees to be charged depending on the area of land, the number of inhabitants of a house, the number of households or the number of containers, whereas single-tier only relates to one of the criteria. An (additional) rental fee may also be charged for refuse containers. Performance fees may be charged on the basis of the volume of the container, the number of collections or the weight or volume of the waste collected. Revenue may also be generated in the downstream steps in the value chain, depending on the treatment of the waste collected. In the case of incineration, for example, the energy generated from the incineration process may be sold. Innovative approaches, for example in São Paolo, generate energy from landfill sites by collecting the gases arising from the seepage water in the deep layers of the site, bringing them to the surface in a controlled manner using vertical pipes and harnessing them for energy production.

Waste utilisation plants also separate out reusable materials such as scrap metal and return them to the market in the form of raw materials. There are three major types of treatment plants – mechanical or biological treatment plants and a combination thereof (mechanical biological treatment plants, MBTs). A key advantage of an MBT is that it can be configured to achieve several different goals. In line with the EU Landfill Directive and national recycling targets, these include: the pre-treatment of waste, diversion of non-biodegradable and biodegradable municipal solid waste through the mechanical sorting of materials for recycling and/or energy recovery as refuse-derived fuel among other functions (DEFRA, 2013).

In France, the municipal waste sector is financed in a variety of ways. One is the collection of a national waste tax, which is then fed into the general budget. This tax, which dates back to the 1920s, is part of the tax levied on developed land. In rural areas, municipalities are entitled to reduce the tax rate to reflect the frequency of collection. In addition to waste tax, a special fee may be levied depending on the quality of the waste disposal services provided.

In Spain, bylaws on fee increases are resolved at municipal level in accordance with the applicable municipal finance legislation. The monthly flat-rate fees charged are broken down on the basis of residential, commercial, office and industrial properties. All natural or legal persons who own or use the corresponding property types are required to pay these fees (Gaßner and Kanngießer, 2002).

Table 4.12 provides an overview of the stages in the value chain to which additional investment opportunities can be allocated. It must be noted that not all the stages in the value chain listed in Table 4.12 are always performed. In many developing and emerging countries, the waste system consists solely of the collection, transportation and disposal stages (Kleiss, 2008). All the intermediate stages may be encountered depending on the respective national strategy and the level of development in the national system, with differences between the individual regions of a country in some cases. The existing stages in the value chain may be covered and implemented by one or more operators (see Section 4.3.1).

Collection is performed individually at the respective point of origin using plastic sacks, bins and containers, which may allow waste to be separated at an early stage, depending on how numerous they are. In many European countries, for example, household and commercial waste is separated into plastics and packaging, waste paper, waste glass, easily biodegradable material (compost) and residual waste. Separation may be performed in the individual households or at local collection points (containers). The methodology varies depending on the region and federal state. Waste collection and the subsequent transfer phase may run seamlessly into one another.

Collection is performed using heavy goods vehicles and other machinery. Private households and commercial enterprises in many countries are mostly served by dustcarts that go from door to door or from container station to container station. The collection phase consists of the collection of waste at the respective point of origin through to its delivery to the transfer stations.

Transfer stations generally take the form of closed buildings in order to prevent dust, noise and smells from reaching the outside world. Transport stations are used to ensure that collection vehicles are not required to travel long distances, as well as to perform functions such as waste pre-treatment, separation for further processing and temporary storage. Sorting and aggregation serve to facilitate the reuse of suitable materials (e.g. metal) and to prepare further treatment. Temporary storage means larger volumes of waste can be transported in a continuous and controlled manner to the relevant treatment facilities using different modes of transportation.

Treatment, however, is only the next-but-one stage in the predominant waste sector value chain in developed countries. Waste must first be transported to the relevant plants using appropriate transport carriers. Depending on the distance and volumes involved, this may involve the road and rail networks and waterways. Once waste arrives at a waste treatment plant, it is treated using various methods with the aim of minimising its negative impact on the environment. The appropriate methods of treatment may vary substantially depending on the type of waste as well as the procedures for further treatment. In the case of thermal procedures, such as combustion, pyrolysis as well as gasification and composting, waste treatment may also serve to generate energy. For example, the heat resulting from incineration can be fed into the network and used for district heating (see also Section 4.6). The materials remaining after treatment may also be transferred for further treatment or, if this is not possible, taken to a landfill site.

In developed nations, disposal – which replaces the treatment stage in a number of countries – is usually the last resort for waste that cannot be treated further using any of the above methods. Landfill sites are established in accordance with the specific physical

TABLE 4.12 Waste disposal infrastructure – value chain elements and investment opportunities

Value chain elements	Investment opportunities	Value chain elements	Investment opportunities
Waste collection and treatment		**Waste recycling and disposal**	
Generation/Separation	– Collecting basin		
– Industrial waste	– Separating (e.g. recovered glass and paper)		
– Municipal waste			
– Building site waste			
– Disassembled demolition waste			
Collection	– Trucks		
– Door-to-door	– Street cleaner		
– Street cleaning	– Other machines		
– Square maintenance			
Transfer	– Collection and sorting halls incl. machines	**Commercialisation**	– Appropriate facilities
– Sorting	– Treating stations	– Recycling products	
– Aggregation			
– Further pre-treatment		⇦	
Transport	– Trucks	**Land filling and processing**	– Landfills
– Common carriers	– Trains	– Collection	– Seepage water plants and landfill gas treatment plants
– Owner-operator	– Ships	– Landfill operation	– Converting plant for recovery of recyclables
– Others		– Further processing	
Treatment	– Combustion plants	**Commercialisation**	– Transmission networks and facilities
– Waste incineration	– Composting plants	– Energy	
– Mechanical/Biological	– Recycling plants	– Electricity	
– Treatment	– Other treatment plants (energy generation, e.g. block heat and power plant)	⇦	
– Composting	– Extraction of energy supply contributes (e.g. pellets) and metals	**Commercialisation**	– Appropriate facilities
– Gasification		– Compost	
– Post treatment		⇦	
– Special treatment			
– Others			

Residuals

Source: Kleiss (2008). Reproduced by permission of T. Kleiss

and chemical properties of the waste materials and the regional, hydrological and climatic characteristics of the location. This generally requires extensive planning and comprehensive expertise. One common variant is the filling of specially created dumps that are then covered with soil or other suitable materials. Alternatively, waste may be stored in abandoned quarries or salt mines, because these offer particular properties with regard to groundwater (Kleiss, 2008).

4.3.3 Competition and regulation

As with the provision of water, electricity and communication, the waste sector forms part of the wider provision of subsistence and was dominated by public structures for a long period. Since the 1990s, however, the sector has seen a growing trend towards liberalisation and the transfer of services to the private sector.

Waste collection and waste treatment are two distinct activities. Economies of density determine whether competition may take place in a market. Few countries rely on in-the-market competition (i.e. continuous market competition as a form of self-regulation) for the collection of household waste, whereas it is possible and common for industrial and commercial waste collection. While waste collection of household waste can be efficiently provided through for-the-market competition (i.e. in the form of individual tenders for individual projects with a certain duration), the actual efficiency results depend on the characteristics of the competitive tendering procedure, the contract itself and its enforcement (OECD, 2013).

The need for regulation in the waste sector results from an understanding of the environment being a public good and the fact that unpolluted land and water have become scarce resources because of environmental contamination from, among other things, waste. Because it is essentially impossible to implement exclusion mechanisms for benefiting from a clean environment, there is no incentive for industry or private households to contribute voluntarily to an improvement in environmental quality, for example by reducing their waste output. This holds particularly if waste producers are not required to pay waste charges.

The tendency of the waste sector to form a natural monopoly and the corresponding disadvantages with regard to potential competition are best examined in terms of the individual steps in the value chain of waste collection and treatment. Its main components consist of gathering (collection, transfer and transportation) and removal (processing, further treatment, disposal and marketing).

For waste collection, the existence of a natural regional monopoly could be justified on account of the significant economies of scale and scope associated with waste collection (German Commission of Monopoly, 2003) and – with the exception of conurbations – competition 'for the market' rather than 'in the market'. But the few sunk costs and small market power of existing providers allow for a high level of competition 'for the market'. They, hence, make external regulation unnecessary. Competitive public tenders of time-based contracts are therefore the predominantly observed form of market regulation for waste collection.

The OECD (2013) identifies the conditions necessary for competitive tendering leading to lower costs than in-house provision by municipalities of local public services. These are:

- Low sunk costs – meaning that key assets are not significantly more valuable within a particular commercial relationship than outside of it;
- No informational advantage to the incumbent;
- Ease of quality monitoring;
- A sufficient number of competitive bidders.

In contrast to waste collection, waste recycling and disposal plants involve high investments and can be used for other purposes only to a limited extent, meaning that investments represent irreversible sunk costs. Economies of scope are offered when different types of waste can be disposed of or recycled using the same facility. In the event of a further liberalisation of municipal waste disposal, irreversible costs will play an important role in terms of competition policy, particularly with regard to combustion plants, mechanical or biological plants and landfill sites.

There is no fundamental barrier to opening up the waste sector to competition at all stages of the value chain, and nor does this liberalisation necessarily endanger the relevant environmental targets. Whatever framework is put in place, it should help to improve efficiency and promote innovation. The resulting (presumably) reduction in waste disposal costs is expected to lead to broader political and public acceptance.

At the same time, the public sector cannot escape potential competition in the waste sector. This presents public waste disposal companies with an opportunity to improve their efficiency and reinforce their market position against the threat of private-service providers entering the market, assuming the latter are given the opportunity to play by the same rules. Examples of this are found in practice and are discussed in the next section (4.3.4).

4.3.4 Private-sector involvement

While the public sector is typically responsible for the disposal of household and commercial waste, private companies are involved in the performance of functions in one form or another throughout the entire value chain around the world.

More and more functions are being transferred to the private sector in various European countries, particularly in the area of waste collection and treatment, with Spain (80% private collection/90% private treatment), Germany (60/90%), the UK (30/80%) and France (50/70%) leading the way. In countries such as the Netherlands (30/40%), Italy (40/30%) and Sweden (40/< 10%), it is notable that, generally, private contribution is lower. In Finland, 100% of collection is outsourced to private contractors while more than 90% of treatment activities remain in public hands (Hall, 2006).

Owing to the high level of revenue achievable in the waste sector, private-sector involvement may be a lucrative opportunity. Power suppliers in particular are entering the waste market because incineration and gasification have a dual function, allowing both waste disposal and energy generation (see also Section 4.6). As such, it is no coincidence that the majority of incinerators are operated by power suppliers. These companies are also increasingly trying to enter the upstream stages of collection and transportation. The resulting (local), (potential) monopolies mean that they may be solely responsible for the disposal of all municipal and commercial waste.

The global players in this market are names that can also be found in largely dominant positions in other infrastructure sectors. Multinational waste disposal companies come in four categories (Hall, 2006). The list is headed by global players such as Veolia (France) or Suez Environnement (France), which are followed by their national competitors, such as Remondis (Germany) and Fomento de Construcciones y Contratas (Spain). The national companies are some two to three times larger than the next 'level' of regional players like Biffa (UK), ALBA (Germany) and AVR/Van Gansewinkel (NL). Other smaller and local companies can be found in many developed countries.

The larger companies in particular are also active in developing and emerging economies, where the waste industry, which was traditionally dominated by the public sector, is increasingly opening up to private companies – although the willingness and ability to pay for waste disposal services is still extremely low.

Various models for the transfer of functions in the waste disposal sector have established themselves internationally. For example, one or more functions may be put out to tender and transferred to private-service providers for a limited period in a competitive process. The public sector pays the private companies for the services performed, giving rise to a service agreement; in international usage, this form of functional privatisation is referred to as the 'contracting model' (see also Chapter 3).

Under the 'franchise model' (see also Chapter 3), a disposal company is granted a local monopoly. The functions transferred may vary from case to case. The company charges consumers for its services in its own right in order to cover its current expenses. Hence, it can be considered as a concession (e.g. functional privatisation model). The charges are usually subject to regulation on account of the monopoly situation. No investments are required in fixed assets under this model, but investments in movable equipment are generally necessary. Typical examples include waste collection or transportation to a landfill site.

The waste sector also uses the 'concept of concessions' (see also Chapter 3) involving major investments, such as the erection of a waste treatment plant, for example an incinerator or a composting plant. The private company is authorised to charge fees to the producers of waste in order to finance its investments and current costs; as in the case of the franchise model, these fees should be regulated. Depending on whether prices that cover the private company's costs can be realistically imposed on the market, the public sector may contribute to start-up funding in the form of subsidies. The investments involved in the construction of incinerators in particular are substantial and irreversible. Therefore, operators often seek to obtain government guarantees for long-term supply contracts, which ensure that the volume and quality of the waste delivered to the plant will use its capacity accordingly.

All three models above may also be structured as institutional PPPs or partial material privatisations with transfer of ownership of the assets according to the classification scheme introduced in Chapter 3. One example of an institutional PPP is Servus Abfall GmbH & CO. KG, which was formed in 2002 in Graz, Austria. The shareholders of Servus Abfall are the municipal company AEVG GmbH (51%) and the private company EBG Abfallentsorgung- und Verwaltungs GmbH (49%, with three private waste service providers each holding 33% of this stake). Italy has also seen the formation of a number of institutional PPPs. The public corporations surrender a portion of their share capital and, as in the Austrian example, form a new company with a private partner that is tasked with performing relevant functions.

Within the waste sector, there are also cases of free competition between several disposal companies operating in the same area. In this case, the companies are granted licences by the public authorities for the same region and offer their services in a competitive market environment, meaning that price regulation is not necessary. Each company is responsible for levying waste disposal fees from the producers of the waste in their own right.

As some older sources show, it may happen that private companies compete with public organisations, even though such a situation is not without controversy from a general market economy perspective. This may, in the short term, lead to more efficiency in the market through more transparency and the possibility of benchmarking. For example, Stockholm City Council shares responsibility for the city's waste collection with several private companies.

This competition has enabled the transparent comparison of costs within the market (Cointreau-Levine, 2000).

In the UK and US, costs have been reduced by more than 25% through the involvement of the private sector by introducing competition between public- and private-service providers. In Phoenix, Arizona, public and private companies participate in a tender procedure for services in the individual zones every seven years. After initially losing out to the private bidders, the public waste disposal companies have improved their efficiency and been able to win back a number of zones. In some countries in Latin America, costs have been cut by as much as 50%. However, fair competition must be ensured at all times. In many cases, public or publicly-dominated companies receive subsidies, giving them a competitive advantage (Cointreau-Levine, 2000).

4.3.5 Sustainability considerations

Solid waste management is a growing environmental issue, in both the developed and the developing world. More than 4 billion tonnes of waste are being generated every year, of which between 1.6 and 2 billion tonnes alone are municipal waste. Urban food waste is expected to almost double from 2005 to 2025, with food waste in landfills to increase the landfill share of global GHG emissions from 8 to 10% (ISWA, 2012). Population pressure, urbanisation and GDP/capital growth contribute to increasing waste, particularly in the developing world. According to World Bank (2012b) estimates, solid waste generation in the Asia-Pacific region alone will more than double from an estimated 1.3 million tonnes/day in 2012 to 3 million tonnes/day by 2025 (World Bank, 2012b). However, properly recycled and disposed-of waste can contribute to the circular economy as a provider of raw materials and energy.

The most relevant ESG factors for investors related to waste disposal are pollution, climate change, poor governance and risk to human health. For a comprehensive overview of ESG risk, please refer to Section 5.2.4.

4.3.5.1 Environmental
Disposing of waste in landfills or by incineration can have significant negative environmental impacts, being mainly the pollution of soil, water or air. Waste rotting in landfill sites produces bad odours and generates large quantities of carbon dioxide and methane gas, which are explosive and contribute to the greenhouse effect. Leachate, the liquid resulting from water seeping through contaminated waste, is a very harmful mixture of chemicals that may result in hazardous substances entering surface water, groundwater or soil. Pollution harms the ecosystems in and near the water, as well as humans and animals that drink it. Hazardous chemicals getting into the soil can affect plants as well as humans and animals. Moreover, landfill sites may attract vermin and rodents, which in turn may spread disease.

Waste incineration produces gases, which may cause air pollution and contribute to acid rain, while the ash from incinerators may contain heavy metals and other toxins. The burning of plastics produces toxic substances, such as dioxins. Air pollution can cause respiratory and other health problems as contaminants are absorbed from the lungs into other parts of the body. Yet, on the positive side, heat produced from incineration is increasingly reused and turned into energy used, for example, in district heating (see Section 4.6).

Climate change can influence solid waste facilities in a number of ways (USAID, 2012): while storms, flooding, rising sea levels and higher temperatures may directly affect waste disposal sites and processes, climate change may also affect waste management operations by limiting access to roads, ports and energy. Flooding is a major threat to solid waste infrastructure. Heavy precipitation and storms may undermine landfill foundation and cause breaks in the containment structure, allowing debris and leachate to escape and contaminate soil and groundwater. Rising sea levels can cause water to flow into the pits of landfills in coastal or low-lying areas, with saltwater to further deteriorate the impermeable lining of sanitary landfill facilities. Higher temperatures change the landfill degradation rates and produce stronger odours. Prolonged droughts may increase the risks of fire.

Adaptation measures are key to protecting human health and the environment from pollution and to mitigating the effects of climate change. They include properly sited, constructed and operated waste disposal facilities in order to decrease climate-change-induced risk of soil and water contamination in addition to physical protection and disaster resilience measures, as well as reducing facility needs through recycling and demand management. More frequent waste collection in residential areas may reduce the health hazards of contaminated waste, especially in high temperatures. Moreover, establishing waste sorting and recycling facilities helps to reduce solid waste. Adaptation measures are generally imposed by environmental regulations.

Long-term-oriented owners of waste disposal assets may pre-empt increasing environmental risk (e.g. from climate change or urbanisation) and the related regulatory changes and take the necessary measures early on to minimise and mitigate future environmental risks. Given the significant environmental issues related to waste management, there is a need for sustainable waste management infrastructure that does not pollute the environment and is futureproof regarding climate-change impacts.

Waste management plays a central role in a circular economy, in which resources are used for as long as possible and products and materials recovered and regenerated. Industry has already begun the transition and is starting to move away from a linear approach to waste disposal towards a resource management approach, whereby it provides raw materials and energy to the rest of the economy. Waste that currently goes to landfills (or is incinerated) can have significant economic value in terms of recoverable material feedstock under a circular economy approach (The Guardian, 2014). Moreover, the EU is spearheading proposals to embed circular economic thinking into the legislative framework (Hayler, 2014). Implementing circular opportunities carry an enormous economic potential, estimated to be worth over US$1 trillion annually in material savings (WEF, 2014b).

4.3.5.2 Social Social aspects related to waste collection and disposal are focused on public health and safety. Poor waste management creates health hazards for people. Uncollected, rotting piles of waste in the street can block drainage channels or, if dumped in watercourses, contaminate water resources and pose significant health risks to those living nearby. In addition to the health aspects, it can negatively affect the social structure of a city as people want to live in, as well as visit, clean and healthy areas instead of being exposed to poor water and air quality and the related health hazards. Cities that smell due to poor sanitation and waste disposal have a low quality of life and fare poorly on attracting investors or tourists.

A further concern are the occupational health and safety risks for solid waste workers and waste pickers (and the related reputational risks for asset owners), mainly related to working with hazardous substances. This applies especially to countries with poor labour standards and environmental regulations.

4.3.5.3 Governance Waste management issues relate to a wide range of aspects of urban governance and can be viewed as an overall indicator of urban development and sustainability. Priorities and standards of waste management services vary between countries and different urban areas. While higher-income countries concentrate on maximising waste recycling, (poorer) developing countries concentrate on providing basic collection, treatment and disposal services to growing cities.

The main groups of stakeholders in a waste management system are the (public or private sector or informal) providers of waste collection and disposal services, the users of waste management services and the (national or local) government, which provides the legal and institutional framework for waste collection and disposal services. Waste management companies are a major (public or private) employer and consume a large proportion of the operational revenue of a city or municipality. In developing countries, waste management may also be a key source of livelihood and social capital, particularly for the urban poor. Governance issues in a solid waste management system relate to management structures, labour practices, contracting procedures and corruption.

In addition, developing countries currently deploy between 20 and 50% of local and regional governmental budgets to solid waste management (UN ESCAP, 2014). Sustainable waste management strategies and infrastructure that focus on source reduction, more efficient collection and transportation, energy and material recovery, toxic and hazardous waste reduction and recycling can not only reduce direct solid waste – and as such weigh less heavily on government budgets – but also reduce the amount of GHG emissions from waste management (via reduced energy use and the capturing of methane from landfill sites). In Europe, on average about 36% of the annual 2.5 billion tonnes of solid waste are currently being recycled, with some countries in the EU still only recycling less than 20% of their solid waste (European Commission, 2010). These results could be further improved if efforts within the EU to include a circular economy approach into EU waste legislation prove successful.

4.4 ENERGY – ELECTRICITY

After a very brief overview of the energy market as a whole, this section will focus on electricity only. To this end, it will present the global electricity market, the structure of the sector as well as its value chain from generation to transmission and storage.

Within generation, this section only covers renewable electricity because of its attractive risk-return profile as well as its sustainability characteristics. It excludes energy generation from coal, oil and thermal nuclear reactors.

First, a number of cross-subsector characteristics of renewable electricity generation are explained, including technical aspects, the regulatory environment and sources of revenues, value chain elements, as well as private-sector involvement. This is followed by a systematic discussion of the individual subsectors of renewable electricity, namely solar (mainly PV), onshore and offshore wind, hydro- and bioenergy/biopower.

Following the value chain of the electricity sector, power networks/grids and the challenge of balancing them in light of the increase in energy generation from renewable sources are explained in some detail. This leads right to the last element of the value chain: power storage, which connects the previous two sections as it addresses the problem faced by transmission grids caused by renewable energy, that is storing enough electricity – predominantly generated from renewable sources – to meet demand without overloading the system.

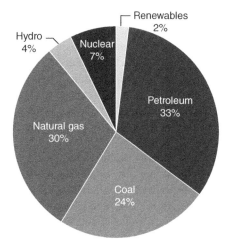

FIGURE 4.5 World energy use by source, 2014
Source: BP (2015)

4.4.1 Overview

Global primary energy consumption (including energy losses) has reached over 151 000 TWh (2014), having increased by over 60% since 1988 (or a compound annual growth rate [CAGR] of 2.5% over 25 years). Fossil fuels (oil, coal, natural gas) currently account for 87% of all energy consumed, with nuclear, hydropower and renewables making up the balance of 13% (see Figure 4.5). When considering how energy is consumed per sector of the economy, 50% is used for industry with transport and residential sectors each using 19% and the commercial sector responsible for the remaining 12% (see Figure 4.6).

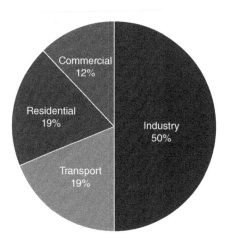

FIGURE 4.6 World energy consumption by sector, 2011
Source: IEA (2012a)

One of the main provision functions of governments involves providing a diverse range of energy products and services to end-users, namely electrical power and district heating/cooling services (from a variety of energy sources) and combustible fuels (mainly natural gas and petroleum liquids). For each of these products and services, a combination of dedicated technologies, standards, inputs and outputs, infrastructures and regulations exist from energy generation to end-use consumption. With this comes an equally diverse range of value chains and business models, which also differentiate the related infrastructure assets. All of these products and services are offered on the global energy market, which comprises a large variety of public and private players.

Although the provision of these energy products and services is undertaken via distinct subsectors within the energy industry (e.g. the electrical power sector, which again has its own related subsectors with their distinct characteristics), they cannot be considered entirely independently of each other. For example, combined heat-and-power plants (CHPs) generate both electricity and heating, new power-to-gas (P2G) technologies convert electricity into storable natural gas, new battery technologies electrify the traditionally fossil-fuel-dominant transport sector and district energy networks provide new ways to integrate electricity, heating/cooling services and energy storage. As such, investors interested in one of these energy sectors or subsectors are well advised not to lose sight of the competing sectors and their various interdependencies, which in turn impact the e.g. renewable energy markets.

4.4.1.1 Global trends in the electricity market Electricity represents around 15% of the total annual global energy consumption and is mainly generated from fossil fuels (68%) and hydropower (16%), nuclear 11% and a small (5%) but growing contribution from other renewable energy sources (RES; mainly wind, solar, biomass/waste); see Figure 4.7.

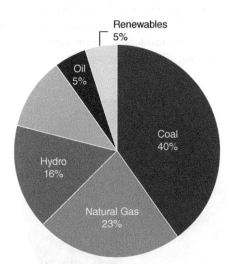

FIGURE 4.7   World electricity use by
primary source, 2013
Source: IEA (2014e)

Growth in the global consumption of electricity is expected to increase by 75% (2011–2030) with renewable energy being the fastest-growing sector which satisfies most of the

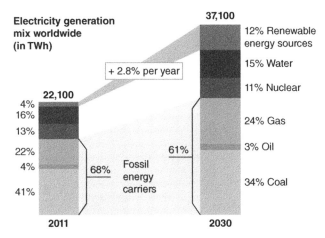

FIGURE 4.8 Power generation by energy source by 2030
Source: Siemens (2015a)

growing demand, according to a forecast by Siemens[9] (see Figure 4.8). The IEA estimates that by 2040 renewable energy plants will meet half of the additional global power demand and that they will continue to increase their share in the energy supply mix even as subsidies for renewables decline.

The development of new generation capacity of all kinds will be different in each region of the world (see Figure 4.9). In China, the demand is projected to increase by 35% by 2030, requiring significant additional generation capacities. In the rest of the world, new power capacities are expected to be crucial to enable the development of these economies.

In summary, the main trends in the global electricity markets are:

- A major increase of global power demand with a stable demand in OECD countries;
- An important increase of renewable power generation in the global energy mix (50% of the added capacities by 2050);
- A shift of new capacity needs from OECD countries to emerging countries, especially China.

4.4.1.2 Structure of electricity sector The structure of the electricity sector is still based largely on centralised power plants, unilateral transmission and distribution (T&D) networks, and minimal energy storage availability. However, the growing use of renewable energy generation plants (solar, wind, etc.) and decentralised networks (district energy), as well as the development of new energy storage technologies, is increasing the complexity of the grid, thereby challenging the existing structure of the sector around the world (see further discussion in Section 4.6).

As part of the generation process, primary energy is transformed into electricity by different conversion processes for different energy sources. Transmission system operators (TSOs) traditionally transport the electricity from the generation facilities using a high voltage

---

[9]The International Energy Agency (IEA) gives similar estimates.

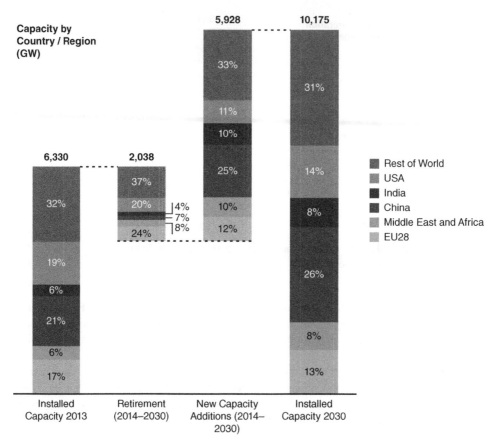

FIGURE 4.9 Power capacity evolution and forecast by region by 2030
Source: Siemens (2015a)

'transmission grid' designed to deliver electricity across long distances (see Figure 4.10). The energy in the transmission grid is sold to the market and delivered to the end-user (or customer) via distribution grids. Distribution encompasses both the medium voltage dispatch regionally and the low-voltage 'last-mile' delivery to the end-user (or customer). Distribution grids are operated by distribution system operators (DSOs), who usually handle any interaction with the end customer (see Figure 4.10). If required, and to the extent storage space is available, electricity can be stored before being fed into the grid.

The TSO together with the DSOs coordinates the dispatch of electricity in order to meet the expected demand of the entire electricity grid. If there is a mismatch between supply and demand, the system operators have to add or remove either generation or load (see Section 4.4.8 for further details).

All three kinds of electricity networks (high/medium/low voltage) are 'natural monopolies', with finite capacity and high barriers to entry. Therefore, in most countries the respective national authorities regulate the provision of these services to ensure open access to market participants.

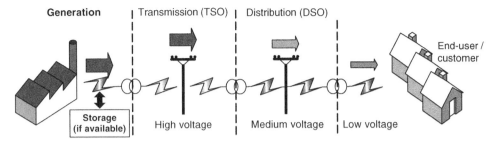

FIGURE 4.10 Current market structure of the electricity industry
Source: Rodríguez-Molina et al. (2014)

Typically, electricity markets comprise wholesalers (via the transmission grid or network), retailers (via the distribution grid) and the ultimate consumers in any geographical area. Markets may extend beyond national boundaries. Three main types of electricity trading can be identified:

- Private bilateral transaction

  Generators and consumers enter into a direct relationship by signing a long-term supplying contract, such as a power purchase agreement (PPA). The consumer, who can also be a public authority, has to take off a certain amount of electricity over a certain period. This mechanism is designed to secure both long-term sufficient electricity supply for the off-taker and predictable cash flows for the seller.
- Wholesale electricity exchange

  Competing electricity producers offer their electricity on the spot market to retail electricity sellers, who then re-price it and deliver it to end-users. The main wholesale electricity exchanges are:
  - Australia: AEMO
  - Canada: IESO in Ontario and AESO in Alberta
  - France: EPEX SPOT
  - Japan: JEPX
  - US: New York Market, Midwest Market and California ISO
- Retail electricity market

  The end-user can choose from competing electricity retailers offering various pricing schemes as well as green energy options. For example, in the UK there is a choice between a number of electricity providers, including several green energy companies that offer up to 100% electricity from renewable sources (Christie, 2015).

4.4.1.3 Value chain The electricity sector covers an enormous range of value chain elements from generation via T&D to storage, the large majority of which is discussed in this section and illustrated in Table 4.13.

Within this value chain, the most important value-added relates to the physical provision and management of the generation plants, dispatch networks and storage facilities, including planning, construction and maintenance. Accordingly, the investments are primarily channeled into this part of the value chain. The other value-added components listed under marketing, such as billing and yield management, are part of operations.

TABLE 4.13 Electricity value chain and investment opportunities

Value chain elements	Investment opportunities
Generation of renewable electricity	
– Generation and sale of electricity from solar power	– Photovoltaic plants – Concentrated solar power plants
– Generation and sale of electricity from wind (onshore and offshore)	– Wind farms (onshore and offshore)
– Generation and sale of electricity from hydropower (reservoirs and run of river)	– Hydropower plants
– Generation and sale of electricity from biomass (wood, agricultural waste, urban waste)	– Biomass plants – Storage facilities for biomass feedstock
Dispatch of electricity	
– High-voltage electricity transmission	– Transmission networks
– Medium- to low-voltage electricity distribution	– Medium-voltage (distribution) networks – Low-voltage (last mile) networks
Storage of electricity/energy	
– Pumped storage hydropower (sale of energy and system services)	– Pumped storage hydropower plants
– Network management (automated demand balancing) and quality-related storage (sale of system services)	– Smart grids – Facilities/equipment based on existing and new technologies (flywheels, batteries, etc.)
Marketing of electricity	
– Billing	– Metering devices
– Yield management (pricing)	– Customer's own storage and energy efficiency investments

4.4.2 Generation – renewable electricity – cross-sector characteristics

Renewable energy sources (RES) have the potential to contribute 50 to 90% of the total global electricity demand by 2030. In some countries, especially those with a traditionally large amount of hydropower, the share of RES of the overall electricity generation is already high. For example, in Iceland and Brazil, RES are responsible for nearly 100 and 85% of total electricity production, respectively (European Commission, 2011; REN21, 2013a). More conservative global estimates show a less dramatic yet still significant increase in RES of up to 12% by 2030 compared to 4% in 2011 (see Figure 4.8 in Section 4.4.1.1). This wide range of estimates for RES in the energy mix is the result of diverse scenarios, each based on different assumptions with respect to future national climate and energy policies and related government support schemes.

A broad variety of RES for electricity generation is available on the market, including hydropower, wind (onshore and offshore), biopower (i.e. electricity produced from biomass), solar photovoltaic (PV), concentrated solar power (CSP), geothermal and ocean (wave and tidal). Hydropower (mainly in the form of large reservoirs/dams) makes up the majority of current renewable electricity generation (74%). However, in the future, most growth will take

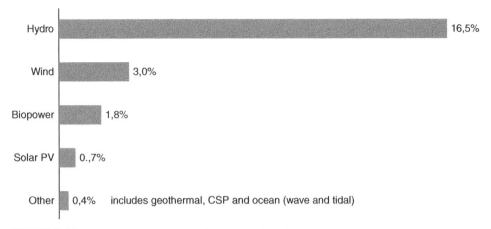

FIGURE 4.11   RES mix in global electricity generation, 2013
Source: REN21 (2014)

place in the three current largest non-hydro RES, namely wind, biopower and solar PV (see Figure 4.11). For this reason, this book will focus on these RES.

4.4.2.1   Characteristics of electricity generation   The unique electricity generation characteristics of each RES must be considered with respect to, among others, their volatility over time as well as balancing and location requirements within the overall electricity grid.

Volatility over time   Renewable electricity generation is usually incremental since it does not have inherent storage power. Most renewable energy plants can only feed electricity into the grid based on the real-time availability of the employed renewable resources (especially wind and solar PV[10]). Therefore, in many advanced electricity markets, the growing share of wind and PV energy has led to increased volatility of power fed into the grid. Wind energy generation displays by far the highest fluctuations in production patterns during the day and during the year.[11] Furthermore, wind farms seldom generate more than 30% of their annual capacities (time-based). PV, while somewhat predictable on daily and yearly cycles, is also relatively volatile, mainly because of its rapid output variations (ramp-up), especially during cloudy days. The amount of water available for hydropower generation depends on seasonal rainfall variation as well as storage capacity (size of reservoir). Biomass production (feedstock) naturally peaks in the summer and autumn, although most feedstock can be stored for later use.

Real-time balancing of electricity supply and demand   Electricity grids need to be continually balanced in order to ensure that the volume of energy fed into the grid corresponds to the volume of energy consumed by end-users. Balancing the grid is the task of TSOs and DSOs and requires forecasting of both power supply and power demand. Because renewable energy

---

[10]Photovoltaic ('PV') power generation is more predictable than wind power generation.
[11]For example, the production of energy by a German wind farm in December is twice the mean average for the year, in July/August it can be as low as half of the annual mean average.

generation (solar and wind in particular) is intermittent – and in order to encourage private investment in renewable energy – in many countries these technologies are given 'priority dispatch' on the grid when generating power. When energy supply exceeds energy demand (as can be the case during peak production of RES), non-RES electricity suppliers may have to wait before being allowed to feed their electricity into the grid. For electrical generators working on long cycles (e.g. large hydropower, nuclear power, coal-fired power), such a situation can be difficult – technically and economically – and may result in the production of power that can neither be sold on the market nor stored for lack of large-scale storage capacities. Similarly, during peaks in demand, these long-cycle sources cannot easily increase electricity production instantly.

In conclusion, energy-related laws and regulations with the aim to promote RES have fulfilled their purpose of increasing the share of renewable energy generation in the overall energy mix. For example, in 2013, the German power production from RES (approximately 150 TWh) was higher than the sum of electricity generated from nuclear and natural gas (BDEW, 2014). As indicated above, the priority dispatch of renewable energy also has negative consequences: Most importantly, it affects the predictability of power sales (and prices) – especially for conventionally generated power from long-cycle sources – as well as the crucial balancing of the grid.

Both consequences could be mitigated with large-scale electricity storage capacity. There is currently a great deal of activity involving the research and development of cost-effective energy storage systems in order to 'smooth out' the incremental nature of renewable energy generation. Many technologies exist and are developing rapidly: electrolysis of hydrogen, fuel cells, pumped storage power stations, batteries and chemical storage being among the more promising ones. However, energy storage development is still in its early stages (see Section 4.4.9 for more information related to energy storage).

Location of generators and grid connection Large-scale renewable energy plants (especially wind and solar) require sizeable land areas – or other surfaces in the case of solar – and are thus often far from urban areas, where most power is consumed. Therefore, the costs for accessing a transmission grid need to be taken into account when assessing the economic feasibility of a project. This is particularly true for offshore wind projects but also for hydro power projects located in remote mountainous areas and some solar projects located in desert areas.

4.4.2.2 Regulatory environment and sources of revenues

Renewable energy technologies, for the most part, are still emerging and therefore still require regulatory intervention (subsidies/incentives) in order to compete effectively with the – often also subsidised – conventional electricity market. The Nationally Appropriate Mitigation Actions (NAMAs) are a set of support schemes developed in 2007 by the United Nations Framework Convention on Climate Change (UNFCCC) in 2007 (see Appendix D).

The two main support schemes (or mechanisms) introduced by regulators around the world are: feed-in tariffs (FITs) and the renewable portfolio standards (RPSs) accompanied by renewable energy certificates/credits (RECs).

Feed-in tariffs (FITs) FITs offer cost-based compensation to renewable energy producers by providing price certainty with long-term contracts, which in turn help to finance and thus promote renewable energy investments. When granting FITs, an authority obligates electric utilities to pay established above-market rates for an agreed period for all renewable power fed into the grid. The utility can pass through these higher rates to either the regional or the national government (budget-financed [see Section 3.3.1–3.3.2], initially used in Spain) or to the end-user (direct user-financed [see Section 3.3.3], used in, for example, Denmark, Finland, France, Germany, Japan and Spain). Hence, the utility itself does not take any price risk. In addition, RES is guaranteed priority to the grid via a priority dispatch mechanism. Two main forms of FIT exist: fixed FITs and premium payment FITs.

Fixed FITs   The regulator guarantees a long-term (12- to 20-year) pricing scheme (or tariff) to the producer for the sale of all electricity generated. Such schemes often include 'tariff digression', a mechanism by which the tariffs offered for new plants decrease over time. The reduction may be related to the point in time a new plant connects to the grid or to the amount of megawatts already connected to the respective grid during a certain period. Such mechanisms aim to encourage investors to enter the market early while accounting for cost reductions of equipment over time. Some fixed FIT schemes also have performance-based rates in order to encourage producers to select optimal locations (for potential sun and wind energy), which maximise the output and efficiency of their plants.

Premium payment FITs   The regulator guarantees a bonus in addition to the market price. The bonus varies based on both the technology used and the amount of installed power capacity on a site. The bonus may vary over time (usually decreasing). This mechanism is applied, for example, in Denmark, Italy, Sweden and Norway. While all electricity produced under such a scheme can be sold above the market price, the latter will vary with the market price, hence impacting the cash flow predictability for the plant operator.

Under premium payment FITs, the investor takes a large part of the market risk, which makes them require higher risk premiums for these kinds of schemes. The remaining risks are the same as those for the fixed FIT scheme.

Renewable portfolio standards (RPSs)   RPSs are renewable electricity production quotas imposed by the regulator on electricity production/distribution companies. These quotas can be met either by the production of renewable (green) energy or by the purchase of renewable energy certificates/credits (RECs) from a third party. When an electricity producer feeds renewable power into the grid, it may either claim the environmental benefits for itself or sell them in the form of RECs to another electricity producer that can then use them to help meet its own RPS obligations. One REC is equal to 1000 kilowatt-hours of renewable (zero-carbon) energy. Figure 4.12 illustrates this process.

Revenue is generated by selling the electricity and the RECs with the electricity producer/investor taking the full volume and price risk for both. Renewable electricity is sold into the grid independently of the RECs at the market price without priority dispatch, and thus has to compete with all other energy sources. The RECs are valid for five years and sold on a dedicated market. Because utility companies under the RPS scheme are required to buy a certain number of RECs a year, the volume of the respective markets is broadly known. However, there is no guarantee RECs will be purchased. Regarding the pricing of RECs, renewable energy producers only make a profit when the price of the RECs is above their marginal costs. In some countries (including Belgium or Sweden), REC minimum prices are granted. It is important to understand that, de facto, the REC maximum price is the fine a utility has to pay if it doesn't meet the regulatory requirements.

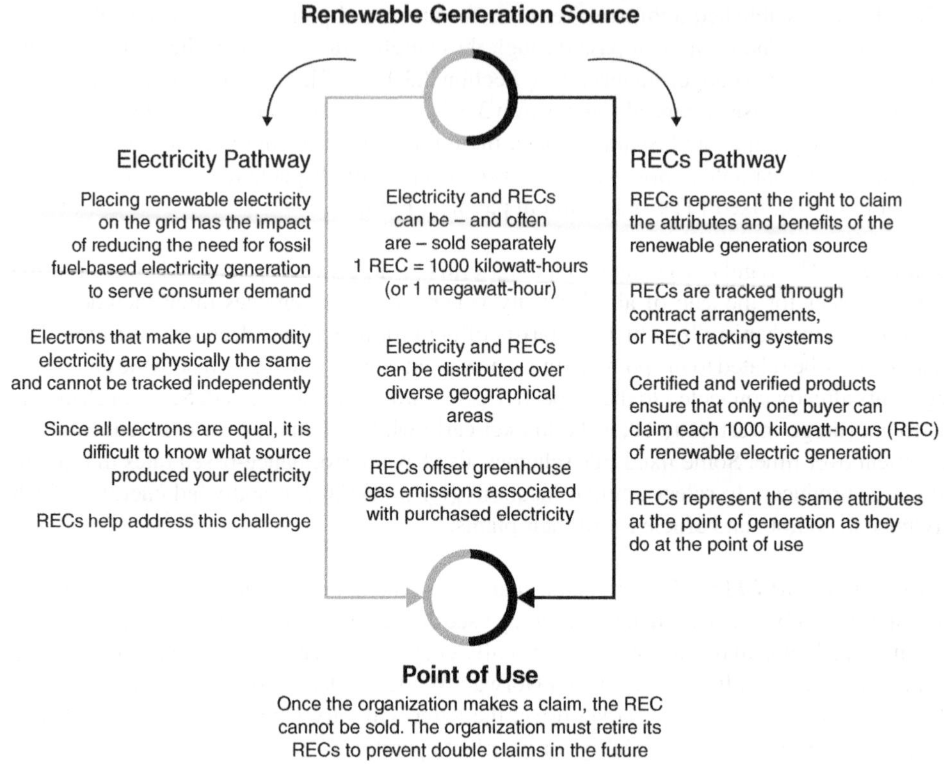

Renewable Generation Source

Electricity Pathway

Placing renewable electricity
on the grid has the impact
of reducing the need for fossil
fuel-based electricity generation
to serve consumer demand

Electrons that make up commodity
electricity are physically the same
and cannot be tracked independently

Since all electrons are equal, it is
difficult to know what source
produced your electricity

RECs help address this challenge

Electricity and RECs
can be – and often
are – sold separately
1 REC = 1000 kilowatt-hours
(or 1 megawatt-hour)

Electricity and RECs
can be distributed over
diverse geographical
areas

RECs offset greenhouse
gas emissions associated
with purchased electricity

RECs Pathway

RECs represent the right to claim
the attributes and benefits of the
renewable generation source

RECs are tracked through
contract arrangements,
or REC tracking systems

Certified and verified products
ensure that only one buyer can
claim each 1000 kilowatt-hours (REC)
of renewable electric generation

RECs represent the same attributes
at the point of generation as they
do at the point of use

Point of Use
Once the organization makes a claim, the REC
cannot be sold. The organization must retire its
RECs to prevent double claims in the future

FIGURE 4.12   Renewable energy certificates
Source: EPA (2008)

This system allows the authority to track and measure the volume of renewable electricity produced and sold on the market. If operators do not meet their obligations, they are fined on a megawatt-hour basis. This scheme is currently in place in Belgium, Italy, Sweden, the UK, 33 out of 50 States in the US and in Chile. The US was the first country to implement RPSs with REC.

Because support mechanisms vary geographically and over time, it is recommended to research data for each country/state when needed in order to get the most up-to-date information on current support programmes.[12]

4.4.2.3   Value chain elements   Table 4.14 illustrates the elements of the electricity value chain relating to renewable energy generation within the entire electricity value chain (see also Table 4.13).

4.4.2.4   Private-sector involvement   Renewable energy generation, with the exception of large-scale hydro energy, is almost entirely in the hands of the private sector globally. The main reason is the small and politically non-strategic nature of these assets.

---

[12]Helpful internet sources are the IEA/IRENA policy database: http://www.iea.org/policiesandmea sures/renewableenergy/, RES Legal: http://www.res-legal.eu as well as the European Commission: http://www.ec.europa.eu/energy

TABLE 4.14 Value chain and investment opportunities – renewable electricity generation

Value chain elements	Investment opportunities
Generation of renewable electricity	
– Generation and sale of electricity from solar power	– Photovoltaic plants (panels, cabling, inverters)
	– CSP plants (similar to PV, with thermal turbines and heat storage units)
– Generation and sale of electricity from wind (onshore and offshore)	– Wind farms (turbines, cabling, transformers)
– Generation and sale of electricity from hydropower (reservoirs and run of the river)	– Hydropower plants (dams, ducts, turbines, cabling, transformers)
– Generation and sale of electricity from biomass (wood, agricultural waste, urban waste)	– Biomass plants (thermal turbines, cabling, transformers)
	– Storage facilities and thermal turbines, cabling and transformers

The profitability of renewable energy generation projects/assets varies strongly. It depends primarily on the following factors:

i. Technical – the ability to produce a significant volume of electricity, which depends on the technology used, the location of the generating facilities and on the ability of the operator to maximise the availability of the assets.
ii. Economic:
 ▪ the marginal cost of the electricity produced
 ▪ the revenue generated per MWh, which depends in turn on:
  – the underlying regulatory support mechanisms (if any)
  – the energy market price
  – the final volume sold into the market.

Under fixed FIT programmes (explained above), the main risks for investors are: (i) development and construction cost, if they enter during development or construction; (ii) resource/volume, that is the amount of electricity produced, which must be assessed for each technology; and (iii) energy price for the period after the expiration of the FIT scheme. Apart from this, investors need to ensure that the expected revenue from energy sold will cover their entire capital costs.

Under an RPS scheme (explained above), the investor takes the full volume and price risks of both the electricity sold as well as the RECs (minimum price may exist). In addition, investors take the same remaining risks as under the fixed FIT scheme. Therefore, assets under RPS schemes are exposed to significantly more risk than those under any of the FIT schemes.

4.4.3 Generation – solar energy

The sunlight reaching the Earth's surface is plentiful, providing almost 7000 times more energy per year than consumed in 2012 by humans (IEA, 2014a). Additionally, the power density of solar electric generation is the highest (global mean of 170 W/m2) among renewable energies.

This suggests that solar energy has the potential to become the world's primary energy source. However, technical barriers (such as the lack of large-scale storage, see Section 4.4.9) and market competition with conventional energy resources will limit the market share in the immediate future.

4.4.3.1 Characteristics and organisation   The global production of solar PV electricity was equal to 0.5% of the global electricity production in 2012. Western Europe (59%) and North America (15%) are the two biggest producers, but Asia is catching up, representing 59% of the installed capacity in 2013. By 2050, PV electricity is expected to represent 10% of global electricity production.

As of the end of 2014, 177 GW of solar PV capacity were installed (a 10-fold increase from 2008) (Greentechmedia, 2015) with an additional 57 GW expected to be added by the end of 2015 (PV-Tech, 2015).

Although solar energy is globally abundant and predictable, its intensity (i.e. the total amount of solar radiation energy received on a particular surface over a specific period) varies geographically and fluctuates during the day and the year.

PV cells can be installed in various scales (from 1 kW to 1000 MW), on various locations (land or existing buildings) and for various purposes (local consumption or feed in the grid). Two kinds of technology are mainly used today: crystalline silicon (85% of the market, high yield and high cost) and thin films (15% of the market, low cost, low yield).

Since 1998, solar PV equipment prices have fallen by 6–8% per year with cost per watt installed down by 60% over the last decade (NREL, 2015). As of 2014, solar PV has reached grid parity in the commercial (large-scale) segment in several countries around the world (Chile, Germany, Italy, Spain) (ECLAREON, 2014). Investment costs are still significant but operating costs are low and the primary energy source (sun) is free. It is important to note that the cells have a short life expectancy (around 25 years) and that, depending on the quality of cells – there are significant differences – the yield may decrease over time (e.g. the warranties of Sunpower corporation have a minimum yield for 25 years).

Solar power can also be used in the form of centralised solar power (CSP). Basically, CSP devices concentrate energy from the sun's rays to heat a receiver to high temperatures. This heat is transformed first into mechanical energy (by turbines or other engines) and then into electricity. The global installed capacity amounted to 4.5 GW in 2014 (up 70% from 2012) with a further 11 GW in the pipeline (Evwind, 2015), and the US and Spain are the leading countries in CSP. A CSP study from IRENA (2012b) entitled *Solar Photovoltaics* explains that the costs of both the construction and the operation of CSP plants are expected to decrease, but so far there are insufficient installations to establish the learning curve. We will not elaborate on CSP in detail here for it is still marginal.[13] However, CSP is discussed further in Section 4.4.9 regarding its potentially important role as an emerging energy storage technology.

4.4.3.2 Sources of revenue and value chain elements   Typically, revenues are generated by selling electricity into the grid on the wholesale market to utility companies, who then provide the retail market for consumers. Other kinds of contractual arrangements, as mentioned in Section 4.4.1 above, are also possible. The price charged per MWh produced

---

[13] Although there is a number of concentrating solar (thermal) power plants (CSP) globally, their combined output represent only 2.3% of total solar electricity generation (REN21, 2013b).

may be determined by the applicable regulatory scheme, if any, rather than the market. In countries using RPS regulation with REC, additional revenues may be generated selling REC on the dedicated market (see Section 4.4.2). The position of solar PV power generation within the electricity value chain is illustrated in Table 4.13 in Section 4.4.2.3.

4.4.3.3 Competition and regulation

Given its relatively high initial capital expense, depending on the location and the size of the plant in question, solar PV may still require ongoing subsidies before it comfortably reaches grid parity.[14] Developers compete for lands with high annual solar potential. However, for PV arrays mounted on new or existing buildings, there is little competition so far.

Regulators mainly oversee the connection to the grid and set the support mechanisms to encourage the development of solar power (see Section 4.4.2.2). In addition, the construction and operation requires various authorisations focusing on environmental regulations, compliance with national and/or international standards and the recycling of solar panels following their use.

4.4.3.4 Private-sector involvement

Solar power plants can represent attractive investments for institutional investors, mainly because their relatively predictable energy output and long-term cash flows can match their long-term liabilities. The main business models and investment considerations which apply to most renewable energy generation plants, including solar PV, are summarised in Sections 4.4.2.2 and 4.4.2.4, respectively.

The levelised cost of solar electricity (LCOE) production is projected to continue to drop in coming years (CleanTechnica, 2015), making PV energy more competitive. According to IEA, global PV power capacity is predicted to exceed 400 GW by 2020, which would be almost twice as much as the capacity installed by end of 2015 (IEA, 2014b). The investments needed globally to get there are expected to amount to an estimated US$60 billion by 2020.

In the coming decades, there will be a shift in demand for solar PV from OECD countries to non-OECD countries (as part of a general shift in energy demand to developing nations). Private investment will be necessary to finance this demand. To this end, it will be essential for solar PV to reach grid parity soon, because non-OECD countries usually cannot afford financial support mechanisms to attract private investment in renewable energy. Without these mechanisms, private capital will only come in if the energy produced can be sold at a price covering the cost of production plus a risk premium asked by investors in these countries. Another possibility would be to look for the warranty of international institutions (the MIGA, the World Bank, regional development banks or ECAs, see also Section 7.4) in order to reduce the exposure to risk and thus the risk premium for the private investor.

4.4.4 Generation – wind energy – onshore

Wind energy (both onshore and offshore) is a major source of electricity: in 2012, wind energy serviced about 30% of electricity consumption in Denmark, 20% in Portugal, 18% in

---

[14]The term grid parity describes the point in time an alternative energy source can generate power at a levelised cost of electricity, which is less than or equal to the price of purchasing electricity from the network.

Spain, 15% in Ireland, 8% in Germany, nearly 4% in the US and 2% in China. The potential production worldwide exceeds the demand of electricity by far (IEA, 2013b).

4.4.4.1 Characteristics and organisation Onshore wind electricity generation is based on a technology, which is well established by now and already cost competitive with conventional power generation in many parts of the world, for example in Australia, Brazil, parts of Europe and the US, among others. No major technological shift is expected. Profitability depends predominantly on:

i. The cost of production, which in turn mainly depends on the accessibility of the site and the country of construction (IRENA, 2012c);
ii. The quality of the location – the intensity (speed and duration) of the wind differs significantly across locations and fluctuates considerably over time (day and year);
iii. The underlying regulatory support mechanism, if any (see Section 4.4.2.2);
iv. The projected energy prices.

4.4.4.2 Sources of revenue and value chain elements Typically, revenues are generated by selling electricity into the grid on the wholesale market to utility companies, who then provide the retail market for consumers. Other kinds of contractual arrangements, as mentioned in Section 4.4.1, are also possible. The price charged per MWh produced may be determined by the applicable regulatory scheme, if any, rather than the market. In countries using RPS regulation with REC, additional revenues may be generated selling REC on the dedicated market (see Section 4.4.2).

The position of onshore wind power generation within the electricity value chain is illustrated in Table 4.13 in Section 4.4.2.3.

4.4.4.3 Competition and regulation Onshore wind competes with any other electricity generation technology. Depending on the location and size of the plant in question, onshore wind may still need subsidies for a while before it comfortably reaches grid parity. Because the location is essential, developers compete for lands with high wind intensity and stability.

The regulator mainly rules the connection to the grid and sets the support mechanisms to enable the development of onshore wind power (see Section 4.4.2.2). In addition, the construction and operation require various authorisations focusing on environmental regulations, compliance with national and/or international standards and the recycling of turbines after their useful life.

4.4.4.4 Private-sector involvement Onshore wind power generation can represent attractive investment opportunities for institutional investors mainly because of their potentially relatively predictable, long-term cash flows able to match their long-term liabilities. The main business models and investment considerations which apply to most renewable energy generation plants, including onshore wind, are summarised in Sections 4.4.2.2 and 4.4.2.4 respectively.

The maintenance costs of wind turbines can be significant, depending on the technology used as well as the weather conditions at the site. Therefore, investors may consider investing in service companies dedicated to the maintenance of onshore turbines even though they are not categorised as infrastructure according to the definition used in this book.

Onshore wind power generation is significantly more volatile than that of solar PV. In order for the average power output to become less variable and, hence, more predictable, investing in turbines across different wind areas to reach a diversification effect may be a good strategy (Neuhoff et al., 2006) to mitigate the volatility risk.

According to IEA, global onshore wind power capacity is predicted to reach 500 GW by 2018 with major players being: China (185 GW), the US (92 GW), Germany (44 GW) and India (34.4 GW). The investment requirements globally are estimated to amount to US\$350 billion by 2018.

4.4.5   Generation – wind energy – offshore

4.4.5.1   Characteristics and organisation

Offshore wind technologies are less mature and the market is less developed than the onshore market, representing only 2% of total installed wind capacity. By the end of 2014, around 8.8 GW of offshore wind had been installed, 91% of which are located in northern European waters (GWEC, 2015).

While wind offshore is stronger and more stable than onshore wind, the development, construction and operation of offshore wind turbines is significantly more expensive, more complex and, hence, more risky than for onshore wind. The maintenance of offshore wind turbines requires special attention because they are located in areas exposed to aggressive conditions (salted water, strong wind) and mechanical parts may suffer from this. Moreover, the costs of interventions offshore will be high as they require special means (boats, helicopters) and safety measures for workers. In addition, they can only take place in certain weather conditions.

New underwater cables (grids) from the offshore turbines to the shore need to be installed to connect the turbines and, hence, the electricity produced, to the transmission grid onshore. These connections must transport considerable power capacities over distances of up to 200 km. The grid connection of offshore wind farms poses a critical challenge from a technical, regulatory, economic and logistical perspective.

4.4.5.2   Sources of revenue and value chain elements

Typically, revenues are generated by selling electricity into the grid on the wholesale market to utility companies, which then provide the retail market for consumers. Other kinds of contractual arrangements, as mentioned in Section 4.4.1, are also possible. The price charged per MWh produced may be determined by the applicable regulatory scheme, if any, rather than the market. In countries using RPS regulation with REC, additional revenues may be generated selling REC on the dedicated market (see Section 4.4.2).

Where offshore wind power generation is situated within the electricity value chain is illustrated in Table 4.13 in Section 4.4.2.3.

4.4.5.3   Competition and regulation

Offshore wind electricity competes with any other electricity generation technology. It is not yet cost-competitive, and nor does it reach grid parity, and its production is equally intermittent as onshore wind. For this reasons, the development of new projects requires the backing of the regulator under a regulatory framework.

Apart from regulatory interventions targeting the construction and operation costs of the off-shore wind farms themselves, the regulator mainly rules the connection from the offshore locations of the parks to the grid and sets the support mechanisms to enable their development (see Section 4.4.2.2). The offshore grid connections are typically subject to a different regulatory scheme from the offshore parks themselves because of their high costs and complexity. Depending on the regulatory scheme of the country in question, offshore grids are built under one of three schemes:

i. The offshore plant operator builds the grid; the construction costs are covered by selling the electricity supported by a special offshore wind FIT (Germany, Ireland, the Netherlands, Sweden);
ii. The TSO builds it; the costs are covered by (higher) transmission fees (France and Denmark);
iii. A tender is launched to award a DBOT contract to a third party, which builds the grid and transfers it to the TSO after commissioning (the UK).

In addition, the construction and operation of offshore windparks require various authorisations focusing on environmental regulations, especially concerning the protection of water and fauna (birds, fishes, etc.), compliance with national and/or international standards and the recycling of equipment.

4.4.5.4 Private-sector involvement   Offshore wind electricity generation can be risky and very expensive – two factors that make it less attractive for private investors than other investments in renewable generation assets. Notwithstanding, once in operation, they are likely to present more predictable, long-term cash flows than onshore wind or solar PV given the rather stable wind environment offshore. Because governments rely heavily on the private sector to finance offshore wind projects, regulation is expected to be the major differentiating factor for private investors to prefer investing in one country over another.

The main business models and investment considerations which apply to most renewable energy generation plants, partially also offshore wind, are summarised in Sections 4.4.2.2 and 4.4.2.4. Additional regulations concerning the offshore grid connections are explained in Section 4.4.5.3 above.

With strong support in several countries, offshore wind power generation is expected to increase significantly by 2018. However, the cost issue is predominant as the levelised cost of energy (LCOE) of offshore wind is still around twice that of onshore wind. Controlling construction, operation and maintenance (O&M) and especially maintenance costs would have to be a crucial part of this given these power plants are located in very difficult environments (storms, water, salt, heavy winds and the like).

The offshore wind energy industry is expected to continue to grow at a CAGR in excess of 15% per year in Europe between 2013 and 2020 (BNEF, 2013). By 2018, offshore wind energy could reach 28 GW globally, delivering 76 GWh of electricity (EWEA, 2014). In 2014 alone, offshore wind power capacity in Europe grew by 1480 MW with 55% of new capacity installed in the UK, 36% in Germany and around 13% in Belgium (GWEC, 2015).

Notwithstanding, offshore wind is not expected to become a significant power supplier on the global scale. The market is likely to be driven by the UK, Denmark and Germany, with France and Sweden having significant projects in the pipeline. According to the European Wind Energy Association (EWEA), in 2014 there were 16 offshore wind farms under development in Europe, which, when all completed, will have a capacity of nearly 4.9 GW. An additional 19 GW of offshore wind power projects have received planning approval, although it remains to be seen how much of this capacity will actually be constructed. The UK has a significant number of offshore projects in the pipeline and could become the largest offshore wind market. The interest in offshore wind is also increasing in China, which already has established around 150 MW and has plans to deploy 5 GW by 2015 and 30 GW by 2020 (GWPMG, 2013). The

US has only discussed significant deployment so far. Offshore wind projects are not expected to develop out of industrialised countries in the near to mid-term.

4.4.6 Generation – hydroelectric energy

Hydroelectric power is the most traditional and largest renewable source of energy generation in the world, representing around 16.2% (3900 TWh[15]) of global electricity production and 1036 GW of installed capacity as of the end of 2014. In 2014, of the 37.4 GW of new installed capacity, only 1.5 GW was pumped storage and the remainder run-of-river plants (IHA, 2015a). (See Section 4.4.9 for more information on electricity storage.) Hydropower capacity is estimated to double before 2050 with the growth being predominantly driven by projects located in emerging countries (Ecoprog, 2015). The largest producers currently are China, Brazil, Canada and the US (IEA, 2012b). Hydropower is heavily regulated because of its strategic importance, and its strong impact on society.

4.4.6.1 Characteristics and organisation
While a hydropower project requires a major upfront investment, operating costs are relatively low (little maintenance and a free and renewable energy source – water) and dams have a very long life expectancy (up to several centuries). Notwithstanding, according to the International Hydropower Association, many of the hydropower facilities around the world will require infrastructure modernisation by 2050 (IHA, 2015b). This may include both replacements of ageing machinery and electronics and upgrades of plants for them to meet changes in usage (e.g. from serving as a base load source to peak-only or vice versa). The need to modernise results in a number of challenges and opportunities, especially when coupling the long lifetimes of civil infrastructure with the uncertainties owing to climate change, constantly changing energy mixes and volatile energy markets (IHA, 2015b).

Most hydropower projects are built under a concessionary agreement in which a public or private organisation takes the full responsibility of designing, building and operating the power plant. The ownership of the plant, especially in the case of large plants, often remains with the public initiator. Some strategic hydropower projects, such as the Three Gorges Dam in China and Itaipu Dam in Brazil, are managed by public authorities.

4.4.6.2 Sources of revenue and value chain elements
Typically, revenues are generated by selling electricity into the grid on the wholesale market to utility companies, who then provide the retail market for consumers. Other kinds of contractual arrangements, as mentioned in Section 4.4.6.1, are also possible. The price charged per MWh produced may be determined by the applicable regulatory scheme, if any, rather than the market, which is the exception rather than the rule in the context of hydro power. In countries using RPS regulation with REC, additional revenues may be generated selling REC on the dedicated market (see Section 4.4.2).

Operators of hydropower plants based on a dam-reservoir system may optimise their revenues by managing both the stock/storage of water and the power generated during peaks of demand. For 'run-of-river' hydropower,[16] revenue optimisation is subject to the operator being capable of predicting the intensity of the river flow and being able to maximise the availability of the generators during peaks of water flows.

---

[15]One TWh (terawatt-hour) is a unit of energy equal to one trillion (1012) watt-hours.
[16]Run-of-river hydropower systems have no (or very minimal) water storage capacity and therefore their power output is directly affected by changes in river flow volumes.

The position of hydropower generation within the electricity value chain is illustrated in Table 4.13 in Section 4.4.2.3. Further, a hydropower plant can add value in a different way by possibly preventing flood damages and being a reliable water resource for the population, farmers and industries.

4.4.6.3 Competition and regulation   Theoretically, competition exists with respect to water resources and with respect to selling electricity into the market. In practice, once the location is determined, competition for water resources is very low. The volume of water needed to produce energy is usually granted by the concession agreement. From a cost-of-production perspective, hydropower easily competes with other sources of energy (with no fuel costs and relatively low maintenance costs compared to fossil fuel plants). However, the energy produced from other RES such as solar and wind may have a first priority into the grid, forcing output from hydropower plants to be scaled back. This priority of dispatch of other renewable sources introduced by the regulator and typically not granted to hydropower has proved to be a major challenge for the profitability of hydropower plants in recent years, despite their low costs of production.

As true for all RES, the regulator also rules the connection to the grid and sets the support mechanisms, if any, for such grid connections (see Section 4.4.2.2). In addition, the construction and operation requires various authorisations, focusing on environmental regulations, compliance with national and/or international standards and recycling of equipment.

4.4.6.4 Private-sector involvement   Some hydropower projects, especially large ones, are considered strategic for the hosting countries (flood management, water and energy supply) and, hence, are financed and managed by public authorities. Notwithstanding, a sufficient number of other, non-strategic hydropower plants, especially small(er) ones, are open for private investment. Generally, hydropower plants offer many characteristics favourable to private capital. These include:

i. Ability to generate relatively predictable, long-term, stable cash flows, hence matching investors' long-term liabilities;
ii. Low- and highly-predictable operating costs;
iii. Mature technology;
iv. No extra or varying costs for the incoming resource used: water.

The main business models and investment considerations which apply to most renewable energy generation plants partially also apply to hydropower. They are summarised in Sections 4.4.2.2 and 4.4.2.4.

In industrialised countries, there is little potential for new hydropower developments – except for small hydropower plants – and, hence, private investments. However, some of the larger hydropower plants may be privatised or partially sold in the coming years.

In France, the hydropower concessions for small hydropower plants are about to be fully or partially privatised. In Austria, hydropower (47% of installed capacity) is already privately held with some owners possibly willing to share investment costs in the future. In Norway, where hydropower accounts for 98.5% of the electricity produced, the potential development of new hydropower plants amounts to 37.7 TWh, that is 30% of the installed capacities (Norwegian Ministry of Petroleum and Energy, 2008, p. 24). However, only 13% of the capacities are privately owned and foreign investors are only allowed to buy hydropower plants with a capacity below 10 MW. Hence, the current legal framework is not particularly favourable to foreign private investment.

In Switzerland, where hydropower accounts for 56% of the production of electricity, plants are operated by privately and publicly majority-owned Swiss utility companies under concession agreements. The Swiss hydropower potential is assumed to have been maximised already, with no new projects expected to be launched in the near future. However, some utilities may be willing to divest minority shares and some concessionary agreements will expire soon, hence providing the (at least theoretical) potential to acquire some of the new concessions launched in the coming years.

The main growth potential for hydropower exists in Asia, South America and Africa (IEA, 2014c). Because the demand for capital for hydropower plants in these countries largely exceeds the investment capacities of these countries, private investment is urgently sought. Many emerging countries (such as Laos, Nepal and the Philippines) recently developed legal frameworks tailored to attract private investment for new hydropower plants.

Prior to the 1990s, the World Bank was the main funding source for large hydropower dam projects. However, widespread public concern in the 1990s over the environmental and social impacts of large dams resulted in the World Bank stepping back from funding such projects. In recent years, only 2% of hydropower projects are funded this way. To take up the slack, national development banks (especially in China, Brazil and India) and private investors (with support from regional development banks) are increasingly funding hydropower projects in emerging markets (Gies, 2014).

4.4.7 Generation – bioenergy

Bioenergy currently provides 14% of the primary energy in the world, with most of it being used directly for heating and cooking and only 1.5% (370 TWh) being converted into electricity (IEA, 2015a). However, by 2018, the electricity generated from bioenergy (biopower) is estimated to increase by over 50% to 560 TWh and to reach 3000 TWh by 2050 per annum (IEA, 2015b). Bioenergy can be generated either directly by the combustion of biomass (plant-based feedstock) in a thermal power plant or indirectly by first converting biomass into biogas or biofuel (liquids), in which form it may be stored as a fuel source to generate power when needed.

The term 'biofuel' is used to describe liquid fuels that are produced from dedicated agriculture products such as corn, sugar-based plants and rapeseed, as well as waste by-products from crop production. Since this section focuses on bioenergy use for electricity (and heat) production, it will focus on biopower and only mention biofuels in passing.

4.4.7.1 Characteristics and organisation
In developed countries, biomass from wood is usually ground and pressed into wood pellets, which can then easily be transported, stored and combusted in commercially available space heaters, combined heat and power (CHP) generators and hot-water boiler systems. CHP systems generate both electricity and usable (waste) heat energy, thus improving the overall efficiency of the primary energy source. Such systems are especially effective when used as part of a district energy system (see Section 4.6).

Biogas generation relies on urban, agricultural and industrial biomass waste that is used to create methane gas through a process known as 'anaerobic digestion'. This gas can be injected directly into a natural gas grid network and can be stored for later use. Such biogas technologies are quite developed with biogas-generated electricity expected to increase dramatically in Germany (18 TWh in 2012 to 28 TWh in 2025) and in the USA (9 TWh in 2012 to 21 TWh in 2025). The global production is estimated to increase by 7.6%/year between 2012 and 2025 (from 50 TWh to 130 TWh).

Biogas needs little investment and the cost of operation is fairly low. The energy sources are usually inexpensive with most of the costs for feedstock resulting from collection and transportation. However, the quality of the biomaterials (feedstock) can vary in quality and quantity, resulting in variable/fluctuating efficiency. The profitability of a biogas generator depends mainly on the proximity of the biomass supply (to reduce transportation costs), the quality of the feedstock and the scale of the plant (a large plant is usually more efficient).

The cost of biomass consisting of wood-based feedstock is low and operational costs are in line with other thermal generation technologies. There is no visibility of price trends of wood products. While the European Climate Foundation predicts a price decrease in Europe, UNECE/FAO expects prices to slightly increase in the coming years. In any case, most potential cost reduction for biopower generation will come from a reduction in the cost of the feedstock (IRENA, 2012d), which, however, is very unpredictable due to many uncontrollable factors like the weather.

Overall, generation costs for biopower are relatively low with little investment needed (mainly the refurbishment of existing generators). Fuel costs account for about 30% of overall generation costs.

4.4.7.2 Sources of revenue and value-added Revenues from bioenergy are generated by selling biogas, heat energy or electricity into the respective grid on the wholesale market to utility companies, which then provide the retail market for consumers. Other kinds of contractual arrangements, as mentioned in Section 4.4.1, are also possible, especially in the case of local district energy systems (see also Section 4.6). The price charged per MWh produced may be determined by the applicable regulatory scheme, if any, rather than the market. In countries using RPS regulation with REC, additional revenues may be generated selling REC on the dedicated market (see Section 4.4.2).

Biogas can either be sold after converting it into electricity or sold directly to an operator for use in the local natural gas grid. Heat energy (hot water or steam) can be sold for industrial use or to provide heating for commercial/residential buildings. Industrial heat is typically sold to an industry located near the power generator. Prices and volumes are defined in a PPA on a mutual agreement basis. Commercial and residential heat are usually sold through a district heating network that is most often managed by the local authority, which sets the price of heat energy. In either case, the heat energy is transported in the form of hot water or steam and distributed via a network of pipes. Renewable/waste heat generated by large-scale plants benefits from specific FITs in many developed countries, including the UK, France, Spain and Switzerland.

The position of bioenergy transformed into power within the electricity value chain is illustrated in Table 4.13 in Section 4.4.2.3. The value-added element of bioenergy in the form of gas and heat are illustrated in their respective value chains: biogas in Section 4.5 and heat generated from biomass in Section 4.6.

RENERGIA WASTE-TO-ENERGY PLANT, SWITZERLAND

Renergia, the waste-to-energy (WtE) plant located in central Switzerland, has a capacity of processing 200 000 tonnes of waste per year. It supplies about 38 000 households with electricity and delivers environmentally sound, carbon-neutral heat from municipal waste for the paper production process of Perlen Papier AG, a paper mill located next to the plant. Owing to the combined heat and power plant, the efficiency factor is very high at approximately 70%. The positive environmental effects are considerable: Perlen Papier AG decreased its CO2 emission by 90 000 tonnes annually by switching from heavy oil to heat for the generation of the steam needed for the paper production. Aerial emissions are reduced dramatically, thanks to a modern flue gas cleaning system. Substantially lower air pollution than with the previous heat production technology based on fuel oil is the result.

The planning process for Renergia started in 2010. It required the involvement of all stakeholders, first and foremost the local community, as residents were afraid of air pollution and heavy traffic to and from the waste incineration plant. The local community was persuaded to consent because, among other things, the management of the paper mill promised to safeguard jobs in the region. The plant went operational as planned in January 2015.

Source: Renergia (2015), management interviews

METRO VANCOUVER'S WASTE-TO-ENERGY FACILITY

The waste-to-energy mass-burn facility of the Greater Vancouver region (Metro Vancouver) treats approximately 25% of the region's garbage and provides electricity to 16 000 households. Every year, approximately 285 000 tonnes of municipal solid waste is converted into 940 000 tonnes of steam and up to 170 000 MWh of electricity, providing both economic and environmental benefits. In addition, about 8000 tonnes of recycled metals are recovered annually. The plant generates approximately $6 million of revenues p.a. from the sale of electricity and $500 000 p.a. from the sale of the recycled metal.

The waste-to-energy facility, operating as Covanta Burnaby Renewable Energy, began commercial operation in 1988. Throughout it's over 25 years in service, the environmental performance of the plant has been exemplary, always meeting or surpassing Canada's stringent regulatory emissions standards. The management of the incineration plant is committed to environmental safety, demonstrated by constant operational improvements and frequent upgrades of emission control systems, which have continually reduced air emissions to today's very low levels. Stack emissions and air quality around the facility have been monitored since the facility opened and are reported monthly to local and regional authorities, the BC Ministry of Environment, the City of Burnaby, and the Fraser Health Authority.

A flue gas cleaning system captures the fine particulates created during the burning process of waste to energy as fly ash. They are then treated to prevent leaching and finally disposed of at a landfill. Furnace grates capture the bottom ash which is tested weekly to ensure it can be safely disposed of at the Vancouver Landfill. After these processes, of the 285 000 tonnes of garbage burnt annually the remaining particulates in the plant's exhaust are equivalent to those emitted by 10 heavy-duty diesel trucks. Not surprisingly, less than 1% of the fine particulate matter and smog-forming nitrogen oxides measured in the Lower Fraser Valley can be attributed to Metro Vancouver's waste-to-energy facility, while the vast majority results from industrial production, heating, road/air/rail transport (see pie charts).

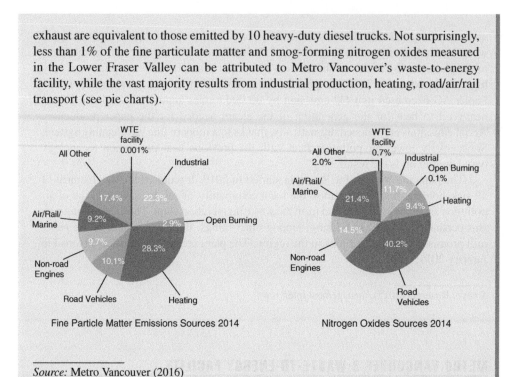

Fine Particle Matter Emissions Sources 2014   Nitrogen Oxides Sources 2014

Source: Metro Vancouver (2016)

4.4.7.3 Competition and regulation

Managing the supply of feedstock is crucial for bioenergy generation because markets are unpredictable and competition for feedstock may be high. When building or acquiring a plant, it is therefore essential to secure the upstream procurement through long-term agreements. This is mainly true for agricultural, urban and industrial wastes because volume and price volatility can be rather high, and this is in part caused by high volatility in supply and demand. A 2014 IRENA biomass whitepaper provides an excellent overview of how critical supply and demand of the biomass in question is and provides an estimate of this balance in six world regions by 2030 (see Figure 4.13).

As true for all RES, the regulator controls the connection to the grid and sets the support mechanisms for the grid for all kinds of energy (electricity, gas and heat) generated from bioenergy of any kind, if any. In addition, the construction and operation of these plants requires various authorisations that focus on environmental regulations, compliance with national and/or international standards and the recycling of equipment.

4.4.7.4 Private-sector involvement

In many geographical areas, the biomass/bioenergy market is a sellers' market. That is, the party having access to or owning the biomass, which can be used for energy production, holds a relatively strong negotiation position in relation to potential plant owners. Against this background, waste disposable operating companies (such as Suez Environnement, Veolia) are entering the power generation market constructing large-scale bioenergy electricity generation plants. With a secured supply in feedstock and FITs (if any), these projects present a very low risk profile for them.

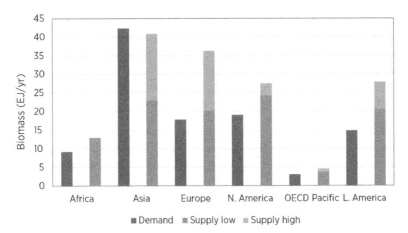

FIGURE 4.13   Comparison of global biomass demand and supply estimates by 2030
Source: IRENA (2014)

Several factors influence the output of a biomass generation plant: most importantly, the availability and quality of the feedstock (affected by seasonal variability except in the case of wood products and waste, see also Section 4.4.7.3 above). This makes the profitable operation of such plants quite challenging. As a result, securing private financing for biomass plants remains difficult.

Institutional private-sector involvement is likely to be requested mainly for large-scale plants (greater than 30 MW) with relatively competitive unitary production costs but with the need for international procurement of feedstock. Large-scale logistics of feedstock are complex and make a plant significantly more vulnerable to external factors – somewhat similar to conventional energy sources.

Notwithstanding these challenges, biopower generation is expected to grow considerably. Cumulative investments (2014–2035) are estimated to amount to US$370–US$450 in OECD countries and US$640–US$890 globally (IEA, 2014c, p. 162). In developing economies, most capital is needed for small, local power plants primarily providing off-grid electricity to local populations. In OECD countries, the growth may be facilitated through dedicated support mechanisms, whereas developing countries may seek public-private partnerships (PPPs).

4.4.8   Transmission and distribution

Within the infrastructure sector, 'transmission and distribution' (T&D) means the 'dispatch' of electricity (high, medium and low voltage), oil or natural gas through dedicated networks.

With respect to electricity T&D, high-voltage dispatch over long distances via the backbone of the network is called 'transmission'. 'Distribution' is understood as being both the medium voltage dispatch regionally and the low-voltage 'last-mile' delivery to the end-user. 'T&D' however, refers not only to the physical grid (powerlines and substations) but also to the system services employed to steer/manage the network and its performance (planning/balance of demand and supply, frequency and voltage control, power continuity, metering, etc.).

All three kinds of electricity networks (high/medium/low voltage) are 'natural monopolies', with finite capacity and high barriers of entry. Therefore, in most countries the respective national authorities regulate these networks, which include substations and their interconnections to the high-voltage grids, to ensure open access to all market participants. The main rule is that T&D, which includes transmission system operators (TSOs) – called regional transmission operators (RTOs) in the US – and district system operators (DSOs), shall not take advantage of their monopoly positions. That is, they shall compete neither in the marketing nor in the generation or production of the resource they dispatch, namely electricity (the same rule applies to oil and gas networks, see Section 4.6 for gas networks). Nonetheless, DSOs under certain regulatory schemes may and must provide energy to consumers at controlled prices when acting as the supplier of last resort. This happens when marketing companies are not available or the private consumer does not want to deal with a marketing company but chooses instead to deal with the DSO directly.

Non-regulated private networks are an exception to the rule. For instance, railroad catenary lines or internal transmission systems of large industrial compounds (like steel mills) usually remain outside regulated T&D activities.

4.4.8.1 Characteristics and organisation Electricity T&D is commonly understood as the delivery of electricity from the generator to the end user. More precisely, it means high-voltage transmission of electricity over long distances from any power generator to any regional, medium-voltage power distribution network, which in turn connects to the final consumption point.

The economic weight of T&D within the electricity value chain is important: in IEA member countries, it represents between 25 and 40% of total electricity supply costs varying significantly by country and regulatory framework.[17] As a rule, approximately one-third of these costs are related to transmission with the majority being caused by distribution.

The IEA forecasts that during 2014–2035, OECD countries will have to invest approximately US$2.2 trillion in T&D to cope with both the ageing of networks and the new low-carbon policies. Seventy-five per cent of the required T&D investments are expected to go into the distribution networks (IEA, 2014c).

SWISS ELECTRICITY T&D SYSTEM

The Swiss electricity T&D system stretches over 250 000 km of network lines (T&D level), through which the electricity is transported and reduced from the extra high-voltage 380/220 kV to the 230 V used by households and businesses:

- Level 1: Extra high-voltage transmission network
  This network operates 246 main trunks at 220 and 380 kV and is responsible for delivering power from power plants – including from Switzerland's neighbouring countries – to the distribution networks. Swissgrid, the monopolistic Swiss TSO, which is majority-controlled by the public sector, owns this network.
- Level 3: High-voltage transregional distribution networks

---

[17]In the US, the economic share of T&D seems to be substantially lower with approximately 14% (EIA, 2012).

These networks operate at between 50 and 150 kV. They distribute power to regional distribution networks and large industrial customers.

- Level 5: Medium voltage regional distribution networks

    These networks operate at between 10 and 35 kV and distribute power to parts of cities, communities and medium-sized industrial customers.

- Level 7: Low-voltage local distribution networks

    These networks operate at 230 or 400 V and supply power to approximately 5.2 million individual households and small businesses. The levels 2, 4 and 6 represent the 'substations', in which the electricity is transformed into a lower voltage.

Switzerland's Level 1 and 2, the part of the network owned and operated by Swissgrid, consist of 6700 km of extra-high-voltage lines (1780 km at 380 kV and 4920 km at 220 kV) that are linked through 50 internal interconnections and 140 substations. The frequency adopted is 50 Hz. It is monitored through approximately 200 000 metering points – remotely connected with the central control room – by increasing and decreasing the supply in line with the demand of the network (switching on and off power plants or exporting/importing energy from abroad). Nine gas-, steam- and pumped-storage hydropower (PSH) plants with over 100 MW capacity each (not owned by Swissgrid) ensure reserve capacity. In addition, the network has 41 cross-border interconnections to Switzerland's neighbours' TSOs, which help balance the system, but also cause more complexity owing to the relevant transit business among neighbouring countries.

The current cost of the 'balancing energy' required to equalise the network is approximately 0.64% of the value of the total energy produced (approximately SFr200 million). This cost has been reduced significantly during the past years (from roughly SFr500 million in 2009) with the savings passed on to the end-users.

DSOs/utilities – and to a lesser extent large customers – own Levels 3–7 of the network. Approximately 680 DSOs and marketers take part in the Swiss market (Germany: 884, France: 150, the UK: 14).

Swiss electricity demand has grown over time. In recent years, demand stabilised slightly above 50 TWh. The quality of the T&D system is the best in Europe (approximately 15 minutes of average annual interruption time for customers connected to distribution networks/SAIDI (System Average Interruption Duration Index), compared to around 61 minutes in the UK) (CEER, 2015).[18] In less than 10 hours per quarter the frequency deviated by at least 0.075 Hz from the target of 50 Hz. Nonetheless, the transmission network is experiencing challenges – partially caused by increasing RES abroad – in coping with current and future changes in the energy generation mix (Switzerland decided not to replace its four nuclear power plants, making up 36% of its current generation). Swissgrid plans to invest approximately SFr2.7 billion by 2024 to refurbish and expand its grid (Swissgrid, 2015).

Transmission system operators (TSOs)   Within T&D, the activities of TSOs are crucial for ensuring a reliable, stable national and international power supply within and across

---

[18] Switzerland ranks second after Luxembourg, which, owing to network size and low complexity, is not a relevant benchmark.

countries/states. In this context, grid balance is fundamental for infrastructure's safety. Even small failures in frequency or voltage can affect a large number of end-users, causing financial damage. A stable and open grid furthermore supports competition in energy trading and market liquidity.[19]

Reserve capacity costs represent approximately 61% of the net operating costs of an electricity network. Given the relative importance of reserve capacity combined with the request for and necessity of grid stability, TSOs have to anticipate both demand and supply, with reserves taking a key position in a network in the form of storage capacity (see also Section 4.4.9). Here the main issue is to meet peak demand at very short notice. To do so, a stringent planning process is required to match supply requirements (e.g. maintenance or upgrades of lines or power plants) and reserves with expected demand levels (10 minutes ahead, one day ahead or longer term).

The main challenge for a TSO is dealing with natural hazards, technical failures and meteorological imbalances since they disrupt the dispatching plans for the generation and consumption of energy. To minimise grid instability or even failure, TSOs are connected and communicate with each other as well as with Distribution Systems Operators, generators and large customers.

Distribution system operators (DSOs)   As exclusive owners of a regional/local network and administrators of the official energy consumption of each single user (meter values), the DSOs play the role of market facilitators and therefore must act in an independent and non-discriminatory way towards all marketers. Their main activities, for which they are regulated and controlled, are: (i) network operations (24h/7 days dispatching control and fault management), (ii) asset management (capacity planning, investments and maintenance) and (iii) demand management (metering, billing and receivables collection, price and revenue controls, new connections and contracts, commercial relationship with traders).

The performance of a DSO may be improved by combining asset and demand management through an optimised timing of investments as well as by the preventing and detecting of network faults. The reliability of the delivery of electricity largely depends on network maintenance, resilience to weather changes and network automation. Asset management activities include increasing the share and size of underground cables (they are considerably more expensive to install than overhead circuits but less expensive to maintain), maintaining substations and poles, but also clearing trees, a major cause of line interruptions.

Automation improves the detection and isolation of network faults through meters/sensors, but also the reliability of the system and its costs. A major improvement of a network can be reached by installing smart meters at the customer's point of delivery.

DSOs aim hard to avoid outages because repair costs, customer compensation and the resulting reduction of allowed returns on the part of the regulator reduce profitability.

---

[19]The pure unit transmission tariff (UTT) averaged €9.40/MWh across Europe (ENTSO, 2015). It includes the recovery of TSO costs (ca. €7.98/MWh) and of non-TSO costs (e.g. renewable energy certifications, regulatory costs, totalling ca. €1.42/MWh). In 21 of 35 European countries, the UTT are charged to the final users. In 14 countries, both power generators and users take a share of the UTT.

On average, the TSO's cost components of the UTT are: infrastructure (57%), system services (32%), and losses (11%) (ENTSO-E, 2015). Typical net operating costs of a TSO (example: Germany 2009) represent ca. 65% of the total cost structure. They comprise: reserve capacity (61%), network losses (34%), reactive power for voltage control power (3%) and sundry (2%). The O&M and asset depreciation expenses count for the residual 35% of the total cost structure.

COMPARING DSOs

The Australian Energy Regulator compared 13 DSOs (AER, 2015). It found differences in comparable productivity ratios of up to 50% between the worst and best performers with the total annual cost per customers ranging from A$1500 to as low as A$400.

The economic fundamentals of a DSO depend on various factors, among which the density of the served area, the relative consumption per point of delivery and the length of the lines, as well as the variations in the weather, are the most important ones.

More than TSOs, DSOs face significant grid loss effects (lost energy caused by wire resistance). By distributing electricity at lower voltages, the loss increases significantly. In Norway, the country with the highest electricity consumption per inhabitant (23 MWh/year, US: 13 MWh/year), for instance, grids of DSOs lose up to 15% (average 8%) (NVE, 2013; World Bank, 2015b). Despite the fact that in most countries losses are recoverable as a cost of the system, regulators incentivise the reduction of grid losses in the interest of consumer.

RES – a challenge for TSOs and DSOs   Traditionally, coal, nuclear and oil-burning power plants, which have low marginal operating costs, formed the 'base-load' of a grid, ensuring a reliable, predictable and cost-effective source of electricity. As such, they were the last plants to be disconnected from the grid in times of low energy demand. Oil- and natural-gas-burning turbines (CCGTs), as well as hydropower, accommodated peak demand, particularly during daytime, thanks to their fast ramp-up and flexibility in sizing power. Environmental considerations were not seriously taken into consideration, neither was renewable electricity generation. This has changed.

The relatively recently established energy policies and regulations (mainly in Europe) supporting sustainable-energy generation (see Sections 4.4.3-4.4.7) have led to distortions in the traditional merit order allocation of capacity. The most important distortions are that they:

i. Artificially impose externalities to the thermal plants (like CO_2 pricing or green certificates) by increasing their marginal costs;

ii. Rule the decommissioning of older thermal plants (specifically oil, coal and nuclear plants);

iii. Subsidise RES (lowering their marginal costs);

iv. Give priority of dispatch to the RES.

The implementation of these RES-supportive policies and regulations has the following consequences on the overall system:

- Conventional plants – coal, nuclear, oil and gas (CCGT) – no longer operate at their peak performance/optimal production level. Therefore, their production cost is higher than it would be if they were running at optimal production levels. Plants with high fix costs suffer particularly under these new regimes. As an example, as of 2013, the four largest German utilities alone cumulatively booked asset impairments in excess of €15 billion (RWE, 2014);

- Power market prices are influenced by the weather, e.g. a windy day translates into high wind energy production, which in turn can lower the electricity market price that day.

This introduces additional price volatility to the market. More importantly, on sunny days, peak hour prices flattened out across Europe because of PV energy generation. Both effects significantly lowered the returns of high fix-cost plants (CCGT and oil-burning plants) as well as for those that rely on price differentials between low off-peak and high peak electricity prices (like PSH), which constitute the capacity reserve for balancing the system.

Traditional power grids function hierarchically by means of different decreasing voltage levels. Energy is generated at high voltage and consumed at low voltage (see above). For several years, ever growing numbers of decentralised RES plants feed increasing amounts of energy directly into the medium-voltage distribution networks rather than into the high-voltage transmission network, which connects all distribution networks. The consequence is that the voltage control function of the TSO and DSOs is severely hindered. Additionally, in the event of short circuits (e.g. owing to a tree falling on a medium-voltage line), strong currents in the medium-voltage network may create serious incidents.

In many advanced electricity markets, the growing share of solar PV and especially wind energy has led to an increased volatility of power fed into the grid (see Section 4.4.2). To give an idea of magnitudes: A 2008 study commissioned by the grid operator of Texas (ERCOT) analysed the imbalances of wind power generation (BDEW, 2014) and found that adding 15GW wind farm capacity requires the equivalent of at least one 18 MW CCGT (combined cycle gas turbine) power plant left idle as reserve to cope with the increased variability in the grid. Similarly, a 2010 EWEA study (BDEW, 2014) forecasts additional balancing costs of up to €4/MWh – mainly for reserves – for wind to have a 20% share of total capacity.

Given the above, the increased volatility caused by RES generation requires: (i) increased reserve capacity (i.e. thermal power plants left idle) with instant availability to cope with low RES generation and (ii) energy storage and RES output management, to flatten out RES generation peaks.

Transmission grids have been dimensioned to accommodate peaks. On average, they only use 20 to 30% of their transmission capacities (McKinsey Quarterly, 2012). Despite these generous overcapacities, meeting recurrent shifts and peaks in power supply caused predominantly by RES remains a challenge for operators these days because the current network architecture was not developed for many small, decentralised (RES) generation plants, but for a few centralised, large ones, which feed their power into the high-voltage transmission grid only.[20] To be able to deal with, and ideally prevent, such issues caused by decentralised RES generation in the future, TSOs and DSOs need to upgrade their networks.

Smart grids   Smart grids, a new T&D concept, address (many of) these challenges. The IEA compared various international studies to benchmark the impact of such system upgrades to RES needs. It concluded that extra T&D costs of US$2–5/MWh in Europe and $1–12/MWh in the US (IEA, 2011) would be required for such upgrades.

Smart grids aim to optimise the efficiency and effectiveness of electricity supply and usage. They do so via a two-way network, which transmits both electric and communication data between large-scale energy plants, distributed energy sources/users and energy storage

---

[20]In RES-intensive countries like Germany, Spain or Italy, the grid manager requires RES plants to be remotely switchable to avoid grid overload in case of high winds or high solar irradiation. This is a clear indication that the system lacks energy storage capacity.

Present day | Future

FIGURE 4.14 The shift from grids to smart grids
Source: IRENA (2013)

systems (see Figure 4.14). The main goal of the additional exchange of information via the communication network is to achieve shared targets among all market players and integrate the renewable energy generated at medium voltage into the grid management.

Smart grid components include smart inverters at RES plants, which are able to ensure power curtailments and precise/fast ramp-up of voltage. For conventional plants, coupling demand changes and forecasts can optimise production management. At the level of T&D, smart applications integrate market data with meter and sensor data, which constantly adapt the requirements of any market participant. These applications are known as 'demand response management systems' and 'automated regulation control systems'.

For end-users, smart applications like smart meters can be installed as well. In some European countries (like Germany), smart meter systems are already fully in place thanks to its advanced metering infrastructure (AMI). An AMI, which is at the heart of any smart grid, consists of a data-collection meter at the point of delivery, a data-gathering device, usually by the secondary substations, and a software platform (a meter data management system) at the DSO site to elaborate demand plans from the instant consumption patterns. Furthermore, end-users may use demand management devices to control and save money on their consumptions. A recent paper of the IEA offers a detailed discussion of smart grid goals, technologies and devices, as well as implementation guidelines (IEA, 2015c).

Assessing the value-added of smart grids is very difficult given no smart grids are being built yet, let alone are in operation. Hence, all estimates are based on theoretical cases only. Notwithstanding, IRENA reports in its *Smart Grids and Renewables* publication that 'a meta-analysis of 30 business cases for smart meter projects in 12 countries representing four continents found that on average the net present value of project benefits exceeded the net present value of costs by nearly two to one' (IRENA, 2015a). A study of the Middle East and North Africa found that smart grid investments could save the region US$300 million to US$1 billion annually while helping to realise the region's large potential for solar power (Northeast Group, 2012). A US study concludes that potential investments in sustainable technologies, including smart grid and renewables, have a net present value of US$20–US$25 billion based solely on benefits to utilities (IRENA, 2013).

Other technology innovations in transmission and distribution   Besides smart grid concepts, significant innovations are likely to increase the efficiency and productivity of T&D assets. Selected new technologies are:

▪ High-voltage direct current (HVDC) systems: New powerlines that can transport two to three times more power than an alternating current (AC) transmission line with the same route width. HVDC lines reduce transmission losses by 30–50% compared to AC lines (Siemens, 2015b).

■ High-speed digital switches: Replace high-voltage transformers; they use 90% less energy, take up only about 1% as much space and are more reliable and flexible than existing transformers (McKinsey Quarterly, 2012).

■ Microgrids in municipal/rural areas: powered by RES and batteries, micro grids feed power in dedicated small grids. Together they constitute self-sufficient systems or units that are integrated into larger smart grids. With these local 'interventions' they help to balance the overall network. These microsystems will enable a significant increase of the stability of local power distribution and reduce future investments in T&D networks.

4.4.8.2 Sources of revenue and value chain elements The sources of revenue of TSOs and DSOs are determined entirely by the national regulatory framework. Almost all frameworks are based on a combination of user-financed, availability-based business models (see Section 4.4.8.3 for a discussion of applicable regulatory frameworks and Section 3.3 for a discussion of the different business models).

The allowed revenues of TSOs and DSOs are calculated on a cost basis or a so-called Regulated Asset Base (RAB) basis by the regulator. TSOs and DSOs charge the marketing companies for their T&D activities. These T&D expenses in turn are passed on to the end-user via the marketing companies/utilities. The fees charged to the end users are annually adjusted downwards or upwards to reflect the true (historical) costs of the TSOs and DSOs.

Irrespective of the regulatory remuneration framework in which a network operator works, significant value-add potential can be materialised via the technological improvements and innovations described in the paragraphs above. Table 4.15 illustrates the two main elements of the electricity value-chain presented above (see Section 4.4.1.3).

TABLE 4.15 Value chain and investment opportunities – electricity dispatch

Value chain elements	Investment opportunities
Dispatch of electricity	
– High-voltage electricity transmission	– Transmission network
– Medium/low-voltage electricity distribution	– Medium-voltage (distribution) network
	– Low-voltage (last mile) network

4.4.8.3 Competition and regulation TSOs/DSOs usually operate within a regulatory framework set by the national regulator. These regulatory frameworks define, among other things: (i) the roles of all parties involved (generator, TSO/DSO, large industrial off-taker), (ii) the business model specifying the remuneration/sources of revenues of the various parties and (iii) the capital requirements (refurbishment and expansion of the network) and quality/performance targets.

For TSOs/DSOs to operate efficiently and effectively within any given regulatory framework, they need to be granted certain (geographical and/or functional) exclusive responsibilities:

■ Independence – act autonomously of any other market participant;
■ Regional focus – serve under exclusivity an appropriately sized area;

- Operational authority – operational authority and responsibility over all supply and demand in its area of coverage;
- System reliability – exclusive authority and responsibility for maintaining the reliability of network assets of the grid it operates.

The intention of the regulation is to foster competition in marketing electricity with the ultimate goal of protecting the end-user from such natural monopolies charging unreasonable rates for their services. Lacking competition, the regulated business models usually include an incentive component to make the network operators become and/or stay economically efficient. Such incentive schemes allow the regulator to penalise the TSOs or DSOs for low availability/quality and to reward them for higher availability/quality than the benchmark or set target. As a rule, the availability/quality rates, which form the basis for the tariffs passed through to the end-users, are set at known intervals, which are based on national/international benchmarking. Some regulatory frameworks (e.g. Greece, Finland, Italy, Poland, Slovakia) tie the tariffs for the T&D industry to the volumes dispatched. This is because the costs of a T&D company depend more on the volume than on the value of supply. The lower the volume of electricity dispatched, the higher the T&D tariffs.

It is beyond the scope of this book to describe the diverse regulatory frameworks for T&D activities prevalent in various countries. Even within the EU, there are significant implementation differences of the EC Directives at all levels, both from an industry structure and from a remuneration point of view. A high level overview of the main industry structures and remuneration schemes is given below.

Industry structure   Three regulatory models are commonly used to warrant fair access to the electricity market for all players:

- *Ownership unbundling (OU)*: generation, transmission, distribution and marketing operations are provided independently by different companies. This model is used in most of Europe except France and some smaller countries such as Switzerland and Austria.
- *Independent transmission operator (ITO)*: the incumbent TSO and the DSO own their respective T&D assets but they still belong to a larger, vertically-integrated company. Only the regulation and authority supervision guarantee that T&D activities are run without causing market distortions. This model is used in France and Austria.
- *Independent system operator (ISO)*: the ISO is fully independent and does not own the T&D assets. The assets can still belong to an integrated company or any other third party (including the state). This model is used in the US, where RTOs have been created to operate existing networks.

Figure 4.15 illustrates which regulatory systems are applied in which country within Europe. Systems can also be combined in various ways.

T&D remuneration schemes   Notwithstanding the many different ways of implementing regulatory systems, two main types of regulatory frameworks are applied in most countries: the cost-plus model and the regulated-asset-based (RAB) model.

Cost-plus model   The regulator sets authorised rates for T&D services based on the actual costs of the companies in question plus an allowed margin. Not all and any costs can be passed

Ownership Unbundling

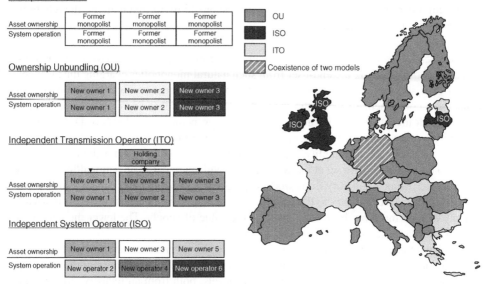

FIGURE 4.15   Transmission System Operators in Europe
Source: Authors' own figure, partially based on the website of the Ministry of Economy, Trade and Industry of Japan (http://www.meti.go.jp/committee/sougouenergy/sougou/denryoku_system_kaikaku/pdf/004_03_02.pdf)

on to the end-user but only those the regulator considers coherent, appropriate and justifiable (or a target standard). Any new investment for maintenance or expansion, for example, needs to be approved beforehand by the national regulator and is ultimately paid for by the end-user via the electricity bill.

Only a very limited number of countries allow TSOs and DSOs to pass on their full costs without limitation to the users by increasing tariffs. The cost-plus model is applied, for example, to TSOs in the US and Belgium. It is fair to say that in both countries various performance-adjustment mechanisms apply.[21]

The regulated-asset-based (RAB) model   The RAB model comes in many varieties. As with the cost-plus model, the authorised T&D tariffs are calculated based on the costs. The latter equally have to be approved by the regulator beforehand. The return on equity, unlike for the cost-plus model, is determined on the basis of the RAB times a weighted average cost of capital (WACC). The WACC is set by the regulator and applied on a standard or actual capital structure (D/E). The RAB in turn comprises only those assets that are technically necessary to the T&D operations and are owned by the network operator. The remuneration structure can be summarised in the expression:

$$\text{Allowed revenue} = \text{Authorised operating expenses (opex)} + \text{Depreciation} + \text{RAB remuneration}$$

---

[21]For the US: FERC (2015).

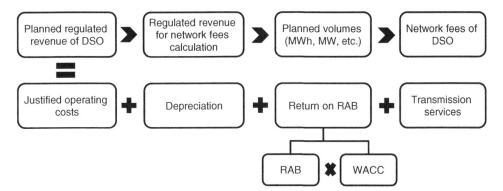

FIGURE 4.16   Revenue-price-income cap mechanism
DSO: distribution system operator; TSO: Transmission system operator; ERO: energy regulatory office ; WACC: weighted average cost of capital; RAB: regulated asset base
Source: Modified from EY (2013a)

Two main business models are prevalent within the RAB framework: incentive-based and revenue-price-income cap. Any RAB model applies one of these two with some variety. The incentive-based model (e.g. in Germany) is characterised by a relative benchmark with its peers. The regulator sets allowed revenues in the form of a revenue cap, which is the sum of three types of costs defined as 'inefficient', 'efficient' and 'non-influenced'. Inefficient and efficient costs are determined via a benchmark of the other TSOs in the country. Non-influenced costs are the fixed costs (employee, grid costs, etc.).

In revenue-price-income cap schemes, the revenue is calculated based on the mechanism illustrated in Figure 4.16.

Switzerland uses an RAB model for its TSO, called Swissgrid, which we describe below as an example.

SWISSGRID (SWISS TSO) – RAB MODEL

Under Swiss law, the tariffs charged to the consumer are based on: (i) projected operating costs, taxes and depreciations derived from historical cost information and (ii) remuneration on the basis of the RAB by means of a WACC.

According to the law, the RAB encompasses three main components: (i) the fixed assets, (ii) net volume and tariff deviations (the timing differences caused by the tariff setting mechanism owing to ex-post cost and volume adjustments to actuals) and (iii) the net working capital.

UVEK, the Swiss regulator, specifies annually which return on capital the owners of Swissgrid are allowed to receive for the RAB. This allowed return is based on the officially set WACC multiplied by the RAB.

In 2014, UVEK introduced a new framework, with all variables such as risk premium for debt and equity components being known. For the calculation of a WACC in any given tariff year, the new regulatory framework only requires UVEK to insert the pricing data for Swiss government bonds. It makes the calculation of the WACC transparent and easy to project. One of the main assumptions of the WACC calculation is a standard pre-defined 40% equity and 60% debt capital structure. For 2015, the WACC was set at 4.70%, resulting from a computed cost of equity of 6.86% (40% weight) and a cost of debt of 3.25% (60% weight). From 2017 going forward, it was reduced to 3.83% (for further information on this revised calculation, refer to ElCom, 2016).

4.4.8.4 Private-sector involvement
Global demand for power continues to increase, providing generally good prospects for the T&D industry. The ongoing shift from centralised to decentralised power generation will further increase the demand for new and upgraded T&D networks, representing around 40% of the total estimated global power investment between 2014 and 2035 (IEA, 2014c). The majority of investments are expected to take place in China, the EU, the US and India (see Figure 4.17).

T&D investment needs are estimated to amount to US$6 trillion between 2014 and 2035 (IEA, 2014c). With public resources being scarce, private investment is expected to fill the gap. Globally, expansion and reinforcement of T&D infrastructure will be necessary to expand services to new customers, to connect new (renewable) sources of power generation (RES) and to maintain or improve the quality of service to existing customers.

For instance, worldwide net additions of 3.2 million kilometres of transmission lines are expected to be required by 2035. About half of the current transmission assets (mainly in Europe and the US) will have reached the end of their technical lifetimes of 40–60 years. This will trigger investment needs for the replacement and refurbishment of such assets. For Europe alone, the European Network of Transmission System Operators for Electricity (ENTSO-E) has identified investment needs of around US$131 billion for the refurbishment or construction of 52 300 km of high-voltage powerlines over the next decade (Ten-Year Network Development Plans – TYNDP). In developing countries, the capital requirements for transmission infrastructure are enormous. They represent almost 65% of the global investment needs in electricity transmission. For private investors to be more inclined to invest in such infrastructure assets in emerging markets, these countries need to upgrade their legal systems and regulatory frameworks.

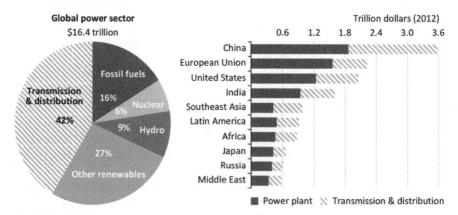

FIGURE 4.17 Cumulative global power sector investment
Source: IEA (2014c), © OECD/IEA 2014, World Energy Investment Outlook 2014, IEA Publishing. Licence: https://www.iea.org/t&c/termsandconditions/

According to a recent report by Edison Electric Institute (EEI), investor-owned electric utilities and stand-alone network companies invested a record US$37.7 billion in T&D infrastructure in 2013, up by 14.2% from 2012. Of this total T&D investment, about 45% went into transmission and 55% into distribution. The report notes that investments in T&D continued to climb in 2014 and are expected to remain at 2014 levels at least through to 2017 (EEI, 2015).

As a rule, electricity T&D lends itself to private investment. Network grids deliver a necessary, basic resource/service to users, which will always be in demand. Their regulated business models 'make it difficult to lose money'. T&D requires high capital expenditures with a very long economic life (up to 60 years). Cash flows are relatively foreseeable over a long period and relatively stable depending on the legal framework introduced by the regulator. The technology of such grids – not considering smart grids and future technological innovations, which are incremental improvements of the existing set-ups, relatively speaking – is mature and operational costs are sufficiently known. Under the concession agreements, new, necessary investments – approved by the regulator – increase the RAB and, as such, increase the costs which the TSO/DSO is allowed to pass on to the off-taker/user via increased tariffs (or financed by the state budget, if applicable). Overall, the risks attached to transmission grids are low compared to most other infrastructure assets.

Up to now, most of the private investments in the T&D segment have been undertaken via the purchase of publicly listed stocks of operators, usually those of large incumbents. Incumbents offered a mixed coverage of many sub-segments of the industry, from generation to trading. More recently, thanks to unbundling, direct investments in T&D assets only, that is separated from all the other typical activities and services of utility companies, are possible (albeit in few countries).

To this end, DSOs, especially those with a good (regional) operator, may be a solid investment if purchased at the right price. Good DSOs should be able to add value in various areas of the network and, in this way, generate extra return from outperforming the benchmark set by the regulator (the benchmark used can be the performance of other DSOs in the country and/or absolute hurdles). Furthermore, investments in these (relatively) small-sized DSOs may offer benefits from aggregation strategies, mainly by leveraging economies of scale in back-office activities in the procurement of capital investments as well as of outsourced services.

Investments in TSOs require a particularly good understanding of the national regulation and in some instances may imply more regulatory risk than DSOs (see Section 5.2.5). At the same time, the control of TSO assets is limited, because the sheer size/valuations of these assets prevent most investors from being able to take majority control.

There may also be slightly more innovative ways for investors to deploy capital in this subsector as indicated above: there is interest from financial investors to fund new electric links dedicated to connect offshore wind farms to the respective national grids in, for example, the UK (called OFTOs, or offshore transmission owners), Germany and Denmark. Another example is the new onshore powerlines in the UK, which serve various purposes. All of these assets, including the offshore connections mentioned above, are built and operated under DBFO contracts (see Section 3.4 for the various contractual models) with Ofgem, the UK regulator, as counterparty. There is significant competition among operators during the tender phase of such long-term concession contracts.

4.4.9 Electricity storage

Utilities – be they publicly or privately owned – are the traditional owners of electricity storage assets. They operate(d) storage capacity as part of their generation and transmission services in order to manage peak demand and optimise their facilities. However, as new storage technologies emerge at various points along the T&D networks, so too will the need for new ownership models.

4.4.9.1 Characteristics and organisation Demand for electrical energy fluctuates in relatively predictable, cyclical patterns over time (during the day and over the year). Conventional, thermal energy power plants (lignite, coal, oil, gas and nuclear) can generate power 'any time on demand', albeit with different ramp-up times, flexibility and marginal costs.

RES do not have inherent energy storage capacities (except for hydropower). They can only feed energy into the grid based on real-time availability of the employed renewable resources (especially wind and solar PV)[22]. As a result, solar- and wind-based generation offer less stable production patterns than hydropower and geothermal energy generation.

Despite their severe storage limitations, in many of the most advanced electricity markets, decentralised RES are given priority access to the grid in order to promote investments in this subsector. This successful promotion from an environmental perspective has several negative side effects, though. First, the resulting growing share of wind and PV energy generation has led to increased volatility of the power capacity fed into the grid. Second, decentralised RES plants feed directly into the medium-voltage distribution networks rather than into the high-voltage transmission network connecting all distribution networks. As a consequence, the voltage control function undertaken by the operators is severely hindered (for a more comprehensive discussion of the challenges TSOs and DSOs face with the volatility of supply caused by increased RES generation and changing usage behaviour of customers, please refer to Section 4.4.8). In order to deal with these limitations and negative side effects, including the volatility of RES, sufficient large-scale storage capacity is urgently needed.

The development of large-scale energy storage systems that allow for the storage of surplus energy generation and make available energy reserves 'to the system' at all times with a short response time may indeed be part of the solution to the above described challenges. The basic functions of storage systems are: they (i) take energy out of the grid at times of oversupply, (ii) store it and (iii) feed it back into the grid at times of high demand. In this way, they provide the flexibility needed to effectively manage the increasing amounts of renewable energy being fed into the grid. In addition, electrical energy storage allows for a precise fine-tuning of the power quality (frequency regulation and voltage control), thus improving the overall efficiency and reliability of the electrical grid.

Key benefits of large-scale energy storage for the electrical grid include:

- Make renewable energy economically viable: maximises resource productivity and enables solar or wind energy to be stored during off-peak hours for use during peak hours;
- Provide an 'electricity reserve' like the national petroleum reserve: critical as a safety net for potential national emergencies;
- Stabilise electricity prices: reduces the disruption of major pricing moves that are due to weather, natural disasters or national emergencies and levels out the large price differences between on-peak and off-peak energy;
- Stabilise the T&D grid: Levels the energy demand profile;

---

[22]Photovoltaic ('PV') power generation is more predictable than wind power.

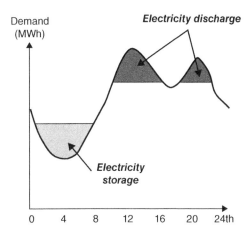

FIGURE 4.18   Load profile of a large-scale
energy storage facility
Source: ESC (2002)

▪ Reduce the need for traditional generation assets: currently, the most polluting power
plants (e.g. coal-fired plants) are still in use – primarily during peak demand.

Figure 4.18 illustrates how energy storage may help to level the energy demand load
profile of the power grid.

All electricity storage devices have two key performance characteristics: (i) the power
rating, which defines the Watt-rate at which electricity can be instantaneously withdrawn and
injected from and to the grid, and (ii) the storage capacity, which defines how much energy
can be stored and for how long. Since storage performance requirements vary depending on
application and location along the electricity grid, a combination of complementary storage
technologies is required to meet the overall storage demand of the electrical grid.

Storage technologies employ physical laws to transform excess electricity into stored
energy via chemical (e.g. batteries, fuel cells, capacitors), mechanical/kinetic (e.g. flywheels,
compressed air, hydropower) and thermal (e.g. molten salt solar, warm water pools) processes.
Following storage, the energy is released to the grid on user demand.

In addition to traditional (existing) storage technologies, different kinds of new electrical
storage technologies are currently at various stages of development. The most common existing
and new electrical energy storage technologies are summarised in Table 4.16.

The predominant electric utility-scale storage technology used is, and has been, pumped
storage hydropower (PSH) with approximately 290 PHSs operational worldwide and 142 GW
of capacity installed (DOE, 2015; IEA, 2014d). In 2013, PSH accounted for 99% of the
installed electrical energy storage capacity globally and 78% of future storage projects under
construction. A 2015 report estimates that more than 100 new PSH plants with an installed
capacity of about 74 GW will be developed by 2020 (a 50% increase over current global
capacity) with an investment volume of about €56 billion (Ecoprog, 2015). However, despite
a potential scale up of global PSH capacity in, for example, Norway, Canada and the United
States as well as many emerging markets, future development of this energy storage technology
is limited because the most suitable (i.e. cost-effective and environmentally friendly) PSH sites

TABLE 4.16   Electrical energy storage technologies (most common)

Technology	Description	Maturity	Advantages	Drawbacks
Pumped hydro (PSH), existing	Water is pumped from lower to higher reserve where it can be used to generate hydropower	Mature	Commercial, large-scale, efficient	Limited locations, low energy density[23]
Compressed air (CAES)	Air is compressed and stored in enclosed volumes and later run through gas turbines to improve efficiency by almost 300%	Demo to mature	Large-scale, low-cost, flexible sizing	Limited locations, low energy density, requires gas to heat air at release
Flywheels (FES)	Energy stored and recovered via massive, fast-spinning rotors connected to a motor-generator	Demo to mature	High power density, efficient, scalable	High cost, low energy density
Lead acid batteries	Conventional electrochemical storage (excludes vehicle batteries)	Demo to mature	Flexible sizing, low cost	Low energy density vs. other batteries, performance degrades above 25°C
Lithium-ion batteries (Li-ion)	High energy density electrochemical storage (excludes electric vehicles)	Demo to mature	Efficient, high energy and power density	High cost, safety (overheating, fire)
Flow batteries	Electrochemical storage using external tanks to store electrolyte material	Develop to deploy	Scalable	High cost (more complex than other batteries)
Sodium–sulfur batteries (NaS)	High temperature electrochemical storage	Demo to deploy	Efficient, high energy and power density	Safety issues, must be kept hot
Hydrogen	Chemical storage via the production of hydrogen (separated from water)	Demo	High energy density	Lower efficiency, high cost, safety
Synthetic natural gas (SNG)	Chemical storage via the production of methane	Demo	High energy density, leverage existing gas infrastructure	Lower efficiency, high cost
Capacitors and superconducting magnetic storage (SMES)	Electromagnetic stored in an electric field between two plates or in a coil (SMES)	Develop to demo	Efficient, high power density, quick response	Lower energy density, higher cost

Sources: Ecofys, 2014; SBC, 2013

---

[23]Energy density is how much total energy can be stored per area or volume. Power density is how much power can be delivered per area or volume.

in most OECD countries have been developed already. Therefore, the consensus is that there is an urgent need (and a race) to develop a variety of new, cost-effective and complementary electrical energy storage technologies on a commercial scale.

Other existing technologies, which are of minor importance in terms of installed base globally, are: (i) compressed air energy storage (CAES), with approximately 435 MW installed; (ii) electro-chemical batteries in various forms, also used to support grids: approximately 300 MW installed in plants over 1 MW; and (iii) flywheels, increasingly used to support frequency regulation of the grid (installed base approximately 150 MW) (DOE, 2015). It is still unclear today which of the technologies will prove to be technically superior, if any, and win the race for large-scale deployment.

In addition to the existing technologies listed above, a broad variety of storage technologies are in (competing) development and some have been for many years (see also Table 4.16). They can be differentiated, among others, by their potential power delivery capacity:

- Capacities under 1 MW:
  - Flywheels;
  - Batteries;
  - Capacitors.
- Capacities between 1 MW and 10 MW:
  - Flywheels;
  - Large scale batteries;
  - Pumped heat storage.
- Capacities between 10 MW and 100 MW:
  - Flow batteries;
  - Sub-surface compressed air energy storage (CAES);
  - Power to gas (P2G);
  - Concentrated solar power (CSP).
- Capacities of 100 MW and above:
  - Pumped-storage hydropower (PSH);
  - Compressed air energy storage (CAES).

Of the existing technologies in utility-scale applications, PSH and CAES are still the most cost-effective large-scale storage systems with high usage cycles.[24] Super-capacitors and flywheels for very short, high-frequency storage and batteries are the lowest cost solution for lower cycle rates. In the following, all of the above technologies will be described briefly on a high level.

Existing energy storage technologies

Pumped-storage hydropower (PSH)   Both river-fed (conventional) hydropower and PSH generate energy using gravity to release the potential energy stored in elevated basins. Unlike river-fed hydropower, which relies on rainfall, PSH pumps back water from an adjacent water basin to the PSH reservoir (at a higher elevation) at night or during weekends, when surplus electricity from base-load plants is available cheaply. In this way, the storage capacity is available for immediate release up to the entire rate of the turbine capacity. The efficiency of a

---

[24] 'Usage cycle' here being the number of times a storage system can be charged and discharged before losing its capacity to store energy.

PSH is always less than that of conventional hydropower, because of the efficiency losses from having to convert hydroelectricity back into stored water (efficiency approximately 70–75%). The economics of PSH hence lies exclusively in its storage function with ability for on-demand release and its ancillary services of balancing the grid.

The storage function describes the amount of energy that can be stored. Its efficiency is determined by: (i) the time it takes to refill water in the upper reservoir (duration of cycle) and (ii) the amount of electricity stored in one refill cycle. Low cycle duration and a high amount of stored power represent high-efficiency PSHs. One other relevant element of a PSH is its speed of energy release.

PSH also offers various ancillary benefits to the frequency regulation (stable Hertz frequency through modulation of active power and fast load gradient) and voltage control of the grid (ensuring that electricity flows from generation to users via management of the reactive power by means of static or synchronous compensation).

Of the approximately 290 PSHs operating currently worldwide (total capacity of approximately 142 GW, IEA, 2014d), 154 plants are located in Europe – the majority in Denmark, France and Austria – with approximately 51.4 GW installed. North America has 37 plants (US 36, Canada 1) with a capacity of 20.6 GW. Japan installed 25.4 GW in 38 plants; China 23.6 GW in 27 plants. The rest of the world accounts for 21.1 GW in 36 plants, mainly in Asia (DOE, 2015).

Compressed air Compressed air energy storage (CAES) uses pre-compressed ambient air instead of water to release energy through expansion turbines. Ambient air is compressed to approximately 70 bar and stored at 40–50°C (100–120°F), (usually) in natural caverns. To compress air, similarly to PSH, cheap excess or off-peak electricity is needed. Current assumed efficiency is slightly above 40% (owing to the inherent inefficiencies of using air (vs. water) as a storage medium), well below the efficiency of PSH.

The CAES technologies are:

- Diabatic (existing): They extract the heat during the compression phase but require re-heating of the air with natural gas before injecting it into the turbines. Hence, these plants need to be close to a thermal power plant and a natural gas pipeline. Diabatic CAES has a medium efficiency (up to 55% if heat is recovered, as in CCGT);
- Adiabatic (under development): They recover the heat from air compression and use it after storage to re-heat the compressed air to be injected into the turbines. This technology aims for a 70% efficiency.

The advantages of CAES over PSH are: (i) no gravity requirement (only a reservoir for the compressed air is required), (ii) no major construction challenges (if a depleted salt/natural gas cavern/reservoir is available) and (iii) reduced risk in terms of earthquakes or geological failure.

The main limitation for utility-scale applications remains the need for the concurrent availability of a large thermal power plant, of a salt cavern and of gas supply. CAES capital expenditure is similar to that of CCGT plants. The main technical developments of CAES are in the type of storage, for instance steel pipes to store the compressed air.

The CAES installed base is currently negligible: worldwide there are five operating plants with a capacity of 435 MW. The largest is a 321 MW cavern/turbine system fed by a nuclear power plant in Germany (Kraftwerk Huntorf) (EON, 2015a). The CAES projects under construction worldwide remain insignificant: nine for an additional 800 MW (DOE, 2015).

Flywheels   Flywheel energy storage (FES) is a mechanical system that transforms electricity into rotational energy and back again. A motor connected to a rotor, which stores the electricity, and a generator, which releases the electricity, comprise the system. Currently 28 plants (920 MW, of which only approximately 150 MW commercial) are in operation worldwide, and five additional plants are under construction (5 MW) (DOE, 2015). FES is particularly efficient as a frequency regulator for electricity transmission quality, because it can store and release energy very quickly.

The two largest applications are in fusion energy research projects (in Germany and the UK, approximately 400 MW each). Large commercial applications exist in a 20 MW-scale (two plants in the US) but the vast majority of installations are below 1 MW in small-scale plants, mainly on islands. FES is also used for continuity purposes (e.g. hospitals and data centres).

Batteries   Batteries use electro-chemical storage systems, which are traditional means to warehouse energy. One broadly differentiates between solid-state and flow batteries. Simply speaking, solid-state rechargeable batteries create electrons by oxidising the positive electrode (cathode), while the anode is reduced, losing electrons. Electrons move from the cathode to the anode to generate DC electricity, when the electrodes are connected to the grid. The various solid-state technologies differ across the type of electrolytes and the electro-chemical electrodes (lead-acid, lithium ions on various supports, nickel–cadmium and sodium–sulfur).

Flow batteries differ from solid-state to the extent that fluid electrolytes contain chemical components that can be charged by oxidation and reduction (redox) in the storage phase. Energy storage capacity and speed of release are similar to the solid-state lithium-ion (Li-ion) batteries. These innovative flow batteries offer significant benefits over solid-state batteries; most importantly, their ability to always remain charged (the charging and the generation process can run in parallel) and their flexible project design and layout.

Worldwide, approximately 390 storage battery plants (for a total of approximately 580 MW) are in operation. Considering only utility-scale batteries in plants over 1 MW, these are mainly solid-state with Li-ion technology (approximately 146 MW worldwide). Li-ion is the prevailing technology, owing to its high storage capacity per volume, fast charging cycles and low environmental impact. Sodium–sulphur ('NaS') and lead-acid batteries (respectively 64 MW and 32 MW installed) are traditional and reliable applications, requiring heat (NaS) and some electrolytes maintenance.

Prices for advanced batteries are likely to continue to fall. Large Li-ion batteries are projected to be the lowest-cost battery technology in 2020 (from US$550 per kWh in 2014 to US$200 by 2020) (EY, 2015). Flow batteries are installed in 34 plants (mainly in Japan and China), totalling 20 MW of installed capacity, of which seven plants with a size between 1 MW and 5 MW use the vanadium redox technology. Twenty new projects are under construction for 7 MW (mainly in the US) (DOE, 2015). The reason for the potential increase of flow batteries is their decreasing cost per unit of power, long life and increased safety (no heating and exhausts).[25]

Energy storage solutions going forward   RES specific storage technologies are wind power to gas (P2G) and molten salt concentrated solar power (CSP). These applications are interesting

---

[25]However, a study of the Webber Energy Group of the University of Texas at Austin in 2013 calculated that the net present value of a flow battery (vanadium redox) can be positive only if the system costs are below US$1.5 million per MW installed (Fares, 2013).

because they expand the paradigm of RES, coping with their main drawback: intermittent energy generation. Both technologies are skewed towards storing energy rather than merely generating electricity.

Power-to-gas (P2G) P2G transforms electricity into gas because gas can be transported and warehoused more easily than electricity. Gas is transported to where there is demand, while concurrently storing the power in the gas pipeline. Hence, gas takes the role of a medium, which dispatches energy in a different chemical status from electricity (moving electrons).

P2G is a two step process using electricity generated by RES to extract hydrogen from water (electrolysis) and then either storing the hydrogen (H_2) by itself or attaching carbon (from CO_2) to obtain methane (CH_4). The conversion process is moderately efficient (electricity to gas: approximately 50–85% efficiency) and compares favourably with other storage technologies. Methane and hydrogen can be re-transformed into electricity via CCGT or fuel cells (albeit with further efficiency loss).

Gas can be transmitted through existing gas pipelines at a fraction of the cost of electricity because the content of energy dispatched through gas pipes is higher than the one through powerlines (EON, 2015b). From a storage point of view, the existing gas pipelines in Europe offer 5000-times more storage capacity than the existing electricity grids. This means with P2G significantly less investment in new electricity storage facilities would be required. The main issue for P2G is still the costs of electrolysis or methanation, which are close to US\$4 million per MW (IEA, 2015d).

RWE POWER-TO-GAS STORAGE

In August 2015, the German utility RWE put online a state-of-the-art 150 kW P2G plant in Ibbenbüren (North Rhine-Westphalia), Germany, as part of a new system that links (for the first time) electricity, natural gas and district heating supply systems. The P2G plant turns surplus power from RES into synthetic natural gas (CH_4) by first separating hydrogen from water and then adding carbon from CO_2, which is then stored in the natural gas network. When needed/at peak demand, the stored gas can be used at a co-generation plant within the local district heating network to generate power.

These kinds of plants, which enable (renewable) energy storage, are critical for meeting Germany's declared goal of doubling the percentage of power generated from renewables (from 25 to 50%) by 2030. At a utilisation rate of 86%, the P2G plant is the most efficient system of its kind in Germany (RWE, 2015).

Concentrated solar power (CSP) Another combined energy generation and storage technology is CSP. Several CSPs are operational in Europe and in the US already (25 plants worldwide for 1.3 GW, of which the vast majority are located in Spain and the US (ESA, 2015a).[26] CSPs collect thermal energy from mirrors concentrating the heat to a boiler filled with molten salt. A steam turbine fed by a heat exchanger generates energy stored by the heated molten salts.

---

[26] According to IRENA (2015b), the installed capacity of CSP reached 3.4 GW in 2013.

TABLE 4.17 Value chain and investment opportunities – energy storage

Value chain elements	Investment opportunities
Storage of electricity/energy – Pumped storage hydropower (sale of energy and system services) – Network management (automated demand balancing) and quality-related storage (sale of system services)	– Storage facilities (dams, ducts, turbines, cabling and transformers) – Smart grids – Facilities/equipment based on existing and new technologies (flywheels, batteries, etc.)

The main drawback of this technology is its requirement to be located on warm sites with high irradiation, hence limiting its diffusion. Desertec, the largest and most ambitious RES undertaking in northern Africa, which is supported by large industrials from different industries and countries, will mainly deploy CSP (DESERTEC, 2015; Desertec has subsequently been massively scaled back, as of December 2015).

4.4.9.2 Sources of revenue and value chain elements As a rule, energy storage providers generate income by buying and storing energy during periods of low demand and low market prices, and selling it back during peaks when demand and market prices are high. The revenues of selling energy at high prices should be higher than the costs of power purchase and energy storage. TSOs and DSOs are an exception for they can pass through to the end-users the costs of the storage assets they own themselves (see Sections 4.4.8.2 and 4.4.8.3).

Apart from this exception, energy storage economics are primarily driven by: (i) arbitrage on electricity prices, (ii) avoidance of network cut-offs at peak supply, (iii) improved quality of supply (frequency regulation and voltage control), (iv) grid capital expenditure, and (v) benefits to end-users (cost of connection, cost of energy at peak, continuity, etc.) Of these five economic drivers, RES operators can generate value from the first two, (i) arbitrage and (ii) via loss of revenue prevention. TSOs and DSOs can generate value and seek economic benefits from (iii) improved quality of supply and (iv) reduced capital expenditure. End-users profit from (v) reduced total cost of supply and reduced risk of power outages. Businesses propositions, which take advantage of the end-users' preparedness to pay for these services, are emerging (mainly in the US). Table 4.17 illustrates the two main storage elements of the value chain, which may add value to different degrees via these five economic drivers explained further below.

(i) Arbitrage Beyond PSH, the economics of hedging energy prices via storage are still uncertain. The spot market pays a premium for large electricity volumes offered at a time. Therefore, to be truly profitable, an arbitrage-based business requires large storage capacities.

(ii) Loss of RES revenue prevention The economics of energy storage investments to prevent revenue losses from renewable assets depend entirely on the applicable RES regulatory framework and the TSO's working practices. In some jurisdictions, lost RES revenues caused by grid outages during overproduction are restored by the TSOs (e.g. Germany). In other jurisdictions (e.g. Italy), TSOs are allowed to order the shutdown or down-rating of RES plants.

(iii) Frequency regulation Apart from structural grid capacity limits, which TSOs need to upgrade, dispatching regulation is needed because of unbalanced supply and demand (typically, this happens on windy and sunny days with low demand). Given that the revenue losses caused by ordered dispatches are insignificant from an economic point of view, at least as of today, it hardly justifies significant storage investment by RES operators.

CSP and P2G are able to decouple power generation and the moment of electricity feed-in into the grid. They hence address and can take advantage of this economical potential.

(iv) Grid capital expenditure   Storage investments for batteries, capacitators or flywheels (not generation plants like PSH or CAES) are traditionally borne by the grid operators (TSOs). TSOs and DSOs may significantly leverage, and hence benefit from, such storage plants themselves, because they reduce their need to invest in new powerlines and substations. Their financial needs (capital expenditure) will accordingly decrease as well.

Irrespective of their own systems benefit, in most jurisdictions, TSOs are allowed to recover system costs for energy storage (investments) by charging them to the end-users, via the marketers/DSOs.

At the same time, most jurisdictions allow regulators to penalise TSOs and DSOs (with fines or lower revenue allowances) for underperformance of the system. This specific aspect (and the related pressure on network managers) may drive future investments by TSOs and DSOs in storage facilities.

(v) Customer benefits   New business models target the need of small RES plants (e.g. residential PV). Essentially, the customer leases or purchases storage capacity coupled with RES power generation (PV or wind). The customer uses its own generated electricity in its entirety without feeding any energy into the grid. Private investors finance and own both generators and storage facilities.

SolarCity, the largest solar energy service provider in the US consumer market, provides a case in point. This company installs and provides leasing and financing options for solar and energy storage services. In December 2013, the company launched DemandLogic, an 'intelligent energy storage system' designed to reduce businesses' peak demand and provide power during outages. The system is able to automate the discharge of stored energy during peak demand, allowing the customer to reduce the amount of electricity purchased at a high price during peak hours and thus reducing its overall electrical utility charges (*Energy Storage Journal*, 2014).

Unless investing via aggregators like SolarCity, this segment will hardly offer investable storage asset opportunities.

4.4.9.3 Competition and regulation   For those storage assets owned by TSOs or DSOs, direct competition does not exist since these operators are natural monopolists (as outlined above), and their storage costs are passed through to the end-users of electricity. PSH and CAES operators, on the contrary, are subject to competition in the sense that the electricity wholesale market, into which they sell their energy, primarily determines their hedging value-added. Furthermore, TSOs can request the stored power from the PSH and CAES operators whenever they need it to balance the grid. This limits the potential business volume and as such the business model of PSH and CAES operators.

In some countries, the regulator compensates conventional power operators for maintaining reserve capacity. However, such compensation is the exception and not the rule. This is particularly relevant for recent combined cycle gas turbine (CCGT) plants, commissioned in the 2005–2009 period, that are now hardly able to recover even the depreciation of investment costs, since they are idle most of the time (RWE, 2014). As of 2014, neither in the EU nor in the US a specific regulatory framework for energy storage assets has been introduced – despite the widely-acknowledged critical position of storage within the energy market. This is a major constraint, which hinders the development of and investment in storage capacity.

Today, most energy storage plants generate electricity while offering ancillary services. As a consequence, energy storage is not easily integrated into existing regulatory frameworks for it can provide value across different segments of the market: it can be part of either the ancillary services (system regulation) provided by both grid managers (TSOs) and local distributors (DSOs) or generation activity. Depending on where it is 'placed', the respective local regulations apply.

While there are no specific legal requirements, the current EU energy directives rule that if a storage plant is an energy-generating one (e.g. PSH) the TSOs and DSOs in charge of the respective network are not allowed to directly sell electricity from this plant into the grid. In other words, hedging electricity prices through storage is legally not possible for network operators, since they are considered to be in competition with private marketers of electricity. Simply put, any plant with a generator/alternator attached to a storage system may be outside of the law.

Network operators are lobbying against this grey area to have at least frequency regulation and voltage control equipment approved (e.g. capacitators and flywheels; Ofgem, 2014). At the other end of the system, RES operators are pushing for a regulatory framework that opens the market for ancillary services as a potential source of extra revenue (EWEA, 2010). Needless to say, the position of storage within the energy market and its regulation is far from clear. There is an evident need for adequate regulatory frameworks, which would render investments in high-quality, large-size energy storage financially attractive (e.g. incentive payments based on reliability, power quality, energy security and efficiency gains from energy storage capacity), irrespective of which market participant within the power value chain benefits.

The European Association for Storage of Energy (EASE) addressed the need to legally define 'energy storage' and design 'a market that monetises the value-added – flexibility and security of supply – that energy storage can bring to the system' (EASE, 2014). The capacity market in the UK may be a way of establishing business models based on storage that rely on hedging the value of the guaranteed supply of energy (UK Department of Energy & Climate Change, 2015). Market participants exchange defined capacity for a defined price for a specific period (e.g. one year). While aimed at giving economic security to conventional generators with idle fleets, capacity markets can also attract storage operators. The UK system has been criticised by RES/storage operators, who have suggested that time horizons are too short to favour new storage investments.

In the US, the Federal Energy Regulatory Commission (FERC) has taken initial steps to open the US electricity markets to energy storage technologies, by funding research and development. It also permitted companies other than large utilities to sell ancillary services (such as energy reliability and security – via energy storage) in the electricity market.

The state of California has asked its three largest utilities to invest in 1.3 GW of new energy storage capacity by 2020 (CPUC, 2015). Notwithstanding, 50% of the storage capacity required will be allotted to private operators not affiliated to utilities (CPUC, 2010). More relevantly, in 2011, FERC established a more advanced pricing for system services (FERC Order 755; FERC, 2011). Under this new tariff scheme, storage operators get paid more than conventional regulation resources (e.g. thermal power plants), the speed and accuracy of which are lower in comparison to energy storage.

The structure, operation and, especially, regulation of electricity markets will ultimately shape incentives to develop and invest in storage. But as long as the political and regulatory risks remain high and a comprehensive regulation for energy storage is missing, potential developers and investors as well as future research and development support for storage will remain limited (EY, 2013b).

4.4.9.4 Private-sector involvement
Beyond PSH, which is a relatively low-cost, traditional, relatively efficient storage technique, and hence a well-known area of investment, the economics of energy storage investments are still uncertain.

There is large development potential for PSH worldwide (approximately 30GW for Europe alone, Eurelectric, 2011). As of today, PSH can provide only a limited amount of the envisaged power storage requirements globally: approximately 2% in North America, 5% in Europe and 10% in Japan (ESA, 2015a). Thirty-one new PSH projects (26 GW) are currently under construction. The majority are located in Japan (six sites and 3.3 GW), China (seven projects for 9.6 GW) and in other developing economies (three projects for 4 GW) (DOE, 2015). As of July 2015, not a single new project is under construction in North America (one contracted, six announced). Apart from six new projects under construction in Portugal and Switzerland, there is almost no greenfield activity in Europe.

Despite this theoretically huge investment potential in PSH and the relative competitive cost of development, the overall interest in new projects located in Europe has decreased significantly, for various reasons:[27]

- Future energy costs are uncertain: uncertainty about a potential introduction of a price on CO2, the ban on nuclear plants in many countries, as well as very volatile oil and gas prices with an unclear future oil and gas supply and demand, which will affect all energy prices (on gas prices, see also Section 4.5.1). Low off-peak energy costs, however, are needed while pumping water back into the reservoirs to profitably operate PSH plants.
- Profitability depends on the absolute spread between peak and off-peak power prices. Low off-peak energy costs, however, are needed to profitably operate the plants, while pumping water back to the reservoirs. With further falling power prices throughout Europe, this spread keeps narrowing. Prices are also sensitive to rainfall: the more rain there is, the lower energy prices will be.
- PSH locations require altitude differences, available in the mountains, which are distant from the main concentration of other power plants and users (located by the sea or in plains). Only large-capacity projects with high absolute capital expenditure have the potential to operate profitably.
- New and repowering projects suffer from drawn-out planning-permission processes and NIMBYism (not in my backyard) and environmental issues, thus few suitable sites for new PSHs exist, at least in Europe.

For the above, the authors believe that scaling up PSH capacity in Europe will be very challenging. In addition, the most cost-effective locations have been developed already in most countries.

Similarly, CAES does not seem to offer a viable solution and, hence, investment proposition for institutional investors, given the requirement of large natural reservoirs and the need

---

[27]The development of new PSH in Europe is estimated to cost approximately €2 million per MW, which is in line with international benchmarks (US$1–3.5 million per MW) and comparable with other RES assets (AXPO, 2015; IRENA, 2012e).

to manage the temperature extremes in the compression and expansion phases. Man-made tanks are still too small to provide for a utility-scale solution without switching to adiabatic technology. For the latter, the costs for insulating the vessels are too high. A US-based company is currently testing a 1.5 MW isothermal CAES plant that does not require caverns for storage or natural gas combustion to reheat the compressed air. The storage of aqueous foam is done in insulated steel pipes at a higher pressure (200 bar), thus requiring less storage volume (SustainX, 2015). Should this pilot case prove successful, it might be an efficient solution and present an interesting investment opportunity for the large-scale storage of energy at RES plants.

Flywheels, capacitors and fluid batteries are significant innovations. They are modular in size and flexible in location and hence of great use in regulating RES power. These technologies are best suited for network managers to regulate frequency response and reserves, given their very fast ramp-up, but time-limited use (IEA, 2013c). McKinsey (McKinsey Quarterly, 2012) forecasts that the cost of these technologies will drop by 2020 to US\$150–200/kWh, allowing for a market of approximately 100 GW in the US alone. To put this into perspective, 100 GW are equivalent to its current fleet of nuclear power plants. Notwithstanding, the authors believe that these technologies are unlikely to be produced in large scale – at least from today's perspective.

Both combined renewable energy generation and storage technologies, P2G and CSP, will emerge as viable innovations and investment opportunities of institutional scale – CSP has already done so to some extent. Nonetheless, both require a great deal of further investment as well as technical skills because they are operationally more complex to manage than RES.

Other interesting technical developments are pumped heat electricity storage (by means of heat pumps) and gravity railcars. Unfortunately, these storage technologies are still not sufficiently proven to be investable.

It is still uncertain whether arbitrage (discussed in Section 4.4.9.2) will become a viable, stand-alone business model for RES operators. This is because they may not be able to afford the costs of installing these large storage capacities if they have to rely on a hedging business model only. The authors tend to believe that only power traders will have the competencies and market access to exploit the benefit of energy arbitrage, within their traditional business model.

The SolarCity 'consumer-centric storage business model' targeting the retail segment (also discussed in Section 4.4.9.2), seems to work irrespective of current regulations. It may get certain large-scale investors seriously interested to invest.

Another, possibly more interesting, investment case is the AES Energy Storage business model. AES Energy Storage is the largest private operator of energy storage, part of the independent power producer AES. It targets network operators delivering integrated battery-based storage solutions (AES, 2015). AES has a fleet of 76 MW in operation in the US and Chile. The business model foresees long-term PPAs with utilities to deliver peak energy on demand. In California, AES is building a 100 MW plant to serve the electricity company Southern California Edison all of its system regulation needs. More recently, TenneT (the Dutch TSO) awarded the company with a 10 MW storage plant, which will be on line at the end of 2015 for primary control reserve.

The authors conclude that the structure, operation and especially regulation of electricity markets will ultimately shape incentives to build and invest in storage. As long as political and regulatory risks remain high, potential developers and investors as well as privately funded research and development will remain limited (EY, 2013b).

4.4.10 Sustainability considerations

The IEA estimates that annual global investments in clean energy infrastructure will need to more than double from US$214 in 2013 up to US$500 in 2020 and then double again to US$1 trillion by 2030 in order to limit global warming to 2°C and avoid the worst impacts of climate change (see also Chapter 1). Correspondingly, the share of renewable electricity generation globally would need to triple from around 20% currently to almost 60% by 2050 (IEA, 2012c). Moreover, the impact on the environment and human health associated with further exploitation of (non-renewable) fossil fuels and with nuclear energy development will ultimately negatively affect economic development as well. Consequently, the large-scale, global development of clean, renewable energy generation sources (RES) is crucial to current sustainable development strategies, despite the fact that some of them, e.g. PSH, may have potentially significant negative environmental and social impacts.

Access to and investment in T&D networks are necessary to foster economic and social development. Investments in new smart grids – together with storage facilities – are likely to significantly reduce the absolute amount of new T&D investments. Either way, close attention needs to be paid to their environmental impact, which, generally speaking, is relatively low. Storage facilities will strongly contribute to increasing grid efficiency, reliability and sustainability, compensating for the fluctuating output from intermittent renewable energy generators like wind and solar plants. Energy storage is seen as a key component to the overall development of sustainable energy systems.

The following sections address the environmental, social and governance (ESG) issues of the entire electricity value chain in the same sequence as discussed above: renewable power generation – solar, wind, hydro, bioenergy – transmission and distribution, and storage. For a comprehensive overview of ESG risk, please refer to Section 5.2.4.

4.4.10.1 Environmental

Electricity generation   Climate change affects power generation assets in many ways. Considerable efforts are made to implement engineering and non-engineering adaptation measures, such as more robust design specifications, refitting or relocating existing infrastructure with the goal to make them more robust to potential negative external (climate change driven) influences and/or to reduce their negative impact on the environment. Decentralised (renewable) power generation plants reduce the need for large facilities in areas exposed to environmental hazards, such as coastal areas. Below, the environmental considerations for solar, wind, hydropower and bioenergy are summarised.

Solar energy   Hail, wind, clouds and extreme temperatures negatively affect the output of solar PV panels. Output decreases significantly with increasing temperatures (e.g. cell temperatures of 50°C result in a 12% lower output than achievable under 'normal conditions'), cloud cover (less 40–80%) and higher wind speeds (which increase the effect of dust particle deposits and abrasion in arid regions) (ADB, 2012). CSP systems and installations, which may increase output by 30–45% compared with a fixed array, are vulnerable to strong winds and storms (e.g. hurricanes/cyclones). Also, as CSP systems require large amounts of cooling water, they can be affected by increased water scarcity caused by prolonged droughts in certain regions.

Adaption measures – engineering and non-engineering – may include designs that improve passive airflow beneath mounting structures, which contribute to reducing the panel temperature, distribution systems to improve grid stability in areas with rapidly fluctuating cloud cover as well as air or waterless cooling for CSP systems in water-restricted areas (ADB, 2012). In addition, PV energy generation systems should be located ideally in locations with moderate cloud cover, snowfall, strong winds or storms.

While solar PV energy generation consumes no fuel and releases no GHG emissions, the manufacturing of solar PV cells is an energy-intensive process requiring large amounts of (mainly fossil fuel) energy and using potentially hazardous materials. Recycling after disposal is critical, yet, in many developing countries, PV panels just get discarded into the environment or burnt, due to a lack of solid waste disposal infrastructure. This in turn results in polluting the environment with toxic gas and CO_2 emissions in the process. Yet, a 2013 news report by Stanford University determined that, owing to efficiency improvements and increased production rates, 'the electricity generated by all of the world's installed solar PV panels in 2012 probably surpassed the amount of energy going into fabricating more modules' (Stanford Report, 2013). This suggests that solar PV is now making a net positive contribution to energy production and GHG emissions reductions.

Notwithstanding, there are still concerns about large-scale solar PV and solar thermal facilities competing for productive land (around 1.5–6.5 hectares per megawatt) and causing habitat loss. Siting such facilities at low-quality locations such as non-productive land or along transportation corridors can address these issues. In addition, smaller-scale systems installed on rooftops will minimise the impact of land use (UCS, 2014).

Wind energy (onshore and offshore)   Cold temperatures, rain, snow, ice and hail can damage blades of wind turbines and reduce power output. Changes in wind patterns (frequency distribution, average speed and timing) can affect turbine performance and therewith wind power output (Baker, Walker and Wade, 1990). Offshore wind farms are affected by rising sea levels, sea ice from melting ice sheets and wind and sea wave loads, which may damage foundations and cause increased corrosion of structures (Pryor and Barthelmie, 2010). An increase in extreme wind (driven by climate change) may result in wind turbines having to be shut down more often in order to avoid damage or overloading the grid. The consequence would be a lower than expected seasonal and annual energy production, despite an overall increase in wind speeds.

Adaptation measures include the design of turbines and structures that can withstand higher wind speeds and gusts and ideally capture the energy of increased wind speeds. Additional protection may be granted by selecting sites that are less prone to, for example, changes in wind speed, storm surges and sea level rises during the lifetime of the turbines.

Large-scale onshore wind farms can occupy between 12 and 60 hectares per megawatt of power output with less than one acre per megawatt being permanently occupied due to the small footprint of each turbine tower. Accordingly, the impact on land use is minimal, allowing the productive use of the land for other purposes such as livestock grazing and food production. Concern over the impact of wind turbines on bird and bat populations because of collisions and changes in air pressure is relatively low and does not pose a threat to species populations' according to a study from the National Wind Coordinating Committee in the US (NWCC, 2010). Offshore wind turbines can have a potentially negative impact on marine wildlife from bird strikes as well as underwater noise disturbances, seabed disturbance and electromagnetic field generation caused by the large cables that carry generated electricity to the land (Bergström et al., 2014).

Hydroelectric energy   Climate change and the related changes in rainfall and temperature patterns may result in surface water evaporation, reduced or increased runoff owing to droughts or flooding and siltation (Mukheibir, 2007). Increased glacial melting and associated glacier flooding, landslides and avalanches can significantly affect hydropower infrastructure. In addition, climate change may also pose a risk of water supply shortages following changes in precipitation patterns and in snow pack levels as well as seasonal runoff flows.

Adaptation measures in areas where water flows are expected to change during the life of the hydropower asset include diverting upstream feeders, building additional water reservoirs, modifying spillways, constructing more robust, or reinforcing existing dams, as well as basin-wide management strategies, which take into account downstream environmental and human water uses (ADB, 2012). Afforestation of the upstream land to reduce the risks of erosion, mudslides, silting and flooding should also be considered.

The negative environmental impacts of hydropower are well known and are often due to the flooding of land for the creation of a large water reservoir. They may include the modification of water procurement for farmers and the local population, impacts on the sensitive flora and fauna in the region and the need to build transmission infrastructure through wilderness areas. The long-term effects of the world's largest dam, China's Three Gorges Dam, have been described as catastrophic. For example, as the dam disrupts heavy silt flows into the river, rapid silt build up is expected, which can lead to an imbalance upstream, depriving agricultural land and fish downstream of essential nutrients. Most new hydropower development is expected to come from large projects in China, India and Brazil, despite the fact that negative social and environmental impacts associated with such large-scale projects may limit the level of development in the affected areas.

The environmental impact of run-of-river projects – and even more so of mini- and micro-hydro projects – is generally much less than that of big dams because they do not affect the downstream flow. Notwithstanding this, the aquatic habitat can still be damaged.

Bioenergy   Extreme weather events (e.g. floods, extended droughts, forest fires, rainfall quantity, increasing CO_2 emissions) can severely affect the supply and quality of feedstock to operate biomass power plants. Adaptation measures include the introduction of more robust feedstock and more efficient irrigation systems than are prevalent today in areas with persistent droughts, early-warning systems to sudden changes in rainfall as well as temperature pattern and crop insurance. In addition, as applies to thermal power generation in general, increasing ambient temperatures may reduce the efficiency of equipment such as generators, boilers and turbines (US Climate Change Science Program, 2008). Water scarcity may affect the fuel processing and cooling processes, which can be addressed with recirculating cooling water systems (open-loop or once through, returning the water to its source or closed loop, recirculating the cooling water) (ADB, 2012).

While bioenergy is considered a renewable (and CO_2-neutral) source of energy, bioenergy production can produce methane gases (in the event of using animal and human waste), which in turn negatively affect the ozone layer. Moreover, bioenergy production may consume large amounts of water and energy both for cultivation and for processing (especially in the case of biofuels). The discharge of hot water in open loop cooling systems back into surface water may negatively affect aquatic life. In addition, bioenergy crops often compete with land for food crops and affect biodiversity by displacing existing wildlife habitat. Pesticide used for biofuel crops may also be harmful to local ecosystems. However, if sustainably managed, bioenergy production has the potential to positively impact sustainable development and reduce GHG emissions. A 2014 report from the International Renewable Energy Agency states that bioenergy could represent 60% of the global renewable energy supply by 2030 with around 40% of the total originating from agricultural residues and waste and another 30% coming from sustainable forestry products (IRENA, 2014).

Current schemes and standards to measure the sustainability of bioenergy production (especially in the case of biofuels) vary considerably. Therefore, organisations such as the World Wildlife Fund and the Global Bioenergy Partnership (GBP), supported by the FAO (Food and Agriculture Organization of the United States), have been working on developing global standards to promote and assess the sustainability of bioenergy. In 2011, the GBP identified 24 sustainability indicators of bioenergy. These indicators are now being used to build domestic policies. In addition, the International Organisation for Standardization (ISO) has developed ISO 12065; sustainability criteria for bioenergy, which provide a practical framework for the consideration of ESG issues in the evaluation of bioenergy projects and assets with the goal of preventing the harmful effects of bioenergy on the environment and society.

Transmission and distribution   The T&D industry is generally clean and forms both the backbone and nervous system of a low-carbon economy. However, electromagnetic emissions or landscape consumption by high-voltage ducts are examples of areas that require attention.

Climate-change-induced environmental hazards (e.g. storms, floods, increasing temperature, prolonged droughts) are sources of potential physical damage to and technical failures of overhead lines, underground cables and their equipment and challenge the operations of transmission network operators (TSO, DSO) (ADB, 2012). Strong winds can damage electric wire and distribution components and cool overhead lines by increasing heat convections; heavy snow, ice and moisture can affect networks, including transformer and switching stations, and reduce line integrity. Increasing temperatures may result in load management issues of transmission lines with capacity constraints; and T&D assets generally are exposed to the risk of physical damage from, for example, flooding or landslides.

Adaptation measures include using multiple routes, relocation, stronger distribution poles and changing overhead line transmission to underground cables to protect against increasing winds and storms, high temperatures and flooding.

Setting up overhead lines and underground cables has a significant impact on the soil and particularly on farmland. Site disruption and potential permanent damage during installation and repair of underground cables is significant (in particular for high-voltage lines), as the soil has to be removed from a large trench with possible disruption to drainage and watercourses or crop growth if installed on farmland. Further, cable fluid leaks from the insulation of underground cables are of concern; yet, generally, do not result in polluting the soil, groundwater or surface waters as biodegradable fluid has been used for decades. For overhead lines, the soil has to be excavated only to set the foundations of the pylons or poles, yet, height restrictions to trees and buildings apply. Overhead lines can be a collision hazard to birds, which can be minimised with brightly coloured attachments fitted to the wires.

Storage   The climate-change-related environmental hazards discussed above for hydropower generation also apply to PSH and CSP, but obviously not to battery production.

PSH, owing to its low energy density (energy stored per volume), requires significant land and water use, which may have environmental impacts, in particular the ones mentioned in connection with dam projects. New storage concepts are being evaluated, such as the use of underground reservoirs, which may help to mitigate such environmental impacts, although investment costs would be significant (ESA, 2015b). The same applies to CAES, from which the environmental impact, especially geological risks, can be significant. From an environmental perspective CAES only makes sense if a natural storage location (e.g. a depleted gas reservoir) eliminates the need for large infrastructural operations or a very long operational lifetime over centuries is expected (Bouman, Øberg and Hertwich, 2013).

Energy storage with flywheels is environmentally friendly but still negligible. The environmental issues related to energy storage in connection with CSP are discussed above.

The production process of most battery storage systems is currently very chemical- and energy-intensive. The sustainability of large-scale production using existing technologies therefore is questionable with respect to mining for raw materials extraction, energy use for manufacturing and toxic waste disposal.

Many energy storage technologies are still in the early stages of development and some promise to be more cost-effective and sustainable than the current ones. For example, a start-up company based out of Carnegie Mellon University brought to the market a large-scale battery technology for electric grid energy storage that claims to be cheaper and cleaner than current commercial scale products. This new battery technology, which uses sodium ions from saltwater, has a lifecycle cost of about half that of a comparable lead–acid battery (Bullis, 2014). Similarly, flow batteries do not cause exhausts or electrode depletion, typical of solid-state batteries. For a more comprehensive summary of how to account for the overall ESG risk, please refer to Section 5.2.4.

Energy storage, at the same time, fosters RES development and contributes to climate-change abatement, while responding to the pressure RES put on the system. It offers relevant benefits since it reduces reserve capacity of CO_2-intensive conventional generation. Redesigning the grid also reduces the need for new powerlines and related human intervention in the environment. For the above, the authors believe that a pragmatic investor will not refrain from evaluating all kinds of energy storage opportunities.

4.4.10.2 Social

Electricity generation   The installation of solar panels causes visual impacts on the landscape – be that land used for recreational or cultural activities, domestic living space or archaeological sites – due to the generally large facilities with numerous, highly geometric and sometimes strongly reflective surfaces. CSP systems could potentially even affect airplane operations if reflected light beams are misdirected into aircraft pathways.

The high temperatures involved in the operation of PV facilities, especially CSP facilities, pose a safety risk for the workforce and the electric and magnetic fields resulting from power generation facilities may affect the quality of life of neighbouring communities. In addition, there are occupational health risks associated with the emission of hazardous substances used to manufacture PV cells, such as solvents and acids used for cleaning the semiconductor parts. Noise emissions from wind turbines on wind farms are often the source of local public concern.

Negative social impacts of hydropower are often related to the expropriation of land and the displacement of (indigenous) communities, a prominent example being the construction of the Three Gorges Dam in China. An effect of forced displacement is the disruption to the traditional way of life and cultural patterns of indigenous communities. For those who can remain, severe impacts may occur from, first, pollution related to industrial activities settling around the power plants and, second, potential diseases imported from foreign workers. The World Commission on Dams – the global multi-stakeholder body established in 1997 by the World Bank and the International Union for Conservation of Nature (IUCN) in response to growing opposition to large dam projects – estimates that 40 to 80 million people have been displaced from their ancestral homes as a result of hydropower projects globally (International

Rivers, 2015). Moreover, in some areas water supply shortages are caused by seasonal runoff flows for communities located downstream of the hydropower infrastructure.

The growing use of food crops for the production of bioenergy can have severe impacts on human health, particularly in the developing world, foremost resulting in deteriorating food security, food and water scarcity and related consequences (e.g. malnutrition, increasing maternal and child mortality, poor public health). Odorous emissions are notable in terms of their negative impact on the quality of life of neighbouring communities. While the odours are not harmful, they can attract unwanted pests, which spread bacteria and infection.

Transmission and distribution   There is significant concern related to electromagnetic emissions and potential related health risks from the electric and magnetic fields (EMFs) near overhead lines and underground cables.

Underground cables are (preferably) installed in dense urban areas, which invariably leads to disturbance of the neighbouring population during construction or repair. The visual impact of overhead lines on sensitive environments (e.g. pristine or lightly populated countryside, archaeological sites, leisure amenity areas) and the potential noise under certain weather conditions can be disturbing and intrusive to local communities. Public resistance can result in long and costly delays to the construction of new lines, hence utility companies pay considerable attention to finding routes that minimise the impact on the natural environment and cultural heritage.

Storage   The social issues related to hydropower and CSP are discussed above. Batteries, as well as hydrogen storage, pose public safety concerns both from their use (risk of potential explosion) and from their disposal.

4.4.10.3   Governance

Electricity generation and storage   Typical governance issues related to large infrastructure projects, such as power generation and storage projects, may concern the regulatory environment, the rule of law and business practices in the host country. The construction, operation and management of infrastructure projects generally are prone to governance risks, in particular lack of transparency and accountability and – as often is the case when government concessions are involved – corruption and bribery. The US$59 billion Three Gorges Dam project, the world's largest hydropower project, serves as an unfortunate example yet again: officials at the Three Gorges Corporation, the company set up to build the dam, were found guilty of nepotism, shady property deals and dodgy bidding procedures (Hui and Blanchard, 2014). In addition, at least US$30 million were embezzled from the project during its first six years of construction and several officials were executed for misappropriating resettlement funds (Wong, 2007).

Political instability with all its known potential consequences on governance more often than not is the primary reason for investors to shy away from investment opportunities in certain countries such as solar projects in Africa (e.g. Libya, Algeria, Tunisia). This is unfortunate as such projects have the potential to support these regions economically and socially, e.g. meet local energy needs and enable income from power export to Europe.

Transmission and distribution   Governance issues in T&D networks, which are characterised by the natural monopolist situation of T&D network operators, relate to the competitive behaviour of industry participants, unfair pricing, market manipulation and potentially corrupt practices. As the largest expansion in power T&D networks (and the related socio-economic benefits) will take place in developing economies, potential investors need to pay particular attention to regulatory readiness, the rule of law and transparency in management. Governance issues need to be addressed, as always, when government licences are handed out to market participants.

4.5 ENERGY – NATURAL GAS NETWORKS

4.5.1 Characteristics and organisation

Gas T&D operators are 'natural monopolies' and, as such, are heavily regulated, also for national security and safety reasons. A well-regulated T&D grid provides a fundamental service to society by granting equal access to gas for industrial and private users.

In 2012, natural gas represented 21% of the global energy demand (IEA, 2014e) and was the third primary source of energy in the world (after oil and coal), and the second in Europe.[28] Global gas demand is estimated at 3500 billion cubic metres (bcm) per year, approximately 70% of the level of oil consumptions. In 2012, the main consumers were the US (approximately 700 bcm), the EU and Russia (each approximately 400 bcm) and the Middle East (cumulatively approximately 400 bcm)[29] with approximately 41% of the gas consumed being used for power generation, 24% for industrial processes and 20% for heating of buildings (Evans and Farina, 2013). Natural gas has a current share of almost one-quarter (23%) of the energy used for electricity generation (Allianz, 2015b).

Gas demand is extremely seasonal (heating during winter and peak power at high temperatures) and variable across the day/week, since it is mainly driven by the electricity peak demand of end-users. Their demand is met by RES to the extent that they generate power at the time it is needed (priority dispatch) and the remainder by combined cycle gas turbine (CCGT) power plants.

Globally, natural gas demand is increasing, while demand for oil is decreasing. In the period from 2012 to 2025, gas demand is expected to grow with a CAGR of 2.8% in bcm (billion cubic meter) terms, 2.4% in MTOE[30]), mainly driven by increased power generation requirements (+3.6% in bcm, +4.4% in TWh). The European gas demand, in contrast, decreased by approximately 17% (2014 vs. 2008) and is expected to stabilise at a slightly higher level than in 2014 by 2030. This has been triggered primarily by: (i) decreased CO_2 certificate prices together with a lack of a market for CO_2 in general and (ii) a significant (and unexpected) increase of coal-fired power generation, especially in the UK, Germany and Spain, plus 'cheap' coal imports from the US (for the coal could no longer compete with the low gas prices in the US). Depressed gas demand and low electricity prices in Europe are the result, hence making running CCGT power plants a loss-making business (CEDIGAZ, 2015a). The decommissioning of old coal-fired power plants both in Europe and the US is expected to happen in the foreseeable future, primarily for environmental reasons. This is likely to restore gas demand for power generation.

Geographically, markets show significant price differences (before local distribution costs), mainly because of logistics costs (from wells up to local distribution). For instance,

---

[28]EU-28; see Eurogas (2014).
[29]Russia, the US and Canada have the highest gas consumption per capita (BP, 2015).
[30]MTOE = million tonnes of oil equivalent (a unit of energy).

in 2014 in Japan, the LNG cif price (price including cost, insurance and freight) was 16.33 US$/MBtu,[31] close to the crude oil average price in the OECD, while in the US and Canada natural gas prices stood at 4.35 and 3.87 US$/MBtu (BP, 2015) respectively. The US government expects the domestic spot prices to increase by 2.8% per annum from 2015 to 2040 in real terms (EIA, 2015a). It is highly difficult to predict a long-term price development for Europe (Rogers, 2015).

Established proven reserves globally of 187 000 bcm of natural gas, which can be economically extracted with current technologies, are expected to meet approximately 50 years of demand (BP, 2015). In 2012, the vast majority (86%) of the natural gas was extracted from sandstone or limestone reservoirs, with only 14% of the gas supply coming from unconventional sources (e.g. coal bed methane, shale gas and tight sands). Since 2000, unconventional production has grown by approximately 20% a year and its share is set to increase further to over 18% in 2025 (+6%/year). Currently, the US accounts for 80% of unconventional gas production (Allianz, 2015b).

Natural gas is usually extracted from oil reservoirs (associated gas) or from gas wells/condensate wells. It requires processing, which is usually done near the well, in order to meet commercial gas quality and purity specification requirements (for transport). These so-called upstream and midstream infrastructure assets are traditionally targeted by strategic investors, such as oil and gas majors or exploration companies. They will not be discussed further in this book because they tend to have rather high-risk profiles from which most institutional investors shy away – at least as direct investments. Instead, this book will focus on so-called downstream assets, which include transportation (pipelines and compression/pumping stations), storage and distribution activities (including meters and control rooms) within the natural gas sector. They tend to have a relatively low-risk profile and hence are sought after by many of whom we believe will be reading this book. These activities are displayed in the levels 6 to 10 of Figure 4.19, which illustrates the entire natural gas value chain.

The T&D elements of the gas value chain can be split into three different businesses: (i) transmission/transportation (high-pressure pipelines and LNG), (ii) storage and (iii) distribution (see also Section 4.5.5).

4.5.2 Transmission

Long-haul high-pressure pipelines transmit and transport approximately 68% of natural gas with the remaining 32% traded by sea or land as liquefied natural gas (LNG). Transmission of gas is around five times more costly than that of oil. They dispatch gas at US$1–US$4/MBTU. Seaborne LNG shipping costs approximately US$2–US$6/MBTU (Evans and Farina, 2013).

Long-haul pipelines are geostrategic assets, connecting producers and consumers. In some cases, consumers in one country are dependent on the production in another country (e.g. Hungary depends on Russia for 80% of its gas), making the reliability of gas being pumped through the pipelines a matter of national security. On this point, Europe is building a new pipeline (Trans-Adriatic Pipeline, or TAP, 10 to 20 bcm/year) connecting the Caspian Sea with Western Europe in order to have access to an alternative gas supply outside of Russia. TAP, which should be ready by 2020, will cost approximately €20 billion and is financed by a number of oil majors (BP, SOCAR, SNAM) and utilities (Axpo, Enagás, Fluxys) with E.ON as a project partner.

The construction of new (international) pipelines is usually a governmental initiative of the hosting countries, typically sponsored by both main gas off-takers and producers. Due

---

[31] MBtu = million British thermal units (equivalent to approximately 27 cubic metres).

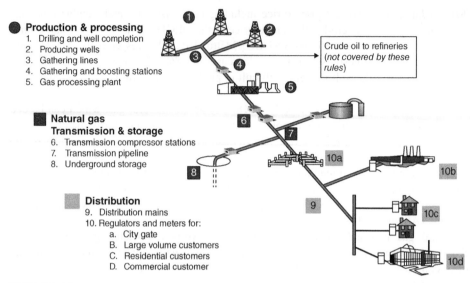

FIGURE 4.19   Natural gas value chain (EPA)
Source: EPA (2015c)

to foreign policy issues surrounding these projects (like the recent Russia–EU crisis), many are delayed or cancelled (e.g. Shtokman gas field links in the Barents Sea; South Stream in the Mediterranean Sea and Nabucco). Still, a large number of projects are currently under construction worldwide. In the US alone, approximately 40 projects are approved or under construction with over US$17 billion of assumed capital expenditure (EIA, 2015b). In Europe, various studies anticipate the need of vast investment programmes in the area of €65–70 billion to solve bottlenecks and increase interconnections (Holz, 2015).

LNG is a reliable means of transporting gas, especially from remote extraction locations to the consumption markets (e.g. from Nigeria and Mozambique) or where a long natural gas pipeline would not be economically feasible. It is possible to ship 600 times more gas in liquid state (cooled down to –168°C/–270°F) than in its natural state. Furthermore, LNG does not ignite easily in the event of spills. LNG technologies are well proven and have been operating commercially since 1964.

Lately, LNG-based logistics have increased in relevance because of supply security issues and in order to diversify gas imports from unstable or geopolitically risky countries (i.e. Russian or North African sources).

4.5.3   Storage

Natural gas storage is required to smooth gas price volatility and buffer seasonal supply and demand swings but also to secure supply (strategic reserves).

Gas is usually stored underground in depleted gas/oil reservoirs; alternative facilities are salt caverns and aquifers. Storage facilities are connected to the main pipeline and employ various wells for injection, measurement, withdrawal as well as dehydration and gathering facilities. The technologies applied in underground storage are known and safe: the first commercial storage facility commenced operations in Ontario in 1915.

Underground storage requires a large amount of gas, which fills the cavern volume necessary to achieve sufficient pressure (cushion gas, which cannot be extracted). Hence, the cost of cushion gas is the single largest investment component of a gas storage facility with up to 50% of the total capital expenditure (IEA, 2014f). Working gas, which can be withdrawn or commercially stored, is only a fraction of the total stored volume. It needs to be recycled in the reservoirs, however, in order not to lose pressure or dissolve in the geological formations. The economics of this business are significantly determined by accurately predicting when to recycle the working gas.

Despite the decreasing gas demand in Europe, storage capacity in Europe grows steadily: 17% between 2014 and 2010. Approximately 20 bcm of additional capacity is under construction with delivery by 2025 (mostly in Germany and Italy) (CEDIGAZ, 2015b). A further 55 bcm are in the planning phase (mostly in the UK and Turkey). To give an indication of the capital requirements involved: the recent development of a small, depleted reservoir in Italy (1.3 bcm, 40-year concession) required capital expenditures of €1.2 billion with 80% leverage.

The main reasons for this (seemingly counterintuitive) development, are:

i. change of gas sales contracts: the market is expected to move from long-term take-or-pay supply contracts, which provide relative stability and predictability to both contractual parties, towards 'hub pricing', where prices are traded at spot terms. This kind of hub pricing, which is common in the US, requires flexibility, and hence more storage capacities close to the hubs,
ii. remoteness of new supply sources and
iii. increased system balancing activities caused by the additional storage.

4.5.4 Distribution

Analogous to electricity distribution, gas DSOs (in the US: local distribution companies, or LDCs) dispatch methane to the end-users. They expand the gas to a lower compression rate (in two stages) to make it usable at the customer's location. While operating their own networks, DSOs/LDCs are also responsible for not just the health and safety of their own operations but also the emergency response to natural disasters or technical failures that affect those operations. A relevant safety aspect is gas losses, which account for approximately 1.7% of consumption in the US and are mostly originated in the low-pressure networks of DSOs caused by leakages or natural accidents (EIA, 2014). DSOs must also ensure open access and metering neutrality to support competition in the marketing of gas to the final user.

Increased volatility of demand, mainly caused by large off-takers, like CCGT plants, requires DSOs to upgrade their networks/pipelines such that they can integrate the exchange of information with the physical supply of gas – similar to smart grids. Traditionally, gas extraction at the wells was designed to match seasonal demand levels, with a relatively small necessity of storage. The increased RES power generation (discussed in Section 4.4.2) combined with Europe's dependency on politically difficult gas sources requires DSOs to respond to demand in the OECD countries differently than in the past. Smart metering and demand planning as well as more physical and digital interconnections among networks – like Edig@s, the common information exchange platform of European TSOs (ENTSOG, 2015; Edigas, 2015) – may help to address these issues.

4.5.5 Sources of revenue and value chain elements

In most countries, the sources of revenue of T&D operators are determined entirely by the national regulator. According to these regulations, operators charge the owners of the gas (i.e. utility/marketing companies) for their dispatching and system services. The owners in turn

TABLE 4.18 Natural gas: Value chain and investment opportunities

Value chain elements	Investment opportunities
Extraction and processing	
– Production and processing	– Drilling and well completion
	– Production wells
	– Gathering lines
– Processing	– Gathering and boosting stations
	– Processing plant
	– LNG liquefaction plants
	– LNG vessels
	– LNG terminals
	– LNG regasification plants
Transmission	
– Transmission (long distance)	– Transmission network (compressor stations, pipeline)
Storage	
– Strategic reserves	– Caverns (underground)
– Balance of system	– LNG storage facilities
	– Distribution facilities
Distribution	
– Distribution (regional and last mile)	– Distribution network (distribution mains, metering system)
Marketing	
– Billing	– Metering devices
– Yield management (pricing)	

are allowed to pass these costs on to the end-users. As such, T&D services are financed by a combination of user payments and availability payments (see Section 3.3 for the three main business models).

On a regular basis, the regulator sets the rates the T&D operators are allowed to charge similar to electricity T&D. The rates are mainly determined by the allowed revenue mechanism, based on the recovery of certain costs and return on capital invested, the so called RAB (see Section 4.4.8.3). In most OECD countries, the mechanism includes adjustment factors – essentially incentives – for quality, availability, level of required investments and system services.

Gas storage revenues are also regulated since in most jurisdictions TSOs must ensure a strategic national reserve, for which they receive an allowed return (in addition to the transmission availability fees).

Table 4.18 provides a summary of the value chain and investment opportunities for natural gas.

4.5.6 Competition and regulation

The gas market in OECD countries is structured similarly to their electricity markets, only that the deregulation of the gas industry and unbundling of the pipelines was already initiated in the 1980s and early 1990s. In essence, producers may sell the resource to marketers, local distributors or directly to end-users. T&D operators (both TSOs and DSOs) must ensure that the owners of the resource are given the possibility to transfer the gas all the way to the final user at a controlled dispatch fee. National regulators oversee the market to ensure competition is not harmed by the natural monopolies.

Direct competition tends to be low or non-existent because a gas pipeline links a single natural gas provider to a single regional network of customers. However, competition on costs exists between producers and gas T&D companies.

The residential and commercial gas markets are less competitive than the ones for electricity (at least for the retail segment). In the US, approximately 10% of the 66.7 million residential users entered into marketing agreements with marketers different from their local distribution companies (LDC). In Europe, in just a few countries there is significant supplier switching (close to 20% in the UK and Spain); Germany represents the average (12.7% in 2013, of which 20% caused by relocation of the consumer) (Bundesnetzagentur, 2014).

As with electricity distribution, last-mile gas players are still not concentrated. In 2008, the US counted more than 1500 LDCs (EIA, 2008). In 2013, Germany had approximately 711 DSOs (Bundesnetzagentur, 2014), of which 683 served fewer than 100 000 customers and 586 with a network shorter than 1000 km. The UK counted 31 players, 10 more than the ones delivering power (CEER, 2013). In contrast, in most European countries the upstream and midstream gas market is in the hands of a few incumbent suppliers/producers that control imports and determine the supply price for DSOs.

4.5.7 Private-sector involvement

The current trend is towards private investors taking positions in gas transmission assets (TSOs). Many European gas networks have been sold partially or entirely by the national incumbents to third-party investors in recent years, including Germany, Norway, Sweden, Switzerland, Austria and Finland. This development is primarily driven by the above-mentioned unbundling of generation and transmission assets and related services in most Western countries.

Global natural gas transmission investments are forecast to amount to US$2633 billion from 2012 to 2035 with a 50/50 split between OECD and non-OECD countries (IEA, 2014c).

The authors consider investments in long-distance gas transmission (international pipelines) as very attractive for financial investors, albeit far from easy given some assets comprise significant market risks in addition to operational complexity, size and regulatory risk exposure.

LNG-related logistics assets like special-purpose tank vessels (approximately 420 worldwide), liquidation plants (54 facilities with 92 trains in operation for export) and regasification plants (for import) do not qualify as infrastructure assets according to this book's definition. Notwithstanding, they represent possibly interesting, investable assets for risk-taking equity or debt investors. However, there are few examples of pure financial investors in this segment so far – possibly for a reason (GIIGNL, 2015). LNG facilities may be particularly attractive for debt investors, as a recent analysis of 26 project-financed LNG plants with an average capital expenditure of US$4.5 billion indicates (Ruester, 2015). Take-or-pay tolling agreements covered most of the expected revenues (LNG plant operators usually do not own the gas).

The two most important risks in this business are market risk (e.g. decreasing LNG prices, competition on vessels calling neighbouring import LNG plants) and country risk (i.e. politically unstable countries). Because of the latter, investors prefer export facilities located in the US, Canada and Australia and import facilities in Europe. Further, LNG plants operate under strict safety and environmental regulations and have long licensing and construction times. Finally, LNG projects tend to be concentrated on a few parties acting as both equity investors and off-takers, which guarantee 70–80% of the sales of the plant's capacity. While these off-take guarantees (tolling agreements) help secure debt financing, they lead to significant counterparty risk.

Natural gas storage can also be of interest for risk-taking investors. There is a good pipeline of assets in safe OECD countries and sufficient demand. Debt investments may be easier to structure for financial investors, even though most opportunities are greenfield/primary with technical complexity and counterparty risk as well.

DSOs are considered attractive investment targets for (also 'smaller') financial investors given size, number of players and business models.

4.5.8 Sustainability considerations

The most relevant ESG factors for investors in natural gas transmission, storage and distribution assets are related to environmental issues including climate change, health and safety and governance practices. They are discussed below. For a comprehensive overview of ESG risks, please refer to Section 5.2.4.

4.5.8.1 Environmental Generally, natural gas is regarded as the cleanest fossil fuel in the context of climate-change risk as its combustion emits less than half the CO_2 that coal does and it operates with a 50–60% efficiency range (NETL, 2007). These results are less favourable, though, when the leakage of methane in connection with drilling and the extraction of natural gas from wells and its transportation in pipelines is taken into account as well, because methane is a far more potent global warming gas than CO_2. As such it has significant global warming potential (Tollefson, 2013). Further, a 2014 IEA report cautions that 'natural gas should be seen only as a "bridge" fuel to cleaner energy technologies unless carbon capture and storage (CCS) is deployed' (IEA, 2014g). The report also notes that, based on possible future energy scenarios, emissions from gas-fired plants will be higher than the average carbon intensity of the global electricity mix after 2025 and thus will lose its status as a low-carbon fuel. The rapid expansion of hydraulic fracturing (or 'fracking') in gas extraction, which requires large amounts of water, sand and chemicals to be pumped deep into the ground, surely does not improve the environmental footprint of gas. As a Stanford University report affirms, fracking poses both environmental and human health risks in the form of local water supply shortages, groundwater contamination and habitat fragmentation (Golden, 2014).

Finally, climate change (specifically, global warming) may also pose physical risks to the stability of underground natural gas pipelines and storage capacities, owing to landslides and changes in hydrology (e.g. melting permafrost in Northern Russia increases the potential for mass movement in soil substructure; Anisimov and Reneva, 2006).

Downstream activities (i.e. the transmission, storage and distribution of natural gas) may have a significant environmental impact, mainly related to air pollution and the infringement of sensitive ecosystems. Air emissions include fugitive air emissions (leakage) but also exhaust fumes from compressor engines and emissions from transporting LNG, posing risks to human health. As more and more offshore and remote production areas are developed (e.g. arctic drilling), transport distances for LNG and the related emissions and negative effects on terrestrial and marine biodiversity will increase.

The construction of pipelines and transport lines requires clearing of vegetation and results in a loss of habitat and fragmentation, changes in species movement, sedimentation and air emissions (e.g. leakage). Fragmentation of large contiguous forest patches is harmful to a wide range of forest species and promotes the spread of invasive species and tree damage from wind and storms. Similar environmental issues apply (albeit possibly to a lesser extent) to natural gas distribution in rural areas. Offshore pipelines affect the surface sediments and their communities and may result in long-lasting changes to the topography (Boesch and Rabalais, 2003).

Environmental issues in gas storage are predominantly related to reservoir management and its safe operations. As natural gas is mostly made up of methane, fugitive emissions of natural gas into the atmosphere can lead to explosions. In underground natural gas storage, migration of natural gas out of the storage formation may result in the contamination of the groundwater (Miyazaki, 2009).

4.5.8.2 Social
The social impacts of natural gas transmission, storage and distribution relate mainly to the health and safety of workers and local communities. Leaks in gas pipelines, gas distribution pipes and storage facilities can lead to explosions and cause fires. In addition, the excavation works for the installation of distribution pipes can be a major inconvenience for local communities, in particular in crowded urban settings and scenic rural environments. Negative aesthetic impacts can be associated with natural gas storage facilities, in particular visual impacts from surface facilities that may include wellhead valve assemblies, gathering lines and compression facilities; moreover, noise emission from compression stations may be an issue (Jellicoe and Delgado, 2014). Pipeline companies depend for their rights of way on good relations with and support from local communities. Negative impacts, accidents and perceived hazards are disruptive to their operations and may prove costly in terms of lost revenues, reputational damage and potential legal damages.

While pipeline operating companies (TSOs and DSOs) focus on ensuring operational safety and maintaining a culture of additional safety among their workers, local utilities focus on customer safety and have put a number of safety measures in place to prevent accidents, among which are sophisticated leak detection equipment with the addition of odorants to the natural gas to make it easier to detect, safety education programmes for customers and local communities, and emergency procedures.

4.5.8.3 Governance
Governance issues in the downstream industry (transmission, storage and distribution) relate to the competitive behaviour of industry participants, unfair pricing, market manipulation and potentially corrupt practices. This is not surprising, as T&D networks are prominent examples of natural monopolies that generally control all the gas transported to and distributed in an area. The aim of any governance activities is to provide safe, efficient and reliable access for all customers.

Corruption risks in the natural gas midstream sector are prevalent and arise, for example, in connection with contract and licence acquisition, joint ventures with state-owned entities and requests to consider specific third parties.

4.6 ENERGY – DISTRICT ENERGY SYSTEMS (DES)[32]

District energy systems (DES) represent a combination of technologies that seek to develop synergies between the production and supply of heat, cooling, hot water, electricity and stored

---

[32]Unless otherwise noted, the two main sources of information for this section are UNEP (2015) and IEA (2014h).

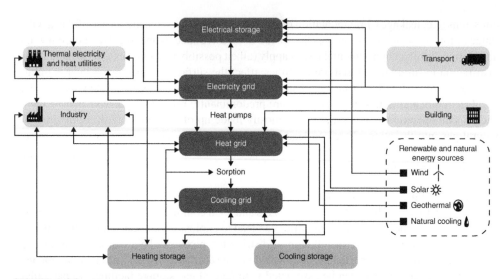

FIGURE 4.20   Illustration of an integrated district energy system
Source: IEA (2014h), © OECD/IEA 2014 Linking Heat and Electricity Systems, Co-generation and District Heating and Cooling Solutions for a Clean Energy. Future, IEA Publishing. Licence: www.iea.org/t&c/termsandconditions

energy, using different energy sources including co-generation, renewable power and heat, including waste heat. The idea behind district energy is to pool energy users (buildings and industrial facilities) in a local network so that energy can be consumed closer to the point of generation, thus avoiding energy losses associated with conventional generation, transmission and distribution systems over long distances (Johnson Controls, 2008). DES predominantly comprises of proven technologies that have been around for many years.

4.6.1   Characteristics and organisation

At the core, DES use a network of (usually underground) insulated pipes to distribute either hot water/steam or chilled water from multiple generation sources to various usage (and storage) points within a geographical district. In addition, they can bridge – and possibly help balance – electrical and thermal energy networks. As such, district energy provides a flexible system for optimising the integration of co-generation and RES (see Figure 4.20).

DES are an excellent tool for supporting the energy transition globally thanks to four key benefits: (i) high energy efficiency, (ii) easy integration of renewable energy, (iii) capability of supporting the balancing of power and gas networks and (iv) easy adaptability to local conditions and supply-demand changes (for challenges of RES integration, see also Section 4.4.8.1).

Such systems are most economical in areas with a high density of energy users, such as cities, as they require less capital cost (length of installed pipe) per unit of energy delivered. At the same time, they offer an ideal solution for local authorities to provide a cost-effective means to meet the strategic goals of increasing energy efficiency and renewable energy contribution while reducing GHG emissions. The successful implementation of district energy systems requires a 'systems thinking' approach, which integrates energy, transport, construction and other industry sectors and takes advantage of synergies as well as new energy storage solutions.

In addition to supplying heating and cooling to buildings, DES provide a number of benefits to society as a whole:

- *High energy efficiency* – ideal for capturing 'waste heat' from co-generation plants, waste incineration or industrial thermal processes.[33] In addition, DES can transfer waste heat from buildings (e.g. from data centres) to other buildings in the network with a heating demand. This way, DES increase energy efficiency unlike most conventional heating and cooling systems, thus saving energy and reducing GHG emissions.
- *Easy integration of renewable energy* – easy integration of local, renewable (thermal and electricity) energy sources (RES) such as geothermal, solar thermal, biomass and waste heat as well as wind and solar. Surplus electricity from RES can be stored in the system, enabling a significantly higher penetration of variable RES, such as wind and solar, in the electricity system. This is accomplished by converting electricity into hot or chilled water and by making use of large-scale heat pumps and thermal storage (IEA, 2014h). 'Free cooling' can also be captured from local lakes or the sea, providing a renewable source of cooling, thus reducing the need for fossil fuels for electrical air conditioning. As such, DES supports the case for energy security boosted through RES and energy efficiency.
- *Support balancing of power and gas networks* – given the capability of DES to easily integrate RES and to generate power and/or gas from biomass on short notice, DES can help level out peaks of supply and demand, which were shown to be among the most severe problems of today's power networks.
- *Easily adaptable to local conditions and changes in supply and demand* – district energy systems can be employed on a global scale while still being locally adaptable to a diverse range of climatic and geographical conditions, owing to their flexible use with a broad range of heating and cooling supply sources.

Globally, the majority of DES is used to supply thermal energy for space heating and hot water. In colder climates they often generate electricity as well. Heating networks can vary in terms of size and load. The largest networks are fuelled by CHPs of 200 MW or more (producing both heat and electricity) and can be found in cities such as Copenhagen, Helsinki, Oslo, Munich, Paris, Toronto, Christchurch (New Zealand) and Tokyo, to name a few. Cooling networks, although not as widespread as those used for heating, have been on the rise recently because of the rapid urban development in warm climates. For example, the city of Dubai, where 70% of electricity demand is from air conditioners, has developed the world's largest district cooling network with plans to meet 40% of its cooling needs through district cooling by 2030 while reducing air conditioning energy by half (UNEP, 2015). Worldwide, the use of DES has been increasing by 12% in Europe, 30% in China and 50% in Russia. In South Korea, district cooling more than tripled between 2009 and 2011.

While first-generation district heating technologies date back to 1900, the latest so-called fourth generation systems (expected to be implemented from 2020 onwards) will be able to operate at low temperatures, resulting in reduced heat loss compared to previous generations, and making connections to areas with low energy density feasible. Such systems will use diverse sources of heat, including low-grade waste heat, and will allow consumers to feed their

---

[33]Globally, thermal power plants achieved a conversion efficiency of 36% in 2011 (IEA, 2011). Co-generation units have an overall yield of 58%, converting the energy input into electricity and heat at the same time. Newer co-generation units can reach conversion efficiencies as high as 90% (IDA, 2015).

heat into the network as well. Heat storage, smart systems and flexible supply will allow high levels of variable renewable energy into the grid.

4.6.2 Sources of revenue and value chain elements

As a rule, district energy is cost-competitive in many climates and economies, thanks to utilising waste heat/cold in many instances. This may be one of the reasons why in many jurisdictions DES do not receive subsidies along the lines of, for example, renewable energy generation plants but instead are directly user-financed. Notwithstanding, parts of the overall district energy system may be eligible for (national) subsidies (budget-financed) of some sort, that is a combination of two of the business models explained above. As such they may be able to contribute to the 'bottom line' for private investors (see also Section 3.3 and Section 4.4.7).

For example, the Scottish government's District Heating Loan Fund is a support scheme that offers low-interest loans to help overcome the high capital costs associated with district heating systems. In Denmark, renewable heat sources (such as heat from CHP plants connected to a district energy system) are exempt from national energy production taxes, while Germany offers low-interest loans for investments in CHP plants and heating boilers that use biomass feedstock (RES LEGAL, 2015). A more indirect example is President Obama's 2012 executive order to put online 40 GW of new CHP systems nationally (a 50% increase) by 2020. This executive order may help to drive state and local legislation support of CHP investments.

More specifically, district energy systems earn revenues from several sources: Heating and cooling, power, ancillary services, connection charges and various other sources of (smaller) revenues.

- *Heating and cooling* – sales are determined by the absolute demand and load profiles of buildings connected to the system. A diversification of consumers as well as of thermal storage may smooth the aggregated load profile, which may allow for attractive heating or cooling offerings. Prices for either service may be regulated or be part of a somewhat liberalised market. Often, the rates have two elements: a capacity charge and a consumption charge.
- *Power* – district energy systems will generally include one or more CHP plants, generating electricity along with heat. The power is typically fed into the distribution or transmission grid and sold on the market at market prices via long-term PPAs or on the spot. In case regulatory support schemes apply (e.g. FITs), these will change the revenue profile (see Section 4.4.2).
- *Ancillary services* – additional revenue may be generated from capacity premiums for being located in a stressed power grid as well as balancing services to the transmission or distribution grid.
- *Connection charges* – to connect to a well-maintained grid users make either a one-off payment or pay a fixed annual/monthly charge.
- *Various of sources* – district energy systems operators may be able to generate additional revenue from subsidies, e.g. for renewable/CHP heat or electricity or from carbon trading.

District energy systems provide value-added by helping to reduce CO_2 emissions and increase local energy security. They do so through improved efficiency and system flexibility that allows for the bridging of, and support of balancing, electricity and thermal systems and the ability to integrate a wide diversity of energy sources (see the box listing the four main benefits).

THE MARSTAL DISTRICT HEATING PLANT, MARSTAL, DENMARK

The Marstal District Heating (DH) Plant, completed in 2011/12 in Marstal, Denmark, provides heating to around 1550 buildings (mostly single family homes). It was developed to demonstrate the potential of using 100% renewable energy for district heating. The system combines 33 365 m^2 of solar thermal energy collectors with biomass (wood chip) boilers, a 4 MW heat and power (CHP) unit, a 1.5 MW compressing heat pump and 87 100 cubic metres (m^3) of local heat storage.

The DH system is very flexible, allowing the conversion of not only surplus electricity into storable thermal energy (power-to-heat) but also stored hot water back into electricity (heat-to-power). In addition, the system can be changed throughout the year for optimal year-round performance. Solar collectors providing most heat and storage throughout the summer. They are supplemented by the heat pump and the wood chip during most of the remaining year, with the back-up waste/bio oil boilers used for a few hours each day to help meet heating demand on the coldest, darkest, winter days.

Denmark's relevant regulatory guidelines support highly efficient, low carbon energy systems such as the Marstal DH by requiring that heat production in municipalities is met by the least-expensive heating option for end-users while meeting national targets of all electricity and heat production using 100% RES by 2035. To support this goal, fossil fuels are heavily taxed while solar energy production is not taxed at all, with reduced tax on electricity used for heat pumps.

In Denmark, DH utilities are non-profit companies. Marstal DH is a consumer-owned cooperative meeting the heating needs of over 95% of the buildings in Marstal. The DH plant is estimated to reduce around 10.5 kilotonnes of CO_2 emissions annually.

Source: Marstal (2013)

CITY OF LONDON COMBINED HEAT AND POWER PLANT

The City of London's district energy system (DES) supplies heat and cooling from a natural gas-fuelled power station via an underground pipe network to nine of the City's large mixed-use properties, which act as anchor customers, as well as to private households. The DES is run as a PPP. The City Corporation is the public partner, and the energy service company, Citigen, the private partner, is responsible for the design, development, financing, and operation. When laying the network's 3.6 km of pipes, Citigen took advantage of existing subways, basements and car parks, which reduced the need to dig up public roads. There was no objection from residents to the development of the scheme. Citigen takes the commercial risk, having invested £70 million to date. Profitability depends on the revenues from both the volume of electricity sold into the grid and the price of gas. Currently, the DES operates at a loss due to electricity prices being lower than assumed.

The DES helps the City of London to achieve its environmental policy and community strategy targets by saving about 3000 tonnes of CO_2 each year. In addition, the City benefits from discounted energy charges for its properties and is freed from paying climate change levy charges. It can avoid installing traditional boilers and chillers and gains additional space from not having to install flues and cooling towers. Currently, the DES runs primarily on natural gas but it can switch to biogas, once it's a more viable option, making it more environmentally friendly in the future.

Source: City of London (2016)

4.6.3 Competition and regulation

Market regulations and the stability of energy policies are key to promoting investments in district energy projects by allowing for a reasonably accurate assessment of a project's ROI, minimising risks for supply plants and grid operators, and rewarding the use of efficient, low-carbon generation technologies. Policy measures may be directed towards reducing the high, upfront capital cost of a district energy system or be used to reduce the costs associated with the operation and maintenance of the system. Local or national policy measures may include a fuel tax exemption system for co-generation, FITs for electricity and heat exported to the distribution network and obligations from distribution grid operators to purchase electricity from efficient, low-carbon sources (see Section 4.4.2).

District energy systems typically compete with natural gas and electricity suppliers for customers (usually building owners or renters). The outcome of the competition between DES services and local gas/electricity service providers depends, in large part, on regulatory measures (both local and national). For example, if a city mandates local building owners to connect to the local DES network for energy efficiency or carbon reduction reasons, it eliminates competition altogether. In such a case, the local authority may put in place tariff regulations to protect building owners from a monopolistic market. Some tariffs are regulated through local or national policies requiring DES to be priced at the cost of the next-alternative technology (such as a gas boiler). In areas with mature DES markets (mainly district heating) such as Scandinavia, Eastern Europe, Germany and major cities in the US and Canada, advanced consumer protection policies are already in place. However, most regions with relatively immature markets (such as the UK) currently lack DES regulations (Business Green, 2015).

Financial and fiscal incentives can also help mitigate the impact of market failure by rewarding the environmental/societal benefits of district energy projects. Several examples of such policy impacts are listed below:

- *Denmark*: the Marstal solar-thermal district heating plant integrating solar thermal generation, large-scale energy storage, heat pump and biomass co-generation was developed under the framework of the Danish government's goal of using 100% renewable heat and electricity generation by 2035 (see the Marstal case study).
- *UK*: policy measures under the Renewable Obligation Certificates (ROC), jointly promoting low-carbon and efficient electricity, were essential for the economic feasibility of the biomass-fuelled co-generation project for the Tullis Russell paper mill in Fife, Scotland.
- *Paris, France*: The city's Climate Action Plan was taken into account in the choice of free cooling technology introduced in the Bercy Climespace cooling plant.

4.6.4 Private-sector involvement

For the majority of DES, the ownership of the heating (and power) or cooling generation plants is separate from the network delivering and storing the heat, cooling or electricity. The three most common ownership models for DES globally are: (i) purely public, (ii) public-private and (iii) purely private (this is in line with many other infrastructure sectors outlined in Section 1.3.4 and Section 3.2). The purely public model, which is the most common for it allows local authorities (or public utilities) to have complete control over the asset during development and operation – and to possibly also meet broader social objectives – is not open for private investment, by definition. However, hybrid ownership models – which include public and private joint venture, concession contracts or community-owned, not-for-profits or cooperatives – as well as purely private structures offer investment opportunities for private investors.

Financing continues to be a limiting factor in efforts to accelerate district energy systems on a global scale. New district energy systems require a high level of capital investment, due to the higher-priced co-generation plants (compared to conventional gas turbine generators), the extensive piping infrastructure and the additional equipment needed to connect the network to a variety of energy supplies and storage systems. Operating expenses (opex), on the other hand, are relatively low. At the same time, network operators (often) cannot charge high prices because of regulation and/or the small price difference for the consumer between DHC (district heating and cooling) and alternative technologies. This combination pushes profitability into the long-term future. However, it is the initial high capital expenditure, which prevents many local municipalities from implementing such widely acknowledged, sustainable local systems rather than a – possibly low – return on investment going forward. This is where private investors may be willing to help close the financing gap if they are offered an appropriate return for the risk they take.

All energy markets globally comprise wholesalers, retailers and ultimate consumers as already elaborated above for the case of electricity markets. The organisational models of district energy systems, however, are more complex than power grids only, because of the addition of heating/cooling services. As such, the business model for the private investor is highly dependent on the technical specifications and organisational structures of the parties involved. The latter can range from conventional supply-and-demand contracts to more complex arrangements involving end-users, distribution markets or generators. For example, the co-generator could have a bilateral contract for heat supply while exporting electricity to the grid operator at market rates. The three most common contractual structures found in DES are listed below.

- *Generator and end-user contract structure (private bilateral transactions)*: bilateral contracts between generators and end-users either through a sale or purchase contract (SPA) providing generators with a stable revenue and end-users with predictable long-term energy prices. However, if the contract requires the supply or purchase of pre-determined amounts of heat or electricity, this structure could limit the flexibility of a DES.
- *Generator and market operator structure (wholesale market)*: this structure can accommodate district energy systems using CHP plants that function as both generators and end-users, allowing bi-directional flows, where the entity producing both power and heating/cooling can either sell surplus power to the market or purchase energy at market rates when needed. Surplus electricity can provide a complementary revenue source. However, fluctuations in electricity prices could make co-generation economically unattractive.
- *End-user and distribution contract structure (retail market)*: end-users choose the most attractive retail electricity supplier on the market while entering into a separate heating/

cooling contract directly with the generator. The majority of these contracts are unidirectional and do not allow the consumer to export energy to the distribution grid.

A private investor will need to analyse the specific contractual situation and possibilities of the DES investment opportunity in question in addition to the regulatory situation in order to understand what the business model may be.

4.6.5 Sustainability considerations

The most relevant ESG factors for investors in district energy systems are environmental and social, yet these are predominantly obvious benefits rather than risks because district heating produces little (if any) pollution. Pollution caused by the waste used for incineration by district heating systems poses an environmental risk, and there are also governance issues to contend with. For a comprehensive overview of ESG risk, please refer to Section 5.2.4.

4.6.5.1 Environmental District energy systems use water (or steam) to *transfer* heat or cooling services from source to end use. The potential negative environmental impacts come more from the primary energy source used to generate the heat rather than the system itself. For example, CHP engine exhaust gases, in particular nitrogen dioxide (NO_2) and particulates, have to be monitored carefully in order to limit air pollution and the related health risks for local communities. Exhaust gas treatment technologies come at a significant cost and as such may compromise the financial viability of smaller CHP systems. Waste-to-energy (WtE) systems include the typical environmental and health risks related to air pollutants potentially emerging from waste incineration processes (see Section 4.3.5).

As DES consist mainly of underground pipes in dense urban areas, they have little negative impact, for example, on local ecosystems, biodiversity or indigenous populations. However, DES that do not recycle the water used to deliver heating or cooling can consume a significant amount of water. Critics point out that CO_2 reductions from DES over conventional heat supply are limited to locations with high heat densities, such as urban areas (Local Government Association, 2015).

DES are well protected from physical risks related to climate change – such as extreme weather, flooding, storms or drought – which affect mainly infrastructure built above ground. However, long-term global warming may create changes in the demand for heating and cooling services and so related demands on capacity. And given the existing energy efficiency of DES and modern technology used to limit CO_2 emissions and prevent pollution (e.g. air, water), climate change will not increase regulatory risk because its potential effects are already addressed.

4.6.5.2 Social Most social sustainability issues of DES are related to the proximity of its energy centre to its users, most typically in densely populated areas. Health risks for the local population arise from exhaust gases and particulates, which may contribute to causing diseases of the human respiratory system (see also Section 4.3.5 on health hazards related to waste combustion). In addition, the delivery of biomass or waste to a DES's energy centre may cause disruption and noise – this is not a problem in the case of gas-powered systems. Operational health and safety issues related to hazardous gases and particulates arise for workers of the DES.

An important social aspect is that some customers may find themselves tied into a monopolistic heating system, which is more expensive than conventionally generated heat (e.g. gas, fuel oil, electricity). This may be a serious issue in times of low prices for fossil fuels, which can only be addressed by market regulation (see below Section 4.6.5.3).

4.6.5.3 Governance DES systems can back government efforts to meet broader societal goals while providing a flexible system that supports local energy development and is adaptable to future supply and demand changes, as mentioned in Section 4.6.1.

Governance issues arise in the context of WtE-based systems, which carry the risk of becoming dependent on society's increasingly wasteful consumption. This, in turn, can create an incentive to increase rather than decrease the amount of waste produced. Similarly, waste as a resource leads to the purchase of waste for energy, often requiring long-distance transport, which further increases the environmental impact (WWF 2015). These potential conflicts of interest need to be addressed and carefully managed by asset owners and authorities.

Market regulations and the stability of energy policies are central to promoting investments in district energy projects (see Section 4.6.3). In urban areas where building owners are obliged to connect to the DES for energy efficiency or GHG reduction reasons, competition with local gas or electricity providers is eliminated and a monopolistic supply situation established. This may result in non-market prices for end-users, which goes against the trend of liberalisation of electricity markets for the benefit of the consumer. Asset owners (government, private sector or PPP) need to address the issue by communicating the benefits and the importance of DES to the affected communities. Nevertheless, non-competitive pricing is not sustainable and will be opposed by consumers with the related negative reputational implications to asset owners.

4.7 SOCIAL INFRASTRUCTURE

The social infrastructure sector is a category of its own (see also Figure 1.6 in Section 1.3). Furthermore, it is so diverse and country-specific that a similar kind of analysis as undertaken in previous chapters may be less fruitful. Notwithstanding, this section gives an overview of the sector with the objective of providing the reader with an initial orientation. The fact is that in some countries, social infrastructure is subsumed under 'public real estate' illustrates as well that it is a 'different animal'.

This book divides the sector into the following subsectors (see Figure 1.6):

- Healthcare facilities
- Elderly housing
- Education facilities
- Administrative facilities
- Cultural centres
- Sport and leisure facilities
- Security facilities

In the following, we will focus on three subsectors of social infrastructure – healthcare, education and administrative facilities – because they are the most relevant ones for infrastructure investors for various reasons. The majority of social infrastructure projects/assets have been realised in one of these three subsectors. Further, these three subsectors cover the most common structural variations and illustrate their limitations as well as their risks and opportunities from an investor's point of view. They also show the highest degree of standardisation in

TABLE 4.19   Sector tasks and services

Non-transferable tasks	Transferable tasks	Facility management (FM) services
– Sovereign tasks and functions	– Non-sovereign tasks and functions	– Technical FM – Economic FM – Infrastructural FM – Space distribution management

project procurement compared to other subsectors, which allows us to highlight the differences and similarities between them.

Before entering into a detailed discussion of the three subsectors, investors need to understand what sets apart social infrastructure from other infrastructure sectors. Typically, social infrastructure shows – compared to economic infrastructure (see Figure 1.6) – a low to very low asset specificity in combination with a great flexibility regarding the transfer of 'asset related tasks and services'. They can be broken down into non-transferable tasks, transferable tasks and facility management (see Table 4.19 and Section 3.1 for further explanation).

Asset specificity in this context means the assets may be designed and used for different purposes (e.g. administrative buildings are used for any kind of office space or sports facilities are increasingly conceived as multipurpose event arenas) without important structural changes or they may be adapted relatively easily to changing requirements and planning parameters.

Any infrastructure project is exposed to a continually changing environment. This is mainly due to three factors. First, demographic change within a society, which leads to structural, age-related changes. This ultimately leads to a change in public demand for specific services, such as homes for the elderly, healthcare facilities or education facilities. Second, innovation and technical development has an impact on the quantity, quality and cost of the services provided, such as security, health or sports facilities. Third, the changing regulatory framework, which can affect the use of a particular social infrastructure asset (e.g. educational policies). These three factors often occur in combination, making infrastructure demand difficult to predict. That is one of the main reasons why investors in the case of the tenant model used in the social infrastructure subsector – even if the related costs are higher – tend to be interested in decreasing the specificity of an asset in this sector in order to increase flexibility of use. This is the case, in particular, if they take the capacity utilisation risk of the building afterwards (see Section 3.3).

Considering these various possible requirements and resulting desirable characteristics of infrastructure projects or assets, a great variety of individual solutions are needed. Given the specific requirements of the social infrastructure subsectors, Table 4.20 illustrates the key characteristics associated with each of them, based on the respective organisational model described in Chapter 3. Characteristics in bold are commonly found among projects/assets in each subsector while aspects in brackets are less common.

4.7.1   Healthcare facilities

4.7.1.1   Characteristics and organisation   The aspects discussed below for healthcare facilities (hospitals in particular) are also found in the elderly housing sector, because many

TABLE 4.20 Social infrastructure sector overview

	Privatisation model	Partnership model	Business model	Contract model	Financing model
Health facilities	**Material** (formal, functional)	**Vertical** (horizontal)/ management of infrastructure **assets** and **tasks and services**	**All tasks and services at own risk** in case of full material privatisation/PSP: PPP owner model, purchase model, lease model, tenant model (= asset based approach in a vertical partnership)	**Design, Build, Operate, Own, Finance** (Transfer, Lease, Rent)	**Corporate finance**, project finance (forfeiting model)/healthcare **service fees** (user fees)
Elderly housing	**Material** (formal, functional)	**Vertical** (horizontal)/ management of infrastructure **assets** and **tasks and services**	**All tasks and services at own risk** in case of full material privatisation/PSP: PPP owner model, purchase model, lease model, tenant model (= asset based approach in a vertical partnership)	**Design, Build, Operate, Own, Finance** (Transfer, Lease, Rent)	**Corporate finance**, project finance (forfeiting model)/senior citizen **service fees** (user fees)
Education facilities	**Functional** (material in case of private education facilities)	**Vertical** (horizontal)/ management of infrastructure **assets** (and Facility management services)	PSP: **PPP owner model, purchase model, lease model, tenant model (= asset based approach** in a vertical partnership)/asset provision and tasks and services at own risk in case of private education facilities	**Design, Build, Operate, Finance, Lease, Rent** (Transfer, Own)	**Project finance, forfeiting model/public budget** (user fees and public subsidies in case of material privatisation)
Administrative facilities	**Material, functional** (formal)	**Vertical, horizontal**/ management of **assets** (and Facility management services)	Asset provision at own risk in case of full material privatisation/PSP: **PPP owner model, purchase model, lease model, tenant model** (= asset based approach in a vertical partnership)	**Design, Build, Operate, Own, Finance, Transfer, Lease, Rent**	**Project finance, forfeiting model** (corporate finance in case of full material privatisation)/**public budget** (rent and service charge)
Sport and leisure facilities	**Material, formal, functional**	**Vertical** (horizontal)/ **urban development** and management of **assets** (and partially tasks and services)	**All tasks and services at own risk** in case of full material privatisation/PSP: PPP owner model, purchase model, lease model, tenant model (= asset based approach in a vertical partnership)	**Design, Build, Operate, Own, Finance, Transfer, Lease, Rent**	**Corporate finance**, project finance (forfeiting model)/**public budget** (subsidies) and **service fees** (user fees)
Cultural centres	**Material, formal, functional**	**Vertical** (horizontal)/ **urban development** and management of **assets** (and partially tasks and services)	**All tasks and services at own risk** in case of full material privatisation/PSP: PPP owner model, purchase model, lease model, tenant model (= asset based approach in a vertical partnership)	**Design, Build, Operate, Own, Finance, Transfer, Lease, Rent**	**Corporate finance**, project finance (forfeiting model)/**public budget** (subsidies) and **service fees** (user fees)
Security facilities	**Functional**	**Vertical, horizontal**/management of **assets**	PSP: **PPP owner model, purchase model, lease model, tenant model (= asset based approach** in a vertical partnership)	**Design, Build, Operate, Finance, Lease, Rent** (Transfer, Own)	**Project finance, forfeiting model/public budget**

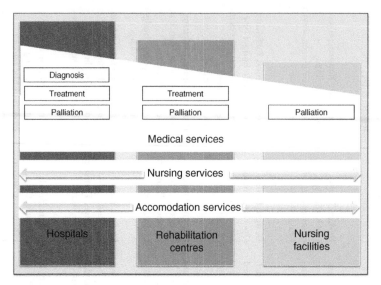

FIGURE 4.21   Healthcare sector overview
Source: Adapted from Wendel (2001)

services provided in the healthcare sector apply to both sectors. The healthcare sector can be broken down into hospitals, rehabilitations centres and nursing facilities (see Figure 4.21).

All three healthcare facilities are currently organised by public, private or non-profit institutions. These three institutional groups have significantly different objectives and vary in their institutional setups. Private investors typically follow economic objectives (for profit). Non-profit operators usually focus on demand (not-for-profit by definition). Public institutions also focus on demand but act within the scope of a certain political interest, while non-profit operators pursue freely chosen, often charitable purposes (Daube, 2011).

As a consequence of public household constraints, many hospitals previously owned and operated by public institutions have been sold in the form of a material privatisation to private investors over the last two decades. According to the Federal Statistical Office in Germany, the share of hospitals owned and operated by private investors increased from 15.2% (1992) to 35.4% (2013) in Germany. In the same period, the share of public hospitals decreased from 46.0% (1992) to 29.9% (2013) (Destatis, 2014). Similar trends can be found in numerous European countries.

4.7.1.2   Sources of revenue and value chain elements   Healthcare facility revenues are generated from three types of services: primary, secondary and tertiary services. Primary services include all medical and nursing services provided by doctors, medical staff and respective equipment. These types of services are at the core of the value chain. The medical or primary services can only be performed together with support services, so-called secondary services, such as patient accommodation or surgery room cleaning (just to name two prominent examples). These secondary services include all services that directly support patient treatment processes (e.g. laboratories, diagnostic radiology). Tertiary services are all non-medical support services that ensure the overall function of the hospital (e.g. administration, general cleaning) (Daube, 2011).

Primary and secondary services are considered transferable services, whereas tertiary services are categorised as facility management services (see Table 4.20). Most countries consider any service provided in a healthcare facility as transferable. This explains the global trend towards material privatisations in this sector.

The revenue stream of a healthcare system can be divided into asset provision (financed in most countries via public budget) and service provision (usually financed by country-specific healthcare systems/funds). The exact financing of the healthcare sector differs significantly in an international context. Therefore, investors are encouraged to become acquainted with the country-specific aspects of healthcare sector finance. Chapter 3, which gives an overview of various business models, may prove to be useful in this context. An in-depth analysis of all kinds of financings prevalent internationally would exceed the scope of this book.

4.7.1.3 Private-sector involvement

Hospital facilities require specific construction features in order to be allowed to provide medical services yet also comprise standard office and logistics construction. The extent to which these features are combined within one building or split between several buildings (hospital campus) is determined during project development by the sponsors (possibly including financial investors). As a result, hospital projects are one-of-a-kind projects. As such, they have probably among the highest asset specificity of all social infrastructure sectors, compared to e.g. administrative facilities. This may also explain why material privatisation tends to be the preferred privatisation model for investors over formal or functional privatisation.

A few examples of formal and functional privatisation exist; however, they usually do not solve the problem of restricted public budgets related to healthcare facilities. Typically, formal privatisation is a step towards selling the asset and thus transferring it into a material privatisation. Only a few PPP projects are designed as functional privatisations. The functional privatisation model is best suited to newly-built hospitals that apply the PPP purchase, lease, tenant or owner model. This model allows forms of private-sector involvement that create opportunities to provide more value for money and transparency for healthcare expenditures of the public budget.

In case the social infrastructure sector in general, and the hospital sector in particular, is opened to private investments, which is not the case in all countries, investors are usually given the option to enter into some sort of public-private 'relationship'. The business model used is typically based on availability payment schemes (see Section 3.3 for further detail). This recognises the fact that social infrastructure – and even more so hospitals and the like – form part of the basic public care provision function and they neither can nor should be run with a primary profitability objective. To this end, public support, that is budget finance, will always be necessary to a larger or lesser extent.

4.7.2 Education facilities

4.7.2.1 Characteristics and organisation

Within the broad range of education facilities, this section focuses particularly on schools and facilities for higher education (see Table 4.21). Day care and kindergarten facilities are not addressed here but typically have similar characteristics.

The education sector is organised by public authorities and the majority of education facilities are also owned and operated by public authorities with few private exceptions. All institutions have to follow a formal education objective set by such public authorities. This is

TABLE 4.21   Education sector overview

Education facilities	
Schools	**Higher education**
– Primary schools	– Universities
– Secondary schools	– Universities of applied science
– Vocational schools	– Art and music schools
– Adult education centres	– Other
– Other	

because providing education to the public is a sovereign function. This, in turn, is manifested in the acknowledgement of professional teachers hired by private education institutions as well as accreditation of the curriculum covered in the school programme of the institution.

The above mentioned demographic change in general, and three major developments in particular continue to significantly affect the education sector, especially school service provision. First, young people tend to move from rural areas to cities, resulting in an increasing average age of the population in rural areas as well as a decreasing number of pupils in the schools there. Education service provision in these areas is increasingly cost-inefficient because of low capacity loads. Second, the opposite trend is found in dense urban areas where a need for new schools owing to a high degree of capacity load applies. This trend in urban areas, however, is not as distinctive because of the third major development: an overall low birth rate in all developed countries.

The education sector is also affected by political education concepts and policies, which (could) influence service provision, for example full-day school programmes that require additional facilities for catering, naptime for younger children and additional staff. Policy changes of this nature often lead to challenging renegotiations of existing PPP contracts or, in the case of private education facilities, re-accreditation issues.

4.7.2.2   Sources of revenue and value chain elements   Education facilities are predominantly budget financed. This applies to both assets as well as service provision. On average, OECD countries spend approximately 6.1% per annum of GDP on education (OECD, 2014b). In most developed countries, parents pay additional school fees for catering, books, workshops and field trips. The exact financing of this sector varies across countries. For Europe, Eurostats publishes data on education that compare current developments of sector finance on a country-by-country basis. For example, Scandinavian countries, including Denmark and the Netherlands, have a much higher public expenditure for education services and enjoy greater freedom of financial management than Germany or southern European countries do. Private funding of education remains marginal, given that the majority of students attend public schools and most private schools are subsidised by public funds as well (Eurostat, 2012).

4.7.2.3   Private-sector involvement   The best way for the private sector to invest in the education sector is twofold: first, via full material privatisation where the private investor fully owns and operates the education institution with the possibility of service provision via accreditation by public authorities. This model applies to all private schools and universities. Second, via functional privatisation where the public sector seeks private investors/partners to build new or to upgrade existing education facilities, such as schools.

The UK introduced the Priority School Building Programme in 2014, as part of which 261 schools will be rebuilt or upgraded to meet current standards set by the respective public authority (Education Funding Agency). The programme is expected to be completed by the end of 2017. Out of the 261 schools, 46 are intended to be delivered via the new British PPP programme named Private Finance 2 (PF2) (Education Funding Agency, 2015).

In Germany, as of 2015 approximately 200 school PPP projects had been realised with a total investment volume of around €2.3 billion. Typically, these projects include several schools within one municipality in order to achieve an attractive investment/effort ratio for private investors (PPP Projektdatenbank, 2015).

In the case of private investments, the business model of the education subsector is typically based on availability payments. The same considerations apply to the health sector, namely hospitals, as mentioned above.

4.7.3   Administrative facilities

4.7.3.1   Characteristics and organisation
Administrative facilities cover a large spectrum of public real estate linked to a wide variety of public-sector organisations on different hierarchical levels and with different levels of solvency. Either the federal, state or municipal authority may be responsible for assets like embassies, ministries, state offices and town halls, among others. To this end, investors need to pay attention to the contractual party in charge of the particular asset in question. This is of particular relevance because – as in almost all social infrastructure subsectors – these facilities are budget financed with the investor receiving 'only' availability payments from their respective contractual counterparty.

The responsibility for needs assessment, planning, approval, procurement, implementation, regulation and budgeting is organised on a sector, federal or regional level, depending on the country-specific regulations.

The 'administrative facility' subsector pursues a stringent asset-based approach because most of the tasks and services provided within these facilities are sovereign and therefore not transferable to the private sector (see Table 4.20).

The construction and functionality of these facilities are very similar at all levels of the public authority hierarchy, i.e. they are among the lowest asset-specific assets within the social infrastructure sector. Therefore, public authorities can take advantage of the overall real estate market (especially for standard office facilities), and are able to buy, rent or build new assets according to their specific needs. Nevertheless, some facilities, owing to their specific function, have a special representative (i.e. an embassy or ministry building) purpose or need to be easily accessible to the public that limits the flexibility of their location. Given these requirements, there is a particular need for output-oriented specifications of functions and services by the responsible public body. The more precise such needs and output objectives are defined, the higher the effectiveness of project implementation. In order to then implement the project efficiently, the public authorities have two options to choose from. They could buy or rent existing assets from the real estate market or plan, design and build a new asset according to their specific needs.

The quintessence of these aspects is that the greater the need for flexibility (future needs), the more expensive it will be for the public authorities to achieve this objective.

4.7.3.2   Sources of revenue and value chain elements
Public administrative facilities are budget-financed and/or (partially) financed by service fees that are part of the general

government revenue (see Table 4.20). In addition to the above mentioned budget-financed availability payments, private investors may be able to generate additional sources of revenue via urban and commercial development, in case the available public property is larger than the property site needed for the public facilities. Private project developments on public property may, for instance, include facilities for residential, shopping or office use, and recreational areas alongside administrative facilities. The development risk of the commercial assets would be assigned to the private investor. The investor offering the highest value for money to the public authorities is likely to win the contract. Value add services could include (in addition to design and build tasks) all facility management services of the administrative facilities.

Debt financing of administrative facilities via project or traditional corporate financing (procured through functional or material privatisation) is often easier than financing other subsectors such as schools, universities, hospitals or even correctional service facilities. This is mainly because administrative facilities are relatively unspecific and show a relatively high residual value as security.

4.7.3.3 Private-sector involvement   The dominant forms of private-sector participation in administrative facilities are material and functional privatisations. Depending on the degree of privatisation, all tasks of project provision (design, build, operate, own, finance, transfer, lease, rent) are applicable within the subsector.

The project track record in several European countries shows that administrative facilities, if realised as a functional privatisation (PPP), tend to apply the tenant model (see Section 3.3.1.5). The tenant model is used for office buildings in particular, since after the contract period between private investor and public authority the utilisation risk is relatively low.

Administrative facility projects are often part of larger urban development because it is difficult to bundle several administrative facility projects – as common in the education sector – in order to reach a decent investment volume. Combining various urban development objectives creates the required synergies. There are numerous examples of large-scale projects, for example the Federal Ministry of Education and Research.

In the case of private investments, the business model of this subsector is typically also based on availability payments only. Different considerations regarding public provision apply to the e.g. health or education sector.

4.7.4 Sustainability considerations

Hospitals, public schools, public housing, community centres and other social infrastructure are among the pillars of a well-functioning, just and prosperous society. Therefore, investments in social infrastructure are vital to global sustainable development.

The most relevant ESG factors for investors in social infrastructure assets are environmental issues in the context of buildings as well as social and governance issues, mainly related to demographic changes and urbanisation, community relations, public policy and stakeholder management. For some investors, ethical considerations may play a role as well. For a comprehensive overview of ESG risk, please refer to Section 5.2.4.

4.7.4.1 Environmental   Climate change can affect social infrastructure facilities in a number of ways. While heavy storms, flooding or rising sea levels may directly affect buildings and their operations, hospitals and elderly care facilities, in particular, will need to consider the risk of the increasing frequency, intensity and duration of extreme heatwaves on such facilities to maintain safe and comfortable interior environment for building occupants.

As the operation of some of these social infrastructure facilities has to be maintained at all times (e.g. emergency rooms and operating theatres in hospitals), adaptation measures such as building flood defences to mitigate climate-change risks may be indispensable. Infrastructure investors will want to own assets that have been built appropriately for designated use and the region in which they are located and with business planning and recovery measures in place.

Regulatory risks related to climate change are relevant for owners of public buildings. Buildings are responsible for about 40% of the global energy consumption, and 25% of the global water use. In addition, they contribute approximately one-third to global CO_2 emissions (UNEP, 2015). Not surprisingly, there is a significant regulatory focus on curtailing the energy use and CO_2 emissions of buildings in general. In the EU, the Energy Performance of Buildings Directive (2010) and the Energy Efficiency Directive (2012) are the main pieces of legislation related to reducing the energy consumption of buildings. Particularly relevant for asset owners is that, under the directive, all new public buildings occupied and/or owned by public authorities must be nearly-zero-energy buildings by the end of 2018, and all buildings by 2020. Furthermore, EU countries have to set minimum energy performance requirements for new buildings and the renovation and retrofit of existing buildings. Nearly-zero- and zero-energy buildings combine energy-efficiency measures (e.g. heating, ventilating and air conditioning (HVAC) technologies) with on-site energy production (e.g. solar panels). In addition, national, sector- and/or project-specific regulations have to be met, which may be more restrictive.

Public and private asset owners of buildings, which host public institutions (e.g. administrative offices, schools), will want to futureproof their assets by implementing the necessary energy efficiency measures in a timely manner for existing and new buildings. Similar considerations apply to the resource efficiency of buildings, that is specifically to water use and waste water disposal as well as air pollution from heating systems. The short-term costs incurred related to implementing the appropriate measures may be offset by the lower risk of vacancies as well as the lower cost of resources (e.g. energy, water) – to what extent depends on the development of global energy prices and local water and waste water prices. The financial burden of implementing resource efficiency measures lies with the asset owner (i.e. the government, institutional or private asset owner), who may or may not – often for short-term financial considerations – decide to take the measures. In certain countries, the requirements for government-owned buildings are stricter than for private assets, as the public sector serves as a role model for the private sector.

Institutional investors see an opportunity in investing in new energy-efficient buildings and refitting existing buildings because they share the savings from lower use of resources (e.g. energy, water). The first institutional investment vehicles for institutional investors, e.g. real estate investment funds, have already been raised in that field. However, the challenge persists to persuade public or private owners of public buildings to enter into a deal, that is, to agree to the implementation of the relevant measures.

In summary, climate protection and resource efficiency measures pay off for asset owners of public buildings – and obviously more so in an environment of rising prices for energy, freshwater supply and waste water disposal.

4.7.4.2 Social Demographic trends such as population growth or ageing societies are relevant aspects for investors in social infrastructure and need to be considered when investing in long-lived assets. Futureproofing social infrastructure assets may require flexible designs of buildings thus ensuring that the space in buildings can be adjusted according to future needs based on demographic shifts in local populations. For example, in the Western world (or Japan, for that matter), with its ageing populations, public education facilities should be built ideally as multifunctional spaces, which may be used for different purposes serving different segments of the population (e.g. education or care facilities for elderly people) in different phases of an asset's life. In addition, investors in healthcare and personal care facilities will seek suitably located (e.g. easily accessible by public transport for patients, staff, suppliers), efficiently designed and well-maintained buildings that can deliver high-quality and cost-effective care. High patient satisfaction and low infection rates may contribute to reducing financial and reputational risks for asset owners.

A well-functioning and well-maintained social infrastructure (e.g. schools, healthcare facilities, administrative services) makes communities attractive for new private residents and corporates, thus adding to the tax base required for further communal investment. Social infrastructure facilities are typically used by the public, and as such are exposed to the potential financial and reputational consequences of casualties resulting from illness, injury or death. Asset owners need to ensure a safe environment for those using the asset.

Further social factors relating to employment do not present material risks but rather opportunities. Social infrastructure may have a positive effect on local employment because of its local presence. Occupational health and safety risks are relatively low in the social sector, with notable exceptions being increased risk of infection in hospitals and care homes and potential safety risks in prisons.

In the case of a PPP, demographic risk usually stays with the – typically – public owner of the building. Other social risks, such as occupational, health, and safety risks, stay with the private service provider (and as such the investor).

4.7.4.3 Governance   Social infrastructure assets generally, and PPPs in particular, tend to have strong links to the communities in which they operate and affect a wide range of stakeholders. It is evident that maintaining positive relationships with government counterparties, local communities, staff and also organisations representing users (e.g. patients, students) is a precondition for well-run facilities.

Moreover, public policy considerations are relevant for long-term oriented infrastructure investors. For example, investors need to address the question of what would happen to the value of their investment in healthcare facilities if governments or individuals can no longer pay for the healthcare and general care costs of a rapidly growing number of old people. Japan may serve as an illustrative example. The country's population began falling in 2004 and is ageing faster than any other in the world. A government report from 2012 expects that by 2060 the number of Japanese will be reduced by over 30% from 127 million to about 87 million, while almost 40% of the population will be 65 or older (The Economist, 2014). As Japan is already shouldering one of the largest public debt burdens, the government is confronted with the insurmountable challenge of finding the tax base to repay its debt in addition to providing pensions and care for its growing elderly population.

Last but not least, ethical considerations need to be mentioned in the context of social infrastructure. In addition to ESG issues, some institutional investors take into account ethical considerations. Many church pension funds, for instance, apply restrictions based on ethical values to their investments and exclude investments in prisons (in addition to investments related to gambling, alcoholic beverages, tobacco, pornography, weapons, etc.).

Risks

A ny investment, of whatever kind, needs to be assessed in light of its potential return as well as its potential risks. Only in combination is it possible and sensible to make an informed investment decision. This chapter focuses on the risks inherent in a potential project or asset, and hence investment, from an equity and debt investor's point of view. To this end, it classifies all risks into two main categories based on their content: (i) general risks and (ii) project/asset-specific risks. Each of these categories is then broken down into six and seven subcategories respectively. Please note that various other ways of how to categorise such risks can be found in the literature (Akintoye, 2001; Akintoye, 2003; Boussabaine, 2007; Tinsley, 2000; Yescombe, 2007). The risks themselves, though, tend to remain the same.

Before discussing each risk subcategory – 13 altogether – in detail, it is important to understand how a professional investor approaches and handles investment risks in principle. Risks are not just observed without doing anything about them. Instead, investors follow a systematic and structured process, as part of which they first and foremost aim to identify every potential risk. Next, they analyse and try to evaluate the risk in question and, if possible, quantify it based on the probability of occurrence and the related financial damage. Once all risks and their potential impact on any given asset have been identified, one can contemplate if and how to mitigate and later on monitor them, that is to manage them. This kind of structured and systematic approach to risks is known in the literature as 'risk management' (Alfen et al., 2010, p. 33; Boussabaine, 2007, p. 23; Merna, Chu and Al-Thani, 2010, p. 42).

The following discussion of the 13 risk subcategories is done with this structured and systematic approach to risk in mind, that is with a risk management mindset. In order for the reader to get a better understanding of this approach and to follow the discussion of the individual risks more easily, the next section gives a brief introduction to risk management.

5.1 RISK MANAGEMENT

Risk management is generally described as a sequence of steps with the objective of managing any identified risks. This book divides this process into four steps: (i) identify, (ii) analyse and evaluate, (iii) allocate and (iv) monitor risks. These four steps need to be followed carefully and repeatedly over time throughout all phases of investing in an infrastructure asset in order to ensure that all risks are identified, evaluated precisely and allocated and/or mitigated

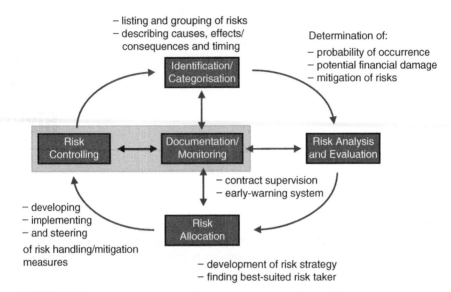

FIGURE 5.1   Risk management process

accordingly (see Figure 5.1). The first step, the correct identification of all potential risks, is critical in order to be able to implement the right mitigating structures that ensure protection of the project/asset and the investment against such identified risks over time to the highest extent possible.

In the *first step*, identification, the asset-specific risk profile is compiled in conjunction with relevant subject matter/technical experts, for example based on checklists. Subsequently, the individual risks are described as precisely as possible in terms of causes, effects and time.

In the *second step*, the identified risks are analysed and evaluated in order to assess their relevance, whether and to what extent the scope of the risks may change over time and how best to handle them. Various instruments may be used to do so, including ABC risk categorisation and sensitivity analyses. Because the evaluation of a risk often changes over time its importance/potential occurrence is continually adjusted accordingly to reflect its actual relevance and/or the emergence of new information. For example, the completion risk becomes less important as the construction phase progresses and is removed from the risk profile altogether upon completion of a project.

During the process of evaluating risks, the probability of occurrence of each risk at any given point in time is multiplied by the potential financial damage it may incur. The ultimate goal of this process is to identify the so-called A risk (i.e. those with the greatest impact on the project). For the purpose of the assessment, the date of potential occurrence is also important. The potential loss and thus the cost of taking a risk (also referred to as 'risk costs') are calculated because they are relevant for any feasibility study that is to be performed, as well as for all negotiations with any of the counter parties.

In the *third step*, the individual risks and the related (payment) obligations if they occur are 'allocated' fully or partially to the various partners as part of the negotiation process in the context of structuring the project or transaction, as applicable. 'Allocation of risk' in this context means a party contractually agrees to bear the risk according to its individual risk strategy. Ideally, each risk is allocated to the party, which is best positioned to take and manage that risk, because it may change its impact on, and hence risk costs for, the project or asset as a whole. These risk costs calculated in the previous phase are crucial for obtaining the most cost-efficient allocation of risk for the project and for all project partners. In this regard, it is important to understand that the cost of taking a risk is not the same for every party involved.

At the highest level, risks can be categorised in terms of their allocation to the contractor (private sector, including all subcontractors and related service providers) or the principal. Within a public–private partnership (PPP) structure, the transfer of 'transferable' risks from the public to the private sector not only serves to optimise the operation of the project but also opens up the possibility of additional efficiency gains by giving the public sector access to the benefits of private risk management. Efficient management can further reduce the project costs and hence improve the bankability and quality of the project (for banks/lenders: greater certainty that debt will be serviced, i.e. the required principal repayments and interest payments will be made; for equity investors: increased return on equity). However, as a rule, the more risks are transferred to the private partner, the more expensive the financing of a project becomes. As such, there is a balancing act to be performed when determining how all the risks inherent to the project/asset as a whole can be allocated to their 'best owner' in a way that generates the greatest efficiency gains for the project/asset.

Irrespective of the characteristics of each individual situation, however, in the case of PPP structures the public sector usually bears the legislative risk and the political risk, whereas the private sector bears the risks related to the planning, technology, construction, operation and financing of the project. The market (price and demand) risk can be allocated to either party, or to both. Its allocation depends on the PPP programme in question, the individual asset and the negotiation skills of the parties involved. Risks relating to *force majeure* are generally borne jointly by both parties (see Section 5.2.6).

Ultimately, though, it is not sufficient merely to identify, analyse and evaluate the risks arising from a project/asset: they must also be monitored and controlled over time in the *fourth step*. Accordingly, risks are systematically tracked as part of contract management. Once the risks have been defined clearly and are allocated to project partners in the project agreements, it is the obligation of the party that bears the respective risk to treat and mitigate it (i.e. limit, prevent or transfer it or to conclude adequate insurance). To this end, the contractual partners must develop, implement and steer appropriate control instruments. In order for all partners to have an interest in fulfilling their respective obligations, an incentive system is mutually agreed in parallel to the risk allocation process (see Section 5.1.1).

The information above shows the potential offered by the systematic implementation of risk management, if only in terms of the conscious handling of risk with a view to preventing unpredictable risks that are difficult to calculate in particular. Based on the principle that 'forewarned is forearmed', this is a vital instrument in ensuring that projects are structured in the most optimal – that is low risk – manner.

As envisaged above, this chapter groups all risks under (i) general risks and (ii) project/asset-specific risks. General risks exist largely independently of the respective project/asset and thus cannot be directly influenced by the project participants, that is the principal or the contractor (this statement applies only conditionally for market risk; see Section 5.2.1). General risks may materialise at any point in the project lifecycle. In contrast, the parties

TABLE 5.1   General risks

General risks	Risk description	Risk allocation
1 Market risk) (See 5.2.1)	Reduction in sales (demand risk) Change in the price of the product/service offered (price risk) Availability of raw materials/primary products (supply risk) Cost increase of production, e.g. raw materials (price risk)	Operator Project SPV Principal[1]
2 Interest rate risk (See 5.2.2)	Risk of changes in interest rates via variable interest rate agreements	Project SPV Debt provider
3 Exchange rate risk (See 5.2.3)	Changes in exchange rate between local currency generated by the project and currency in which project costs/loans are denominated	Project SPV Debt provider
4 Environmental, social and governance (ESG) risk (See 5.2.4)	Environmental risks: climate change, resource scarcity, environmental degradation, changes in environmental regulations, etc. Social risks: human rights, labour rights, health and safety risks for employees and local communities, consumer protection, public resistance to project, etc. Governance risks: corrupt business practices, weak public and corporate governance structures, management incentive systems, weak rule of law, government and stakeholder relations, etc.	National Government Project SPV Principal
5 Political, legal and regulatory risk (See 5.2.5)	Changes in legislation/(de)regulation Nationalisation/seizure Expropriation Breach of contract/concession Currency transfer and conversion Changes in tax rates and tax legislation Public acceptance	Principal Project SPV Sponsors Debt provider Multilateral institutions Export credit agencies (ECA) Insurer
6 *Force majeure* (See 5.2.6)	Strikes War/terrorism Earthquakes and other natural disasters Increased extreme weather events from climate change	Principal Project SPV Insurers

[1]The Principal can be identical with the National Government as is often the case for PPP assets.

involved can address project/asset-specific risks directly and possibly assess them separately for the various project phases, if applicable.

Table 5.1 lists the main types of *general risks*, including the most relevant factors affecting each risk, and the different partners, to which the risk may be allocated. Table 5.2 breaks down the most significant *project/asset-specific risks* during their lifecycles, as applicable, from the

TABLE 5.2 Asset-specific risks

Asset-specific risks		Risk description	Risk allocation
1	Planning, construction and completion risk (See 5.3.1)	Planning amendments by the principal Excess costs owing to delays in the planning or construction phase Construction overruns not attributable to planning errors Existence of transport/infrastructure	General contractor Project SPV Principal[1]
2	Technical and performance risk (See 5.3.2)	Use of tried-and-tested technology from known manufacturers that is adequate for the operating process Suitable climate or soil quality (for the construction of large plants)	Producer Operator Project SPV
3	Financial risk (See 5.3.3)	Changes in contractual conditions between the signature date and the provision of financing	Project SPV Debt provider Sponsors
4	Syndication risk (See 5.3.4)	Ability to syndicate/place loans	Debt provider
5	Operational risk (See 5.3.5)	Excess operating/ maintenance costs Interruption of operation Selection of operator/partner	Operator
6	Contractual and counterparty risk (See 5.3.6)	Failure to receive approvals, licences and concessions Effectiveness and enforceability of contracts and agreements Poor functionality of the judicial system Ability of contractual partners to provide products, services and payments	All contractual parties National Government Project SPV Sponsors Debt provider Multilateral institutions Export credit agencies (ECA) Insurer
7	Realisation risk (See 5.3.7)	For projects to be transferred back to the principal	Sponsors Project SPV

[1]The Principal can be identical with the National Government as is often the case for PPP assets.

perspective of debt and/or equity investors. The following Sections 5.2 and 5.3 present each risk and discuss the key factors affecting it. Also see Section 5.4 for a brief overview of sector-specific risks.

For clarity, the following discussion does not address the individual risks that can result in delinquency, default or even liquidation, either individually or in combination, throughout the four phases of the risk management process.

Category of risk	Risk description	Consequence of risk	Tolerance	Probability	Worth of risk	Transferable	Non-transferable
			Asset-specific risk				
Technical							
Operative				100%		85%	15%
	Risk of disruption in operation	Higher operational costs, higher staff costs	−10%	10%	8.50%	7.23%	1.28%
			0%	15%			
			5%	25%			
			15%	35%			
			20%	15%			
Economic							
Legal/Tax							
			General risk				
Political/ Jurisdiction							
Variation in price							
Demand							
Change in interest rates							
Currency							
Environment							
Force Majeure							

FIGURE 5.2 Risk matrix – sample risk score calculation

Risk matrices may be used in order to provide a better overview of the individual risks and the accumulated overall risk of a project or company. They are prepared at the end of the risk analysis process in order to categorise and quantify all the risks identified along with their likelihood of occurrence (see Figure 5.2), thereby enabling a risk score to be calculated for every project/asset and/or company. This procedure allows different projects/assets to be compared in a relatively structured manner, as well as to be categorised into various risk classes at a later date. This kind of model can also be used by investors and banks for internal risk classification purposes, although it is rather complex and work-intensive.

Risks invariably change over the course of a project; for example, operating costs may be higher or lower than forecast. Additional information obtained over time is included in the risk matrix in order to refine the risk quantification.

The categorisation of a risk as 'transferable' or 'non-transferable' within the matrix is not always conclusive. For example, the risk of soil contamination – unless fully excluded by a preliminary study – cannot be reasonably transferred in full to the private partner. However, it may be classified as 'transferable' in such a risk matrix. The appropriate level of presentation detail must be decided individually over time.

As a matter of principle, the aim should be to ensure appropriate risk allocation based on the experience of the project developer, if applicable, the potential for risk distribution, the nature of the project/asset, the willingness of the market to assume risk and the public interest. In order to facilitate improved risk estimation and hedging, sensitivity scenarios that take into account the likelihood of occurrence and the potential impact of such risks are developed during the structuring of the financing.

Based on these analyses, a decision is taken as to whether financing should be pursued in the form of project finance if financing is desired and if the asset has not been financed previously. If these analyses confirm that the project is economically viable, financially sustainable and entails an acceptable level of risk, the group of sponsors (often with the assistance of a financial advisor) and the financing bank(s) implement the envisaged, previously modelled financing structure (see Chapter 6).

5.2 GENERAL RISKS

5.2.1 Market risk

Developments in relevant markets (commodity, raw material prices, etc.) cannot be influenced by the (project) company (see Section 1.3.1 for the use of the terminology 'project company', '(project) company' and 'company', as well as Section 6.1 for an explanation of the overall legal structure of most infrastructure projects, which have project financing in place). Accordingly, market risks are classified as a type of general risk. They are the decisive factor in the financial success or failure of a large number of, if not most, projects.

Market risks are generally borne by the (project) company. They relate to the sale of the goods produced and the services provided in the forecast volume (demand risk) at the planned price (price risk) and the adequate supply (supply risk) and purchase prices of raw materials and other production factors (price risk). Therefore, it is particularly crucial to control market risk to the greatest possible extent. This is made possible by (i) careful analysis and market studies prior to investing as well as (ii) the conclusion of long-term minimum purchase and supply agreements at an early stage.

When analysing and calculating future market risks using market studies, it is important to ascertain the extent to which customers have realistic alternatives to purchasing the goods provided by the project/asset company, that is if there is competition (e.g. alternative telecom operators) or an effective monopoly (e.g. in the case of water or power supply). Based on experience, calculations of market risk often fail to take fully into account the alternative actions, products or services available to potential customers or correctly assess their future consumer behaviour, including their price sensitivity. This means forecast demand as predicted by the project sponsor (see Section 6.1 for a definition of 'project sponsor') or the seller of an asset or company, as the case may be, is often too optimistic, for example because of a failure to recognise the extent to which potential users could avoid toll roads or tunnels by using existing alternative routes or means of transport (e.g. Eurotunnel and the introduction of tolls for heavy goods vehicles in Germany).

Regarding risk reduction via long-term contracts: the market risk associated with the product/service offered or demanded may be reduced on the part of the company by agreeing minimum purchase or supply volumes at specific conditions with the purchasers/suppliers of the products/services prior to investing. This may take the form of long-term purchase or supply agreements or minimum off-take/payment guarantees from creditworthy parties (see also Section 1.3.9). Prices are often fixed within a specific range. Examples can be found in the road sector with traffic bands, in the oil and gas (generally commodity) sector, or in the renewable energy sector, where producers are guaranteed the off-take of the entire volume produced (by priority dispatch laws) at statutory feed-in tariffs (FITs) (see Chapter 4 for details). Typically, companies establish long-term purchase agreements.

Long-term purchase agreements are typically used for raw materials and commodities, such as power purchase or oil supply. They mostly take the form of throughput agreements in which the respective customers guarantee the producer a minimum utilisation or a minimum volume for a specific period at a specific price. Payments for contractually agreed volumes need to be made irrespective of whether the customer utilises this volume (in full) or not. In the case of take-or-pay agreements, the customer is obliged to make periodical payments for the purchase of a contractually defined volume of a product at a fixed price irrespective of whether the products are actually purchased/supplied or not. This guarantee protects the project operator not only from market risk but also from other risks that could prevent delivery.

In the case of PPP projects, the public principal may offer purchase guarantees in connection with the payment of fixed performance fees. For example, the public sector may undertake to make compensation payments to the operators of toll road projects if traffic fails to reach the agreed volume, or it may pay the operator on an availability basis in order to eliminate the market risk for the operator altogether. Service agreements may be concluded with the private service providers for projects in areas such as public services, prisons or healthcare. Agreeing on a minimum purchase volume or minimum utilisation level and fixing prices within a specific range serves to provide the operator with a reliable basis of calculation prior to investing. As well as significantly reducing the demand risk for the private parties, this provides customers and consumers with assurance as to the long-term availability of the goods offered, which in turn prevents the need for risk premiums on the part of the provider.

Projects/assets involving pure user-financed payments have a significantly higher market risk for the project/asset. For the purposes of risk structuring and allocation, this risk may remain with private investors in full, or be shared by the private and public sectors in various forms, as outlined above. The extent to which the retention of individual market risks by the principal (risk sharing) is more appropriate from a macroeconomic perspective must be examined on a project-specific basis and discussed with all parties. Studies performed by independent advisors in the course of the due diligence process provide equity investors and debt providers (banks) with a basis for their assessment of market risk.

In the same way as for customers, it must be ensured that the project/asset has sufficient access to the necessary resources from its suppliers (physical availability of raw materials; *price risk*). For investments where procurement volume largely comprises raw materials, this means guaranteeing an adequate supply of the necessary raw materials. For example, a mining company requires the existence of corresponding ore deposits, whereas power plants need an adequate supply of gas, oil or biomass, including waste-to-energy power plants. This requires not only evidence of a sufficient volume of raw materials in general but also their availability, quality and geographical or geological location (if applicable). The extent to which, based on these factors, raw material, including biomass and waste, can be obtained and delivered at a reasonable price over a specified period is of the utmost importance. For example, the cost of extraction and supply may vary considerably depending on the location of a mine or oilfield. Long-term supply agreements at prices that are fixed to the greatest possible extent – such as the contractual structures used for customers – are a tried-and-tested method of reducing risk. Studies by independent advisors, particularly geologists, on the existence and quality of sources of raw materials and the costs involved in their extraction or supply provide the parties involved with the basis for a corresponding risk assessment.

The availability of adequate infrastructure and logistics for the delivery of raw materials and the distribution/transportation of end products also needs to be assessed, including the question of supplier and customer creditworthiness. This form of supply-side guarantee is not necessary for a number of PPP projects/assets, for example, in the service industry. Here, the risk factors are not based on physically scarce commodities or technical equipment but rather on human resource costs. Dependency on raw materials or technical equipment exists only for companies in industrial sectors, such as energy or water supply, wind turbines or waste disposal. In these cases, long-term supply agreements can ensure the availability of oil, gas, fresh water, wind turbines or also sufficient waste for the operation of a waste incinerator throughout the term of the project/asset, thereby increasing the likelihood of its profitable operation.

Investors and financing banks require an as reliable basis of calculation as possible and hence long-term planning security on the supply and demand side with respect to the expected cash flows (for dividend payments or debt service). An in-depth analysis can be performed only on the basis of detailed price/volume information. With this in mind, the providers of debt typically insist on long-term agreements – ideally going beyond the term of the loan – that prescribe the quantity and quality of the sales and raw material supply volumes and the respective prices.

In order to better illustrate the individual risks, reference will be made throughout this book to two case studies that highlight selected risks during the different phases of a greenfield project due diligence/risk analysis: İskenderun, a 'traditional' project finance in an emerging-market country, which was structured with a partial government guarantee for market price risk and the Warnow Tunnel, a project finance within a PPP structure without a third-party market risk guarantee.

ISKENDERUN (TURKEY)

With a project volume of US$1.4 billion, this 1210 MW coal-fired power station on the Mediterranean coast of south-eastern Turkey near the city of İskenderun was then the largest hard coal power station realised in the country at the time. The power plant – which consists of two 605 MW units fired with imported coal, coal processing and transfer infrastructure – was responsible for almost 8% of Turkey's electricity requirements at the time. Due to the rapid growth in demand for electricity in Turkey, the Turkish government provided support for a total of five energy projects in 1996/97. The power plant went operational in November 2003 after a construction phase of only 39 months.

A 20-year power purchase agreement concluded in March 1999 between the Turkish state power authority (TEAS) and the project company ISKEN ensured the purchase of 85% of the electricity generated annually on the basis of a take-or-pay arrangement. The project company received a fixed price per unit produced that covered the costs of operation, maintenance and energy, a minimum rate of return on capital employed and debt service. This long-term agreement eliminates most of the undesirable market risk for the private investors. At the end of the 20-years, the power plant will remain in the hands of the project company. In order to make the power purchase agreement bankable, that is acceptable for the financing banks, TEAS agreed to renegotiate material contractual elements with the parties involved, particularly the guaranteed power purchase volumes and the precautionary measures for cases of *force majeure*. This led to changes in the tariff structure as well as provisions regarding the extension of the term of the purchase agreement. All of TEAS's payment obligations under the power purchase agreement were fixed in US dollars and guaranteed by the Turkish Undersecretariat of Treasury. The contractual relationships with ISKEN are regulated by Turkish law, whereas the law of the State of New York applies to the banks involved. The project company concluded long-term coal supply agreements with RAG Trading GmbH and Rheinbraun Brennstoff GmbH, two of the world's largest coal suppliers at the time.

In accordance with these agreements, the suppliers were responsible for the purchase, shipping and transportation of the coal and its handover at the project jetty. The costs of the coal were contained in the raw material factor included in the calculation of the electricity price under the terms of the power purchase agreement. In order to ensure maximum supply, the suppliers may obtain the coal from various approved sources. The obligations set out in the coal supply agreement were sufficiently flexible to meet the requirements of the state power authority in terms of power supply. In order to meet the requirements for the reloading of the coal from the coal ships to a chain of barges in shallow coastal waters, the project sponsors formed an independent transportation company in conjunction with local partners. Concerning ESG aspects, İskenderun complied with the environmental standard of the World Bank/IFC at the time. The authors do not have any information about the criteria back then.

Sources: From various public and private confidential sources.

WARNOW TUNNEL, ROSTOCK (GERMANY)

The Warnow tunnel was the first privately-financed road project in Germany with an operational concession to be constructed in accordance with the German Federal Highway Private Finance Act (FStrPrivFinG). The tunnel connects the east and west bank of the Warnow river in the Hanseatic City of Rostock. A private investor and operator, Warnowquerung Rostock GmbH & Co. KG (the project company formed by Bouygues), charges a fee (toll) for the use of the tunnel. Construction for the project began on 1 December 1999 and the tunnel was opened on 12 September 2003. The Warnow Tunnel consists of six watertight concrete elements that were positioned in the bed of the Warnow river using an immersed tube construction, a technique that is far from common in Germany. Including the entrance and exit portals, the tunnel has a total length of 790 m, a width of 22.5 m with four lanes and a height of 8.5 m.

The 30-year concession agreement between the Hanseatic City of Rostock and Warnowquerung Rostock GmbH & Co. KG assumed that the project would be operable based on an average starting toll of €1.50 per passenger car unit (at 1995 prices) during the 30-year concessionary period, including covering its financing and current operating costs. A socially and economically acceptable toll level was determined in conjunction with the Hanseatic City of Rostock. Tolls are levied only for the use of the tunnel itself and not for the access routes and junctions created as part of the overall project. Buses serving scheduled public transport routes can use the tunnel without any additional cost to the passenger. A discount was offered to the large number of regular users that were expected on account of the significant volume of inner-city traffic using the Warnow Tunnel.

In contrast to the fixed, long-term purchase agreement forming part of the İskenderun project, which is backed by a guarantee from the Turkish government, the Warnow tunnel is purely direct user-financed, which involves a significant degree of market risk for the investor, because the revenues depend entirely on the actual utilisation of the tunnel. Price increases aimed at offsetting the – actually experienced – lower than expected volume of traffic are only politically expedient and legally enforceable to a limited extent and are not particularly rational from the perspective of the project.

Sources: Among others, Hehenberger, 2003

5.2.2 Interest rate risk

In addition to the traditional market-related risks described above, developments on the financial markets can also affect the financial performance of an infrastructure project/asset or company. This primarily relates to interest rate risk and, for investments in foreign currencies, exchange rate risk, which is discussed in the next section.

Loans forming part of traditional project finance and involving commercial banks only (i.e. no involvement from the development banks, see Section 7.4) generally do not have a term of more than 10–12 years and are mostly negotiated with variable interest rates consisting of two components (see also Section 7.3.1):

- The reference interest rate, i.e. the costs payable by the banks to refinance loans on the capital markets, which is determined based on a reference interest rate. Depending on the currency in which the loan is denominated, this may be the three- or six-month Euribor (for the euro) or Libor (for the US dollar).
- The interest margin, i.e. the interest rate corresponding to current market and industry standards and yield expectations of the lenders as well as their evaluation of the project/asset risks, and yield expectations of the lenders. In the case of greenfield projects as opposed to operational assets or companies, their risk usually declines as the project progresses and predefined key financial indicators (*financial covenants*) are achieved, thereby reflecting the gradual reduction in project risk.

Whereas the interest margin may be fixed and, if so, can be calculated in advance, the reference interest rate always varies depending on developments in the global capital markets. Hence, the project/asset may be exposed to significant additional financing costs, that is the risk that the cash flows will be adversely affected due to higher than planned interest payments in periods of rising interest rates in particular (*interest rate risk*). In most cases, interest rate risk is borne by the (project) company.

One way of mitigating interest rate risks is to borrow at a fixed rate for the entire term of the loan. Alternatively, the interest rate can be fixed for a specified period – this implies, though, that it needs to be renegotiated in the future when this period expires – or hedged using interest rate derivatives (*hedging*). Either measure enables the (project) company to fix its interest payments in the medium to long term, thereby allowing planning security of future cash flows. The mechanics of derivatives are discussed in greater detail in Section 7.7 using the examples of interest rate and exchange rate risk.

For projects/assets with a long duration (25–30 years from the outset), interest rate risk also arises from the fact that commercial banks alone are usually reluctant to provide loans that go beyond a term of 10–12 years. Consequently, loans are often divided into multiple loan and interest periods (e.g. two periods of 10 years plus the remaining duration). At the end of each interest period, interest rate conditions will be renegotiated. Depending on capital market conditions, the new loan may be significantly more or less expensive, thereby affecting the profitability of the project/asset or company. In the case of a PPP the sponsor may agree in advance with the principal that the cost of this potentially more expensive follow-up finance (*interest rate risk*) will be passed on directly to the public project developer, either in full or in part, via a corresponding increase in the performance fee. This serves to spread the interest rate risk of the project across several parties. In exchange, the project company may offer to negotiate improved interest rate conditions with a corresponding positive effect on the level of the principal's performance fee. In traditional project finance, sharing the interest rate risk of refinancing between the parties is generally possible but less common. In order to mitigate this interest rate risk, development banks often provide longer-term financing for the outstanding portion of the loan, which in turn allows commercial banks to borrow at longer terms as well as at better conditions.

5.2.3 Exchange rate risk

In addition to interest rate risk, projects/assets are often subject to exchange rate risk if the currency of the loans provided is different from the currency of the project revenue. This situation applies in particular to investments in countries with soft currencies. For example, if the revenue is denominated in local (soft) currency because of the nature of the project/asset (toll road revenue, price of water or power supply) but the financing and/or a portion of the project or operating costs are provided or incurred in hard currencies such as the US dollar or the euro.

One way of reducing exchange rate risk is to take out loans to pay for costs in the same local currency as those costs, especially if that currency is weak. The drawback of this structure is that capital on the local markets is often extremely limited, due to a lack of liquidity and/or the weak external value of the local currency, thus resulting in high interest rates. Accordingly, when a project or transaction is structured, its revenue should be paid in a hard currency – ideally in the same currency in which the loans are provided – or linked to the development of the respective hard currency by means of price adjustment or rate hedging clauses in the contracts in order to ensure that the loans can be serviced. For power plant projects in countries with soft currencies, for example, electricity prices are often tied to the fluctuations between the local currency and the currency of the loans (i.e. the US dollar) within a specific range. Although solutions of this nature are technically feasible, the question arises as to whether price increases in response to significant exchange rate fluctuations would be welcomed at a political level or whether they could be realistically implemented given the average national income in emerging economies. For example, in the spring of 2005, power suppliers in Argentina were forced to reverse the price adjustments they had imposed. A similar issue – which could arise in many (lower income) countries in the context of the statutory FITs guarantees for renewable energy – is the higher prices utilities have to pay (due to FITs) for renewable energy, which they are obliged to take off but are allowed to pass on to the end consumer.

Obtaining a guarantee for exchange rate risk from the government of the host country provides the greatest possible protection, but is itself subject to political risk in the form of the creditworthiness of the government and the relevance of the project/asset for the host country. The exchange rate is generally borne and hedged by the (project) company.

As for interest rate transactions, exchange rate hedging instruments exist for foreign currency transactions; these primarily relate to currency futures and currency options (see Section 7.7).

5.2.4 Environmental, social and governance (ESG) risk

Environmental, social and governance (ESG) risks, as introduced in Section 2.2, take into account non-financial (externalised) risk factors that can nevertheless affect the financial performance of an infrastructure asset. When ESG risks materialise, in addition to potential financial damage, often a significant reputational damage occurs to the project/asset and its shareholders, be it the project sponsors or its partners. Which ESG risk factors need to be considered in any given risk assessment depends on both the nature of the particular investment strategy, and, more importantly, the unique characteristics of the project/asset in question

TABLE 5.3   Selected ESG risks related to infrastructure investments

Environmental	Social	Governance
Climate change (physical and policy risks)	Human rights, labour rights	Corruption related to government approvals, licensing
Resource scarcity (e.g. water and other natural resources)	Safety and health risks	Public and corporate governance structures
Environmental degradation	Consumer protection	Executive compensation, incentive systems
Pollution (e.g. hazardous waste, contamination)	Public resistance of local communities and/or indigenous populations to projects	Local rule of law Government and stakeholder relations

(infrastructure sector, business model, location, etc.). All three risk aspects (environmental, social and governance) need to be assessed individually in order to evaluate the overall ESG risk profile related to a particular infrastructure investment.

ESG risks are often interrelated. For example, a large infrastructure project/asset that disrupts an environmentally sensitive ecosystem (environmental risk) may engender protest from the local community or advocacy groups (social risk) at the same time. As government approvals are always necessary preconditions of any infrastructure project, governance issues related to corruption often emerge in the context of environmental and social risks. Hence, all three of them need to be considered carefully in any infrastructure investment, but especially in jurisdictions with a weak rule of law.

The main benefit of considering ESG risks as part of evaluating infrastructure projects or assets is risk reduction. In the case of environmental risk, the focus lies on reducing financial risk resulting from physical damage of the assets and from non-compliance with environmental regulations as well as related reputational risk. Social issues, such as poor labour practices, or governance aspects, such as unethical management practices resulting in corruption, may have negative economic consequences as well and additionally can cause lasting reputational damage to a project's partners.

Table 5.3 illustrates selected ESG risks for infrastructure projects. A detailed discussion of the three ESG risks follows.

Depending on the infrastructure sector in question and the physical location of a specific asset, the ESG risks affecting it can differ a lot in scope and relevance. To this end, the most important, sector-specific ESG risks are discussed in Chapter 4. It is beyond the scope of this book to systematically analyse all geographies. The examples throughout this book aim to give some guidance.

5.2.4.1   Environmental risk   Environmental risk has become an increasingly important issue because of the depletion of finite natural resources and the irreversible damage to ecosystem services, such as clean water and waste decomposition, constraining the ability of existing infrastructure to meet the increased demands of population growth and human development. This risk category contains all environment-related matters that could potentially lead to additional costs or delays of a project or prevent its completion altogether. Risks result either *from* the infrastructure asset *affecting the environment* (e.g. pollution of the environment) or they result *from the environment on* the asset. The latter could be either directly through environmental hazards such as storms or floods caused by, for example, climate change, damaging built infrastructure, or indirectly through changes in environmental policies and regulations, which in turn may lead to the failure to receive all necessary government approvals, or through changed environmental conditions. An infrastructure asset that is built in a sustainable way – to, for example, weather heavy storms, operate resource efficiently and take into account foreseeable regulatory changes likely to affect it – is more likely to be resilient and futureproof in the long term than an asset that is not. Furthermore, it may reduce or eliminate potentially negative impacts on the environment (including natural resources and wildlife) and society more easily.

Examples of common environmental risks associated with infrastructure include:

- On the asset
  - Physical risk from climate change
  - Policy risks resulting from changes in environmental regulation (e.g. carbon tax)
- From the asset
  - Climate-change risk (greenhouse gas emissions)
  - Unsustainable use of scarce resources (e.g. water)
  - Damage to ecosystem services (such as food and water production, control of climate and disease, nutrient cycles and crop pollination)
  - Negative impact on biodiversity and ecosystem services
  - Negative impact on prime habitats, wetlands, surface water, farmland and forests
  - Chemical and other hazardous waste
  - Water contamination
  - Gaseous emissions (air pollution), including dust
  - Generally, non-compliance with effective environmental regulations.

The potentially severe impact from climate change on any infrastructure (from a physical and regulatory perspective) across all sectors and the related effects on the risk profile, return perspectives and future value of such assets are of increasing concern to investors. Therefore, climate-change risk, unlike all the other environmental risks, is discussed comprehensively in a special section below.

CLIMATE CHANGE

Climate change is a growing global risk with high potential impact for infrastructure investors whose long-term assets are particularly vulnerable to both the physical and the policy risks associated with a changing climate. According to the International Institute for Sustainable Development, climate-change risk to infrastructure is defined as 'the exposure and vulnerability of infrastructure systems to climate hazards (floods, hurricanes, droughts, etc.). Exposure refers to the presence of infrastructure in a climate-hazard prone area whereas vulnerability is based on the sensitivity of infrastructure to climate hazards and its adaptive capacity (both technically and financially) to minimise the negative impacts to such hazards' (Boyle, Cunningham and Dekens, 2013, see also www.IISD.org). Infrastructure resilience, on the other hand, refers to the ability of a system to anticipate, absorb, accommodate or recover from the effects of a hazardous event in a timely and effective manner (IPCC, 2012).

Infrastructure assets are exposed to two types of climate change-related risks as introduced above: *physical risk* (direct physical exposure to increased frequency and intensity of extreme weather (e.g. floods, hurricanes, droughts), sea level changes, etc.) and *policy risk* (uncertainty in climate and energy policy changes in carbon tax, subsidies, FITs, etc.). Both physical and policy risks may have an important negative effect on the returns and thus the valuation of an infrastructure asset.

Physical risk to infrastructure from climate change is a growing concern around the world with many local, regional and national governments developing adaptation plans and protocols to cope with the current and future impacts of extreme weather, such as rising sea levels, river flooding, long-term drought and extreme heatwaves. Such impacts cut across all sectors of infrastructure from coastal roads and ports to inland power plants, buildings and water supply systems, putting both new and existing infrastructure at risk.

Direct damage from extreme weather is just one of the physical risks to infrastructure and society caused by climate change. Others are relative sea-level rises, river flooding, long-term regional droughts and extreme heatwaves, all of which are predicted to increase in the coming decades, mostly because of climate change (US Department of Transportation, 2011). The rapid increase in weather-related catastrophes in recent years (refer to Figure 1.5) has resulted in measurable negative impacts on infrastructure, which is also reflected in increased insurance premiums. For example, in the US there has been a rapid rise in major power outages (50 000 customers or more) over the last decade, with the number of weather-related outages doubling from 2003 to 2012 (see Figure 5.3).

The extent to which climate-change risks physically affect a particular infrastructure asset depends on its unique conditions. For example, a road, bridge or airport built near a coastline may be more prone to physical risk caused by an increase in severe storms than a similar project/asset located further inland. Water scarcity resulting from prolonged droughts will not only affect water supply and disposal systems but also energy generation systems such as hydropower or conventional thermal and nuclear power plants, which require large volumes of cooling water during operations.

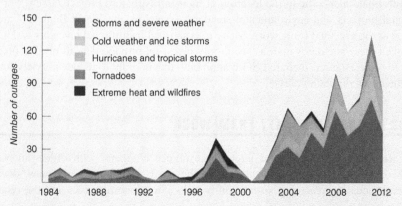

FIGURE 5.3 Major power outages in the US owing to extreme weather events (major = at least 50 000 customers affected)
Source: Kenward and Raja (2014)

In addition to climate-change-related physical risks to the assets, policy risks are a concern. They manifest themselves in a growing body of environmental regulations and requirements relating to, for example, government targets on greenhouse gas reduction, carbon taxes or changes in investment subsidies targeting certain sectors. Assets/projects in the energy and transport sectors are likely to be more exposed to *climate policy* risks than those in other infrastructure sectors.

Certain environmental risks are thus closely linked to political and regulatory risks. This is underlined by the discussion on stranded fossil fuel assets and renewable energy regulations (see Sections 5.2.5.2 and 5.2.5.3).

Moreover, there are significant reputational risks involved in operating an infrastructure asset that does not comply with environmental regulations but rather has a negative impact on the environment, be that by depleting natural resources and damaging ecosystem services or by hurting biodiversity or wildlife. NGO activists may even fight certain activities of infrastructure operators that are legally unquestionable yet to some extent detrimental to the environment. Negative media attention may result in serious reputational damage, which is to be avoided. This is especially true for infrastructure companies listed on a public stock exchange with the potentially negative effect on their market value.

Prior to any investment, these aspects must be examined in detail. Environmental studies are generally performed by specialists in the field. Their primary objective is to ensure that potential environmental and related reputational risks are minimised prior to construction and, hence, prior to providing significant equity capital and debt financing (e.g. with regard to air and soil contamination, the use of dangerous building materials in the project construction phase or the consideration of conservation areas). Obtaining government approvals is an essential part of this process.

Although environmental risks are global issues, their specific impacts on infrastructure can be very local. For this reason, investors should seek out information on environmental risks at the subnational and municipal level whenever possible in order to get the most accurate and detailed information specific to the location of their infrastructure projects/assets. For major international projects, the environmental standards issued by the World Bank/IFC are long recognised as the accepted framework. Many international institutional investors and insurers have adopted these standards and, as such, only invest in, provide debt to or give insurance coverage to projects/assets that are ESG-compliant – this in order to reduce not only financial but also their own reputational risk.

SWISS RE SUSTAINABILITY FRAMEWORK

Swiss Re is the world's second largest reinsurance company with offices in more than 25 countries. It is also ranked one of the most sustainable companies,[1] due to its strong focus on managing sustainability risks. Sustainability risks and the related

---

[1] For example, Swiss Re was ranked as the 2015 RobecoSAM insurance sector leader in sustainability in the Dow Jones Sustainability Indices (http://www.swissre.com/investors/ratings/sustainability_ratings/).

reputational risks arise in the context of business activities, which create tangible economic benefits while damaging the environment with disruptive effects on society. Swiss Re's Sustainability Risk Framework (SRF) addresses such sustainability risks with an exemplary and clear approach. In particular, the framework assesses any potential negative environmental effects a company's policy has on society, and therefore the attendant reputational risk for that company. It comprises the following elements: (i) eight policies on sensitive sectors or issues; (ii) the Sensitive Business Risks process, a due diligence tool for case-by-case assessments; (iii) company and country exclusions.

Swiss Re applies this framework to all business transactions, that is (re)insurance as well as investments. The eight sensitive sectors and issues are: the defence industry, oil and gas, mining, dams, animal testing, forestry and logging, nuclear weapons proliferation as well as overarching human rights and environmental protection policies. Transactions in these sectors are subject to the Sensitive Business Risks process, which results in three options for action: to proceed as normal, proceed with conditions or abstain from the transaction. The number of Sensitive Business Risk referrals more than doubled in five years, increasing from around 90 cases in 2008 to over 200 cases in 2013. Excluded are business transactions with companies, which conduct activities such as the manufacturing of antipersonnel mines; the verifiable complicity in systemic, repeated and severe human rights violations; the infliction of repeated, severe and unmitigated damage to the environment; and the proliferation of nuclear weapons (Swiss Re, 2015).

For example, Swiss Re's risk assessment of a hydropower plant (dam) construction project – one of the sensitive sectors – in an emerging country involved the evaluation of the following risk criteria: project governance, environmental and social impacts (and the mitigation of these impacts), public perception and funding. Concerns were found in all parameters. In particular, the project governance was found to have 'serious shortcomings' such as not adhering to recognised standards (such as the IFC Performance Standards; see IFC, 2012) and having an incomplete/arbitrary process for environmental licensing. These issues resulted in a highly critical response from the public. In addition, the financial viability of the project was questioned by some of the potential private funders. For these reasons, Swiss Re chose to abstain from providing reinsurance to the project.

The SRF does not directly address all key ESG risk factors covered in this book, such as stranded (fossil-fuel) assets, changes in regulations affecting sustainability (e.g. renewable energy regulations, physical climate-change risks resulting from increases in extreme weather events, increased flooding and droughts and changes in the available water supply). However, it analyses these risks as part of its economic viability assessment it undertakes for any commercial transaction within Swiss Re. The risks are reflected in the pricing for the respective insurance coverage.

Environmental factors in general and climate risks in particular also have an impact on several aspects of infrastructure project/asset appraisals, including: planning, construction and completion risk; technology risks; financing and syndication risk; operational risks; and residual value risk. Adaptation measures designed to minimise a project's or asset's environmental vulnerability and to make it more resilient may include both structural measures to fortify the asset against physical damage and policy measures for disaster preparedness such as emergency procedures. With respect to upfront investment costs for such measures, the net cost of adapting infrastructure to, for example, climate change has been calculated to add up to 1–2% to the total *upfront* investment costs (European Policy Center, 2012). The uncertainty surrounding the long-term implications of climate change may make the immediate need for the additional investment in structural adaptation measures challenging to justify. However, climate resilient infrastructure adaptation measures should lead to lower long-term costs as they help to prevent damage to and interruption of infrastructure. From this perspective, the overall cost of adaptation appears small in relation to other factors that may influence overall lifecycle costs (World Bank, 2012b).

Moreover, as sustainable infrastructure should generate at least the same returns as traditional infrastructure, and yet is more resilient to certain risks, it implies that sustainable infrastructure is less risky while providing comparable returns. Consequently, risk-adjusted returns of sustainable infrastructure are relatively higher than those of conventional infrastructure, which in turn should result in higher valuations and lower borrowing rates for sustainable infrastructure assets. In essence, the potential de-risking characteristics of sustainable infrastructure are value drivers of infrastructure assets. Also, in this respect, the additional costs incurred at the outset of an investment to ensure an infrastructure project/asset meets all relevant current and foreseeable future ESG standards may well pay off.

Like political risk, environmental risk is multifaceted in its nature. Depending on the extent to which it can be limited (e.g. the environmental approval process can be controlled by the public partner), environmental risk is usually borne both by the (project) company and by the public-sector sponsor.

5.2.4.2 Social risk   The Three Gorges Dam in central China (completed in 2006), which resulted in the displacement of millions of inhabitants from the Yangtze River region and led to high-level international protests, provides a stark example of the potential social risk related to infrastructure. Social risks are often linked to environmental or governance risk. Construction of infrastructure projects in areas that may permanently alter or damage local ecosystems (environmental risk) can lead to high-level protests from advocacy groups (social risk). Poor labour conditions and increased exposure to occupational hazards (social risk) are often the results of poor management practices (governance risk).

Social risks in large infrastructure projects predominantly relate to human and labour rights as well as to health and safety risks for workers and local communities. The risks manifest themselves in public and NGO resistance to a project and the related reputational risk of negative media attention. Examples of social risks associated with infrastructure projects/assets may include:

- General safety risks associated with large construction projects
- Worker and community exposure to hazardous substances
- Poor living conditions for workers at remote sites
- Child labour, forced labour
- Negative impacts on indigenous populations and cultural heritage sites.

Social impact varies not only by infrastructure sector (energy, transport, etc.) but also by the size and location of a particular project/asset: more risks are associated with larger-scale projects/assets built in environmentally or culturally sensitive areas than smaller-scale ones located in urbanised areas.

5.2.4.3 Governance risk 'Governance', broadly defined, refers to the processes and procedures put in place to manage any type of organisation or project. In the context of ESG risks related to infrastructure projects/assets, it also entails all aspects of government relations, in particular involving government approvals, licences and concessions (closely related to Section 5.2.5). Examples of governance risks include:

- Corrupt business practices
- Failure to obtain proper permits, certifications
- Improper payments to contractors or subcontractors
- Weak public and corporate governance structures
- Management incentive systems unaligned with interests of project sponsors
- Failure to achieve the necessary level of stakeholder engagement and buy-in.

Like environmental and social risk, governance risk may vary considerably based on the type, size and location of an infrastructure asset. For example, occupational hazards for workers may be more of a risk in countries where labour laws are weak with little regulatory oversight. Governance risk is often associated with poor management practices (at corporate, contractor or subcontractor level), be it during the planning, approval, construction or management phase of an infrastructure project. Typically, investors in infrastructure projects in developing countries with a poor rule of law need to put a strong emphasis on governance issues and related reputational risks.

5.2.5 Political, legal and regulatory risk

Political, legal and regulatory risk is a multifaceted and wide-ranging risk category. It is probably among the most critical ones together with market risk. It arises from the extent to which local governments and jurisdictions are able to affect the development of a project or operation of an asset during its usually very long lifetime through significant changes in legislation, deregulation, nationalisation, seizure and expropriation, the failure to obtain necessary approvals, licences and concessions or even then a breach of concession. The consequences of such risks are particularly severe for industries where profitability depends (almost) entirely on government provisions. Additional risks falling into this category include restrictions on currency movement (conversion and transfer risk), payment freezes and payment holidays, changes in tax rates and breach of contract by government bodies. The functionality of the court system and the unenforceability of contracts may also lead to significant problems, particularly in countries with little developed constitutional structures.

Given the above, it goes without saying that political, legal and regulatory risks are particularly relevant in emerging economies, some of which have relatively poorly-developed legal cultures and respective administrative systems but should not be underestimated in countries with constitutional security either. In developed countries, for example, significant risks may occur because of conflicts of interest within federal structures, changes in legislation affecting the tax system, the investment regulations, the environmental regulations and/or investment incentives/subsidies, as well as other bureaucratic obstacles. Some specific examples are discussed in Sections 5.2.5.1–3.

Depending on the capabilities of the individual participants involved, these risks are allocated to the various partners (public sector, (project) company, credit and investment insurers, multilateral organisations, export credit agencies; see also Figure 5.1 and Chapter 6).

An alliance involving several strong partners and including international guarantors increases the possibility of being able to influence the authorities in the respective country in the event of growing political uncertainty. The involvement of local banks and the timely application for and receipt of all necessary approvals can also help to limit political risk at an early stage of an investment.

In addition to the risks outlined above, public acceptance is a key factor in the successful implementation of any new infrastructure investment. This is influenced by considerations such as environmental protection, noise pollution, protection of historical buildings or the often unjustified fears of the population that the involvement of private investors will result in inferior product quality, price increases, job losses or a higher degree of dependency in general. From the perspective of a private capital provider (equity or debt), a lack of public acceptance may endanger a project severely. The early involvement of the public sector and a targeted, open information policy is advisable in order to at least minimise any objections, which are often unsubstantiated and the result of a lack of knowledge.

A number of means or ways may prevent or contain political risks in emerging economies. The involvement of multilateral banks and institutions – such as the European Investment Bank (EIB), the European Bank for Reconstruction and Development (EBRD), the African Development Bank, the Asian Development Bank, or the World Bank and its subsidiary operations like the IFC and the MIGA – in the financing of a project offers a de facto umbrella, albeit in relative terms (see also Section 7.4). This umbrella functions primarily via the political relevance of these banks for financing all kinds of local projects rather than via legally enforceable provisions. Any impairment of the credit rating of the host country because of political risk could dramatically reduce its future access to these crucial sources of development finance.

In addition to these multilateral banks, a project may also seek to involve governmental and private export credit agencies (ECAs), which to some extent operate as, or offer, a kind of insurance. They support the export transactions of national companies by providing export loan guarantees as part of the (indirect) promotion of exports. Depending on the respective export transaction, the assumption of economic and political risk by these quasi-insurers may differ in terms of the type of goods being insured, the definition of the insured event and the amount and structure of the cover provided.

Insurance of direct foreign investments offers specific protection against political risk. This relates to long-term investment guarantees for non-commercial risks, which are offered by all industrialised nations, by some large private insurance groups and the World Bank subsidiary the Multilateral Investment Guarantee Agency (MIGA). All three alternatives essentially cover the same political risks. Finally, it became apparent in the financial crisis that sufficient diversification of insurance providers is advisable to mitigate the concentration risk of the insurers themselves. Section 7.4.4 provides further information on export promotion and export credit guarantees.

Including this form of risk coverage in a project or an investment structure serves to increase political security, thereby improving the basis of calculation of financial projections for the investment. Accordingly, private sector banks involved in project finance often demand such an investment guarantee, with the claims from the insurance cover provided assigned to the banks as security for the loans extended.

Hedging against political, legal and regulatory risk is not only advisable in countries with a comparatively low degree of constitutional security. Capital protection in regions with relative political stability and stable regulatory frameworks may also be appropriate for investments in politically and economically sensitive sectors (e.g. finance, media, infrastructure). This is because various government approvals are required for such investments and the project sponsors rely to a large extent on obtaining legally enforceable approvals from the relevant government bodies. Along the same lines, in politically stable economies investors rely on coherent, predictable regulations. A breach of approval or a change of regulation, especially when affecting past investments, poses a significant risk to the economic success of existing infrastructure assets as well as future projects in planning.

A relatively recent example of an unexpected regulatory change with significant economic implications for the investors took place in the least expected place: Norway, an extremely stable, AAA-rated country. In 2012, a consortium of foreign institutional investors bought Gasled, the Norwegian national gas network from the Norwegian state. Within only a few months of the transaction, Norway changed the regulatory system of its gas network. Going forward, the tariff the new owners were allowed to charge was reduced by almost 90%! Needless to say, such a severe tariff reduction had a dramatic impact on revenues and, hence, the economics of the project. Interesting about this case – and somewhat of an irony – is that a very rich country such as Norway as project partner may also constitute a political risk as it has enough capital not to care if it offends foreign investors.

In the following three sections, we discuss three kinds of political and regulatory risk in more detail, which may be of particular interest to investors.

5.2.5.1 Solvency II   Since January 2016, the European Union (EU) introduced risk-based capital requirements for insurance companies, known as Solvency II. The intent of this new regulation is to reduce the risk of insolvency of insurers (as happened during the financial crisis in 2007) by requiring EU insurance companies to hold at all times a risk-adjusted amount of capital on their balance sheets. The insurance industry is concerned because this new directive, among others, will make investments by European insurance companies in infrastructure assets prohibitively expensive, owing to the high capital requirements of equity and long-term debt.

Within this framework, investments in any infrastructure are captured by the market risk sub-module of the standard model used by almost all insurers, except very large ones, to calculate the risk adjusted capital. This category also includes investments in hedge funds, private equity and venture capital. Infrastructure equity is considered 'type 2 equity' under the standard model and, as such, requires 49% of equity capital, irrespective of the specific risk profile of the asset in question. Even relatively low-risk infrastructure assets – such as a solar PV plant regulated by a 20-year guaranteed, fixed-price FIT regime in a safe country like Germany, the risk and cash-flow profile of which resembles that of a government bond – fall under these capital requirements.

The capital requirements for infrastructure debt are captured under the spread risk sub-module, regardless of the debt being held as bonds or long-term loans. They are calculated in relation to the duration and credit rating of the instrument whereby long-term, non-sovereign debt is penalised with relatively high capital charges. This is the case despite the fact that this is exactly the kind of debt infrastructure assets seek and life insurers need to match their very long-term liabilities. For unrated infrastructure debt, the spread risk charge to be applied falls between that for A- and BBB-rated bonds and loans (JP Morgan, 2013).

As a result of these regulations, many insurance companies that are principally interested to invest in the equity and/or debt of infrastructure projects or assets and thereby support national governments in financing the necessary infrastructure, will refrain from doing so. This holds in particular for equity. This is likely to jeopardise the realisation of many infrastructure assets, which are in the interest of the public and could otherwise be financed.

In March 2013, the German Insurance Association (GDV) published a position paper recommending the creation of a separate risk category for infrastructure under Solvency II capital requirements with a risk factor of 20%, as opposed to the current 49%. The European Insurance and Occupational Pensions Authority (EIOPA) rejected this proposal based on a lack of data to substantiate the claim that such investments pose a lower risk than other investments in this risk class (Chief Investment Officer, 2014).

5.2.5.2 Renewable energy regulations Global investors express a strong interest in significantly increasing their exposure to clean energy assets. Notwithstanding, global clean energy investments are declining, according to the BNEF (2015). This hesitation is due to several factors, among them Solvency II (see Section 5.2.5.1) and uncertainty surrounding national and international regulations affecting the energy industry. More specifically, the latter relates to potential changes in the regulatory frameworks targeted at renewable energy investments. Going forward, decreasing financial support for renewable energy is expected – and even explicitly intended in all countries – with renewable energy generation costs reaching network parity and new investments eventually becoming profitable without subsidies. The explicit aim is to reduce the financial burden on consumers and/or the public budget (depending on the regulations in the respective countries) of these support programmes. While the right thing to do in the medium-term, it is unfortunate that these changes and reductions come at a time of highly-volatile energy prices.

While pre-announced legal or regulatory changes going forward have been the norm for centuries across all industry sectors, during the past years some countries have introduced regulatory changes addressing renewable energy generation assets retrospectively. Spain is the most prominent example. This has caused not only economic losses for investors but also, most importantly, a decrease of investor confidence in the governments of developed countries in general, which understandably leads to investment hesitation.

REGULATORY CHANGES IN RENEWABLE ENERGY

In 2007/08, *Spain* experienced a boom in solar PV investment owing to what was perceived then as a generous, budget-financed FIT and to related policies to promote renewable energy investments. However, these policies were unsustainable for the government budget, even more so following the subsequent global financial crisis, resulting in the Spanish government retroactively cutting FITs and altering related policies for both investments in solar and wind energy development. The result was a 75% cut in PV sector jobs from 2008 to 2012 (from around 42 000 to 10 000) and a decrease of investor confidence in the reliability of such government policy frameworks (del Río and Mir-Artigues, 2014).

A different example is *Australia*. Despite a global trend towards policies that favour renewable energy over fossil fuels, Australia became the first nation in 2015 to recall an existing levy on CO_2 emissions and is currently looking to cut its 2020 renewable energy targets, in addition to eliminating the current 30% tax on coal mining profits. This is despite the fact that the government itself has already invested over US$17 billion through subsidies in renewables. These policy changes threaten several renewable energy projects, including a US$340 million wind farm investment by a privately-held company (Bloomberg, 2014). Moreover, such changes send conflicting signals and may severely harm the environment in and around Australia with coal being among the most pollutive energy sources.

The *UK's* FIT scheme (introduced in 2010) is part of a set of initiatives (which also include the Renewables Obligation and Contract for Difference regime) designed to encourage the deployment of renewable energy across the UK. The FIT scheme, which was meant to target small farmers, firms and private individuals, aims to support small-scale renewable energy generation (5 MW or less) by providing an incentive for total energy *generated*, plus an additional incentive for the portion of energy generated that is *exported* to the grid (i.e. not used on-site). Subsidies for electricity generation are paid for through additions to consumer bills. As part of this scheme, the UK government set in place a budgetary limit on low-carbon energy subsidies, known as LCF.

In July 2015, it was announced that the LCF budget would have a forecasted overspend of 20% by 2020/21, blamed in part on a greater-than-anticipated participation of developers and institutional investors in the FIT programme and changes in wholesale energy prices. This prompted the government to propose cost-control measures for the FIT scheme through a consultation published in August 2015, with the aim of preventing budget overrun (DECC, 2015). In the government consultation response of 17 Dec 2015, it was finally determined to maintain the FIT scheme beyond January 2016, yet first to reduce, and ultimately phase-out, generation FITs for low-carbon energy generation. Ex-post FITs will not be affected. Proposed measures include a more stringent degression mechanism (reductions in FITs over time) and deployment caps (limiting the scheme once the total capacity of deployed energy generation (per technology) has been reached in the UK) with an eventual phasing-out of the generation FIT scheme entirely by 2018/19. If further analysis during this consultation indicates that such measures cannot keep the budget in check, the government also proposes to end generation FITs for all new applicants, starting in January 2016. All existing installations, as well as those for which the FIT review impact assessment has been completed by August 2015, were not affected by the proposed changes to tariffs and caps. These policy changes threaten the various ongoing renewable energy developments of small, entrepreneurial developers and private individuals in particular. The reduced deployment caps, which were exhausted for 2016 in no time, combined with related tariff degressions going forward, have significantly changed the economics of many infrastructure developments.

5.2.5.3 Stranded (fossil-fuel) assets   Stranded assets are defined as 'assets that have suffered from unanticipated or premature write-downs, devaluations, or conversion to liabilities, which can be caused by a variety of risks', according to the Stranded Assets Programme at Oxford University (Ansar A. et al., 2013). The main risk of stranded fossil fuel assets is that energy companies will no longer be able to exploit all their known reserves. As a consequence, impairments will have to be made on the balance sheets with the related negative impact on company valuations and shareholder value.

The risk of stranded assets is caused by several factors, such as potential policy changes (carbon pricing, air pollution regulations), changing social norms (e.g. the current fossil-fuel divestment movement) and falling costs for clean energy technologies (wind, solar PV, etc.). A 2012 IEA report estimates that two-thirds of the world's proven reserves of fossil fuels may be unusable ('unburnable'), once the regulations to cut carbon emissions to limit global temperature increases to 2°C are enacted (IEA, 2012c). One scenario projected that US$120 billion new fossil-fuel capacity in the power sector, US$180 billion in upstream oil and gas and US$4 billion in coal mining investment will become stranded by 2035 (IEA, 2014g).

Mercer (2015) contends that the average annual returns from coal could fall by anywhere between 18 and 74%. A 2013 HSBC report warns that future action to mitigate climate change may devalue fossil fuel companies (especially oil and coal) by as much as 60–80% (Spedding, Mehta and Robins, 2013). If such estimates prove to be right – due to governments restricting energy use or taxing carbon emissions to mitigate climate change – then reducing exposure to the sector would be perfectly rational and in line with the fiduciary duty of investors.

The risk of stranded assets is twofold, though. The straightforward one is discussed above: owning capital-intensive, long-term assets and fossil fuel reserves, the value of which may decrease significantly because of regulatory changes. The second aspect is that current owners and new investors do not know if and when regulatory changes targeting fossil fuel assets will be introduced. Investors run the risk of negating their fiduciary duty of earning the highest possible return for beneficiaries when excluding fossil fuel assets 'too early', well before a major devaluation of the assets in question occurs, hence leaving 'money on the table'. Denigrators of divestment call attention to the fact that selling a security does not materially lower its price if there are many buyers still out there (The Economist, 2015a). Also, it is unclear whether divestment will make any difference to firms' behaviour.

Pressure groups record increasing success in getting investors to move out of fossil fuels. The most remarkable recruit to date is Norway's sovereign wealth fund, with total assets of almost US$900 billion. It agreed to sell US$9 billion worth of shares in firms that mine coal and tar sands (The Economist, 2015b). A number of the largest pension funds globally have followed suit or are considering to do so.

It will be interesting to see whether a tipping point will be reached. With tougher regulations emerging to stem climate change, investors who defend their fossil fuel positions with the argument of fiduciary duty and a focus on maximising short-term returns may run into difficulties down the road.

5.2.6 Force majeure

'*Force majeure*' refers to extraordinary events or circumstances beyond the control of the parties, such as war, terrorism, strikes or an event described by the legal term 'act of God', such as earthquakes, extreme weather events or other natural disasters preventing one or both parties from fulfilling their obligations under the contract. During the project analysis phase, these risks require close attention because they may result in the total loss of the capital employed. For example, it is essentially impossible to attract investors and implement project finance in troubled regions, such as war-torn countries. In Western Europe, thanks to the region's geographical and political stability, these risks are not relevant. In some cases, private insurers and, to a lesser extent, public insurers, cover *force majeure* risks. The remaining risks are borne by the (project) company and/or the public sector.

The expected increase of *force majeure* events from extreme weather (caused by climate change, see Figure 5.3) may increase the ongoing costs and/or reduce the return of infrastructure investments owing to their life-long exposure to nature. In addition to the risk of

TABLE 5.4   Natural catastrophes in the US, 2003–2012

(2003–2012, US$ billions)

			Overall losses	Insured losses	
	Number of events	Fatalities		Total	10-year average
Earthquake/tsunami	29	6	$1	$0.3	$0.03
Tropical cyclone (2)	46	1,975	378	204.0	20.40
Severe thunderstorm (3)	775	1,630	169	107.0	10.70
Heatwave/drought	21	425	48	20.0	2.00
Wildfire	253	112	15	8.0	0.80
Winter events (4)	114	765	22	13.0	1.30
River flood/flash flood (5)	162	245	23	4.0	0.40

(1) As of July 2013.
(2) Includes flooding caused by hurricanes and other tropical cyclones. Includes National Flood Insurance Program losses.
(3) Includes tornadoes.
(4) Includes winter storms, winter damage and blizzards.
(5) Excludes flood damage losses caused by tropical cyclones and hurricanes.
Sources: Munich RE, Geo Risks Research, NatCalSERVICE

revenue loss of the asset in question following operational disruptions, the prices for insurance policies covering extreme weather events may rise rapidly if their annual payouts to cover natural catastrophes increase. For example, in the US, over 90% of total insured losses from natural catastrophes (2003–2012) were from climate-related events such as tropical cyclones, severe thunderstorms, heatwaves and droughts (see Table 5.4 and climate-change risk in Section 5.2.4.1). Rising insurance premia should be the logical consequence of these developments even though the authors do not have publicly available data to support this.

5.3   PROJECT/ASSET-SPECIFIC RISKS

Project/asset-specific risks differ from the general risks discussed above insofar as some or all of the participants can influence and, in most cases, insure these risks, be that through specific insurance guarantees or through the involvement of suitable partners (see Table 5.2 in Section 5.1). Further, general risks may occur throughout the entire term or lifetime of a project or asset, whereas project/asset-specific risks may occur and hence be allocated to the various phases of a project or asset to a varying extent, depending on the level of impact of the project/asset-specific risks and the likelihood of their occurrence.

The most important principle in the context of risk assessment and mitigation is: any contracts among the parties are structured in such a way as to ensure that the party best positioned to assess, control and manage a specific risk is given responsibility for its minimisation.

While general ESG risks are covered above (see Section 5.2.4), ESG risks typically also arise in combination with other project/asset-specific risks. Naturally, there is a significant overlap with general ESG risks. Therefore, the authors suggest the relevant ESG risks be addressed specifically in the context of performing due diligence on project/asset-specific risks (e.g. technology risk, operational risk). To this end, we provide some examples below.

5.3.1 Planning, construction and completion risk

Planning, construction and completion risk is generally relevant only for development projects (greenfield). In the case of brownfield projects with assets that are already operational, the risks are either irrelevant or of only secondary importance, for example in the case of capacity expansion or substantial replacement investments.

The planning phase of a project requires significant preliminary organisational and engineering work in order to ensure the timing as well as logistical and technical feasibility of the project. All factors affecting its realisation phase must be examined in detail (see Section 6.4.2). In addition, all necessary approvals and expert appraisals must be obtained and efficient project management performed in order to ensure that the project is commissioned smoothly, on budget and on schedule.

The contract for the construction of a project is typically awarded to a general contractor, which transfers individual elements of the construction work to subcontractors but itself bears all the completion risk for the project as a whole with respect to the project sponsors and financiers (see Section 6.3 for an explanation of their roles). Accordingly, the experience and reputation of the general contractor are relevant factors when assessing the overall planning, construction and completion risk. Its creditworthiness and financial resources may also play an important role if it is to be held responsible for defects or delays in the completion of the project or it is required to provide preliminary financing during the construction phase. The analysis of planning, construction and completion risk should also encompass aspects such as future capacity expansions or additional infrastructure measures, such as access roads, power lines or pipes for the supply of electricity, gas, water or other primary products.

In order to evaluate construction and completion risk, the sponsors and other providers of capital require independent appraisals prepared by specialist engineering offices. This is intended to ensure that:

- The forecast project costs are realistic (e.g. cost overruns during the construction phase or as a result of excess costs or delays in completion; any additional contributions typically have to be covered by the providers of equity);
- The project can be completed on schedule;
- The planned operating performance of the project is achievable after completion;
- Any capacity expansions or increased utilisation can be implemented as planned.

The risk of failing to meet the required performance standards or cost increases because of changes in internal planning is borne by the general contractor, because it is in a position to control and manage this risk. As a rule, all capital providers (debt and equity) expect the general contractor or the project developer to provide a guarantee of completion.

The (public) principal retains the risk of changes in planning or additional costs due to delays in the approval process caused by the principal itself.

ESG-related project/asset-specific risks to be considered during the planning, construction and completion phases include:

- Risk of project site being exposed to environmental hazards resulting from climate change;
- Risk of contaminated soil on construction site from previous assets or industrial activity or project construction;
- Risk of negative/unsatisfactory results of environmental impact assessment for the project;

- Risk of delays in the approval process owing to environmental issues, interference of interest groups or NGOs;
- Risk of improper contractual arrangements between contractor and subcontractor on ESG issues, such as adherence to environmental standards in the construction phase, work conditions on building site (application of labour laws, health and safety) etc.

EVALUATION OF PLANNING, CONSTRUCTION AND COMPLETION RISK

İskenderun: All environmentally relevant aspects of the project were examined in detail by the parties involved. Independent advisors prepared an environmental impact assessment in accordance with the applicable standards issued by the World Bank at the time and the Turkish government. The study confirmed that the project was admissible from an environmental perspective. Following more than a decade of operations, significant negative environmental impact and the related concerns of the local community can be observed.

Warnow: Prior to the project, the developer performed an environmental impact assessment and different scenarios for various route layouts. Adherence to the accompanying landscape preservation plan that was prepared in advance was reviewed as part of the individual construction measures and found to meet the relevant requirements. Another important task, the disposal of the soil excavated in the course of the underground mining and construction work, was also performed in accordance with the requirements of the planning approval process.

5.3.2 Technical risk

Extensive preliminary work with respect to procedural feasibility during the planning phase of a project is crucial in order to prevent a scenario where the project assets fail to operate at the planned level of performance or, in extreme circumstances, don't operate at all or are unavailable. When selecting the technical partners, it should generally be ensured that tried-and-tested technologies from known manufacturers are used rather than new, untested technologies, unless this is an essential aspect of the project. An analysis is also performed to determine the extent to which the chosen technology has already been used successfully in similar projects and whether potential changes in geographical or climactic conditions could affect its functionality and effectiveness.

Equipment that has been used in cool, dry regions may not meet the relevant requirements in a warm, humid climate. For example, a power turbine may perform less efficiently at higher altitudes than at sea level. New or rarely-used technologies offering cost or efficiency benefits should be tested in pilot projects before being rolled out for large-scale operations. In principle, all technologies should undergo a test phase prior to construction. In this context, it is also important that the technologies used offer the necessary operating performance to facilitate planned capacity expansions. All risks related to these aspects are borne by the (project) company or, depending on the supply guarantees provided, the manufacturer of the equipment used.

The manufacturer guarantees the contractual performance of the technology supplied and assumes responsibility for any defects or inefficiencies and resulting costs for a certain period to the extent required under a standard guarantee. However, this manufacturer guarantee does not cover the incorrect use or maintenance of the equipment supplied; in such cases, the corresponding liability lies with the operator. With these considerations in mind, the establishment of an experienced operating team that is intimately familiar with the technology used is vital in order to ensure that production processes run smoothly (see Section 5.3.5).

It is in the interests of the operator to use the most cost-effective technology solution in the long term. Accordingly, the risk of using relatively new technologies may be acceptable for the operator in light of the anticipated cost savings over the term of the project. From the perspective of the debt providers, however, using new technology with a limited testing history increases the risk of operational downtime, and hence the insolvency risk. This in turn increases the lending costs for the project.

Instead of higher failure rates, a sensitivity analysis may simulate this technology risk by assuming lower efficiency on the part of the technologies used. Either option serves to reduce the expected cash flow, which usually results in a lower amount of debt provision. Alternatively, the providers of equity may undertake to make additional payments in the event of the cash flow from the project being insufficient to service the debt. This example again shows how varied, interrelated and complex the interests of the project participants are and how difficult it can be to reconcile these interests within appropriate contractual structures.

MANAGEMENT OF TECHNICAL RISK

İskenderun: The project company concluded a US$812.5 million turnkey construction agreement with a fixed completion date with a consortium consisting of Siemens, SIMKO, Gama Tekfen and BBO Energy. The contract also included the coal unloading facilities, the jetty and a 380 kV transformer station. The project used tried-and-tested technologies based on historical data from many years of successful operation. Siemens Power Generation is an experienced general contractor that typically hands over projects on schedule and as planned.

Warnow Tunnel: An experienced construction consortium was used, managed by Bouygues Travaux Publics SA (France) and Macquarie Infrastructure (Australia) in conjunction with several small and medium-sized enterprises from the region. In some areas, new construction techniques and technologies were used.

ESG risks in the context of technology risks become manifest in the project sponsors' dilemma (and the related conflicts of interest) between little-tested and established technologies. Aspects of this multifaceted issue include:

- Risk of using established and proven but not futureproof technologies (costs related to upgrading technology with futureproof technologies during the life of the project/asset);
- Risk of implementing new and little-tested but potentially futureproof, environmental technologies (anticipated lower negative ESG impact) for the more-efficient resource use and the related potential cost savings may not materialise;
- Risk of (environmental) technologies used becoming obsolete once more cost- and/or resource-efficient technologies come to the market (costs related to upgrading to technologies that have less negative environmental impact).

5.3.3 Financing risk

Financing risk occurs when the assurances provided in the financing agreements no longer apply before all the available capital has been drawn down or one of the parties involved is no longer able or willing to meet its contractual obligations, with the result that the project is underfinanced. In the case of greenfield projects, this typically occurs during the planning and construction phase.

Loan agreements generally contain a clause stating that the project sponsors must contribute their capital to the (project) company in full before any funds can be drawn down under the credit agreements. The creditworthiness of the project sponsors and the general contractor are relevant for all lenders, that is their ability and/or willingness to make additional payments for debt service in the event the project fails to generate the amounts required.

The general contractor may be one of the sponsors or a subsidiary thereof. This allows the sponsor to assess reliably the quality of the services provided, which may be beneficial for the other providers of equity and debt. However, although often stated and assumed to be the case, such a constellation does not always ensure that the interests of all sponsors including the general contractor are aligned. Under certain circumstances, for example in the case of construction changes borne by the sponsors, the general contractor can charge rather high prices and generate decent additional revenue, because at this stage it is in a monopoly position within the consortium. All sponsors share the costs; only the general contractor has the benefit.

Lenders generally tie loan disbursements to the achievement of specific milestones. These may be physical (e.g. construction progress in the construction phase) or financial (such as revenue or EBITDA targets). The loan agreements typically contain assurances on the precise use of the funds provided, which is subsequently controlled and monitored by the banks. If the borrower does not meet the assurances, the debt providers are entitled to terminate the loan agreements. There is a fundamental consideration as to whether this is actually appropriate in any given case or whether lenders merely use the threat of termination as a tool for facilitating the assertion of their claims with respect to the project sponsors. Termination may trigger a genuinely critical situation and seriously endanger the completion of the project.

Banks often offer bridge loans to cover temporary financing bottlenecks, provided that a third party or the timely commissioning of the project guarantee repayment.

In order to control the cash flow set out in the repayment schedule, the loan agreements contain clauses on the achievement of defined key financial indicators (*financial covenants*), the breach of which may also result in the termination of the agreements. These primarily consist of key indicators that compare the available cash flow with the outstanding debt service obligations (interest and principal) and ensure that they exceed contractual obligations to a sufficient extent. If a covenant is breached but the lenders do not consider this as evidence of the borrower's inability to repay the loan in the long term, this generally 'only' results in the renegotiation of the financial covenants based on a revised business plan, and not the termination of the loan itself. Equity investors, including financial sponsors, may use similar key financial indicators or milestones to control and monitor a project's development.

For the project sponsors, the most critical moment in the financing process is the period between the signing of the credit agreements and the financial close, that is the date on which the funds are actually made available and can be drawn down. Generally, several weeks lie between these two dates: the financing must be available to the project sponsors at the earliest possible date but at the same time the debt providers demand evidence of the necessary approvals and the initial progress in the construction of the project. The requirements the borrower has to meet are compiled in a catalogue of disbursement or closing conditions. Loans may be disbursed only when all the conditions set out in the catalogue have been met.

For this period between signing and closing, the credit agreements contain a material adverse change (MAC) clause that requires the project to progress without sustained impairment, that is fulfilment of all disbursement conditions. The risk for the (project) company and the sponsors lies in the interpretation of the term 'sustained impairment'. This may include project delays, the withdrawal of one of the parties to the project, environmental hazards (floods, storms etc.) or negative developments on the capital markets or in the host country (e.g. there has been some debate as to whether the subprime crisis constituted a MAC event). The project sponsors should aim to define the term 'impairment' as precisely as possible and assign certain events in order to ensure that the success of the project is not dependent on general trends or short-term market developments. Accordingly, depending on the terms of the contract, financial risk, while primarily borne by the (project) company and the sponsors (owing to potential obligations to make additional payments if the financing cannot be drawn) is also borne by the lenders.

Project/asset-specific ESG risks to be considered when assessing the financing risk are:

- Risk of project not meeting ESG requirements of equity and/or debt providers, e.g. reputational risks due to infrastructure project/asset being in a sensitive area (environment, indigenous populations etc.);
- MAC risk from environmental hazards (storms, floods, etc.) affecting the site before or during construction phase.

5.3.4 Syndication risk

Loans for major financial transactions are typically initially negotiated and, in some cases, signed by one bank or a small number of banks and other debt providers. Generally, the banks, not so the other debt providers, then sell a predetermined portion of their interest in the loan or bond issue to other market participants (*syndication*). Traditionally, these were predominantly other banks. More recently, institutional investors represent a significant part, if not the majority, of the buyers of such syndicated loans and bonds.

Syndication risk, which is usually borne entirely by the syndicating banks, describes the risk that it will not be possible to sell the loans/bonds on the market at the conditions at which they were signed with the borrower. In this case, the banks would have to keep a greater portion of the respective loans or bonds on their books than desired. The infrastructure market immediately following the outbreak of the subprime crisis was a case in point. Until the crisis – and worryingly now (2015/2016) again – banks (but also other institutional debt providers) financed major infrastructure transactions under increasingly aggressive conditions. Shortly after the onset of the crisis, however, it became clear that the banks would no longer be able to place (i.e. syndicate) the securities – some of which had already been signed with the borrowers – at the conditions originally negotiated. The banks attempted to trigger the MAC clause (see Section 5.3.3) in order to renegotiate the conditions. When this failed, some banks were prepared to pay high break-up fees rather than expose themselves to the risk of taking the loans onto their books under the conditions originally negotiated.

At the time, some banks were able to transfer a portion of the syndication risk to the equity investors because of their strong bargaining position, despite the fact that legally the syndication risk was to be borne solely by them. This was achieved through various combinations of measures, such as the renegotiation of conditions for debt, lower leverage provided, the transfer of portions of the loans to the equity providers and so on. In most cases though, the banks did not succeed and had to provide the loans as agreed.

The asset-specific ESG risks mentioned in the context of financing (see Section 5.3.3) equally apply to the syndication risk.

5.3.5 Operational risk

The ability to operate a project/asset efficiently is another key element in ensuring its economic feasibility. Accordingly, the associated risk – known as 'operational risk', which consists of the interruption of operations, excess operating and maintenance costs, etc. – covers the operation, management, servicing and maintenance of a project/asset and is borne by the operator.

When analysing these operational risks, the experience and creditworthiness of the future operator is the primary consideration. The operator is usually a company with a connection to the sponsors or the general contractor; it is less common to retain an external operator. Long before the physical assets are constructed and a project becomes operational, the operator and the project company enter into an operating agreement, which mainly sets out the rights and obligations of the management with regard to the project company and its shareholders, including assurances and assumptions of liability. The operator should be familiar with the available technology, all operating processes and the related products as well as other internal and external conditions. The manufacturer must guarantee the long-term efficiency of the technology used and facilitate it through appropriate servicing and maintenance. Regular maintenance serves to reduce the risk significantly. Accordingly, suppliers must ensure the availability, efficiency and absence of technical defects of their equipment by concluding corresponding maintenance agreements. Risks arising from the nature of the raw materials and primary products used and their provision in sufficient quantities may be passed on to the manufacturer or the supplier, if applicable.

The operator must be able to ensure not only the technical operation of the assets but also the company's economic operation – at least within the initial project plan. Operational risk may be covered by concluding insurance for operational downtime.

In order to examine the quality of the operator, the providers of equity and debt obtain references, perform evaluations of the management team and analyse its experience. As the operator is often a subsidiary of one of the sponsors, information on its quality and experience will be available, and there is a certain alignment of interests between the sponsors and the operator regarding the successful implementation of the project, which also benefits the other providers of capital. Warranty claims against the operator for the non-fulfilment of the agreed performance standards may take the form of contractual penalties. For example, the operator shall be held liable if incorrect calculations or a failure to perform certain steps result in higher infrastructural or technical operation/management costs, price and/or volume adjustments or deviations from performance standards in future.

The project/asset-specific ESG risks to be assessed during the due diligence of operational risk are predominantly related to violating environmental, health or safety regulations, and the physical impact on the environment, which may prompt pressure groups to become involved. However, they also include the impact of the environment on the asset:

- Risk of operations violating environmental standards or regulations (e.g. soil and water contamination, air pollution, noise-generating wind turbines);
- Risk of operations violating health and safety of workforce and/or local communities;

- Risk of inefficient use of natural resources caused by 'old' technology (e.g. excessive water use competing with the water needs of local communities and agriculture);
- Risk of operations disturbing the natural habitat of wildlife and sea life (e.g. birds caught in wind turbines, noise impacting animal mating behaviour, roads to block game passes etc.) resulting in costly restructuring measures;
- Risk of climate change induced environmental hazards, disrupting the operations of the asset.

5.3.6 Contractual and counterparty risk

Contractual risk primarily describes the risk of inadequately structured agreements and a failure to observe the basis of legislation or legal loopholes that could result in the invalidity or differing interpretations of contracts and agreements. Potential contractual risk caused by a counterparty is borne by all parties in accordance with the respective agreements. The SPV invariably bears the greatest risk because it is the central contractual partner.

A detailed discussion of contractual and counterparty risk can be found by reference to the comprehensive body of legal literature on the topic of infrastructure investments, PPP and project finance. Accordingly, this section will not examine these risks in detail.

In the context of ESG risks, counterparty risks may arise with contractors (and subcontractors) and suppliers that do not observe ESG standards and the related reputational risks.

5.3.7 Realisation risk

Realisation risk relates to the residual or terminal value of the assets (buildings, equipment, etc.) that can be realised from disposal, transfer or further utilisation at the end of the project term or lifetime of the assets. The risk is that at this point in time their market value or their functionality may be lower than initially expected or forecast at the outset.

The terminal value of assets depends on a number of project/asset-specific factors. The most important ones are: the remaining duration of their land lease and permits beyond their projected lifetime, if applicable, the age of the assets, their general condition, the need for repairs or future investment, the up-to-datedness and efficiency of the technologies used, the management expertise of the operator and, in particular, the existence of long-term concessions, licences and supply and purchase agreements. In addition, general aspects, such as the overall economic and capital market environment at the time of the realisation, have a strong influence on the residual value as well, which is difficult to predict many years in advance, if at all.

From the perspective of the debt providers, realisation risk is relatively unimportant, because the residual value is low compared with the principal and interest payments received over the years. Moreover, a potential sale of the assets typically lies so far in the future that the discounted net present value of the assets (see Section 6.4.4.1) is negligible in its function as payment security. Instead, loans must be repayable from current income. Although unimportant for calculation purposes, the saleability of the assets in question may be relevant for the banks in the event of payment arrears or insolvency of the (project) company. While port facilities constructed specifically for the operation of a mine in the Chilean desert will struggle to find an external buyer, for example, turbines of a modern gas power station or the presses used in a steel plant can achieve attractive resale prices.

From the perspective of equity investors, however, the residual value of a project company or infrastructure asset can be a key factor when calculating the investment return. The relevance of the residual value depends on both the nature of the asset and, most importantly, the intended holding period. As to the nature of the asset, a distinction is made between assets the equity investors own and assets that are only licensed or are concessions but ultimately remain in the possession of the government (e.g. certain PPP projects). As a rule, the residual value only matters for the former. Regarding the intended holding period, the residual value is crucial for those (short-term) investors who intend to pass on the asset after only few years because it is an important factor when determining the expected return on their initial investment.

In the case of PPPs, it should be defined which kind of PPP is being used (see Chapter 3). Depending on the contract model, any realisation risk may be transferred to the private partner at the end of the contractual term (e.g. PPP purchaser model). Alternatively, the private partner may have no realisation risk at the end of the term (e.g. PPP owner model) because the public principal always remains the owner of the property throughout the term of the concession or licence contract and beyond. This is the case for most road infrastructure projects as roads constitute a common asset.

In traditional purely private transaction structures, some kind of realisation risk applies. This is either because the expected lifetime of a project/asset has been reached or because the sponsors/initial investors do not intend to hold it during its entire technical or projected lifetime (this may be determined by the licence/concession) but instead sell it, for example, shortly after it goes operational (saleability risk). The sale price of an asset before the end of its projected lifetime is driven essentially by the same factors as the residual value.

Project/asset-specific ESG risks may turn out to be particularly relevant in the context of realisation because a futureproofed infrastructure asset that is resilient to ESG risks will be able to demand a higher residual value than an asset which is not. For example:

■ Risk that the technology used is not futureproof and no longer meets environmental standards at the end of its lifetime, lowering the residual value for potential buyers;
■ Risk that the chosen location of the project is not futureproof, e.g. the location does not meet contamination standards or the location is in an area with a high risk of environmental hazards and hence requires costly protection measures.

5.4 SECTOR-SPECIFIC RISKS

In addition to the general and project/asset-specific risks across sectors described above, there are also sector-specific risks. Table 5.5 below contains some examples of these risks for selected subsectors, namely: transport and traffic, water supply and disposal, renewable energy generation and energy transmission/distribution/storage, as well as social infrastructure.

Chapter 5 covered the main risks inherent in infrastructure projects/assets. To this end, risks were categorised into two main categories – general risks and project/asset specific risks – and then broken down into 13 subcategories. While, as a rule, every project/asset needs to be assessed individually, each infrastructure sector has certain sector-specific risks.

Throughout the entire risk discussion above, the key role of the financing of any infrastructure endeavour and how the financing is structured has become apparent. It can make or break its success. The following Chapter 6 scrutinises the topic of project finance, which is the most common form of infrastructure financing, in the context of traditional infrastructure projects/assets as well as those in PPP settings.

TABLE 5.5 Sector-specific risks

Sector	Sector-specific risk	Comments and examples
Transport		
Roadways	– Composition of traffic	Increased operational costs due to higher maintenance costs from more wear and tear
	– Traffic volume/toll price (market risk)	E.g., less revenues due to deviations in traffic volumes and/or lower than projected toll increases
	– Capture, charging and collection (revenue risk)	E.g., lower than forecasted revenues from not correctly captured users or captured users not paying
	– Unforeseeable parallel infrastructure affecting traffic volumes (see above)	E.g., additional non-toll river crossing or bridge or parallel route to a toll motorway
	– Changes in toll road access affecting traffic volumes	E.g., road works or closures reduce revenues
	– Capacity	E.g., available road cross-section may be or become insufficient in size
	– Amendments to the Highway Code of the respective country affecting the volume and composition of traffic	E.g., axle loads, emission limits
	– Climate change	E.g., risk of damage from soil erosion resulting from increased flooding in coastal areas (physical areas)
Railways	– Volume of traffic/revenue	Depends on contractual structure, e.g. user finance/availability fee model, and the line or sub-network
	– Interface between network and operation	Depends on the structure of the concession (integrated, route only or operation only)
	– Development of wheel/rail technology	Rapid technological developments and breakthroughs
	– Development of high-tech system elements/change in traffic control rules	Higher (operating) costs due to expenditure for new control and signal technology
	– General network development affecting volume of revenue	Volume developments difficult to estimate, interdependencies within the network as a whole
	– Climate change	E.g., risk of damage from soil erosion resulting from increased flooding in coastal areas (physical areas)
Airports	Traffic volume/pricing (intermodal, national, international)	Complex global competition for landing rights, slots, landing fees, etc.
	– Changing regulations	Revenues from regulated activities related to air traffic may be affected
	– Retail revenue (market risk)	Retail revenue is a key source of income, which entirely depends on passenger volumes
	– Technological development (operators, users)	Higher operating costs due to expenditure for necessary technology upgrades
	– Interface between operators, airlines, passengers, etc.	Complex and volatile interface between the various stakeholders leading to unforeseeable consequences
	– Utilisation/dimensioning of buildings/equipment	Passenger volumes affect spatial planning, technical equipment, retail areas, connection concepts, etc.
	– Transport connections	For example, new road and rail connections required
	– Climate change	Increased frequency of extreme weather events causing physical damage to airport facilities
Waterways	– Traffic volume/capacity	E.g., insufficiently deep/wide waterways, existing locks/pumping stations unable to cope with the traffic volume
	– Water levels	Waterways may be impossible to navigate at low/high tide due to flooding or drought impacting water levels
	– Transport connections	For example, new road and rail connections via ports may be required
	– Climate change	Increased frequency of flooding or drought affecting water levels (physical risk)
Ports	– Volume of traffic/prices (market risk)	Revenues affected by strong international/national/intermodal competition, particularly between seaports
	– Utilisation/dimensioning of buildings/equipment	E.g., ports may no longer be able to process certain ships owing to their size or inadequate water levels
	– Transport connections	For example, new road and rail connections may be required
	– Climate change	Physical damage from more frequent and intense coastal storms, droughts lowering water levels in ports
Water supply and disposal		
Water supply	– Capture, charging and collection (revenue risk)	E.g., lower than forecasted revenues from not correctly captured users or captured users not paying
	– Number of customers and consumption per customer	More/less customers due to demographic change/changing consumption patterns due to e.g. weather, price
	– Hydrology/Climate change	E.g., insufficient future water supply due to resource depletion, less rainfall/snowpack in catchment area
	– Water loss	Technical (equipment) failure may result in water loss

	– Dimensioning (network, pipelines, etc.)	Demographic changes, development of new residential/industrial areas or other kinds of usage may result in higher than forecasted costs for adapting pipelines and/or distribution networks
	– Regulatory framework (quality and network connection, payment scheme)	Regulatory changes in consumer standards, environmental requirements, and/or the regulated payment scheme affecting the (forecasted) regulated revenue
	– Pollution of the environment	For instance, pollution of catchment area with substances from agriculture (e.g. nitrates from extensive agriculture) or other industries and violations of limits, resulting in higher water treatment costs,
	– Climate change	Physical damage to water treatment facilities in coastal areas due to more frequent extreme weather events
Water disposal	– Capture, charging and collection (revenue risk)	E.g., lower than forecasted revenues from not correctly captured users or captured users not paying
	– Political acceptance	Contractually agreed/allowed increase of charges may not be possible politically
	– Waste water volume	Dependent on demographic changes, behavioural changes
	– Dimensioning (network, pipelines, treatment plants, etc.)	E.g., incorrectly estimated volumes and degree of contamination, demographic changes, development of new residential/industrial areas may increase costs for adapting pipelines, networks and treatment plants
	– Network connection/obligation/measurement basis	Investment in new equipment to ensure accurate metering and billing
	– Regulatory changes (e.g. quality, payment scheme)	Regulatory changes in e.g. quality requirements, which may increase operational costs, or payment schemes, which are the basis for regulatory revenues
	– Water contamination and degree of contamination	Changes in agricultural or industrial activity may increase purification costs
	– Climate change	Physical damage to water treatment purification facilities due to more frequent extreme weather events
Renewable energy generation		
Cross-sector	– Regulatory changes	Regulatory changes related to environmental regulations/policies (e.g carbon pricing, feed-in tariffs, generation caps) may impact demand for and (regulated) pricing of renewable energy. Capacity caps may impact ongoing developments
	– (Natural) resource (volume risk)	E.g., lower than forecasted volume of resources (e.g. wind, sun, water) required for energy production
	– Energy prices (price risk)	Volatile and extremely interrelated energy markets (both across energy sources e.g oil, gas, electricity, and across geographies) combined with changing user behaviour - partially due to environmental considerations – may result in lower than forecasted revenues
Solar PV	– Climate change	Climate change may result in either an increase or decrease in the annual sunshine hours resulting in changes in energy output, hence impacting forecasted revenues; rising average temperatures reduce the productivity of solar panels, extreme weather events, e.g. hailstorms, cause damage to panels
Wind – onshore and offshore	– Climate change	Higher frequency of extreme windstorms (i.e. >20m/sec) results in lower than expected energy generation and hence revenues, since, wind turbines must be (partially) shut down to avoid physical damage
	– Technical issues and costs overruns (offshore)	Technical challenges (and resulting increased operating costs) of constructing and maintaining massive wind turbines in ocean environments.
	– Procurement risks	Rising operating costs for equipment or spare parts, (partially) caused by e.g. rising costs of raw materials
Hydropower	– Water availability	Water supply shortages due to changes in precipitation patterns, changes in snow pack levels and seasonal runoff flows or increased upstream industrial or agricultural activity
	– Environmental/public acceptance	Hydropower projects may (strongly) impact local ecosystems and (indigenous) communities leading to public/NGO opposition and resulting in challenges to obtain environmental permits
	– Climate change	Water supply shortages due to e.g. extreme weather events such as droughts, persistent changes in precipitation patterns, snow pack levels and seasonal runoff flows
Bioenergy	– Feedstock supply/public acceptance	Bioenergy crops competing with food production for access to productive land resulting in limited access to biomass feedstock supply

(*continued*)

TABLE 5.5 (*Continued*)

Sector	Sector-specific risk	Comments and examples
Energy transmission and storage		
Electricity transmission	– Capture, charging and collection	E.g., lower than forecasted revenues from not correctly captured users or captured users not paying
	– Dimensioning (network)	Correct estimation of volume and technology requirements; demographic changes, development of new residential/industrial areas may result in higher than forecasted costs for adapting networks or obsolete facilities
	– Regulatory changes (environmental)	Stricter environmental requirements may lead to higher construction costs for new lines and higher operating and maintenance costs
	– Regulatory changes (user charges/payment scheme)	Changes in regulatory payment schemes may reduce the share of (forecasted) revenue from regulatory revenue, which may be up to 100% of total revenues
	– Demand in volume (market risk)	Demographic changes and decentralised energy generation (district heating) may lead to reduced electricity demand via transmission (and even distribution) networks
	– Technological developments	For example, cost-intensive area-wide coverage with smart grids
	– Climate change	Physical risk to network facilities due extreme weather events
Natural gas transmission	– Weather	Warmer temperatures may lead to lower revenues from the sale of natural gas for heating
	– Regulatory changes (environmental)	E.g., carbon taxes or similar climate chang-related charges could reduce profits; stricter environmental requirements may increase construction costs for new lines and operating/maintenance costs
	– Regulatory changes (user charges/payment scheme)	Changes in the regulatory payment scheme may reduce the share of (forecasted) revenue from regulatory revenue, which may be up to 100%
	– Dimensioning (network, pipelines)	Incorrectly estimated volumes and technology requirements, demographic changes, development of new residential/industrial areas may lead to higher adaptation costs or obsolete facilities
	– Climate change	E.g., physical damage to facilities (e.g., Arctic supply pipeline substructure due to melting permafrost)
Energy storage	– Regulatory risk/capture, charging and collection	Lack of a clearly-defined regulatory framework for storage facilities (ownership/primary function etc.) hinders the development of reliable business models for the provision and charging of storage services
	– Technological risk	Except for PHS, mostly new/still developing technologies or unproven on commercial scale
Social infrastructure		
Healthcare facilities	– Regulatory risk (costs and tariffs)	Changes in healthcare regulations and policies (e.g. medical standards) may impact operating costs and/or allowed user charges/payment schemes
	– Technological development (operators)	Technological development, resulting in increased investment/operating cost for medical equipment
	– Utilisation/demographics	Fewer (or more) people use the facility, changes in required services due to e.g. ageing populations
	– Realisation risk	Limited third party usability of the building
	– Liability risks/reputational risk	E.g., financial consequences of lawsuits resulting from treatment mistakes in hospitals
	– Climate change	Physical risk to buildings due to increased frequency of extreme weather events
Educational facilities	– Vandalism	Physical and financial damage from wilful destruction of facilities
	– Technology (particularly IT systems)	E.g., replacement costs from earlier than forecasted obsolescence of technical equipment
	– Syllabus changes affecting spatial planning	E.g., higher investment/operating costs due to more visual instruction for technical/scientific subjects
	– Utilisation/demographics	Fewer (or more) people using the facility
	– Changes in requirements affecting spatial planning or facility management	For instance, space requirements/number of pupils, air conditioning requirements
Administrative facilities	– Regulatory changes (utilisation/demographics)	Administrative reforms/increased efficiency from digitalisation may lead to lower demand for office space
	– Representation/visibility of the building	E.g. design of the building may no longer meet the requirements in the planning phase
	– Vandalism	Physical and financial damage from destruction of facilities.
	– Climate change	Physical risk to buildings due increased frequency of extreme weather events

CHAPTER 6

Project Finance

Project finance is a way of providing debt financing that differs from a straightforward loan. Historically, individual elements of what is now called 'project finance' were used to fund mercantile expeditions. The loans granted were serviced exclusively using the revenue generated from the sale of the respective goods. As early as the 17th century, for example, trade expeditions to India were being funded using this form of project finance, with the risk of loss (i.e. shipwreck) borne by the financiers. One of the most frequently cited examples of the use of project finance in recent history is the construction of the Suez Canal.

In the US, however, the concept of project finance has evolved only over the last century. During the oil boom of the 1930s, it was banks that provided the funding for the acquisition of oil exploration technology, securing their loans against rights to use the oil reserves exploited as a result. Loans were repaid solely from current oil income. Therefore, loan approval was granted based on forecasted revenues from the oil extracted, that is the expected cash flows. As part of the growing trend towards globalisation, financing was subsequently provided for projects in the raw materials industry, such as mining (from the 1960s onwards) and offshore oil and gas drilling. Over the past two decades, project finance has also been used to fund the development and creation of cross-sector, cross-border solutions in infrastructure areas such as transportation, energy and water supply, telecommunications, as well as 'social infrastructure' – schools, hospitals and administrative buildings, for example.

6.1 PROJECT FINANCE BASICS

Project finance is defined as the financing of a standalone, clearly demarcated economic unit (project). The key characteristics of project finance are:

- *Special purpose company/vehicle (SPV)* – Contractual partner is a (usually newly created and clearly demarcated) project company. It can also be an existing company with operational assets though (on the use of the terms 'project company', 'company' and 'SPV', see Section 1.3.1).
- *Cash-flow-based lending* – Loan approval is based on the expected cash flow from the respective project/asset, i.e. the loans extended are repaid solely from the cash flows generated by the project/asset.

- *Risk sharing structures* – The different partners assume risks related to the project/asset based on their ability to influence and control the risks.
- *Limitation of liability* – Liability is limited to the capital contribution of the sponsors and the assets of the company; providers of debt have no or only limited recourse to the sponsors.
- *Off-balance sheet finance* – Providers of equity are required only to recognise project finance in their balance sheets if they have an interest in the company of 50% or greater.

Strictly speaking, forms of financing that do not possess these characteristics should not be labelled project finance. Accordingly, financing structures that are merely similar to project finance in certain respects are mentioned in this book in passing, but not discussed in detail; for that we recommend readers consult *Working Paper on the Internal Ratings-based Approach to Specialised Lending Exposures* (Basel Committee on Banking Supervision, 2001).

Project finance differs from conventional loan finance in that it has a large number of structural characteristics that, though complex, are beneficial to the sponsors. In the case of project finance, the borrower is often not an established company – as is usually the case for traditional lending – but may be a (newly-created) special-purpose vehicle (SPV) with no history and no significant fixed assets of its own in the case of greenfield development projects. From a lender's and an equity investor's perspective, however, the main difference between project finance and traditional lending is not how long the company has been in existence and whether it has pre-existing fixed assets but the basis on which the loan or the investment decision is reached. In the case of conventional loan finance, it is taken on the basis of an analysis of historical income statements, balance sheets and cash flows, which are an indicator for the creditworthiness of the company. The total freely available assets of the company serve to secure the loan. In contrast, project finance is largely granted on the basis of the available future cash flows of the company, which depend on the development of the project/asset and the underlying business plan. In the event of default, liability is largely limited to the (more or less valuable) assets of the company.

In light of this heightened financing risk, detailed risk analysis and comprehensive risk structuring are essential. These require an in-depth investigation and evaluation of the technical, economic, legal and organisational aspects of the project and their inherent risks (see Section 5.3). Although project assets are also pledged as security in project finance, they play a comparatively minor role in the lending decision. Ultimately, the allocation of the various risks arising from a project to the participants in accordance with the overall structure is far more relevant. This in turn depends largely on the interests of the respective participants, and is therefore highly project-specific. For example, if a government is interested in the implementation of a new infrastructure development or a substantial renovation or expansion of an existing infrastructure asset, it may be prepared to guarantee minimum payments in the event of a low level of utilisation, for example if the traffic on a toll road falls below a defined minimum level or the energy purchase prices achieved are insufficient to cover the costs. This type of guarantee changes the risk level and, as a consequence, the financing structure of a project substantially: as the risk is reduced, private financiers will be more willing to come in and provide loans at better conditions.

Furthermore, from a lender's perspective, the results of a comprehensive study by Standard & Poor's (2014) are interesting. Standard & Poor's default and recovery statistics indicate that the creditworthiness of infrastructure projects is strong and is expected to remain strong in the future. Since the first default of a rated project in 1998, the average annual default rate for all project finance debt rated by Standard & Poor's is just 1.5% and thus considerably below the 1.8% default rate for corporate issuers in the same period (Standard & Poor's, 2014). In addition, a study from Moody's concluded that corporate infrastructure project debt (1983–2012) not only has lower default rates than traditional corporate lending but also significantly higher recovery rates (see Figure 2.2 and Figure 2.3 in Section 2.1.2.3). The reasons stated include larger debt cushions, stricter structuring and tighter monitoring on the part of lenders and management. All in all, the complexity of project finance requires banks to possess a considerably higher degree of expertise, analytical skills and specialist knowledge than is the case for conventional loan finance.

From the perspective of the equity investors, and in particular the project sponsors, project finance is beneficial in that the creditworthiness of their own company is not formally relevant and their assets are pledged only as security for the loans provided in the amount of their obligation to make additional payments, if at all (see Section 6.3.2.2 for details). Depending on the sponsor's share in the project company, however, an equity investor may be required to include the project finance in its consolidated balance sheet (this is the case with interests of 50% or more).

Purely privately financed project finance has been used as a financing solution for certain types of infrastructure investment projects for a number of years. By now, it has become a common form of financing in public–private partnerships (PPPs) as well, with the public sector acting as the principal and not merely as a licensor, for example. In some respects, the PPP constellation has led to a shift in the interests of the parties involved within the project structure. However, because the fundamental structure and methodology of traditional project finance – that is a private-sector company acts as principal – remain the same for PPP project finance – that is the principal is a public sector institution instead – both types of project finance are discussed jointly in this book. We will particularly focus on the latter variant, as this has relatively rarely been the subject of financial literature to date.

6.2 PROJECT FINANCE AND PPP

Although financing is only one of the many tasks to be performed by the private contractor within the realisation of an infrastructure project in general and a PPP project in particular – along with planning, construction, operation and maintenance – its political relevance and impact on lifecycle costs, risk structure and (effective) risk allocation make it a core element and, in many cases, the key factor when structuring infrastructure projects.

The financing of PPP projects is a frequent topic of public discussion in particular. Debate often centres on whether the private provision of the necessary capital is viable or whether it would ultimately be more economic for the public principal to use a comparatively lower-interest form of financing, such as a municipal loan (Horn and Alfen, 2003).

A PPP project could be structured in such a way as to avoid the need for private finance. If the necessary loans were provided solely by the public partner (e.g. a municipality), the project could even benefit from the improved interest rates available in the public sector. As in this case, the private project partners would not bear any financing burden (repayment of debt and dividends on equity); however, their readiness to ensure the highest degree of efficiency and their commitment to cost optimisation throughout the entire project lifecycle (total costs) would likely be lower. On the contrary, without the responsibility of having to finance the project themselves it would be in the private partners' interest to actually increase the scope of services provided – and hence the remuneration they receive – rather than limiting it to the necessary elements. If the partners had this kind of diverging incentive structure, there would be a risk that the cost savings from favourable interest rate conditions in the public sector were eliminated by above-average lifecycle costs and, in some cases, rising maintenance and availability risks across a longer lifecycle. In other words, financing projects exclusively via public budgets could result in a failure to harness potential cost reduction and optimisation factors from the very start (Horn and Alfen, 2003).

This situation also applies to the forfeiting arrangements with declarations of waiver of defence, objection and offsetting: these can be found today in many countries, including Germany and France.

Project finance can make a vital contribution to optimising a project as a whole from both the perspective of the (public) project developer and the users. This is because it requires, and thus includes, certain steps of analysis, evaluation, quantification, structuring and monitoring by the providers of debt and additional equity, if applicable, from which the developer can benefit tremendously – while possibly experiencing it as painful at the time. These services include:

- Dedicated project evaluation on the basis of detailed technical, economic, organisational and legal due diligence up until the financial close;
- Recommendations regarding the optimal structure from a technical and economic perspective;
- Recommendations related to the optimal financing structure;
- Systematic risk and quality management;
- Project monitoring across all project phases.

In other words, the transfer of financing to private partners in the context of project finance may constitute an economically rational approach to the question of structuring an infrastructure project. It allows for the maximum alignment of interests of the parties, while simultaneously increasing the chance of uncovering all project risks and transferring to the party that is best positioned to bear and manage them.

Not all infrastructure projects, however, are suitable for project finance. The decisive criteria include:

- The economic potential, i.e. the likelihood that the forecast revenues will be sufficient to meet the return expectations of the providers of equity and debt with an acceptable degree of risk;
- The risk profile of the project, i.e. the likelihood of achieving a balanced risk profile as described above;
- The scale of the project or the financing requirements.

The project developer may positively influence all these criteria during the development process, if it intends to leverage the benefits of project finance.

The availability of sufficient economic potential is primarily determined by the project selection. As a case in point, in Germany the PPP programmes in the road traffic infrastructure or container ports sectors initially suffered from the public bodies' mistake of selecting projects that were likely to generate a comparatively low level of traffic, whereas projects with high traffic volumes were generally financed in a conventional manner.

To achieve a balanced risk allocation, the (public) sponsor must first define and analyse all the risks it intends to transfer to the private partners with the aim of determining whether the private partners will be suited and capable of managing them and what price tag can be attached to each risk transfer. The less the private partners can influence the risk and the more the public principal is in charge, the more expensive the risk transfer will become and hence less viable and less financeable.

The scale of a project is also a decisive factor in project finance, because the upfront costs remain relatively fixed and do not increase proportionately with the financing volume. Project finance is worthwhile only above a certain financing volume of at least €50 million, and preferably above €100 million. Accordingly, developers should seek to obtain such financing or establish the conditions for project finance only for projects above a certain volume or else bundle several projects together. This route is chosen, for example, to finance a growing number of schools and hospitals as well as renewable energy plants across Europe.

BAM PPP PGGM INFRASTRUCTURE COOPERATIVE

In May 2011, BAM PPP formed a joint venture with the Dutch pension fund administrator PGGM which combines the capabilities of a proven developer of PPP concessions with the skills of a major long-term investor. This JV, known as BAM PPP PGGM Infrastructure Cooperative, constitutes a long-term, cooperative partnership for investments in the social and transport PPP markets in the Netherlands, Belgium, the UK, Ireland, Germany and Switzerland. Apart from BAM PPP bringing into the JV a portfolio of existing PPP assets, providing an acceptable initial investment size for PGGM, it continuously delivers newly developed assets into the JV. It usually does so in a bundled form for the above mentioned reason of scale, among others. As a case in point, in July 2014, this JV was selected to deliver four new post-primary schools in Ireland. Known as 'Bundle 4', this is the fourth 'bundled' PPP project in the Irish Schools PPP Programme. BAM PPP is an operating company of the Royal BAM Group, a worldwide construction services company. PGGM is a Dutch pension fund service provider with €167 billion in assets.

6.3 BASIC STRUCTURE OF PROJECT FINANCE

There is no such thing as a standard structure for project finance – whether traditional or within a PPP – because each situation has its own special features that must be incorporated into the structure. The concrete structuring of a financing depends on the legal and geographical conditions, the industry/sector, its underlying business model – and in particular the allocation of risks and responsibilities among the partners. Despite the large number of contractual options and financial instruments, however, all forms of project finance share certain fundamental characteristics.

6.3.1 Key characteristics

The key characteristics of project financing as opposed to traditional corporate loans were introduced briefly in Section 6.1 and are described in more detail in the following subsections.

6.3.1.1 Special-purpose vehicle (SPV) Project finance is generally – though not necessarily – used in the context of (time-limited) legally-independent investment projects. To this end, independent (project) companies – known as special-purpose companies or vehicles (SPVs) – are formed. Newly-created project companies generally take the legal form of a limited-liability company. The (project) company bears all the rights and obligations arising from the project and hence assumes the overall business responsibility for it. Risks are borne by the (project) company to the extent that they are not contractually transferred to other parties, such as the sponsors backing it or the general contractors executing the project. Project sponsors usually provide the company's equity capital, complemented in some cases by external financial investors.

In the context of PPPs, the public sector may also become a shareholder of the project company in order to be able to exercise influence and to control the PPP project developer.

6.3.1.2 Cash-flow-based lending   Within project finance, the project company not only receives equity from the sponsors but also takes on debt from third parties – typically in the form of bank loans and sometimes (though rarely) bonds. The debt financing is primarily based on the forecast cash flows from the project. Therefore, they form the basis for the capital procurement of the project. This means the key criterion for project finance from the perspective of the financing banks is the ability of the project to generate sufficient cash flows to cover not only the investment and operating costs but also the interest and principal payments (debt service) under the planned financing structure. In contrast, the equity investors are not interested in debt service but rather in generating an appropriate return on their investment, be it in terms of value appreciation (capital gain) or current income (yield). In this context, the fact that the amount and term of the interest and principal payments can be structured flexibly to reflect the projected cash flows over time is one of the major benefits of project finance. Cash flow models are developed to determine the feasibility and bankability of a project.

6.3.1.3 Risk-sharing structures   The core concept of project finance is that all risks are allocated to the partners based on their competencies and resources. The ultimate goal is to ensure that each risk will ultimately be borne by the party best positioned to manage it and thus will assume the risk most cost efficiently. As the risk allocation is achieved solely through structuring of the transaction, structure is the core element of project finance. The aim is to identify a resource-efficient structure that optimises the total costs of the project and ensures that the actual occurrence of a risk does not result in the failure of the project as a whole. This is particularly important in light of the standard limitation of liability to the SPV and the corresponding higher level of financing risk. In order to achieve optimal risk allocation among the partners, all risks must first be identified, analysed and quantified based on a rigorous and extensive risk management (see Section 5.1). Risk allocation is performed as part of the development of the structure in question, which takes into account the distribution of the responsibilities and risks during the planning, construction, financing and operating phases. These are specified in a comprehensive contractual arrangement, which forms the legal basis for a resilient structure that adequately reflects the various interests of the partners.

In the case of PPP project finance, all risks are grouped into two categories: (i) *transferable risks* that can be transferred to the private sector and (ii) *retained risks* that are retained by the public sector. This allocation is an important element of economic feasibility studies[1] because it allows an economic assessment and enables the comparability of PPP project solutions with conventional solutions residing solely in the public sector.

An additional, though less important, benefit of a comprehensive risk structuring of project finance is the flexibility in determining the terms and conditions of the financing compared with conventional lending, although this applies only to loans and to a limited extent to project bonds (see Section 7.3.2). It should also be noted that project finance allows for longer loan periods than is the case for traditional corporate loans.

6.3.1.4 Limitation of liability

Under these types of contractual structures, recourse to the sponsors is possible only to an extremely limited extent – when previously agreed in the contracts – if at all. Standard bank collateral is less relevant for the financing. As a matter of principle, the recoverable assets of the (project) company are limited to the capital contribution of the shareholders (sponsors) and the financial investors (if any) and, where applicable, the assets attributable to the project itself, providing they are owned by the project company. Sponsors are generally liable only up to the amount of their capital contribution (in what is called *non-recourse* financing, which is rarely seen in practice) or to a limited extent above and beyond this amount (in *limited recourse* financing, which is the most widely used form).

In general, there are two common methods of limiting the liability of the sponsors: (i) *time-limited liability*, for example only between the construction and ramp-up phases with no subsequent liability after this date, and (ii) *liability limited to a maximum amount* (the *cap*) in the form of additional payments/contributions. These two forms of limited liability may be used individually or combined in various ways. They are specified separately in the contractual arrangements. There is no *full recourse* in project finance, because such a structure would be incompatible with the performance incentive concept.

6.3.1.5 Off-balance-sheet finance

The legally independent project company is the debtor of the external capital raised for the project. The sponsors providing equity are not required to consolidate their interests in the project company in their balance sheets (off-balance-sheet financing) unless they are majority shareholders in it ($\geq 50\%$). The benefits of this syndicate structure are twofold: first, the sponsors are able to avoid a potential deterioration in their balance sheet ratios – and hence their return on equity – due to the potentially significant debt component of the project company. Second, the projects can be structured in a way that would otherwise exceed the capacity of the individual sponsors. In any case, project finance expands the financing options available to investors.

In addition to the reasons derived directly from the characteristics of project finance, aspects such as a greater return on equity thanks to a high debt component (known as the 'leverage effect') and, in some cases, more favourable capital costs may be of relevance if the project company is able to achieve better conditions than the sponsor.

---

[1]For more information on feasibility studies, see German Federal Ministry of Finance (2007), which contains a manual developed by working parties at federal and state level and the German audit courts and was made binding by a circular issued by the same Ministry of Finance on 20 August 2007.

This list of key characteristics underlines the fact that project finance involves complex structures with a large number of participants. The following section discusses the main groups involved in a project's financing in detail.

6.3.2 Participants and other stakeholders

Major infrastructure projects capitalised via project finance generally bring together a large number of participants and other stakeholders with differing – and often opposing – objectives and interests. Private investors and companies generally get involved in infrastructure projects for economic reasons, whereas government bodies do so in order to exercise sovereign functions (e.g. provision of subsistence) or to implement economic policy (e.g. stimulus measures or improvements in the balance of payments). Suitable structures help to combine these diverging interests in a partnership and generate value for all parties involved. Accordingly, the optimal structuring of the individual interests and responsibilities within a partnership forms the basis for a project's success, which also explains why each project structure is different and needs to be adapted to the specific situation.

The aim and the challenge of project finance is to incorporate the interests of all the participants within a contractual arrangement that ensures the repayment of the debt raised to finance the project with reasonable certainty while allowing the sponsors to achieve the desired yield and return.

Infrastructure projects generally have an extremely high public profile, owing to the fact that they affect the sphere of other interested parties/stakeholders above and beyond the immediate project participants. This is particularly the case if they are realised as PPPs. Figure 6.1 shows an example of the interaction between the direct project participants and additional stakeholders.

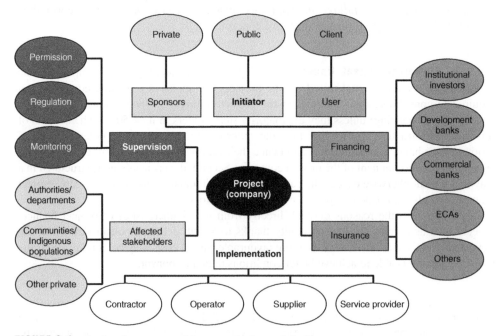

FIGURE 6.1 Project finance – participants and other stakeholders

Interested groups that are not directly involved in the project may exercise a significant influence on its objectives, composition and the scope of services to be provided though, and therefore on its economic success. The identity of these stakeholders, however, can vary substantially depending on the respective sector, and so Figure 6.1 should be taken only as an example. Stakeholders may include the responsible authorities to the same extent as private users, trade unions, the local community and other public and private agencies. The sponsors must identify potential stakeholders and their particular interests as early as possible and consider and address them in the project development process.

The participants are described as follows (note that this list includes only those groups that are directly involved in the project to the extent that they perform services and have a contractual relationship with the project company):

- *Public-sector bodies:* role of principals (in the case of PPP structure) or role of licensors/concession grantors (in the case of traditional project finance);
- *Providers of equity:* sponsors and financial investors as shareholders;
- *Providers of debt:* commercial banks, institutional investors and development banks;
- *Various service providers:* contracted by the project company to perform planning and consulting, construction, maintenance, operation and other tasks.

In the case of user-financed PPPs (see Section 3.3) – but also any traditional purely private project finance structure, which involves revenue streams from end-users – this list of contractual relationships should also include paying customers. Even if no written agreement exists between the user and the project company, such as in the case of toll roads, there is a contractual relationship between them in a legal sense every time a user uses the toll road.

In the case of traditional, purely private project financings, the project sponsors usually also act as the initiators and principals of the project. This means they exercise control over the project and dictate the course of action. The public sector may act as a licensor or concession grantor in such cases. The basic structure outlined in Figure 6.2 provides an overview of the participants and cash flows in a typified project financing (traditional and PPP structure).

For the avoidance of doubt, the main difference between PPP project finance and traditional project finance is that the government – rather than private sponsors – performs the key principal role, that is it exercises a more extensive function than, for example, that of licensor or concession grantor only. Accordingly, the standards and requirements of the public sector are decisive. They must be embedded within the system of the public-sector structure. In this arrangement, the sponsors 'merely' act as bidders for the project tendered by the public sector. After being awarded the contract, the sponsors act as 'agents' of the public-sector principal or – in the case of user-financed PPPs (see Section 3.3) – as *Beliehene* (natural or legal persons statutorily entrusted with specific sovereign or administrative functions under German law) for a limited period. In any case, they must observe and uphold the requirements and special characteristics of the government throughout all project phases. It goes without saying that, due to the difference in the configuration, the transition from traditional project finance to a PPP structure also changes the interests of the project partners and the desired risk allocation.

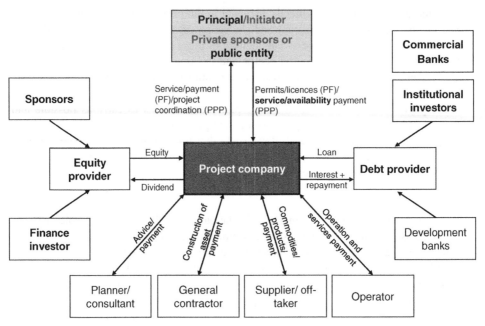

FIGURE 6.2   Typified structure of (PPP) project finance – payment streams

RENERGIA WASTE-TO-ENERGY PLANT, SWITZERLAND

The ownership and project finance structure of the waste-to-energy plant Renergia in Switzerland (see introduction to case study in Section 4.6.5.1) represents a combination of a traditional, purely private one and a PPP. This is because Renergia has public and private owners and yet does not have typical PPP-like contractual structures. The public owners are cantons (member states of the Swiss Confederation), which hold their altogether 90% interest in Renergia via their typically 100% owned waste associations. Perlen Papier AG, the private partner, owns 10% of the equity. Please refer to Chapter 7 for details of the financing structure.

Renergia was established in 2012 as a Swiss limited-liability corporation (*Aktiengesellschaft*) with public and private shareholders. The project costs of SFr320 million were funded with SFr100 million equity, of which 90% was provided by all waste associations of central Switzerland, which in turn are owned by their respective cantons. Every association participated in the funding in proportion to its waste contribution, the paper mill Perlen Papier AG contributed the land on which the WtE plant was built in return for a 10% ownership in the share capital of Renergia. SFr220 million in debt was provided on a project finance basis by a consortium of banks led by Zürcher Kantonalbank, Switzerland's largest cantonal bank, and other local banks.

6.3.2.1 Public entities   Public-sector bodies have a legislative function in the sense that they can influence the legal environment in which all the project partners operate equally.

The public sector also acts as the body responsible for granting approvals for essentially any project in the areas of planning, construction, operation, environmental considerations and so on. In the case of infrastructure projects in particular, it may also act as a concession grantor or assume responsibility for sector-specific supervisory and regulatory functions.

In the case of traditional project finance, the public sector plays a comparatively subordinate role as a contractual partner, issuing licences, approvals and so on for concrete projects as described above; however, it may still play a decisive role in the realisation of a concrete project in this function even if it does not perform any additional tasks.

In the PPP context, the public sector is at the heart of every contractual structure. It acts as the principal for the project, with the private sector applying for the award of contractual partner status. In the role of project developer, the government issues a tender for a project including all the specifications relating to the planned business model, performance standards, financing requirements and other features for the benefit of the public. The tender forms the basis for the development of concrete PPP bids by interested parties.

6.3.2.2 Equity providers Each project starts with a small core of one or several equity providers, known as 'sponsors'. They jointly advance the project, yet with each of them pursuing the aim of achieving their own business objectives. In the case of traditional project finance, the members of this core group also act as initiators and principals of the project (see Figure 6.2). In PPP structures, however, they act as bidders for projects tendered by the public sector. In both cases, sponsors provide significant amounts of equity and jointly assume full responsibility for the organisation and implementation of the project (see Figure 6.3 for a detailed illustration of all equity providers).

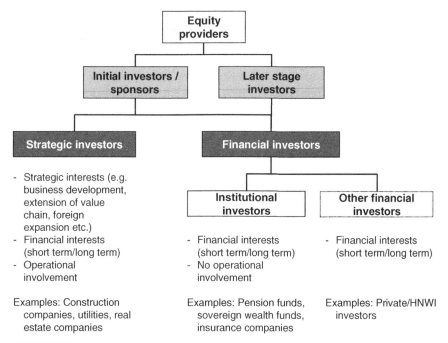

FIGURE 6.3 Equity providers

Sponsors traditionally take the form of *strategic sponsors*. This applies in particular to companies operating in areas related to the infrastructure sector, such as construction, energy or real estate, and their customers and suppliers, as well as facility management and other specialist service industries. As well as providing financial support, they contribute to the project by performing services, meaning they are actively involved in the project development and operation process because of their specialist expertise. Strategic investors pursue financial objectives as well as long-term strategic business development targets such as the generation of internal growth, the extension of their value chain, foreign expansion, the sale and distribution of their own products and services, together with the development of new markets and segments and new sources of raw materials. These types of project investments also offer strategic sponsors the opportunity to diversify their asset portfolio and risk structure.

In addition, there are a growing number of *financial sponsors*. These include insurance companies, pension funds, sovereign wealth funds, and investment funds specialising in infrastructure and energy investments. Unlike strategic sponsors, financial sponsors do not generally become involved in projects at an operational level and have no performance-based project interests or tasks; instead, they seek primarily to achieve an adequate return on the capital employed by getting involved early on in the project. In some exceptional cases, however, financial sponsors may be engaged in operating activities, whether via their own specialist infrastructure departments or subsidiaries or specialised infrastructure fund managers.

Financial investors can therefore be distinguished from financial and strategic sponsors by their later entry date as well as the lower level of operational involvement. Financial sponsors typically invest when the project has been fully structured, has successfully overcome the high-risk ramp-up phase and/or is operational and generating current income.

Generally, financial sponsors play a less important role than strategic sponsors at the outset of a project when primarily specialist sector expertise is required. For larger projects in particular, however, their involvement may be crucial to the realisation of a project, for example if the strategic sponsors do not have the means to provide sufficient capital in their own right. Financial investors (vs. financial sponsors) may become involved if large amounts of capital are required at a later stage of the project and these requirements cannot be (or are not) met by the existing investors and/or lenders or if any of the sponsors wants to sell.

In order to obtain capital from financial investors, it is important to ensure that international standards for project development and structuring are observed. The structures must offer investors a sufficiently attractive risk-return profile and in terms of governance, the opportunity to intervene in the project at an operational level, whether directly or via their partners. Simultaneously, the contractual structures must also provide them with assurance in the case of project alterations falling outside the scope of the project that significantly alter its economic viability, for example changes in legislation (see also Section 7.1 for further information on equity provision).

Owing to their strict investment criteria and stringent requirements with regard to professional project structuring, financial investors indirectly perform the function of quality auditors in the same way as banks. As such, their involvement can significantly improve the quality of a project for all participants.

6.3.2.3 Commercial banks Providers of debt are usually the most important, that is the largest, source of financing of a project financing. This group is composed of commercial banks and development banks, and increasingly also the aforementioned financial investors (e.g. insurance companies, pension funds, investment companies). Depending on the volume and risk profile of the project, the debt component of a financing structure may be up to 90%

(see Section 6.3.2 and Figure 6.1). The banks' role is not necessarily limited to their function as a provider of capital. It may also include consultation on and support for project and risk analysis, structuring, placement of capital with investors, etc. In the same way as financial investors, their critical feasibility studies serve to ensure a minimum quality standard with regard to the preparation and implementation of the project.

While the consulting and structuring fees of banks may be significant, the key objective of all debt providers is to recover the capital provided, including the interest payments, from the cash flow of the company once in operation. The interest margin of the financing reflects the banks' assessment of an appropriate return in light of the overall market and the respective project risks involved. Typically, creditors only participate in the positive development of the project/asset to the extent they receive interest payments, whereas they may be subject to significant losses in the event of the insolvency of the company (see also Section 7.3 for further information on debt provision).

6.3.2.4 Development banks

In addition to commercial banks, a number of development banks may act as creditors for project finance depending on the respective project. As providers of debt, they perform a similar function to commercial banks, but differ primarily in that they pursue different business goals in part, and hence may apply different criteria when deciding upon financing certain transactions. Development banks do not normally focus on maximising their returns from a project but rather place greater value on other aspects, such as promoting the economy in specific geographical areas and industries or social considerations when making lending decisions. Therefore, the lending conditions (e.g. interest margins on loan terms, etc.) of development banks are generally more favourable than those offered by commercial banks. Most development banks have AAA credit ratings (the highest level available) due to being supported by government guarantees, meaning that they can obtain capital market finance at extremely favourable conditions. These conditions are then largely passed on to borrowers (more information on development banks and their tasks can be found in Section 7.4).

Over the past few years, a number of development banks (e.g. World Bank, the Asian Development Bank, KfW) have issued so-called climate bonds or green bonds. These securities have been developed to fund infrastructure projects that have a positive impact on the environment, particularly on climate change both in developed and developing countries. Proceeds from these bonds are earmarked for green projects but are backed by the issuer's entire balance sheet. See Section 7.3.2.1 for more information on green and climate bonds.

6.3.2.5 General contractors, operators and other participants

General contractors and operators perform key functions within project finance. The general contractor is the party contracted with the construction of the asset. In most instances, the assets to be constructed by the general contractor represent the majority, if not all, of the investment value of the project. Accordingly, it is vital to find a reliable and experienced partner that can guarantee the scheduled completion of the project as well as the desired technical quality.

The general contractor typically assumes all risks relating to the construction of the asset, particularly with respect to the contractual completion at the agreed cost and the construction quality, in accordance with a turnkey or EPC (engineering, procurement and construction) contract. Accordingly, the general contractor bears considerable responsibility for the functionality of the project assets. As such, the credit rating of the general contractor is an important element, because it must be sufficiently strong to ensure that the contractor is able to cover potential cost overruns or other damages in case it is held liable by the project partners.

Depending on the scope of the construction, the general contractor often commissions a number of subcontractors to perform individual tasks within it. Between themselves, the subcontractors are responsible to the general contractor for the services performed. However, only the general contractor is liable externally to the SPV and ultimately to the principal, irrespective of whether the general contractor or one of its subcontractors is responsible for the respective services.

The operator is responsible for the successful operational management of the project after commissioning. In many cases, the operator has a relationship with any of the sponsors, for example, a subsidiary of a sponsor. Less frequently, an external management team may be contracted to operate the project. The decisive selection criterion is that the operator must have extensive and broad expertise in the operation of similar assets.

The suppliers and/or customers of the project company also play a key role in the successful realisation of a project. Depending on the industry, it is essential to conclude long-term fixed supply and/or purchase agreements prior to construction in order to ensure the company is provided with the necessary raw materials, primary products and services, or that these are purchased, thereby enabling the planning of future cash flows. In the case of PPP projects, these contracts may be replaced in part by service agreements and/or fixed performance fees (for information on the relevance of long-term supply and purchase agreements for project risk, see also Sections 5.2.1 and 5.3).

6.3.3 Objectives and contributions of project participants

It is important to always bear in mind that the participants in project finance – particularly when embedded in a PPP structure – have different objectives and requirements in terms of the (project) company and its financing. As a matter of principle, it must be possible to meet these objectives in order to justify the establishment of a partnership in the first place. Conflicting interests should be reconciled, ideally by creating win–win situations in the interest of maximising the success potential of the project.

The same applies to the members of individual groups of participants. A group of sponsors, which initially come together to form a bidder consortium and later become the shareholders of the company, often consists of a number of construction companies, suppliers and service providers whose expectations and contributions are not necessarily congruent in terms of their content, timing and scope. Their interests in the company may differ accordingly. Depending on the size of the project, banks may also participate in consortia/syndicates or other contractual arrangements with a view to risk sharing or the structuring of the project finance (see also Section 7.3.1.2).

Furthermore, the public-sector partner itself is not always a homogeneous institution. In countries with federal structures, in particular, often a number of different public partners, sometimes with extremely differing objectives and interests, need to be involved. This may give rise to objectives and additional risks for the private partners, which must be identified and evaluated. Particular care should be exercised when the principal and contractual partner is composed of multiple administrations. Germany is a case in point, where this scenario often arises in connection with PPP projects, such as federal highways, for which the national government delegates its responsibility to the federal states in accordance with constitutional law. The larger the number of participants in a project, the greater the complexity and the more difficult it becomes to create a joint platform for all parties.

TABLE 6.1 Objectives and contributions of project participants

Objectives	Contributions
Public sector	
– Efficiency benefits	– Concessions/licences
– Leveraging of public funds	– Performance fees
– Earlier and rapid project implementation	
– Good service quality	
– Adherence to statutory requirements and provisions	
Sponsors (strategic)	
– Adequate return	– Equity
– Strategic potential (expansion of business activities)	– Project development expertise (technical expertise)
	– Management expertise
Sponsors (financial) and financial investors	
– Maximisation of returns (equity provider)	– Equity (private equity)
– Full captial and interest payments (debt provider)	– Debt
	– Quality control
– High long-term current income	– Financing expertise
	– Expertise in financial project structuring
	– Long-term partner
Commercial banks	
– Full repayment and interest payments	– Debt
– Financial analysis and modelling	– Quality control
– Income from various kinds of fees	– Financing expertise
– Cross-selling of other products and services	– Expertise in financial project structuring
Development banks	
– Full repayment and interest payments	– Debt
– Promotion of development objectives	– Quality control
	– Financing expertise
	– Expertise in financial project structuring
	– Political risk reduction/insurance
General contractors/construction firms	
– Adequate margins	– Required construction services
	– Fixed turnkey price
Operators (facility managers and other service providers)	
– Adequate margins	– Required services
	– Fixed prices

Table 6.1 shows the key parties in a typical project finance and their main objectives and contributions. Whereas the public sector primarily expects efficiency benefits and additional funding, the private participants give priority to generating an adequate return and achieving strategic objectives.

6.3.4 Typical contractual framework for project finance

The legal documentation of a project financing serves to document the risk structure previously developed. This structure forms the nucleus of any project finance arrangement. Accordingly, the negotiation and preparation of the contractual framework is governed by a basic general rule: first the structure, then the contract! The development of an appropriate structure starts with determining the contractual parties and their role within the overall structure and ends in a contract after the completion of term sheet negotiations.

In order to determine the rights, obligations and risk allocation of the individual project partners, a set of contracts is developed with the aim of steering away risks from the company to the partners as much as possible. In a (PPP) tender process or an auction process of a private transaction, generally, the project company is formed only once the project/asset is awarded to the winning bidder (sponsor), that is shortly before the contracts are signed. Accordingly, the bidder and developer consortium must ensure that this contractual framework is prepared and negotiated 'back to back' during the bid and (PPP) contract negotiation phase.

The following sections contain a brief presentation of the main agreements forming part of the contractual framework of a project financing (see also Figure 6.4).

6.3.4.1 PPP project and concession agreement
The (PPP) project or concession agreement sets out the rights and obligations of the (project) company with respect to the public principal or private initiator and the risk allocation between the parties during the entire term of the agreement, making it a comprehensive contractual arrangement. The particular challenge is to identify all eventualities to the greatest possible extent and agree on them by mutual consent. This is impossible to achieve in full for agreements, which may have a term of

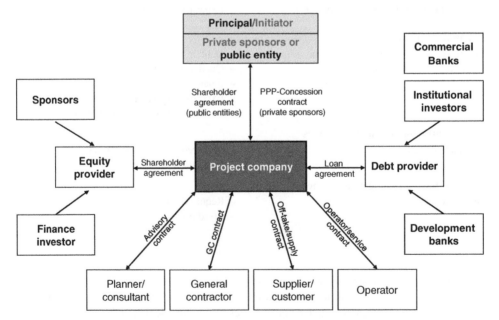

FIGURE 6.4   Basic structure of (PPP) project finance – contractual relations

more than 25 years in the case of a PPP, because legislation, statutory provisions, standards and other parameters such as the nature and extent of the need for project services will inevitably change over time. Accordingly, it is far more important to establish acceptable and balanced rules and mechanisms for dealing with unforeseeable situations and conflict resolution than is the case for conventional project agreements.

6.3.4.2 Shareholder agreement The shareholder agreement sets out the rights and obligations and the risk allocation between the sponsors and, at a later stage, any financial investors of the project company, if applicable, (please note that the 'Shareholder agreement' is displayed in Figure 6.4 twice in order to be able to differentiate between private initiators and public principals in the graphic). Areas requiring particular contractual provision include the equity capitalisation of the project company, voting rights and the composition of the supervisory bodies of the company, as well as any obligations to make additional payments. Shareholder agreements often also provide for the nature and extent of any performance-based relationship between the company and the sponsors.

6.3.4.3 General contractor agreement The general contractor agreement serves to transfer the typical risks arising in connection with the construction process – and often a significantly more extensive body of risks beyond this – to the company that is responsible for construction. It mostly takes the form of a turnkey contract. Since the general contractor is often part of a construction group, which is a sponsor and as such also a shareholder of the project company (conflict of interest), the public-sector principal (PPP) or the remaining shareholders (traditional), as the case may be, and the financing banks have an equal interest in ensuring that any service provided by any of the shareholders is contracted on an arm's-length basis.

6.3.4.4 Operation and service agreements The services to be performed in the operating phase must be assigned to the corresponding service providers in various forms of operation and maintenance (O&M) and service agreements. A management company may be formed in order to bundle the various tasks or the project company may contract third parties to perform these tasks in lots and carry out the resulting interface management itself. The contracted service providers often also have an equity interest in the project company.

Construction groups with an involvement in PPP projects are increasingly expanding their business activities to include operational management services. Their goal is to increase their value added and thus establish themselves as system providers. More importantly, they want to establish a source of long-term cash flows that are not capital-intensive and independent of acquiring new construction projects and do not contain typical construction risks. Moreover, this model allows construction companies to offer the full range of services from a single source. Such in-house solutions are often advantageous in terms of value engineering and greater flexibility of contractual performance.

6.3.4.5 Loan agreement Banks (including development banks), and lately also financial investors, usually provide 60–90% of the investment volume of the total project financing needs in the form of debt. The precise risk allocation and the rights and obligations of the company with respect to the debt providers are set out in corresponding loan agreements. Depending on the nature and complexity of the project/asset, these generally take the form of structured finance arrangements, that is the loans are tailored to the specific project. On the lender side, depending on the scale of the financing, this often involves cooperation between several lenders within a syndicate or club deals (see Section 7.3.1.3).

As this discussion clearly shows, it is vital that the developer/sponsor consortium selects the potential contractual partners – and particularly the financing partners – at an early stage, in order to allow for the risk allocation within the full contractual framework in good time prior to the signing of the contracts. This applies irrespective of whether the contractual parties are shareholders of the company or are contracted by the company to perform services on its behalf.

6.4 STRUCTURING PROJECT FINANCINGS – TRADITIONAL AND IN PPPS

This section provides a detailed description of the individual phases of a project financing. Before doing so, it gives an overview of the way in which a project finance structure is embedded in the overall process of a PPP, which is slightly different from traditional structures. To this end, this section also points to the differing objectives and expectations of the various parties involved and the conditions required by public principals, strategic sponsors and financial investors/sponsors with the explicit aim to enable these groups to overcome the 'language issues' they largely encounter as a result of extreme cultural differences.

The PPP process forms the framework, in which the various project finance phases – shown in *italics* in Table 6.2 – are embedded accordingly.[2]

PPP projects involving project finance can be broken down into a number of sub-processes depending on the perspective of the respective party. From the perspective of the public principal, the project sponsors and the various service providers, typically four phases can be identified:

- *Project definition and advisory* by the project developer. This includes considerations on the economic feasibility and bankability of the planned measures and the fundamental suitability of PPP as a method of procurement, as well as an investigation of its economic feasibility compared with traditional procurement, including the necessary technical forecasts. Already at this early stage, the project developer who is part of or hired by the public principal, generally calls upon the services of financial consultants as well as the typical technical, economic and legal consultants in order to establish whether the project is fundamentally suited to a project finance model.
- *Tender procedure, project and risk analysis.* The tender procedure involves a structured negotiation process that generally needs to be followed for PPP projects for governance reasons. This takes the form of a competition in which a limited number of bidders is

---

[2]This section does not contain a detailed presentation of the phases of the PPP procurement process, because it is rather country-specific. Relevant information can be found in country-specific procurement law and/or corresponding literature.

TABLE 6.2 Phases of a PPP project with project finance

Participants	Project definition and advisory	Tender project and risk analysis	Awarding and financing	Implementation and monitoring

Client	– Selection of project
	– PPP-suitability test
	  →*Suitable PPP/PF*
	– Value for money test
	  →Announcement
		– Request for information
		– Invitation to offer
		– *Guidelines/specifications for PF*
			– Bid assessment
			– Negotiation process
			– Awarding
				– Monitoring of services

Sponsors	– Suitability test – Search of partners – Application	– Application – Preparation offer: financial, technical, economical – *Assessment of PF* – *Business plan* – *Cash flow model* – Submission of bid	– Contract negotiations – *Modification offer (PF)* – *Establishment of SPC* – PPP contract – *Equity provision* – *Financial close*	– Control of assets
Banks	– *Clarification of general suitability for PF, i.e. bankability*	– *Assessment of specific bankability* – *Due diligence (technical, economical, legal)* – *Risk analysis and distribution* – *Cash flow model* – *Structuring PF (incl. term sheet)*	– *Support sponsors* – *Firm commitments* – *Info memo* – *Loan contracts, arranging, syndication* – *Financial close*	– *Drawdown of debt tranches* – *Monitoring of financial covenants and milestones* – *Refinancing, rating, other financial services*
Contractor and other service provider		– Offer to consortium of sponsors (services, prices) for construction and service contracts	– Possible modification of services, prices (value engineering)	– Completion – Guarantee – Services
SPC			– Establishment of SPC – Signing and takeover contracts – *Financial close*	– Project and risk management. – Point of contact for all stakeholders

Note: PF = project finance, SPC = Special Purpose Company.

invited from the pool of applicants. Following initial project and risk analysis, these bidders are asked to deliver their bids followed by a subsequent reworking and resubmission period. This includes the results of concrete due diligence on the project as well as its bankability, risk allocation and the preparation of a cash flow model.

- *Contract award and financing.* This phase begins with the evaluation and ranking of the bids, the selection of the bidders with whom negotiations will be opened – in some cases including the best and final offer (BAFO) by the preferred bidder(s), the award of the contract and the signature of the corresponding agreements. This is generally followed by the financial close, i.e. the closing of the project financing as a prerequisite for the implementation of the project. This phase is particularly important for the sponsors, i.e. the winning bidder, because it is now that the fine-tuning of the overall contractual framework is negotiated 'back to back' and ultimately developed into a financeable structure.
- *Implementation and monitoring.* This phase is generally broken down into implementation, which consists of construction and operation, including maintenance, throughout the agreed term of the PPP contract, and monitoring once the transaction has been completed.

The elements printed in *italics* in Table 6.2 show how the financing aspects of a PPP span across all four phases of the project. Given the financing focus of this book – as opposed to a public-sector or industry focus, for example – it makes sense to examine the entire PPP process from the perspective of the financiers. On this basis, it may be more appropriate to let the financing guide the process and classify it into the following five phases of project finance that form the basis for any PPP finance (see Table 6.3):

- Advisory
- Project assessment
- Risk analysis and allocation
- Financing
- Implementation and monitoring.

Table 6.3 shows that the individual sub-phases of the project finance process for an infrastructure project largely occur sequentially and pursue different objectives. The risks and responsibilities are spread broadly across the project participants over the lifetime of a project. The course and outcome of each sub-process serves as the basis for deciding whether the project finance should be continued or whether it is to be abandoned or will be rejected by the banks. All five phases are described in detail in the following sections.

As previously mentioned, traditional project finance for infrastructure projects does not differ fundamentally from project finance in PPP structures. The most notable structural difference is that, in the latter case, the principal is the public sector and hence not the same person as the sponsor. This generally results in more extensive project requirements, more complicated structures and a shift in the interests of the involved public and private project participants (see Section 6.3.2). Accordingly, the following overview of the various phases of the project finance process distinguishes between traditional and PPP project finance only when there are significant differences.

TABLE 6.3 Phases of project finance

Criteria	Advisory	Project assessment	Risk analysis and allocation	Financing	Implementation and monitoring
Goals	– Clarification/ analysis of general bankability/financial and economic viability – Structuring of financing	– Specific bankability and economic viability/sustainability – Assess essential precondition for PF	– Detailed risk analysis – Optimal risk distribution – Cost minimisation	– Development of viable financing	– Implement project – Monitor if project develops according to plan and meets all covenants and milestones
Participants	– Consultants – Sponsors – State/government	– Consultants – Sponsors and state – Banks (and finance investors) – Experts	– Consultants – Sponsors and state – Experts – Insurances – Banks (and finance investors)	– Consultants – Sponsors and state – Banks and finance investors	– Sponsors and state – Banks and finance investors
Time required	– 6–12 months	– 2–6 months (standalone); 3–9 months (integrated)	– 1–3 months	– 1–3 months	– Term of project and of financing
Results	– PF not suited for financing the project or: – PF suited for financing the project – Address/approach suitable investors with DD material	– PF of potentially involved parties not considered doable or: – Continue risk analysis	– Abandon project or: – Structure financing	– Financing not viable/sustainable and/or economical or: – Implement project	– Implementation according to plan and finalise project

Note: PF = project finance; DD = due diligence.

6.4.1   Phase I – Advisory

When providing consulting services to a (project) company, the task of the financial advisor is to perform a fundamental due diligence of the economic viability, and hence the bankability, of a concrete infrastructure project/asset, as well as to identify the most suitable form of financing for the project/asset and to structure it accordingly. For PPP projects, this consulting activity takes place at the level of the public sector, that is identical with the project developer in this case. This serves largely to exclude the possibility of the public sector putting a PPP project which involves project finance out to tender despite its being fundamentally unsuitable for a project finance solution. However, consulting services may also be required at the level of the sponsor or the financial investor. Sponsors and financial investors with little experience in the area of PPP projects and project finance generally find it difficult to perform a detailed calculation of the bankability of a tendered project, submit an adequately structured financing request to third-party banks and/or financial investors or assess the proposed financing structure.

In addition to the economic viability of a project, consultants perform an initial ESG analysis with the goal of determining whether an infrastructure project meets the sustainability requirements (environmental, social and governance standards) of its key stakeholders (private and public project sponsors [equity providers], financing banks and financial investors if any [debt providers] and insurers).

If the public sector is the principal, the prerequisites for financing in general, and project finance involving a PPP structure in particular, are examined during this initial phase in order to determine whether the planned project can fundamentally be privately financed (see also Table 6.3). In the case of traditional project finance with a private principal, the latter is responsible for examining the project not only in a general sense but also in terms of its own strategic objectives and economic conditions, the existing portfolio and its risk profile. In both cases, this analysis must include the technical and operational conditions, economic feasibility, risk structure and potential political, legal and tax aspects of the project.

The project analysis in the advisory phase (phase 1) differs from the analysis in the project assessment, also called due diligence, phase (phase 2), primarily in terms of the level of detail. Otherwise, the areas of assessment are essentially identical. Therefore, it is discussed extensively only in phase 2 in the next section.

The outcome of the advisory phase, answers, among others, the question as to which alternative forms of finance would be suitable for the project in question and whether project finance is a suitable option. The conclusion may be that another form of financing is more suitable, such as traditional financing. If so, the traditional route will be followed.

6.4.2   Phase II – Project assessment

Once it is determined that an infrastructure project/asset is fundamentally suitable for project finance, the project assessment phase seeks to assess the economic long-term viability of the project/asset – and hence its bankability – in detail for the parties involved. This includes an examination of the key preconditions for successful project finance, and in particular technical and economic feasibility, the operating concept and the structuring of the risk profile (see Figure 6.5). An in-depth sustainability assessment that focuses on potential ESG risks, is an integral part of it. In practice, the assessments and concepts described below typically take place simultaneously.

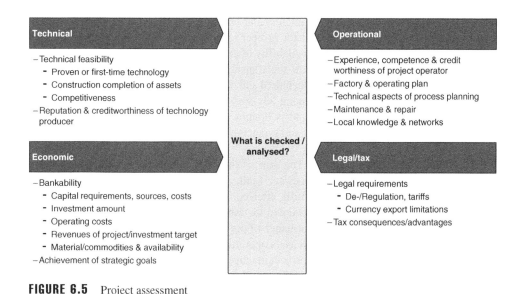

Technical

−Technical feasibility
 - Proven or first-time technology
 - Construction completion of assets
 - Competitiveness
−Reputation & creditworthiness of technology
 producer

Economic

−Bankability
 - Capital requirements, sources, costs
 - Investment amount
 - Operating costs
 - Revenues of project/investment target
 - Material/commodities & availability
−Achievement of strategic goals

What is checked / analysed?

Operational

−Experience, competence & credit
 worthiness of project operator
−Factory & operating plan
−Technical aspects of process planning
−Maintenance & repair
−Local knowledge & networks

Legal/tax

−Legal requirements
 - De-/Regulation, tariffs
 - Currency export limitations
−Tax consequences/advantages

FIGURE 6.5   Project assessment

6.4.2.1   Technical assessment   The technical assessment, which also includes a structural survey, primarily seeks to ascertain whether a project is feasible in terms of its completion within the agreed schedule, the technical equipment and the performance of the systems employed after it goes operational. One relevant factor may be whether the necessary construction measures and the technologies used are proven procedures and products or whether they are being used for the first time in connection with the project. The reputation and credit rating of the technology supplier, other suppliers and selected subcontractors are also key aspects requiring examination. This means the feasibility of the project and hence its financial sustainability depend to a large extent on typical engineering considerations. As such, the analysis also seeks to determine the extent to which the infrastructure and assets employed ensure the smooth progress of the operating processes and workflows from a technical perspective and whether the systems involved are adequately connected, for example. Independent external advisors usually perform the technical analysis of the project.

6.4.2.2   Economic assessment   There is a strong reciprocal effect between technical and economic feasibility, in other words changes in the technical structure of a project generally have a direct impact on its economic viability, and hence its bankability. From the point of view of the project sponsor(s), the economics (i.e. the financial profitability of a project) may be less important than achieving strategic objectives, such as tapping new sales markets or sources of raw materials.

For the debt providers, be it banks or financial investors, the economic assessment is a crucial factor in determining the 'bankability' or 'finance-ability' of a project or an asset, as the case may be. The key points covered by the economic assessment are: (i) capital requirements, sources and costs; (ii) the investment volume for the construction and commissioning of the project; (iii) running operating costs; (iv) the income generated by the project, which determines the cash flows available for interest and principal payments to the debt providers and ultimately the return on investment for project sponsors and other providers of equity; (v) cost of materials/raw materials and availability of the necessary raw materials; and (vi) cost of project analysis and the structuring of the transaction, including all necessary advisory activities such as legal and tax advisors, technical and financial advisors. The analysis of points (i)–(v) is usually performed by the financial advisors of the project sponsors in conjunction with external consultants and experts and is documented in the information memorandum prepared for the financiers, that is banks and financial investors, if any.

6.4.2.3 Operational assessment The aim of the operational assessment is to ensure the general ability of the designated operator (and, in some cases, these are the sponsors themselves) to operate an asset successfully after completion. This includes an examination of the credit rating, expertise and experience of the (sponsors and) operators by, for example, obtaining references, analysing the performance of previous projects and evaluating the future management team (its experience as well as its operating budget). The operational assessment also includes an analysis of the planned project management processes and workflows, factory and operational planning, dimensioning and networking of the systems, preparatory work and the existence of suitable instruments for reporting and controlling tasks.

For projects abroad, established, long-standing relationships with government bodies and knowledge of the local situation may be decisive for the successful operation of the asset.

Maintenance and repair work can make considerable demands on the expertise of the operating company and may require specific logistical solutions, depending on the project/asset type and its geographical location. The successful operation of the asset also depends largely on strong management skills, such as the optimal coordination of all parties involved and the early resolution of potential conflict situations. In addition, optimal insurance cover with a structure and volume typical for the industry is a standard requirement for the operation of such assets. The assessment of operational risk is also usually performed with the assistance of an external consultant.

6.4.2.4 Legal/tax assessment The legal, regulatory, contractual and tax assessment of project finance are additional key components of the overall analysis process. Legal and tax aspects, which may initially appear secondary in nature, can severely affect the profitability of a project finance. Examples are contract award law, labour law, subsidy law, municipal law and public assistance law, as well as tax law. These considerations are all the more important for projects/assets situated in emerging economies, for example where aspects such as (de)regulation, collective bargaining agreements, customs duties and restrictions on currency movement may be particularly relevant. Tax advisors and lawyers primarily cover the tax and legal aspects of project finance within the analysis process. For detailed legal and tax information, readers are referred to the extensive legal literature related to project finance.

6.4.3 Phase III – Risk analysis and allocation

Infrastructure projects/assets are subject to a large number of different risks. A thorough understanding of all risk inherent in and related to an infrastructure project or asset is central to any equity or debt investment decision by any party. The accurate identification of all risks is the first step. This seemingly trivial insight is critical in order to understand which aspects require further analysis and evaluation. During the comprehensive technical, operational, legal and tax due diligence, a large number of risks are typically identified whereby only relatively few tend to be serious, so-called 'red flags'. Notwithstanding, all of them must be investigated, evaluated and mitigated in one way or another. None of the project participants could bear all these risks alone, nor would anyone want to do so.

Only after thorough risk analysis and evaluation – and ideally also quantification – is it possible to implement corresponding structures that mitigate them, and hence ensure protection. An optimal risk structure seeks to allocate the individual risks to those participants who are best positioned to assume the respective risk. The aim is to ensure that each participant ultimately bears the risks that it is best able, and thus most cost-efficiently, to manage or control. This allows the greatest possible benefit for the project as a whole and the minimisation of the potential costs arising to the company as a result.

Please refer to Chapter 5 for an extensive discussion of the most relevant risks, which anybody interested in investing in infrastructure projects/assets – equity or debt – should be aware of and may come across. As such, Chapter 5 essentially takes the reader through a broad risk analysis including options/possibilities of coverage and optimal risk allocation among the project participants.

6.4.4 Phase IV – Financing

A realistic, long-term financing concept forms the basis for the success of any infrastructure endeavour. The aspects to be taken into consideration are as follows (they are summarised in Figure 6.6 and discussed in greater detail in the following four sections):

- *Bankability:* The project must be fundamentally financeable, i.e. must have a positive net present value.

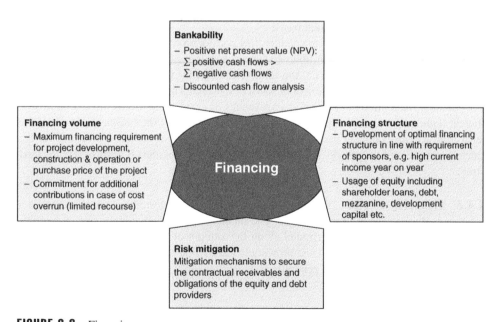

FIGURE 6.6 Financing

- *Financing volume:* Maximum financing needs to meet the purchase price of the asset or the cost of development, construction and the initial operation of the project.
- *Financing structure:* Proportion of equity and debt financing using various instruments, e.g. shareholder loans, mezzanine, development capital, considering the annual current income requirements of the sponsors.
- *Risk mitigation:* Mitigation mechanisms to secure the contractual receivables and obligations of the equity and debt providers.

6.4.4.1 Bankability While it may be stating the obvious, the bankability of a project/asset is a fundamental prerequisite for all financiers to establish a successful financing structure. A project is only bankable if it has a positive net present value over the term of the financing and the project. The financing is generally shorter than the (calculated) duration of the project, determined by, for example the term of a concession or the lifetime of the existing asset, as the case may be. The net present value is calculated as the total of all positive and negative cash flows discounted[3] to the reference date. Thereby, negative cash flows – in the case of already existing (brownfield) assets – primarily relate to the purchase price, including various ancillary expenses, financing costs (debt service), potential expansion or replacement investments and the operation of the facilities.

For greenfield projects, negative cash flows encompass project development and construction costs, including potential investments in infrastructure (e.g. access roads, transmission lines), the cost of facilities and technical equipment and in most cases the operating costs incurred in the years immediately after commissioning (see below), capital interest charges and other ancillary financing. Transaction costs, such as advisory fees or taxes, apply to both greenfield projects and operational assets.

Positive cash flows arise from revenues generated by the asset, such as user paid tolls (motorway), sale or transmission of commodities (e.g. coal, oil and gas) or the sale of electricity generated from such commodities, as well as availability payments (schools, hospitals), all of which are accounted for on an annual basis.

The providers of debt determine whether they consider a project/asset to be bankable. To this end, they require positive cash flows to exceed negative cash flows amply over the term of the loans. The coverage ratio (i.e. the relative amount by which the positive cash flows exceed the negative cash flows *before* debt service) represents a contingency reserve that may offset potential fluctuations in project/asset revenues or costs, and ensures the availability of sufficient liquidity for the scheduled repayment of the loans plus interest payments from the free cash flow *before* debt service. As such, the coverage ratio serves as an indicator for the financial robustness of the project. The position of the equity providers is discussed in the next section.

6.4.4.2 Financing volume The provision of sufficient long-term financial resources is a key factor in the success of projects/assets. The financing volume, that is the capital requirements of the project/asset, is determined along the amount of the total investment required (see previous section for greenfield and brownfield calculation basis). As a rule, sponsors (and any additional financial investors) generally provide the equity capital, including shareholder

---

[3]Discounting is performed based on a discount rate.

loans, whereas banks (and any additional financial investors) provide the debt (i.e. in the form of a loan or bond). The nature and scope of the project determine which of the various financing instruments available might be most suitable. These are discussed in Chapter 7.

When determining the maximum financing volume that a project/asset can support, it needs to be remembered that the cash flow required for debt service is often – in the case of greenfield projects always – generated in full only in the second or third year of operation, rather than immediately upon purchase of the assets or completion of the construction phase. Accrued interest up until this date must be included when calculating the total capital requirements. It is also important to add contingency premiums to account for eventualities such as cost increases, delays in completion or exchange rate fluctuations.

In addition to the cash flow available to repay the debt over the entire term of the loan (the loan life coverage ratio, or LLCR), providers of debt may be even more interested in the cash flow available to pay the debt service in each individual year (debt service coverage ratio, or DSCR) when determining the adequate financing volume. The latter serves to ensure that the project can meet its interest and principal payment obligations on a year-by-year basis.

The providers of equity also require a positive net present value, which allows them to receive an appropriate return on their capital employed. Unlike the lender(s), for whom the cash flow *before* debt service (interest and principal payments) is the relevant parameter for measuring net present value, equity investors care about the free cash flow *after* debt service both on an annual basis to ensure a sufficient annual current income (from e.g. interest on shareholder loans or dividends) as well as over the term of the entire project, which determines their ultimate return.

The time horizon for the equity providers typically is beyond the term of the loan and as such, longer than that of debt providers. Only if the strategy of the equity provider(s) is the maximisation of short-term returns rather than generating a high level of current income (yield) over the long term, the calculation of net present value may be based on a significantly shorter period than the term of the loan or the duration of the project. An example is IRR-oriented equity investors seeking to maximise their returns via the resale/terminal value by selling a greenfield project right after it has been successfully commissioned (please also refer to Chapter 2 and Section 5.3.7).

6.4.4.3 Financing structure

Once the capital requirements of a project or asset, as the case may be, have been determined, the sponsors/equity providers establish a financing structure that takes into account the characteristics of the project/asset and the expected cash flow profile. The aim is to ensure the viability of the project finance in light of both the debt service paid to the debt providers as well as the return requirements of the sponsors.

The following sources of funding are usually considered when structuring a financing solution: (i) equity from sponsors or financial investors in the form of share capital and shareholder loans; (ii) instruments with both the characteristics of equity or debt, such as mezzanine capital; (iii) debt in the form of traditional loans, divided into various tranches and terms; (iv) bonds; and (v) development capital, including subsidies. For overseas projects, (vi) export finance may represent an additional source of funding for export transactions. Development capital and export finance are provided by government (related) institutions.

The assets as such may be used to optimise the available liquidity, including for asset-backed structures under which future receivables (parts of its current assets) are bundled, securitised and passed on to investors. This allows the (project) company to obtain the cash flows from the receivables in advance, while the buyers of these securities recover their capital and generate a return on the capital employed following the settlement of the receivables.

Sale and leaseback solutions are another option to optimise liquidity: the (project) company sells parts of its valuable (project) fixed assets to a leasing company and leases back the same assets. The direct inflow of liquidity is offset by future lease instalments, which are paid for from the (project) cash flow generated. Derivatives, such as futures and options, are often employed to hedge the aforementioned interest rate and exchange rate risks. All these sources of funding are discussed in Chapter 7.

When establishing the funding structure, as well as selecting the appropriate financing instruments, it is important to match the maturities and repayment schedules of the underlying financing with the expected cash flows from the project/asset. In the case of traditional project loans (as opposed to bonds sold on the capital market), for example, the operating cash flow for a given period is taken into account when calculating the debt service for that period. A repayment schedule sets out lower repayment instalments at first, with higher instalments as the project progresses and the generated revenue increases. The precise reconciliation of the available cash flows (revenue) and the debt service thereby help to optimise the cost of capital.

As well as the absolute amount of funding, the relative volume (i.e. the debt/equity ratio) is an important factor when defining the optimal financing volume. From the perspective of the providers of equity, a high debt/equity ratio is usually desirable – especially in times of low interest rates – because the leverage effect (expensive equity is replaced by less expensive debt) serves to increase the return on equity. Yet maximising the debt/equity ratio may not be optimal for all equity investors alike, because a high debt/equity ratio increases the annual debt service and as such reduces, or often entirely eliminates the free cash flow available to the equity sponsors via dividends or shareholder loan interest payments. If current income is a high priority for sponsors, a low leverage may be preferable.

Further, a high leverage may reduce the creditworthiness of the borrower, thereby increasing its cost of debt financing. In addition, the risk arising from changes in interest rates or exchange rate fluctuations increases because such fluctuations have a greater impact on highly leveraged projects. For projects/assets that could be subject to extreme fluctuations in revenue, the risk of defaulting on debt service obligations in the event of a deterioration in revenues increases; this is what happened to many highly leveraged companies during the financial crisis. As such, the optimal debt/equity ratio for an infrastructure project or asset depends not only on the level of cash flow generated but also on the extent of the overall risks, in particular the market (price and demand) and the political, regulatory, currency and interest rate risks.

Irrespective of the expected available cash flows, the lenders – as mentioned above – generally require the equity providers to maintain an equity ratio of 10–40% of the total financing volume depending on the risk profile of the respective project/asset. Under unusually tight financing conditions, as for example, during the subprime crisis, this quota can easily rise to 50% or higher.

6.4.4.4 Risk mitigation Project finance is all about structuring and risk mitigation. To this end, financings generally contain certain inherent mitigation mechanisms in order to secure the contractual receivables and obligations of the equity and debt providers. These may be combined in different permutations to form an adequate mitigation concept. In addition to the allocation of risks to various parties, potential clauses include:

- Sufficient equity in the company from the start, while obtaining commitments from the sponsors/equity providers for predefined additional payments to cover excess costs or unexpectedly low levels of revenue in the first years of operation (limited recourse of sponsors);
- Turnkey construction agreement with a general contractor with an adequate credit rating;
- Corporate or bank guarantees/warranties (advance payment and retention guarantees);
- Capital maintenance and operational guarantees by the sponsors;
- Contractual penalties;
- Insurance for the most relevant risks (country and/or political risk, planning and employer's liability, construction services, technical or operational interruption), and export credit agencies (ECAs).

The specific structure of guarantees and insurance cover is flexible and may be adjusted to reflect individual requirements. The cornerstones of such guarantees are the amount, term and approval of the guarantee commitment. Similarly, insurance cover may generally be tailored to the requirements of the project/asset and its participants. However, there are only a handful of insurance companies in the market that cover the long duration of PPP projects. If the insurance period is shorter than the calculated duration/lifetime of the project, this gives rise to a risk in terms of the conditions at which a new insurance cover can be taken out after the initial cover expires (this is similar to the interest rate risk discussed in Section 5.2). This risk of potential additional costs should ideally be reflected in the project structure – analogous to the interest rate risk – by agreeing price adjustment clauses or ensuring that it is included in the bid submission process and passed on to the developer as part of the performance fee.

The risk of the insurer going into default must be taken into account. In light of the experience of established private insurance groups going into default, it is advisable not only to undertake a thorough due diligence of the insurers in question but also to diversify across different insurance providers.

RISK MITIGATION

İskenderun: The financing volume of the project was US$1.4 billion, broken down into US$1.0 billion of debt and US$370 million of equity. The investor appetite was limited at the time because of the country risk inherent to Turkey, and so the project sponsors pursued a multi-sourcing strategy to secure financing. Its objective was to involve a limited number of export insurers in the financing process and thereby generate a sufficient degree of cover for the political risk. A total of US$639 million was raised via three ECAs: Hermes (Germany), OeKB (Austria) and CGIC (South Africa). With the first-time involvement of CGIC in a project of this nature, the South African government provided its domestic industry with the opportunity to supply the global energy market with its own technology. The GKA programme of the Federal Republic

of Germany (guarantees for foreign investments and federal guarantees for direct foreign investments) was selected for the remaining debt finance volume (US$386 million),
which also provided insurance against political risk, including cover for specific contractual breaches in connection with the power purchase agreement. The term of the
various debt tranches was 16 years (final maturity in 2016) with an average term of
eight years. The loans were structured as limited recourse during the construction phase
(with a completion guarantee provided by STEAG) and reclassified as non-recourse
after completion. The lead arranger for the European component of the debt finance was
a banking syndicate consisting of Dresdner Kleinwort Benson, KfW and West LB. The
transaction was three times oversubscribed. The tranche covered by CGIC was financed
by ABSA (Amalgamated Banks of South Africa) and fully syndicated on the African
market.

Warnow: The total volume of the project was around €219 million, of which €43 million
(20%) was provided in the form of equity by a construction consortium managed
by the sponsor Bouygues Travaux Publics SA and the financial investor Macquarie
Infrastructure. A global banking syndicate headed by Deutsche Bank, Nord/LB, KfW
and EIB, provided loans totalling €148 million (68%) with terms of between 23 and
25 years. The loans were syndicated to a consortium of 13 national and international
banks. A 12% subsidy (€28 million), including a contribution from the EU as part of
the promotion of the TEN (Trans-European Network), underlined the importance of the
project in terms of joint European interests and helped to facilitate its financing.

6.4.5   Phase V – Implementation and monitoring

After a satisfactory due diligence has taken place and appropriate financing has been secured,
the project transaction is executed. Once an SPV has been set up, if applicable, and the
preconditions for injecting the equity and drawing down the debt have been demonstrably met,
the equity and credit providers deliver the capital accordingly. Thereafter, the financing partners
are generally not deeply involved in the implementation and monitoring of the operational
steps leading to the start of operations. This holds unless significant delays occur (e.g. failure to
achieve milestones) that could affect the future cash flows generated by the project/asset. Given
this book predominantly targets investors, the rest of this section focuses on the subsequent
financial rather than operational monitoring function.

Monitoring by the equity and debt providers is primarily based on the debt-related coverage
ratios agreed during the financing process, additional contractually agreed financial covenants,
ratios or milestones and the current course of the business. The aim of monitoring is to
recognise emerging problems at an early stage and resolve them in cooperation with all the
relevant parties. All equity investors and lenders alike are ultimately interested in recovering
their capital plus a corresponding return. They normally receive the following documents from
the company for the purpose of their monitoring activity:

■ Monthly reports (management accounts) by the company, primarily consisting of the
income statement, balance sheet and cash flow statement;

- Quarterly reports including financial data and explanatory remarks by the management of the company;
- Audited annual financial statements that meet the requirements of the relevant accounting legislation.

The company agrees in advance with the capital providers on format and content of the respective reports. As part of the monitoring process, actual business performance is compared with the original budgets and forecasts; any deviations are analysed and will require an explanation, and possibly short-term action, from the management at the least, and in the case of a renegotiation of the agreements.

TOLL ROAD PROJECTS

For toll road projects, one of the aspects monitored is whether the number of motor vehicles per month and the average toll paid are consistent with forecasts. This indicates whether motorists have accepted the toll road or prefer to make a detour to avoid it, and whether the original volume and price estimates were realistic. Both aspects directly affect the level of cash flows, and as such the coverage ratios.

In addition to the analysis of the financial reports, monitoring takes the form of joint or individual meetings between the equity investors, the lenders and the company on several occasions during the course of the year. These meetings primarily occur in conjunction with shareholder meetings (three or four times a year) and supervisory board or advisory board meetings. Meetings also take place with the representatives of the lender or lender syndicate, as the case may be. Meetings on specific topics, for example strategic issues, may be convened at short notice as well.

If project monitoring establishes that the actual revenue and cash flow are lower than the original forecast, which constitutes the basis of calculation for the financing structure and hence the coverage ratios, the following actions may be taken – focusing primarily on the financing side:

- Improvement of revenue by own means (if possible); if economically and politically justifiable, this may also be achieved by adjusting the purchase/off-take agreements;
- Optimisation of the cost structure;
- Redefinition of the coverage ratios if the debt can still be serviced from the cash flow but the projected ratios are 'broken', that is, the actual ratios are lower than originally forecast;
- Restructuring of the project financing, e.g. by adjusting or redefining the interest payments, if the cash flow is insufficient to meet the debt service obligations.

The aim of this chapter was to provide an overview of project finance in general and in the context of PPP in particular. In view of the finance focus of this book and the central status of the financing within any transaction, the necessary financing instruments for such transactions are examined further in the next chapter, Chapter 7.

Financing Instruments

Infrastructure assets generally lend themselves to debt financing because of both the (often large) amounts of capital required given the nature of the assets and their (ideally long-term) contracted cash flows. Financing of infrastructure assets can take the form of traditional (corporate) finance, project finance or asset-backed finance. Which kind of financing, or which combination of financings, is most suitable predominantly depends on the stage/maturity of the asset (e.g. large, new infrastructure projects typically take project finance), the timing of the financing requirements and the nature of the contracts – which in turn depend on the nature of the infrastructure asset in question.

Most financings employ various financing instruments to ensure an optimal structure. The instruments and the form and extent to which they are used depend on a number of factors. In particular, these factors include the size of the project/asset, the amount and viability of the available cash flows, the preferences and requirements of the sponsor or principal, if any, the risk-return expectations of the equity providers, the risk and collateral structure of the project, the political and economic conditions in the (host) country and the creditworthiness of the sponsors, if applicable. Taken together, these factors determine the volume and structure of a financing, including the selection of the appropriate financing instruments.

This section classifies financing instruments broadly based on the type of capital provided. It distinguishes between two main categories: equity (covered in Section 7.1), debt (discussed in Section 7.3), with mezzanine capital being a hybrid of these two (see Section 7.2); see Figure 7.1 for a graphic representation of the different financing instruments. Equity and debt instruments manifest themselves in different ways.

Sponsors and investors may also call upon national/regional public-sector development banks or multilateral institutions such as the World Bank Group for additional equity or debt financing (see Section 7.4). Many national and international development banks run industry-specific loan programmes in order to support investments in certain sectors, such as renewable energy generation or energy efficiency. In the broader area of climate protection, they relatively recently also set-up 'green bonds' and early stage specific 'greenfield debt' programmes. The former is done partially through dedicated 'Green Banks', which focus on climate issues (see Section 7.3.2).

It is also possible to benefit from indirect subsidies by involving state-owned or private export credit agencies (ECAs), which support the export transactions of companies by providing export credit guarantees. Instruments such as asset-backed securities (ABSs) and sale and

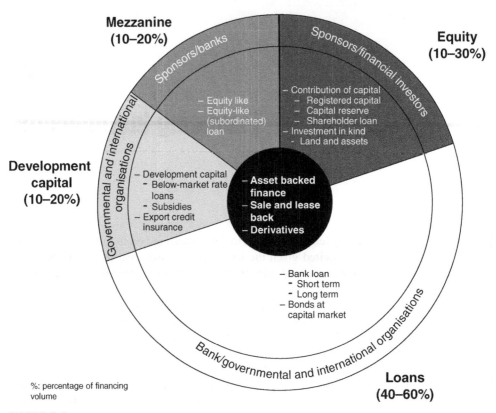

FIGURE 7.1 Financing instruments

leaseback transactions may also be included in the financing structure (see Sections 7.5 and 7.6). Finally, Section 7.7 briefly touches upon the derivatives that can be used to hedge interest rate and exchange rate risk within the financing structure (see also Section 5.2 for interest rate and exchange rate risks).

The various forms of capital differ in terms of their risk profile with the level of risk taken generally determining the level of the expected return. Equity is the form of financing with the highest risk, because it is subordinate to all other financing instruments, such as mezzanine capital and debt.

7.1 EQUITY

Equity is usually provided to a company for an unlimited period and may be contributed in different forms:

- As a cash contribution in the form of cash and cash equivalents;
- As a non-cash contribution in kind, i.e. project assets such as land and equipment.

RENERGIA – FINANCING STRUCTURE

The total project costs of the publicly- (90%) and privately- (10%) owned waste-to-energy plant Renergia in Switzerland (see also Sections 4.4.7.2 and 6.3.2) totalled SFr320 million, of which SFr100 million were funded in equity. The waste associations of central Switzerland contributed 90% of the equity capital for a total share of 90% in the company. Every association participated in the funding in proportion to its waste contribution. The privately-held paper mill Perlen Papier AG received 10% ownership in return for contributing the land on which the WtE plant was built. SFr220 million in debt was provided on a project finance basis by a consortium of banks led by Zürcher Kantonalbank, Switzerland's largest cantonal bank, and other local banks.

Cash contributions may take various forms and be structured with various components. The share capital corresponds to the subscribed shares in the project company combined with voting rights in proportion to the respective shareholding. The capital reserve – or premium – is a contribution by the shareholders that does not constitute subscribed capital and corresponds to the excess over the nominal amount of the share capital when the shares are issued. Contributions may also be made in the form of preferred capital (e.g. in exchange for the receipt of a preferred dividend) and/or via shareholder loans. Although the latter instruments are classified as loans, and hence debt, for legal purposes and bear some kind of interest, they are treated as subordinate to the claims of all other creditors and thus carry the qualities of an equity investment. The interest accrued for shareholder loans in each period is often capitalised (i.e. not paid out but added to the existing principal amount) depending on the current yield requirements of the shareholders.

In order to reconcile the interests of the sponsors with those of the lenders, the equity ratio generally amounts to between 10 and 40% of the total financing volume of a project depending on its (perceived) risk profile. In unusual times, a higher share may be requested by the creditors (see also Section 5.2.1).

Every investor on any level of the capital structure is interested in minimising its risks and limiting its liability. The same holds for equity investors, even though they are most exposed. Accordingly, many – while by no means all – equity investors prefer to keep the share of equity as low as possible, which serves to increase the return on capital employed (leverage effect). By increasing the level of debt instead of allowing/asking for additional equity contributions from third parties, equity providers also prevent the dilution of their own interests. However, in principal, a high level of debt increases the level of risk of any investment by making it more vulnerable to unexpected revenue or cost irregularities. The irony is that risk averse investors in certain instances may be better advised to increase their equity share if they aim to reduce their level of risk.

The goals of the providers of equity and debt differ when it comes to the optimal level of leverage. Lenders usually insist on an equity ratio that provides a comfortable coverage for their loan. They further prefer the equity to be fully paid in before any debt is drawn upon, despite the fact that it is also possible for the equity to be contributed alongside the debt on a pro rata basis. A sufficient financial commitment by the providers of equity is a sign of confidence for the financing parties regarding the seriousness of the project sponsors and the feasibility of the project. Further, it helps to align the interests of all project participants.

The public sector is subject to a conflict of interests in respect to the optimal equity share in PPP projects. On the one hand, it has an interest in minimising its total costs by minimising the equity ratio, because this serves to reduce the subsequent annual fee (e.g. availability payments) payable by the public sector to the project company. (Given that equity is generally more expensive than debt, a lower equity ratio reduces the overall costs of the project for the equity providers; the public sector may or may not be among the equity providers, depending on the contractual model applied/chosen; see Chapter 3.) On the other hand, the public sector has to reconcile the interests of the private partners to the greatest possible extent with its own in order to secure the provision of services and achieve economic stability within the project. In this context, a high equity share represents a credible commitment to secure the contractual agreements and prevent opportunistic behaviour.

Although equity investors generally share certain financial goals, they do not form a homogeneous group. Their individual interests may differ regarding their investment horizon, among others (see also Sections 1.2 and 1.3.8). To this end, a good financing structure is often considered to include long-term capital tie-up, as sought after by most long-term oriented yield investors, short- to medium-term-oriented, return-maximising IRR investors, in contrast, require the possibility of an early exit option. Therefore, to attract both kinds of investors, the financing structure must allow the option to sell the interest in a project/asset after a certain date prior to, for example, the end of the project lifetime or prior to the repayment of the debt without jeopardising the long-term success of the financing or the entire project/asset. Such an arrangement does not contradict the principle of reconciliation of the interests of the sponsors, the principal and the lenders, provided that the contractual agreements are made accordingly and the sale of an equity interest is contingent on the fulfilment of certain conditions and/or milestones, for example scheduled project/asset development and/or economic success.

As a matter of principle, the following exit strategies may come into consideration for equity investors in infrastructure (see also Chapter 1):

- *Sale via the secondary market*, i.e. some or all of the investors involved in the transaction may and/or must sell their interests in the company to one or several new (*financial*) investor(s) – individually or simultaneously.[1]
- *Trade sale*, i.e. some (mostly all) of the investors invested in the asset can and/or must sell their interests to one or several new (*strategic*) investor(s) individually or simultaneously.
- *IPO:* an individual infrastructure project, a portfolio of infrastructure projects or an infrastructure investment vehicle may be listed on the stock exchange. Bundling several infrastructure project companies can create sizeable portfolios with stable revenue streams, attractive returns and a diversified risk structure (for a discussion of some of the issues in respect to listed infrastructure assets/funds, see Sections 2.1 and 2.3).

7.2 MEZZANINE CAPITAL

Mezzanine capital legally qualifies as an interest-bearing loan that is subordinate to senior debt given its terms and conditions. In practice, however, mezzanine is a hybrid of debt and

---

[1] In the market for secondary funds interests, investors usually can and do sell their shares independently of the remaining fund investors.

equity financing; it is debt capital that gives the lender the right to convert the debt into equity ownership under certain conditions. Closely examined, any specific hybrid instrument of such subordinated capital can be allocated relatively clearly to either equity or debt. Mezzanine capital may be an appropriate solution when liable equity capital cannot be obtained from investors in the required volume or is too expensive and conventional commercial loans can only be granted to a limited extent.

Accordingly, a fundamental distinction is made between mezzanine capital with the characteristics of equity (interest-bearing instruments which include a participation in the value appreciation of the project) and debt (interest only, often divided into a cash relevant, i.e. a current interest-paying portion and a capitalised portion). Innovative mezzanine structures such as payment in kind (e.g. movable and immovable assets) are growing in importance.

In terms of risk, mezzanine finance is placed somewhere between traditional loans against collateral and equity. Typically, mezzanine finance is subordinate to traditional senior loans, tax-deductible, terminable, flexible with respect to terms and conditions and has a wide range of potential uses. For the purposes of project finance, mezzanine capital usually bears a portion of the project risks and hence assumes a certain liability function.

In the same way as providers of debt, issuers of mezzanine capital base their investment decision on the expected project cash flows and the covenants issued by the borrower, which grant certain rights of information, participation or control.

7.3 DEBT

Debt is the most important source of finance for infrastructure projects and assets in general. It typically accounts for between 60 and 90% of (project) financing (including mezzanine capital and subsidies where applicable; see Section 7.1 for exceptions). This section primarily addresses the long-term financing instruments of senior, possibly syndicated, loans and bonds, because these are central to the realisation of any financing. Short-term instruments, such as working capital facilities, supplier loans, trade credit and leases, will be mentioned only in passing for the sake of completeness.

7.3.1 Senior loans

Senior (bank) loans are the traditional debt instrument for any financing, including project finance. Senior loans that are provided by a consortium of banks and/or financial investors (syndicate or club), are also referred to as 'syndicated (bank) loans' (discussed in Section 7.3.1.2) or club deals (see Section 7.3.1.3). In contrast to bonds, the terms and conditions of senior loans can be tailored to the individual requirements of each project or asset to a large extent. Most importantly, the interest and principal payments can be adjusted to reflect the cash flows of the (project) company.

The interest rate for any debt is determined based on a reference interest rate (e.g. Euribor is applied for euro-denominated loans and Libor for dollar-denominated ones) and a project/asset-specific margin. The level of the margin is based on current market and industry standards and the risk profile of the respective infrastructure project/asset (project/asset- and sponsor-specific risks), as well as the yield expectations of the lenders. The interest rate for the term of the debt may be variable, fixed or tied to a specific corridor (interval). In the event of fixed interest rates, banks generally refinance them using swap transactions while financial investors very often do not (for more information on interest rate structures and interest rate swaps, see Sections 5.2.1 and 7.7). Interest rate conditions may also be fixed over a period of more than 10 years, usually involving interest rate hedges.[2]

7.3.1.1 Traditional senior loan

The average term of a traditional senior (project finance) loan provided by banks is 7–12 years. Renewable energy or PPP projects, for example, generally require loan durations of 20–30 years, or longer in exceptional cases. For these kinds of maturities, usually development banks come in and provide substantial parts of the financing (see Section 7.4 for details). Lately, long-term-oriented financial yield investors have entered this segment of the debt market, which is favourable for the financing of long-term infrastructure assets.

Irrespective of the term, lenders usually insist on repayment of their loans approximately two to five years before the end of the calculated project term, which is, for instance, when a granted concession or licence for a motorway or hospital runs out (see Section 5.4 and Chapter 6, for the interest rate and financing risk resulting from such a situation). The purpose of leaving a so-called 'tail' of several years is to ensure that there is sufficient time to get the (project) company back on track or restructure the loan in case the borrower encounters difficulties repaying the loan. The main goal of the lenders is that the loan will be repaid in full by the end of the concession or licence of the (project) company.

Senior loans have the lowest level of risk of all financing instruments. They are secured by way of standard collateral, such as:

- Assigning all present and future claims of the (project) company arising from the material (project) agreements/contracts;
- Pledging the shares in the (project) company held by the equity owners and the balances on the (project) company accounts;
- Ensuring sufficient capitalisation;
- Maintaining reserve and liquidity accounts (e.g. debt service and/or maintenance reserves);
- Achieving defined financial covenants;
- Granting defined rights of subrogation to the financiers.

Interest and principal payments on the loan are senior to all other debt financings. The repayment of the loan is usually not tied to the success of the project, meaning the lenders are not generally liable for the inherent business risk. Notwithstanding, they are affected if a (project) company does not succeed according to plan and will need to engage in renegotiations.

---

[2]This option, however, is not normally offered in Germany; instead, the loan is divided into several loans spread across the overall term of the finance, for example 25 years (which may be two loans with a term of 10 years plus one loan with a term of five years). This procedure is enshrined in German law (section 489 of the new version of the German Civil Code and section 609a of the old version of the German Civil Code), which states that a borrower may partially or fully terminate a fixed-rate loan after 10 years by giving six months' notice, irrespective of the contractual term originally agreed. This right is exercised by borrowers if interest rates are lower at the end of a 10-year period than when the loan was initially offered. In order to prevent the risk of termination – because this could result in significant costs for the bank if it has already conducted refinancing transactions – German banks do not generally offer loans with a term of more than 10 years.

In the case of larger transaction volumes, there are often tranches of senior and junior (or subordinated) debt. The difference primarily relates to the order (priority) of capital repayment. Subordinated debt will be serviced after the senior debt and generally has a greater likelihood of default. Therefore, junior debt requires a higher interest rate in order to reflect this increased level of risk.

7.3.1.2 Syndicated loan

The main difference between traditional senior loans by a single debt provider, typically a bank, and syndicated loans is that the latter are made available by a group of debt providers, typically a group of banks (the syndicate) and then placed on/sold down to the wider debt market by this syndicate. The goal is to diversify credit risk – and earn money on arranger fees. Syndications are commonly chosen for large transactions because of the significant exposure of individual lenders: in some cases, even major international banks would be temporarily overextended if required to underwrite these sizeable loans in their own right or be unwilling to do so, owing to potential cluster risks.[3] Several debt providers may form a syndicate under the management of one bank (or, in some cases, a group of banks) – known as the 'lead arranger' or the 'lead manager' – to structure and arrange the financing of a large transaction. The financing offer submitted by the lead arranger to the borrower contains all the terms and conditions and the planned structure of the financing. Similar to a traditional bank loan, the structure is tailored to the respective project/asset, particularly with regard to positive and negative future cash flows, debt service and options for flexible loan disbursement. In the financing offer, the lead arranger indicates the amount of the loan, which it will keep on its own books after syndication is complete (final take). This is usually around 10% of the total volume. From the borrower's perspective, but also from the perspective of the other debt providers, who ultimately participate in the loan, the final take is relevant because it reflects the long-term commitment and conviction of the arranger to the transaction and its long-term sustainability.

The lead arranger forms the aforementioned arranging group in conjunction with other lenders (co-arrangers or managers), whose underwriting primarily depends on the attractiveness of the respective transaction, the structure of the financing as well as the fee structure offered to them by the lead arranger (the lead arranger usually receives the largest share of the commission because it is responsible for acquiring the project and overseeing the structuring and arrangement of the financing). The commitment of these co-arrangers or managers to the financing completes the first phase of the syndication, known as 'underwriting'. That is, the individual debt providers firmly commit to underwrite defined amounts of the overall loan (underwriting commitment). Up to this point, the lead arranger is contractually obliged to provide the full amount of the loan to the borrower itself.

From the lead arranger's perspective, it is advantageous to attract prestigious banks to the syndicate, which can further place the loan in question on the debt market following the underwriting. During the next stage, the syndicate offers smaller tranches of the overall loan (usually less than the final take of the lead arranger and the managers) to other interested lenders, (co-) managers or participants. When placing loans for foreign projects, it may become necessary to involve local banks in the financing alongside international banks, primarily for political considerations.

---

[3]Collection of risk of the same type (e.g. same geographical location, same industry) or with the same structure.

Financial, long-term, yield-oriented investors, who have long bought infrastructure bonds in private (or public) placements (see Section 7.3.2), are now also moving into the loan market. They are buyers of syndicated tranches but may also enter loan syndicates from the start alongside banks. Financial investors who make the extra effort to enter such syndicates early on will likely want to hold the loan until maturity.

Syndicated loans are characterised by a quite comprehensive set of contractual agreements covering, among others, the nature and extent of the collateral demanded by the lenders. Three types of lending terms and conditions are of particular importance: covenants, representations and warranties and events of default. The lenders may also request certain control rights in the credit agreement.

SYNDICATED LOAN

Bank A is commissioned to structure and arrange a €400 million financing package for a project/company. The desired final take of Bank A after successful syndication is €50 million. For the underwriting phase, Bank A (lead arranger) includes three banks (managers) in the banking syndicate, each of which initially underwrites €100 million, as does Bank A. The aim of each of the managers is to keep a final take of €40 million on their books after syndication. In the course of syndication, a further 10 banks (co-managers) are invited to participate in the overall loan amount with an average interest of €23 million.

7.3.1.3 Club deal A club deal in this debt context describes a scenario in which several lenders – as opposed to one lead manager – gather early on during the structuring phase of a financing. They jointly negotiate and mutually agree on the terms and the structure and underwrite together the entire loan amount. This approach – often causing financing to take longer to put together – may be selected when any individual lender considers the risk of underwriting the entire loan amount as arranger in its own right to be too high, or when the prospect of finding other banks to underwrite the transaction afterwards is not particularly promising. Also, the borrower may be the one interested in involving certain banks in the syndicate from the start in order to establish business relationships or to reflect local customs.

7.3.2 Bonds

For large transactions (project volume in excess of €200 million) and long durations, a bond may be issued instead of, in addition to or after obtaining a loan. As opposed to loans, which may be tailored to the borrower's financing needs, bonds must have a specific term and a specific form of interest and principal repayment. The term and the interest rate of a bond depend on the quality and requirements of the (project) company as well as the current situation in the capital markets and, hence, the investor appetite.

Generally speaking, there are two types of bonds: (i) fixed-interest and (ii) variable-interest bonds. Fixed interest bonds are the rule. Exceptions excluded, they provide investors with planning security regarding the annual current yields. For insurance groups and other investors whose liabilities tend to be fixed in absolute amounts, fixed interest bonds thus tend to be a perfect investment. For pension fund type investors whose liabilities are inflation linked, variable interest bonds, the margins of which are equally linked to inflation, are more suitable. Therefore, the disadvantage of cash flows of variable-interest bonds being more difficult to forecast, due to the inherent interest rate risk, is not a major issue for pension funds in contrast to e.g. insurance groups (see Sections 2.1, 5.2.2 and 7.3.1).

A bond may be placed via one or several banks privately or on the open market. Private placements are primarily offered directly to institutional investors, such as insurance companies and pension funds. Private placements have the advantage of allowing issuers to circumvent the time-consuming and costly initial listing, prospectus preparation, rating, placement on the market and ongoing capital market communications. In addition, funds can be generated more quickly.

Compared with syndicated loans, bonds are advantageous in that they generally have longer terms, sometimes as long as 50 years, and superior interest rate conditions (depending on the respective rating). However, bonds offer little or no flexibility in the event of a change in the borrower's conditions requiring adjustments to the available debt finance, for example an unexpectedly severe fall of projected revenues, early redemption or amendments to the interest and repayment structure. Among other things, this lack of flexibility is due to the broad distribution of the bond in public, and hence the large number of bondholders. In contrast, in the case of loan financings, the limited number of syndicate lenders means the providers of debt tend to have a direct relationship to the borrower and hence can be contacted easily in order to initiate negotiations if needed.

A further drawback of bonds may be the fact that the capital from the bond is provided in a lump sum at a fixed point in time (e.g. at the start of the construction phase) even if the capital is required only successively in tranches in line with the construction progress of the project. This means the interest burden for the borrower is higher, because interest must be paid on the full amount of the bond from provision, whereas loan interest is only payable incrementally based on the amounts drawn down.

In Anglo-Saxon countries, and the UK, Canada and Australia in particular, bond issues to finance infrastructure projects/assets, including PPPs are relatively common, with the result that there is a relatively liquid market for shares in PPP bonds. The buyers are primarily insurance companies and private or corporate pension funds. In the rest of the world, only a few bonds of this type have been issued to date, meaning that no real corresponding market exists. Bond financing is expected to become increasingly important globally, however, as the number and volume of infrastructure transactions grow.

GREEN AND CLIMATE BONDS

Within the US$100 trillion global bond universe (Bank for International Settlements, 2014) develops a small but rapidly growing 'green' and 'climate' bond market.[4] 'Labelled' green or climate bonds, which are only a small part of this market so far, are characterised by the fact that their proceeds are officially earmarked for eligible climate

---

[4]The terms 'green bond' and 'climate bond' are often used interchangeable in media publications since standards are still being developed to specifically define these two new bond products.

protection projects while the pricing is comparable to non-green bonds from the same issuer. Green bonds are used to finance projects devoted to climate protection (low-carbon investments and climate adaptation) as well as other environmental protection measures, such as renewable energy and energy-efficiency measures, climate-related flood protection infrastructure and other endeavours to reduce greenhouse gas emissions (UNEP, 2014). Climate bonds allow investors to increase the sustainability of their bond portfolio while meeting their fixed-income yield and risk requirements (Climate Bond Initiative, 2015a).

The green and climate bond market developed rapidly since its humble beginnings in 2007, when the European Investment Bank issued a first environmental-themed bond, the Climate Awareness Bond (EIB, 2015). In 2008, the Swedish bank SEB partnered with the International Bank for Reconstruction and Development (IBRD) – one of five institutions that make up the World Bank Group – and issued the world's first independently reviewed green bond (AAA rated fixed income product). In 2015, $US41.8 billion labelled green bonds have been issued (see Figure 7.2) (Climate Bond Initiative, 2016). The largest issuers of green bonds to date are the development banks, mainly the European Investment Bank, the World Bank and the German development bank KfW. Similar to 2014, corporate issuers, banks and municipalities have been important issuers of climate bonds as well, the latter to finance green property projects for universities and sustainable water projects. There was also a widening of the type of projects financed by green bonds, with more capital targeting the green sector outside of the

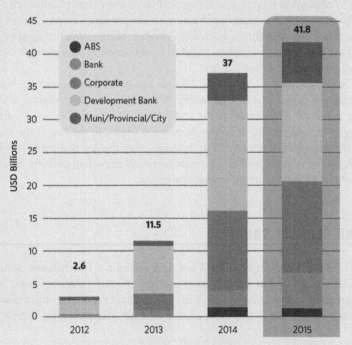

FIGURE 7.2   The 'labelled' green bond market, 2012–2015
Source: Replicated from Climate Bond Initiative (2015a)

renewable energy space, namely low carbon transport and sustainable water (Climate Bond Initiative, 2016).

Green ABSs (Asset Backed Securities) have emerged in 2013 with the first municipal ABS issued in 2014. Local governments issue municipal bonds and use the proceeds, for example, to make loans to building owners that want to make renewable energy or energy-efficiency upgrades and installations (e.g. the US Property Assessed Clean Energy, or PACE, bond). The loan is then repaid through a property tax assessment.

In May 2015, the German real estate and mortgage bank BerlinHyp issued the first labelled green 'Pfandbrief', a covered bond (FT, 2015), meaning a bond with a dual recourse to the issuer and a cover pool of assets (Climate Bond Initiative, 2015a). Proceeds of the €500m bond issue have been earmarked for green assets within the cover pool (i.e. mortgages of certified green buildings in Europe). The issue was four times oversubscribed and it is expected that further green covered bond issuances will follow as real estate accounts for the largest part of the €2400 billion covered bond market. (Climate Bond Initiative, 2015b).

In 2015, almost half of all labelled green bond proceeds financed renewable energy projects (46%); the second biggest use of proceeds relates to energy efficiency (20%), followed by transport (13%), water (9%) and waste (6%) projects (Climate Bond Initiative, 2015b) (see Figure 7.3).

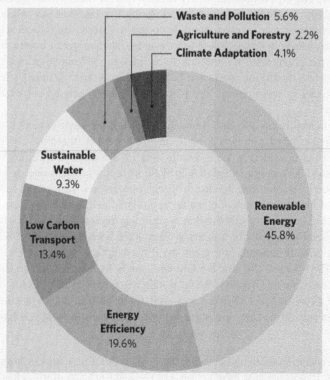

FIGURE 7.3 Green bonds use of proceeds (2015)
Source: Replicated from Climate Bond Initiative (2015a)

Investor demand for labelled green bonds is strong. Issuances are regularly strongly oversubscribed or upsized. An example is the offering of KfW, which in 2015 doubled a A$300m green bond issue to A$600m (Climate Bonds Initiative, 2015b) as well as the Third EUR Climate Awareness Bond (CAB) issuance of the EIB of above €1.5bn, which amounts to €13bn of Green Bonds issued by EIB to date via 59 CABs in 11 currencies (EIB, 2016). Moreover, large institutional investors such as Zurich Insurance, Deutsche Bank and Barclays Treasury pledged to build billion-euro green bond portfolios and several green bond funds are being established by some of the world's largest asset managers (World Bank, 2015c).

Yet, green-labelled bonds make up only close to 10% of the much larger universe of estimated US$531.8 billion unlabelled climate-aligned bonds as defined by the Climate Bonds Taxonomy (Climate Bond Initiative, 2015c). Unlabelled climate-aligned bonds are bonds issued by companies with over 95% of revenues derived from climate-aligned assets. The largest theme is transport (e.g. rail transport) with over US$400 billion bonds outstanding since 2005. So-called low-carbon rail bonds in China account for the majority of the transport theme. The second-largest sector is energy, with close to US$120 billion in bonds outstanding (Climate Bond Initiative, 2015b).

The vast majority of climate-aligned bonds are investment grade (BB– or above) and they are denominated in 37 different currencies, mainly though in Chinese Yuan, USD, EUR and GBP. The report notes that only around 47% of the US$500 billion in bonds (US$236.6 billion) would likely meet the grade rating, currency and size requirements of the majority of mainstream investment grade portfolios. Moreover, issuers of unlabelled climate-aligned bonds are expected to start issuing labelled green bonds, thus taking advantage of the green label by attracting new investors. Companies are required to track and report on qualifying assets and be certified by a credible independent review. The market leader in wind power, Vestas, chose to label a general corporate purpose bond as green.

There is currently no universal standard to ensure the environmental integrity of green and climate bond products in this emerging market, therefore investors must be cautious when considering such investments as a means of meeting sustainable investment goals. As recommended in a 2014 Ceres report on clean energy investment, 'standardization will minimize the due diligence burden on investors and reduce transaction costs of investing in newer clean energy-related investment products [and] will also increase the liquidity of climate bonds and other products' (Ceres, 2014a). In the meantime, several standards for voluntary usage have been developed to assist issuers and investors alike in entering the green bond marketplace, such as the Green Bond Principles (GBP) (Ceres, 2014b), the Climate Bonds Standard (Climate Bond Initiative, 2015d) and China's Green Financial Bonds Directive (GFBD). Ceres' GBP were developed by a coalition of 13 banks,[5] and over 100 institutions have signed up to these principles as of July 2015. They provide issuers with guidance on the key components of a

---

[5]This coalition comprises the following banks: Bank of America, Citigroup, Crédit Agricole CIB, Deutsche Bank, JPMorgan Chase, BNP Paribas, Daiwa, Goldman Sachs, HSBC, Mizuho, Morgan Stanley, Rabobank and SEB.

credible green bond and support investors by ensuring the availability of the information needed to evaluate the environmental impact of their investments. In addition to the 'Climate Bond Standard', the Climate Bond Initiative developed a certification scheme that provides investors and governments assurance of the environmental integrity of so-called climate bonds. End of 2015, the People's Bank of China released the GFBD, which outlines standards on how to use 'green bonds'. The directive is the country's first guideline on green bonds, which should help significantly scale up their use and ensure increased development of low-carbon projects like renewable energy and public transit systems in China (World Resources Institute, 2016).

7.3.3 Short-term finance

7.3.3.1 Working capital facilities Banks provide short-term funds for the financing of day-to-day operations. These take the form of flexible working capital facilities and are primarily used for the advance financing of stocks and inventories as well as customer receivables.

7.3.3.2 Supplier loans Traditional supplier loans need to be mentioned for the sake of completeness. The suppliers or customers of the (project) company may choose to grant it more favourable payment terms. This form of credit is normally comparatively expensive and should be used only to resolve temporary liquidity bottlenecks.

7.4 GOVERNMENT SUPPORT SCHEMES

Government support schemes are and have been a crucial source for the financing of infrastructure in addition to equity, debt and mezzanine capital. This holds for both industrial nations, to a lesser extent, and more importantly for emerging markets and developing countries. A wide range of possible development schemes may come into consideration depending on the nature of the project and a number of additional factors. These may be incorporated into the overall financing structure in various ways. Repayable grants, low-interest loans and guarantees are particularly relevant in the context of infrastructure assets as they tend to require financing over very long terms, which commercial banks usually are not prepared to provide — or only alongside development banks.

Sources for support programmes are made available on a national level by state-owned development banks such as KfW in Germany, the Japanese Bank for International Cooperation (JBIC) or the Overseas Private Investment Corporation (OPIC) in the US, to name a few. The European Investment Bank (EIB), the European Bank for Reconstruction and Development (EBRD) and the European Union (EU) provide capital at the European level. The usage of these funds does not necessarily have to happen within the geography of the respective institutions.

Global or international organisations comparable to the EIB or EBRD on a European level primarily include multilateral institutions such as the World Bank Group and its subsidiaries: the International Finance Corporation (IFC), the International Bank for Reconstruction and Development (IBRD), as well as the International Development Agency (IDA), the Inter-American Development Bank (IDB), the Asian Development Bank (ADB) and the African

Development Bank (AfDB), among others. It is also possible to use indirect support programmes by involving state-owned or private ECAs, which support the export transactions of domestic companies by providing export credit guarantees. In the same way, support programmes for direct foreign investments are offered both by the respective national governments as well as international organisations such as the Multilateral Investment Guarantee Agency (MIGA), a subsidiary of the World Bank.

The various, above-mentioned economic development activities cannot always unambiguously be allocated to a specific kind of institution. Each country tends to have its own, somewhat unique, way of organising and structuring its development activities using different kinds of institutions. Germany, for instance, has the public development bank (KfW) and the ECA (Hermes). The US is similarly organised with the OPIC and the US EXIM Bank. Japan in turn takes a different approach altogether and combines almost all support activities under one roof in the JBIC. In the following sections, these three national development banks are briefly introduced: the German KfW, the American OPIC and the Japanese JBIC. In addition, the EIB and its various support programmes are highlighted. EPEC, the European PPP Expertise Centre, is briefly mentioned, given the relevance of PPP within the infrastructure context. Finally, the role of ECAs and some of their national representatives are introduced. The large number and variety of extraordinary support schemes developed by governments and the ECB in the wake of the subprime crisis, are not the subject of this book.

7.4.1   National development banks

7.4.1.1   Kreditanstalt für Wiederaufbau (KfW) – Germany   As a bank owned by the German federal government (80%) and the federal states (20%), the KfW Bankengruppe, headquartered in Frankfurt, supports the economy, the society and the environment in Germany and abroad. The KfW Group encompasses a total of four brands/subsidiaries with different objectives:

- *KfW-IPEX Bank* is a wholly owned subsidiary of KfW, responsible for project and export financing.
- *KfW-Development Bank* provides finance and support programmes mainly to public-sector players in developing countries and emerging economies.
- *DENA* (German Energy Agency) is Germany's centre of expertise for energy efficiency, renewable energy sources (RES) and intelligent energy systems. It promotes energy generation, networks, storage and use with maximum efficiency, safety, affordability and climate protection both nationally and internationally.
- *DEG* (*Deutsche Entwicklungs- und Investitionsgesellschaft*) provides structuring and finance for investments by private companies in developing countries.

DEG, in addition to providing finance, serves as one of the three official public partners of a special PPP programme (develoPPP.de) of the Federal German Ministry for Economic Cooperation and Development (BMZ). The programme targets companies that invest in developing countries and are seeking ways to shape their corporate commitment in the long term. BMZ provides up to €200 000 and maximum 50% of the project cost out of public funds. Partnerships with the private sector may last up to a maximum of three years and cover a wide variety of areas and topics (KfW-Förderbank, 2015).

7.4.1.2 Overseas Private Investment Corporation (OPIC) – USA

OPIC supports US foreign policy by primarily helping American businesses invest overseas and complementing the private sector in managing risks associated with foreign direct investment. OPIC services are available for new and expanding business enterprises in more than 150 countries worldwide. OPIC pursues three main areas of business: financing, political risk insurance and investments in private equity funds.[6]

OPIC provides medium- to long-term funding through direct loans and investment guaranties to eligible investment projects in developing countries and emerging markets. It does so through certificates of participation (COPs) and via third-party lenders. In 2014, OPIC introduced 'Green Guaranties' for projects that adhere to the GBP (Green Bond Policies), developed in 2014. Examples of potential eligible projects include renewable energy plants, clean transportation and sustainable waste management facilities (also see Section 7.3.2.1). In addition to financial products, OPIC offers risk-mitigation products, which protect against losses to tangible assets, investment value and earnings that result from political perils such as war, political violence (including terrorism) and government-imposed restrictions (Overseas Private Investment Corporation, 2009).

7.4.1.3 Japanese Bank for International Cooperation (JBIC) – Japan

JBIC[7] is a policy-based financial institution of Japan that conducts lending, investment and guarantee operations while complementing private-sector financial institutions. The aim of JBIC is to promote overseas business development and securement of important resources as well as to preserve the global environment, prevent disruptions in the international financial system or take appropriate measures with respect to damages caused by such disruption.

JBIC's main financing activities include: import and export loans, overseas investment loans, united loans, bridge loans, equity participation and research activities. In addition, guarantees are offered for: performance bonds, product import, corporate bonds issued by Japanese companies and overseas syndicated loads/government bonds. JBIC also extends credit by acquiring loan receivables by assignment as well as government bonds and corporate debentures issued for funding their projects (JBIC, 2015).

7.4.2 European Investment Bank (EIB)

The EIB was created by the Treaty of Rome in 1958 as the long-term lending bank of the EU. The task of the EIB is to contribute towards the integration, balanced development and economic and social cohesion of EU Member States. The EIB raises substantial volumes of funds on the capital markets that it lends on favourable terms to projects furthering EU policy objectives. To this end, it continuously adapts its activity to reflect developments in EU policies (EIB, 2015).

---

[6]Private equity investments outside of infrastructure are not the subject of this book and, hence, are not discussed further.

[7]The International Financial Operations (IFOs) of the JBIC, National Life Finance Corporation (NLFC), Agriculture, Forestry and Fisheries Finance Corporation (AFC) and Japan Finance Corporation for Small and Medium Enterprise (JASME) merged in 2008, to become a new policy-based financing institution: the Japan Finance Corporation (JFC). However, in order to maintain the international trust and confidence gained by JBIC, the international department of JFC continues to use the name JBIC when conducting international finance operations.

The EIB finances a broad range of projects in a number of geographical regions, focusing on Europe in particular, in all sectors of the economy. The projects promoted by its public- or private-sector clients and eligible for EIB funding must be economically, financially, technically and environmentally sound and adhere to at least one of its seven lending objectives, which are directly derived from the EU economic policy objectives (EIB, 2015).

The EIB enjoys financial autonomy within the EU and operates in keeping with strict banking practice in close collaboration with the wider banking community, both when borrowing on the capital markets and when financing capital projects (EIB, 2015). Notwithstanding, it cooperates with other EU institutions, especially the European Commission, the European Parliament and the Council of the EU.

In the same way as development banks, the EIB does not provide subsidies but primarily extends loans and increasingly equity. The EIB is rated triple-A, which allows it to achieve favourable refinancing terms on the capital markets, which it passes on to borrowers by offering loans at cost, thereby substantially reducing the overall financing costs of selected projects.

As a rule, the EIB lends up to 50% of the investment costs of any given project. To this end, it has two main financing facilities: *individual loans*, which are provided directly to projects and programmes in both the public and private sectors, costing more than €25 million and *intermediated loans*, which are credit lines to banks and financial institutions to help them provide finance to small and medium-sized enterprises (SMEs) with eligible investment programmes or projects costing less than €25 million.

The EIB also has a range of specialised lending instruments:

- *Structured Finance Facility:* created to provide funding to projects with a high-risk profile and to pursue equity financing and guarantee operations in favour of large-scale infrastructure schemes.
- *Risk-Sharing Finance Facility:* created in conjunction with the European Commission to expand the EIB's basis for providing higher-risk financing for innovative projects in the sectors of technology platforms and research and development.
- *Carbon Credit Funds:* created in collaboration with institutions such as the EBRD and the World Bank to develop the carbon market in transition countries and to encourage private-sector participation.

In 2014 the EIB disbursed €65 billion in support of its EU economic policy objectives, €59.3 billion of which went to countries in the Member States of the EU and EFTA. The total outstanding volume of signed loans as of the end of 2014 amounted to €549bn (end-2013: €522bn), of which 89% were for projects within the EU (end-2013: 90%). The volume of loans actually disbursed by the end of the year amounted to €450bn (end-2013: €428bn) of which €63.6 was invested in infrastructure (transport, energy, water, severage, telecommunications and social infrastructure) (EIB, 2015).

Furthermore, the EIB has a dedicated infrastructure funding program under which it has committed over €1 billion to 25 equity and two debt funds (EIB, 2015).

In October 2014, the EIB agreed to partner with some of the world's largest asset management and private equity firms, pension funds, insurance groups and commercial banks – under the leadership of the Word Bank – on the new Global Infrastructure Facility (GIF) that has the potential to unlock billions of dollars for infrastructure investment in the developing world.

In 2015, the EIB announced that the European Fund for Strategic Investment (EFSI) would be the key instrument of the European Commission's 'Juncker Plan for Investment in Europe' – intended to reverse the trends of falling investment within Europe (European Commission, 2015). The goal is to inject at least €315 billion in the real economy over three years (2015–2017) promoting PPP solutions. The Plan consists of three strategic directions: (1) mobilising capital without creating public debt; (2) supporting projects and investments in key areas such as infrastructure, education, research and innovation; and (3) removing sector-specific and other non-financial barriers to investment. Targeted infrastructure includes broadband and energy networks, renewable energy generation and energy efficiency as well as transport infrastructure in industrial centres (see www.eib.org for further information).

7.4.3   European PPP Expertise Centre (EPEC)

The EIB together with the European Commission took a lead on PPP expertise and launched EPEC in 2008. EPEC is designed to strengthen the organisational capacity of the public sector to engage in PPP transactions and thereby to help grow the European PPP market (EPEC, 2015).

EPEC's aims to enable public authorities in the EU Member and Candidate Countries to become more effective participants in PPPs and thereby identifying best practice in issues of common concern as well as to reduce costs and increase deal flow. To this end, EPEC offers structured network activities and policy programme support, sharing experience as well as pooling and synthesising information from across the EU on requirements for transactions and skill sets. EPEC does not offer advice on individual projects (EPEC, 2015).

Membership of EPEC is free, limited to public authorities whose role includes policy responsibility and the promotion of PPP projects or programmes at the national or regional level. EPEC currently has 41 members (2014), including the EIB, the European Commission and national or regional authorities responsible for PPP policy or programmes in their jurisdictions (EPEC, 2015).

7.4.4   Governmental export credit and direct investment insurance – ECAs

In addition to national, regional and multilateral development banks and institutions, a project may seek to hedge political and economic risk by calling on governmental and private ECAs, which support the export transactions of companies by providing export loan guarantees as part of the (indirect) promotion of exports (see also Section 5.2.1). Depending on the respective export transaction, the assumption of economic and political risk by these insurers may differ in terms of the type of goods being insured, the definition of the insured event and the amount and structure of the cover provided. In the case of export promotion by the German federal government (Hermes cover), for example, guarantees are provided only to exporters domiciled in Germany or the domestic banks financing the export transaction. The goods or services underlying the cover must also be primarily German in origin.

Most countries have comparable schemes and programmes that follow the same principle, this is support their respective national industries. The Export Credits Guarantee Department (ECGD) of the UK's official ECA, for instance, aims to help UK exporters of capital equipment and project-related goods and services win business. In addition, it provides insurance to UK exporters against non-payment by their overseas buyers, guarantees for bank loans to facilitate the provision of finance to buyers of goods and services from UK companies and political risk insurance to UK investors in overseas markets.

In the USA, the US Export-Import Bank (EXIM Bank) is the principal government agency responsible for supporting the export of American goods and services, and thereby creating and sustaining jobs through a variety of loan, guarantee and insurance programmes. Generally, its programmes are available to any American export firm regardless of size. The Japanese provide these kinds of services under the roof of the JBIC (see Section 7.4.1.3).

In addition to the insurance of export transactions for risk-hedging purposes, direct foreign investments may be specifically insured against political risk. This insurance takes the form of long-term investment guarantees for the non-commercial risks of foreign investors. Insurance of this nature is provided by all industrialised nations as well as the World Bank subsidiary MIGA. Both insurance alternatives essentially cover the same political risks. In Germany, for example, the federal government offers political risk guarantees for direct foreign investments that are eligible for promotion (*Bund für förderungswürdige Direktinvestitionen*). This includes investments in foreign companies, the capitalisation of foreign branches and production premises of German companies and loans extended to foreign companies that are similar to investments.

Guarantees may also cover contributions distributed as dividends or payable as interest on guaranteed investments as well as loans that are similar to investments for a specific period. In providing coverage for investment projects, MIGA works in close cooperation with investors, public and private credit insurers and development policy lenders (KfW and DEG in Germany). Contracts guaranteed by MIGA are also refinanced by ECAs in the context of export finance transactions. Obtaining this form of risk cover serves to reduce political risk, and hence improve the basis of calculation for many investment projects. Accordingly, private banks involved in project finance often demand an investment guarantee, the claims of which are assigned to the financing banks (see www.miga.org).

7.5 ASSET-BACKED SECURITIES

Structures such as ABSs are financing instruments that seek to generate additional liquidity through the sale of company assets. This primarily relates to current assets of the same type – particularly receivables – that can demonstrate a sustainable cash flow (see Figure 7.4).

The assets are sold to a special-purpose vehicle (SPV), which bundles them and refinances them on the credit or money market by issuing securities that are backed by the assets acquired. In other words, ABSs serve to securitise the future cash flows of the underlying receivables. The seller receives a direct cash injection less a discount the moment the assets are sold, whereas the buyer receives a security with broad risk diversification and usually a guaranteed minimum return. The purchase price of the receivables is often settled in more than one instalment. The first instalment corresponds to the discounted present value of the receivables purchased, reduced by a risk discount calculated on the basis of the historical default rate. Subsequent instalments are paid when the cash receipts of the debtor exceed the first purchase price instalment.

ABS structures are a highly flexible financing instrument that may be used in a more efficient and versatile manner than many other forms of financing, such as traditional loans, corporate bonds or share issues. Generally speaking, any asset with a regular cash flow can be securitised, for example loan receivables (from companies, project finance, mortgages

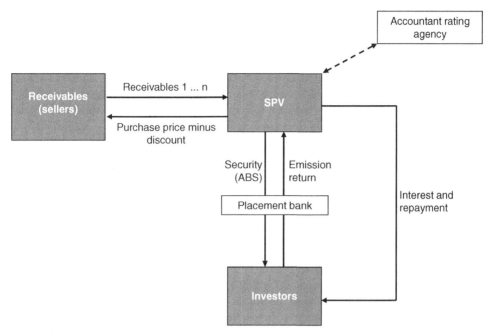

FIGURE 7.4   Asset-backed financing

or consumers), lease agreements, credit card transactions, licence and franchise agreements and all forms of goods and services. Rather than merely securitising and selling assets on a single occasion, the SPV can constantly incorporate new, bundled receivables, resulting in continuous liquidity for the seller and the long-term receipt of interest and principal payments for the buyer of the securities. Forms of collateral in ABS transactions include the cash flow structure of the transaction (e.g. over-collateralisation via the quantitative and qualitative selection of receivables, subordinated funds of the SPV, reserve funds), collateralisation by the seller of the receivables (limited recourse, letters of comfort) and collateralisation by third parties (letters of credit, warranties/guarantees, insurance, assignment of contributions).

As well as the liquidity effect, the benefits for the seller of the securities include a stronger balance sheet, favourable financing conditions due to the involvement of the capital markets, diversified sources of financing and reduced refinancing risk, as well as potential positive tax effects. Disadvantages may include the significant time and effort required to prepare the portfolio of receivables for the sale and to perform due diligence and credit checks as well as the constant flow of documentation subsequently required by the rating agencies in the form of portfolio monitoring and risk management. Furthermore, before structuring an ABS transaction, it must be ensured that the advising bank is capable of placing the securities on the capital markets.

ABS financing solutions may be used in project finance when the receivables held by the project company have a corresponding minimum volume (€30–€35 million), are sufficiently diversified and expect to generate a sufficiently sustainable cash flow (i.e. where possible, the portfolio should encompass a range of debtors with excellent credit ratings). Long-term purchase agreements with creditworthy partners may be sufficient for the structuring of an

ABS transaction even if the receivables relate to a small number of debtors. In this case, however, the potential default risk of the receivables increasingly resembles the credit risk of one or a small number of contractual partners, with the acquisition of the securities more akin to the extension of a loan to the debtors from an investor perspective. In the case of projects in the oil sector, for example, one single customer may be responsible for all the receivables of the project company. On the other hand, oil is a fungible resource, meaning that the purchasing company is under greater pressure to settle the outstanding receivables, because the project company could otherwise find a different buyer on the global market for the extracted oil.

7.6 SALE AND LEASEBACK

Sale and leaseback structures can also increase liquidity for the asset owner. In a sale and leaseback transaction, which is a special form of lease, a company sells movable or immovable fixed assets (land, buildings, machinery) to a leasing company and simultaneously leases the assets back for continued use with the option of repurchasing them after a certain period. The leasing company becomes the economic owner of the assets, whereas the cost of maintenance, insurance and operation generally remains with the lessee.

As is typical for all leasing models, the initial benefit of sale and leaseback structures is that they allow companies to generate a short-term increase in liquidity and free up capital without surrendering the rights to use the respective assets. The seller's equity base also improves as a result of the reduction in balance sheet assets. Depending on their structure, the use of sale and leaseback transactions may also have tax benefits in terms of the identification of hidden reserves in a company's fixed assets. Hidden reserves arise when the market or resale value of an asset is higher than its carrying amount in the seller's balance sheet. The identification of hidden reserves results in the seller realising a profit, which can be offset by tax loss carry-forwards where available.

The lessee (company) pays regular lease instalments for the lease of the asset and recognises these instalments as expenses on its own books, while the leasing company capitalises the acquired asset in its balance sheet, resulting in tax deductible depreciation. As these benefits can be passed on in the amount of the lease instalments, this form of funding is often cheaper than conventional bank loans. One potential drawback is the future impact on the seller's cash flow due to the lease installments. In addition, because the company is no longer the owner of the asset, it will also be unable to participate in any future increase in its value.

As a general rule, the selection of an adequate sale and leaseback structure should focus not only on achieving a short-term improvement in liquidity but also on establishing a long-term overall concept that takes into account all cash flows and tax options, as well as all the related risks.

7.7 DERIVATIVES

Among other things, project cash flows are exposed to interest rate risk and, in the case of projects abroad, exchange rate risk (see Section 5.2.1). Both of these forms of risk can be hedged using derivatives. Derivatives (also known as 'derivative instruments') are tradable financial products such as futures, options, swaps, certificates and so on, and non-standardised forward contracts, the own value of which is derived from the value of the underlying traditional assets (e.g. shares, bonds or gold). Derivatives may also be based on other traded 'objects' or products such as currencies or commodities. The term 'derivative' (from the Latin *derivativus*) generally describes a structure that is derived from another structure, that is, in this case, the price of the instrument generally depends on the established transaction underlying the instrument.

The fundamental principle of a derivative is that the performance and the consideration are not exchanged concurrently as in the case of a spot transaction but instead are agreed in advance for a later date. As such, there is a significant delay between the conclusion of the contract and its fulfilment.

The appeal of trading in derivative instruments is often the fact that they enable full participation in market developments while committing a relatively low level of funds (leverage effect). However, derivatives may also be used to hedge against fluctuations in interest rates and exchange rates, sharp rises in the cost of goods or fluctuations in the price of securities in exchange for the payment of a risk premium.

The most important derivatives exchanges in the world are the CME Group (CME, CBOT, NYMEX and COMEX), Intercontinental Exchange in the US, and the German–Swiss EUREX (Statista, 2015).

When referring to derivatives, a basic distinction is made between futures and options. The following sections provide a simple overview of the functionality of these instruments using interest rate and currency transactions as examples.

7.7.1 Futures

An interest rate future is an agreement to fix an interest rate in future periods with symmetrical risk allocation; that is, the potential gains and losses are identical for each of the parties involved. This category of derivatives includes:

- *Forward rate agreements (FRA):* An FRA is an agreement between two parties to pay or receive a defined interest payment at a fixed date in the future without exchanging the underlying principal amount.
- *Interest rate futures:* An interest rate future is a standardised, exchange-traded futures contract based on an agreement to purchase or sell a specified interest-bearing instrument at a predefined price in the future. Accordingly, FRAs and futures are used to hedge standardised future interest periods. The agreement entails an obligation – rather than an option – to deliver or purchase the relevant securities.
- *Interest rate swaps:* An interest rate swap is an agreement between two parties on the exchange of interest payments (fixed versus variable) in the same currency over a defined term based on a fixed principal amount that is not exchanged (see Figure 7.5).

From the buyer of futures' perspective, the conditions of an exchange transaction of this nature should be determined following an in-depth analysis of the underlying credit structure and cash flows and the related cost of refinancing the credit exposure. The interest rate hedge must serve to ensure structurally congruent refinancing for the buyer at each future interest and principal payment date; that is, the cash flows from asset-side and liability-side transactions must match. Swaps are concluded on the basis of current fixed interest rate quotations.

In the same way as for interest rate hedges, exchange rate risk can be hedged using currency forwards. Currency forwards are agreements to purchase or sell a specific amount of a foreign currency on a defined date in the future at an exchange rate that is fixed in advance. The transaction is only fulfilled at the agreed future date. The difference between the forward

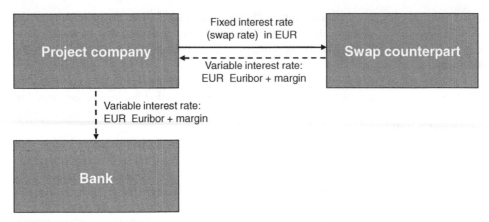

FIGURE 7.5 Interest rate swap

rate and the spot rate – also referred to as the 'swap rate' – is due to the interest rate differentials between the respective currencies.

7.7.2 Options

An interest rate option is the contractual right to receive or pay a defined interest rate at a future date. The buyer obtains the right – but not the obligation – to exercise the option in exchange for the payment of an option premium. In contrast to futures, options have an asymmetrical risk profile, that is, whereas the potential losses are limited to the amount of the option premium, the potential gains are unlimited. Options include:

- A *cap* is an agreement between two parties under which an interest rate cap is defined for an underlying principal amount. If the effective interest rate exceeds this cap, the buyer of the option is entitled to demand the payment of the difference between the effective interest rate and the interest rate cap by the seller.
- A *floor* is the opposite of a cap, i.e. an interest rate floor is defined.
- A *collar* combines the purchase of a cap and the sale of a floor in order to hedge against rising interest rates while reducing the cost of the cap.
- A *swaption* gives the buyer of the option the right to enter into an interest rate swap at a predetermined date.

As for interest rate options, currency options embody the contractual right to purchase or sell a specific amount of a foreign currency on a future date at a defined exchange rate. The buyer obtains the right – but not the obligation – to exercise the option in exchange for the payment of an option premium. The cost of the option premium is generally greater than the cost of a similar currency forward. The difference lies in the value of the option, which gives the buyer the right to choose between exercising the option and realising the corresponding gains depending on the development of the respective exchange rate.

A hybrid interest rate and exchange rate hedge is offered by the cross-currency swap, under which interest rate payments in various currencies are hedged. This agreement may also involve the exchange of the principal amounts underlying the transaction, which are denominated in various currencies.

Concluding Remarks

E conomic and social infrastructure appear to be key elements of robust and sustainable growth in economies globally. Notwithstanding, the past decades have been characterised by insufficient investment in new and inadequate maintenance of existing facilities. Exacerbated by budget deficits and population growth, an enormous global investment shortfall in infrastructure of at least US$1 trillion per annum has been the result (WEF, 2014a). Recently, renewed government interest and explicit investor demand have turned this negative trend around with private investors increasingly filling the gap. Adding global challenges like resource scarcity, social unrest, ageing societies and climate change to the equation explains why sustainability and infrastructure have become intrinsically interconnected. The authors are convinced that environmental, social and governance (ESG) factors will strongly determine the long-term financial viability of infrastructure investments.

Infrastructure represents an important investment opportunity for institutional investors, such as pension funds, insurance companies and sovereign wealth funds, who seek lasting and stable returns to match their long-term liabilities as well as portfolio diversification, among others. Infrastructure investments can provide both, thanks to the often cited long-term contractual structures of infrastructure assets and their potentially low correlation with traditional asset classes. They enable investors to improve the overall risk-return profile of their portfolios. From a sustainability perspective, assets like renewable energy plants, resource-efficient water supply facilities and climate-change-resilient transportation systems and buildings, to mention just a few, all positively contribute to sustainable development.

The aim of this book has been to comprehensively guide investors through the basic, as well as advanced, essential concepts of infrastructure investing. To this end, we started with an overview providing a definition for and describing the main characteristics of infrastructure. In Chapter 2, we comprehensively covered all aspects of infrastructure investing, as it is important for institutional investors to define their individual and integrated infrastructure investment strategies. They included: a discussion on risk-return profiles, benchmarking (sustainable) infrastructure, portfolio diversification potential of infrastructure assets, sustainable infrastructure investing, and investment approaches to infrastructure. We shed light on different organisational models of infrastructure in Chapter 3, including their 'sub-models', which addressed – partially complex – aspects of private sector involvement, ownership, business models, contractual structures and financing. In Chapter 4, we provided an extensive overview of the characteristics of the infrastructure sectors and subsectors which are the most relevant for financial investors: transport, water, waste and energy (electricity, natural gas, and district energy systems); social infrastructure is covered only on a high level. We dedicated the entirety of Chapter 5 to risks inherent in infrastructure assets, providing a detailed discussion of general risks and project/asset specific risks, as well as a list of sector-specific risks with numerous examples. Readers will appreciate the profound coverage of all critical aspects of project finance in Chapter 6, as well as the overview of the most common financing instruments used within the context of infrastructure in Chapter 7.

How infrastructure is designed and managed today will play a key role in how it will affect society and the environment tomorrow and for decades to come. This is why we have placed particular emphasis on sustainability aspects and considerations throughout this second edition. The explicit intention of this extra effort has been to help and motivate investors to incorporate ESG (risk) factors into their infrastructure investment decision-making processes.

Sample Page from CDC[1] Toolkit on ESG for Fund Managers

TABLE A.1 Rating Risks - The Environment

Risk category	Description of category	Examples
Category A **High risk**	A proposed investment is classified as Category A if it is likely to have significant adverse environmental impacts that are sensitive, diverse or unprecedented.	– Large dams and reservoirs – Forestry (large scale) – Agro-industries (large scale) – Industrial plants (large-scale) – Major new industrial estates – Extractive industries, including mining, major oil and gas developments and major pipelines – Large ferrous and non-ferrous metal operations – Large port and harbour developments – Developments with large resettlement components – Large thermal and hydropower development – Projects that include the manufacture, use or disposal of environmentally significant quantities of pesticides or herbicides – Manufacture, transportation and use of hazardous and/or toxic materials – Domestic and hazardous waste disposal operations

(continued)

---

[1]CDC is the UK's Development Finance Institution (DFI) wholly owned by the UK Government.

TABLE A.1 (*Continued*)

Risk category	Description of category	Examples
Category B **Medium risk**	A proposed investment is classified as Category B if its potential adverse impacts on environmentally important areas including wetlands, forests, grasslands and other natural habitats are less adverse than those of Category A investments but more adverse than Category C investments. These impacts are site-specific; few if any of them are irreversible and in most cases mitigating measures can be designed more readily than for Category A investments.	– Agro-industries (small scale) – Electrical transmission – Aquaculture – Renewable energy (except large hydroelectric power projects) – Tourism (including hotel projects) – Rural water supply and sanitation – Rehabilitation, maintenance and modernisation projects (small scale) – Manufacture of construction materials – General manufacturing – Telecommunications – Greenfield projects in existing industrial estate
Category C **Low risk**	A proposed investment is classified as Category C if it is likely to have minimal or no adverse environmental impacts.	– Advisory assignments – Media and information technology – Life insurance companies – Securities underwriters and broker/dealers – Technical assistance

Credit List for Envision's Sustainable Infrastructure Rating System

TABLE B.1 Credit List

QUALITY OF LIFE
13 Credits

1 PURPOSE
QL1.1 Improve Community Quality of life
QL1.2 Stimulate Sustainable Growth & Development
QL1.3 Develop Local Skills & Capabilities

2 WELLBEING
QL2.1 Enhance Public Health & Safety
QL2.2 Minimize Noise and Vibration
QL2.3 Minimize Light Pollution
QL2.4 Improve Community Mobility & Access
QL2.5 Encourage Alternative Modes of Transportation
QL2.6 Improve Site Accessibility, Safety & Wayfinding

3 COMMUNITY
QL3.1 Preserve Historic & Cultural Resources
QL3.2 Preserve Views & Local Character
QL3.3 Enhance Public Space

QL0.0 Innovate or Exceed Credit Requirements

LEADERSHIP
10 Credits

1 COLLABORATION
LD1.1 Provide Effective Leadership & Commitment
LD1.2 Establish A Sustainability Management System
LD1.3 Foster Collaboration & Teamwork
LD1.4 Provide for Stakeholder Involvement

2 MANAGEMENT
LD2.1 Pursue By-Product Synergy Opportunities
LD2.2 Improve Infrastructure Integration

3 PLANNING
LD3.1 Plan For Long-Term Monitoring & Maintenance
LD3.2 Address Conflicting Regulations & Policies
LD3.3 Extend Useful Life

LD0.0 Innovate or Exceed Credit Requirements

RESOURCE ALLOCATION
14 Credits

1 MATERIALS
RA1.1 Reduce Net Embodied Energy
RA1.2 Support Sustainable Procurement Practices
RA1.3 Use Recycled Materials
RA1.4 Use Regional Materials
RA1.5 Divert Waste From Landfills
RA1.6 Reduce Excavated Materials Taken Off Site
RA1.7 Provide For Deconstruction & Recycling

2 ENERGY
RA2.1 Reduce Energy Consumption
RA2.2 Use Renewable Energy
RA2.3 Commission & Monitor Energy Systems

3 WATER
RA3.1 Protect Fresh Water Availability
RA3.2 Reduce Potable Water Consumption
RA3.3 Monitor Water Systems

RA0.0 Innovate or Exceed Credit Requirements

NATURAL WORLD
15 Credits

1 SITING
NW1.1 Preserve Prime Habitat
NW1.2 Protect Wetlands & Surface Water
NW1.3 Preserve Prime Farmland
NW1.4 Avoid Adverse Geology
NW1.5 Preserve Floodplain Functions
NW1.6 Avoid Unsuitable Development on Steep Slopes
NW1.7 Preserve Greenfields

2 LAND+WATER
NW2.1 Manage Stormwater
NW2.2 Reduce Pesticide & Fertilizer Impacts
NW2.3 Prevent Surface & Groundwater Contamination

3 BIODIVERSITY
NW3.1 Preserve Species Biodiversity
NW3.2 Control Invasive Species
NW3.3 Restore Disturbed Soils
NW3.4 Maintain Wetland & Surface Water Functions

NW0.0 Innovate or Exceed Credit Requirements

CLIMATE AND RISK
8 Credits

1 EMISSIONS
CR1.1 Reduce Greenhouse Gas Emissions
CR1.2 Reduce Air Pollutant Emissions

2 RESILIENCE
CR2.1 Assess Climate Threat
CR2.2 Avoid Traps & Vulnerabilities
CR2.3 Prepare For Long-Term Adaptability
CR2.4 Prepare For Short-Term Hazards
CR2.5 Manage Heat Island Effects

CR0.0 Innovate or Exceed Credit Requirements

Infrastructure Sustainability Rating System (Australia) – Themes and Categories

TABLE C.1   Themes and Categories for ISRS

Theme	Category	Theme	Category
Management & Governance	Management Systems	**Ecology**	Ecology
	Procurement & Purchasing	**People & Places**	Community Health, Wellbeing & Safety
	Climate Change Adaptation		Heritage
Using Resources	Energy & Carbon		Stakeholder Participation
	Water		Urban & Landscape Design
	Materials	**Innovation**	Innovation
Emission, Pollution & Waste	Discharges to Air, Land & Water		
	Land	**Economic Performance***	Future Development
	Waste	**Workforce***	Future Development

National Appropriate Mitigation Actions (NAMAs)

TABLE D.1 Policy-Based National Appropriate Mitigation Actions (NAMAs)

	NAMA	Definition
Non-market-based		
Fiscal incentives	Grant	Monetary assistance that does not have to be repaid and that is bestowed by a government for specified purposes to an eligible recipient
	Energy production payment	Direct payment from the government per unit of RE production
	Rebate	One-time direct payment from the government to a private party to cover a percentage or specified amount of the investment cost of a RE system or service
	Tax credit (production or investment)	Annual income tax credit based on the amount of money invested in that facility or the amount of energy that it generates during the relevant year
	Tax reduction/exemption	Reduction in tax – including sales, value-added, energy or carbon tax
	Variable or accelerated depreciation	Allows for reduction in income tax burden in first years of operation of RE equipment
Public Finance	Investment	Financing provided in return for an equity ownership interest in a RE company or project
	Guarantee	Risk-sharing mechanism aimed at mobilizing domestic lending from commercial banks for RE companies and projects that have high perceived credit (i.e. repayment) risk

(continued)

TABLE D.1   (*Continued*)

	NAMA	Definition
	Loan	Financing provided to a RE company or project in return for a debt (i.e. repayment) obligation
	Public procurement	Public entities preferentially purchase RE services (such as electricity) and/or RE equipment
Regulations	Renewable Portfolio Standard/Quota obligation or mandate	Obliges designated parties (generators, suppliers, consumers) to meet minimum (often gradually increasing) RE targets
	Tendering/Bidding	Public authorities organize tenders for given quota of RE supplies or supply capacities, and remunerate winning bids at prices mostly above standard market levels
	Fixed payment FIT	Guarantees RE supplies with priority access and dispatch, and sets a fixed price varying by technology per unit delivered during a specified number of years
	Premium payment FIT	Guarantees RE supplies an additional payment on top of their energy market price or end-use value
	Net metering (also net billing)	Allows a two-way flow of electricity between the electricity distribution grid and customers with their own generation
	Priority or guaranteed access to network	Provides RE supplies with unhindered access to established energy networks
	Priority dispatch	Mandates that RE supplies are integrated into energy systems before supplies from other sources
Market-based		
Regulations	RECs	Tradable Certificates, need to be based on regulation defining a Renewable Energy Target (RET) obligation such as a Renewables Portfolio Standards (RPS)
	Carbon trading	Fossil energy producers need to surrender GHG emission allowances, increasing the competitive position of RET
	Carbon offsets	RET projects generate GHG emission credits that can be sold on the market
	Green energy purchasing	Regulates the supply of voluntary RE purchases by consumers, beyond existing RE obligations

TABLE D.1 *(Continued)*

NAMA	Definition
Green labelling	Government-sponsored labelling (there are also some private sector labels) that guarantees that energy products meet certain sustainability criteria to facilitate voluntary green energy purchasing; some governments require labelling on consumer bills, with full disclosure of the energy mix (or share of RE)

Source: IRENA, 2012a.

TABLE 0.1   (Continued)

References

ABP (2009). http://www.abp.nl/abp/abp/english/, accessed 10 September 2009.

ADB (2012). Climate Risk and Adaptation in the Electric Power Sector, Asian Development Bank (ADB), http://www.adb.org/sites/default/files/publication/29889/climate-risks-adaptation-power-sector.pdf, accessed 25 November 2015.

AER (2015). Annual Benchmarking Report, Australian Energy Regulator (AER), November 2014, https://www.aer.gov.au/networks-pipelines/guidelines-schemes-models-reviews/annual-benchmarking-report, accessed 25 November 2015.

AES (2015). AES Energy Storage, http://www.aesenergystorage.com, accessed 25 November 2015.

Airbus (2014). Global Market Forecast 2015–2034, http://www.airbus.com/company/market/forecast/, accessed 25 November 2015.

Akintoye, A. (2001). *Framework for Risk Assessment and Management of Private Finance Initiative Projects*, Glasgow Caledonian University, Glasgow.

Akintoye, A. (2003). *Public-Private Partnerships Managing Risks and Opportunities*, Oxford: Blackwell Science.

Albalate, D., Bel, G. and Fageda, X. (2007). *Privatisation and Regulation of Toll Motorways in Europe*, University of Barcelona, Spain, March.

Alfen, H.W., Riemann, A., Leidel, K. et al. (2010). *Lebenszyklusorientiertes Risikomanagement für PPP-Projekte im öffentlichen Hochbau: Abschlussbericht zum Forschungsprojekt*, Bauhaus-Universität Weimar, Weimar, Germany (in German).

Allianz (2015a). Allianz Group Annual Report 2014, https://www.allianz.com/v_1426595532000/media/investor_relations/en/results_reports/annual_report/ar2014/ar2014_group.pdf, accessed 25 November 2015.

Allianz (2015b). *Energy Factsheets*, Allianz Climate Solutions GmbH, 17 June 2015, Munich, Germany.

American Society of Civil Engineers (2015). Aims & Scope of Journal of Infrastructure Systems, http://ascelibrary.org/page/jitse4/editorialboard, accessed 25 November 2015.

Ammermann, H. (2015). *Squaring the Circle: Improving European Infrastructure Financing*, Study by Roland Berger Strategy Consultants and United Europe, March 2015, http://www.united-europe.eu/wp-content/uploads/2015/03/RB-Study.pdf, accessed 25 November 2015.

AMP Capital (2014a). Listed Infrastructure: Have investors missed the boat?, AMP Capital Investors Limited, http://www.ampcapital.com/ampcapitalglobal/media/contents/news-and-research/insights/pdf/20140210-insights-listed-infrastructure%E2%80%93have-investors-missed-the-boat.pdf?ext=.pdf, accessed 25 November 2015.

AMP Capital (2014b). Understanding Infrastructure, AMP Capital Investors Limited, http://www.ampcapital.com.au/AMPCapitalAU/media/contents/Contents/Resources/Understanding-Infrastructure.pdf, accessed 25 November 2015.

AMP Capital (2013c). Transport and ESG: Watch out for bumps along the road, http://www.ampcapital.com.au/article-detail?alias=/site-assets/articles/insights-papers/2013/2013-04/transport-and-esg-%E2%80%93-watch-out-for-bumps-along-the&audience=1, accessed 25 November 2015.

361

Ang, G. and Marchal, V. (2013). *Mobilising Private Investment in Sustainable Transport: The Case of Land-Based Passenger Transport Infrastructure*, OECD Environment Working Papers, No. 56.

Anisimov, O. and Reneva, S. (2006). Permafrost and changing climate: The Russian perspective, *Royal Swedish Academy of Sciences*, 35(4).

Ansar, A., Caldecott, B., and Tilbury, J. (2013). Stranded Assets, Smith School of Enterprise and the Environment, Oxford: University of Oxford, http://www.smithschool.ox.ac.uk/research/stranded-assets/SAP-divestment-report-final.pdf, accessed 1 October 2015.

APM Terminals (2009). Company Brochure, www.apmterminals.com, accessed 25 November 2015.

Arlanda Express (2015). A-Train AB, https://www.arlandaexpress.com/atrainorganisation.aspx, accessed 25 November 2015.

ASFiNAG (2009). PPP-Projekt Ostregion Paket 1, http://www.ots.at/presseaussendung/OTS_20061221_OTS0178/asfinag-auch-financial-closing-im-ppp-projekt-ostregion-abgeschlossen, accessed 25 November 2015.

ASFiNAG (2014). Geschäfts- und Nachhaltigkeitsbericht 2014, http://www.asfinag.at/documents/10180/10018088/ASFINAG+Geschaeftsbericht+2014+de.pdf/ec4c1ea6-f0fa-44c4-a3a6-f1e0e855f3eb, accessed 25 November 2015.

Averch, H. and Johnson, L.L. (1962). Behaviour of the firm under regulatory constraint, *American Economic Review* 52.

AviAlliance (2014). Athens International Airport Eleftherios Venizelos Annual Report 2014, http://avialliance.de/avia_de/data/pdf/AIA_Annual_Report_2014.pdf, accessed 25 November 2015.

AviAlliance (2015a). Düsseldorf Airport Geschäftsbericht 2014, http://avialliance.de/avia_de/data/pdf/dus_gb_2014_de.pdf, accessed 25 November 2015.

AviAlliance (2015b). Chronik (in German), http://www.avialliance.de/avia_de/24.jhtml#a, accessed 25 November 2015.

AXPO (2015). Zukunft Wasserkraft: Linthal 2015: Kraftwerke Linth-Limmern AG, Axpo Power AG, Hydroenergie, https://www.axpo.com/content/dam/axpo/switzerland/erleben/dokumente/130429_Axpo_Zukunft_Wasserkraft_5Aufl.pdf, accessed 25 November 2015.

Baker, R.W., Walker, S.N. and Wade, J.E. (1990). Annual and seasonal variations in mean wind speed and wind turbine energy production, *Solar Energy* 45(5), 285–289.

Bank for International Settlements (2014). International banking, and financial market developments, *BIS Quarterly Review* March, https://www.bis.org/publ/qtrpdf/r_qt1403.pdf, accessed 25 November 2015.

Basel Committee on Banking Supervision (2001). *Working Paper on the Internal Ratings-based Approach to Specialised Lending Exposures*, Bank for International Settlement, A part of Basel II.

BBC News (2014). Thames Water to Pay £86m Package after Mis-reporting Data, http://www.bbc.com/news/business-27710187, accessed 25 November 2015.

BDEW (2014). Erneuerbare Energien und das EEG: Zahlen, Fakten, Grafiken (2014) - Anlagen, installierte Leistung, Stromerzeugung, EEG-Auszahlungen, Marktintegration der Erneuerbaren Energien und regionale Verteilung der EEG-induzierten Zahlungsströme, Bundesverband der Energie- und Wasserwirtschaft e.V. (BDEW), 24 February 2014, Berlin, Germany (in German).

Bergström, L., Kautsky, L., Malm, T., Rosenberg, R., Wahlberg, M. et al. (2014). Effects of offshore wind farms on marine wildlife: A generalized impact assessment, *Environmental Research Letters*, 9, http://iopscience.iop.org/article/10.1088/1748-9326/9/3/034012/pdf, accessed 25 November 2015.

Bloomberg (2014). 'Appalling' Windfarms Risk Being Blown Away as Abbott Lauds Coal, 19 November 2014, http://www.bloomberg.com/news/articles/2014-11-19/-appalling-windfarms-risk-being-blown-away-as-abbott-lauds-coal, accessed 25 November 2015.

Bloomberg Business (2012). Middle Class in Emerging Markets Means Growth: Cutting research, 19 October 2012, http://www.bloomberg.com/news/articles/2012-10-18/middle-class-in-emerging-markets-means-growth-cutting-research, accessed 25 November 2015.

Bloomberg Business (2014a). Peru Seeks Private Funding for $19 Billion of Water Works, 17 September 2014, http://www.bloomberg.com/news/articles/2014-09-17/peru-seeks-private-funding-for-19-billion-of-water-works, accessed 25 November 2015.

Bloomberg Business (2014b). New Rules May Hurt $11.2 Trillion EU Insurer Investment, 1 September 2014, http://www.bloomberg.com/news/articles/2014-09-01/new-rules-may-hurt-11-2-trillion-eu-insurer-investments, accessed 25 November 2015.

BNEF (2015). Bloomberg New Energy Finance http://about.bnef.com, accessed 18 September 2015.

Boeing (2015). Current Market Outlook 2015–2034, http://www.boeing.com/commercial/market/long-term-market/traffic-and-market-outlook/, accessed 25 November 2015.

Boesch, D.F. and Rabalais, N.N. (2003). *Long-term Environmental Effects of Offshore Oil and Gas Development*, London: Elsevier Applied Science.

Bouman, E.A., Øberg, M.M. and Hertwich, E.G. (2013). *Life Cycle Assessment of Compressed Air Energy Storage (CAES), The Sixth International Conference on Life Cycle Management, 2013*, Gothenburg, Sweden.

Boussabaine, H.A. (2007). *Cost Planning of PFI and PPP Building Projects*, New York: Taylor & Francis.

Boyle, J., Cunningham, M. and Dekens, J. (2013). *Climate Change Adaptation and Canadian Infrastructure*: A review of the literature, IISD Report November 2013, The International Institute for Sustainable Development, Winnipeg, Canada.

BP (2015). *BP Statistical Review of World Energy June 2015*, London: British Petroleum (BP).

Brisa (2009). 2009 Annual Report, http://www.brisa.com.tr/English/Download/FaaliyetRaporu2009.pdf, accessed 25 November 2015.

Brisa (2013). Brisa Annual Report 2013, http://www.brisa.com.tr/English/Download/Brisa_Annual_Report_2013.pdf, accessed 25 November 2015.

Buhr, W. (2007). General considerations on infrastructure: Essence of the term, role of the state, impacts of population decline and aging, in X. Feng and A.M. Popescu (eds), *Infrastrukturprobleme bei Bevölkerungsrückgang: Schriften zur öffentlichen Verwaltung und öffentlichen Wirtschaft*, Berlin: Berliner Wissenschafts-Verlag.

Bullis, K. (2014). A Battery to Prop Up Renewable Power Hits the Market, *MIT Technology Review*, 14 November, http://www.technologyreview.com/news/532311/a-battery-to-prop-up-renewable-power-hits-the-market, accessed 25 November 2015.

Bundesnetzagentur (2014). *Monitoringbericht 2014, Bundesnetzagentur für Elektrizität, Gas, Telekommunikation, Post und Eisenbahnen, Bonn*, Germany: Bundeskartellamt.

Business Green (2015). Should the District Heating Industry Be Regulated? http://www.businessgreen.com/bg/analysis/2402251/should-the-district-heating-industry-be-regulated, accessed 25 November 2015.

CEDIGAZ (2015a). Gas and Coal Competition in EU Power Sector, Presentation by Cornot-Gandolphe, S., 13 June 2014, http://www.cedigaz.org/documents/2014/CEDIGAZ%20-%2013%20June%202014%20General%20meeting.pdf, accessed 25 November 2015.

CEDIGAZ (2015b). Gas Storage in Europe: Recent developments and outlook to 2035, Presentation by Hureau, G., European Gas Conference, 27–29 January 2015, Vienna, http://www.cedigaz.org/documents/2015/Gas%20Storage%20in%20Europe,%20recent.pdf, accessed 25 November 2015.

CEER (2013). Status Review on the Transposition of Unbundling Requirements for DSOs and Closed Distribution System Operators, Council of European Energy Regulators, 16 April 2013, Brussels, Belgium.

CEER (2015). *CEER Benchmarking Report 5.2 on the Continuity of Electricity Supply*, Brussels, Belgium: Council of European Energy Regulators.

CER (2015). *Annual Report 2014–2015*, Brussels, Belgium, http://www.cer.be/cer-annual-report-2014-2015, accessed 25 November 2015.

Ceres (2013). The 21st Century Investor: Ceres blueprint for sustainable investing, http://www.ceres.org/resources/reports/the-21st-century-investor-ceres-blueprint-for-sustainable-investing-summary, accessed 25 November 2015.

Ceres (2014a). Investing in the Clean Trillion: Closing the clean energy investment gap: A Ceres report, http://www.ceres.org/resources/reports/investing-in-the-clean-trillion-closing-the-clean-energy-investment-gap, accessed 25 November 2015.

Ceres (2014b). Green Bond Principles 2014: Voluntary process guidelines for issuing green bonds, https://www.ceres.org/resources/reports/green-bond-principles-2014-voluntary-process-guidelines-for-issuing-green-bonds/view, accessed 25 November 2015.

CFA Institute (2012). Benchmarks for Unlisted Infrastructure, https://www.cfainstitute.org/learning/products/publications/ipmn/Pages/ipmn.v2012.n1.2.aspx, accessed 25 November 2015.

Chief Investment Officer (2014). Capital Adequacy Blow for Infrastructure Projects, Asset International, http://www.ai-cio.com/channel/regulation,-legal/capital-adequacy-blow-for-infrastructure-projects/, accessed 25 November 2015.

China Water Risk (2010). China's Water Crisis, http://chinawaterrisk.org/wp-content/uploads/2011/06/Chinas-Water-Crisis-Part-1.pdf, accessed 25 November 2015.

Christie, S. (2015). The best energy companies you've never heard of, http://www.telegraph.co.uk/finance/personalfinance/household-bills/10583986/The-best-energy-companies-youve-never-heard-of.html, accessed 25 November 2015.

City of Düsseldorf (1997). http://www.duesseldorf.de/stadtarchiv/stadtgeschichte/chronik/1997.shtml, accessed 25 November 2015.

City of London (2016). City of London's combined heat and power plant, Local Government Association, http://www.local.gov.uk/climate-change/-/journal_content/56/10180/3510883/ARTICLE, accessed 28 February 2016.

Civil Aviation Authority (2015). Economic Regulation, http://www.caa.co.uk/default.aspx?catid=2345&pagetype=90&pageid=12994, accessed 25 November 2015.

CleanTechnica (2015). Solar PV Costs to Fall Another 25% in Three Years, 26 May 2015, http://cleantechnica.com/2015/05/26/solar-pv-costs-to-fall-another-25-per-cent-in-three-years, accessed 25 November 2015.

Climate Bond Initiative (2015a). The Review: First ever green covered bond (Pfandbrief) issued by German giant BerlinHyp: EUR500m, 7yr, 0.125%, AAA and 4x oversubscribed! Wunderbar!, 8 May 2015, https://www.climatebonds.net/2015/05/review-first-ever-green-covered-bond-pfandbrief-issued-german-giant-berlinhyp-eur500m-7yr, accessed 25 November 2015.

Climate Bond Initiative (2015b). Bonds and Climate Change: The state of the market in 2015, https://www.climatebonds.net/files/files/CBI-HSBC%20report%207July%20JG01.pdf, accessed 25 November 2015.

Climate Bond Initiative (2015c). Climate Bonds Taxonomy, http://www.climatebonds.net/standards/taxonomy, accessed 25 November 2015.

Climate Bond Initiative (2015d). About the Climate Bonds Standard, http://www.climatebonds.net/standards/about2, accessed 25 November 2015.

Climate Bond Initiative (2016). 2015 Year End Review – From tall trees to many green shoots: the evolution of the green bond market continues with 2015 seeing $41.8bn green bonds issued – that's the biggest ever! http://www.climatebonds.net/2016/01/2015-year-end-review-tall-trees-many-green-shoots-evolution-green-bond-market-continues-2015#sthash.Pjq9nS9D.dpuf, accessed 28 February 2016.

CNT (2013). The Case for Fixing the Leaks, Center for Neighborhood Technology, http://www.cnt.org/publications/the-case-for-fixing-the-leaks-protecting-people-and-saving-water-while-supporting, accessed 25 November 2015.

Cohen, B.R. (2012). Fixing America's Crumbling Underground Water Infrastructure, *Issue Analysis* 4.

Cointreau-Levine, S. (2000). *Private Sector Participation in Municipal Solid Waste Management, Part II Guidance Note*, St. Gallen, Switzerland: SKATE, Swiss Centre for Development Cooperation Technology and Management.

Colonial First State (2007). *A Look at Wholesale Infrastructure Fund Benchmarks. Infrastructure Research*, Colonial First State Global Asset Management, 2007.

Colonial First State (2010). *Setting the Goalposts: A review of infrastructure fund benchmarks*, Infrastructure Research Note, Colonial First State Global Asset Management, November 2010.

Colonial First State (2014). *Infrastructure Comes of Age*, Infrastructure Insight Series, Part 1, Colonial First State: Global Asset Management, June 2014.

CPUC (2010). Decision Adopting Energy Storage Procurement Framework and Design Program, California Public Utilities Commission, http://docs.cpuc.ca.gov/PublishedDocs/Published/G000/M078/K912/78912194.pdf, accessed 25 November 2015.

CPUC (2015). California Public Utilities Commission, www.cpuc.ca.gov/PUC/energy.htm, accessed 28 February 2016.

Credit Suisse (2010). Can Infrastructure Investing Enhance Portfolio Efficiency?, https://www.credit-suisse.com/pwp/am/downloads/marketing/infrastructure_ch_uk_lux_ita_scandinavia.pdf, accessed 25 November 2015.

Danish Ministry of the Environment (2015). Adapting Railways to Climate Change, http://en.klimatilpasning.dk/recent/cases/items/adaptingrailwaystoclimatechange.aspx, accessed 25 November 2015.

Daube, D. (2011). Public Private Partnership (PPP) für Immobilien öffentlicher Krankenhäuser – Entwicklung eines PPP-Eignungstests als Entscheidungshilfe für kommunale Krankenhäuser und Universitätsklinika, Weimar.

DECC (2015). *Consultation on a Review of the Feed-in Tariffs Scheme*, London: Department of Energy and Climate Change (DECC).

DEFRA (2013). Mechanical Biological Treatment of Municipal Solid Waste, https://www.gov.uk/government/publications/mechanical-biological-treatment-of-municipal-solid-waste, accessed 25 November 2015.

del Río, P. and Mir-Artigues, P. (2014). *A Cautionary Tale: Spain's solar PV investment bubble*, Winnipeg, Canada: The International Institute for Sustainable Development.

DESERTEC (2015). DESERTEC Foundation, http://www.desertec.org, accessed 25 November 2015.

Destatis (2014). Grundaten der Krankenhäuser 2014, Statistisches Bundesamt, Gesundheitswesen, Fachserie 12, Reihe 6.1.1, Wiesbaden.

DOE (2015). Global Energy Storage Database, US Department of Energy, http://www.energystorageexchange.org, accessed 25 November 2015.

EASE (2014). Regulation for Energy Storage in the EU Update from Brussels, The European Association for Energy Storage, Energy Storage Europe Conference, 11 March 2014, Düsseldorf, Germany.

ECLAREON (2014). PV Grid Parity Monitor: Commercial Sector, 1st issue, ECLAREON SL, http://www.leonardo-energy.org/sites/leonardo-energy/files/documents-and-links/pv_gpm_3_commercial_2014.pdf, accessed 25 November 2015.

Ecofys (2014). Energy Storage: Opportunities and challenges: A West Coast Perspective White Paper, Ecofys, 4 April 2014, http://www.ecofys.com/files/files/ecofys-2014-energy-storage-white-paper.pdf, accessed 25 November 2015.

The Economist (2014). The Incredible Shrinking Country, *The Economist*, 25 March, http://www.economist.com/blogs/banyan/2014/03/japans-demography, accessed 25 November 2015.

The Economist (2015a). No Smoking, *The Economist*, 27 June 2015, www.economist.com, accessed 1 October 2015.

The Economist (2015b). Fight the power, *The Economist*, 27 June 2015, p. 62.

Ecoprog (2015). The World Market for Pumped-Storage Power Plants, Ecoprog GmbH, March 2015, http://www.researchandmarkets.com/reports/2556862/the_world_market_for_pumpedstorage_power_plants, accessed 25 November 2015.

EDHEC (2013). Towards Efficient Benchmarks for Infrastructure Equity Investments: A review of the literature on infrastructure equity investment and directions for future research, EDHEC-Risk Institute, http://www.edhec-risk.com/edhec_publications/all_publications/RISKReview.2013-01-15.4142/attachments/EDHEC_Publication_Towards_Efficient_Benchmarks.pdf, accessed 25 November 2015.

EDHEC (2014). Benchmarking Long-Term Investment in Infrastructure: Objectives, roadmap and recent progress, EDHEC-Risk Institute, http://www.edhec-risk.com/edhec_publications/all_publications/RISKReview.2014-06-18.1812/attachments/EDHEC_Position_Paper_Benchmarking_Long_Term_Investment_in_Infrastructure.pdf, accessed 25 November 2015.

Edigas (2015). http://www.edigas.org, accessed 25 November 2015.

Education Funding Agency (2015). Priority School Building Programme, https://www.gov.uk/government/collections/priority-school-building-programme-psbp, accessed 25 November 2015.

EEI (2015). Actual and Planned Transmission Investment By Shareholder-owned Utilities (2008–2017), Edison Electric Institute, http://www.eei.org/issuesandpolicy/transmission/documents/bar_transmission_investment.pdf, accessed 25 November 2015.

EIA (2008). Distribution of Natural Gas: The Final Step in the Transmission Process, US Energy Information Administration, http://www.eia.gov/pub/oil_gas/natural_gas/feature_articles/2008/ldc2008/ldc2008.pdf, accessed 25 November 2015.

EIA (2012). Electric Power Annual 2012, US Energy Information Administration, http://www.eia.gov/electricity/annual/archive/03482012.pdf, accessed 25 November 2015.

EIA (2014). Natural Gas Annual 2014: Natural gas losses and unaccounted for by state, US Energy Information Administration, http://www.eia.gov/naturalgas/annual/pdf/table_a01.pdf, accessed 25 November 2015.

EIA (2015a). *Annual Energy Outlook 2015 with projections to 2040*, Washington: US Energy Information Administration, April 2015.

EIA (2015b). Natural Gas: Pipelines, U.S. Energy Information Administration, http://www.eia.gov/naturalgas/data.cfm#pipelines, accessed 25 November 2015.

EIB Papers (2010). Inderst, G., *Infrastructure as An Asset Class,* Vol 15 (1).

EIB (2015). European Investment Bank, 2014 Financial Report, http://www.eib.org/attachments/general/reports/fr2014en.pdf, accessed 28 February 2016.

EIB (2016). Climate Awareness Bond Hits 100th Green Bond listing on LuxSE, http://www.eib.org/investor_relations/press/2016/fi-2016-007-climate-awareness-bond-hits-100th-green-bond-listing-on-luxse.htm, accessed 28 February 2016.

EIOPA (2015). Discussion Paper on Infrastructure Investments by Insurers, European Insurance and Occupational Pensions Authority, https://eiopa.europa.eu/Publications/Consultations/EIOPA-CP-15-003_Discussion_paper_on_Infrastructure_Investments_for_public.pdf, accessed 25 November 2015.

Eiswirth, M. and Hölzl, H. (1997). *The Impact of Leaking Sewers on Urban Groundwater*, University of Karlsruhe, Germany, Department of Applied Geology, http://users.ipfw.edu/ISIORHO/G300Eiswirth-Hoetzl_IAH_Nottingham_1997.pdf, accessed 25 November 2015.

Elcom (2016). Eidgenössische Elektrizitätskommission (ElCom), https://www.elcom.admin.ch/elcom/de/home.html, accessed 28 February 2016.

Elliott, C. (2009). Investing in Social Infrastructure, in C. Lutyens (ed.), *Infrastructure*, London: PEI Media Ltd.

Energy Storage Journal (2014). Energy Storage Takes Shape, http://www.energystoragejournal.com/storage-services-take-shape/, accessed 1 October 2015.

ENTSO-E (2015). Overview of Transmission Tariffs in Europe: Synthesis 2015, European Network of Transmission System Operators for Electricity (ENTSO-E), June 2015.

ENTSOG (2015). http://www.entsog.eu, accessed 25 November 2015.

Environment Agency (2009). Britain's Largest Water Company Prosecuted for 5km River Pollution, http://waterbriefing.org/home/company-news/item/710-thames-water-prosecuted-for-5km-river-pollution, accessed 25 November 2015.

EON (2015a). Kraftwerk Huntorf, http://www.eon.com/de/ueber-uns/struktur/asset-finder/huntorf-power-station.html, accessed 25 November 2015.

EON (2015b). The Energy-World in Transition: Changing customer needs and new products, Dr.-Ing. Leonhard Birnbaum, Eurogas, Annual Conference, 3 March 2015, Brussels, Belgium.

EPA (2008). *EPA's Green Power Partnership: Renewable energy certificates*, Washington: Environmental Protection Agency.

EPA (2015a). Addressing Climate Change in the Water Sector, United States Environment Protection Agency, www2.epa.gov/climate-change-water-sector, accessed 25 November 2015.

EPA (2015b). Water Impacts of Climate Change, http://water.epa.gov/scitech/climatechange/Water-Impacts-of-Climate-Change.cfm, accessed 25 November 2015.

EPA (2015c). Emissions from the Oil & Natural Gas Industry, www.epa.gov/airquality/oilandgas/basic.html, accessed 25 November 2015.

EPEA (2009). About Cradle to Cradle, http://www.epea.com/en/content/about-cradle-cradle, accessed 25 November 2015.

EPEC (2015). European PPP Expertise Centre, http://www.eib.org/epec/index.htm, accessed 1 October, 2015.

ESC (2002). Energy Storage: The Missing Link in the Electricity Value Chain, ESC White Paper, http://www.energystoragecouncil.org/ESC%20White%20Paper%20.pdf, accessed 25 November 2015.

Eurelectric (2011). Hydro in Europe: Powering renewables: Full report, http://www.eurelectric.org/media/26690/hydro_report_final-2011-160-0011-01-e.pdf, accessed 25 November 2015.

Eurofound (2005). Privatisation and Decentralisation of the French Motorways, http://www.eurofound.europa.eu/observatories/eurwork/articles/privatisation-and-decentralisation-of-the-french-motorways, accessed 25 November 2015.

Eurogas (2014). Eurogas Statistical Report 2014, http://www.eurogas.org/uploads/media/Eurogas_Statistical_Report_2014.pdf, accessed 25 November 2015.

Euromed Transport Project (2008). European Commission, Main Contract: Micro study on public private partnerships in the transport sector, October 2008, http://www.enpi-info.eu/files/publications/ppp_study_en.pdf, accessed 25 November 2015.

European Commission (1999). Council Directive 99/31/EC of 26 April 1999 on the landfill of waste entered into force on 16.07.1999, Brussels, Belgium.

European Commission (2000a). *Green Paper on Public Private Partnerships and Community Law on Public Contracts and Concessions*, Brussels, Belgium: European Commission.

European Commission (2000b). *Water Directive*, Directive 2000/60/EC of the European Parliament and of the Council Establishing a Framework for the Community Action in the Field of Water Policy or, in short, the EU Water Framework Directive (WFD) adopted on 23 October 2000, Brussels, Belgium: European Commission.

European Commission (2006). *Waste Directive*, Directive 2006/12/EC of the European Parliament and of the Council of 5 April 2006 on waste, Brussels, Belgium: European Commission.

European Commission (2008). *Directorate-General for Transport and Energy: Modern Rail – Modern Europe – Towards an integrated European railway area*, Brussels, Belgium: European Commission, http://ec.europa.eu/transport/publications/doc/modern_rail_en.pdf, accessed 25 November 2015.

European Commission (2011). *Communication from the Commission to the European Parliament, the Council, the European economic and social committee and the Committee of the regions: Energy Roadmap 2015*, 15 December 2011, Brussels, Belgium: European Commission.

European Commission (2013a). *Adapting Infrastructure to Climate Change*, Commission Staff Working Document, European Commission, Brussels, Belgium: European Commission.

European Commission (2015). Investment Plan, http://ec.europa.eu/priorities/jobs-growth-investment/plan/index_en.htm, accessed 25 November 2015.

European Commission (2010). Waste, http://ec.europa.eu/environment/waste/, accessed 25 November 2015.

European Commission Mobility and Transport (2015). Inland Waterways, http://ec.europa.eu/transport/modes/inland/index_en.htm, accessed 25 November 2015.

European Policy Center (2012). *The climate Is Changing: Is Europe ready? Building a common approach to adaptation*, Issue paper No. 70, Brussels, Belgium: European Policy Center (EPC).

European PPP Expertise Centre (2009). http://www.eib.org/epec/index.htm, 28 February 2016.

Eurosif (2014). *European SRI Study*, Brussels, Belgium: Eurosif AISBL.

Eurostat (2004). Press release STAT/04/18, 2004. New Decision of Eurostat on Deficit and Debt Treat ment of Public Private Partnerships, http://europa.eu/rapid/press-release_STAT-04-18_en.htm? locale=en#, accessed 25 November 2015.

Eurostat (2012). Key Data on Education in Europe 2012, http://ec.europa.eu/eurostat/documents/3217 494/5741409/978-92-9201-242-7-EN.PDF/d0dcb0da-5c52-4b33-becb-027f05e1651f, accessed 25 November 2015.

Eurostat (2013). Municipal Waste Statistics 2003 to 2013, http://ec.europa.eu/eurostat/statistics-explain ed/index.php/File:Municipal_waste_generated_by_country_in_2003_and_2013,_sorted_by_2013 _level_(kg_per_capita)nw.png, accessed 25 November 2015.

Evans, P.C. and Farina, M.F. (2013). The Age of Gas & the Power of Networks, General Electric Company, https://www.ge.com/sites/default/files/GE_Age_of_Gas_Whitepaper_20131014v2.pdf, accessed 25 November 2015.

Evwind (2015). http://www.evwind.es/2015/03/06/installed-concentrated-solar-power-csp-capacity-now-over-4-5-gw/50831, Quarterly Update March 2015, accessed 28 February 2016.

EWEA (2010). Powering Europe: Wind Energy and the Electricity Grid, http://www.ewea.org/ grids2010/fileadmin/documents/reports/grids_report.pdf, 25 November 2015.

EWEA (2014). The European Offshore Wind Industry: Key Trends and Statistics 1st Half 2014, http:// www.ewea.org/fileadmin/files/library/publications/statistics/European_offshore_statistics_1st-half _2014.pdf, 25 November 2015.

EY (2013a). Mapping Power and Utilities Regulation in Europe, Ernst & Young, http://www.ey.com/ Publication/vwLUAssets/Mapping_power_and_utilities_regulation_in_Europe/$FILE/Mapping_ power_and_utilities_regulation_in_Europe_DX0181.pdf, accessed 25 November 2015.

EY (2013b). Business Pulse: Exploring dual perspectives on the top 10 risks and opportunities in 2013 and beyond: Power and utilities report, http://www.ey.com/Publication/vwLUAssets/Business_Pulse :_power_and_utilities/$FILE/Business_Pulse_Power_and_Utilities.pdf, accessed 25 November 2015.

EY (2015). Renewable Energy Country Attractiveness Index (RECAI), *Ernst & Young* 43, March 2015, http://www.ey.com/Publication/vwLUAssets/Renewable_Energy_Country_Attractiveness_Index_ 43/$FILE/RECAI%2043_March%202015.pdf, accessed 25 November 2015.

Fares, R. (2013). *Cost–Benefit Analysis of Grid Energy Storage*, Austin, TX: Webber Energy Group, University of Texas.

Fayard, A., Gaeta, F. and Quinet, E. (2004). *French Motorways: Experience and assessment, conference on highways: Cost and regulation in Europe*. 26–27 November 2004. University of Bergamo, Italy.

FERC (2011). Frequency Regulation Compensation in the Organized Wholesale Power Markets, https://www.ferc.gov/whats-new/comm-meet/2011/102011/E-28.pdf, accessed 25 November 2015.

FERC (2015). Transmission Planning and Cost Allocation, http://www.ferc.gov/industries/electric/ indus-act/trans-plan.asp, accessed 25 November 2015.

Finkenzeller, K., Dechant, T. and Shepherd, W. (2010). Infrastructure: A new dimension of real estate? An asset allocation analysis. *Journal of Property Investment & Finance*, 28(4), 263–274.

Freudenstein, S. and Obieray, D. (2005). Lebenszykluskosten und strikte Regie entscheidend – PPP – Projekte für die Schieneninfrastruktur am Beispiel der HSL-ZUID in *den Niederlanden in PPP for Infrastructure 01/2005; Hamburg*, Germany: Deutsche Verkehrs-Verlag GmbH (in German).

Frey, R.L. (1978). Art. Infrastruktur, in Albers, W. et al. (eds.), *Handwörterbuch der Wirtschaftswissenschaft*, Stuttgart, Germany: Gustav Fischer (in German).

FT (2015). Climate bonds still modest, but touching at $560bn, http://www.ftseglobalmarkets.com/ news/climate-bonds-still-modest-but-touching-at-$560bn.html#sthash.f3e1gtjs.dpuf, accessed 1 October, 2015.

Fulmer, J.E. (2009). In *Infrastructure Investor*, July/August 2009, PEI Media.

Gambino, L. (2015). California Restricts Water as Snowpack Survey Finds 'No Snow Whatsoever', http://www.theguardian.com/us-news/2015/apr/01/california-governor-orders-mandatory-water-re strictions-drought, accessed 25 November 2015.

Gaβner, H. and Kanngieβer, A. (2002). *Structures of Waste Management: Case study comparison on structures of waste management in France, Italy and Spain* (Ländervergleich zu den Strukturen der Entsorgungswirtschaft in Frankreich, Italien und Spanien), Berlin.

German Commission of Monopoly (2003).Wettbewerbsfragen der Kreislauf- und Abfallwirtschaft – Sondergutachten 37, http://www.monopolkommission.de/images/PDF/SG/s37_volltext.pdf, accessed 25 November 2015 (in German).

German Federal Ministry of Finance (2007). Wirtschaftlichkeitsuntersuchungen bei PPP-Projekten: Manual developed by working parties at federal and state level and the German audit courts and made binding by a circular issued by the German Federal Ministry of Finance on 20 August 2007; http://www.vifg.de/_downloads/service/infrastrukturfinanzierung-und-ppp/2007-09_Leitfaden_-_ WU_bei_PPP-Projekten.pdf, accessed 28 February 2016.

German Federal Ministry of Transport, Building and Urban Affairs (2003). Former Federal Ministry for Transport, Construction and Housing, PricewaterhouseCoopers; Freshfields Bruckhaus Deringer; VBD; Bauhaus-Universität Weimar; Creativ Concept. PPP im öffentlichen Hochbau, Volume 1 (in German).

Gies, E (2014). A Dam Revival, Despite Risks: Private funding brings a boom in hydropower, with high costs, http://www.nytimes.com/2014/11/20/business/energy-environment/private-funding-brings-a -boom-in-hydropower-with-high-costs.html?_r=0, accessed 25 November 2015.

GIIGNL (2015). The LNG Industry in 2014, http://www.giignl.org/sites/default/files/PUBLIC_AREA/Pu blications/giignl_2015_annual_report.pdf, accessed 25 November 2015.

Golden, M. (2014). Stanford-led Study Assesses the Environmental Costs and Benefits of Fracking, *Stanford News Service*, 12 September 2014, Stanford, CA: Stanford University.

Graetz, H. (2008). Water Management: *Synergy potential of a fragmented Water Management System (Synergiepotenzial einer fragmentierten Wasserwirtschaft), series of Chair Construction Economics (Schriftenreihe der Professur Betriebswirtschaftslehre im Bauwesen), Vol. 3*, Weimar, Germany.

Greenery Theme (2008). European Landfill Directive, http://recyclerubber.wordpress.com/2008/02/10/eu ropean-landfill-directive, accessed 25 November 2015.

Greentechmedia (2015). The Global Solar PV Market Hit 177GW in 2014: A tenfold increase from 2008, 31 March 2015, http://www.greentechmedia.com/articles/read/The-Global-Solar-PV-Market-Hit-177GW-in-2014-A-Tenfold-Increase-From-2008, accessed 25 November 2015.

GSIA (2015). Global Sustainable Investment Review 2014, http://www.gsi-alliance.org/wp-content/ uploads/2015/02/GSIA_Review_download.pdf, accessed 25 November 2015.

Gurría, A. (2009). Crisis and Water: The financial and economic crisis and water, Remarks by the OECD Secretary-General, delivered at the 5th World Water Forum High Level Panel on Finance, Istanbul, 17 March 2009, http://www.oecd.org/newsroom/thefinancialandeconomiccrisisandwater.htm, accessed 25 November 2015.

GWEC (2015). Global Wind Energy Council, www.gwec.net, accessed 25 November 2015.

GWP (2015). www.gwp.org, accessed 1 October 2015.

GWPMG, (2013). Global wind power market guide, http://www.reportlinker.com/p01099838/Global-Wind-Power-Market-Guide-Economics-Technologies-and-Opportunities.html#utm_source= prnewswire&utm_medium=pr&utm_campaign=Renewable_energy, accessed 1 October 2015.

Hall, D. (2006). Waste Management Companies in Europe, Public Services International Research Unit (PSIRU), http://www.psiru.org/reports/2006-02-G-EUwaste.doc, accessed 25 November 2015.

Hartigan, L.R., Prasad, R. and De Francesco, A.J. (2011). Constructing an investment return series for the UK unlisted infrastructure market: Estimation and application. *Journal of Property Research* 28(1), 35–58.

Hayler, J. (2014). Circular Economy Is Turning the Old Waste Sector into a Resource Industry, http://www.theguardian.com/sustainable-business/circular-economy-old-waste-sector-resource-management, accessed 25 November 2015.

Hehenberger, P. (2003). Der Warnow Tunnel – Absenktunnel und Konzessionsprojekt, Häfen und Wasser straßen, HANSA, Schiffahrt-Schiffbau-Hafen (*Hansa International Maritime Journal*), 140(3) (in German).

Holz, F. (2015). *Supply Security in Natural Gas Networks: The European situation*, DIW Berlin: German Institute for Economic Research, IEB Symposium Barcelona, http://www.ieb.ub.edu/files/Holz.pdf, accessed 25 November 2015.

Horn, K. U. and Alfen, H.W. (2003). *Public Private Partnership im Hochbau:* Leitfaden Wirtschaf tlichkeitsvergleich, PPP-Task Force of Ministry of Finance of the Federal State North Rhine Westphalia, Düsseldorf, November.

HPH (2015). Experience, https://www.hph.com/en/webpg-87.html, accessed 25 November 2015.

HSL-Zuid (2009). www.hslzuid.nl/, accessed 27 April 2009.

Hui, L. and Blanchard, B. (2014). Chinese Criticize State Firm Behind Three Gorges Dam Over Graft Probe, Reuters.com, 28 February 2014, http://www.reuters.com/article/2014/02/28/us-china-corruption-dam-idUSBREA1R0AJ20140228, accessed 25 November 2015.

Huibers (2012). Do infrastructure equities offer structural benefits to the institutional investor?, *ASRE Research Papers*, http://www.vastgoedkennis.nl/docs/publicaties/ASRE_research_paper_12_04_Do_infrastructure_equities.pdf, accessed 25 November 2015.

IBM – Business Consulting Services (2006). Rail Regulation in Europe: Comparison of the status quo of the regulation of rail network access in the EU-25 countries, March 2006, Zurich, Switzerland.

IEA (2011). Methodology Used to Calculate T&D Investment, http://www.worldenergyoutlook.org/media/weowebsite/energymodel/Methodology_TransmissionDistribution.pdf, accessed 25 November 2015.

IEA (2012a). World Energy Outlook 2012, https://www.iea.org/newsroomandevents/speeches/130326FuturewEnergyTrendsWEO2012NZrev.pdf, accessed 25 November 2015.

IEA (2012b). Technology Roadmap: Hydropower, https://www.iea.org/publications/freepublications/publication/2012_Hydropower_Roadmap.pdf, accessed 25 November 2015.

IEA (2012c). Energy Technology Perspectives 2012: Pathways to a clean energy system, https://www.iea.org/publications/freepublications/publication/ETP2012_free.pdf, accessed 25 November 2015.

IEA (2013a). Global EV Outlook: Understanding the electric vehicle landscape to 2020, Paris, 2013.

IEA (2013b). Technology Roadmap: Wind energy 2013 edition, https://www.iea.org/publications/freepublications/publication/Wind_2013_Roadmap.pdf, 25 November 2015.

IEA (2013c). Electricity Networks: Infrastructure and operations, https://www.iea.org/publications/insights/insightpublications/ElectricityNetworks2013_FINAL.pdf, 25 November 2015.

IEA (2014a). Key World Energy Statistics 2014, http://www.iea.org/publications/freepublications/publication/keyworld2014.pdf, accessed 25 November 2015.

IEA (2014b). Technology Roadmap: Solar photovoltaic energy 2014 edition, https://www.iea.org/publications/freepublications/publication/TechnologyRoadmapSolarPhotovoltaicEnergy_2014edition.pdf, accessed 25 November 2015.

IEA (2014c). World Energy Investment Outlook 2014, https://www.iea.org/publications/freepublications/publication/WEIO2014.pdf, accessed 25 November 2015.

IEA (2014d). Technology Roadmap: Energy storage, https://www.iea.org/publications/freepublications/publication/TechnologyRoadmapEnergystorage.pdf, accessed 25 November 2015.

IEA (2014e). Gas Market Trends and Developments in Global and Regional Trade, Ashgabat, December 2014, http://www.energycharter.org/fileadmin/DocumentsMedia/Events/IME_Ashgabat_2014_S2_Mazzega.pdf, accessed 25 November 2015.

IEA (2014f). Energy Supply Security 2014, https://www.iea.org/publications/freepublications/publication/energy-supply-security-the-emergency-response-of-iea-countries-2014.html, accessed 25 November 2015.

IEA (2014g). *Energy Technology Perspectives 2014: Harnessing electricity's potential*, Paris: International Energy Agency.

IEA (2014h). *Linking Heat and Electricity Systems: Co-generation and district heating and cooling solutions for a clean energy future*, Paris: International Energy Agency.

IEA (2015a). Bioenergy, https://www.iea.org/topics/renewables/subtopics/bioenergy/, accessed 25 November 2015.

IEA (2015b). International Energy Agency, http://www.iea.org, accessed 25 November 2015.

IEA (2015c). How2guide for: Smart grids in distribution networks: Roadmap development and implementation, https://www.iea.org/publications/freepublications/publication/TechnologyRoadmapHow2GuideforSmartGridsinDistributionNetworks.pdf, accessed 25 November 2015.

IEA (2015d). Technology Roadmap: Hydrogen and fuel cells, https://www.iea.org/publications/freepublications/publication/TechnologyRoadmapHydrogenandFuelCells.pdf, accessed 25 November 2015.

IFC (2012). *Performance Standards on Environmental and Social Sustainability*, Washington: International Finance Corporation, World Bank Group.

IHA (2015a). *2015 Hydropower Status Report*, London: International Hydropower Association.

IHA (2015b). Modernisation, https://www.hydropower.org/topics/business/modernisation, accessed 25 November 2015.

Inderst, G. and Della Croce, R. (2013). *Pension Fund Investment in Infrastructure: A comparison between Australia and Canada*, OECD Working Papers on Finance, Insurance and Private Pensions, No. 32, OECD Publishing.

Institutional Investor (2014). Why Investors Are Returning to Infrastructure Bonds, *Institutional Investor*, 8 January 2014, www.institutionalinvestor.com, accessed 25 November 2015.

International Rivers (2015). Human impact of dams, https://www.internationalrivers.org, accessed 1 October 2015.

Investor Platform for Climate Change (2015). Global Investor Statement on Climate Change, http://investorsonclimatechange.org/portfolio/global-investor-statement-climate-change/, accessed 25 November 2015.

IPCC (2012). *Managing the Risks of Extreme Events and Disasters to Advance Climate Change Adaptation: Special Report of the Intergovernmental Panel on Climate Change (IPCC)*, Cambridge: Cambridge University Press, p. 582, https://www.ipcc-wg2.gov/SREX/images/uploads/SREX-All_FINAL.pdf, accessed 25 November 2015.

IRENA (2012a). IRENA Handbook on Renewable Energy Nationally Appropriate Mitigation Actions (NAMAs) for Policy Makers and Project Developers, http://www.irena.org/DocumentDownloads/Publications/Handbook_RE_NAMAs.pdf, accessed 28 February 2016.

IRENA (2012b). Renewable Energy Technologies: Cost Analysis Series: Solar photovoltaics, https://www.irena.org/DocumentDownloads/Publications/RE_Technologies_Cost_Analysis-SOLAR_PV.pdf, accessed 25 November 2015.

IRENA (2012c). Renewable Energy Technologies: Cost analysis series: Wind power, https://www.irena.org/DocumentDownloads/Publications/RE_Technologies_Cost_Analysis-WIND_POWER.pdf, 25 November 2015.

IRENA (2012d). Renewable Energy Technologies: Cost analysis series: Biomass for power generation, https://www.irena.org/DocumentDownloads/Publications/RE_Technologies_Cost_Analysis-BIOMASS.pdf, accessed 25 November 2015.

IRENA (2012e). Renewable Energy Technologies: Cost analysis series: Hydropower, https://www.irena.org/DocumentDownloads/Publications/RE_Technologies_Cost_Analysis-HYDROPOWER.pdf, accessed 25 November 2015.

IRENA (2013). Smart Grids and Renewables: A guide for effective deployment, Ruud Kempener (IRENA), Paul Komor and Anderson Hoke (University of Colorado), Working Paper, November 2013.

IRENA (2014). Global Bioenergy: Supply and demand projections: A working paper for REmap 2030, September 2014, https://www.irena.org/remap/IRENA_REmap_2030_Biomass_paper_2014.pdf, accessed 25 November 2015.

IRENA (2015a). Smart grids and renewables – a cost-benefit analysis guide for developing countries, Kempener, R., Komor, P. and Hoke, A. The International Renewable Energy Agency (IRENA), Colorado: University of Colorado.

IRENA (2015b). Renewable Power Generation Costs in 2014, http://www.irena.org/Document Downloads/Publications/IRENA_RE_Power_Costs_2014_report.pdf, accessed 25 November 2015.

ISWA (2012). Globalization and Waste Management, http://www.iswa.org/index.php?eID=tx_iswatfg_download&fileUid=36, accessed 25 November 2015.

IUCN (2009). Perspectives on Water and Climate Change Adaption: Environment as infrastructure: Resilience to climate change impacts on water through investments in nature, http://www.world watercouncil.org/fileadmin/wwc/Library/Publications_and_reports/Climate_Change/PersPap_02._ Environment_as_Infrastructure.pdf, accessed 25 November 2015.

JBIC (2015). http://www.jbic.go.jp/en, accessed 3 October 2015.

Jellicoe, M. and Delgado, M. S. (2014). Quantifying the Risks of Underground Natural Gas Storage, National Agricultural & Rural Development Policy Center (NARDEP), Policy Brief 24, June 2014.

Jochimsen, R. (1966). *Theorie Der Infrastruktur, Grundlagen Der Marktwirtschaftlichen Entwicklung*, Tübingen, Germany: J.C.B. Mohr (Paul Siebeck) (in German).

Johannessen, C. (2008). Prepayment at the Water Tap (Vorkasse am Wasserhahn, Prepaid-Wasserzähler gefährden die Ärmsten der Armen), http://www.oikoumene.org/ewn/de/whatwedo/news-events/vorkasse-am-wasserhahn-prepaid-wasserzaehler-gefaehrden-die-aermsten-der-armen?set_langua ge=de, accessed 25 November 2015.

Johnson Controls (2008). Application Opportunities for Absorption Chillers, http://www .johnsoncontrols.com/content/dam/WWW/jci/be/integrated_hvac_systems/hvac_equipment/chiller _products/absorption_single/Absorption_Single_Stage_Application_Guide_PDF.pdf, accessed 25 November 2015.

JPMorgan (2015). JPMorgan Asset Management: Global real asset: Client presentation: 'Infrastructure portfolio construction: Key considerations for institutional investors', August 2015.

Källenfors, D. (2005). Nordea: Innovative Financing at Innovative Financing of Transnational Transport Projects Conference, Stockholm, Sweden, 18 October.

Kaminker, C., Kawanishi, O., Stewart, F., Caldecott, B. and Howarth, N. (2013). *Institutional Investors and Green Infrastructure Investments: Selected case studies*, OECD Working Papers on Finance, Insurance and Private Pensions, No. 35, Geneva: OECD Publishing.

Kenward, A. and Raja, U. (2014). *Blackout: Extreme weather, climate change and power outages*, Princeton, NJ: Climate Central.

KfW-Förderbank (2015). KfW, https://www.kfw.de/kfw.de-2.html, accessed 25 November 2015.

Kleiss, T. (2008). *Institutional Arrangements for Municipal Solid Waste Combustion Projects, series of Chair Construction Economics (Schriftenreihe der Professur Betriebswirtschaftslehre im Bauwesen), Vol. 6*, Weimar, Germany.

Kraemer, R.A. and Jäger, F. (1997). Deutschland, in: F.N. Correia and R.A. Kraemer (eds), *Dimensionen Europäischer Wasserpolitik*, Berlin: Springer.

Lavigne-Delville, J. (2014). Marine Transportation: Research brief, http://www.sasb.org/wp-content/uploads/2014/09/TR0301_Marine_Industry_Brief.pdf, accessed 25 November 2015.

Linklaters (2014). Set to Revive: Investing in Europe's infrastructure, http://www.linklaters.com/pdfs/mkt/london/6380_LIN_Infrastructure%20Report%20FINAL_WEB.PDF, accessed 25 November 2015.

List, F. (1841). *Das Nationale System der Politischen Ökonomie*, Stuttgart, Germany: Cotta Verlag (1841); Volksausgabe, Basel, Switzerland: Kyklos Verlag (1959) (in German).

Local Government Association (2015). www.local.gov.uk, accessed on 25 November 2015.

Malinowski, B. (1944/2006). *A Scientific Theory of Culture and Other Essays*, Chapel Hill, NC: The University of North Carolina Press (1944); *Eine wissenschaftliche Theorie der Kultur und andere Aufsätze*, 4. Aufl. Frankfurt, Germany: Suhrkamp Verlag.

Marques, R.C. (2010). *Regulation of Water and Wastewater Services: An international comparison*, London: IWA Publishing.

Marstal (2013). Dannemand Andersen, J., Bødker, L., Jensen, M.V., *Large Thermal Energy Storage at Marstal District Heating*, Proceedings of the 18th International Conference on Soil Mechanics and Geotechnical Engineering, Paris.

McKinsey (2009). Charting Our Water Future: Economic frameworks to inform decision making, www.mckinsey.com/client_service/sustainability/latest_thinking/charting_our_water_future, accessed 25 November 2015.

McKinsey Global Institute (2013). Infrastructure Productivity: How to save $1 trillion a year, http://www.mckinsey.com/insights/engineering_construction/infrastructure_productivity, accessed 25 November 2015.

McKinsey Quarterly (2012). Five Technologies to Watch, http://www.mckinsey.com/insights/energy_resources_materials/five_technologies_to_watch, accessed 25 November 2015.

MEAG (2015). MEAG MUNICH ERGO Asset Management GmbH, https://www.meag.com/reddot/html/de/unternehmen/ud_aum-konzern.asp, accessed 28 February 2016.

Mercer (2009). Shedding Light on Responsible Investment: Approaches, returns and impacts, http://www.law.harvard.edu/programs/lwp/pensions/conferences/cm_europe12_09/Shedding_light_on_responsible_investment_free_version.pdf, accessed 25 November 2015.

Mercer (2013). 2012 Global Investor Survey Report, http://www.mercer.com/content/dam/mercer/attachments/asia-pacific/australia/2013_Global_Investor_Survey_Report_Final.pdf, accessed 25 November 2015.

Mercer (2015). Investing in a Time of Climate Change, http://www.mercer.com/services/investments/investment-opportunities/responsible-investment/investing-in-a-time-of-climate-change-report-2015.html, accessed 28 February 2016.

Merna, A., Chu, Y. and Al-Thani, F. (2010). *Project Finance in Construction: A structured guide to assessment*, Chichester: Wiley-Blackwell.

Metro Vancouver (2016). https://www.metrovancouver.org, accessed 13 March 2015.

Meyer, T. and Matthonet, P.-Y. (2006). *Beyond the J-curve: Managing a portfolio of venture capital and private equity funds*, Chichester: John Wiley & Sons, Ltd.

Mintz, J. (2014). Jack M. Mintz: Canada's 'strategic asset' tactic makes for bad foreign investment policy, *Financial Post* (10 July 2014), http://business.financialpost.com/fp-comment/jack-m-mintz-canadas-strategic-asset-tactic-makes-for-bad-foreign-investment-policy, accessed 25 November 2015.

Miyazaki, B. (2009). Well Integrity: An overlooked source of risk and liability for underground natural gas storage: Lessons learned from incidents in the USA, London Geological Society, *Special Publications* 313, 163–172, http://sp.lyellcollection.org/content/313/1/163, accessed 25 November 2015.

Moody's (2012). Infrastructure Default and Recovery Rates, 1983–2012, 18 December 2012, http://cib.natixis.com/flushdoc.aspx?filename=Infrastructure_Default_and_Recovery_Rates_1983_2012h1_Moodys.pdf, accessed 25 November 2015.

Moody's (2014). Infrastructure Default and Recovery Rates, 1983–2013, https://www.moodys.com/research/Infrastructure-Default-and-Recovery-Rates-1983-2013–PBC_168013, accessed 25 November 2015.

Morgan Stanley (2015). Sustainable Reality: Understanding the performance of sustainable investment strategies, Morgan Stanley Institute for Sustainable Investing, https://www.morganstanley.com/sustainableinvesting/pdf/sustainable-reality.pdf, accessed 25 November 2015.

Mukheibir, P. (2007). Possible climate change impacts on large hydroelectricity schemes in Southern Africa, *Journal of Energy in Southern Africa*, 18(1).

Munich, RE (2013). 2012 Natural Catastrophe Year in Review, https://www.munichre.com/site/mram/get/documents_E1227251636/mram/assetpool.mr_america/PDFs/4_Events/MunichRe_III_NatCat 01032013.pdf, accessed 25 November 2015.

NBIM (2013). NBIM Discussion Notes: Infrastructure investments, http://www.nbim.no/globalassets/documents/dicussion-paper/2013/discussionnote_2-13-final.pdf, accessed 25 November 2015.

NETL (2007). *Cost and Performance Baseline for Fossil Energy Plants, Volume 1: Bituminous coal and natural gas to electricity*, Final Report, National Energy Technology Laboratory (NETL).

Newell, G., Peng, H.W. and De Francesco, A. (2011). The performance of unlisted infrastructure investment portfolios, *Journal of Property Research*, 28(1), 59–74.

Neuhoff, K., Ehrenmann, A., Butler, L., Cust, J., Hoexter, H. et al. (2006). Space and Time: Wind in an investment planning model, http://www.dspace.cam.ac.uk/bitstream/1810/131660/1/eprg0603.pdf, accessed 25 November 2015.

Northeast Group (2012) http://www.northeast-group.com/reports/MENA_Smart_Grid_Market_ Forecast_2012-2022_Brochure.pdf, accessed 28 February 2016.

Norwegian Ministry of Petroleum and Energy (2008). Fact 2008: Energy and water resources in Norway, https://www.regjeringen.no/en/dokumenter/fact-2008---energy-and-water-resources-i/id536186, accessed 25 November 2015.

NREL (2015). 'U.S. Photovoltaic Prices and Cost Breakdowns: Q1 2015 Benchmarks for Residential, Commercial, and Utility-Scale Systems', Donald Chung, Carolyn Davidson, Ran Fu, Kristen Ardani, and Robert Margolis, National Renewable Energy Laboratory (NREL), US Department of Energy.

NVE (2013). Energy in Norway, http://www.nve.no/Global/Energi/Analyser/Energi%20i%20Norge%20 folder/FOLDE2013.pdf, accessed 25 November 2015.

NWCC (2010). Wind Turbine Interactions with Birds, Bats, and Their Habitats: A summary of research results and priority questions, https://www1.eere.energy.gov/wind/pdfs/birds_and_bats_fac t_sheet.pdf, accessed 25 November 2015.

OECD (2006). Infrastructure to 2030: Vol. 1, Telecom, land transport, water and electricity, http://www.oecd.org/futures/infrastructureto2030/37182873.pdf, accessed 25 November 2015.

OECD (2007). Infrastructure to 2030: Vol. 2: Mapping policy for electricity, water and transport, http://www.oecd.org/futures/infrastructureto2030/40953164.pdf, accessed 25 November 2015.

OECD (2011). *Benefits of Investing in Water and Sanitation: An OECD perspective*, OECD Studies on Water, OECD Publishing, Paris, DOI: http://dx.doi.org/10.1787/9789264100817-en, accessed 25 November 2015.

OECD (2012). OECD Environmental Outlook to 2050: The consequences of inaction, http://www.oecd .org/env/indicators-modelling-outlooks/49846090.pdf, accessed 25 November 2015.

OECD (2013). Waste Management Services 2013: OECD policy roundtables, http://www.oecd.org/daf/competition/Waste-management-services-2013.pdf, accessed 25 November 2015.

OECD (2014a). Pooling of Institutional Investors Capital: Selected case studies in unlisted equity infrastructure, http://www.oecd.org/finance/OECD-Pooling-Institutional-Investors-Capital-Unlisted-Equity-Infrastructure.pdf, accessed 25 November 2015.

OECD (2014b). Education at a Glance 2014: OECD indicators, http://www.oecd.org/edu/Education-at-a-Glance-2014.pdf, accessed 25 November 2015.

OECD/ITF (2008). *Transport Infrastructure Investment: Options for efficiency*, Paris: Joint Transport Research Centre of the OECD and the International Transport Forum.

OECD/ITF (2013). *Spending on Transport Infrastructure 1995–2011: Trends, policies and data*, Paris: Organization for Economic Cooperation and Development and International Transport Forum (ITF).

OECD/World Water Council (2015). Water: Fit to finance? Catalyzing national growth through water security, World Water Council, Marseille, 2015, http://www.worldwatercouncil.org/fileadmin/world _water_council/documents/publications/forum_documents/WWC_OECD_Water-fit-to-finance_ Report.pdf, accessed 25 November 2015.

Ofgem (2014). Working Documents: Work Stream Six, https://www.ofgem.gov.uk/publications-and-updates/working-documents-work-stream-six, accessed 25 November 2015.

OFWAT (2015). Annual Reports: Thames Water, https://www.ofwat.gov.uk/aboutofwat/reports/annual reports/, accessed 25 November 2015.

Osborne, A. (2014). Political risk is main barrier to investment, says L&G chief, *The Telegraph* (5 March), http://www.telegraph.co.uk/finance/newsbysector/banksandfinance/insurance/10679055/Political-risk-is-main-barrier-to-investment-says-LandG-chief.html, accessed 25 November 2015.

Oxford Economics (2012). *The Economic Impact of Physics Research in the UK: Satellite navigation case study*, Oxford, Oxford Economics.

PCA/IPD (2006). *Investment Performance Index: June 2006*, Melbourne, Australia: IPD.

Peng, H.W. and Newell, G. (2007). The Significance of Infrastructure in Investment Portfolios, Pacific RIM Real Estate Society Conference, Fremantle 21–24 January 2007, University of Western Sydney, Australia.

Port Finance International (2015). APM Terminals acquire Grup Maritim TCB and 11 terminal portfolio, http://www.portfinanceinternational.com/categories/finance-deals/item/2311-apm-terminals-to-acquire-grup-maritim-tcb-and-11-terminal-portfolio, accessed 25 November 2015.

PPP Projektdatenbank (2015). Project List and Contract Volume, http://www.ppp-projektdatenbank.de/index.php?id=9, accessed 25 November 2015.

Preqin (2014a). Europe-Based Infrastructure Investors, https://www.preqin.com/blog/0/10085/europe-infrastructure-investor, accessed 25 November 2015.

Preqin (2014b). Comparing Infrastructure Investments among US and Canadian Public Pensions, https://www.preqin.com/blog/101/8338/us-canada-public-pensions,%20February%202014, accessed 25 November 2015.

Preqin (2015a). 2015 Preqin Global Infrastructure Report, Preqin Ltd, https://www.preqin.com/item/2015-preqin-global-infrastructure-report/4/10606, accessed 25 November 2015.

Preqin (2015b). *Preqin Q4-2014 Infrastructure Factsheet*, Prequin Ltd.

Private Participation in Infrastructure Project Database (2014). World Bank Group, http://ppi.worldbank.org/customquery, accessed 25 November 2015.

Probitas (2014). *Real Assets Presentation*, London: Probitas Partners, Probitas Funds Management.

Pryor, S.C. and Barthelmie, R.J. (2010). Climate change impacts on wind energy: A review, *Renewable and Sustainable Energy Reviews* 14(1), 430–437.

PSA International (2015). Annual Report 2014, http://www.internationalpsa.com/home/default.html, accessed 18 September 2015.

PSIRU (2006). Waste Management Companies in Europe, http://gala.gre.ac.uk/3615/1/PSIRU_9615_-_2006-02-G-EUwaste.pdf, accessed 25 November 2015.

PV-Tech (2015). Global Solar Demand in 2015 to Hit 57GW on Strong 30% Growth Rate: IHS, http://www.pv-tech.org/news/global_solar_demand_in_2015_to_hit_57gw_on_strong_30_growth_rate_ihs, accessed 25 November 2015.

RARE (2009). *Direct vs Listed Infrastructure*, RARE Infrastructure Special Fund Update, RARE Research, 2009.

RARE (2013). *RARE Guide to Listed and Unlisted Infrastructure*, RARE Research, January 2013.

REN21 (2013a). Renewables Global Futures Report 2013, http://www.ren21.net/Portals/0/documents/activities/gfr/REN21_GFR_2013.pdf, accessed 25 November 2015.

REN21 (2013b). Renewables 2013: Global status report, http://www.ren21.net/Portals/0/documents/Resources/GSR/2013/GSR2013_lowres.pdf, accessed 25 November 2015.

REN21 (2014). Renewables 2014: Global status report, http://www.ren21.net/Portals/0/documents/Resources/GSR/2014/GSR2014_full%20report_low%20res.pdf, accessed 25 November 2015.

Renergia (2015). https://www.renergia.ch, accessed 13 October 2015.

RES LEGAL (2015). Legal Sources on Renewable Energy, http://www.res-legal.eu/home, accessed 25 November 2015.

Reuters (2014). Gas Pipeline Partner Sues Norway Government over Tariff Cut, http://www.reuters.com/article/2014/01/16/norway-gas-idUSL5N0KQ15S20140116, accessed 25 November 2015.

Rodrigue, J.P. (2013). *The Geography of Transport Systems*, 3rd edition, New York: Routledge.

Rodríguez-Molina, J., Martínez-Núñez, M., Martínez, J.-F. and Pérez-Aguiar, W. (2014). Business Models in the Smart Grid: Challenges, opportunities and proposals for prosumer profitability, *MDPI, Energies 2014* 7(9), 6142–6171, http://www.mdpi.com/1996-1073/7/9/6142/pdf, accessed 25 November 2015.

Rogers, H. (2015). *The Impact of Lower Gas and Oil Prices on Global Gas and LNG Markets*, Oxford: Oxford Institute for Energy Studies.

Rogers, P. and Hall, A. (2003). *Effective Water Governance*, Global Water Partnership Technical Committee, Background Paper No. 7, http://www.gwp.org/Global/ToolBox/Publications/Background%20papers/07%20Effective%20Water%20Governance%20(2003)%20English.pdf, accessed 25 November 2015.

RTE (2015). Transmission System Operators: The 3 models in Europe, http://www.meti.go.jp/committee/sougouenergy/sougou/denryoku_system_kaikaku/pdf/004_03_02.pdf, accessed 25 November 2015.

Ruester, S. (2015). *Financing LNG Projects and the Role of Long-Term Sales-and-Purchase Agreements*, DIW Berlin: German Institute for Economic Research, http://www.diw.de/documents/publikationen/73/diw_01.c.494837.de/dp1441.pdf, accessed 25 November 2015.

RWE (2014). *The German Energiewende and Implications for Utilities*, RWE AG, 25 April 2014.

RWE (2015). RWE Tests Innovative Energy Storage Solution, http://www.rwe.com/web/cms/en/113648/rwe/press-news/press-release/?pmid=4013698, accessed 25 November 2015.

SANRAL (2009). About SANRAL, http://www.nra.co.za/live/content.php?Category_ID=6, accessed 25 November 2015.

SBC (2013). Leading the Energy Transition: Fact book electricity storage, https://www.sbc.slb.com/~/media/Files/SBC%20Energy%20Institute/SBC%20Energy%20Institute_Electricity_Storage%20Factbook_vf1.pdf, accessed 25 November 2015.

Schubert, H. (1995). Soziale infrastruktur, in: *Handwörterbuch der Raumordnung*, Hannover, Germany.

Siemens (2015a). Sustainable Power Generation: Facts and forecasts: Global support for renewable energy sources, http://www.siemens.com/innovation/en/home/pictures-of-the-future/energy-and-efficiency/sustainable-power-generation-facts-and-forecasts.html, accessed 25 November 2015.

Siemens (2015b). Power Transmission: Electricity superhighways, http://www.siemens.com/innovation/en/home/pictures-of-the-future/energy-and-efficiency/power-transmission-electrictiy-superhighways.html, accessed 25 November 2015.

SNIFFER (2008). Human Health and the Environmental Impacts of Using Sewage Sludge on Forestry and for Restoration of Derelict Land, www.sniffer.org.uk/files/7713/4183/7997/UKLQ09_Task_1_Report_Final.pdf, accessed 25 November 2015.

Sorgenfrei, J. (2013). *Port Business*, Norderstedt, Germany: BoD.

Sovereign Wealth Center (2015). Fund Profiles, http://www.sovereignwealthcenter.com/fund-profiles.html, accessed 25 November 2015.

Spedding, P., Mehta, K. and Robins, N. (2013). Oil & Carbon Revisited: Value at risk from 'unburnable' reserves, *HSBC Global Research*, 25 January 2013, London.

Standard & Poor's (2014). Global Infrastructure: How to fill a $500 billion hole, *Standard & Poor's Ratings Direct*, January 16, 2014.

Stanford Report (2013). Global Solar Photovoltaic Industry Is Likely Now a Net Energy Producer, Stanford Researchers Find, http://news.stanford.edu/news/2013/april/pv-net-energy-040213.html, accessed 25 November 2015.

Statista (2015). Largest Derivatives Exchanges Worldwide in 2014, by number of contracts traded (in millions), http://www.statista.com/statistics/272832/largest-international-futures-exchanges-by-number-of-contracts-traded, accessed 25 November 2015.

Staub-Bisang, M. (2012). *Sustainable Investing for Institutional Investors: Risk, regulations and strategies*, Singapore: John Wiley & Sons, Ltd.

SustainX (2015). SustainX Begins Startup of World's First Grid-Scale Isothermal Compressed Air Energy Storage System, http://www.sustainx.com/e9c13ca1-134c-49e9-9031-036592c1b37a/about-us-news-events-detail.htm, accessed 25 November 2015.

Swissgrid (2015). Data and Facts about the Swiss Transmission System, http://www.swissgrid.ch/swissgrid/en/home/reliability/griddata.html, accessed 25 November 2015.

Swiss Re (2014). *Infrastructure Investing: It matters*, Swiss Re: Zurich, Switzerland.

Swiss Re (2015). Our Sustainability Risk Framework, http://www.swissre.com/corporate_responsibility/managing_env_risks.html, accessed 25 November 2015.

Tahzib, B. and Zvijakova, L. (2012). Environmental impact of land transport, Transfer inovacii 24/2012., 70-77.

Thames Tideway Tunnel (2015). http://www.thamestidewaytunnel.co.uk/, accessed 25 November 2015.

TIAA-CREF (2014). Socially Responsible Investing: Delivering competitive performance, TIAA-CREF Asset Management, https://www.tiaa-cref.org/public/pdf/C19224_SRI_White_Paper_v13.pdf, accessed 25 November 2015.

Tinsley, R. (2000). *Advanced Project Financing: Structuring risk*. London: Euromoney Books.

Tollefson, J. (2013). Methane Leaks Erode Green Credentials of Natural Gas, *Nature*, 2 January.

Top1000funds (2015). CalPERS Gives Its Managers ESG Ultimatum, http://www.top1000funds.com/news/2015/05/22/calpers-gives-its-managers-esg-ultimatum, accessed 25 November 2015.

Transnational Institute (2014). Here to Stay: Water remunicipalisation as a global trend, https://www.tni.org/files/download/heretostay-en.pdf, accessed 25 November 2015.

UBS (2006). Q-Series: Infrastructure and utilities. UBS Investment Research, November.

UCS (2014). 'Solar Power on the Rise: The Technologies and Policies behind a Booming Energy Sector' Union of Concerned Scientists (UCS), http://www.ucsusa.org/clean_energy/our-energy-choices/renewable-energy/solar-power-technologies-and-policies.html#.VtLvQeZ0eUQ, accessed 28 February 2016.

UK Department of Energy & Climate Change (2015). Capacity Market Will Ensure Security of Electricity Supply by Providing a Payment for Reliable Sources of Capacity, 15 June 2015, https://www.gov.uk/government/collections/electricity-market-reform-capacity-market, accessed 25 November 2015.

UK Waste (2014). UK Resource Efficiency & Waste Management Market Report, http://www.rwmexhibition.com/files/rwm_market_report_2014v3.pdf, accessed 25 November 2015.

Umweltdatenbank (2009). Waste, http://www.umweltdatenbank.de/lexikon/abfall.htm, accessed 25 November 2015.

UN (2003). *Water for People, Water for Life: United Nations World Water Development Report*, http://www.un.org/esa/sustdev/publications/WWDR_english_129556e.pdf, accessed 25 November 2015.

UN (2013). UN Water Scarcity Factsheet, http://www.unwater.org/publications/publications-detail/en/c/204294, accessed 25 November 2015.

UN (2015a). World Population Prospects: The 2015 Revision, issued by the United Nations (UN), Department of Economic and Social Affairs, 2015, https://www.un.org/development/desa/en/, accessed 25 November 2015.

UN (2015b). *Private Sector Investment and Sustainable Development: The current and potential role of institutional investors, companies, banks and foundations in sustainable development*, Geneva: UN Global Compact.

UN ESCAP (2014). Pro-poor and Sustainable Solid Waste Management in Secondary Cities and Small Towns in Asia-Pacific, http://www.unescap.org/resources/pro-poor-and-sustainable-solid-waste-management-secondary-cities-and-small-towns-asia, accessed 25 November 2015.

UN Water (2013). UN Water Scarcity Factsheet, http://www.unwater.org/downloads/water_scarcity.pdf, accessed 25 November 2015.

UN Water (2014a). Global Water Statistics, http://www.unwater.org/statistics/statistics-detail/en/c/211801/, accessed 25 November 2015.

UN Water (2014b). The United Nations World Water Development Report 2014: Water and energy, unesdoc.unesco.org/images/0022/002257/225741E.pdf, accessed 25 November 2015.

UNCTAD (2014). *Review of Maritime Transport 2014*, Geneva: UNCTAD.

UNEP (2014). Financial institutions taking action on climate change, http://www.unepfi.org/fileadmin/ documents/FinancialInstitutionsTakingActionOnClimateChange.pdf, accessed 1 October, 2015.

UNEP (2015). *District Energy in Cities: Unlocking the potential of energy efficiency and renewable energy*, United Nations Energy Programme.

UNICEF (2014). Progress on Drinking Water and Sanitation: World Health Organization and UNICEF Joint Monitoring Programme, www.wssinfo.org/fileadmin/user_upload/resources/JMP_report_ 2014_webEng.pdf, accessed 25 November 2015.

UNPRI (2015). Responsible Investment and Fiduciary Duty, www.unpri.org, accessed 25 November 2015.

US Climate Change Science Program (2008). Effects of Climate Change on Energy Production and Use in the United States, Synthesis and Assessment Product 4.5, http://science.energy.gov/~/ media/ber/pdf/Sap_4_5_final_all.pdf, accessed 25 November 2015.

US Department of Transportation (2011). Impacts of Climate Change and Variability on Transportation Systems and Infrastructure, *The Gulf Coast Study*, March 2011.

USAID (2012). Solid Waste Management: Addressing climate change impacts on infrastructure, https:// www.usaid.gov/sites/default/files/documents/1865/Infrastructure_SolidWasteManagement.pdf, accessed 25 November 2015.

Wackerbauer, J. (2003). Regulierungsmodelle für die öffentliche Wasserversorgung und ihre Wettbewerbseffekte, 'ifo Schnelldienst 21/2003', ifo Institut für Wirtschaftsforschung, München, 2003.

Water.org (2015). Billions Affected Daily by Water and Sanitation Crisis, http://www.water.org/water-crisis/one-billion-affected/, accessed 25 November 2015.

WCED (1987). Brundtland Report: Our common future. *The World Commission on Environment and Development (WCED)*. Oxford: Oxford University Press.

Weber, B., Alfen, H.W. and Maser, S. (2006). *Projektfinanzierung und PPP – Praktische Anleitung für PPP und andere Projektfinanzierungen*, Köln: Bank-Verlag.

Weber, B. (2009). What you don't see is what you get: The real risks and reasonable terms of infrastructure investment, in *Investing in Infrastructure*, Lutyens, C. (ed.), London: PEI Media Ltd.

Weber, B. (2013). *Benchmarking Infrastructure, European Bond Commission Conference*, 14–15 October 2013, London.

Weber, B. and Alfen, H.W. (2010). *Infrastructure as an Asset Class*, John Wiley & Sons Ltd.

WEF (2014a). Infrastructure Investment: Policy blueprint, http://www3.weforum.org/docs/WEF_II_ InfrastructureInvestmentPolicyBlueprint_Report_2014.pdf, accessed 28 February 2016.

WEF (2014b). Towards the Circular Economy: Accelerating the scale-up across global supply chains, http://www3.weforum.org/docs/WEF_ENV_TowardsCircularEconomy_Report_2014.pdf, accessed 25 November 2015.

WEF (2015). WEF 2015 Global Risks Report, http://www3.weforum.org/docs/WEF_Global_Risks_2015 _Report15.pdf, accessed 25 November 2015.

Wendel, V. (2001). Controlling in Non-Profit-Unternehmen des stationären Gesundheitssektors, Diss., Universität Mannheim, Bd. 170 der Schriften zur öffentlichen Verwaltung und öffentlichen Wirtschaft, Mannheim.

WHO (2011). Global Health and Ageing, http://www.who.int/ageing/publications/global_health.pdf?ua =1, accessed 25 November 2015.

Wong, S. (2007). Three Gorges resettlers lose out to corruption, *International Rivers* 1 (February), http:// www.internationalrivers.org/resources/three-gorges-resettlers-lose-out-to-corruption-1751, accessed 25 November 2015.

World Bank (2006). Good Governance for Good Water Management, http://siteresources.worldbank .org/INTENVMAT/64199955-1162240805462/21127276/8GoodGovernance.pdf, accessed 29 September 2015.

World Bank (2007). *Port Reform Toolkit*, second edition – Module 3 – Alternative Port Management Structures and Ownership Models.

World Bank (2012a). Transformation Through Infrastructure, www.siteresources.worldbank.org, accessed 25 September 2015.

World Bank (2012b). What a Waste: A global review of solid waste management, http://siteresources .worldbank.org/INTURBANDEVELOPMENT/Resources/336387-1334852610766/What_a_Was te2012_Final.pdf, accessed 30 September 2015.

World Bank (2012c). *The Costs of Adapting to Climate Change for Infrastructure*, Washington, World Bank Group.

World Bank (2015a). The World Bank Private Participation in Infrastructure Database, ppi.worldbank .org, accessed 29 September 2015.

World Bank (2015b). Electric Power Transmission and Distribution Losses, http://data.worldbank.org/ indicator/EG.ELC.LOSS.ZS, accessed 25 November 2015.

World Bank (2015c). New World Bank Green Bond Is a Story of Market Growth and Innovation, http:// www.worldbank.org/en/news/feature/2015/02/25/green-bond-story-market-growth-innovation, accessed 25 November 2015.

World Bank Database (2015). Data, http://data.worldbank.org/region/WLD, accessed 25 November 2015.

World Resources Institute (2016). 'With New Guidelines, China's Green Bond Market Poised to Take Off in the Year of the Monkey', Zhu, S., http://www.wri.org/blog/2016/01/new-guidelines-china%E2%80%99s-green-bond-market-poised-take-year-monkey, accessed 28 February 2016.

World Shipping Council (2013). Top 50 World Container Ports, http://www.worldshipping.org/about-the-industry/global-trade/top-50-world-container-ports, accessed 25 November 2015.

WWF (2015). Denmark waste to energy, www.wwf.panda.org, accessed 1 October 2015.

Yescombe, E.R. (2007). *Public–Private Partnerships*, Oxford: Butterworth-Heinemann.

World Bank, 2007. *Port Reform Toolkit*, second edition – Module 3 – Alternative Port Management Structures and Ownership Models.

World Bank, 2013. *Transformation Through Infrastructure*. www.worldbank.org (accessed 29 November 2013).

Index

Compiled by Michelle Baker at INDEXING SPECIALISTS (UK) Ltd., Indexing House, 306A Portland Road, Hove, East Sussex BN3 5LP United Kingdom